MRS. BEETON'S

DICTIONARY OF EVERY-DAY COOKERY.

THE "ALL ABOUT IT" BOOKS.

MRS. BEETON'S DICTIONARY OF EVERY-DAY COOKERY.

LONDON:
S. O BEETON, 248, STRAND, W.C.
1865.

London:
Cox & Wyman, Classical and General Printers,
Great Queen Street, W.C.

PREFACE.

The reasons for the publication of this Volume—the First of a Series of Practical Manuals which were to be called the "All About It" Books—were thus explained in a Prospectus issued a few months ago, and approved by the late Mrs. S. O. Beeton :—

MANY wishes have been expressed to the Authoress of the "Book of Household Management" that a volume of Recipes in Cookery should be written which could be sold at a price somewhere between the seven-and-sixpenny "Household Management" and the Shilling Cookery Book. Accordingly Mrs. Beeton has prepared a Collection of Recipes, and of other Practical Information concerning the Dressing and Serving of Family Fare, which, when completed, will be published, in serviceable binding, at the price of Three Shillings and Sixpence.

As Mistress, Cook, and Critic have declared that the details in Mrs. Beeton's larger work are *so easy to understand*, the Authoress has followed, in every Recipe printed in the present Dictionary, the same simple plan she originally used. Regarding, however, the *arrangement* of the Recipes, the Authoress has chosen the Dictionary form, believing an alphabetical arrangement to be the best for a book that is being constantly referred to. By the adoption of a very intelligible system, all *cross* reference, and that very disagreeable parenthesis (*See* So-and-so) is avoided, except in a very few instances. Where any warning as to what should *not* be done is likely to be needed, it is given, as well as advice as to what ought to be done. No pains have been thought too great to make *little things* clearly understood. Trifles constitute perfection. It is just the knowledge or ignorance of little things that usually makes the difference between the success of the careful and experienced housewife or servant, and the failure of her who is careless and inexperienced.' Mrs. BEETON has brought to her new offering to the Public a most anxious care to describe plainly and fully all the more difficult and recondite portions of Cookery, whilst the smallest items have not been "unconsidered trifles," but each Recipe and preparation have claimed minute attention.

THE

DICTIONARY OF COOKERY.

ALMOND CAKE.

Ingredients.—½ lb. of sweet almonds, 1 oz. of bitter almonds, 6 eggs, 8 tablespoonfuls of sifted sugar, 5 tablespoonfuls of fine flour, the grated rind of 1 lemon, 3 oz. of butter. *Mode.*—Blanch and pound the almonds to a paste; separate the whites from the yolks of the eggs; beat the latter, and add them to the almonds. Stir in the sugar, flour, and lemon-rind; add the butter, which should be beaten to a cream; and, when all these ingredients are well mixed, put in the whites of the eggs, which should be whisked to a stiff froth. Butter a cake-mould, put in the mixture, and bake in a good oven from 1¼ to 1¾ hour. *Time.*—1¼ to 1¾ hour. *Average cost,* 2*s.* 6*d.* *Seasonable* at any time.

ALMOND CHEESECAKES.

Ingredients.—¼ lb. of sweet almonds, 4 bitter ones, 3 eggs, 2 oz. of butter, the rind of ¼ lemon, 1 tablespoonful of lemon-juice, 3 oz. of sugar. *Mode.*—Blanch and pound the almonds smoothly in a mortar, with a little rose or spring water; stir in the eggs, which should be well beaten, and the butter, which should be warmed; add the grated lemon-peel and juice, sweeten, and stir well until the whole is thoroughly mixed. Line some patty-pans with puff-paste, put in the mixture, and bake for 20 minutes, or rather less, in a quick oven. *Time.*—20 minutes, or rather less. *Average cost,* 10*d.* *Sufficient* for about 12 cheesecakes.

ALMOND PASTE, for Second-Course Dishes.

Ingredients.—1 lb. of sweet almonds, 6 bitter ones, 1 lb. of very finely-sifted sugar, the whites of 2 eggs. *Mode.*—Blanch the almonds, and dry them thoroughly; put them into a mortar, and pound them well, wetting them gradually with the whites of 2 eggs. When well pounded, put them into a small preserving-pan, add the sugar, and place the pan on a small but clear fire (a hot plate is better); keep stirring until the paste is dry, then take it out of the pan, put it between two dishes, and, when cold, make it into any shape that fancy may dictate. *Time.*—½ hour. *Average cost,* 2*s.* 8*d.* for the above quantity. *Sufficient* for 3 small dishes of pastry. *Seasonable* at any time.

ALMOND PUDDING, Baked (very rich).

Ingredients.—¼ lb. of almonds, 4 bitter ditto, 1 glass of sherry, 4 eggs, the rind and juice of ½ lemon, 3 oz. of butter, 1 pint of cream, 2 tablespoonfuls of sugar. *Mode.*—Blanch and pound the almonds to a smooth paste with the water; mix these with the butter, which should be melted; beat up the eggs, grate the lemon-rind, and strain the juice; add these, with the cream, sugar, and wine, to the other ingredients, and stir them well together. When well mixed, put it into a pie-dish lined with puff-paste, and bake for ½ hour. To make this pudding more economically, substitute milk for the cream; but then add rather more than 1 oz. of finely-grated bread. *Time.*—½ to ¾ hour. *Average cost,* 3*s.*, with cream at 1*s.* 6*d.* per pint. *Sufficient* for 4 or 5 persons. *Seasonable* at any time.

ALMOND PUDDINGS, Small.

Ingredients.—½ lb. of sweet almonds, 6 bitter ones, ¼ lb. of butter, 4 eggs, 2 tablespoonfuls of sifted sugar, 2 tablespoonfuls of cream, 1 tablespoonful of brandy. *Mode.*—Blanch and pound the almonds to a smooth paste with a spoonful of water; warm the butter, mix the almonds with this, and add the other ingredients, leaving out the whites of 2 eggs, and be particular that these are well beaten. Mix well, butter some cups,

SMALL ALMOND PUDDINGS.

half fill them, and bake the puddings from 20 minutes to ½ hour. Turn them out on a dish, and serve with sweet sauce, or with sifted sugar only. *Time.*—20 minutes to ½ hour. *Average cost*, 2*s*. *Sufficient* for 4 or 5 persons. *Seasonable* at any time.

ALMOND PUFFS.

Ingredients.—2 tablespoonfuls of flour, 2 oz. of butter, 2 oz. of pounded sugar, 2 oz. of sweet almonds, 4 bitter almonds. *Mode.*—Blanch and pound the almonds in a mortar to a smooth paste; melt the butter, dredge in the flour, and add the sugar and pounded almonds. Beat the mixture well, and put it into cups or very tiny jelly-pots, which should be well buttered, and bake in a moderate oven for about 20 minutes, or longer, should the puffs be large. Turn them out on a dish, the bottom of the puff uppermost, and serve. *Time.*—20 minutes. *Average cost*, 8*d*. *Sufficient* for 2 or 3 persons. *Seasonable* at any time.

ALMOND SOUP.

Ingredients.—4 lbs. of lean beef or veal, a few vegetables as for Stock (*see* STOCK), 1 oz. of vermicelli, 4 blades of mace, 6 cloves, ½ lb. of sweet almonds, the yolks of 6 eggs, 1 gill of thick cream, rather more than 3 quarts of water. *Mode.*—Boil the beef or veal, vegetables, and spices gently in water that will cover them, till the gravy is very strong, and the meat very tender; then strain off the gravy, and set it on the fire with the specified quantity of vermicelli to 2 quarts. Let it boil till sufficiently cooked. Have ready the almonds, blanched and pounded very fine; the yolks of the eggs boiled hard; mixing the almonds, whilst pounding, with a little of the soup, lest the latter should grow oily. Pound them to a pulp, and keep adding to them, by degrees, a little soup, until they are thoroughly mixed together. Let the soup be cool when mixing, and do it perfectly smooth. Strain it through a sieve, set it on the fire, stir frequently, and serve hot. Just before taking it up, add the cream. *Time.*—From 4 to 5 hours to simmer meat and vegetables; 20 minutes to cook the vermicelli. *Average cost* per quart, 2*s*. 3*d*. *Seasonable* all the year. *Sufficient* for 8 persons.

ANCHOVY BUTTER.

Ingredients.—To every lb. of butter allow 6 anchovies, 1 small bunch of parsley. *Mode.*—Wash, bone, and pound the anchovies well in a mortar; scald the parsley, chop it, and rub through a sieve; then pound all the ingredients together, mix well, and make the butter into pats immediately. This makes a pretty dish, if fancifully moulded, for breakfast or supper, and should be garnished with parsley. *Average cost*, 1*s*. 8*d*. *Sufficient* to make 2 dishes, with 4 small pats each. *Seasonable* at any time.

ANCHOVY SAUCE, for Fish.

Ingredients.—4 anchovies, 1 oz. of butter, ½ pint of melted butter, cayenne to taste. *Mode.*—Bone the anchovies, and pound them in a mortar to a paste, with 1 oz. of butter. Make the melted butter hot, stir in the pounded anchovies and cayenne; simmer for 3 or 4 minutes; and, if liked, add a squeeze of lemon-juice. A more general and expeditious way of making this sauce is to stir in 1½ tablespoonfuls of anchovy essence to ½ pint of melted butter, and to add seasoning to taste. Boil the whole up for 1 minute, and serve hot. *Time.*—5 minutes. *Average cost*, 6*d*. for ½ pint. *Sufficient*, this quantity, for a brill, small turbot, 2 soles, &c.

ANCHOVY TOAST.

Ingredients.—Toast 2 or 3 slices of bread, or, if wanted very savoury, fry them in clarified butter, and spread on them the paste made by recipe for potted anchovies. Made mustard, or a few grains of cayenne, may be added to the paste before laying it on the toast.

ANCHOVIES, Fried.

Ingredients.—1 tablespoonful of oil, ½ a glass of white wine, sufficient flour to thicken; 12 anchovies. *Mode.*—Mix the oil and wine together, with sufficient flour to make them into a thickish paste; cleanse the anchovies, wipe them, dip them in the paste, and fry of a nice brown colour. *Time.*—½ hour. *Average cost*, for this quantity, 9*d.* *Sufficient* for 2 persons. *Seasonable* all the year.

ANCHOVIES, Potted, or Anchovy Butter.

Ingredients.—2 dozen anchovies, ½ lb. of fresh butter. *Mode.*—Wash the anchovies thoroughly; bone and dry them, and pound them in a mortar to a paste. Mix the butter gradually with them, and rub the whole through a sieve. Put it by in small pots for use, and carefully exclude the air with a bladder, as it soon changes the colour of anchovies, besides spoiling them. To potted anchovies may be added pounded mace, cayenne, and nutmeg to taste.

APPLE CHARLOTTE, a very simple.

Ingredients.—9 slices of bread and butter, about 6 good-sized apples, 1 tablespoonful of minced lemon-peel, 2 tablespoonfuls of juice, moist sugar to taste. *Mode.*—Butter a pie-dish; place a layer of bread and butter, without the crust, at the bottom; then a layer of apples, pared, sored, and cut into thin slices; sprinkle over these a portion of the lemon-peel and juice, and sweeten with moist sugar. Place another layer of bread and butter, and then one of apples, proceeding in this manner until the dish is full; then cover it up with the peel of the apples, to preserve the top from browning or burning; bake in a brisk oven for rather more than ¾ hour; turn the charlotte on a dish, sprinkle sifted sugar over, and serve. *Time.*—¾ hour, or a few minutes longer. *Average cost*, 1*s.* *Sufficient* for 5 or 6 persons. *Seasonable* from August to March.

APPLE CHEESECAKES.

Ingredients.—½ lb. of apple pulp, ¼ lb. of sifted sugar, ¼ lb. of butter, 4 eggs, the rind and juice of 1 lemon. *Mode.*—Pare, core, and boil sufficient apples to make ½ lb. when cooked; add to these the sugar, the butter, which should be melted, the eggs, leaving out 2 of the whites, and the grated rind and juice of 1 lemon; stir the mixture well; line some patty-pans with puff-paste; put in the mixture, and bake about 20 minutes.—*Time.*—About 20 minutes. *Average cost*, for the above quantity, with the paste, 1*s.* 6*d.* *Sufficient* for about 18 or 20 cheesecakes. *Seasonable* from August to March.

APPLE CUSTARD, Baked.

Ingredients.—1 dozen large apples, moist sugar to taste, 1 small teacupful of cold water, the grated rind of 1 lemon, 1 pint of milk, 4 eggs, 2 oz. of loaf sugar. *Mode.*—Peel, cut, and core the apples; put them into a lined saucepan with the cold water, and, as they heat, bruise them to a pulp; sweeten with moist sugar, and add the grated lemon-rind. When cold, put the fruit at the bottom of a pie-dish, and pour over it a custard, made with the above proportion of milk, eggs, and sugar; grate a little nutmeg over the top, place the dish in a moderate oven, and bake from 25 to 35 minutes. The above proportions will make rather a large dish. *Time.*—25 to 35 minutes. *Average cost*, 1*s.* 6*d.*, if fruit has to be bought. *Sufficient* for 6 or 7 persons. *Seasonable* from August to March.

APPLE DUMPLINGS, Baked (a Plain Family Dish).

Ingredients.—6 apples, suet-crust, sugar to taste. *Mode.*—Pare and take out the cores of the apples with a scoop, and make a suet-crust with ¾ lb. of flour to 6 oz. of suet; roll the apples in the crust, previously sweetening them with moist sugar, and taking care to join the paste nicely. When they are formed into round balls, put them on a tin, and bake them for about ½ hour, or longer, should the apples be very large; arrange them pyramidically on a dish, and sift over them some pounded white sugar. These may be made richer by using puff-paste instead of suet-crust. *Time.*—From ½ to ¾ hour, or longer. *Average cost*, 1½*d.* each. *Sufficient* for 4 persons. *Seasonable* from August to March, but flavourless after the end of January.

APPLE DUMPLINGS, Boiled.

Ingredients.—6 apples, suet-crust, sugar to taste. *Mode.*—Pare and take out the cores of the apples with a scoop; sweeten, and roll each apple in a piece of crust, made with ¾ lb. of flour to 6 oz. of suet, and be particular that the paste is nicely joined. Put the dumplings into floured cloths, tie them securely, and place them in boiling water. Keep them boiling from ¾ to 1 hour; remove the cloths, and send them hot and quickly to table. Dumplings boiled in knitted cloths have a very pretty appearance when they come to table. The cloths should be made square, just large enough to hold one dumpling, and should be knitted in plain knitting, with *very coarse* cotton. *Time.*—¾ to 1 hour, or longer should the dumplings be very large. *Average cost*, 1½*d.* each. *Sufficient* for 4 persons. *Seasonable* from August to March, but flavourless after the end of January.

APPLE FRITTERS.

Ingredients.—For the batter, 2 tablespoonfuls of flour, ½ oz. of butter, ½ saltspoonful of salt, 2 eggs, milk, 4 medium-sized apples, hot lard or clarified beef-dripping. *Mode.*—Break the eggs, dividing the whites from the yolks, and beat them separately. Put the flour into a basin, stir in the butter, which should be melted to a cream; add the salt, and moisten with sufficient warm milk to make it of a proper consistency, that is to say, a batter that will drop from the spoon. Stir this well, rub down any lumps that may be seen, add the yolks and then the whites of the eggs, which have been previously well whisked; beat up the batter for a few minutes, and it is ready for use. Now peel and cut the apples into rather thick whole slices, without dividing them, and stamp out the middle of each slice, where the core is, with a cutter. Throw the slices into the batter; have ready a pan of boiling lard or clarified dripping; take out the pieces of apple one by one, put them into the hot lard, and fry a nice brown, turning them when required. When done, lay them on a piece of blotting-paper before the fire, to absorb the greasy moisture; then dish on a white d'oyley, piling the fritters one above the other; strew over them some pounded sugar, and serve very hot. The flavour of the fritters would be very much improved by soaking the pieces of apple in a little wine, mixed with sugar and lemon-juice, for 3 or 4 hours before wanted for table; the batter, also, is better for being mixed some hours before the fritters are made. *Time.*—From 7 to 10 minutes to fry the fritters; 5 minutes to drain them. *Average cost*, 9*d.* *Sufficient* for 4 or 5 persons. *Seasonable* from August to March.

APPLE JAM.

Ingredients.—To every lb. of fruit weighed after being pared, cored, and sliced, allow ¾ lb. of preserving-sugar, the grated rind of 1 lemon, the juice of ½ lemon. *Mode.*—Peel the apples, core and slice them very thin, and be particular that they are all the same sort. Put them into a jar, stand this in a saucepan of boiling water, and let the apples stew until quite tender. Previously to putting the fruit into the jar, weigh it, to ascertain the proportion of sugar that may be required. Put the apples into a preserving-pan, crush the sugar to small lumps, and add it, with the grated lemon-rind and juice, to the apples. Simmer these over the fire for ½ hour, reckoning from the time the jam begins to simmer properly; remove the scum as it rises, and, when the jam is done, put it into pots for use. Place a piece of oiled paper over the jam, and, to exclude the air, cover the pots with tissue paper dipped in the white of an egg, and stretched over the top. This jam will keep good for a long time. *Time.*—From 3 to 4 hours to stew in the jar; ½ hour to boil after the jam begins to simmer. *Average cost*, for this quantity, 5*s.* *Sufficient.*—7 or 8 lbs. of apples for 6 pots of jam. *Seasonable.*—Make this in September, October, or November, when apples can be bought at a reasonable price.

APPLE JELLY.

Ingredients.—To 6 lbs. of apples allow 3 pints of water; to every quart of juice allow 2 lbs. of loaf sugar;—the juice of ½ lemon. *Mode.*—Pare, core, and cut the apples into slices, and put them into a jar, with water in the above proportion. Place them in a cool oven, with the jar well covered, and, when the juice is thoroughly drawn and the apples are quite soft, strain them through a jelly-bag. To every quart of juice allow 2 lbs. of loaf sugar, which should be crushed to small lumps, and put into a preserving-pan with the juice. Boil these together for rather more than ½ hour, remove the scum as it rises, add the lemon-juice just before it is done, and put the jelly into pots for use. This preparation is useful for garnishing sweet dishes, and may be turned out for dessert. *Time.*—The apples to be put in the oven over-night, and left till morning; rather more than ½ hour to boil the jelly. *Average cost*, for this quantity, 3*s*. *Sufficient* for 6 small pots of jelly. *Seasonable*.—This should be made in September, October, or November.

APPLE JELLY.

Ingredients.—Apples, water; to every pint of syrup allow ¾ lb. of loaf sugar. *Mode*.—Pare and cut the apples into pieces, remove the cores, and put them in a preserving-pan with sufficient cold water to cover them. Let them boil for an hour; then drain the syrup from them through a hair sieve or jelly-bag, and measure the juice; to every pint allow ¾ lb. of loaf sugar, and boil these together for ¾ hour, removing every particle of scum as it rises, and keeping the jelly well stirred, that it may not burn. A little lemon-rind may be boiled with the apples, and a small quantity of strained lemon-juice may be put in the jelly just before it is done, when the flavour is liked. This jelly may be ornamented with preserved greengages, or any other preserved fruit, and will turn out very prettily for dessert. It should be stored away in small pots. *Time*.—1 hour to boil the fruit and water; ¾ hour to boil the juice with the sugar. *Average cost*, for 6 lbs. of apples, with the other ingredients in proportion, 3*s*. *Sufficient* for 6 small pots of jelly. *Seasonable*.—Make this in September, October, or November.

APPLE JELLY, Clear, for immediate Eating.

Ingredients.—2 dozen small apples, 1½ pint of spring-water; to every pint of juice allow ½ lb. of loaf sugar, ½ oz. of isinglass, the rind of ½ lemon. *Mode*.—Pare, core, and cut the apples into quarters, and boil them, with the lemon-peel, until tender; then strain off the apples, and run the juice through a jelly-bag; put the strained juice, with the sugar and isinglass, which has been previously boiled in ½ pint of water, into a lined saucepan or preserving-pan; boil all together for about ¼ hour, and put the jelly into moulds. When this jelly is clear, and turned out well, it makes a pretty addition to the supper-table, with a little custard or whipped cream round it: a little lemon-juice improves the flavour, but it is apt to render the jelly muddy and thick. If required to be kept any length of time, rather a larger proportion of sugar must be used. *Time*.—About 1 hour to boil the apples; ¼ hour the jelly. *Average cost*, 2*s*. *Sufficient* for 1½-pint mould. *Seasonable* from August to March.

APPLE JELLY, Thick, or Marmalade, for Entremets or Dessert Dishes.

Ingredients.—Apples; to every lb. of pulp allow ¾ lb. of sugar, ½ teaspoonful of minced lemon-peel. *Mode*.—Peel, core, and boil the apples with only sufficient water to prevent them from burning; beat them to a pulp, and to every lb. of pulp allow the above proportion of sugar in lumps. Dip the lumps into

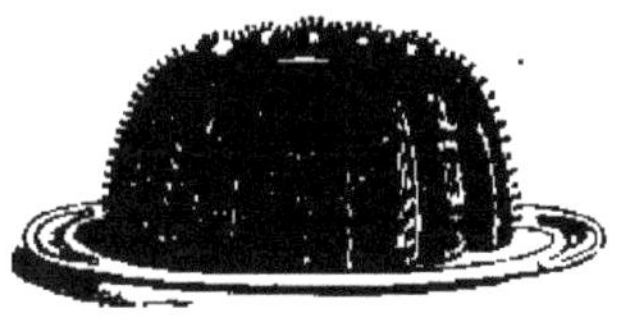

APPLE JELLY, STUCK WITH ALMONDS.

water; put these into a saucepan, and boil till the syrup is thick and can be well skimmed; then add this syrup to the apple pulp, with the minced lemon-peel, and stir it over a quick fire for about 20 minutes, or till the apples cease to stick to the bottom of the pan. The jelly is then done, and may be poured into moulds which have been previously dipped in water, when it will turn out nicely for dessert or a side dish; for the latter, a little custard should be poured round, and it should be garnished with strips of citron or stuck with blanched almonds. *Time*.—From ½ to ¾ hour to reduce the apples to a pulp; 20 minutes to boil after the sugar is added. *Sufficient*.—1½ lb. of apple pulp sufficient for a small mould. *Seasonable* from August to March; but is best and cheapest in September, October, or November.

APPLE PUDDING, Rich Baked.

Ingredients.—½ lb. apple pulp, ½ lb. of loaf sugar, 6 oz. of butter, the rind of 1 lemon, 6 eggs, puff-paste. *Mode.*—Peel, core, and cut the apples, as for sauce; put them into a stewpan, with only just sufficient water to prevent them from burning, and let them stew until reduced to a pulp. Weigh the pulp, and to every ½ lb. add the sifted sugar, grated lemon-rind, and 6 well-beaten eggs. Beat these ingredients well together; then melt the butter, stir it to the other things, put a border of puff-paste round the dish, and bake for rather more than ½ hour. The butter should not be added until the pudding is ready for the oven. *Time.*—½ to ¾ hour. *Average cost,* 1*s.* 10*d.* *Sufficient* for 5 or 6 persons. *Seasonable* from August to March.

APPLE PUDDING, Baked.

Ingredients.—12 large apples, 6 oz. of moist sugar, ¼ lb. of butter, 4 eggs, 1 pint of bread crumbs. *Mode.*—Pare, core, and cut the apples, as for sauce, and boil them until reduced to a pulp; then add the butter, melted, and the eggs, which should be well whisked. Beat up the pudding for 2 or 3 minutes; butter a pie-dish; put in a layer of bread crumbs, then the apple, and then another layer of bread crumbs; flake over these a few tiny pieces of butter, and bake for about ½ hour. A very good economical pudding made be made merely with apples, boiled and sweetened, with the addition of a few strips of lemon-peel. A layer of bread crumbs should be placed above and below the apples, and the pudding baked for ½ hour. *Time.*—About ½ hour. *Average cost,* 1*s.* 6*d.* *Sufficient* for 5 or 6 persons. *Seasonable* from August to March.

APPLE PUDDING, Baked (Very Good).

Ingredients.—5 moderate-sized apples, 2 tablespoonfuls of finely-chopped suet, 3 eggs, 3 tablespoonfuls of flour, 1 pint of milk, a little grated nutmeg. *Mode.*—Mix the flour to a smooth batter with the milk; add the eggs, which should be well whisked, and put the latter into a well-buttered pie-dish. Wipe the apples clean, but do not pare them; cut them in halves, and take out the cores; lay them in the batter, rind uppermost; shake the suet on the top, over which also grate a little nutmeg; bake in a moderate oven for an hour, and cover, when served, with sifted loaf sugar. This pudding is also very good with the apples pared, sliced, and mixed with the batter. *Time.*—1 hour. *Average cost,* 9*d.* *Sufficient* for 5 or 6 persons.

APPLE PUDDING, Boiled.

Ingredients.—Suet crust, apples, sugar to taste, 1 small teaspoonful of finely-minced lemon-peel, 2 tablespoonfuls of lemon-juice. *Mode.*—Make a butter or suet crust by either of the given recipes, using for a moderate-sized pudding from ¾ to 1 lb. of flour, with the other ingredients in proportion. Butter a basin; line it with some paste; pare, core, and cut the apples into slices, and fill the basin with these; add the sugar, the lemon-peel and juice, and cover with crust; pinch the edges together, flour the cloth, place it over the pudding, tie it securely, and put it into plenty of fast-boiling water; let it boil from 2½ to 3 hours; then turn it out of the basin and send to table quickly. Apple puddings may also be boiled in a cloth without a basin; but, when made in this way, must be served without the least delay, as the crust soon becomes heavy. Apple pudding is a very convenient dish to have when the dinner-hour is rather uncertain, as it does not spoil by being boiled an extra hour; care, however, must be taken to keep it well covered with water all the time, and not to allow it to stop boiling. *Time.*—From 2½ to 3 hours, according to the quality of the apples. *Average cost,* 10*d.* *Sufficient*, made with 1 lb. of flour, for 7 or 8 persons. *Seasonable* from August to March; but the apples become flavourless and scarce after February.

APPLE SAUCE, for Geese, Pork, &c.

Ingredients. — 6 good-sized apples, sifted sugar to taste, a piece of butter the size of a walnut; water. *Mode.*—Pare, core, and quarter the apples, and throw them into cold water to preserve their whiteness. Put them in a saucepan, with sufficient water to moisten them, and boil till soft enough to pulp. Beat them up, adding sugar to taste, and a small piece of butter. This quantity is sufficient for a good-sized tureen. *Time.*—According to the apples, about ¾ hour. *Average cost,* 4*d.* *Sufficient,* this quantity, for a goose or couple of ducks.

APPLE SNOW (a pretty Supper Dish).

Ingredients. — 10 good-sized apples, the whites of 10 eggs, the rind of 1 lemon, ½ lb. of pounded sugar. *Mode.* —Peel, core, and cut the apples into quarters, and put them into a saucepan with the lemon-peel, and sufficient water to prevent them from burning,—rather less than ½ pint. When they are tender, take out the peel, beat them into a pulp, let them cool, and stir them to the whites of the eggs, which should be previously beaten to a strong froth. Add the sifted sugar, and continue the whisking until the mixture becomes quite stiff, and either heap it on a glass dish or serve it in small glasses. The dish may be garnished with preserved barberries or strips of bright-coloured jelly, and a dish of custards should be served with it, or a jug of cream. *Time.*—From 30 to 40 minutes to stew the apples. *Average cost*, 1*s*. 6*d*. *Sufficient* to fill a moderate-sized glass dish. *Seasonable* from August to March.

APPLE SNOWBALLS.

Ingredients. — 2 teacupfuls of rice, apples, moist sugar, cloves. *Mode.*—Boil the rice and milk until three-parts done; then strain it off, and pare and core the apples without dividing them. Put a small quantity of sugar and a clove into each apple, put the rice round them, and tie each ball separately in a cloth. Boil until the apples are tender; then take them up, remove the cloths, and serve. *Time.*—½ hour to boil the rice separately; ½ to 1 hour with the apple. *Seasonable* from August to March.

APPLE SOUFFLE.

Ingredients.—6 oz. of rice, 1 quart of milk, the rind of ½ lemon, sugar to taste, the yolks of 4 eggs, the whites of 6, 1½ oz. of butter, 4 tablespoonfuls of apple marmalade. *Mode.*—Boil the milk with the lemon-peel until the former is well flavoured; then strain it, put in the rice, and let it gradually swell over a slow fire, adding sufficient sugar to sweeten it nicely. Then crush the rice to a smooth pulp with the back of a wooden spoon; line the bottom and sides of a round cake-tin with it, and put it into the oven to set; turn it out of the tin dexterously, and be careful that the border of rice is firm in every part. Mix with the marmalade the beaten yolks of eggs and the butter, and stir these over the fire until the mixture thickens. Take it off the fire; to this add the whites of the eggs, which should be previously beaten to a strong froth; stir all together, and put it into the rice border. Bake in a moderate oven for about ½ hour, or until the soufflé rises very light. It should be watched, and served instantly, or it will immediately fall after it is taken from the oven. *Time.* — ½ hour. *Average cost*, 1*s*. 8*d*. *Sufficient* for 4 or 5 persons. *Seasonable* from August to March.

APPLE TART or PIE.

Ingredients. — Puff-paste, apples; to every lb. of unpared apples allow 2 oz. of moist sugar, ½ teaspoonful of finely-minced lemon-peel, 1 tablespoonful of lemon-juice. *Mode.*—Make puff-paste by either of the given recipes, with ½ lb. of flour; place a border of it round the edge of a pie-dish, and fill the dish with apples pared, cored, and cut into slices; sweeten with moist sugar, add the lemon-peel and juice, and 2 or 3 tablespoonfuls of water; cover with crust, cut it evenly round close to the edge of the pie-dish, and bake in a hot oven from ½ to ¾ hour, or rather longer, should the pie be very large. When it is three-parts done, take it out of the oven, put the white of an egg on a plate, and, with the blade of a knife, whisk it to a froth; brush the pie over with this, then sprinkle upon it some sifted sugar, and then a few drops of water. Put the pie back into the oven, and finish baking, and be particularly careful that it does not catch or burn, *which it is very liable to do after the crust is iced.* If made with a plain crust, the icing may be omitted. Many things are suggested for the flavouring of apple pie; some say 2 or 3 tablespoonfuls of beer, others the same quantity of sherry, which very much improve the taste; whilst the old-fashioned addition of a few cloves is, by many persons, preferred to anything else, as also a few slices of quince. *Time.*—½ hour before the crust is iced; 10 to 15 minutes afterwards. *Average cost*, 9*d*. *Sufficient.*—Allow 2 lbs. of apples to a tart for 6 persons. *Seasonable* from August to March; but the apples become flavourless after February.

APPLE TART (Creamed).

Mode.—Make an apple tart by the preceding recipe, with the exception of omitting the icing. When the tart is baked, cut out the middle of the lid or crust, leaving a border all round the dish. Fill up with a nicely-made boiled custard, grate a little nutmeg over the top, and the pie is ready for table. This tart is usually eaten cold; is rather an old-fashioned dish, but, at the same time, extremely nice. *Time.*—½ to ¾ hour. *Average cost,* 1*s.* 3*d.* *Sufficient* for 5 or 6 persons. *Seasonable* from August to March.

APPLE TRIFLE (a Supper Dish).

Ingredients.—10 good-sized apples, the rind of ½ lemon, 6 oz. of pounded sugar, ½ pint of milk, ½ pint of cream, 2 eggs, whipped cream. *Mode.*—Peel, core, and cut the apples into thin slices, and put them into a saucepan with 2 tablespoonfuls of water, the sugar, and minced lemon-rind. Boil all together until quite tender, and pulp the apples through a sieve; if they should not be quite sweet enough, add a little more sugar, and put them at the bottom of the dish to form a thick layer. Stir together the milk, cream, and eggs, with a little sugar, over the fire, and let the mixture thicken, but do not allow it to reach the boiling-point. When thick, take it off the fire; let it cool a little, then pour it over the apples. Whip some cream with sugar, lemon-peel, &c., the same as for other trifles; heap it high over the custard, and the dish is ready for table. It may be garnished as fancy dictates, with strips of bright apple jelly, slices of citron, &c. *Time.*—From 30 to 40 minutes to stew the apples; 10 minutes to stir the custard over the fire. *Average cost,* 2*s.*, with cream at 1*s.* 6*d.* per pint. *Sufficient* for a moderate-sized trifle. *Seasonable* from August to March.

APPLES à la Portugaise.

Ingredients.—8 good boiling apples, ½ pint of water, 6 oz. of sugar, a layer of apple marmalade, 8 preserved cherries, garnishing of apricot jam. *Mode.*—Peel the apples, and, with a scoop, take out the cores; boil the fruit in the above proportion of sugar and water, without being too much done, and take care the apples do not break. Have ready some apple marmalade; cover the bottom of a glass dish with this, level it, and lay the apples in a sieve to drain; pile them neatly on the marmalade, raising them in the centre, and place a preserved cherry in the middle of each. Garnish with strips of candied citron or apricot jam, and the dish is ready for table. *Time.*—From 20 to 30 minutes to stew the apples. *Average cost,* 1*s.* 3*d.* *Sufficient* for 1 entremets. *Seasonable* from August to March.

APPLES, Buttered (Sweet Entremets).

Ingredients.—Apple marmalade or 7 good boiling apples, ½ pint of water, 6 oz. of sugar, 2 oz. of butter, a little apricot jam. *Mode.*—Pare the apples, and take out the cores with a scoop; boil up the sugar and water for a few minutes; then lay in the apples and simmer them very gently until tender, taking care not to let them break. Have ready sufficient marmalade made by the recipe for APPLE MARMALADE, flavoured with lemon, to cover the bottom of the dish; arrange the apples on this with a piece of butter placed in each, and in between them a few spoonfuls of apricot jam or marmalade; put the dish in the oven for 10 minutes, then sprinkle over the top sifted sugar, and either brown it before the fire or with a salamander, and serve hot. The syrup that the apples were boiled in should be saved for another time. *Time.*—From 20 to 30 minutes to stew the apples very gently, 10 minutes in the oven. *Average cost,* 1*s.* 6*d.* *Sufficient* for 1 entremets.

APPLES and RICE (a Plain Dish).

Ingredients.—8 good-sized apples, 3 oz. of butter, the rind of ½ lemon minced very fine, 6 oz. of rice, 1½ pints of milk, sugar to taste, ½ teaspoonful of grated nutmeg, 6 tablespoonfuls of apricot jam. *Mode.*—Peel the apples, halve them, and take out the cores; put them into a stewpan with the butter, and strew sufficient sifted sugar over to sweeten them nicely, and add the minced lemon-peel. Stew the apples very gently until tender, taking care they do not break. Boil the rice, with the milk, sugar, and nutmeg, until soft, and, when thoroughly done, dish it, piled high in the centre; arrange the apples on it, warm the apricot jam, pour it over the whole, and serve hot. *Time.*—About 30 minutes to stew the apples very gently; about ¾ hour to cook the rice. *Average cost*, 1*s*. 6*d*. *Sufficient* for 5 or 6 persons. *Seasonable* from August to March.

APPLES AND RICE (a pretty Dish of).

Ingredients.—6 oz. of rice, 1 quart of milk, the rind of ½ lemon, sugar to taste, ½ saltspoonful of salt, 8 apples, ¼ lb. of sugar, ¼ pint of water, ½ pint of boiled custard. *Mode.*—Flavour the milk with lemon-rind, by boiling them together for a few minutes; then take out the peel, and put in the rice, with sufficient sugar to sweeten it nicely, and boil gently until the rice is quite soft; then let it cool. In the meantime pare, quarter, and core the apples, and boil them until tender in a syrup made with sugar and water in the above proportion; and, when soft, lift them out on a sieve to drain. Now put a middling-sized gallipot in the centre of a dish; lay the rice all round till the top of the gallipot is reached; smooth the rice with the back of a spoon, and stick the apples into it in rows, one row sloping to the right, and the next to the left. Set it in the oven to colour the apples; then, when required for table, remove the gallipot, garnish the rice with preserved fruits, and pour in the middle sufficient custard, made by the recipe for boiled custard, to be level with the top of the rice, and serve hot. *Time.*—From 20 to 30 minutes to stew the apples; ¾ hour to simmer the rice; ¼ hour to bake. *Average cost*, 1*s*. 6*d*. *Sufficient* for 5 or 6 persons. *Seasonable* from August to March.

APPLES, Compote of (Soyer's Recipe,—a Dessert Dish).

Ingredients.—6 ripe apples, 1 lemon, ½ lb. of lump sugar, ½ pint of water. *Mode.*—Select the apples of a moderate size, peel them, cut them in halves, remove the cores, and rub each piece over with a little lemon. Put the sugar and water together into a lined saucepan, and let them boil until forming a thickish syrup, when lay in the apples with the rind of the lemon cut thin, and the juice of the same. Let the apples simmer till tender; then take them out very carefully, drain them on a sieve, and reduce the syrup by boiling it quickly for a few minutes. When both are cold, arrange the apples neatly on a glass dish, pour over the syrup, and garnish with strips of green angelica or candied citron.

COMPOTE OF APPLES.

Smaller apples may be dressed in the same manner: they should not be divided in half, but peeled, and the cores pushed out with a vegetable-cutter. *Time.*—10 minutes to boil the sugar and water together; from 20 to 30 minutes to simmer the apples. *Average cost*, 6*d*. *Sufficient* for 4 or 5 persons. *Seasonable* from August to March.

APPLES, Flanc of; or Apples in a raised Crust. (Sweet Entremets.)

Ingredients.—¾ lb. of short crust, 9 moderate-sized apples, the rind and juice of ½ lemon, ½ lb. of white sugar, ¾ pint of water, a few strips of candied citron. *Mode.*—Make a plain stiff short crust, roll it out to the thickness of ½ inch, and butter an oval mould; line it with the crust, and press it carefully all round the sides, to obtain the form of the mould, but be particular not to break the paste. Pinch the part that just rises above the mould with the paste-pincers, and fill the case with flour; bake it for about ¾ hour; then take it out of the oven, remove the flour, put the case back in the oven for another ¼ hour, and do not allow it to get scorched. It is now ready for the apples, which should be prepared in the following manner: peel, and take out the cores with a small knife, or a scoop for the purpose, without dividing the apples; put them into a small lined saucepan, just capable of holding them, with sugar, water, lemon-juice and rind, in the above proportion. Simmer them very gently until tender; then take out the apples, let them cool, arrange them in the flanc or case, and boil down the syrup until reduced to a thick jelly; pour it over the apples, and garnish with a few slices of candied citron.

A more simple flanc may be made by rolling out the paste, cutting the bottom of a round or oval shape, and then a narrow strip for the sides: these should be stuck on with the white of an egg to the bottom piece, and the flanc then filled with raw fruit, with sufficient sugar to sweeten it nicely. It will not require so long baking as in a mould; but the crust must be made everywhere of an equal thickness, and so perfectly joined that the juice does not escape. This dish may also be served hot, and should be garnished in the same manner, or a little melted apricot jam may be poured over the apples, which very much improves their flavour. *Time.*—Altogether, 1 hour to bake the flanc; from 30 to 40 minutes to stew the apples very gently. *Average cost*, 1*s.* 6*d.* *Sufficient* for 1 entremets or side-dish. *Seasonable* from August to March.

APPLES, Ginger (a pretty Supper or Dessert Dish).

Ingredients.—1½ oz. of whole ginger, ¼ pint of whiskey, 3 lbs. of apples, 2 lbs. of white sugar, the juice of 2 lemons. *Mode.*—Bruise the ginger, put it into a small jar, pour over sufficient whiskey to cover it, and let it remain for 3 days; then cut the apples into thin slices, after paring and coring them; add the sugar and the lemon-juice, which should be strained; and simmer all together *very gently* until the apples are transparent, but not broken. Serve cold, and garnish the dish with slices of candied lemon-peel or preserved ginger. *Time.*—3 days to soak the ginger; about ¾ hour to simmer the apples very gently. *Average cost*, 2*s.* 6*d.* *Sufficient* for 3 dishes. *Seasonable* from August to March.

APPLES Iced, or Apple Hedgehog.

Ingredients. — About 3 dozen good boiling apples, 1 lb. of sugar, ½ pint of water, the rind of ½ lemon minced very fine, the whites of 2 eggs, 3 tablespoonfuls of pounded sugar, a few sweet almonds. *Mode.*—Peel and core a dozen of the apples without dividing them, and stew them very gently in a lined saucepan with ½ lb. of the sugar and ½ pint of water, and when tender lift them carefully on to a dish. Have ready the remainder of the apples, pared, cored, and cut into thin slices; put them into the same syrup with the other ½ lb. of sugar, the lemon-peel, and boil gently until they are reduced to a marmalade; keeping them stirred, to prevent them from burning. Cover the bottom of the dish with some of the marmalade, and over that a layer of the stewed apples, in the insides of which, and between each, place some of the marmalade; then place another layer of apples, and fill up the cavities with marmalade as before, forming the whole into a raised oval shape. Whip the whites of the eggs to a stiff froth, mix with them the pounded sugar, and cover the apples very smoothly all over with the icing; blanch and cut each almond into 4 or 5 strips; place these strips at equal distances over the icing, sticking up; strew over a little rough pounded sugar, and put the dish in a very slow oven, to colour the almonds, and so allow the apples to get warm through. This entremets may also be served cold, and makes a pretty supper-dish. *Time.*—From 20 to 30 minutes to stew the apples. *Average cost*, 2*s.* to 2*s.* 6*d.* *Sufficient* for 5 or 6 persons. *Seasonable* from August to March.

APPLES in Red Jelly (a pretty Supper Dish).

Ingredients.—6 good-sized apples, 12 cloves, 6 oz. of pounded sugar, 1 lemon, 2 teacupfuls of water, 1 tablespoonful of gelatine, a few drops of prepared cochineal. *Mode.*—Choose rather large apples; peel them and take out the cores, either with a scoop or a small silver knife, and put into each apple 2 cloves and as much sifted sugar as they will hold. Place them, without touching each other, in a large pie-dish; add more white sugar, the juice of 1 lemon, and 2 teacupfuls of water. Bake in the oven, with a dish over them, until they are done. Look at them frequently, and, as each apple is cooked, place it in a glass dish. They must not be left in the oven after they are done, or they will break, and so would spoil the appearance of the dish. When the apples are neatly arranged in the dish without touching each other, strain the liquor in which they have been stewing into a lined saucepan; add to it the rind of the lemon, and a tablespoonful of gelatine which has been previously dissolved in cold water, and, if not sweet, a little more sugar, and 6 cloves. Boil till quite clear; colour with a few drops of prepared cochineal, and strain the jelly through a double muslin into a jug; let it cool *a little;* then pour it into the dish round the apples. When quite cold, garnish the tops of the apples with a bright-coloured marmalade, jelly, or the white of an egg beaten to a strong froth, with a little sifted sugar. *Time.*—From 30 to 50 minutes to bake the apples. *Average cost,* 1*s.*, with the garnishing. *Sufficient* for 4 or 5 persons. *Seasonable* from August to March.

APPLES, to preserve, in Quarters (in imitation of Ginger).

Ingredients.—To every lb. of apples allow ¾ lb. of sugar, 1½ oz. of the best white ginger; 1 oz. of ginger to every ½ pint of water. *Mode.*—Peel, core, and quarter the apples, and put the fruit, sugar, and ginger in layers into a wide-mouthed jar, and let them remain for 2 days; then infuse 1 oz. of ginger in ½ pint of boiling water, and cover it closely, and let it remain for 1 day: this quantity of ginger and water is for 3 lbs. of apples, with the other ingredients in proportion. Put the apples, &c., into a preserving-pan with the water strained from the ginger, and boil till the apples look clear and the syrup is rich, which will be in about an hour. The rind of a lemon may be added just before the apples have finished boiling; and great care must be taken not to break the pieces of apple in putting them into the jars. Serve on glass dishes for dessert. *Time.*—2 days for the apples to remain in the jar with sugar, &c.; 1 day to infuse the ginger; about 1 hour to boil the apples. *Average cost,* for 3 lbs. of apples, with the other ingredients in proportion, 2*s.* 3*d.* *Sufficient.*—3 lbs. should fill 3 moderate-sized jars. *Seasonable.*—This should be made in September, October, or November.

APPLES, Stewed, and Custard (a pretty Dish for a Juvenile Supper).

Ingredients.—7 good-sized apples, the rind of ½ lemon or 4 cloves, ½ lb. of sugar, ¾ pint of water, ½ pint of custard. *Mode.*—Pare and take out the cores of the apples, without dividing them, and, if possible, leave the stalks on; boil the sugar and water together for 10 minutes; then put in the apples with the lemon-rind or cloves, whichever flavour may be preferred, and simmer gently until they are tender, taking care not to let them break. Dish them neatly on a glass dish, reduce the syrup by boiling it quickly for a few minutes, let it cool a little; then pour it over the apples. Have ready quite ½ pint of custard made by the recipe for Boiled Custard; pour it round, but not over, the apples when they are quite cold, and the dish is ready for table. A few almonds blanched and cut into strips, and stuck in the apples, would improve their appearance. *Time.*—From 20 to 30 minutes to stew the apples. *Average cost,* 1*s.* *Sufficient* to fill a large glass dish. *Seasonable* from August to March.

APRICOT CREAM.

Ingredients.—12 to 16 ripe apricots, ½ lb. of sugar, 1½ pint of milk, the yolks of 8 eggs, 1 oz. of isinglass. *Mode.*—Divide the apricots, take out the stones, and boil them in a syrup made with ¼ lb. of sugar and ¼ pint of water, until they form a thin marmalade, which rub through a sieve. Boil the milk with the other ¼ lb. of sugar, let it cool a little, then mix with it the yolks of eggs which have been previously well beaten; put this mixture into a jug, place this jug in boiling water, and stir it one way over the fire until it thickens; but on no account let it boil. Strain through a sieve, add the isinglass, previously boiled with a small quantity of water, and keep stirring it till nearly cold; then mix the cream with the apricots; stir well, put it into an oiled mould, and, if convenient, set it on ice; at any rate, in a very cool place. It should turn out on the dish without any difficulty. In winter-time, when fresh apricots are not obtainable, a little jam may be substituted for them. *Time.*—From 20 to 30 minutes to boil the apricots. *Average cost,* 3*s.* 6*d.* *Sufficient* to fill a quart mould. *Seasonable* in August, September, and October.

APRICOT JAM, or Marmalade.

Ingredients.—To every lb. of ripe apricots, weighed after being skinned and stoned, allow 1 lb. of sugar. *Mode.*—Pare the apricots, which should be ripe, as thinly as possible, break them in half, and remove the stones. Weigh the fruit, and to every lb. allow the same proportion of loaf sugar. Pound the sugar very finely in a mortar, strew it over the apricots, which should be placed on dishes, and let them remain for 12 hours. Break the stones, blanch the kernels, and put them with the sugar and fruit into a preserving-pan. Let these simmer very gently until clear; take out the pieces of apricot singly as they become so, and, as fast as the scum rises, carefully remove it. Put the apricots into small jars, pour over them the syrup and kernels, cover the jam with pieces of paper dipped in the purest salad-oil, and stretch over the top of the jars tissue paper, cut about 2 inches larger and brushed over with the white of an egg: when dry, it will be perfectly hard and air-tight. *Time.*—12 hours, sprinkled with sugar; about ¾ hour to boil the jam. *Average cost.*—When cheap, apricots may be purchased for preserving at about 1*s.* 6*d.* per gallon. *Sufficient.*—10 lbs. of fruit for 12 pots of jam. *Seasonable.*—Make this in August or September.

APRICOT PUDDING, Baked.

Ingredients.—12 large apricots, ¾ pint of bread crumbs, 1 pint of milk, 3 oz. of pounded sugar, the yolks of 4 eggs, 1 glass of sherry. *Mode.*—Make the milk boiling hot, and pour it on to the bread crumbs; when half cold, add the sugar, the well-whisked yolks of the eggs, and the sherry. Divide the apricots in half, scald them until they are soft, and break them up with a spoon, adding a few of the kernels, which should be well pounded in a mortar; then mix the fruit and other ingredients together, put a border of paste round the dish, fill with the mixture, and bake the pudding from ½ to ¾ hour. *Time.*—½ to ¾ hour. *Average cost*, in full season, 1*s.* 6*d.* *Sufficient* for 4 or 5 persons. *Seasonable* in August, September, and October.

APRICOT TART.

Ingredients.—12 or 14 apricots, sugar to taste, puff-paste or short crust. *Mode.*—Break the apricots in half, take out the stones, and put them into a pie-dish, in the centre of which place a very small cup or jar, bottom uppermost; sweeten with good moist sugar, but add no water. Line the edge of the dish with paste, put on the cover, and ornament the pie in any of the usual modes. Bake from ½ to ¾ hour, according to size; and if puff-paste is used, glaze it about 10 minutes before the pie is done, and put it into the oven again to set the glaze. Short crust merely requires a little sifted sugar sprinkled over it before being sent to table. Green apricots make very good tarts, but they should be boiled with a little sugar and water before they are covered with the crust. *Time.*—½ to ¾ hour. *Average cost*, in full season, 1*s.* *Sufficient* for 4 or 5 persons. *Seasonable* in August, September, and October; green ones rather earlier.

APRICOTS, Compote of (an elegant Dish).

Ingredients.—½ pint of syrup (*see* SYRUP), 12 green apricots. *Mode.*—Make the syrup by the given recipe, and, when it is ready, put in the apricots whilst the syrup is boiling. Simmer them very gently until tender, taking care not to let them break; take them out carefully, arrange them on a glass dish, let the syrup cool a little, pour it over the apricots, and, when cold, serve. *Time.*—From 15 to 20 minutes to simmer the apricots. *Average cost*, 9*d.* *Sufficient* for 4 or 5 persons. *Seasonable* in June and July, with green apricots.

APRICOTS, Flanc of, or Compote of Apricots in a Raised Crust (Sweet Entremets).

Ingredients.—¾ lb. of short crust (*see* CRUST), from 9 to 12 good-sized apricots, ¾ pint of water, ½ lb. of sugar. *Mode.*—Make a short crust by the given recipe, and line a mould with it. Boil the sugar and water together for 10 minutes; halve the apricots, take out the stones, and simmer them in the syrup until tender; watch them carefully, and take them up, for fear they should break. Arrange them neatly in the flanc or case; boil the syrup until reduced to a jelly; pour it over the fruit, and serve either hot or cold. Greengages, plums of all kinds, peaches, &c., may be done in the same manner, as also currants, raspberries, gooseberries, strawberries, &c.; but with the last-named fruits, a little currant-juice added to them will be found an improvement. *Time.*—Altogether, 1 hour to bake the flanc, from 15 to 20 minutes to simmer the apricots. *Average cost*, 1*s.* 6*d.* *Sufficient* for 1 entremets or side-dish. *Seasonable* in July, August, and September.

The pretty appearance of this dish depends on the fruit being whole; as each apricot is done, it should be taken out of the syrup immediately.

APRIL—BILLS OF FARE.

Dinner for 18 persons.

First Course.

Spring Soup,
removed by
Salmon and Lobster Sauce.

Fillets of Mackerel. — Vase of Flowers. — Fried Smelts.

Soles à la Crême.

Second Course.

Roast Ribs of Lamb.

Larded Capon.

Stewed Beef à la Jardinière. — Vase of Flowers. — Boiled Ham.

Spring Chickens.

Braised Turkey.

Entrées.

Lamb Cutlets,
Asparagus and Peas.

Curried Lobster. — Vase of Flowers. — Oyster Patties.

Grenadines de Veau.

Third Course.

Ducklings,
removed by
Cabinet Pudding.

Raspberry-Jam Tartlets. — Rhubarb Tart.

Charlotte à la Parisienne.

Clear Jelly. — Vase of Flowers. — Orange Jelly.

Victoria Sandwiches. — Cheese-cakes.

Raspberry Cream.

Nesselrode Pudding.

Dessert and Ices.

Dinner for 12 persons.

First Course.—Soup à la reine; julienne soup; turbot and lobster sauce; slices of salmon à la genévése. *Entrées.*—Croquettes of leveret; fricandeau de veau; vol-au-vent; stewed mushrooms. *Second Course.*—Fore-quarter of lamb; saddle of mutton; boiled chickens, asparagus and peas; boiled tongue garnished with tufts of broccoli; vegetables. *Third Course.*—Ducklings; larded guinea-fowls; charlotte à la parisienne; orange jelly; meringues; ratafia ice pudding; lobster salad; sea-kale; dessert and ices.

Dinner for 10 persons.

First Course.—Gravy soup; salmon and dressed cucumber; shrimp sauce; fillets of whitings. *Entrées.*—Lobster cutlets; chicken patties. *Second Course.*—Roast fillet of veal; boiled leg of lamb; ham, garnished with broccoli; vegetables. *Third Course.*—Ducklings; compôte of rhubarb; custards; vanilla cream; orange jelly; cabinet pudding; ice pudding; dessert.

Dinner for 8 persons.

First Course.—Spring soup; slices of salmon and caper sauce; fried filleted soles. *Entrées.*—Chicken vol-au-vent; mutton cutlets and tomato sauce. *Second Course.*—Roast loin of veal; boiled fowls à la béchamel; tongue; vegetables. *Third Course.*—Guinea-fowls; sea-kale; artichoke bottoms; cabinet pudding; blancmange; apricot tartlets; rice fritters; macaroni and Parmesan cheese; dessert.

Dinners for 6 persons.

First Course.—Tapioca soup; boiled salmon and lobster sauce. *Entrées.*—Sweetbreads; oyster patties. *Second Course.*—Haunch of mutton; boiled capon and white sauce; tongue; vegetables. *Third Course.*—Soufflé of rice; lemon cream; charlotte à la parisienne; rhubarb tart; dessert.

First Course.—Julienne soup; fried whitings; red mullet. *Entrées.*—Lamb cutlets and cucumbers; rissoles. *Second Course.*—Roast ribs of beef; neck of veal à la béchamel; vegetables. *Third Course.*—Ducklings; lemon pudding; rhubarb tart; custards; cheesecakes; dessert.

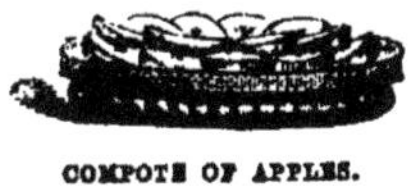

First Course.—Vermicelli soup; brill and shrimp sauce. *Entrées.* — Fricandeau of veal; lobster cutlets. *Second Course.*—Roast fore-quarter of lamb; boiled chickens; tongue; vegetables. *Third Course.*—Goslings; sea-kale; plum pudding; whipped cream; compôte of rhubarb; cheesecakes; dessert.

First Course.—Ox-tail soup; crimped salmon. *Entrées.*—Croquettes of chicken; mutton cutlets and soubise sauce. *Second Course.* — Roast fillet of veal; boiled bacon-cheek, garnished with sprouts; boiled capon; vegetables. *Third Course.*—Sea-kale; lobster salad; cabinet pudding; ginger cream; raspberry-jam tartlets; rhubarb tart; macaroni; dessert.

APRIL, Plain Family Dinners for.

Sunday. — 1. Clear gravy soup. 2. Roast haunch of mutton, sea-kale, potatoes. 3. Rhubarb tart, custards in glasses.

Monday.—1. Crimped skate and caper sauce. 2. Boiled knuckle of veal and rice, cold mutton, mashed potatoes. 3. Baked plum-pudding.

Tuesday.—1. Vegetable soup. 2. Toad-in-the-hole, made from remains of cold mutton. 3. Stewed rhubarb and baked custard puddings.

Wednesday.—1. Fried soles, anchovy sauce. 2. Boiled beef and carrots, suet dumplings. 3. Lemon pudding.

Thursday.—1. Pea-soup, made with liquor that beef was boiled in. 2. Cold beef, mashed potatoes, mutton cutlets and tomato sauce. 3. Macaroni.

Friday.—1. Bubble-and-squeak made with remains of cold beef, roast shoulder of veal stuffed, spinach and potatoes. 2. Boiled batter pudding and sweet sauce.

Saturday.—1. Stewed veal with vegetables, made of remains of cold shoulder, broiled rump-steak and oyster sauce. 2. Yeast dumplings.

Sunday.—Boiled salmon and dressed cucumber, anchovy sauce. 2. Roast fore-quarter of lamb, spinach, potatoes, and mint sauce. 3. Rhubarb tart and cheese-cakes.

Monday.—Curried salmon, made with remains of salmon, dish of boiled rice. 2. Cold lamb, rump-steak and kidney pudding, potatoes. 3. Spinach and poached eggs.

Tuesday.—1. Scotch mutton broth with pearl barley. 2. Boiled neck of mutton, caper sauce, suet dumplings, carrots. 3. Baked rice puddings.

Wednesday.—1. Boiled mackerel and melted butter and fennel sauce, potatoes. 2. Roast fillet of veal, bacon and greens. 3. Fig pudding.

Thursday.—1. Flemish soup. 2. Roast loin of mutton, broccoli, potatoes, veal rolls made from remains of cold veal. 3. Boiled rhubarb pudding.

Friday.—1. Irish stew or haricot for cold mutton, minced veal. 2. Half-pay pudding.

Saturday.—1. Rump-steak pie, broiled mutton chops. 2. Baked arrowroot pudding.

APRIL, Things in Season.

Fish.—Brill, carp, cockles, crabs, dory, flounders, ling, lobsters, red and grey mullet, mussels, oysters, perch, prawns, salmon (but rather scarce and expensive), shad, shrimps, skate, smelts, soles, tench, turbot, whitings.

Meat.—Beef, lamb, mutton, veal.

Poultry.—Chickens, ducklings, fowls, pigeons, pullets, rabbits.

Game.—Leverets.

Vegetables.—Broccoli, celery, lettuces, young onions, parsnips, radishes, small salad, sea-kale, spinach, sprouts, various herbs.

Fruit.—Apples, nuts, pears, forced cherries, &c. for tarts, rhubarb, dried fruits, crystallized preserves.

ARROWROOT BISCUITS, or Drops.

Ingredients.—½ lb. of butter, 6 eggs, ½ lb. of flour, 6 oz. of arrowroot, ½ lb. of pounded loaf sugar. *Mode.*—Beat the butter to a cream; whisk the eggs to a strong froth, add them to the butter, stir in the flour a little at a time, and beat the mixture well. Break down all the lumps from the arrowroot, and add that with the sugar to the other ingredients. Mix all well together, drop the dough on a buttered tin, in pieces the size of a shilling, and bake the biscuits about ¼ hour in a slow oven. If the whites of the eggs are separated from the yolks, and both are beaten separately before being added to the other ingredients, the biscuits will be much lighter. *Time.*—¼ hour. *Average cost,* 2*s.* 6*d.* *Sufficient* to make from 3 to 4 dozen biscuits. *Seasonable* at any time.

ARROWROOT BLANCMANGE (an inexpensive Supper Dish).

Ingredients.—4 heaped tablespoonfuls of arrowroot, 1½ pint of milk, 3 laurel-leaves or the rind of ½ lemon, sugar to taste. *Mode.*—Mix to a smooth batter the arrowroot with ½ pint of the milk; put the other pint on the fire, with laurel-leaves or lemon-peel, whichever may be preferred, and let the milk steep until it is well flavoured; then strain the milk, and add it, boiling, to the mixed arrowroot; sweeten it with sifted sugar, and let it boil, stirring it all the time, till it thickens sufficiently to come from the saucepan. Grease a mould with pure salad-oil, pour in the blancmange, and, when quite set, turn it out on a dish, and pour round it a compôte of any kind of fruit, or garnish it with jam. A tablespoonful of brandy, stirred in just before the blancmange is moulded, very much improves the flavour of this sweet dish. *Time.*—Altogether, ½ hour. *Average cost*, 6*d.* without the garnishing. *Sufficient* for 4 or 5 persons. *Seasonable* at any time.

ARROWROOT PUDDING, Baked or Boiled.

Ingredients.—2 tablespoonfuls of arrowroot, 1½ pint of milk, 1 oz. of butter, the rind of ½ lemon, 2 heaped tablespoonfuls of moist sugar, a little grated nutmeg. *Mode.*—Mix the arrowroot with as much cold milk as will make it into a smooth batter, moderately thick; put the remainder of the milk into a stewpan with the lemon-peel, and let it infuse for about ½ hour; when it boils, strain it gently to the batter, stirring it all the time to keep it smooth; then add the butter; beat this well in until thoroughly mixed, and sweeten with moist sugar. Put the mixture into a pie-dish, round which has been placed a border of paste; grate a little nutmeg over the top, and bake the pudding from 1 to 1½ hour, in a moderate oven, or boil it the same length of time in a well-buttered basin. To enrich this pudding, stir to the other ingredients, just before it is put in the oven, 3 well-whisked eggs, and add a tablespoonful of brandy. For a nursery pudding, the addition of the latter ingredients will be found quite superfluous, as also the paste round the edge of the dish. *Time.*—1 to 1½ hour, baked or boiled. *Average cost*, 7*d.* *Sufficient* for 5 or 6 persons. *Seasonable* at any time.

ARROWROOT SAUCE, for Puddings.

Ingredients.—2 small teaspoonfuls of arrowroot, 4 dessertspoonfuls of pounded sugar, the juice of 1 lemon, ¼ teaspoonful of grated nutmeg, ½ pint of water. *Mode.*—Mix the arrowroot smoothly with the water; put this into a stewpan; add the sugar, strained lemon-juice, and grated nutmeg. Stir these ingredients over the fire until they boil, when the sauce is ready for use. A small quantity of wine, or any liqueur, would very much improve the flavour of this sauce: it is usually served with bread, rice, custard, or any dry pudding that is not very rich. *Time.*—Altogether, 15 minutes. *Average cost*, 4*d.* *Sufficient* for 6 or 7 persons.

ARROWROOT, to make.

Ingredients.—Two teaspoonfuls of arrowroot, 3 tablespoonfuls of cold water, ½ pint of boiling water. *Mode.*—Mix the arrowroot smoothly in a basin with the cold water, then pour on it the *boiling water, stirring* all the time. The water must be *boiling* at the time it is poured on the mixture, or it will not thicken; if mixed with hot water only, it must be put into a clean saucepan, and boiled until it thickens; but this occasions more trouble, and is quite unnecessary, if the water is boiling at first. Put the arrowroot into a tumbler, sweeten it with lump sugar, and flavour it with grated nutmeg or cinnamon, or a piece of lemon-peel, or, when allowed, 3 tablespoonfuls of port or sherry. As arrowroot is in itself flavourless and insipid, it is almost necessary to add the wine to make it palatable. Arrowroot made with milk instead of water is far nicer, but is not so easily digested. It should be mixed in the same manner, with 3 tablespoonfuls of cold water, the boiling milk then poured on it, and well stirred. When made in this manner, no wine should be added, but merely sugar, and a little grated nutmeg or lemon-peel. *Time.*—If obliged to be boiled, 2 minutes. *Average cost*, 2*d.* per pint. *Sufficient* to make ½ pint of arrowroot.

ARTICHOKES, Boiled.

Ingredients.—To each ½ gallon of water,

allow 1 heaped tablespoonful of salt, a piece of soda the size of a shilling; artichokes. *Mode.*—Wash the artichokes well in several waters; see that no insects remain about them, and trim away

ARTICHOKES.

the leaves at the bottom. Cut off the stems and put them into *boiling* water, to which has been added salt and soda in the above proportion. Keep the saucepan uncovered, and let them boil quickly until tender; ascertain when they are done by thrusting a fork in them, or by trying if the leaves can

JERUSALEM ARTICHOKES.

be easily removed. Take them out, let them drain for a minute or two, and serve in a napkin, or with a little white sauce poured over. A tureen of melted butter should accompany them. This vegetable, unlike any other, is considered better for being gathered two or three days; but they must be well soaked and washed previous to dressing. *Time.*—20 to 25 minutes, after the water boils. *Sufficient,*—a dish of 5 or 6 for 4 persons. *Seasonable* from July to the beginning of September.

ARTICHOKES, a French Mode of Cooking.

Ingredients.—5 or 6 artichokes; to each ½ gallon of water allow 1 heaped tablespoonful of salt, ½ teaspoonful of pepper, 1 bunch of savoury herbs, 2 oz. of butter. *Mode.*—Cut the ends of the leaves, as also the stems; put the artichokes into boiling water, with the above proportion of salt, pepper, herbs, and butter; let them boil quickly until tender, keeping the lid of the saucepan off, and when the leaves come out easily, they are cooked enough. To keep them a beautiful green, put a large piece of cinder into a muslin bag, and let it boil with them. Serve with plain melted butter. *Time.*—20 to 25 minutes. *Sufficient,*—5 or 6 sufficient for 4 or 5 persons. *Seasonable* from July to the beginning of September.

ARTICHOKES, Fried (Entremets, or small dish to be served with the Second Course).

Ingredients.—5 or 6 artichokes, salt and water: for the batter,—¼ lb. of flour, a little salt, the yolk of 1 egg, milk. *Mode.*—Trim and boil the artichokes, and rub them over with lemon-juice, to keep them white. When they are quite tender, take them up, remove the chokes, and divide the bottoms; dip each piece into batter, fry them into hot lard or dripping, and garnish the dish with crisped parsley. Serve with plain melted butter. *Time.*—20 minutes to boil the artichokes, 5 to 7 minutes to fry them. *Sufficient,*—5 or 6 for 4 or 5 persons. *Seasonable* from July to the beginning of September.

ARTICHOKES à l'Italienne.

Ingredients.—4 or 5 artichokes, salt and butter, about ½ pint of good gravy. *Mode.*—Trim and cut the artichokes into quarters, and boil them until tender in water mixed with a little salt and butter. When done, drain them well, and lay them all round the dish, with the leaves outside. Have ready some good gravy, highly flavoured with mushrooms; reduce it until quite thick, and pour it round the artichokes, and serve. *Time.*—20 to 25 minutes to boil the artichokes. *Sufficient* for one side-dish. *Seasonable* from July to the beginning of September.

ARTICHOKES, Boiled Jerusalem.

Ingredients.—To each ½ gallon of water allow 1 heaped tablespoonful of salt; artichokes. *Mode.*—Wash, peel, and shape the artichokes in a round or oval form, and put them into a saucepan with sufficient *cold* water to cover them salted in the above proportion. Let them boil gently until tender; take them up, drain them, and serve them in a napkin, or plain, whichever mode is preferred; send to table with them a tureen of melted butter or cream sauce, a little of which may be poured over the artichokes when they are *not* served in a napkin. *Time.*—About twenty minutes after the water boils. *Average cost,* 2*d.* per lb.

Sufficient,—10 for a dish for 6 persons. *Seasonable*.—from September to June.

ARTICHOKES, Mashed Jerusalem.

Ingredients.—To each ½ gallon of water allow 1 oz. of salt, 15 or 16 artichokes, 1 oz. butter, pepper and salt to taste. *Mode*.—Boil the artichokes as in the preceding recipe until tender; drain and press the water from them, and beat them up with a fork. When thoroughly mashed and free from lumps, put them into a saucepan with the butter and a seasoning of *white* pepper and salt; keep stirring over the fire until the artichokes are quite hot, and serve. A pretty way of serving Jerusalem artichokes as an entremets, or second course dish, is to shape the artichokes in the form of a pear, and to serve them covered with white sauce, garnished with Brussels sprouts. *Time*.—About 20 minutes. *Average cost*, 2*d*. per lb. *Sufficient* for 6 or 7 persons. *Seasonable* from September to June.

ARTICHOKE (Jerusalem) SOUP, sometimes called Palestine Soup (a White Soup).

Ingredients.—3 slices of lean bacon or ham, ½ a head of celery, 1 turnip, 1 onion, 3 oz. of butter, 4 lbs. of artichokes, 1 pint of boiling milk, or ½ pint of boiling cream, salt and cayenne to taste, 2 lumps of sugar, 2½ quarts of white stock. *Mode*.—Put the bacon and vegetables, which should be cut into thin slices, into the stewpan with the butter. Braise these for ¼ of an hour, keeping them well stirred. Wash and pare the artichokes, and after cutting them into thin slices, add them, with a pint of stock, to the other ingredients. When these have gently stewed down to a smooth pulp, put in the remainder of the stock. Stir it well, adding the seasoning, and when it has simmered for five minutes, pass it through a strainer. Now pour it back into the stewpan, let it again simmer five minutes, taking care to skim it well, and stir it to the boiling milk or cream. Serve with small sippets of bread fried in butter. *Time*.—1 hour. *Average cost* per quart, 1*s*. 2*d*. *Seasonable* from June to October. *Sufficient* for 8 persons.

ASPARAGUS, Boiled.

Ingredients.—To each ½ gallon of water allow 1 heaped tablespoonful of salt; asparagus. *Mode*.—Asparagus should be dressed as soon as possible after it is cut, although it may be kept for a day or two by putting the stalks into cold water; yet to be good, like every other vegetable, it cannot be cooked too fresh. Scrape

BOILED ASPARAGUS.

the white part of the stems, *beginning* from the *head*, and throw them into cold water; then tie them into bundles of about 20 each, keeping the heads all one way, and cut the stalks evenly, that they may all be the same length; put them into *boiling* water, with salt in the above

ASPARAGUS TONGS.

proportion; keep them boiling quickly until tender, with the saucepan uncovered. When the asparagus is done, dish it upon toast, which should be dipped in the water it was cooked in, and leave the white ends outward each way, with the points meeting in the middle. Serve with a tureen of melted butter. *Time*.—15 to 18 minutes after the water boils. *Average cost*, in full season, 2*s*. 6*d*. the 100 heads. *Sufficient*.—Allow about 50 heads for 4 or 5 persons. *Seasonable*.—May be had forced from January, but cheapest in May, June and July.

ASPARAGUS-PEAS (Entremets, or to be served as a Side Dish with the Second Course).

Ingredients.—100 heads of asparagus, 2 oz. of butter, a small bunch of parsley, 2 or 3 green onions, flour, 1 lump of sugar, the yolks of 2 eggs, 4 tablespoonfuls of cream, salt. *Mode*.—Carefully scrape the asparagus, cut it into pieces of an equal size, avoiding that which is in the least hard or tough, and throw them into cold water. Then boil the asparagus in salt and water until three-parts done; take it out, drain, and place it on a cloth to dry the moisture away from it. Put it into a stewpan with the butter, parsley, and onions, and shake over a brisk fire for 10 minutes. Dredge in a little flour, add the sugar, and moisten with boiling water. When boiled a short time and reduced, take out the parsley and onions, thicken with the yolks of 2 eggs beaten with the cream; add a seasoning of salt, and when the whole is on the point of simmering, serve. Make the sauce sufficiently thick to adhere to the vegetable. *Time.*—Altogether, ½ hour. *Average cost*, 1*s*. 6*d*. a pint. *Seasonable* in May, June, and July.

ASPARAGUS PUDDING (a delicious Dish, to be served with the Second Course).

Ingredients.—½ pint of asparagus peas, 4 eggs, 2 tablespoonfuls of flour, 1 tablespoonful of *very finely* minced ham, 1 oz. of butter, pepper and salt to taste, milk. *Mode.*—Cut up the nice green tender parts of asparagus, about the size of peas; put them into a basin with the eggs, which should be well beaten, and the flour, ham, butter, pepper, and salt. Mix all these ingredients well together, and moisten with sufficient milk to make the pudding of the consistency of thick batter; put it into a pint buttered mould, tie it down tightly with a floured cloth, place it in *boiling water*, and let it boil for 2 hours; turn it out of the mould on to a hot dish, and pour plain melted butter *round*, but not over, the pudding. Green peas pudding may be made in exactly the same manner, substituting peas for the asparagus. *Time.*—2 hours. *Average cost*, 1*s*. 6*d*. per pint. *Seasonable* in May, June, and July.

ASPARAGUS SOUP.

Ingredients.—100 heads of asparagus, 2 quarts of medium stock (see STOCK), 1 pint of water, salt. *Mode.*—Scrape the asparagus, but do not cut off any of the stems, and boil it in a pint of water salted, *until the heads are nearly done*. Then drain the asparagus, cut off the green heads very neatly, and put them on one side until the soup is ready. If the stock is not made, add the stems of asparagus to the rest of the vegetables; if, however, the stock is ready, boil the stems a little longer in the same water that they were first cooked in. Then strain them off, add the asparagus water to the stock, and when all is boiling drop in the green heads (or peas as they are called), and simmer for 2 or 3 minutes. If the soup boils long after the asparagus is put in, the appearance of the vegetable would be quite spoiled. A small quantity of sherry, added after the soup is put into the tureen, would improve this soup very much. Sometimes a French roll is cut up and served in it. *Time.*—*To nearly cook* the asparagus, 12 minutes. *Average cost*, 1*s*. 9*d*. per quart. *Sufficient* for 6 or 8 persons. *Seasonable* from May to August.

ASPIC, or Ornamental Savoury Jelly.

Ingredients.—4 lbs. of knuckle of veal, 1 cow-heel, 3 or 4 slices of ham, any poultry trimmings, 2 carrots, 1 onion, 1 faggot of savoury herbs, 1 glass of sherry, 3 quarts of water; seasoning to taste of salt and whole white pepper; 3 eggs. *Mode.*—Lay the ham on the bottom of a stewpan, cut up the veal and cow-heel into small pieces, and lay them on the ham; add the poultry trimmings, vegetables, herbs, sherry, and water, and let the whole simmer very gently for 4 hours, carefully taking away all scum that may rise to the surface; strain through a fine sieve, and pour into an earthen pan to get cold. Have ready a clean stewpan, put in the jelly, and be particular to leave the sediment behind, or it will not be clear. Add the whites of 3 eggs, with salt and pepper, to clarify; keep stirring over the fire till the whole becomes very white; then draw it to the side, and let it stand till clear. When this is the case, strain it through a cloth or jelly-bag, and use it for moulding poultry, &c. Tarragon vinegar may be added to give an additional flavour. *Time.*—Altogether 4½ hours. *Average cost* for this quantity, 4*s*.

AUGUST—BILLS OF FARE.

Dinner for 18 persons.

First Course.

Red Mullet.	Mock-Turtle Soup, removed by Broiled Salmon and Caper Sauce. Vase of Flowers. Soup à la Julienne, removed by Brill and Shrimp Sauce.	Perch.

August—Bills of Fare

Second Course.

Capon à la Financière.

Haunch of Venison.

Ham, garnished.

Vase of Flowers.

Leveret Pie.

Saddle of Mutton.

Roast Fowls.

Entrées.

Curried Lobster.

Fricandeau de Veau à la Jardinière.

Vase of Flowers.

Fillets of Ducks and Peas.

Lamb Cutlets à la Purée de Pommes de Terre.

Third Course.

Lobster Salad.

Raspberry Tartlets.

Charlotte à la Vanille.

Grouse removed by Cabinet Pudding.

Fruit Jelly.

Vase of Flowers.

Vol-au-Vent of Pears.

Larded Peahen, removed by Iced Pudding.

Custards.

Cheesecakes.

Prawns.

Dessert and Ices.

Dinner for 12 persons.

First Course.—Vermicelli soup; soup à la reine; boiled salmon; fried flounders; trout en matelot. *Entrées.* — Stewed pigeons; sweetbreads; ragoût of ducks; fillets of chickens and mushrooms. *Second Course.* — Quarter of lamb; cotellette de bœuf à la jardinière; roast fowls and boiled tongue; bacon and beans. *Third Course.*—Grouse; wheatears; greengage tart; whipped cream; vol-au-vent of plums; fruit jelly; iced pudding; cabinet pudding; dessert and ices.

Dinner for 8 persons.

First Course.—Julienne soup; fillets of turbot and Dutch sauce; red mullet. *Entrées.* — Riz de veau aux tomates; fillets of ducks and peas. *Second Course.* —Haunch of venison; boiled capon and oysters; ham, garnished; vegetables. *Third Course.* — Leveret; fruit jelly; compôte of greengages; plum tart; custards, in glasses; omelette soufflé; dessert and ices.

Dinner for 6 persons.

First Course.—Macaroni soup; crimped salmon and sauce Hollandaise; fried fillets of trout. *Entrées.* — Tendrons de veau and stewed peas; salmi of grouse. *Second Course.*—Roast loin of veal; boiled bacon, garnished with French beans; stewed beef à la jardinière; vegetables. *Third Course.*—Turkey poult; plum tart; custard pudding; vol-au-vent of pears; strawberry cream; ratafia soufflé; dessert.

First Course.—Vegetable-marrow soup; stewed mullet; fillets of salmon and ravigotte sauce. *Entrées.*—Curried lobster; fricandeau de veau à la jardinière. *Second Course.*—Roast saddle of mutton; stewed shoulder of veal, garnished with forcemeat balls; vegetables. *Third Course.*—Roast grouse and bread sauce; vol-au-vent of greengages; fruit jelly; raspberry cream; custards; fig pudding; dessert.

AUGUST, Plain Family Dinners for.

Sunday.—1. Vegetable-marrow soup. 2. Roast quarter of lamb, mint sauce; French beans and potatoes. 3. Raspberry-and-currant tart, custard pudding.

Monday.—1. Cold lamb and salad, small meat-pie, vegetable marrow, and white sauce. 2. Lemon dumplings.

Tuesday.—1. Boiled mackerel. 2. Stewed loin of veal, French beans and potatoes. 3. Baked raspberry pudding.

Wednesday.—1. Vegetable soup. 2. Lamb cutlets and French beans; the remains of stewed shoulder of veal, mashed vegetable marrow. 3. Black-currant pudding.

Thursday.—1. Roast ribs of beef, Yorkshire pudding, French beans and potatoes. 2. Bread-and-butter pudding.

Friday.—1. Fried soles and melted butter. 2. Cold beef and salad, lamb cutlets and mashed potatoes. 3. Cauliflowers and white sauce instead of pudding.

Saturday.—1. Stewed beef and vegetables, with remains of cold beef; mutton pudding. 2. Macaroni and cheese.

Sunday.—1. Salmon pudding. 2. Roast fillet of veal, boiled bacon-cheek garnished with tufts of cauliflowers, French beans and potatoes. 3. Plum tart, boiled custard pudding.

Monday.—1. Baked soles. 2. Cold veal and bacon, salad, mutton cutlets and tomato sauce. 3. Boiled currant pudding.

Tuesday.—1. Rice soup. 2. Roast fowls and water-cresses, boiled knuckle of ham, minced veal garnished with croûtons; vegetables. 3. College pudding.

Wednesday.—1. Curried fowl with remains of cold fowl; dish of rice, stewed rump-steak and vegetables. 2. Plum tart.

Thursday.—1. Boiled brisket of beef, carrots, turnips, suet dumplings, and potatoes. 2. Baked bread pudding.

Friday.—1. Vegetable soup, made from liquor that beef was boiled in. 2. Cold beef and dressed cucumber, veal cutlets and tomato sauce. 3. Fondue.

Saturday.—1. Bubble-and-squeak, made from remains of cold beef; cold veal-and-ham pie, salad. 2. Baked raspberry pudding.

AUGUST, Things in Season.

Fish.—Brill, carp, chub, crayfish, crabs, dory, eels, flounders, grigs, herrings, lobsters, mullet, pike, prawns, salmon, shrimps, skate, soles, sturgeon, thornback, trout, turbot.

Meat.—Beef, lamb, mutton, veal, buck venison.

Poultry.—Chickens, ducklings, fowls, green geese, pigeons, plovers, pullets, rabbits, turkey poults, wheatears, wild ducks.

Game.—Leverets, grouse, blackcock.

Vegetables. — Artichokes, asparagus, beans, carrots, cabbages, cauliflowers, celery, cresses, endive, lettuces, mushrooms, onions, peas, potatoes, radishes, sea-kale, small salading, sprouts, turnips, various kitchen herbs, vegetable marrows.

Fruit.—Currants, figs, filberts, gooseberries, grapes, melons, mulberries, nectarines, peaches, pears, pineapples, plums, raspberries, walnuts.

BACON, Boiled.

Ingredients.—Bacon; water. *Mode.*—As bacon is frequently excessively salt, let it be soaked in warm water for an hour or two previous to dressing it; then pare off the rusty parts, and scrape the under-side and rind as clean as possible. Put it into a saucepan of cold water; let it come gradually to a boil, and as fast as the scum rises to the surface of the water, remove it. Let it simmer very gently until it is *thoroughly* done; then take it up, strip off the skin, and sprinkle over the bacon a few bread raspings, and garnish with tufts of cauliflower or Brussels sprouts. When served alone, young and tender broad beans or green peas are the usual accompaniments. *Time.*—1 lb. of bacon, ¾ hour; 2 lbs., 1½ hour. *Average cost*, 10*d.* to 1*s.* per lb. for the primest parts. *Sufficient.*—2 lbs., when served with poultry or veal, sufficient for 10 persons. *Seasonable* at any time.

BOILED BACON.

BACON, Broiled Rashers of.

Before purchasing bacon, ascertain that it is perfectly free from rust, which may easily be detected by its yellow colour; and for broiling, the streaked part of the thick flank is generally the most esteemed. Cut it into *thin* slices, take off the rind, and broil over a nice clear fire; turn it two or three times, and serve very hot. Should there be any cold bacon left from the previous day, it answers very well for breakfast, cut into slices, and broiled or fried. *Time.*—3 or 4 minutes. *Average cost*, 10*d.* to 1*s.* per lb. for the primest parts. *Seasonable* at any time.

Note.—When the bacon is cut very thin, the slices may be curled round and fastened by means of small skewers, and fried or toasted before the fire.

BACON and HAMS, Curing of.

The carcass of the hog, after hanging over-night to cool, is laid on a strong bench or stool, and the head is separated from the body at the neck close behind the ears; the feet and also the internal fat are removed. The carcass is next divided into two sides in the following manner:—The ribs are divided about an inch from the spine on each side, and the spine, with the ends of the ribs attached, together with the internal flesh between it and the kidneys, and also the flesh above it, throughout the whole length of the sides, are removed. The portion of the carcass thus cut out is in the form of a wedge—the breadth of the interior consisting of the breadth of the spine, and about an inch of the ribs on each side, being diminished to about half an inch at the exterior or skin along the back. The breast-bone, and also the first anterior rib, are also dissected from the side. Sometimes the whole of the ribs are removed; but this, for reasons afterwards to be noticed, is a very bad practice. When the hams are cured separately from the sides, which is generally the case, they are cut out so as to include the hock-bone, in a similar manner to the London mode of cutting a haunch of mutton. The carcass of the hog thus cut up is ready for being salted, which process, in large curing establishments, is generally as follows:—The skin side of the pork is rubbed over with a mixture of fifty parts by weight of salt, and one part of saltpetre in powder, and the incised parts of the ham or flitch, and the inside of the flitch, covered with the same. The salted bacon, in pairs of flitches with the insides to each other, is piled one pair of flitches above another on benches slightly inclined, and furnished with spouts or troughs to convey the brine to receivers in the floor of the salting-house, to be afterwards used for pickling pork for navy purposes. In this state the bacon remains a fortnight, which is sufficient for flitches cut from hogs of a carcass weight less than 15 stone (14 lbs. to the stone). Flitches of a larger size, at the expiration of that time, are wiped dry and reversed in their place in the pile, having, at the same time, about half the first quantity of fresh, dry, common salt sprinkled over the inside and incised parts; after which they remain on the benches for another week. Hams being thicker than flitches, will require, when less than 20 lbs. weight, 3 weeks; and when above that weight, 4 weeks to remain under the above described process. The next and last process in the preparation of bacon and hams, previous to being sent to market, is drying. This is effected by hanging the flitches and hams for 2 or 3 weeks in a room heated by stoves, or in a smoke-house, in which they are exposed for the same length of time to the smoke arising from the slow combustion of the sawdust of oak or other hard wood. The latter mode of completing the curing process has some advantages over the other, as by it the meat is subject to the action of *creosote*, a volatile oil produced by the combustion of the sawdust, which is powerfully antiseptic. The process also furnishing a thin covering of a resinous varnish, excludes the air not only from the muscle, but also from the fat—thus effectually preventing the meat from becoming rusted; and the principal reasons for condemning the practice of removing the ribs from the flitches of pork are, that by so doing the meat becomes unpleasantly hard and pungent in the process of salting, and, by being more exposed to the action of the air, becomes sooner and more extensively rusted. Notwithstanding its superior efficacy in completing the process of curing, the flavour which smoke-drying imparts to meat is disliked by many persons, and it is therefore by no means the most general mode of drying adopted by mercantile curers. A very impure variety of *pyroligneous* acid, or vinegar made from the destructive distillation of wood, is sometimes used, on account of the highly preservative power of the creosote which it contains, and also to impart the smoke-flavour; in which latter object, however, the coarse flavour of tar is given, rather than that derived from the smoke from combustion of wood. A considerable portion of the bacon and hams salted in Ireland is exported from that country packed amongst salt, in bales, immediately from the salting process, without having been in any degree dried. In the process of salting above described, pork loses from 8 to 10 per cent. of its weight, according to the size and quality of the meat; and a further diminution of weight, to the extent of 5 to 6 per cent. takes place in drying during the first fortnight after being taken out of salt; so that the total loss in weight occasioned by the preparation of bacon and hams in a proper state for market, is not less on an average than 15 per cent. on the weight of the fresh pork.

BACON, to Cure and Keep it free from Rust (Cobbett's Recipe).

The two sides that remain, and which are called flitches, are to be cured for bacon. They are first rubbed with salt on their insides, or flesh sides, then placed one on the other, the flesh sides uppermost, in a salting-trough which has a gutter round its edges to drain away the brine; for, to have sweet and fine bacon, the flitches must not be sopping in brine, which gives it the sort of vile taste that barrel and sea pork have. Every one knows how different is the taste of fresh dry salt from that of salt in a dissolved state; therefore change the salt often,—once in 4 or 5 days; let it melt and sink in, but not lie too long; twice change the flitches, put that at bottom which was first on the top: this mode will cost you a great deal more in salt than the sopping mode, but without it your bacon will not be so sweet and fine, nor keep so well. As for the time required in making your flitches sufficiently salt, it depends on circumstances. It takes a longer time for a thick than a thin flitch, and longer in dry than in damp weather, or in a dry than in a damp place; but for the flitches of a hog of five score, in weather not very dry or damp, about 6 weeks may do; and as yours is to be fat, which receives little injury from over-salting, give time enough, for you are to have bacon until Christmas comes again. The place for salting should, like a dairy, always be cool, but well ventilated; confined air, though cool, will taint meat sooner than the midday sun accompanied by a breeze. With regard to smoking the bacon, two precautions are necessary: first, to hang the flitches where no rain comes down upon them; and next, that the smoke must proceed from wood, not peat, turf, or coal. As to the time required to smoke a flitch, it depends a good deal upon whether there be a constant fire beneath; and whether the fire be large or small: a month will do, if the fire be pretty constant and rich, as a farm-house fire usually is; but over-smoking, or rather too long hanging in the air, makes the bacon rust; great attention should therefore be paid to this matter. The flitch ought not to be dried up to the hardness of a board, and yet it ought to be perfectly dry. Before you hang it up, lay it on the floor, scatter the flesh side pretty thickly over with bran, or with some fine sawdust, not of deal or fir; rub it on the flesh, or pat it well down upon it: this keeps the smoke from getting into the little openings, and makes a sort of crust to be dried on. To keep the bacon sweet and good, and free from hoppers, sift fine some clean and dry wood ashes. Put some at the bottom of a box or chest long enough to hold a flitch of bacon; lay in one flitch, then put in more ashes, then another flitch, and cover this with six or eight inches of the ashes. The place where the box or chest is kept ought to be dry, and, should the ashes become damp, they should be put in the fireplace to dry, and when cold, put back again. With these precautions, the bacon will be as good at the end of the year as on the first day. For simple general rules, these may be safely taken as a guide; and those who implicitly follow the directions given, will possess at the expiration of from 6 weeks to 2 months well-flavoured and well-cured bacon.

BACON or HAMS, to Cure in the Devonshire way.

Ingredients.—To every 14 lbs. of meat allow 2 oz. of saltpetre, 2 oz. of salt prunella, 1 lb. of common salt. For the pickle, 3 gallons of water, 5 lbs. of common salt, 7 lbs. of coarse sugar, 3 lbs. of bay salt. *Mode.*—Weigh the sides, hams, and cheeks, and to every 14 lbs. allow the above proportion of saltpetre, salt prunella, and common salt. Pound and mix these together, and rub well into the meat; lay it in a stone trough or tub, rubbing it thoroughly, and turning it daily for two successive days. At the end of the second day, pour on it a pickle made as follows:—Put the above ingredients into a saucepan, set it on the fire, and stir frequently; remove all the scum, allow it to boil for ¼ hour, and pour it hot over the meat. Let the hams, &c., be well rubbed and turned daily; if the meat is small, a fortnight will be sufficient for the sides and shoulders to remain in the pickle, and the hams 3 weeks; if from 30 lbs. and upwards, 3 weeks will be required for the sides, &c., and from 4 to 5 weeks for the hams. On taking the pieces out, let them drain for an hour, cover with dry sawdust, and smoke from a fortnight to three weeks. Boil and carefully skim the pickle after using, and it will keep good, closely corked, for 2 years. When boiling it for use, add about 2 lbs. of common salt, and the same of treacle, to allow for waste. Tongues are excellent put into this pickle cold, having been first rubbed well with saltpetre and salt, and allowed to remain 24 hours, not forgetting to make a deep incision under the thick part of the tongue, so as to allow the pickle to penetrate more readily. A fortnight or three weeks, according to the size of the tongue, will be sufficient. *Time.*—Small meat to remain in the pickle a fortnight, hams 3 weeks; to be smoked from a fortnight to 3 weeks.

BACON, to Cure in the Wiltshire way.

Ingredients.—1½ lb. of coarse sugar ½ lb. of bay salt, 6 oz. of saltpetre, 1 lb. of common salt. *Mode.*—Sprinkle each flitch with salt, and let the blood drain off for 24 hours; then pound and mix the above ingredients well together and rub it well into the meat, which should be turned every day for a month; then hang it to dry, and afterwards smoke it for 10 days. *Time.*—To remain in the pickle from three to four weeks, to be smoked 10 days, or rather longer.

BACON, Fried Rashers of, and Poached Eggs.

Ingredients. — Bacon; eggs. *Mode.*— Cut the bacon into thin slices, trim away the rusty parts, and cut off the rind. Put it into a *cold* frying-pan, that is to say, do not place the pan on the fire before the bacon is in it. Turn it 2 or 3 times, and dish it on a very hot dish. Poach the eggs and slip them on to the bacon without breaking the yolks, and serve quickly. *Time.*—3 or 4 minutes. *Average cost,* 10*d.* to 1*s.* per lb. for the primest parts. *Sufficient.*—Allow 6 eggs for 3 persons. *Seasonable* at any time. *Note.* — Fried rashers of bacon, curled, serve as a pretty garnish to many dishes; and, for small families, answer very well as a substitute for boiled bacon, to serve with a small dish of poultry, &c.

The Bain Marie. — It is an open kind of vessel, as shown in the engraving, and is a utensil much used in modern

THE BAIN MARIE.

cookery, both in English and French kitchens. It is filled with boiling or nearly boiling water; and into this water should be put all the stewpans containing those ingredients which it is desired to keep hot. The quantity and quality of the contents of these vessels are not at all affected; and if the hour of dinner is uncertain in any establishment, by reason of the nature of the master's business, nothing is so sure a means of preserving the flavour of all dishes as the employment of the bain marie.

BARBEL.

Ingredients.—½ pint of port wine, a saltspoonful of salt, 2 tablespoonfuls of vinegar, 2 sliced onions, a faggot of sweet herbs, nutmeg and mace to taste, the juice of a lemon, 2 anchovies; 1 or 2 barbels, according to size. *Mode.* —Boil the barbels in salt and water till done; pour off some of the water, and to the remainder put the ingredients mentioned above. Simmer gently for ½ hour or rather more, and strain. Put in the fish, heat it gradually, but do not let it boil, or it will be broken. *Time.*—Altogether 1 hour. *Sufficient* for 4 persons. *Seasonable* from September to November.

BARBERRIES (Berberris vulgaris).

A fruit of such great acidity, that even birds refuse to eat it. In this respect, it nearly approaches the tamarind. When boiled with sugar, it makes a very agreeable preserve or jelly, according to the different modes of preparing it. Barberries are also used as a dry sweetmeat, and in sugarplums or comfits; are pickled with vinegar, and are used for various culinary purposes. They are well calculated to allay heat and thirst in persons afflicted with fevers. The berries, arranged on bunches of nicely curled parsley, make an exceedingly pretty garnish for supper dishes, particularly for white meats, like boiled fowl à la Béchamel, the three colours, scarlet, green, and white, contrasting well, and producing a very good effect.

BARBERRIES, to preserve in Bunches.

Ingredients.—1 pint of syrup, barberries. *Mode.*—Prepare some small pieces of clean white wood, 3 inches long and ¼ inch wide, and tie the fruit on to these in nice bunches. Have ready some clear syrup (*see* SYRUP); put in the barberries, and simmer them in it for 2 successive days, boiling them for nearly ½ hour each day, and covering them each time with the syrup when cold. When the fruit looks perfectly clear it is sufficiently done, and should be stowed away in pots, with the syrup poured over, or the fruit may be candied. *Time.*—½ hour to simmer each day. *Seasonable* in autumn.

BARLEY SOUP.

Ingredients.—2 lbs. of shin of beef, ¼ lb. of pearl barley, a large bunch of parsley, 4 onions, 6 potatoes, salt and pepper, 4 quarts of water. *Mode.*—Put in all the ingredients, and simmer gently for 3 hours. *Time.*—3 hours. *Average cost*, 2½*d.* per quart. *Seasonable* all the year, but more suitable for winter.

BARLEY-SUGAR, to make.

Ingredients.—To every lb. of sugar allow ½ pint of water, ½ the white of an egg. *Mode.*—Put the sugar into a well-tinned saucepan, with the water, and, when the former is dissolved, set it over a moderate fire, adding the well-beaten egg before the mixture gets warm, and stir it well together. When it boils, remove the scum as it rises, and keep it boiling until no more appears, and the syrup looks perfectly clear; then strain it through a fine sieve or muslin bag, and put it back into the saucepan. Boil it again like caramel, until it is brittle, when a little is dropped in a basin of cold water: it is then sufficiently boiled. Add a little lemon-juice and a few drops of essence of lemon, and let it stand for a minute or two. Have ready a marble slab or large dish, rubbed over with salad-oil; pour on it the sugar, and cut it into strips with a pair of scissors: these strips should then be twisted, and the barley-sugar stored away in a very dry place. It may be formed into lozenges or drops, by dropping the sugar in a very small quantity at a time on to the oiled slab or dish. *Time.*—¼ hour. *Average cost*, 7*d.* *Sufficient* for 5 or 6 sticks.

BARLEY-WATER, to make.

Ingredients.—2 oz. of pearl barley, 2 quarts of boiling water, 1 pint of cold water. *Mode.*—Wash the barley in cold water; put it into a saucepan with the above proportion of cold water, and when it has boiled for about ¼ hour, strain off the water, and add the 2 quarts of fresh boiling water. Boil it until the liquid is reduced one half; strain it, and it will be ready for use. It may be flavoured with lemon-peel, after being sweetened, or a small piece may be simmered with the barley. When the invalid may take it, a little lemon-juice gives this pleasant drink in illness a very nice flavour; as does also a small quantity of port wine. *Time.*—To boil until the liquid is reduced one half. *Sufficient* to make 1 quart of barley-water.

BATTER PUDDING, Baked.

Ingredients.—1½ pint of milk, 4 tablespoonfuls of flour, 2 oz. of butter, 4 eggs, a little salt. *Mode.*—Mix the flour with a small quantity of cold milk; make the remainder hot, and pour it on to the flour, keeping the mixture well stirred; add the butter, eggs, and salt; beat the whole well, and put the pudding into a buttered pie-dish; bake for ¾ hour, and serve with sweet sauce, wine sauce, or stewed fruit. Baked in small cups, very pretty little puddings may be made; they should be eaten with the same accompaniments as above. *Time.*—¾ hour. *Average cost*, 9*d.* *Sufficient* for 5 or 6 persons. *Seasonable* at any time.

BATTER PUDDING, Baked, with Dried or Fresh Fruit.

Ingredients.—1½ pint of milk, 4 tablespoonfuls of flour, 3 eggs, 2 oz. of finely-shredded suet, ¼ lb. of currants, a pinch of salt. *Mode.*—Mix the milk, flour, and eggs to a smooth batter; add a little salt, the suet, and the currants, which should be well washed, picked, and dried;

put the mixture into a buttered pie-dish, and bake in a moderate oven for 1¼ hour. When fresh fruits are in season, this pudding is exceedingly nice, with damsons, plums, red currants, gooseberries, or apples; when made with these, the pudding must be thickly sprinkled over with sifted sugar. Boiled batter pudding, with fruit, is made in the same manner, by putting the fruit into a buttered basin, and filling it up with batter made in the above proportion, but omitting the suet. It must be sent quickly to table, and covered plentifully with sifted sugar. *Time.*—Baked batter pudding, with fruit, 1¼ to 1½ hour; boiled ditto, 1½ to 1¾ hour, allowing that both are made with the above proportion of batter. Smaller puddings will be done enough in ¾ or 1 hour. *Average cost,* 10*d.* *Sufficient* for 7 or 8 persons. *Seasonable* at any time, with dried fruits.

BATTER PUDDING, Boiled.

Ingredients.—3 eggs, 1 oz. of butter, 1 pint of milk, 3 tablespoonfuls of flour, a little salt. *Mode.*—Put the flour into a basin, and add sufficient milk to moisten it; carefully rub down all the lumps with a spoon, then pour in the remainder of the milk, and stir in the butter, which should be previously melted; keep beating the mixture, add the eggs and a pinch of salt, and, when the batter is quite smooth, put it into a well-buttered basin, tie it down very tightly, and put it into boiling water; move the basin about for a few minutes after it is put into the water, to prevent the flour settling in any part, and boil for 1¼ hour. This pudding may also be boiled in a floured cloth that has been wetted in hot water: it will then take a few minutes less than when boiled in a basin. Send batter puddings very quickly to table, and serve with sweet sauce, wine sauce, stewed fruit, or jam of any kind: when the latter is used, a little of it may be placed round the dish in small quantities, as a garnish. *Time.* 1¼ hour in a basin, 1 hour in a cloth. *Average cost,* 7*d.* *Sufficient* for 5 or 6 persons. *Seasonable* at any time.

BATTER PUDDING, with Orange Marmalade.

Ingredients.—4 eggs, 1 pint of milk, 1½ oz. of loaf sugar, 3 tablespoonfuls of flour. *Mode.*—Make the batter with the above ingredients, put it into a well-buttered basin, tie it down with a cloth, and boil for 1 hour. As soon as it is turned out of the basin, put a small jar of orange marmalade all over the top, and send the pudding very quickly to table. It is advisable to warm the marmalade to make it liquid. *Time.*—1 hour. *Average cost,* with the marmalade, 1*s.* 3*d.* *Sufficient* for 5 or 6 persons. *Seasonable* at any time; but more suitable for a winter pudding.

BEANS, Boiled Broad or Windsor.

Ingredients. — To each ½ gallon of water, allow 1 heaped tablespoonful of salt; beans. *Mode.*—This is a favourite vegetable with many persons, but, to be nice, should be young and freshly gathered. After shelling the beans, put them into *boiling* water, salted in the above proportion, and let them boil rapidly until tender. Drain them well in a colander; dish, and serve with them separately a tureen of parsley and butter. Boiled bacon should always accompany this vegetable, but the beans should be cooked separately. It is usually served with the beans laid round, and the parsley and butter in a tureen. Beans also make an excellent garnish to a ham, and when used for this purpose, if very old, should have their skins removed. *Time.* — Very young beans, 15 minutes; when a moderate size, 20 to 25 minutes, or longer. *Average cost,* unshelled, 6*d.* per peck. *Sufficient.*—Allow one peck for 6 or 7 persons. *Seasonable* in July and August.

BROAD BEANS.

BEANS, Broad, à la Poulette.

Ingredients.—2 pints of broad beans ½ pint of stock or broth, a small bunch of savoury herbs, including parsley, a small lump of sugar, the yolk of 1 egg, ¼ pint of cream, pepper and salt to taste. *Mode.*—Procure some young and freshly-gathered beans, and shell sufficient to make 2 pints; boil them, as in the preceding recipe, until nearly done; then drain them and put them into a stewpan with the stock, finely-minced herbs, and sugar. Stew the beans until perfectly tender, and the liquor has dried away a little; then beat up the yolk of an egg with the cream, add this to the beans, let the whole get thoroughly hot, and when on the point of simmering, serve. Should the beans be very large, the skin should be removed previously to boiling them. *Time.*—10 minutes to boil the beans, 15 minutes to stew them in the stock. *Average cost*, unshelled, 6*d*. per peck. *Seasonable* in July and August.

BEANS, Boiled French.

Ingredients.—To each ½ gallon of water allow 1 heaped tablespoonful of salt, a *very small* piece of soda. *Mode.*—This vegetable should always be eaten young, as when allowed to grow too long it tastes stringy and tough when cooked. Cut off the heads and tails, and a thin strip on each side of the beans to remove the strings; then divide each bean into 4 or 6 pieces, according to size, cutting them lengthways in a slanting direction, and as they are cut put them into cold water, with a small quantity of salt dissolved in it. Have ready a saucepan of boiling water, with salt and soda in the above proportion; put in the beans, keep them boiling quickly, with the lid uncovered, and be careful that they do not get smoked. When tender, which may be ascertained by their sinking to the bottom of the saucepan, take them up, pour them into a colander, and when drained, dish and serve with plain melted butter. When very young, beans are sometimes served whole: thus dressed, their colour and flavour are much better preserved, but the more general way of sending them to table is to cut them into thin strips. *Time.*—Very young beans, 10 to 12 minutes; moderate size, 15 to 20 minutes, after the water boils. *Average cost*, in full season, 1*s*. 4*d*. per peck, but when forced very expensive. *Sufficient.*—Allow ½ peck for 6 or 7 persons. *Seasonable* from the middle of July to the end of September, but may be had forced from February to the beginning of June.

BEANS, French Mode of Cooking French.

Ingredients.—A quart of French beans, 3 oz. of fresh butter, pepper and salt to taste, the juice of ½ lemon. *Mode.*—Cut and boil the beans by the preceding recipe, and when tender, put them into a stewpan, and shake over the fire, to dry away the moisture from the beans. When quite dry and hot, add the butter, pepper, salt, and lemon-juice; keep moving the stewpan, without using a spoon, as that would break the beans; and when the butter is melted, and all is thoroughly hot, serve. If the butter should not mix well, add a tablespoonful of gravy, and serve very quickly. *Time.*—About ½ hour to boil the beans; 10 minutes to shake them over the fire. *Average cost*, in full season, about 1*s*. 4*d*. per peck. *Sufficient* for 3 or 4 persons. *Seasonable* from the middle of July to the end of September.

BEANS, to Boil Haricots Blancs, or White Haricot.

Ingredients.—1 quart of white haricot beans, 2 quarts of soft water, 1 oz. of butter, 1 heaped tablespoonful of salt. *Mode.*—Put the beans into cold water, let them soak from 2 to 4 hours, according to their age; then put them into cold water salted in the above proportion, bring them to boil, and let them simmer very slowly until tender; pour the water away from them, let them stand by the side of the fire, with the lid of the saucepan partially off, to allow the beans to dry; then add 1 oz. of butter and a seasoning of pepper and salt. Shake the beans about for a minute or two, and serve: do not stir them with a spoon, for fear of breaking them to pieces. *Time.*—After the water boils, from 2 to 2½ hours. *Average cost*, 4*d*. per quart. *Sufficient* for 4 or 5 persons. *Seasonable* in winter, when other vegetables are scarce.

Note.—Haricots blancs, when new and fresh, should be put into boiling water, and do not require any soaking previous to dressing.

BEANS, Haricots Blancs & Minced Onions.

Ingredients.—1 quart of white haricot beans, 4 middling-sized onions, ¼ pint of good brown gravy, pepper and salt to taste, a little flour. *Mode.*—Peel and mince the onions not too finely, and fry them in butter of a light brown colour; dredge over them a little flour, and add the gravy and a seasoning of pepper and salt. Have ready a pint of haricot beans well boiled and drained; put them with the onions and gravy, mix all well together, and serve very hot. *Time.*—From 2 to 2½ hours to boil the beans; 5 minutes to fry the onions. *Average cost*, 4*d.* per quart. *Sufficient* for 4 or 5 persons. *Seasonable* in winter.

BEANS, Haricots Blancs à la Maître d'Hôtel.

Ingredients.—1 quart of white haricot beans, ¼ lb. of fresh butter, 1 tablespoonful of minced parsley, pepper and salt to taste, the juice of ½ lemon. *Mode.*—Should the beans be very dry, soak them for an hour or two in cold water, and boil them until perfectly tender, as in the preceding recipe. If the water should boil away, replenish it with a little more cold, which makes the skin of the beans tender. Let them be very thoroughly done; drain them well; then add to them the butter, minced parsley, and a seasoning of pepper and salt. Keep moving the stewpan over the fire without using a spoon, as this would break the beans; and, when the various ingredients are well mixed with them, squeeze in the lemon-juice, and serve very hot. *Time.*—From 2 to 2½ hours to boil the beans. *Average cost*, 4*d.* per quart. *Sufficient* for 4 or 5 persons. *Seasonable* in winter.

HARICOT BEANS.

BECHAMEL, or French White Sauce.

Ingredients.—1 small bunch of parsley, 2 cloves, ½ bay-leaf, 1 small bunch of savoury herbs, salt to taste; 3 or 4 mushrooms, when obtainable; 2 pints of white stock, 1 pint of milk or cream, 1 tablespoonful of arrowroot. *Mode.*—Put the stock into a stewpan, with the parsley, cloves, bay-leaf, herbs, and mushrooms; add a seasoning of salt, but no pepper, as that would give the sauce a dusty appearance, and should be avoided. When it has boiled long enough to extract the flavour of the herbs, &c., strain it, and boil it up quickly again, until it is nearly half reduced. Now mix the arrowroot smoothly with the milk or cream, and let it simmer very gently for 5 minutes over a slow fire; pour to it the stock, and continue to simmer slowly for 10 minutes, if the sauce be thick. If, on the contrary, it be too thin, it must be stirred over a sharp fire till it thickens. Always make it thick, as it can easily be thinned with cream, milk, or white stock. This sauce is excellent for pouring over boiled fowls. *Time.*—Altogether, 2 hours. *Average cost*, 3*s.* per quart, with cream at 1*s.* 6*d.* per pint.

BECHAMEL MAIGRE, or Without Meat.

Ingredients.—2 onions, 1 blade of mace, mushroom trimmings, a small bunch of parsley, 1 oz. of butter, flour, ½ pint of water, 1 pint of milk, salt, the juice of ½ lemon, 2 eggs. *Mode.*—Put in a stewpan the milk and ½ pint of water, with the onions, mace, mushrooms, parsley, and salt. Let these simmer gently for 20 minutes. In the meantime, rub on a plate 1 oz. of flour and butter; put it to the liquor, and stir it well till it boils up; then place it by the side of the fire, and continue stirring until it is perfectly smooth. Now strain it through a sieve into a basin, after which put it back in the stewpan, and add the lemon-juice. Beat up the yolks of the eggs with about 4 dessertspoonfuls of milk; strain this to the sauce, keep stirring it over the fire, *but do not let it boil, or it will curdle. Time.*—Altogether, ¾ hour. *Average cost*, 5*d.* per pint.

This is a good sauce to pour over boiled fowls when they are a bad colour.

BEEF, Aitchbone of, Boiled.

Ingredients. — Beef, water. *Mode.*—After this joint has been in salt 5 or 6 days, it will be ready for use, and will not take so long boiling as a round, for it is not so solid. Wash the meat, and, if too salt, soak it for a few hours, changing the water once or twice, till the required freshness is obtained. Put into a saucepan, or boiling-pot, sufficient water to cover the meat; set it over the fire, and when it boils, plunge in the joint, and let it boil up quickly. Now draw the pot to the side of the fire, and let the process be very gradual, as the water must only simmer, or the meat will be hard and tough. Carefully remove the scum from the surface of the water, and

AITCH-BONE OF BEEF.

continue doing this for a few minutes after it first boils. Carrots and turnips are served with this dish, and sometimes suet dumplings, which may be boiled with the beef. Garnish with a few of the carrots and turnips, and serve the remainder in a vegetable-dish. *Time.*—An aitch-bone of 10 lbs., 2½ hours after the water boils; one of 20 lbs., 4 hours. *Average cost*, 6*d*. per lb. *Sufficient.*—10 lbs. for 7 or 8 persons. *Seasonable* all the year, but best from September to March.

Note.—The liquor in which the meat has been boiled may be easily converted into a very excellent pea-soup. It will require very few vegetables, as it will be impregnated with the flavour of those boiled with the meat.

BEEF A LA MODE.

Ingredients.—6 or 7 lbs. of the thick flank of beef, a few slices of fat bacon, 1 teacupful of vinegar, black pepper, allspice, 2 cloves well mixed and finely pounded, making altogether 1 heaped teaspoonful; salt to taste, 1 bunch of savoury herbs, including parsley, all finely minced and well mixed; 3 onions, 2 large carrots, 1 turnip, 1 head of celery, 1½ pint of water, 1 glass of port wine. *Mode.*—Slice and fry the onions of a pale brown, and cut up the other vegetables in small pieces, and prepare the beef for stewing in the following manner:—Choose a fine piece of beef, cut the bacon into long slices, about an inch in thickness, dip them into vinegar, and then into a little of the above seasoning of spice, &c., mixed with the same quantity of minced herbs. With a sharp knife make holes deep enough to let in the bacon; then rub the beef over with the remainder of the seasoning and herbs, and bind it up in a nice shape with tape. Have ready a well-tinned stew-pan (it should not be much larger than the piece of meat you are cooking), into which put the beef, with the vegetables, vinegar, and water. Let it simmer *very gently* for 5 hours, or rather longer, should the meat not be extremely tender, and turn it once or twice. When ready to serve, take out the beef, remove the tape, and put it on a hot dish. Skim off every particle of fat from the gravy, add the port wine, just let it boil, pour it over the beef, and it is ready to serve. Great care must be taken that this does not boil fast, or the meat will be tough and tasteless; it should only just bubble. When convenient, all kinds of stews, &c. should be cooked on a hot plate, as the process is so much more gradual than on an open fire. *Time.*—5 hours, or rather more. *Average cost*, 7*d*. per lb. *Sufficient* for 7 or 8 persons. *Seasonable* all the year, but more suitable for a winter dish.

BEEF A LA MODE (Economical).

Ingredients.—About 3 lbs. of clod or sticking of beef, 2 oz. of clarified dripping, 1 large onion, flour, 2 quarts of water, 12 berries of allspice, 2 bay-leaves, ½ teaspoonful of whole black pepper, salt to taste. *Mode.*—Cut the beef into small pieces, and roll them in flour; put the dripping into a stewpan with the onion, which should be sliced thin. Let it get quite hot; lay in the pieces of beef, and stir them well about. When nicely browned all over, add *by degrees* boiling water in the above proportion, and, as the water is added, keep the whole well stirred. Put in the spice, bay-leaves, and seasoning, cover the stewpan closely, and set it by the side of the fire to stew very *gently*, till the meat becomes quite tender, which will be in about 3 hours, when it will be ready to serve. Remove the bay-leaves before it is sent to table. *Time.*—3 hours. *Average cost*, 1*s*. 3*d*. *Sufficient* for 6 persons. *Seasonable* at any time.

BEEF, Baked.

[COLD MEAT COOKERY. 1.] *Ingredients.* About 2 lbs. of cold roast beef, 2 small onions, 1 large carrot or 2 small ones, 1 turnip, a small bunch of savoury herbs, salt and pepper to taste, quite

½ pint of gravy, 3 tablespoonfuls of ale, crust or mashed potatoes. *Mode.*—Cut the beef in slices, allowing a small amount of fat to each slice; place a layer of this in the bottom of a pie-dish, with a portion of the onions, carrots, and turnips, which must be sliced; mince the herbs, strew them over the meat, and season with pepper and salt. Then put another layer of meat, vegetables, and seasoning; and proceed in this manner until all the ingredients are used. Pour in the gravy and ale (water may be substituted for the former, but it is not so nice), cover with a crust or mashed potatoes, and bake for ½ hour, or rather longer. *Time.*—Rather more than ½ hour. *Average cost,* exclusive of the meat, 6*d.* *Sufficient* for 5 or 6 persons. *Seasonable* at any time.

Note.—It is as well to parboil the carrots and turnips before adding them to the meat, and to use some of the liquor in which they were boiled as a substitute for gravy; that is to say, when there is no gravy at hand. Be particular to cut the onions in very *thin* slices.

[COLD MEAT COOKERY. 2.] *Ingredients.*—Slices of cold roast beef, salt and pepper to taste, 1 sliced onion, 1 teaspoonful of minced savoury herbs, 12 tablespoonfuls of gravy or sauce of any kind, mashed potatoes. *Mode.*—Butter the sides of a deep dish, and spread mashed potatoes over the bottom of it; on this place layers of beef in thin slices (this may be minced, if there is not sufficient beef to cut into slices), well seasoned with pepper and salt, and a very little onion and herbs, which should be previously fried of a nice brown; then put another layer of mashed potatoes, and beef, and other ingredients, as before; pour in the gravy or sauce, cover the whole with another layer of potatoes, and bake for ½ hour. This may be served in the dish, or turned out. *Time.*—½ hour. *Average cost,* exclusive of the cold beef, 6*d.* *Sufficient.*—A large pie-dish full for 5 or 6 persons. *Seasonable* at any time.

BEEF-BONES, Broiled.

[COLD MEAT COOKERY.] *Ingredients.*—The bones of ribs or sirloin; salt, pepper and cayenne. *Mode.*—Separate the bones, taking care that the meat on them is not too thick in any part; sprinkle them well with the above seasoning, and broil over a very clear fire. When nicely browned, they are done; but do not allow them to blacken.

BEEF, Brisket of, à la Flamande.

Ingredients.—About 6 or 8 lbs. of the brisket of beef, 4 or 5 slices of bacon, 2 carrots, 1 onion, a bunch of savoury herbs, salt and pepper to taste, 4 cloves, 4 whole allspice, 2 blades of mace. *Mode.*—Choose that portion of the brisket which contains the gristle, trim it, and put it into a stewpan with the slices of bacon, which should be placed under and over the meat. Add the vegetables, herbs, spices, and seasoning, and cover with a little weak stock or water; shut the stewpan-lid as closely as possible, and simmer very gently for 4 hours. Strain the liquor, reserve a portion of it for sauce, and the remainder boil quickly over a sharp fire until reduced to a glaze, with which glaze the meat. Garnish the dish with scooped carrots and turnips, and, when liked, a little cabbage; all of which must be cooked separately. Thicken and flavour the liquor that was saved for sauce, pour it round the meat, and serve. The beef may also be garnished with glazed onions, artichoke-bottoms, &c. *Time.*—4 hours. *Average cost,* 7*d.* per lb. *Sufficient* for 6 or 8 persons. *Seasonable* at any time.

BEEF, Brisket of, Stewed.

Ingredients.—7 lbs. of the brisket of beef, vinegar and salt, 6 carrots, 6 turnips, 6 small onions, 1 blade of pounded mace, 2 whole allspice pounded, thickening of butter and flour, 2 tablespoonfuls of ketchup; stock, or water. *Mode.*—About an hour before dressing it, rub the meat over with vinegar and salt; put it into a stewpan, with sufficient stock to cover it (when this is not at hand, water may be substituted for it), and be particular that the stewpan is not much larger than the meat. Skim well, and when it has simmered very gently for 1 hour, put in the vegetables, and continue simmering till the meat is perfectly tender. Draw out the bones, dish the meat, and garnish either with tufts of cauliflower or braised cabbage cut in quarters. Thicken as much gravy as required, with a little butter and flour; add spices and ketchup in the above proportion, give one boil, pour some of it over the meat, and the remainder send in a tureen. *Time.*—Rather more than 3 hours. *Average cost*, 7*d.* per lb. *Sufficient* for 7 or 8 persons. *Seasonable* at any time.

Note.—The remainder of the liquor in which the beef was boiled may be served as a soup, or it may be sent to table with the meat in a tureen.

BEEF, Broiled, and Mushroom Sauce.

[COLD MEAT COOKERY.] *Ingredients.*—2 or 3 dozen small button mushrooms, 1 oz. of butter, salt and cayenne to taste, 1 tablespoonful of mushroom ketchup, mashed potatoes, slices of cold roast beef. *Mode.*—Wipe the mushrooms free from grit with a piece of flannel, and salt; put them in a stewpan with the butter, seasoning, and ketchup; stir over the fire until the mushrooms are quite done, when pour it in the middle of mashed potatoes, browned. Then place round the potatoes slices of cold roast beef, nicely broiled over a clear fire. In making the mushroom sauce the ketchup may be dispensed with, if there is sufficient gravy. *Time.*—½ hour. *Average cost*, exclusive of the meat, 8*d.* *Seasonable* from August to October.

BEEF, Broiled, and Oyster Sauce.

[COLD MEAT COOKERY.] *Ingredients*—2 dozen oysters, 3 cloves, 1 blade of mace, 2 oz. of butter, ½ teaspoonful of flour, cayenne and salt to taste, mashed potatoes, a few slices of cold roast beef. *Mode.*—Put the oysters in a stewpan, with their liquor strained; add the cloves, mace, butter, flour, and seasoning, and let them simmer gently for 5 minutes. Have ready in the centre of a dish round walls of mashed potatoes, browned; into the middle pour the oyster sauce quite hot, and round the potatoes place, in layers, slices of the beef, which should be previously broiled over a nice clear fire. *Time.*—5 minutes. *Average cost*, 1*s.* 6*d.*, exclusive of the cold meat. *Sufficient* for 4 or 5 persons. *Seasonable* from September to April.

BEEF BUBBLE-AND-SQUEAK.

[COLD MEAT COOKERY.] *Ingredients.*—A few thin slices of cold boiled beef; butter, cabbage, 1 sliced onion, pepper and salt to taste. *Mode.*—Fry the slices of beef gently in a little butter, taking care not to dry them up. Lay them on a flat dish, and cover with fried greens. The greens may be prepared from cabbage sprouts or green savoys. They should be boiled till tender, well drained, minced, and placed till quite hot in a frying-pan, with butter, a sliced onion, and seasoning of pepper and salt. When the onion is done it is ready to serve. *Time.*—Altogether, ½ hour. *Average cost*, exclusive of the cold beef, 3*d.* *Seasonable* at any time.

BEEF CAKE.

[COLD MEAT COOKERY.] *Ingredients.*—The remains of cold roast beef; to each pound of cold meat allow ¼ lb. of bacon or ham; seasoning to taste of pepper and salt, 1 small bunch of minced savoury herbs, 1 or 2 eggs. *Mode.*—Mince the beef very finely (if underdone it will be better), add to it the bacon, which must also be chopped very small, and mix well together. Season, stir in the herbs, and bind with an egg, or 2 should 1 not be sufficient. Make it into small square cakes, about ½ inch thick, fry them in hot dripping, drain them, and serve in a dish with good gravy poured round. *Time.*—10 minutes. *Average cost*, exclusive of the cold meat, 6*d.* *Seasonable* at any time.

BEEF, Collared.

Ingredients.—7 lbs. of the thin end of the flank of beef, 2 oz. of coarse sugar, 6 oz. of salt, 1 oz. of saltpetre, 1 large handful of parsley, minced, 1 dessert-spoonful of minced sage, a bunch of savoury herbs, ½ teaspoonful of pounded allspice; salt and pepper to taste. *Mode.*—Choose fine tender beef, but not too fat; lay it in a dish, rub in

COLLARED BEEF.

the sugar, salt, and saltpetre, and let it remain in the pickle for a week or ten days, turning and rubbing it every day. Then bone it, remove all the gristle and the coarse skin of the inside part, and sprinkle it thickly with parsley, herbs, spice, and seasoning in the above proportion, taking care that the former are finely minced, and the latter well pounded. Roll the meat up in a cloth as tightly as possible; bind it firmly with broad tape, and boil it gently for 6 hours. Immediately on taking it out of the pot put it under a good weight, without undoing it, and let it remain until cold. This dish is a very nice addition to the breakfast-table. *Time.*—6 hours. *Average cost,* for this quantity, 4*s*. *Seasonable* at any time.

Note.—During the time the beef is in pickle it should be kept cool, and regularly rubbed and turned every day.

BEEF COLLOPS.

Ingredients. — 2 lbs. of rump-steak, ¼ lb. of butter, 1 pint of gravy (water may be substituted for this), salt and pepper to taste, 1 shalot, finely minced, ½ pickled walnut, 1 teaspoonful of capers. *Mode.*—Have the steak cut thin, and divide it in pieces about 3 inches long; beat these with the blade of a knife, and dredge with flour. Put them in a frying-pan with the butter, and let them fry for about 3 minutes; then lay them in a small stewpan, and pour over them the gravy. Add a piece of butter kneaded with a little flour, put in the seasoning and all the other ingredients, and let the whole simmer, but not boil, for 10 minutes. Serve in a hot covered dish. *Time.*—10 minutes. *Average cost,* 1*s*. per lb. *Sufficient* for 4 or 5 persons. *Seasonable* at any time.

BEEF CARVING.

Beef, Aitchbone of. — A boiled aitchbone of beef is not a difficult joint

to carve, as will be seen on reference to the accompanying engraving. By following with the knife the direction of the line from 1 to 2, nice slices will be easily cut. It may be necessary, as in a round of beef, to cut a thick slice off the outside before commencing to serve.

Beef, Brisket of. — There is but little description necessary to add to show the carving of a boiled brisket of beef beyond the engraving here inserted.

The only point to be observed is, that the joint should be cut evenly and firmly quite across the bones, so that on its reappearance at table it should not have a jagged and untidy look.

Beef, Ribs of.—This dish resembles the sirloin, except that it has no fillet or undercut. As explained in the recipes, the end piece is often cut off, salted and boiled. The mode of carving is similar to

that of the sirloin, viz., in the direction of the dotted line from 1 to 2. This joint will be the more easily cut if the plan be pursued which is suggested in carving the sirloin; namely, the inserting of the knife immediately between the bone and the meat, before commencing to cut it into slices. All joints of roast beef should be cut in even and thin slices. Horseradish, finely scraped, may be served as a garnish; but horseradish sauce is preferable for eating with the beef.

Beef, a Round of. — A round of beef is more easily carved than any other

joint of beef, but, to manage it properly, a thin-bladed and very sharp knife is necessary. Off the outside of the joint, at its top, a thick slice should first be cut, so as to leave the surface smooth: then thin and even slices should be cleverly carved in the direction of the line 1 to 2; and with each slice of the lean a delicate morsel of the fat should be served.

Beef, Sirloin of. — This dish is served differently at various tables, some preferring it to come to table with the fillet, or, as it is usually called, the undercut, uppermost. The reverse way, as shown in the cut, is that most usually adopted. Still the undercut is best eaten

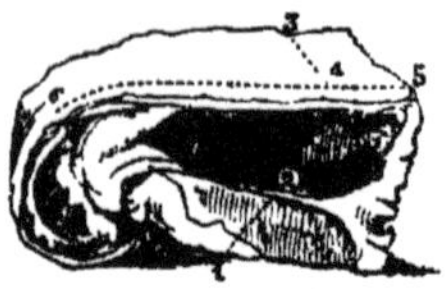

when hot; consequently, the carver himself may raise the joint, and cut some slices from the under side, in the direction of from 1 to 2, as the fillet is very much preferred by some eaters. The upper part of the sirloin should be cut in the direction of the line from 5 to 6, and care should be taken to carve it evenly and in thin slices. It will be found a great assistance, in carving this joint well, if the knife be first inserted just above the bone at the bottom, and run sharply along between the bone and meat, and also to divide the meat from the bone in the same way at the side of the joint; the slices will then come away more readily. Some carvers cut the upper side of the sirloin across, as shown by the line from 3 to 4; but this is a wasteful plan, and one not to be recommended. With the sirloin, very finely-scraped horseradish is usually served, and a little given, when liked, to each guest. Horseradish sauce is preferable, however, for serving on the plate, although the scraped horseradish may still be used as a garnish.

Beef Tongue.—Passing the knife

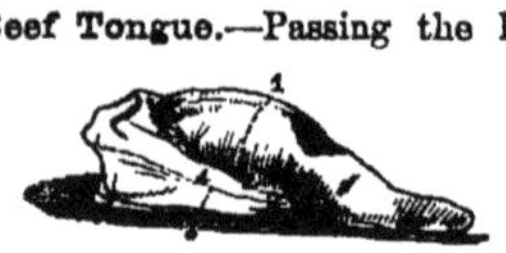

down in the direction of from 1 to 2, a not too thin slice should be helped; and the carving of a tongue may be continued in this way until the best portions of the upper side are served. The fat which lies about the root can be served by turning the tongue, and cutting in the direction of from 3 to 4.

BEEF, Curried.

[COLD MEAT COOKERY.] *Ingredients.* —A few slices of tolerably lean cold roast or boiled beef, 3 oz. of butter, 2 onions, 1 wineglassful of beer, a dessert-spoonful of curry powder. *Mode.*—Cut up the beef into pieces about 1 inch square, put the butter into a stewpan with the onions sliced, and fry them of a light-brown colour. Add all the other ingredients, and stir gently over a brisk fire for about 10 minutes. Should this be thought too dry, more beer, or a spoonful or two of gravy or water, may be added; but a good curry should not be very thin. Place it in a deep dish, with an edging of dry boiled rice, in the same manner as for other curries. *Time.*—10 minutes. *Average cost,* exclusive of the meat, 4*d.* *Seasonable* in winter.

BEEF, Roast Fillet of (Larded).

Ingredients.—About 4 lbs. of the inside fillet of the sirloin, 1 onion, a small bunch of parsley, salt and pepper to taste, sufficient vinegar to cover the meat, glaze, Spanish sauce (*see* SAUCE *Mode.*—Lard the beef with bacon, and put it into a pan with sufficient vinegar to cover it, with an onion sliced, parsley, and seasoning, and let it remain in this pickle for 12 hours. Roast it before a nice clear fire for about 1¼ hour, and, when done, glaze it. Pour some Spanish sauce round the beef, and the remainder serve in a tureen. It may be garnished with Spanish onions boiled and glazed. *Time.*—1¼ hour. *Average cost,* exclusive of the sauce, 4*s.* *Sufficient* for 6 or 8 persons. *Seasonable* at any time.

BEEF, Fricandeau of.

Ingredients.—About 3 lbs. of the inside fillet of the sirloin (a piece of the rump may be substituted for this), pepper and salt to taste, 3 cloves, 2 blades of mace, 6 whole allspice, 1 pint of stock (*see* STOCK), or water, 1 glass of sherry, 1 bunch of savoury herbs, 2 shalots, bacon. *Mode.*—Cut some bacon into thin strips, and sprinkle over them a seasoning of pepper and salt, mixed with cloves, mace, and allspice, well pounded. Lard the beef with these, put it into a stewpan with the stock or water, sherry, herbs, shalots, 2 cloves, and more pepper and salt. Stew the meat gently until tender, when take it out, cover it closely, skim off all the fat from the gravy, and strain it. Set it on the fire, and boil, till it becomes a glaze. Glaze the larded side of the beef with this, and serve on sorrel sauce, which is made as follows:—Wash and pick some sorrel, and put it into a stewpan with only the water that hangs about it. Keep stirring, to prevent its burning, and when done, lay it in a sieve to drain. Chop it, and stew it with a small piece of butter and 4 or 5 tablespoonfuls of good gravy, for an hour, and rub it through a sieve. If too acid, add sugar; a little cabbage-lettuce boiled with the sorrel will be found an improvement. *Time.*—2 hours to gently stew the meat. *Average cost*, for this quantity, 4*s*. *Sufficient* for 6 persons. *Seasonable* at any time.

BEEF, Fried Salt.

[COLD MEAT COOKERY.] *Ingredients.*—A few slices of cold salt beef, pepper to taste, ¼ lb. of butter, mashed potatoes. *Mode.*—Cut any part of cold salt beef into thin slices, fry them gently in butter, and season with a little pepper. Have ready some very hot mashed potatoes, lay the slices of beef on them, and garnish with 3 or 4 pickled gherkins. Cold salt beef, warmed in a little liquor from mixed pickle, drained, and served as above, will be found good. *Time.*—About 5 minutes. *Average cost*, exclusive of the meat, 4*d*. *Seasonable* at any time.

BEEF FRITTERS.

[COLD MEAT COOKERY.] *Ingredients.*—The remains of cold roast beef, pepper and salt to taste, ¾ lb. of flour, ½ pint of water, 2 oz. of butter, the whites of 2 eggs. *Mode.*—Mix very smoothly, and, by degrees, the flour with the above proportion of water; stir in 2 oz. of butter, which must be melted but not oiled, and, just before it is to be used, add the whites of two well-whisked eggs. Should the batter be too thick, more water must be added. Pare down the cold beef into thin shreds, season with pepper and salt, and mix it with the batter. Drop a small quantity at a time into a pan of boiling lard, and fry from 7 to 10 minutes, according to the size. When done on one side, turn and brown them on the other. Let them dry for a minute or two before the fire, and serve on a folded napkin. A small quantity of finely-minced onions, mixed with the batter, is an improvement. *Time.*—From 7 to 10 minutes. *Average cost*, exclusive of the meat, 6*d*. *Seasonable* at any time.

BEEF, Hashed.

[COLD MEAT COOKERY. 1.] *Ingredients.*—Gravy saved from the meat, 1 teaspoonful of tomato sauce, one teaspoonful of Harvey's sauce, one teaspoonful of good mushroom ketchup, ½ glass of port wine or strong ale, pepper and salt to taste, a little flour to thicken, 1 onion finely minced, a few slices of cold roast beef. *Mode.*—Put all the ingredients but the beef into a stewpan with whatever gravy may have been saved from the meat the day it was roasted; simmer these gently for 10 minutes, then take the stewpan off the fire; let the gravy cool and skim off the fat. Cut the beef into thin slices, dredge them with flour, and lay them in the gravy; let the whole simmer gently for 5 minutes, but not boil, or the meat will be tough and hard. Serve very hot, and garnish with sippets of toasted bread. *Time.*—20 minutes. *Average cost*, exclusive of the cold meat, 4*d*. *Seasonable* at any time.

[COLD MEAT COOKERY. 2.] *Ingredients.*—The remains of ribs or sirloin of beef, 2 onions, 1 carrot, 1 bunch of savoury herbs, pepper and salt to taste, ½ blade of pounded mace, thickening of flour, rather more than 1 pint of water. *Mode.*—Take off all the meat from the bones of ribs or sirloin of beef; remove the outside brown and gristle; place the meat on one side, and well stew the bones and pieces, with the above ingredients, for about 2 hours, till it becomes a strong gravy, and is reduced to rather more than ½ pint; strain this, thicken with a teaspoonful of flour, and let the gravy cool; skim off all the fat; lay in the meat, let it get hot through, but do not allow it to boil; and garnish with sippets of toasted bread. The gravy should be flavoured as in the preceding recipe. *Time.*—Rather more than 2 hours. *Average cost*, exclusive of the cold meat, 6*d*. *Seasonable* at any time.

BEEF-TEA, Savoury (Soyer's Recipe).

Ingredients.—1 lb. of solid beef, 1 oz. of butter, 1 clove, 2 button onions or ½ a large one, 1 saltspoonful of salt, 1 quart of water. *Mode.*—Cut the beef into very small dice; put it into a stewpan with the butter, clove, onion, and salt; stir the meat round over the fire for a few minutes until it produces a thin gravy, then add the water, and let it simmer gently from ½ to ¾ of an hour, skimming off every particle of fat. When done, strain it through a sieve, and put it by in a cool place until required. The same, if wanted quite plain, is done by merely omitting the vegetables, salt, and clove; the butter cannot be objectionable, as it is taken out in skimming. *Time.*—½ to ¾ hour. *Average cost*, 8*d.* per pint. *Sufficient.*—Allow 1 lb. of beef to make 1 pint of good beef-tea.

Note.—The meat left from beef-tea may be boiled a little longer, and pounded with spices, &c., for potting. It makes a very nice breakfast dish.

BEETROOT, Boiled.

Ingredients.—Beetroot; boiling water. *Mode.*—When large, young, and juicy, this vegetable makes a very excellent addition to winter salads, and may easily be converted into an economical and quickly-made pickle. (*See* BEETROOT, PICKLED.) Beetroot is more frequently served cold than hot: when the latter mode is preferred, melted butter should be sent to table with it. It may also be stewed with button onions, or boiled and served with roasted onions. Wash the beets thoroughly; but do not prick or break the skin before they are cooked, as they would lose their beautiful colour in boiling. Put them into boiling water, and let them boil until tender, keeping them well covered. If to be served hot, remove the peel quickly, cut the beetroot into thick slices, and send to table melted butter. For salads, pickle, &c., let the root cool, then peel, and cut it into slices. *Time.*—Small beetroot, 1½ to 2 hours; large, 2½ to 3 hours. *Average cost*, in full season, 2*d.* each. *Seasonable.*—May be had at any time.

BEETROOT, Pickled.

Ingredients.—Sufficient vinegar to cover the beets, 2 oz. of whole pepper, 2 oz. of allspice to each gallon of vinegar. *Mode.*—Wash the beets free from dirt, and be very careful not to prick the outside skin, or they would lose their beautiful colour. Put them into boiling water, let them simmer gently, and when about three parts done, which will be in 1½ hour, take them out and let them cool. Boil the vinegar with pepper and allspice, in the above proportion, for 10 minutes, and when cold, pour it on the beets, which must be peeled and cut into slices about ½ inch thick. Cover with bladder to exclude the air, and in a week they will be fit for use.

BISCUITS, Crisp.

Ingredients.—1 lb. of flour, the yolk of 1 egg, milk. *Mode.*—Mix the flour and the yolk of the egg with sufficient milk to make the whole into a very stiff paste; beat it well, and knead it until it is perfectly smooth. Roll the paste out *very thin*; with a round cutter shape it into small biscuits, and bake them a nice brown in a slow oven from 12 to 18 minutes. *Time.*—12 to 18 minutes. *Average cost*, 4*d.* *Seasonable* at any time.

BISCUITS, Dessert, which may be flavoured with Ground Ginger, Cinnamon, &c.

Ingredients.—1 lb. of flour, ½ lb. of butter, ½ lb. of sifted sugar, the yolks of 6 eggs, flavouring to taste. *Mode.*—Put the butter into a basin; warm it, but do not allow it to oil; then with the hand beat it to a cream. Add the flour by degrees, then the sugar and flavouring, and moisten the whole with the yolks of the eggs, which should previously be well beaten. When all the ingredients are thoroughly incorporated, drop the mixture from a spoon on to a buttered paper, leaving a distance between each cake, for they spread as soon as they begin to get warm. Bake in rather a slow oven from 12 to 18 minutes, and do not let the biscuits acquire too much colour. In making the above quantity, half may be flavoured with ground ginger and the other half with essence of lemon or currants, to make a variety. With whatever the preparation is flavoured, so are the biscuits called, and an endless variety may be made in this manner. *Time.*—12 to 18 minutes, or rather longer, in a very slow oven. *Average cost*, 1*s.* 6*d.*

Sufficient to make from 3 to 4 dozen cakes. *Seasonable* at any time.

BISCUITS, Simple Hard.

Ingredients.—To every lb. of flour allow 2 oz. of butter, about ½ pint of skimmed milk. *Mode.*—Warm the butter in milk until the former is dissolved, and then mix it with the flour into a very stiff paste; beat it with a rolling-pin until the dough looks perfectly smooth. Roll it out thin; cut it with the top of a glass into round biscuits; prick them well, and bake them from 6 to 10 minutes. The above is the proportion of milk which we think would convert the flour into a stiff paste; but should it be found too much, an extra spoonful or two of flour must be put in. These biscuits are very nice for the cheese course. *Time.*—6 to 10 minutes. *Seasonable* at any time.

BLACK-COCK, to Roast.

Ingredients.—Black-cock, butter, toast. *Mode.*—Let these birds hang for a few days, or they will be tough and tasteless, if not well kept. Pluck and draw them, and wipe the insides and outsides with a damp cloth, as washing spoils the flavour. Cut off the heads, and truss them, the same as a roast fowl, cutting off the toes, and scalding and peeling the feet. Trussing them with the head on, as shown in the engraving, is still practised by many cooks, but the former method

ROAST BLACK-COCK.

is now considered the best. Put them down to a brisk fire, well baste them with butter, and serve with a piece of toast under, and a good gravy and bread sauce. After trussing, some cooks cover the breast with vine-leaves and slices of bacon, and then roast them. They should be served in the same manner and with the same accompaniments as with the plainly-roasted birds. *Time.*—45 to 50 minutes. *Average cost,* from 5*s.* to 6*s.* the brace; but seldom bought. *Sufficient,*—2 or 3 for a dish. *Seasonable* from the middle of August to the end of December.

BLACK-COCK, to Carve.

Skilful carving of game undoubtedly adds to the pleasure of the guests at a dinner-table; for game seems pre-eminently to be composed of such delicate limbs and tender flesh that an inapt practitioner appears to more disadvantage when mauling these pretty and favourite dishes, than larger and more robust *pièces de résistance.* This bird is variously served with or without the head on; and, although we do not personally object to the appearance of the head as shown in the woodcut, yet it seems to be more in vogue to serve it without. The carving is not difficult, but should be ele-

BLACK-COCK.

gantly and deftly done. Slices from the breast, cut in the direction of the dotted line from 2 to 1, should be taken off, the merrythought displaced, and the leg and wing removed by running the knife along from 3 to 4, reserving the thigh, which is considered a great delicacy, for the most honoured guests, some of whom may also esteem the brains of this bird.

BLANC-MANGE (a Supper Dish).

Ingredients. — 1 pint of new milk, 1¼ oz. of isinglass, the rind of ½ lemon, ¼ lb. of loaf sugar, 10 bitter almonds, ½ oz. of sweet almonds, 1 pint of cream. *Mode.* — Put the milk into a saucepan, with the isinglass, lemon-rind, and sugar, and let these ingredients stand by the side of the fire until the milk is well flavoured; add the almonds, which should be blanched and pounded in a mortar to a paste, and let the milk just boil up; strain it through a fine sieve or muslin into a jug, add the cream, and stir the mixture occasionally until nearly cold. Let it stand for a few minutes, then pour it into the mould, which should be previously oiled with the purest salad-oil, or dipped in cold water. There will be a sediment at the bottom of the jug, which must not be poured into the mould, as, when turned out, it would very much disfigure the appearance of the blanc-mange. This blanc-mange may be made very much richer by using 1½ pint of cream, and melting the isinglass in ½ pint of boiling water. The flavour may also be very much varied by adding bay-leaves, laurel-leaves, or essence of vanilla, instead of the lemon-rind and almonds. Noyeau, Maraschino, Curaçoa, or any favourite liqueur, added in small proportions, very much enhances

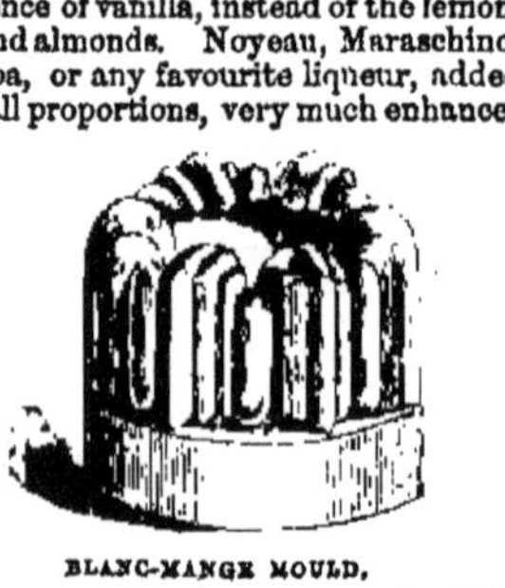

BLANC-MANGE MOULD.

the flavour of this always favourite dish. In turning it out, just loosen the edges of the blanc-mange from the mould, place a dish on it, and turn it quickly over: it should come out easily, and the blanc-mange have a smooth glossy appearance when the mould is oiled, which it frequently has not when it is only dipped in water. It may be garnished as fancy dictates. *Time.*—About 1½ hour to steep the lemon-rind and almonds in the milk. *Average cost*, with cream at 1*s.* per pint, 3*s.* 6*d.* *Sufficient* to fill a quart mould. *Seasonable* at any time.

BLANC-MANGE, Cheap.

Ingredients.—¼ lb. of sugar, 1 quart of milk, 1½ oz. of isinglass, the rind of ½ lemon, 4 laurel-leaves. *Mode.*—Put all the ingredients into a lined saucepan, and boil gently until the isinglass is dissolved; taste it occasionally to ascertain when it is sufficiently flavoured with the laurel-leaves; then take them out, and

BLANC-MANGE.

keep stirring the mixture over the fire for about 10 minutes. Strain it through a fine sieve into a jug, and, when nearly cold, pour it into a well-oiled mould, omitting the sediment at the bottom. Turn it out carefully on a dish, and garnish with preserves, bright jelly, or a compôte of fruit. *Time.*—Altogether, ½ hour. *Average cost*, 8*d.* *Sufficient* to fill a quart mould. *Seasonable* at any time.

BOUDIN à la REINE (an Entrée; M. Ude's Recipe).

Ingredients.—The remains of cold roast fowls, 1 pint of Béchamel, salt and cayenne to taste, egg and bread crumbs. *Mode.*—Take the breasts and nice white meat from the fowls; cut it into small dice of an equal size, and throw them into some good Béchamel (*see* BÉCHAMEL); season with salt and cayenne, and put the mixture into a dish to cool. When this preparation is quite cold, cut it into 2 equal parts, which should be made into boudins of a long shape, the size of the dish they are intended to be served on; roll them in flour, egg and bread-crumb them, and be careful that the ends are well covered with the crumbs, otherwise they will break in the frying-pan; fry them a nice colour, put them before the fire to drain the greasy moisture from them, and serve with the remainder of the Béchamel poured round: this should be thinned with a little stock. *Time.*—10 minutes to fry the boudins. *Average cost*, exclusive of the fowl, 1*s.* 3*d.* *Sufficient* for 1 entrée.

BRAWN, to make.

Ingredients.—To a pig's head weighing 6 lbs. allow 1½ lb. lean beef, 2 tablespoonfuls of salt, 2 teaspoonfuls of pepper, a little cayenne, 6 pounded cloves. *Mode.*—Cut off the cheeks and salt them, unless the head be small, when all may be used. After carefully cleaning the head, put it on in sufficient cold water to cover it, with the beef, and skim it just before it boils. A head weighing 6 lbs. will require boiling from 2 to 3 hours. When sufficiently boiled to come off the bones easily, put it into a hot pan, remove the bones, and chop the meat with a sharp knife before the fire, together with the beef. *It is necessary to do this as quickly as possible to prevent the fat settling in it.* Sprinkle in the seasoning, which should have been previously mixed. Stir it well and put it quickly into a brawn-tin if you have one; if not, a cake-tin or mould will answer the purpose, if the meat is well pressed with weights, which must not be removed for several hours. When quite cold, dip the tin into boiling water for a minute or two, and the preparation will turn out and be fit for use. *Time.*—From 2 to 3 hours. *Average cost,* for a pig's head, 4½*d.* per lb. *Seasonable* from September to March.

Note.—The liquor in which the head was boiled will make good pea soup, and the fat, if skimmed off and boiled in water, and afterwards poured into cold water, answers the purpose of lard.

BREAD-MAKING.

PANIFICATION, or bread-making, consists of the following processes, in the case of Wheaten Flour. Fifty or sixty per cent. of water is added to the flour, with the addition of some leavening matter, and preferably, of yeast from malt and hops. All kinds of leavening matter have, however, been, and are still used in different parts of the world: in the East Indies, "toddy," which is a liquor that flows from the wounded cocoa-nut tree; and in the West Indies, "dunder," or the refuse of the distillation of rum. The dough then undergoes the well-known process called *kneading.* The yeast produces fermentation, a process which may be thus described:—The dough reacting upon the leavening matter introduced, the starch of the flour is transformed into saccharine matter, the saccharine matter being afterwards changed into alcohol and carbonic acid. The dough must be well "bound," and yet allow the escape of the little bubbles of carbonic acid which accompany the fermentation, and which, in their passage, cause the numerous little holes which are seen in light bread.

The yeast must be good and fresh, if the bread is to be digestible and nice. Stale yeast produces, instead of vinous fermentation, an acetous fermentation, which flavours the bread and makes it disagreeable. A poor thin yeast produces an imperfect fermentation, the result being a heavy, unwholesome loaf.

When the dough is well kneaded, it is left to stand for some time, and then, as soon as it begins to swell, it is divided into loaves; after which it is again left to stand, when it once more swells up, and manifests for the last time the symptoms of fermentation. It is then put into the oven, where the water contained in the dough is partly evaporated, and the loaves swell up again, while a yellow crust begins to form upon the surface. When the bread is sufficiently baked, the bottom crust is hard and resonant if struck with the finger, while the crumb is elastic, and rises again after being pressed down with the finger. The bread is, in all probability, baked sufficiently if, on opening the door of the oven, you are met by a cloud of steam, which quickly passes away.

One word as to the unwholesomeness of new bread and hot rolls. When bread is taken out of the oven, it is full of moisture; the starch is held together in masses, and the bread, instead of being crusted so as to expose each grain of starch to the saliva, actually prevents their digestion by being formed by the teeth into leathery poreless masses, which lie on the stomach like so many bullets. Bread should always be at least a day old before it is eaten; and, if properly made, and kept in a *cool dry* place, ought to be perfectly soft and palatable at the end of three or four days. Hot rolls, swimming in melted butter, and new bread, ought to be carefully shunned by everybody who has the slightest respect for that much-injured individual—the Stomach.

AERATED BREAD.—It is not unknown to some of our readers that Dr. Dauglish, of Malvern, has recently patented a process for making bread "light," without the use of leaven. The ordinary process of bread-making by fermentation is tedious, and much labour of human hands is requisite in the kneading, in order that the dough may be thoroughly interpenetrated with the leaven. The new process impregnates the bread, by the application of machinery, with carbonic acid gas, or fixed air. Different opinions are expressed about the bread; but it is curious to note, that, as corn is now reaped by machinery, and dough is baked by machinery, the whole process of bread-making is probably in course of undergoing changes which will emancipate both the housewife and the professional baker from a large amount of labour.

In the production of Aërated Bread, wheaten flour, water, salt, and carbonic acid gas (generated by proper machinery), are the only materials employed. We need not inform our readers that carbonic acid gas is the source of the effervescence, whether in common water coming from a depth, or in lemonade, or any aërated drink. Its action, in the new bread, takes the place of fermentation in the old.

In the patent process, the dough is mixed in a great iron ball, inside which is a system of paddles, perpetually turning, and doing the kneading part of the business. Into this globe the flour is dropped till it is full, and then the common atmospheric air is pumped out, and the pure gas turned on. The gas is followed by the water, which has been aërated for the purpose, and then begins the churning or kneading part of the business.

Of course, it is not long before we have the dough, and very "light" and nice it looks. This is caught in tins, and passed on to the floor of the oven, which is an endless floor, moving slowly through the fire. Done to a turn, the loaves emerge at the other end of the apartment,—and the Aërated Bread is made.

It may be added, that it is a good plan to change one's baker from time to time, and so secure a change in the quality of the bread that is eaten.

MIXED BREADS.—Rye bread is hard of digestion, and requires longer and slower baking than wheaten bread. It is better when made with leaven of wheaten flour rather than yeast, and turns out lighter. It should not be eaten till two days old. It will keep a long time.

A good bread may be made by mixing rye-flour, wheat-flour, and rice-paste, in equal proportions; also by mixing rye, wheat, and barley. In Norway, it is said that they only bake their barley bread once a year, such is its "keeping" quality.

Indian-corn flour mixed with wheat-flour (half with half) makes a nice bread, but it is not considered very digestible, though it keeps well.

Rice cannot be made into bread, nor can potatoes; but one-third potato-flour to three-fourths wheaten flour makes a tolerably good loaf.

A very good bread, better than the ordinary sort, and of a delicious flavour, is said to be produced by adopting the following recipe:—Take ten parts of wheat-flour, five parts of potato-flour, one part of rice-paste; knead together, add the yeast, and bake as usual. This is, of course, cheaper than wheaten bread.

Flour, when freshly ground, is too glutinous to make good bread, and should therefore not be used immediately, but should be kept dry for a few weeks, and stirred occasionally until it becomes

dry, and crumbles easily between the fingers.

Flour should be perfectly dry before being used for bread or cakes; if at all damp, the preparation is sure to be heavy. Before mixing it with the other ingredients, it is a good plan to place it for an hour or two before the fire, until it feels warm and dry.

Yeast from home-brewed beer is generally preferred to any other: it is very bitter, and on that account should be well washed, and put away until the thick mass settles. If it still continues bitter, the process should be repeated; and, before being used, all the water floating at the top must be poured off. German yeast is now very much used, and should be moistened, and thoroughly mixed with the milk or water with which the bread is to be made.

The following observations are extracted from a valuable work on Bread-making, and will be found very useful to our readers:—

The first thing required for making wholesome bread is the utmost cleanliness; the next is the soundness and sweetness of all the ingredients used for it; and, in addition to these, there must be attention and care through the whole process.

An almost certain way of spoiling dough is to leave it half-made, and to allow it to become cold before it is finished. The other most common causes of failure are using yeast which is no longer sweet, or which has been frozen, or has had hot liquid poured over it.

Too small a proportion of yeast, or insufficient time allowed for the dough to rise, will cause the bread to be heavy.

Heavy bread will also most likely be the result of making the dough very hard, and letting it become quite cold, particularly in winter.

If either the sponge or the dough be permitted to overwork itself, that is to say, if the mixing and kneading be neglected when it has reached the proper point for either, sour bread will probably be the consequence in warm weather, and bad bread in any. The goodness will also be endangered by placing it so near the fire as to make any part of it hot, instead of maintaining the gentle and equal degree of heat required for its due fermentation.

MILK OR BUTTER.—Milk which is not

perfectly sweet will not only injure the flavour of the bread, but, in sultry weather, will often cause it to be quite uneatable; yet either of them, if *fresh and good*, will materially improve its quality.

To keep bread sweet and fresh, as soon as it is cold it should be put into a clean earthen pan, with a cover to it: this pan should be placed at a little distance from the ground, to allow a current of air to pass underneath. Some persons prefer keeping bread on clean wooden shelves without being covered, that the crust may not soften. Stale bread may be freshened by warming it through in a gentle oven. Stale pastry, cakes, &c., may also be improved by this method.

The utensils required for making bread on a moderate scale, are a kneading-trough or pan, sufficiently large that the dough may be kneaded freely without throwing the flour over the edges, and also to allow for its rising; a hair sieve for straining yeast, and one or two strong spoons.

Yeast must always be good of its kind, and in a fitting state to produce ready and proper fermentation. Yeast of strong beer or ale produces more effect than that of milder kinds; and the fresher the yeast, the smaller the quantity will be required to raise the dough.

As a general rule, the oven for baking bread should be rather quick, and the heat so regulated as to penetrate the dough without hardening the outside. The oven door should not be opened after the bread is put in until the dough is set, or has become firm, as the cool air admitted, will have an unfavourable effect on it.

Brick ovens are generally considered the best adapted for baking bread: these should be heated with wood faggots, and then swept and mopped out, to cleanse them for the reception of the bread. Iron ovens are more difficult to manage, being apt to burn the surface of the bread before the middle is baked. To remedy this, a few clean bricks should be set at the bottom of the oven, close together, to receive the tins of bread. In many modern stoves the ovens are so much improved that they bake admirably; and they can always be brought to the required temperature, when it is higher than is needed, by leaving the door open for a time.

BREAD, to make good Home-made (Miss Acton's Recipe).

Ingredients.—1 quartern of flour, 1 large tablespoonful of solid brewer's yeast, or nearly 1 oz. of fresh German yeast, 1¼ to 1½ pint of warm milk-and-water. *Mode.*—Put the flour into a large earthenware bowl or deep pan; then, with a strong metal or wooden spoon, hollow out the middle; but do not clear it entirely away from the bottom of the pan, as, in that case, the sponge, or leaven (as it was formerly termed) would stick to it, which it ought not to do.

COTTAGE LOAF.

Next take either a large table-spoonful of brewer's yeast which has been rendered solid by mixing it with plenty of cold water, and letting it afterwards stand to settle for a day and night; or nearly an ounce of German yeast; put it into a large basin, and proceed to mix it, so that it shall be as smooth as cream, with ¾ pint of warm milk-and-water, or with water only; though even a very little milk will much improve the bread. Pour the yeast into the hole made in the flour, and stir into it as much of that which lies round it as will make a thick batter, in which there must be no lumps. Strew plenty of flour on the top, throw a thick clean cloth over, and set it where the air is warm; but do not place it upon

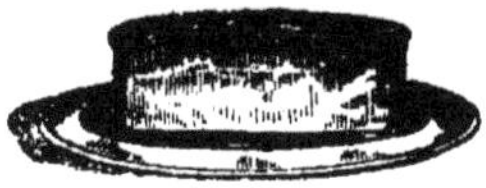

TIN BREAD.

the kitchen fender, for it will become too much heated there. Look at it from time to time: when it has been laid for nearly an hour, and when the yeast has risen and broken through the flour, so that bubbles appear in it, you will know that it is ready to be made up into dough. Then place the pan on a strong chair, or dresser, or table, of convenient height; pour into the sponge the remainder of the warm milk-and-water;

stir into it as much of the flour as you can with the spoon; then wipe it out clean with your fingers, and lay it aside. Next take plenty of the remaining flour, throw it on the top of the leaven, and begin, with the knuckles of both hands, to knead it well. When the flour is nearly all kneaded in, begin to draw the edges of the dough towards the middle, in order to mix the whole thoroughly; and when it is free from flour and lumps and crumbs, and does not stick to the hands when touched, it will be done, and may be covered with the cloth, and left to rise a second time. In ¾ hour look at it, and should it have swollen very much and begin to crack, it will be light enough to bake. Turn it then on to a paste-board or very clean dresser, and with a large sharp knife divide it in two; make it up quickly into loaves, and despatch it to the oven: make one or two incisions across the tops of the loaves, as they will rise more easily if this be done. If baked in tins or pans, rub them with a tiny piece of butter laid on a piece of clean paper, to prevent the dough from sticking to them. All bread should be turned upside down, or on its side, as soon as it is drawn from the oven: if this be neglected, the under part of the loaves will become wet and blistered from the steam, which cannot then escape from them. *To make the dough without setting a sponge*, merely mix the yeast with the greater part of the warm milk-and-water, and wet up the whole of the flour at once after a little salt has been stirred in, proceeding exactly, in every other respect, as in the directions just given. As the dough will *soften* in the rising, it should be made quite firm at first, or it will be too lithe by the time it is ready for the oven. *Time*.—To be left to rise an hour the first time, ¾ hour the second time; to be baked from 1 to 1¼ hour, or baked in one loaf from 1½ to 2 hours.

BREAD, to make a Peck of good.

Ingredients.—3 lbs. of potatoes, 6 pints of cold water, ½ pint of good yeast, a peck of flour, 2 oz. of salt. *Mode*.—Peel and boil the potatoes; beat them to a cream while warm; then add 1 pint of cold water, strain through a colander, and add to it ½ pint of good yeast, which should have been put in water over-night to take off its bitterness. Stir all well together with a wooden spoon, and pour the mixture into the centre of the flour; mix it to the substance of cream, cover it over closely, and let it remain near the fire for an hour; then add the 5 pints of water, milk-warm, with 2 oz. of salt; pour this in, and mix the whole to a nice light dough. Let it remain for about 2 hours; then make it into 7 loaves, and bake for about 1½ hour in a good oven. When baked, the bread should weigh nearly 20 lbs. *Time*.—About 1½ hour.

BREAD-AND-BUTTER FRITTERS.

Ingredients.—Batter, 8 slices of bread and butter, 3 or 4 tablespoonfuls of jam. *Mode*.—Make a batter, the same as for apple fritters; cut some slices of bread and butter, not very thick; spread half of them with any jam that may be preferred, and cover with the other slices; slightly press them together, and cut them out in square, long, or round pieces. Dip them in the batter, and fry in boiling lard for about 10 minutes; drain them before the fire on a piece of blotting-paper or cloth. Dish them, sprinkle over sifted sugar, and serve. *Time*.—About 10 minutes. *Average cost*, 1*s*. *Sufficient* for 4 or 5 persons. *Seasonable* at any time.

BREAD-AND-BUTTER PUDDING, Baked.

Ingredients.—9 thin slices of bread and butter, 1½ pint of milk, 4 eggs, sugar to taste, ¼ lb. of currants, flavouring of vanilla, grated lemon-peel, or nutmeg. *Mode*.—Cut 9 slices of bread and butter, not very thick, and put them into a pie-dish, with currants between each layer, and on the top. Sweeten and flavour the milk, either by infusing a little lemon-peel in it, or by adding a few drops of essence of vanilla; well whisk the eggs, and stir these to the milk. *Strain* this over the bread and butter, and bake in a moderate oven for 1 hour, or rather longer. This pudding may be very much enriched by adding cream, candied peel, or more eggs than stated above. It should not be turned out, but sent to table in the pie-dish, and is better for being made about two hours before it is baked. *Time*.—1 hour, or rather longer. *Average cost*, 9*d*. *Sufficient* for 6 or 7 persons. *Seasonable* at any time.

BREAD CRUMBS, Fried.

Cut the bread into thin slices, place them in a cool oven overnight, and when thoroughly dry and crisp, roll them down into fine crumbs. Put some lard, or clarified dripping, into a frying-pan; bring it to the boiling-point, throw in the crumbs, and fry them very quickly. Directly they are done, lift them out with a slice, and drain them before the fire from all greasy moisture. When quite crisp, they are ready for use. The fat they are fried in should be clear, and the crumbs should not have the slightest appearance or taste of having been, in the least degree, burnt.

BREAD, Fried, for Borders.

Proceed by frying some slices of bread, cut in any fanciful shape, in boiling lard. When quite crisp, dip one side of the sippet into the beaten white of an egg mixed with a little flour, and place it on the edge of the dish. Continue in this manner till the border is completed, arranging the sippets a pale and a dark one alternately.

BREAD, Fried Sippets of, for Garnishing many Dishes.

Cut the bread into thin slices, and stamp them out in whatever shape you like,—rings, crosses, diamonds, &c. &c. Fry them in the same manner as the bread crumbs, in clear boiling lard or clarified dripping, and drain them until thoroughly crisp before the fire. When variety is desired, fry some of a pale colour, and others of a darker hue.

BREAKFASTS.

It will not be necessary to give here a long bill of fare of cold joints, &c., which may be placed on the sideboard, and do duty at the breakfast-table. Suffice it to say, that any cold meat the larder may furnish should be nicely garnished and be placed on the buffet. Collared and potted meats or fish, cold game or poultry, veal-and-ham pies, game-and-rumpsteak pies, are all suitable dishes for the breakfast-table; as also cold ham, tongue, &c. &c.

The following list of hot dishes may perhaps assist our readers in knowing what to provide for the comfortable meal called breakfast. Broiled fish, such as mackerel, whiting, herrings, dried haddocks, &c.; mutton chops and rumpsteaks, broiled sheep's kidneys, kidneys à la maître d'hôtel, sausages, plain rashers of bacon, bacon and poached eggs, ham and poached eggs, omelets, plain boiled eggs, œufs-au-plat, poached eggs on toast, muffins, toast, marmalade, butter, &c. &c.

In the summer, and when they are obtainable, always have a vase of freshly-gathered flowers on the breakfast-table, and, when convenient, a nicely-arranged dish of fruit: when strawberries are in season, these are particularly refreshing; as also grapes, or even currants.

BRILL.

Ingredients.—¼ lb. of salt to each gallon of water; a little vinegar. *Mode.*—Clean the brill, cut off the fins, and rub it over with a little lemon-juice, to preserve its whiteness. Set the fish in sufficient cold water to cover it; throw in salt, in the above proportions, and a little vinegar, and bring it gradually to boil: simmer very gently till the fish is done, which will be in about 10 minutes for a small brill, reckoning from the time the water begins to simmer. It is difficult to give the *exact* number of minutes required for cooking a brill, as the fish varies somewhat in thickness, but the cook can always bear in mind that fish of every description should be *very thoroughly dressed*, and never come to table in the *least degree underdone*. The time for boiling of course depends entirely on the size of the fish. Serve it on a hot napkin, and garnish with cut lemon, parsley, horseradish, and a little lobster coral sprinkled over the fish. Send lobster or shrimp sauce and plain melted butter to table with it. *Time.*—After the water boils, a small brill, 10 minutes; a medium sized brill, 15 to 20 minutes; a large brill, ½ hour. *Average cost*, from 4*s.* to 8*s.*; but when the market is plentifully supplied, may be had from 2*s.* each. *Seasonable* from August to April.

To choose Brill.—The flesh of this fish, like that of turbot, should be of a yellowish tint, and should be chosen on account of its thickness. If the flesh has a bluish tint, it is not good.

A Brill and John Dory are carved in the same manner as a Turbot.

Note.—The thick parts of the middle of the back are the best slices in a tur-

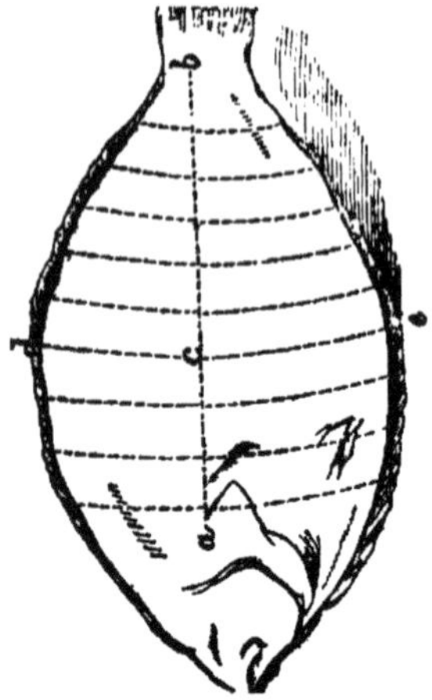

HOW TO CARVE A BRILL.

bot; and the rich gelatinous skin covering the fish, as well as a little of the thick part of the fins, are dainty morsels, and should be placed on each plate.

BROWNING, for Stock.

Ingredients.—2 oz. of powdered sugar, and ½ a pint of water. *Mode.*—Place the sugar in a stewpan over a slow fire until it begins to melt, keeping it stirred with a wooden spoon until it becomes black, when add the water, and let it dissolve. Cork closely, and use a few drops when required.

Note.—In France, burnt onions are made use of for the purpose of browning. As a general rule, the process of browning is to be discouraged, as apt to impart a slightly unpleasant flavour to the stock, and consequently all soups made from it.

BROWNING for Gravies and Sauces.

The browning for stock answers equally well for sauces and gravies, when it is absolutely necessary to colour them in this manner; but where they can be made to look brown by using ketchup, wine, browned flour, tomatoes, or any coloured sauce, it is far preferable. As, however, in cooking so much depends on appearance, perhaps it would be as well for the inexperienced cook to use the artificial means. When no browning is at hand, and you wish to heighten the colour of your gravy, dissolve a lump of sugar in an iron spoon close to a sharp fire; when it is in a liquid state, drop it into the sauce or gravy quite hot. Care, however, must be taken not to put in too much, as it would impart a very disagreeable flavour to the preparation.

BRUSSELS-SPROUTS, Boiled.

Ingredients.—To each ½ gallon of water allow 1 heaped tablespoonful of salt; a *very small* piece of soda. *Mode.*—Clean the sprouts from insects, nicely wash them, and pick off any dead or discoloured leaves from the outsides; put them into a saucepan of *boiling* water, with salt and soda in the above proportion; keep the pan uncovered, and let them boil quickly over a brisk fire until tender; drain, dish, and serve with a tureen of melted butter, or with a maître d'hôtel sauce poured over them. Another mode of serving them is, when they are dished, to stir in about 1½ oz. of butter and a seasoning of pepper and salt. They must, however, be sent to table very quickly, as, being so very small, this vegetable soon cools. Where the cook is very expeditious, this vegetable when cooked may be arranged on the dish in the form of a pineapple, and so served has a very pretty appearance. *Time.*—from 9 to 12 minutes after the water boils. *Average cost*, 1*s*. 4*d*. per peck. *Sufficient.*—Allow between 40 and 50 for 5 or 6 persons. *Seasonable* from November to March.

BUBBLE-AND-SQUEAK.

[COLD MEAT COOKERY.] *Ingredients.*—A few thin slices of cold boiled beef; butter, cabbage, 1 sliced onion, pepper and salt to taste. *Mode.*—Fry the slices of beef gently in a little butter, taking care not to dry them up. Lay them on a flat dish, and cover with fried greens. The greens may be prepared from cabbage sprouts or green savoys. They should be boiled till tender, well drained, minced, and placed, till quite hot, in a frying-pan, with butter, a sliced onion, and seasoning of pepper and salt. When the onion is done, it is ready to serve. *Time.*—Altogether, ½ hour. *Average cost*, exclusive of the cold beef, 3*d*. *Seasonable* at any time.

BULLOCK'S HEART, to Dress a.

Ingredients.—1 heart, stuffing of veal forcemeat. *Mode.*—Put the heart into warm water to soak for 2 hours; then wipe it well with a cloth, and, after cutting off the lobes, stuff the inside with a highly-seasoned forcemeat. Fasten it in, by means of a needle and coarse thread; tie the heart up in paper, and set it before a good fire, being very particular to keep it well basted, or it will eat dry, there being very little of its own fat. Two or three minutes before dishing remove the paper, baste well, and serve with good gravy and red-currant jelly or melted butter. If the heart is very large, it will require 2 hours, and, covered with a caul, may be baked as well as roasted. *Time.*—Large heart, 2 hours. *Average cost*, 2*s*. 6*d*. *Sufficient* for 6 or 8 persons. *Seasonable* all the year.

Note.—This is an excellent family dish, is very savoury, and, though not seen at many good tables, may be recommended for its cheapness and economy.

BUNS, Light.

Ingredients.—½ teaspoonful of tartaric acid, ½ teaspoonful of bicarbonate of soda, 1 lb. of flour, 2 oz. of butter, 2 oz. of loaf sugar, ¼ lb. of currants or raisins,—when liked, a few caraway seeds, ½ pint of cold new milk, 1 egg. *Mode.*—Rub the tartaric acid, soda, and flour all together through a hair sieve; work the butter into the flour; add the sugar, currants,

BUNS.

and caraway seeds, when the flavour of the latter is liked. Mix all these ingredients well together; make a hole in the middle of the flour, and pour in the milk, mixed with the egg, which should be well beaten; mix quickly, and set the dough, with a fork, on baking-tins, and bake the buns for about 20 minutes. This mixture makes a very good cake, and if put into a tin, should be baked 1½ hour. The same quantity of flour, soda, and tartaric acid, with ½ pint of milk and a little salt, will make either bread or teacakes, if wanted quickly. *Time.*—20 minutes for the buns; if made into a cake, 1½ hour. *Sufficient* to make about 12 buns.

BUNS, Plain.

Ingredients.—1 lb. of flour, 6 oz. of good butter, ¼ lb. of sugar, 1 egg, nearly ¼ pint of milk, 2 small teaspoonfuls of baking-powder, a few drops of essence of lemon. *Mode.*—Warm the butter, without oiling it; beat it with a wooden spoon; stir the flour in gradually with the sugar, and mix these ingredients well together. Make the milk lukewarm, beat up with it the yolk of the egg and the essence of lemon, and stir these to the flour, &c. Add the baking-powder, beat the dough well for about 10 minutes, divide it into 24 pieces, put them into buttered tins or cups, and bake in a brisk oven from 20 to 30 minutes. *Time.*—20 to 30 minutes. *Average cost*, 1*s*. *Sufficient* to make 12 buns. *Seasonable* at any time.

BUNS, Victoria.

Ingredients. — 2 oz. of pounded loaf sugar, 1 egg, 1½ oz. of ground rice, 2 oz. of butter, 1½ oz. of currants, a few thin slices of candied-peel, flour. *Mode.* — Whisk the egg, stir in the sugar, and beat these ingredients both together; beat the butter to a cream, stir in the ground rice, currants, and candied-peel, and as much flour as will make it of such a consistency that it may be rolled into 7 or 8 balls. Place these on a buttered tin, and bake them for ½ to ¾ hour. They should be put into the oven immediately or they will become heavy, and the oven should be tolerably brisk. *Time.*—½ to ¾ hour. *Average cost*, 6*d*. *Sufficient* to make 7 or 8 buns. *Seasonable* at any time.

BUTTER, Browned.

Ingredients.—¼ lb. of butter, 1 tablespoonful of minced parsley, 3 tablespoonfuls of vinegar, salt and pepper to taste. *Mode.*—Put the butter into a fryingpan over a nice clear fire, and when it smokes, throw in the parsley, and add the vinegar and seasoning. Let the whole simmer for a minute or two, when it is ready to serve. This is a very good sauce for skate. *Time.*—¼ hour.

BUTTER, Clarified.

Put the butter in a basin before the

fire, and when it melts, stir it round once or twice, and let it settle. Do not strain it unless absolutely necessary, as it causes so much waste. Pour it gently off into a clean dry jar, carefully leaving all sediment behind. Let it cool, and carefully exclude the air by means of a bladder, or piece of wash-leather, tied over. If the butter is salt, it may be washed before melting, when it is to be used for sweet dishes.

BUTTER, Curled.

Tie a strong cloth by two of the corners to an iron hook in the wall; make a knot with the other two ends, so that a stick might pass through. Put the butter into the cloth; twist it tightly over a dish, into which the butter will fall through the knot, so forming small and pretty little strings. The butter may then be garnished with parsley, if to serve with a cheese course; or it may be sent to table plain for breakfast, in an ornamental dish. Squirted butter for garnishing hams, salads, eggs, &c., is made by forming a piece of stiff paper in the shape of a cornet, and squeezing the butter in fine strings from the hole at the bottom. Scooped butter is made by dipping a teaspoon or scooper in warm water, and then scooping the butter quickly and thin. In warm weather, it would not be necessary to heat the spoon.

BUTTER, Fairy.

Ingredients.—The yolks of 2 hard-boiled eggs, 1 tablespoonful of orange-flower water, 2 tablespoonfuls of pounded sugar, ¼ lb. of good fresh butter. *Mode.*—Beat the yolks of the eggs smoothly in a mortar, with the orange-flower water and the sugar, until the whole is reduced to a fine paste; add the butter, and force all through an old but clean cloth by wringing the cloth and squeezing the butter very hard. The butter will then drop on the plate in large and small pieces, according to the holes in the cloth. Plain butter may be done in the same manner, and is very quickly prepared, besides having a very good effect.

BUTTER, to keep Fresh.

Butter may be kept fresh for ten or twelve days by a very simple process. Knead it well in cold water till the buttermilk is extracted; then put it in a glazed jar, which invert in another, putting into the latter a sufficient quantity of water to exclude the air. Renew the water every day.

BUTTER, Maître d'Hôtel, for putting into Broiled Fish just before it is sent to Table.

Ingredients.—¼ lb. of butter, 2 dessert-spoonfuls of minced parsley, salt and pepper to taste, the juice of 1 large lemon. *Mode.*—Work the above ingredients well together, and let them be thoroughly mixed with a wooden spoon. If this is used as a sauce, it may be poured either under or over the meat or fish it is intended to be served with. *Average cost*, for this quantity, *5d.*

Note.—4 tablespoonfuls of Béchamel, 2 do. of white stock, with 2 oz. of the above maître d'hôtel butter stirred into it, and just allowed to simmer for 1 minute, will be found an excellent hot maître d'hôtel sauce.

BUTTER, Melted.

Ingredients.—¼lb. of butter, a dessert-spoonful of flour, 1 wineglassful of water, salt to taste. *Mode.*—Cut the butter up into small pieces, put it into a saucepan, dredge over the flour, and add the water and a seasoning of salt; stir it *one way* constantly till the whole of the ingredients are melted and thoroughly blended. Let it just boil, when it is ready to serve. If the butter is to be melted with cream, use the same quantity as of water, but omit the flour; keep stirring it, but do not allow it to boil. *Time.*—1 minute to simmer. *Average cost* for this quantity, *4d.*

BUTTER, Melted (more Economical).

Ingredients.—2 oz. of butter, 1 dessert-spoonful of flour, salt to taste, ½ pint of water. *Mode.*—Mix the flour and water to a smooth batter, which put into a saucepan. Add the butter and a seasoning of salt, keep stirring *one way* till all the ingredients are melted and perfectly smooth; let the whole boil for a minute or two, and serve. *Time.*—2 minutes to simmer. *Average cost* for this quantity, *2d.*

BUTTER, Rancid, What to do with.

When butter has become very rancid,

it should be melted several times by a moderate heat, with or without the addition of water, and as soon as it has been well kneaded, after the cooling, in order to extract any water it may have retained, it should be put into brown freestone pots, sheltered from the contact of the air. The French often add to it, after it has been melted, a piece of toasted bread, which helps to destroy the tendency of the butter to rancidity.

BUTTER, Melted (the French Sauce Blanche).

Ingredients.—¼ lb. of fresh butter, 1 tablespoonful of flour, salt to taste, ½ gill of water, ½ spoonful of white vinegar, a very little grated nutmeg. *Mode.*—Mix the flour and water to a smooth batter, carefully rubbing down with the back of a spoon any lumps that may appear. Put it in a saucepan with all the other ingredients, and let it thicken on the fire, but do not allow it to boil, lest it should taste of the flour. *Time.*—1 minute to simmer. *Average cost*, 5*d.* for this quantity.

BUTTER, Melted, made with Milk.

Ingredients.—1 teaspoonful of flour, 2 oz. of butter, ⅓ pint of milk, a few grains of salt. *Mode.*—Mix the butter and flour smoothly together on a plate, put it into a lined saucepan, and pour in the milk. Keep stirring it *one way* over a sharp fire; let it boil quickly for a minute or two, and it is ready to serve. This is a very good foundation for onion, lobster, or oyster sauce: using milk instead of water makes it look much whiter and more delicate. *Time.*—Altogether, 10 minutes. *Average cost* for this quantity, 3*d.*

CABBAGE, Boiled.

Ingredients.—To each ½ gallon of water allow 1 heaped tablespoonful of salt; a *very small* piece of soda. *Mode.*—Pick off all the dead outside leaves, cut off as much of the stalk as possible, and cut the cabbages across twice, at the stalk end; if they should be very large, quarter them. Wash them well in cold water, place them in a colander, and drain; then put them into *plenty* of *fast-boiling* water, to which have been added salt and soda in the above proportions. Stir them down once or twice in the water, keep the pan uncovered, and let them boil quickly until tender. The instant they are done, take them up into a colander, place a plate over them, let them thoroughly drain, dish, and serve. *Time.*—Large cabbages, or savoys, ½ to ¾ hour, young summer cabbage, 10 to 12 minutes, after the water boils. *Average cost*, 2*d.* each in full season. *Sufficient.*—2 large ones for 4 or 5 persons. *Seasonable.*—Cabbages and sprouts of various kinds at any time.

CABBAGE, Red, Pickled.

Ingredients.—Red cabbages, salt and water; to each quart of vinegar, ½ oz. of ginger well bruised, 1 oz. of whole black pepper, and, when liked, a little cayenne. *Mode.*—Take off the outside decayed leaves of a nice red cabbage, cut it in quarters, remove the stalks, and cut it across in very thin slices. Lay these on a dish, and strew them plentifully with salt, covering them with another dish. Let them remain for 24 hours, turn into a colander to drain, and, if necessary, wipe lightly with a clean soft cloth. Put them in a jar; boil up the vinegar with spices in the above proportion, and, when cold, pour it over the cabbage. It will be fit for use in a week or two, and, if kept for a very long time, the cabbage is liable to get soft and to discolour. To be really nice and crisp, and of a good red colour, it should be eaten almost immediately after it is made. A little bruised cochineal boiled with the vinegar adds much to the appearance of this pickle. Tie down with bladder, and keep in a dry place. *Seasonable* in July and August, but the pickle will be much more crisp if the frost has just touched the leaves.

CABBAGE, Red, Stewed.

Ingredients.—1 red cabbage, a small slice of ham, ½ oz. of fresh butter, 1 pint of weak stock or broth, 1 gill of vinegar, salt and pepper to taste, 1 tablespoonful of pounded sugar. *Mode.*—Cut the cabbage into very thin slices, put it into a stewpan, with the ham cut in dice, the butter, ½ pint of stock, and the vinegar; cover the pan closely, and let it stew for 1 hour. When it is very tender, add the remainder of the stock, a seasoning of salt and pepper, and the pounded sugar; mix all well together, stir over the fire until nearly all the liquor is dried away, and serve. Fried sausages are usually sent to table with this dish: they should be laid round and on the cabbage, as a garnish. *Time.*—Rather more than 1 hour. *Average cost*, 4*d*. each. *Sufficient* for 4 persons. *Seasonable* from September to January.

CABBAGE SOUP.

Ingredients.—1 large cabbage, 3 carrots, 2 onions, 4 or 5 slices of lean bacon, salt and pepper to taste, 2 quarts of medium stock. *Mode.*—Scald the cabbage, cut it up and drain it. Line the stewpan with the bacon, put in the cabbage, carrots, and onions; moisten with skimmings from the stock, and simmer very gently, till the cabbage is tender; add the stock, stew softly for half an hour, and carefully skim off every particle of fat. Season and serve. *Time.* 1½ hour. *Average cost*, 1*s*. per quart. *Seasonable* in winter. *Sufficient* for 8 persons.

CABINET or CHANCELLOR'S PUDDING.

Ingredients.—1½ oz. of candied peel, 4 oz. of currants, 4 dozen sultanas, a few slices of Savoy cake, sponge cake, a French roll, 4 eggs, 1 pint of milk, grated lemon-rind, ¼ nutmeg, 3 tablespoonfuls of sugar. *Mode.*—Melt some butter to a paste, and with it, well grease the mould or basin in which the pudding is to be boiled, taking care that it is buttered in every part. Cut the peel into thin slices, and place these in a fanciful device at the bottom of the mould, and fill in the spaces between with currants and sultanas; then add a few slices of sponge cake or French roll; drop a few drops of melted butter on these, and between each layer sprinkle a few currants. Proceed in this manner until the mould is nearly full; then flavour the milk with nutmeg and grated lemon-rind; add the sugar, and stir to this the eggs, which should be well beaten. Beat this mixture for a few minutes; then strain it into the mould, which should be quite full; tie a piece of buttered paper over it, and let it stand for two hours; then tie it down with a cloth, put it into

CABINET PUDDING.

boiling water, and let it boil slowly for 1 hour. In taking it up, let it stand for a minute or two before the cloth is removed; then quickly turn it out of the mould or basin, and serve with sweet sauce separately. The flavouring of this pudding may be varied by substituting for the lemond-rind essence of vanilla or bitter almonds; and it may be made much richer by using cream; but this is not at all necessary. *Time.*—1 hour. *Average cost*, 1*s*. 3*d*. *Sufficient* for 5 or 6 persons. *Seasonable* at any time.

CABINET or BOILED BREAD-AND-BUTTER PUDDING, Plain.

Ingredients.—2 oz. of raisins, a few thin slices of bread and butter, 3 eggs, 1 pint of milk, sugar to taste, ¼ nutmeg. *Mode.*—Butter a pudding-basin, and line the inside with a layer of raisins that have been previously stoned; then nearly fill the basin with slices of bread and butter with the crust cut off, and, in another basin, beat the eggs; add to them the milk, sugar, and grated nutmeg; mix all well together, and pour the whole on to the bread and butter; let it stand ½ hour, then tie a floured cloth over it; boil for 1 hour, and serve with sweet sauce. Care must be taken that the basin is quite full before the cloth is tied over. *Time.*—1 hour. *Average cost*, 9*d*. *Sufficient* for 5 or 6 persons. *Seasonable* at any time.

CAFÉ AU LAIT.

This is merely very strong coffee added to a large proportion of good hot milk; about 6 tablespoonfuls of strong coffee being quite sufficient for a breakfast-cupful of milk. Of the essence which answers admirably for *café au lait*, so much would not be required. This preparation is infinitely superior to the weak watery coffee so often served at English tables. A little cream mixed with the milk, if the latter cannot be depended on for richness, improves the taste of the coffee, as also the richness of the beverage. *Sufficient.*—6 tablespoonfuls of strong coffee, or 2 tablespoonfuls of the essence, to a breakfast-cupful of milk.

CAFÉ NOIR.

This is usually handed round after dinner, and should be drunk well sweetened, with the addition of a little brandy or liqueurs, which may be added or not at pleasure. The coffee should be made very strong, and served in very small cups, but never mixed with milk or cream. *Café noir* may be made of the essence of coffee by pouring a tablespoonful into each cup, and filling it up with boiling water. This is a very simple and expeditious manner of preparing coffee for a large party, but the essence for it must be made very good, and kept well corked until required for use.

CAKES, Making and Baking of.

Eggs should always be broken into a cup, the whites and yolks separated, and they should always be strained. Breaking the eggs thus, the bad ones may be easily rejected without spoiling the others, and so cause no waste. As eggs are used instead of yeast, they should be very thoroughly whisked; they are generally sufficiently beaten when thick enough to carry the drop that falls from the whisk.

Loaf Sugar should be well pounded, and then sifted through a fine sieve.

Currants should be nicely washed, picked, dried in a cloth, and then carefully examined, that no pieces of grit or stone may be left amongst them. They should then be laid on a dish before the fire, to become thoroughly dry; as, if added damp to the other ingredients, cakes will be liable to be heavy.

Good Butter should always be used in the manufacture of cakes; and, if beaten to a cream, it saves much time and labour to warm, but not melt, it before beating.

Less butter and eggs are required for cakes when yeast is mixed with the other ingredients.

The heat of the oven is of great importance, especially for large cakes. If the heat be not tolerably fierce, the batter will not rise. If the oven is too quick, and there is any danger of the cake burning or catching, put a sheet of clean paper over the top: newspaper, or paper that has been printed on, should never be used for this purpose.

To know when a cake is sufficiently baked, plunge a clean knife into the middle of it; draw it quickly out, and if it looks in the least sticky put the cake back, and close the oven door until the cake is done.

Cakes should be kept in closed tin canisters or jars, and in a dry place. Those made with yeast do not keep so long as those made without it.

CAKES, nice Breakfast.

Ingredients.—1 lb. of flour, ½ teaspoonful of tartaric acid, ½ teaspoonful of salt, ½ teaspoonful of carbonate of soda, 1½ breakfast-cupful of milk, 1 oz. of sifted loaf sugar, 2 eggs. *Mode.*—These cakes are made in the same manner as the soda bread, with the addition of eggs and sugar. Mix the flour, tartaric acid, and salt well together, taking care that the two latter ingredients are reduced to the finest powder, and stir in the sifted sugar, which should also be very fine. Dissolve the soda in the milk, add the eggs, which should be well whisked, and with this liquid work the flour, &c. into a light dough. Divide it into small cakes, put them into the oven immediately, and bake for about 20 minutes. *Time.*—20 minutes.

CAKE, Christmas.

Ingredients.—5 teacupfuls of flour, 1 teacupful of melted butter, 1 teacupful of cream, 1 teacupful of treacle, 1 teacupful of moist sugar, 2 eggs, ½ oz. of powdered ginger, ½ lb. of raisins, 1 teaspoonful of carbonate of soda, 1 tablespoonful of vinegar. *Mode.*—Make the butter sufficiently warm to melt it, but do not allow it to oil; put the flour into a basin, add to it the sugar, ginger, and raisins, which should be stoned and cut into small pieces. When these dry ingredients are thoroughly mixed, stir in the butter, cream, treacle, and well-whisked eggs, and beat the mixture for a few minutes. Dissolve the soda in the vinegar, add it to the dough, and be particular that these latter ingredients are well incorporated with the others; put the cake into a buttered mould or tin, place it in a moderate oven immediately, and bake it from 1¾ to 2¼ hours. *Time.*—1¾ to 2¼ hours. *Average cost,* 1*s.* 6*d.*

CAKE, Common (suitable for sending to Children at School).

Ingredients.—2 lbs. of flour, 4 oz. of butter or clarified dripping, ½ oz. of caraway seeds, ¼ oz. of allspice, ½ lb. of pounded sugar, 1 lb. of currants, 1 pint of milk, 3 tablespoonfuls of fresh yeast.

Mode.—Rub the butter lightly into the flour; add all the dry ingredients, and mix these well together. Make the milk warm, but not hot; stir in the yeast, and with this liquid mix the whole into a light dough; knead it well, and line the cake-tins with strips of buttered paper: this paper should be about 6 inches higher than the top of the tin. Put in the dough; stand it in a warm place to rise for more than an hour, then bake the cakes in a well-heated oven. If this quantity be divided into two, they will take from 1½ to 2 hours' baking. *Time.*—1½ to 2 hours. *Average cost*, 1*s*. 9*d*. *Sufficient* to make 2 moderate-sized cakes.

CAKE, Economical.

Ingredients.—1 lb. of flour, ¼ lb. of sugar, ¼ lb. of butter or lard, ½ lb. of currants, 1 teaspoonful of carbonate of soda, the whites of 4 eggs, ½ pint of milk. *Mode.*—In making many sweet dishes, the whites of eggs are not required, and if well beaten and added to the above ingredients, make an excellent cake with or without currants. Beat the butter to a cream, well whisk the whites of the eggs, and stir all the ingredients together but the soda, which must not be added until all is well mixed, and the cake is ready to be put into the oven. When the mixture has been well beaten, stir in the soda, put the cake into a buttered mould, and bake it in a moderate oven for 1½ hour. *Time.*—1½ hour. *Average cost*, 1*s*. 3*d*.

CAKE-MOULD.

CAKE, Good Holiday.

Ingredients.—1½*d*. worth of Borwick's German baking-powder, 2 lbs. of flour, 6 oz. of butter, ¼ lb. of lard, 1 lb. of currants, ½ lb. of stoned and cut raisins, ¼ lb. of mixed candied peel, ½ lb. of moist sugar, 3 eggs, ¾ pint of cold milk. *Mode.*—Mix the baking-powder with the flour; then rub in the butter and lard; have ready the currants, washed, picked, and dried, the raisins stoned and cut into small pieces (not chopped), and the peel cut into neat slices. Add these with the sugar to the flour, &c., and mix all the dry ingredients well together. Whisk the eggs, stir to them the milk, and with this liquid moisten the cake; beat it up well, that all may be very thoroughly mixed; line a cake-tin with buttered paper, put in the cake, and bake it from 2¼ to 2¾ hours in a good oven. To ascertain when it is done, plunge a clean knife into the middle of it, and if, on withdrawing it, the knife looks clean, and not sticky, the cake is done. To prevent it burning at the top, a piece of clean paper may be put over whilst the cake is soaking, or being thoroughly cooked in the middle. A steamer, such as is used for steaming potatoes, makes a very good cake-tin, if it be lined at the bottom and sides with buttered paper. *Time.*—2¼ to 2¾ hours. *Average cost*, 2*s*. 6*d*. *Seasonable* at any time.

CAKE, Luncheon.

Ingredients.—½ lb. of butter, 1 lb. of flour, ½ oz. of caraway seeds, ¼ lb. of currants, 6 oz. of moist sugar, 1 oz. of candied peel, 3 eggs, ½ pint of milk, 1 small teaspoonful of carbonate of soda. *Mode.*—Rub the butter into the flour until it is quite fine; add the caraway seeds, currants (which should be nicely washed, picked, and dried), sugar, and candied peel cut into thin slices; mix these well together, and moisten with the eggs, which should be well whisked. Boil the milk, and add to it, whilst boiling, the carbonate of soda, which must be well stirred into it, and, with the milk, mix the other ingredients. Butter a tin, pour the cake into it, and bake it in a moderate oven from 1 to 1½ hour. *Time.*—1 to 1½ hour. *Average cost*, 1*s*. 8*d*. *Seasonable* at any time.

CAKE, a nice useful.

Ingredients.—¼ lb. of butter, 6 oz. of currants, ¼ lb. of sugar, 1 lb. of dried flour, 2 teaspoonfuls of baking-powder, 3 eggs, 1 teacupful of milk, 2 oz. of sweet almonds, 1 oz. of candied peel. *Mode.*—Beat the butter to a cream; wash, pick, and dry the currants; whisk the eggs; blanch and chop the almonds, and cut the peel into neat slices. When all these are ready, mix the dry ingredients together; then add the butter, milk, and eggs, and beat the mixture well for a few minutes. Put the cake into a buttered mould or tin, and bake it for rather more than 1½ hour. The currants and candied peel may be omitted, and a little lemon or almond flavouring substituted for them; made in this manner, the cake will be found very good. *Time.*—Rather more than 1½ hour. *Average cost,* 1s. 9d.

CAKE, a Pavini.

Ingredients.—½ lb. of flour, ½ lb. of ground rice, ½ lb. of raisins stoned and cut into small pieces, ¼ lb. of currants, ¼ lb. of butter, 2 oz. of sweet almonds, ¼ lb. of sifted loaf sugar, ½ nutmeg grated, 1 pint of milk, 1 teaspoonful of carbonate of soda. *Mode.*—Stone and cut the raisins into small pieces; wash, pick, and dry the currants; melt the butter to a cream, but without oiling it; blanch and chop the almonds, and grate the nutmeg. When all these ingredients are thus prepared, mix them well together; make the milk warm, stir in the soda, and with this liquid make the whole into a paste. Butter a mould, rather more than half fill it with the dough, and bake the cake in a moderate oven from 1½ to 2 hours, or less time should it be made into 2 cakes. *Time.*—1½ to 2 hours. *Average cost,* 1s. 8d. *Seasonable* at any time.

CAKE, a nice Plain.

Ingredients.—1 lb. of flour, 1 teaspoonful of Borwick's baking-powder, ¼ lb. of good dripping, 1 teacupful of moist sugar, 3 eggs, 1 breakfast-cupful of milk, 1 oz. of caraway seeds, ½ lb. of currants. *Mode.* Put the flour and the baking-powder into a basin; stir these together; then rub in the dripping, add the sugar, caraway seeds, and currants; whisk the eggs with the milk, and beat all together very thoroughly until the ingredients are well mixed. Butter a tin, put in the cake, and bake it from 1½ to 2 hours. Let the dripping be quite clean before using: to insure this, it is a good plan to clarify it. Beef dripping is better than any other for cakes, &c., as mutton dripping frequently has a very unpleasant flavour, which would be imparted to the preparation. *Time.*—1½ to 2 hours. *Average cost,* 1s. *Seasonable* at any time.

CAKE, a nice Plain, for Children.

Ingredients.—1 quartern of dough, ¼ lb. of moist sugar, ¼ lb. of butter or good beef dripping, ¼ pint of warm milk, ½ grated nutmeg or ½ oz. of caraway seeds. *Mode.*—If you are not in the habit of making bread at home, procure the dough from the baker's, and as soon as it comes in put it into a basin near the fire; cover the basin with a thick cloth, and let the dough remain a little while to rise. In the mean time, beat the butter to a cream, and make the milk warm; and when the dough has risen, mix with it thoroughly all the above ingredients, and knead the cake well for a few minutes. Butter some cake-tins, half fill them, and stand them in a warm place, to allow the dough to rise again. When the tins are three parts full, put the cakes into a good oven, and bake them from 1¾ to 2 hours. A few currants might be substituted for the caraway seeds when the flavour of the latter is disliked. *Time.*—1¾ to 2 hours. *Average cost,* 1s. 2d. *Seasonable* at any time.

CAKE, Queen.

Ingredients.—1 lb. of flour, ½ lb. of butter, ½ lb. of pounded loaf sugar, 3 eggs, 1 teacupful of cream, ½ lb. of currants, 1 teaspoonful of carbonate of soda, essence of lemon, or almonds to taste. *Mode.*—Work the butter to a cream; dredge in the flour, add the sugar and currants, and mix the ingredients well together. Whisk the eggs, mix them with the cream and flavouring, and stir these to the flour; add the carbonate of soda, beat the paste well for 10 minutes, put it into small buttered pans, and bake the cake from ¼ to ½ hour. Grated lemon-rind may be substituted for the lemon and almond flavouring, which will make the cakes equally nice. *Time.*—¼ to ½ hour. *Average cost,* 1s. 9d. *Seasonable* at any time.

CAKE, Saucer, for Tea.

Ingredients.—¼ lb. of flour, ¼ lb. of *tous-les-mois,* ¼ lb. of pounded white sugar, ¼ lb. of butter, 2 eggs, 1 oz. of candied orange or lemon-peel. *Mode.*—Mix the flour and *tous-les-mois* together; add the sugar, the candied peel cut into thin slices, the butter beaten to a cream, and the eggs well whisked. Beat the mixture for 10 minutes, put it into a buttered cake-tin or mould, or, if this is not obtainable, a soup-plate answers the purpose, lined with a piece of buttered paper. Bake the cake in a moderate oven from 1 to 1½ hour, and when cold, put it away in a covered canister. It will remain good some weeks, even if it be cut into slices. *Time.*—1 to 1¼ hour. *Average cost*, 1*s.* *Seasonable* at any time.

CAKES, Scrap.

Ingredients.—2 lbs. of leaf, or the inside fat of a pig; 1½ lb. of flour, ¼ lb. of moist sugar, ½ lb. of currants, 1 oz. of candied lemon-peel, ground allspice to taste. *Mode.*—Cut the leaf, or flead, as it is sometimes called, into small pieces; put it into a large dish, which place in a quick oven; be careful that it does not burn, and in a short time it will be reduced to oil, with the small pieces of leaf floating on the surface; and it is of these that the cakes should be made. Gather all the scraps together, put them into a basin with the flour, and rub them well together. Add the currants, sugar, candied peel, cut into thin slices, and the ground allspice. When all these ingredients are well mixed, moisten with sufficient cold water to make the whole into a nice paste; roll it out thin, cut it into shapes, and bake the cakes in a quick oven from 15 to 20 minutes. These are very economical and wholesome cakes for children, and the lard, melted at home, produced from the flead, is generally better than that you purchase. To prevent the lard from burning, and to insure its being a good colour, it is better to melt it in a jar placed in a saucepan of boiling water; by doing it in this manner, there will be no chance of its discolouring. *Time.*—15 to 20 minutes. *Sufficient* to make 3 or 4 dozen cakes. *Seasonable* from September to March.

CALF.

The manner of cutting up a calf for the English market is to divide the carcase into four quarters, with eleven ribs to each fore quarter; which are again subdivided into joints, as exemplified on the cut.

Hind quarter:—

1. The loin.
2. The chump, consisting of the rump and hock-bone.
3. The fillet.
4. The hock, or hind knuckle.

Fore quarter:—

5. The shoulder.
6. The neck.
7. The breast.
8. The fore knuckle.

The several parts of a moderately-sized well-fed calf, about eight weeks old, are nearly of the following weights:—loin

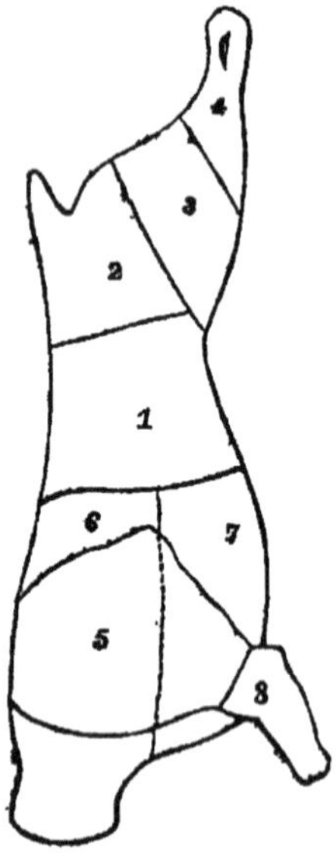

SIDE OF A CALF, SHOWING THE SEVERAL JOINTS.

and chump 18 lbs., fillet 12½ lbs., hind knuckle 5½ lbs., shoulder 11 lbs., neck 11 lbs., breast 9 lbs., and fore knuckle 5 lbs.; making a total of 144 lbs. weight. The London mode of cutting the carcase is considered better than that pursued in Edinburgh, as giving three roasting joints and one boiling in each quarter; besides the pieces being more equally divided, as regards flesh, and from the handsomer appearance they make on the table.

CALF'S FEET, Baked or Stewed.

Ingredients.—1 calf's foot, 1 pint of milk, 1 pint of water, 1 blade of mace, the rind of ½ lemon, pepper and salt to taste. *Mode.* Well clean the foot, and either stew or bake it in the milk-and-water with the other ingredients from 3 to 4 hours. To enhance the flavour, an onion and a small quantity of celery may be added, if approved; ½ a teacupful of cream, stirred in just before serving, is also a great improvement to this dish. *Time.*—3 to 4 hours. *Average cost,* in full season, 9*d.* each. *Sufficient* for 1 person. *Seasonable* from March to October.

CALF'S FEET, Boiled, and Parsley and Butter.

Ingredients.—2 calf's feet, 2 slices of bacon, 2 oz. of butter, two tablespoonfuls of lemon-juice, salt and whole pepper to taste, 1 onion, a bunch of savoury herbs, 4 cloves, 1 blade of mace, water, parsley, and butter. *Mode.*—Procure 2 white calf's feet; bone them as far as the first joint, and put them into warm water to soak for 2 hours. Then put the bacon, butter, lemon-juice, onion, herbs, spices, and seasoning into a stewpan; lay in the feet, and pour in just sufficient water to cover the whole. Stew gently for about three hours; take out the feet, dish them, and cover with parsley and butter. The liquor they were boiled in should be strained and put by in a clean basin for use: it will be found very good as an addition to gravies, &c. *Time.*—Rather more than 3 hours. *Average cost,* in full season, 9*d.* each. *Sufficient* for 4 persons. *Seasonable* from March to October.

CALF'S-FOOT BROTH.

Ingredients.—1 calf's foot, 3 pints of water, 1 small lump of sugar, nutmeg to taste, the yolk of 1 egg, a piece of butter the size of a nut. *Mode.*—Stew the foot in the water with the lemon-peel *very gently,* until the liquid is half wasted, removing any scum, should it rise to the surface. Set it by in a basin until quite cold, then take off every particle of fat. Warm up about ½ pint of the broth, adding the butter, sugar, and a very small quantity of grated nutmeg; take it off the fire for a minute or two, then add the beaten yolk of the egg; keep stirring over the fire until the mixture thickens, but do not allow it to boil again after the egg is added, or it will curdle, and the broth will be spoiled. *Time.*—To be boiled until the liquid is reduced one half. *Average cost,* in full season, 9*d.* each. *Sufficient* to make 1½ pint of broth. *Seasonable* from March to October.

CALF'S FEET, Fricasseed.

Ingredients.—A set of calf's feet; for the batter, allow for each egg 1 tablespoonful of flour, 1 tablespoonful of bread-crumbs, hot lard, or clarified dripping, pepper and salt to taste. *Mode.*—If the feet are purchased uncleaned, dip them into warm water repeatedly, and scrape off the hair, first one foot and then the other, until the skin looks perfectly clean, a saucepan of water being kept by the fire until they are finished. After washing and soaking in cold water, boil them in just sufficient water to cover them, until the bones come easily away. Then pick them out, and after straining the liquor into a clean vessel, put the meat into a pie-dish until the next day. Now cut it down in slices about ½ inch thick, lay on them a stiff batter made of egg, flour, and bread-crumbs in the above proportion; season with pepper and salt, and plunge them into a pan of boiling lard. Fry the slices a nice brown, dry them before the fire for a minute or two, dish them on a napkin, and garnish with tufts of parsley. This should be eaten with melted butter, mustard, and vinegar. Be careful to have the lard boiling to *set* the batter, or the pieces of feet will run about the pan. The liquor they were boiled in should be saved, and will be found useful for enriching gravies, making jellies, &c. *Time.*—About 3 hours to stew the feet, 10 or 15 minutes to fry them. *Average cost,* in full season, 9*d.* each. *Sufficient* for 8 persons. *Seasonable* from March to October.

Note.—This dish can be highly recommended to delicate persons.

CALF'S-FEET JELLY.

Ingredients.—1 quart of calf's-feet stock, ½ lb. sugar, ½ pint of sherry, 1 glass of brandy, the shells and whites of 5 eggs, the rind and juice of 2 lemons, ½ oz. of isinglass. *Mode.*—Prepare the stock as directed in recipe for stock, taking care to leave the sediment, and to remove all the fat from the surface. Put it into a saucepan cold, without clarifying it; add the remaining ingredients, and stir them well together before the saucepan is placed on the fire. Then simmer the mixture gently for ¼ hour, *but do not stir it after it begins to warm.* Throw in a teacupful of cold water, boil for another 5 minutes, and keep the saucepan covered by the side of the fire for about ½ hour, but do not let it boil again. In simmering, the head or scum may be carefully removed as it rises; but particular attention must be given to the jelly, that it be not stirred in the slightest degree after it is heated. The isinglass should be added when the jelly begins to boil: this assists to clear it, and makes it firmer for turning out. Wring out a jelly-bag in hot water; fasten it on to a stand, or the back of a chair; place it near the fire with a basin underneath it, and run the jelly through it. Should it not be perfectly clear the first time, repeat the process until the desired brilliancy is obtained. Soak the moulds

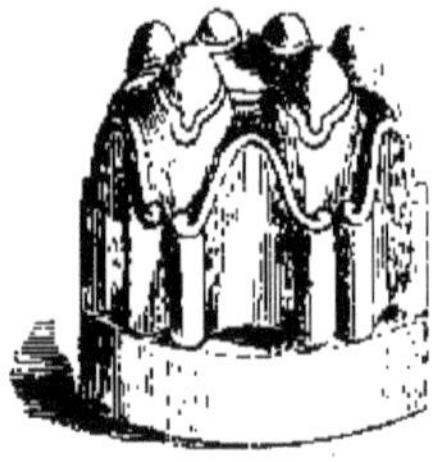

JELLY-MOULD.

in water, drain them for half a second, pour in the jelly, and put it in a cool place to set. If ice is at hand, surround the moulds with it, and the jelly will set sooner, and be firmer when turned out. In summer it is necessary to have ice in which to put the moulds, or the cook will be, very likely, disappointed, by her jellies being in too liquid a state to turn out properly, unless a great deal of isinglass is used. When wanted for table, dip the moulds in hot water for a minute, wipe the outside with a cloth, lay a dish on the top of the mould, turn it quickly over, and the jelly should slip out easily. It is sometimes served broken into square lumps, and piled high in glasses. Earthenware moulds are preferable to those of pewter or tin for red jellies, the colour and transparency of the composition being often spoiled by using the latter. To make this jelly more economically, raisin wine may be substituted for the sherry and brandy, and the stock made from cow-heels, instead of calf's feet. *Time.*—20 minutes to simmer the jelly, ½ hour to stand covered. *Average cost,* reckoning the feet at 6*d.* each, 5*s.* 6*d.* *Sufficient* to fill two 1½-pint moulds. *Seasonable* at any time.

Note.—As lemon-juice, unless carefully strained, is liable to make the jelly muddy, see that it is clear before it is added to the other ingredients. Omit the brandy when the flavour is objected to.

CALF'S HEAD à la Maître d'Hotel.

[COLD MEAT COOKERY.] *Ingredients.*—The remains of a cold calf's head, rather more than ½ pint of maître d'hôtel sauce. *Mode.*—Make the sauce by the given recipe, and have it sufficiently thick that it may nicely cover the meat; remove the bones from the head, and cut the meat into neat slices. When the sauce is ready, lay in the meat; *gradually* warm it through, and, after it boils up, let it simmer very gently for 5 minutes, and serve. *Time.*—Rather more than 1½ hour. *Average cost,* exclusive of the meat, 1*s.* 2*d.* *Seasonable* from March to October.

CALF'S HEAD, Boiled (with the Skin on).

Ingredients. — Calf's head, boiling water, bread crumbs, 1 large bunch of parsley, butter, white pepper and salt to taste, 4 tablespoonfuls of melted butter, 1 tablespoonful of lemon juice, 2 or 3 grains of cayenne. *Mode.*—Put the head into boiling water, and let it remain by the side of the fire for 3 or 4 minutes; take it out, hold it by the ear, and with the back of a knife, scrape off the hair (should it not come off easily, dip the head again into boiling water). When perfectly clean, take the eyes out, cut off the ears, and remove the brain, which soak for an hour in warm water. Put the head into hot water to soak for a few minutes, to make it look white, and then have ready a stewpan, into which lay the head; cover it with cold water, and bring it gradually to boil. Remove the scum, and add a little salt, which assists to throw it up. Simmer it very gently from 2½ to 3 hours, and when nearly done, boil the brains for ¼ hour; skin and chop them, not too finely, and add a tablespoonful of minced parsley which has been previously scalded. Season with pepper and salt, and stir the brains, parsley, &c., into about 4 tablespoonfuls of melted butter; add the lemon-juice and cayenne, and keep these hot by the side of the fire. Take up the head, cut out the tongue, skin it, put it on a small dish with the brains round it; sprinkle over the head a few bread crumbs mixed with a little minced parsley; brown these before the fire, and serve with a tureen of parsley and butter, and either boiled bacon, ham, or pickled pork as an accompaniment. *Time.*—2½ to 3 hours. *Average cost*, according to the season, from 3*s.* to 7*s.* 6*d.* *Sufficient* for 8 or 9 persons. *Seasonable* from March to October.

CALF'S HEAD, Boiled (without the Skin).

Ingredients.—Calf's head, water, a little salt, 4 tablespoonfuls of melted butter, 1 tablespoonful of minced parsley, pepper and salt to taste, 1 tablespoonful of lemon-juice. *Mode.*—After the head has been thoroughly cleaned, and the brains removed, soak it in warm water to blanch it. Lay the brains also into warm water to soak, and let them remain

CALF'S HEAD.

for about an hour. Put the head into a stewpan, with sufficient cold water to cover it, and, when it boils, add a little salt; take off every particle of scum as it rises, and boil the head until perfectly tender. Boil the brains, chop them, and mix with them melted butter, minced parsley, pepper, salt, and lemon-juice in the above proportion. Take up the head,

HALF A CALF'S HEAD.

skin the tongue, and put it on a small dish with the brains round it. Have ready some parsley and butter, smother the head with it, and the remainder send to table in a tureen. Bacon, ham, pickled pork, or a pig's cheek, are indispensable with calf's head. The brains are sometimes chopped with hard-boiled eggs, and

mixed with a little Béchamel or white sauce. *Time.*—From 1½ to 2¼ hours. *Average cost*, according to the season, from 3*s.* to 5*s.* *Sufficient* for 6 or 7 persons. *Seasonable* from March to October.

Note.—The liquor in which the head was boiled should be saved: it makes excellent soup, and will be found a nice addition to gravies, &c. Half a calf's head is as frequently served as a whole one, it being a more convenient-sized joint for a small family. It is cooked in the same manner, and served with the same sauces, as in the preceding recipe.

CALF'S HEAD, Collared.

Ingredients.—A calf's head, 4 tablespoonfuls of minced parsley, 4 blades of pounded mace, ½ teaspoonful of grated nutmeg, white pepper to taste, a few thick slices of ham, the yolks of 6 eggs boiled hard. *Mode.*—Scald the head for a few minutes; take it out of the water, and with a blunt knife scrape off all the hair. Clean it nicely, divide the head and remove the brains. Boil it tender enough to take out the bones, which will be in about 2 hours. When the head is boned, flatten it on the table, sprinkle over it a thick layer of parsley, then a layer of ham, and then the yolks of the eggs cut into thin rings and put a seasoning of pounded mace, nutmeg, and white pepper between each layer; roll the head up in a cloth, and tie it up as tightly as possible. Boil it for 4 hours, and when it is taken out of the pot, place a heavy weight on the top, the same as for other collared meats. Let it remain till cold; then remove the cloth and binding, and it will be ready to serve. *Time.*—Altogether, 6 hours. *Average cost*, 5*s.* to 7*s.* each. *Seasonable* from March to October.

CALF'S HEAD, Fricasseed (an Entrée).

[COLD MEAT COOKERY.] *Ingredients.*—The remains of a boiled calf's head, 1½ pint of the liquor in which the head was boiled, 1 blade of pounded mace, 1 onion minced, a bunch of savoury herbs, salt and white pepper to taste, thickening of butter and flour, the yolks of 2 eggs, 1 tablespoonful of lemon-juice, forcemeat balls. *Mode.*—Remove all the bones from the head, and cut the meat into nice square pieces. Put 1½ pint of the liquor it was boiled in into a saucepan, with mace, onions, herbs, and seasoning in the above proportion: let this simmer gently for ¾ hour, then strain it and put in the meat. When quite hot through, thicken the gravy with a little butter rolled in flour, and, just before dishing the fricassee, put in the beaten yolks of eggs, and lemon-juice; but be particular, after these two latter ingredients are added, that the sauce does not boil, or it will curdle. Garnish with forcemeat balls and curled slices of broiled bacon. To insure the sauce being smooth, it is a good plan to dish the meat first, and then to add the eggs to the gravy: when these are set, the sauce may be poured over the meat. *Time.*—Altogether, 1¼ hour. *Average cost*, exclusive of the meat, 6*d.*

CALF'S HEAD, Hashed.

[COLD MEAT COOKERY.] *Ingredients.*—The remains of a cold boiled calf's head, 1 quart of the liquor in which it was boiled, a faggot of savoury herbs, 1 onion, 1 carrot, a strip of lemon-peel, 2 blades of pounded mace, salt and white pepper to taste, a very little cayenne, rather more than 2 tablespoonfuls of sherry, 1 tablespoonful of lemon-juice, 1 tablespoonful of mushroom ketchup, forcemeat balls. *Mode.*—Cut the meat into neat slices, and put the bones and trimmings into a stewpan with the above proportion of liquor that the head was boiled in. Add a bunch of savoury herbs, 1 onion, 1 carrot, a strip of lemon-peel, and 2 blades of pounded mace, and let these boil for 1 hour, or until the gravy is reduced nearly half. Strain it into a clean stewpan, thicken it with a little butter and flour, and add a flavouring of sherry, lemon-juice, and ketchup, in the above proportion; season with pepper, salt, and a little cayenne; put in the meat, let it *gradually* warm through, but not boil more than *two* or *three* minutes. Garnish the dish with forcemeat balls and pieces of bacon rolled and toasted, placed alternately, and send it to table very hot. *Time.*—Altogether 1½ hour. *Average cost*, exclusive of the remains of the head, 6*d.* *Seasonable* from March to October.

CALF'S HEAD, Moulded.

[COLD MEAT COOKERY.] *Ingredients.*—The remains of a calf's head, some thin slices of ham or bacon, 6 or 8 eggs boiled hard, 1 dessertspoonful of salt, pepper, mixed spice, and parsley, ½ pint of good white gravy. *Mode.*—Cut the head into thin slices. Butter a tin mould, cut the yolks of eggs in half, and put some of them round the tin; sprinkle some of the parsley, spice, &c., over it; then put in the head and the bacon in layers, adding occasionally more eggs and spice till the whole of the head is used. Pour in the gravy, cover the top with a thin paste of flour and water, and bake ¾ of an hour. Take off the paste, and, when cold, turn it out. *Time.*—From ¾ to 1 hour to bake the preparation. *Seasonable* from March to October.

CALF'S HEAD, to Carve.

This is not altogether the most easy-looking dish to cut when it is put before a carver for the first time; there is not much real difficulty in the operation, however, when the head has been attentively examined, and, after the manner of a phrenologist, you get to know its bumps, good and bad. In the first place, inserting the knife quite down to the bone, cut slices in the direction of the line 1 to 2; with each of these should be helped a piece of what is called the throat sweetbread, cut in the direction of from 3 to 4. The eye, and the flesh round, are favourite morsels with many, and should be given to those at the table who are known to be the greatest connoisseurs. The jawbone being removed, there will then be found some nice lean; and the palate, which is reckoned by some a titbit, lies under the head. On a separate dish there is always served the tongue and brains, and each guest should be asked to take some of these.

CALF'S HEAD.

CALF'S LIVER aux Fines Herbes and Sauce Piquante.

Ingredients.—A calf's liver, flour, a bunch of savoury herbs, including parsley; when liked, 2 minced shalots; 1 teaspoonful of flour, 1 tablespoonful of vinegar, 1 tablespoonful of lemon-juice, pepper and salt to taste, ¼ pint water. *Mode.*—Procure a calf's liver as white as possible, and cut it into slices of a good and equal shape. Dip them in flour, and fry them of a good colour in a little butter. When they are done, put them on a dish, which keep hot before the fire. Mince the herbs very fine, put them in the frying-pan with a little more butter; add the remaining ingredients, simmer gently until the herbs are done, and pour over the liver. *Time.*—According to the thickness of the slices, from 5 to 10 minutes. *Average cost,* 10*d.* per lb. *Sufficient* for 7 or 8 persons. *Seasonable* from March to October.

CALF'S LIVER and BACON.

Ingredients.—2 or 3 lbs. of liver, bacon, pepper and salt to taste, a small piece of butter, flour, 2 tablespoonfuls of lemon-juice, ¼ pint of water. *Mode.*—Cut the liver in thin slices, and cut as many slices of bacon as there are of liver; fry the bacon first, and put that on a hot dish before the fire. Fry the liver in the fat which comes from the bacon, after seasoning it with pepper and salt and dredging over it a very little flour. Turn the liver occasionally to prevent its burning, and when done, lay it round the dish with a piece of bacon between each. Pour away the bacon fat, put in a small piece of butter, dredge in a little flour, add the lemon-juice and water, give one boil, and pour it in the *middle* of the dish. It may be garnished with slices of cut lemon, or forcemeat balls. *Time.*—According to the thickness of the slices, from 5 to 10 minutes. *Average cost,* 10*d.* per lb. *Sufficient* for 6 or 7 persons. *Seasonable* from March to October.

CALF'S LIVER, Larded and Roasted (an Entrée).

Ingredients.—A calf's liver, vinegar, 1 onion, 3 or 4 sprigs of parsley and thyme, salt and pepper to taste, 1 bay-leaf, lardoons, brown gravy. *Mode.*—Take a fine white liver, and lard it the same as a fricandeau; put it into vinegar with an onion cut in slices, parsley, thyme, bay-leaf, and seasoning in the above proportion. Let it remain in this pickle for 24 hours, then roast and baste it frequently with the vinegar, &c.; glaze it, serve under it a good brown gravy, or sauce piquante, and send it to table very hot. *Time.*—Rather more than 1 hour. *Average cost,* 10*d.* per lb. *Sufficient* for 7 or 8 persons. *Seasonable* from March to October.

Note.—Calf's liver stuffed with forcemeat (*see* FORCEMEAT), to which has been added a little fat bacon, will be found a very savoury dish. It should be larded or wrapped in buttered paper, and roasted before a clear fire. Brown gravy and currant jelly should be served with it.

CAMP VINEGAR.

Ingredients.—1 head of garlic, ½ oz. cayenne, 2 teaspoonfuls of soy, 2 ditto walnut ketchup, 1 pint of vinegar, cochineal to colour. *Mode.*—Slice the garlic, and put it, with all the above ingredients, into a clean bottle. Let it stand to infuse for a month, when strain it off quite clear, and it will be fit for use. Keep it in small bottles well sealed, to exclude the air. *Average cost for this quantity,* 8*d.*

CANARY PUDDING (very good).

Ingredients.—The weight of 3 eggs in sugar and butter, the weight of 2 eggs in flour, the rind of 1 small lemon, 3 eggs. *Mode.*—Melt the butter to a liquid state, but do not allow it to oil; stir to this the sugar and finely-minced lemon-peel, and gradually dredge in the flour, keeping the mixture well stirred; whisk the eggs; add these to the pudding; beat all the ingredients until thoroughly blended, and put them into a buttered mould or basin; boil for 2 hours, and serve with sweet sauce. *Time.*—2 hours. *Average cost,* 9*d.* *Sufficient* for 4 or 5 persons. *Seasonable* at any time.

CANNELONS, or Fried Puffs (Sweet Entremets).

Ingredients.—½ lb. of puff-paste; apricot, or any kind of preserve that may be preferred; hot lard. *Mode.*—Cannelons, which are made of puff-paste rolled very thin, with jam inclosed, and cut out in long narrow rolls or puffs, make a very pretty and elegant dish. Make some good puff-paste by the recipe given; roll it out very thin, and cut it into pieces of an equal size, about 2 inches wide and 8 inches long; place upon each piece a spoonful of jam, wet the edges with the white of egg, and fold the paste over *twice*; slightly press the edges together, that the jam may not escape in the frying; and when all are prepared, fry them in boiling lard until of a nice brown, letting them remain by the side of the fire after they are coloured, that the paste may be thoroughly done. Drain them before the fire, dish on a d'oyley, sprinkle over them sifted sugar, and serve. These cannelons are very delicious made with fresh instead of preserved fruit, such as strawberries, raspberries, or currants: it should be laid in the paste, plenty of pounded sugar sprinkled over, and folded and fried in the same manner as stated above. *Time.*—About 10 minutes. *Average cost*, 1*s*. *Sufficient.*—½ lb. of paste for a moderate-sized dish of cannelons. *Seasonable*, with jam, at any time.

CAPER SAUCE, for Fish.

Ingredients.—½ pint of melted butter, 3 dessertspoonfuls of capers, 1 dessert-spoonful of their liquor, a small piece of glaze, if at hand (this may be dispensed with), ¼ teaspoonful of salt, ditto of pepper, 1 tablespoonful of anchovy essence. *Mode.*—Cut the capers across once or twice, but do not chop them fine; put them in a saucepan with ½ pint of good melted butter, and add all the other ingredients. Keep stirring the whole until it just simmers, when it is ready to serve. *Time.*—1 minute to simmer. *Average cost* for this quantity, 5*d*. *Sufficient* to serve with a skate, or 2 or 3 slices of salmon.

CAPER SAUCE, for Boiled Mutton.

Ingredients.—½ pint of melted butter, 3 tablespoonfuls of capers or nasturtiums, 1 tablespoonful of their liquor. *Mode.*—Chop the capers twice or thrice, and add them, with their liquor, to ½ pint of melted butter, made very smoothly with milk; keep stirring well; let the sauce just simmer, and serve in a tureen. Pickled nasturtium-pods are fine-flavoured, and by many are eaten in preference to capers. They make an excellent sauce. *Time.*—2 minutes to simmer. *Average cost* for this quantity, 8*d*. *Sufficient* to serve with a leg of mutton.

CAPER SAUCE, a Substitute for.

Ingredients.—½ pint of melted butter, 2 tablespoonfuls of cut parsley, ½ teaspoonful of salt, 1 tablespoonful of vinegar. *Mode.*—Boil the parsley slowly to let it become a bad colour; cut, but do not chop it fine. Add it to ½ pint of smoothly-made melted butter, with salt and vinegar in the above proportions. Boil up and serve. *Time.*—2 minutes to simmer. *Average cost* for this quantity, 3*d*.

CAPSICUMS, Pickled.

Ingredients.—Vinegar, ¼ oz. of pounded mace, and ¼ oz. of grated nutmeg, to each quart; brine. *Mode.*—Gather the pods with the stalks on, before they turn red; slit them down the side with a small-pointed knife, and remove the seeds only; put them in a strong brine for 3 days, changing it every morning; then take them out, lay them on a cloth, with another one over them, until they are perfectly free from moisture. Boil sufficient vinegar to cover them, with mace and nutmeg in the above proportions; put the pods in a jar, pour over the vinegar when cold, and exclude them from the air by means of a wet bladder tied over.

CARP, Baked.

Ingredients.—1 carp, forcemeat, bread crumbs, 1 oz. butter, ½ pint of stock (*see* STOCK), ½ pint of port wine, 6 anchovies, 2 onions sliced, 1 bay-leaf, a faggot of sweet herbs, flour to thicken, the juice of 1 lemon; cayenne and salt to taste; ½ teaspoonful of powdered sugar. *Mode.*—Stuff the carp with a delicate forcemeat, after thoroughly cleansing it, and sew it up, to prevent the stuffing from falling out. Rub it over with an egg, and sprinkle it with bread crumbs, lay it in a deep earthen dish, and drop the butter, oiled, over the bread crumbs. Add the stock, onions, bay-leaf, herbs, wine, and anchovies, and bake for 1 hour. Put 1 oz. of butter into a stewpan, melt it, and dredge in sufficient flour to dry it up; put in the strained liquor from the carp, stir frequently, and when it has boiled, add the lemon-juice and seasoning. Serve the carp on a dish garnished with parsley and cut lemon, and the sauce in a boat. *Time.*—1¼ hour. *Average cost.* Seldom bought. *Seasonable* from March to October. *Sufficient* for 1 or 2 persons.

CARP, Stewed.

Ingredients. — 1 carp, salt, stock, 2 onions, 6 cloves, 12 peppercorns, 1 blade of mace, ½ pint of port wine, the juice of ½ lemon, cayenne and salt to taste, a faggot of savoury herbs. *Mode.*—Scale the fish, clean it nicely, and, if very large, divide it; lay it in the stewpan, after having rubbed a little salt on it, and put in sufficient stock to cover it; add the herbs, onions and spices, and stew gently for 1 hour, or rather more, should it be very large. Dish up the fish with great care, strain the liquor, and add to it the port wine, lemon-juice, and cayenne; give one boil, pour it over the fish, and serve. *Time.* 1¼ hour. *Average cost.* Seldom bought. *Seasonable* from March to October. *Sufficient* for 1 or 2 persons.

Note.—This fish can be boiled plain, and served with parsley and butter. Chub and Char may be cooked in the same manner as the above, as also Dace and Roach.

CARROT JAM, to Imitate Apricot Preserve.

Ingredients.—Carrots; to every lb. of carrot pulp allow 1 lb. of pounded sugar, the grated rind of 1 lemon, the strained juice of 2, 6 chopped bitter almonds, 2 tablespoonfuls of brandy. *Mode.*—Select young carrots; wash and scrape them clean, cut them into round pieces, put them into a saucepan with sufficient water to cover them, and let them simmer, until perfectly soft; then beat them through a sieve. Weigh the pulp, and to every lb. allow the above ingredients. Put the pulp into a preserving-pan with the sugar, and let this boil for 5 minutes, stirring and skimming all the time. When cold, add the lemon-rind and juice, almonds and brandy; mix these well with the jam; then put it into pots, which must be well covered and kept in a dry place. The brandy may be omitted, but the preserve will then not keep: with the brandy it will remain good for months. *Time.*—About ¾ hour to boil the carrots; 5 minutes to simmer the pulp. *Average cost,* 1*s.* 2*d.* for 1 lb. of pulp, with the other ingredients in proportion. *Sufficient* to fill 3 pots. *Seasonable* from July to December.

CARROT PUDDING, Baked or Boiled.

Ingredients.—½ lb. of bread crumbs, 4 oz. suet, ¼ lb. of stoned raisins, ¾ lb. of carrot, ¼ lb. of currants, 3 oz. of sugar, 3 eggs, milk, ¼ nutmeg. *Mode.*—Boil the carrots, until tender enough to mash to a pulp; add the remaining ingredients, and moisten with sufficient milk to make the pudding of the consistency of thick batter. If to be boiled, put the mixture into a buttered basin, tie it down with a cloth, and boil for 2½ hours: if to be baked, put it into a pie-dish, and bake for nearly an hour; turn it out of the dish, strew sifted sugar over it, and serve. *Time.*—2½ hours to boil; 1 hour to bake. *Average cost,* 1*s.* 2*d.* *Sufficient* for 5 or 6 persons. *Seasonable* from September to March.

CARROT SOUP.

Ingredients.—4 quarts of liquor in which a leg of mutton or beef has been boiled, a few beef-bones, 6 large carrots, 2 large onions, 1 turnip; seasoning of salt and pepper to taste; cayenne. *Mode.*—Put the liquor, bones, onions, turnip, pepper, and salt, into a stewpan, and simmer for 3 hours. Scrape and cut the carrots thin, strain the soup on them, and stew them till soft enough to pulp through a hair sieve or coarse cloth; then boil the pulp with the soup, which should be of the consistency of pea-soup. Add cayenne. Pulp only the red part of the carrot, and make this soup the day before it is wanted. *Time.*—4½ hours. *Average cost,* per quart, 1½*d.* *Seasonable* from October to March. *Sufficient* for 8 persons.

CARROT SOUP.

Ingredients.—2 lbs. of carrots, 3 oz. of butter, seasoning to taste of salt and cayenne, 2 quarts of stock or gravy soup. *Mode.*—Scrape and cut out all specks from the carrots, wash, and wipe them dry, and then reduce them into quarter-inch slices. Put the butter into a large stewpan, and when it is melted, add 2 lbs. of the sliced carrots, and let them stew gently for an hour without browning. Add to them the soup, and allow them to simmer till tender,—say for nearly an hour. Press them through a strainer with the soup, and add salt and cayenne if required. Boil the whole gently for 5 minutes, skim well, and serve as hot as possible. *Time* 1¼ hour. *Average cost,* per quart, 1*s.* 1*d.*

CARROTS, Boiled.

Ingredients.—To each ½ gallon of water, allow one heaped tablespoonful of salt; carrots. *Mode.*—Cut off the green tops, wash and scrape the carrots, and should there be any black specks, remove them. If very large, cut them in halves, divide them lengthwise into four pieces, and put them into boiling water, salted in the above proportion; let them boil until tender, which may be ascertained by thrusting a fork into them: dish, and serve very hot. This vegetable is an indispensable accompaniment to boiled beef. When thus served, it is usually boiled with the beef; a few carrots are placed round the dish as a garnish, and the remainder sent to table in a vegetable-dish. Young carrots do not require nearly so much boiling, nor should they be divided: these make a nice addition to stewed veal, &c. *Time.*—Large carrots, 1¾ to 2¼ hours; young ones, about ½ hour. *Average cost*, 6*d.* to 8*d.* per bunch of 18. *Sufficient.*—4 large carrots for 5 or 6 persons. *Seasonable.* — Young carrots from April to July, old ones at any time.

CARROTS, to dress, in the German way.

Ingredients.—8 large carrots, 3 oz. of butter, salt to taste, a very little grated nutmeg, 1 tablespoonful of finely-minced parsley, 1 dessertspoonful of minced onion, rather more than 1 pint of weak stock or broth, 1 tablespoonful of flour. *Mode.*—Wash and scrape the carrots, and cut them into rings of about ¼ inch in thickness. Put the butter into a stewpan; when it is melted, lay in the carrots, with salt, nutmeg, parsley, and onion in the above proportions. Toss the stewpan over the fire for a few minutes, and when the carrots are well saturated with the butter, pour in the stock, and simmer gently until they are nearly tender. Then put into another stewpan a small piece of butter; dredge in about a tablespoonful of flour; stir this over the fire, and when of a nice brown colour, add the liquor that the carrots have been boiling in; let this just boil up, pour it over the carrots in the other stewpan, and let them finish simmering until quite tender. Serve very hot. This vegetable, dressed as above, is a favourite accompaniment to roast pork, sausages, &c., &c. *Time.*—About ¾ hour. *Average cost*, 6*d.* to 8*d.* per bunch of 18. *Sufficient* for 6 or 7 persons. *Seasonable.* — Young carrots from April to July, old ones at any time.

CARROTS, Sliced (Entremets, or to be served with the Second Course, as a Side-Dish).

Ingredients.—5 or 6 large carrots, a large lump of sugar, 1 pint of weak stock, 3 oz. of fresh butter, salt to taste. *Mode.*—Scrape and wash the carrots, cut them into slices of an equal size, and boil them in salt and water until half done; drain them well, put them into a stewpan with the sugar and stock, and let them boil over a brisk fire. When reduced to a glaze, add the fresh butter and a seasoning of salt; shake the stewpan about well, and when the butter is well mixed with the carrots, serve. There should be no sauce in the dish when it comes to table, but it should all adhere to the carrots. *Time.* — Altogether, ¾ hour. *Average cost*, 6*d.* to 8*d.* per bunch of 18. *Sufficient* for 1 dish. *Seasonable.*—Young carrots from April to July, old ones at any time.

CARROTS, Stewed.

Ingredients.—7 or 8 large carrots, 1 teacupful of broth, pepper and salt to taste, ½ teacupful of cream, thickening of butter and flour. *Mode.*—Scrape the carrots nicely; half-boil, and slice them into a stewpan; add the broth, pepper and salt, and cream; simmer till tender, and be careful the carrots are not broken. A few minutes before serving, mix a little flour with about 1 oz. of butter; thicken the gravy with this; let it just boil up, and serve. *Time.*—About ¾ hour to boil the carrots, about 20 minutes to cook them after they are sliced. *Average cost*, 6*d.* to 8*d.* per bunch of 18. *Sufficient* for 5 or 6 persons. *Seasonable.*—Young carrots from April to July, old ones at any time.

CAULIFLOWERS à la SAUCE BLANCHE (Entremets, or Side-dish, to be served with the Second Course).

Ingredients.—3 cauliflowers, ½ pint of sauce blanche, or French melted butter, 3 oz. of butter, salt and water. *Mode.*—Cleanse the cauliflowers as in the succeeding recipe, and cut the stalks off flat at the bottom; boil them until tender in salt and water, to which the above proportion of butter has been added, and be careful to take them up the moment they are done, or they will break, and the appearance of the dish will be spoiled. Drain them well, and dish them in the shape of a large cauliflower. Have ready ½ pint of sauce made by recipe, pour it over the flowers, and serve hot and quickly. *Time.*—Small cauliflowers, 12 to 15 minutes; large ones, 20 to 25 minutes, after the water boils. *Average cost,* large cauliflowers, in full season, 6*d.* each. *Sufficient,* 1 large cauliflower for 3 or 4 persons. *Seasonable* from the beginning of June to the end of September.

CAULIFLOWERS, Boiled.

Ingredients.—To each ½ gallon of water allow 1 heaped tablespoonful of salt. *Mode.*—Choose cauliflowers that are close and white; trim off the decayed outside leaves, and cut the stalk off flat at the bottom. Open the flower a little in places to remove the insects, which are generally found about the stalk, and let the cauliflowers lie in salt and water for an hour previous to dressing them, with their heads downwards: this will effectually draw out all the vermin. Then put them into fast-boiling water, with the addition of salt in the above proportion, and let them boil briskly over a good fire, keeping the saucepan uncovered, and the water well skimmed. When the cauliflowers are tender, take them up with a slice; let them drain, and, if large enough, place them upright in the dish. Serve with plain melted butter, a little of which may be poured over the flower. *Time.*—Small cauliflower 12 to 15 minutes, large one 20 to 25 minutes, after the water boils. *Average cost,* for large cauliflowers, 6*d.* each. *Sufficient.* — Allow 1 large cauliflower for 3 persons. *Seasonable* from the beginning of June to the end of September.

BOILED CAULIFLOWER.

CAULIFLOWERS, with Parmesan Cheese (Entremets, or Side-dish, to be served with the Second Course).

Ingredients.—2 or 3 cauliflowers, rather more than ½ pint of white sauce, 2 tablespoonfuls of grated Parmesan cheese, 2 oz. of fresh butter, 3 tablespoonfuls of bread crumbs. *Mode.*—Cleanse and boil the cauliflowers by the preceding recipe, drain them, and dish them with the flowers standing upright. Have ready the above proportion of white sauce; pour sufficient of it over the cauliflowers just to cover the top; sprinkle over this some rasped Parmesan cheese and bread crumbs, and drop on these the butter, which should be melted, but not oiled. Brown with a salamander, or before the fire, and pour round, but not over, the flowers the remainder of the sauce, with which should be mixed a small quantity of grated Parmesan cheese. *Time.*—Altogether, ½ hour. *Average cost,* for large cauliflowers, 6*d.* each. *Sufficient.*—3 small cauliflowers for 1 dish. *Seasonable* from the beginning of June to the end of September.

CAYENNE CHEESES.

Ingredients.—½ lb. of butter, ½ lb. of flour, ½ lb. of grated cheese, ⅓ teaspoonful of cayenne, ⅓ teaspoonful of salt; water. *Mode.*—Rub the butter in the flour; add the grated cheese, cayenne, and salt, and mix these ingredients well together. Moisten with sufficient water to make the whole into a paste; roll out, and cut into fingers about 4 inches in length. Bake them in a moderate oven a very light colour, and serve very hot. *Time.*—15 to 20 minutes. *Average cost,* 1*s.* 4*d.* *Sufficient* for 6 or 7 persons. *Seasonable* at any time.

CAYENNE VINEGAR, or Essence of Cayenne.

Ingredients.—½ oz. of cayenne pepper, ½ pint of strong spirit, or 1 pint of vinegar. *Mode.*—Put the vinegar, or spirit, into a bottle, with the above proportion of cayenne, and let it steep for a month, when strain off and bottle for use. This is excellent seasoning for soups or sauces, but must be used very sparingly.

CELERY.

With a good heart, and nicely blanched, this vegetable is generally eaten raw, and is usually served with the cheese. Let the roots be washed free from dirt, all the decayed and outside leaves being cut off, preserving as much of the stalk as possible, and all specks or blemishes being carefully removed. Should the celery be large, divide it lengthwise into quarters, and place it, root downwards, in a celery-glass, which should be rather more than half filled with water. The top leaves may be curled, by shredding them in narrow strips with the point of a clean skewer, at a distance of about 4 inches from the top. *Average cost*, 2*d*. per head. *Sufficient*. — Allow 2 heads for 4 or 5 persons. *Seasonable* from October to April.

CELERY, IN GLASS.

Note.—This vegetable is exceedingly useful for flavouring soups, sauces, &c., and makes a very nice addition to winter salad.

CELERY SAUCE, for Boiled Turkey, Poultry, &c.

Ingredients.—6 heads of celery, 1 pint of white stock, 2 blades of mace, 1 small bunch of savoury herbs; thickening of butter and flour, or arrowroot, ½ pint of cream, lemon-juice. *Mode*. —Boil the celery in salt and water until tender, and cut it into pieces 2 inches long. Put the stock into a stewpan with the mace and herbs, and let it simmer for ½ hour to extract their flavour. Then strain the liquor, add the celery, and a thickening of butter kneaded with flour, or, what is still better, with arrowroot; just before serving, put in the cream, boil it up, and squeeze in a little lemon-juice. If necessary, add a seasoning of salt and white pepper. *Time*.—25 minutes to boil the celery. *Average cost*, 1*s*. 3*d*. *Sufficient*, this quantity for a boiled turkey.

Note.—This sauce may be made brown by using gravy instead of white stock, and flavouring it with mushroom ketchup or Harvey's sauce.

CELERY SAUCE (a more simple Recipe).

Ingredients.—4 heads of celery, ½ pint of melted butter made with milk, 1 blade of pounded mace; salt and white pepper to taste. *Mode*.—Wash the celery, boil it in salt and water till tender, and cut

it into pieces 2 inches long; make ½ pint melted butter by recipe; put in the celery, pounded mace, and seasoning; simmer for 3 minutes, when the sauce will be ready to serve. *Time*.—25 minutes to boil the celery. *Average cost*, 6*d*. *Sufficient*, this quantity for a boiled fowl.

CELERY SOUP.

Ingredients.—9 heads of celery, 1 teaspoonful of salt, nutmeg to taste, 1 lump of sugar, ½ pint of strong stock, a pint of cream, and 2 quarts of boiling water. *Mode*.—Cut the celery into small pieces; throw it into the water, seasoned with the nutmeg, salt, and sugar. Boil it till sufficiently tender; pass it through a sieve, add the stock, and simmer it for half an hour. Now put in the cream, bring it to the boiling-point, and serve immediately. *Time*.—1 hour. *Average cost*, 1*s*. per quart. *Seasonable* from September to March. *Sufficient* for 8 persons.

Note.—This soup can be made brown instead of white, by omitting the cream, and colouring it a little. When celery cannot be procured, half a drachm of the seed, finely pounded, will give a flavour to the soup, if put in a quarter of an hour before it is done. A little of the essence of celery will answer the same purpose.

CELERY, Stewed, à la Crême.

Ingredients.—6 heads of celery; to each ½ gallon of water allow 1 heaped tablespoonful of salt, 1 blade of pounded mace, ⅓ pint of cream. *Mode*. —Wash the celery thoroughly; trim, and boil it in salt and water until tender. Put the cream and pounded mace into a stewpan, shake it over the fire until the cream thickens, dish the celery, pour over the sauce, and serve. *Time*.—Large heads of celery, 25 minutes; small ones, 15 to 20 minutes. *Average cost*, 2*d*. per head. *Sufficient* for 5 or 6 persons. *Seasonable* from October to April.

CELERY, Stewed (with White Sauce).

Ingredients.—6 heads of celery, 1 oz. of butter; to each half gallon of water allow 1 heaped teaspoonful of salt, ½ pint of white sauce (*see* WHITE SAUCE). *Mode*. —Have ready sufficient boiling water just to cover the celery, with salt and butter in the above proportion. Wash the celery well, cut off the decayed outside leaves, trim away the green tops, and shape the root into a point; put it into the boiling water, let it boil rapidly until tender, then take it out, drain well, place it upon a dish, and pour over it about ½ pint of white sauce, made by recipe. It may also be plainly boiled as above, placed on toast, and melted butter poured over, the same as asparagus is dished. *Time.*—Large heads of celery 25 minutes, small ones 15 to 20 minutes, after the water boils. *Average cost*, 2*d.* per head. *Sufficient* for 5 or 6 persons. *Seasonable* from October to April.

CELERY, Stewed (with White Sauce).

Ingredients.—6 heads of celery, ½ pint of white stock or weak broth, 4 tablespoonfuls of cream, thickening of butter and flour, 1 blade of pounded mace, a *very little* grated nutmeg; pepper and salt to taste. *Mode.*—Wash the celery, strip off the outer leaves, and cut it into lengths of about 4 inches. Put these into a saucepan, with the broth, and stew till tender, which will be in from 20 to 25 minutes; then add the remaining ingredients, simmer altogether for 4 or 5 minutes, pour into a dish, and serve. It may be garnished with sippets of toasted bread. *Time.*—Altogether, ½ hour. *Average cost*, 2*d.* per head. *Sufficient* for 5 or 6 persons. *Seasonable* from October to April.

Note.—By cutting the celery into smaller pieces, by stewing it a little longer, and, when done, by pressing it through a sieve, the above stew may be converted into a Purée of Celery.

CELERY VINEGAR.

Ingredients.—¼ oz. of celery-seed, 1 pint of vinegar. *Mode.*—Crush the seed by pounding it in a mortar; boil the vinegar, and when cold, pour it to the seed; let it infuse for a fortnight, when strain and bottle off for use. This is frequently used in salads.

CHAMPAGNE-CUP.

Ingredients.—1 quart bottle of champagne, 2 bottles of soda-water, 1 liqueur-glass of brandy or Curaçoa, 2 tablespoonfuls of powdered sugar, 1 lb. of pounded ice, a sprig of green borage. *Mode.*—Put all the ingredients into a silver cup; stir them together, and serve the same as claret-cup. Should the above proportion of sugar not be found sufficient to suit some tastes, increase the quantity. When borage is not easily obtainable, substitute for it a few slices of cucumber-rind. *Seasonable.*—Suitable for pic-nics, balls, weddings, and other festive occasions.

CHARLOTTE-AUX-POMMES.

Ingredients.—A few slices of rather stale bread ½ inch thick, clarified butter, apple marmalade, with about 2 dozen apples, ½ glass of sherry. *Mode.*—Cut a slice of bread the same shape as the bottom of a plain round mould, which has been well buttered, and a few strips the height of the mould, and about 1½ inch wide; dip the bread in clarified butter (or spread it with cold butter, if not wanted quite so rich); place the round piece at the bottom of the mould, and set the narrow strips up the sides of it, overlapping each other a little, that no juice from the apples may escape, and that they may hold firmly to the mould. Brush the *interior* over with the white of egg (this will assist to make the case firmer); fill it with the apple marmalade, with the addition of a little sherry, and cover them with a round piece of bread, also brushed over with egg, the same as the bottom; slightly press the bread down to make it adhere to the other pieces; put a plate on the top, and bake the *charlotte* in a brisk oven, of a light colour. Turn it out on the dish, strew sifted sugar over the top, and pour round it a little melted apricot jam. *Time.*—40 to 50 minutes. *Average cost*, 1*s.* 9*d.* *Sufficient* for 5 or 6 persons. *Seasonable* from July to March.

CHARLOTTE-AUX-POMMES.

CHARLOTTE-AUX-POMMES, an easy method of making.

Ingredients.—½ lb. of flour, ¼ lb. of butter, ¼ lb. of powdered sugar, ½ teaspoonful of baking-powder, 1 egg, milk, 1 glass of raisin-wine, apple marmalade, ¼ pint of cream, 2 dessert-spoonfuls of pounded sugar, 2 tablespoonfuls of lemon-juice. *Mode.*—Make a cake with the flour, butter, sugar, and baking-powder; moisten with the egg and sufficient milk to make it the proper consistency, and bake it in a round tin. When cold, scoop out the middle, leaving a good thickness all round the sides, to prevent them breaking; take some of the scooped-out pieces, which should be trimmed into neat slices; lay them in the cake, and pour over sufficient raisin-wine, with the addition of a little brandy, if approved, to soak them well. Have ready some apple marmalade, made by recipe; place a layer of this over the soaked cake, then a layer of cake and a layer of apples; whip the cream to a froth, mixing with it the sugar and lemon-juice; pile it on the top of the *charlotte*, and garnish it with pieces of clear apple jelly. This dish is served cold, but may be eaten hot by omitting the cream, and merely garnishing the top with bright jelly just before it is sent to table. *Time.*—1 hour to bake the cake. *Average cost*, 2*s.* *Sufficient* for 5 or 6 persons. *Seasonable* from July to March.

CHARLOTTE, Russe (an elegant Sweet Entremet).

Ingredients.—About 18 Savoy biscuits, ¾ pint of cream, flavouring of vanilla, liqueurs, or wine, 1 tablespoonful of pounded sugar, ½ oz. of isinglass. *Mode.* Procure about 18 Savoy biscuits, or ladies'-fingers, as they are sometimes called; brush the edges of them with the white of an egg, and line the bottom of a plain round mould, placing them like a star or rosette. Stand them upright all round the edge, carefully put them so closely together that the white of egg connects them firmly, and place this case in the oven for about 5 minutes, just to dry the egg. Whisk the cream to a stiff froth, with the sugar, flavouring, and melted isinglass; fill the charlotte with it, cover with a slice of sponge-cake cut in the shape of the mould; place it in ice, where let it remain till ready for table; then turn it on a dish, remove the mould, and serve. 1 tablespoonful of liqueur of any kind, or 4 tablespoonfuls of wine, would nicely flavour the above proportion of cream. For arranging the biscuits in the mould, cut them to the shape required, so that they fit in nicely, and level them with the mould at the top, that, when turned out, there may be something firm to rest upon. Great care and attention is required in the turning out of this dish, that the cream does not burst the case; and the edges of the biscuits must have the smallest quantity of egg brushed over them, or it would stick to the mould, and so prevent the charlotte from coming away properly. *Time.* —5 minutes in the oven. *Average cost*, with cream at 1*s.* per pint, 2*s.* 6*d.* *Sufficient* for 1 charlotte. *Seasonable* at any time.

CHEESE.

Cheese is the curd formed from milk by artificial coagulation, pressed and dried for use. Curd, called also casein and caseous matter, or the basis of cheese, exists in the milk, and not in the cream, and requires only to be separated by coagulation: the coagulation, however, supposes some alteration of the curd. By means of the substance employed to coagulate it, it is rendered insoluble in water. When the curd is freed from the whey, kneaded and pressed to expel it entirely, it becomes cheese; this assumes a degree of transparency, and possesses many of the properties of coagulated albumen. If it be well dried, it does not change by exposure to the air; but if it contain moisture, it soon putrefies; it therefore requires some salt to preserve it, and this acts likewise as a kind of seasoning. All our cheese is coloured more or less, except that made from skim milk. The colouring substances employed are arnatto, turmeric, or marigold, all perfectly harmless unless they are adulterated; and it is said that arnatto sometimes contains red lead.

Cheese varies in quality and richness according to the materials of which it is composed. It is made—1. Of entire milk, as in Cheshire; 2. of milk and cream, as at Stilton; 3. of new milk mixed with skim milk, as in Gloucestershire; 4. of skimmed milk only, as in Suffolk, Holland, and Italy.

The principal varieties of cheese used in England are the following: *Cheshire cheese*, famed all over Europe for its rich quality and fine piquante flavour. It is made of entire new milk, the cream not being taken off. *Gloucester cheese* is much milder in its taste than the Cheshire. There are two kinds of Gloucester cheese, single and double:—*Single Gloucester* is made of skimmed milk, or of the milk deprived of half the cream; *Double Gloucester* is a cheese that pleases almost every palate: it is made of the whole milk and cream. *Stilton cheese* is made by adding the cream of one day to the entire milk of the next: it was first made at Stilton, in Leicestershire. *Sage cheese* is so called from the practice of colouring some curd with bruised sage, marigold-leaves, and parsley, and mixing this with some uncoloured curd. With the Romans, and during the middle ages, this practice was extensively adopted. *Cheddar cheese* much resembles Parmesan. It has a very agreeable taste and flavour, and has a spongy appearance. *Brickbat cheese* has nothing remarkable except its form. It is made by turning with rennet a mixture of cream and new milk; the curd is put into a wooden vessel the shape of a brick, and is then pressed and dried in the usual way. *Dunlop cheese* has a peculiarly mild and rich taste: the best is made entirely from new milk. *New cheese* (as it is called in London) is made chiefly in Lincolnshire, and is either made of all cream, or, like Stilton, by adding the cream of one day's milking to the milk that comes immediately from the cow: they are extremely thin, and are compressed gently two or three times, turned for a few days, and then eaten new with radishes, salad, &c. *Skimmed Milk cheese* is made for sea voyages principally. *Parmesan cheese* is made in Parma and Piacenza. It is the most celebrated of all cheese: it is made entirely of skimmed cows' milk; the high flavour which it has is supposed to be owing to the rich herbage of the meadows of the Po, where the cows are pastured. The best Parmesan is kept for three or four years, and none is carried to market till it is at least six months old. *Dutch cheese* derives its peculiar pungent taste from the practice adopted in Holland of coagulating the milk with muriatic acid instead of rennet. *Swiss cheeses*, in their several varieties, are all remarkable for their fine flavour; that from *Gruyère*, a bailiwick in the canton of Fribourg, is best known in England; it is flavoured by the dried herb of *Melilotos officinalis* in powder. Cheese from milk and potatoes is manufactured in Thuringia and Saxony. *Cream cheese*, although so called, is not properly cheese, but is nothing more than cream dried sufficiently to be cut with a knife.

CHEESE.

In families where much cheese is consumed, and it is bought in large quantities, a piece from the whole cheese should be cut, the larger quantity spread with a thickly-buttered sheet of white paper, and the outside occasionally wiped. To keep cheeses moist that are in daily use, when they come from table a damp cloth should be wrapped round them, and the cheese put into a pan with a cover to it, in a cool but not very dry place. To ripen cheeses, and bring them forward, put them into a damp cellar; and to check too large a production of mites, spirits may be poured into the parts affected. Pieces of cheese which are too near the rind, or too dry to put on table, may be made into Welsh rarebits, or grated down and mixed with macaroni. Cheeses may be preserved in a perfect state for years, by covering them with parchment made pliable by soaking in water, or by rubbing them over with a coating of melted fat. The cheeses selected should be free from cracks or bruises of any kind.

CHEESE, Mode of Serving.

The usual mode of serving cheese at good tables is to cut a small quantity of it into neat square pieces, and to put them into a glass cheese-dish, this dish being handed round. Should the cheese crumble much, of course this method is rather wasteful, and it may then be put on the table in the piece, and the host may cut from it. When served thus, the cheese must always be carefully scraped, and laid on a white d'oyley or napkin, neatly folded. Cream cheese is often served in a cheese course, and, sometimes, grated Parmesan: the latter should be put into a covered glass dish. Rusks, cheese-biscuits, pats or slices of butter, and salad, cucumber, or water-cresses, should always form part of a cheese-course.

CHEESE-GLASS.

CHEESE, Pounded.

Ingredients.—To every lb. of cheese allow 3 oz. of fresh butter. *Mode.*—To pound cheese is an economical way of using it if it has become dry; it is exceedingly good spread on bread, and is the best way of eating it for those whose digestion is weak. Cut up the cheese into small pieces, and pound it smoothly in a mortar, adding butter in the above proportion. Press it down into a jar, cover with clarified butter, and it will keep for several days. The flavour may be very much increased by adding mixed mustard (about a teaspoonful to every lb.), or cayenne, or pounded mace. Curry-powder is also not unfrequently mixed with it.

CHEESE, Toasted, or Scotch Rarebit.

Ingredients. — A few slices of rich cheese, toast, mustard, and pepper. *Mode.*—Cut some nice rich sound cheese into rather thin slices; melt it in a cheese-toaster on a hot plate or over steam, and, when melted, add a small quantity of mixed mustard and a seasoning of pepper; stir the cheese until it is completely dissolved, then brown it before the fire, or with a salamander. Fill the bottom of the cheese-toaster with hot water, and serve with dry or buttered toasts, whichever may be preferred. Our engraving illustrates a cheese-toaster with hot-water reservoir: the cheese is melted in the upper tin, which is placed in another vessel of boiling water, so keeping the preparation beautifully hot. A small quantity of porter, or port wine, is sometimes mixed with the cheese; and, if it be not very rich, a few pieces of butter may be mixed with it to great advantage. Sometimes the melted cheese is spread on the toasts, and then laid in the cheese-dish at the top of the hot water. Whichever way it is served, it is highly necessary that the mixture be very hot, and very quickly sent to table, or it will be worthless. *Time.*—About 5 minutes to melt the cheese. *Average cost,* 1½*d.* per slice. *Sufficient.*—Allow a slice to each person. *Seasonable* at any time.

HOT-WATER CHEESE-DISH.

CHEESE, Toasted, or Welsh Rarebit.

Ingredients.—Slices of bread, butter, Cheshire or Gloucester cheese, mustard, and pepper. *Mode.*—Cut the bread into slices about ½ inch in thickness; pare off the crust, toast the bread slightly without hardening or burning it, and spread it with butter. Cut some slices, not quite so large as the bread, from a good rich fat cheese; lay them on the toasted bread in a cheese-toaster; be careful that the cheese does not burn, and let it be equally melted. Spread over the top a little made mustard and a seasoning of pepper, and serve very hot, with very hot plates. To facilitate the melting of the cheese, it may be cut into thin flakes, or toasted on one side before it is laid on the bread. As it is so essential to send this dish hot to table, it is a good plan to melt the cheese in small round silver or metal pans, and to send these pans to table, allowing one for each guest. Slices of dry or buttered toast should always accompany them, with mustard, pepper, and salt. *Time.*—About 5 minutes to melt the cheese. *Average cost,* 1½*d.* per slice. *Sufficient.*—Allow a slice to each person. *Seasonable* at any time.

Note.—Should the cheese be dry, a little butter mixed with it will be an improvement.

CHEESE SANDWICHES.

Ingredients. —Slices of brown bread-and-butter, thin slices of cheese. *Mode.* —Cut from a nice fat Cheshire, or any good rich cheese, some slices about ½ inch thick, and place them between some slices of brown bread-and-butter, like sandwiches. Place them on a plate in the oven, and, when the bread is toasted, serve on a napkin very hot and very quickly. *Time.*—10 minutes in a brisk oven. *Average cost,* 1½*d.* each sandwich. *Sufficient.*—Allow a sandwich for each person. *Seasonable* at any time.

CHEESECAKES.

Ingredients.—8 oz. of pressed curds, 2 oz. of ratafias, 6 oz. of sugar, 2 oz. of butter, the yolks of 6 eggs, nutmegs, salt, rind of 2 oranges or lemons. *Mode.* —Rub the sugar on the orange or lemon rind, and scrape it off. Press the curd in a napkin, to get rid of moisture; pound it thoroughly in a mortar with the other ingredients till the whole becomes a soft paste. Line 2 dozen, or more, tartlet-pans with good puff-paste, garnish these with the cheese-custard, place a strip of candied-peel on the top of each, and bake in a moderate oven a light colour; when done, shake a little sifted sugar over them. Currants, dried cherries, sultanas, and citron may be used instead of candied-peel. *Time.*—20 minutes to bake. *Average cost*, 6*d.* per dozen. *Seasonable* at any time.

CHEROKEE, or Store Sauce.

Ingredients.—½ oz. of cayenne pepper, 5 cloves of garlic, 2 tablespoonfuls of soy, 1 tablespoonful of walnut ketchup, 1 pint of vinegar. *Mode.*—Boil all the ingredients *gently* for about ½ hour; strain the liquor, and bottle off for use. *Time.*—½ hour. *Seasonable.*—This sauce can be made at any time.

CHERRIES, Dried.

Cherries may be put into a slow oven and thoroughly dried before they begin to change colour; they should then be taken out of the oven, tied in bunches, and stored away in a dry place. In the winter, they may be cooked with sugar for dessert, the same as Normandy pippins. Particular care must be taken that the oven be not too hot. Another method of drying cherries is to stone them, and to put them into a preserving-pan, with plenty of loaf sugar strewed amongst them. They should be simmered till the fruit shrivels, when they should be strained from the juice. The cherries should then be placed in an oven cool enough to dry without baking them. About 5 oz. of sugar would be required for 1 lb. of cherries, and the same syrup may be used again to do another quantity of fruit.

CHERRIES, Morello, to Preserve.

Ingredients.—To every lb. of cherries allow 1¼ lb. of sugar, 1 gill of water. *Mode.*—Select ripe cherries, pick off the stalks, and reject all that have any blemishes. Boil the sugar and water together for 5 minutes; put in the cherries, and boil them for 10 minutes, removing the scum as it rises. Then turn the fruit, &c., into a pan, and let it remain until the next day, when boil it all again for another 10 minutes, and, if necessary, skim well. Put the cherries into small pots, pour over them the syrup, and, when cold, cover down with oiled papers, and the tops of the jars with tissue-paper brushed over on both sides with the white of an egg, and keep in a dry place. *Time.*—Altogether, 25 minutes to boil. *Average cost*, from 8*d.* to 10*d.* per lb. pot. *Seasonable.*—Make this in July or August.

CHERRIES, to Preserve in Syrup (very delicious).

Ingredients.—4 lbs. of cherries, 3 lbs. of sugar, 1 pint of white-currant juice. *Mode.*—Let the cherries be as clear and as transparent as possible, and perfectly ripe; pick off the stalks, and remove the stones, damaging the fruit as little as you can. Make a syrup with the above proportion of sugar, mix the cherries with it, and boil them for about 15 minutes, carefully skimming them; turn them gently into a pan, and let them remain till the next day, then drain the cherries on a sieve, and put the syrup and white-currant juice into the preserving-pan again. Boil these together until the syrup is somewhat reduced and rather thick, then put in the cherries, and let them boil for about 5 minutes; take them off the fire, skim the syrup, put the cherries into small pots or wide-mouthed bottles; pour the syrup over, and, when quite cold, tie them down carefully, so that the air is quite excluded. *Time.*—15 minutes to boil the cherries in the syrup; 10 minutes to boil the syrup and currant-juice; 5 minutes to boil the cherries the second time. *Average cost* for this quantity, 3*s.* 6*d.* *Seasonable.*—Make this in July or August.

CHERRY BRANDY, to make.

Ingredients. — Morello cherries, good brandy; to every lb. of cherries allow 3 oz. of pounded sugar. *Mode.*—Have ready some glass bottles, which must be perfectly dry. Ascertain that the cherries are not too ripe and are freshly gathered, and cut off about half of the stalks. Put them into the bottles, with the above proportion of sugar to every lb. of fruit; strew this in between the cherries, and, when the bottles are nearly full, pour in sufficient brandy to reach just below the cork. A few peach or apricot kernels will add much to their flavour, or a few blanched bitter almonds. Put corks or bungs into the bottles, tie over them a piece of bladder, and store away in a dry place. The cherries will be fit to eat in 2 or 3 months, and will remain good for years. They are liable to shrivel and become tough if too much sugar be added to them. *Average cost*, 1*s.* to 1*s.* 6*d.* per lb. *Sufficient*.—1 lb. of cherries and about a ¼ pint of brandy for a quart bottle. *Seasonable* in August and September.

CHERRY JAM.

Ingredients. — To every lb. of fruit, weighed before stoning, allow ½ lb. of sugar; to every 6 lbs. of fruit allow 1 pint of red-currant juice, and to every pint of juice 1 lb. of sugar. *Mode*.—Weigh the fruit before stoning, and allow half the weight of sugar; stone the cherries, and boil them in a preserving-pan until nearly all the juice is dried up, then add the sugar, which should be crushed to powder, and the currant-juice, allowing 1 pint to every 6 lbs. of cherries (original weight), and 1 lb. of sugar to every pint of juice. Boil all together until it jellies, which will be in from 20 minutes to ½ hour; skim the jam well, keep it well stirred, and, a few minutes before it is done, crack some of the stones, and add the kernels: these impart a very delicious flavour to the jam. *Time*.—According to the quality of the cherries, from ¾ to 1 hour to boil them; 20 minutes to ½ hour with the sugar. *Average cost*, from 7*d.* to 8*d.* per lb. pot. *Sufficient*.—1 pint of fruit for a lb. pot of jam. *Seasonable*.—Make this in July or August.

CHERRY SAUCE, for Sweet Puddings (German Recipe).

Ingredients.—1 lb. of cherries, 1 tablespoonful of flour, 1 oz. of butter, ½ pint of water, 1 wineglassful of port wine, a little grated lemon-rind, 4 pounded cloves, 2 tablespoonfuls of lemon-juice, sugar to taste. *Mode*.—Stone the cherries, and pound the kernels in a mortar to a smooth paste; put the butter and flour into a saucepan, stir them over the fire until of a pale brown, then add the cherries, the pounded kernels, the wine, and the water. Simmer these gently for ¼ hour, or until the cherries are quite cooked, and rub the whole through a hair sieve; add the remaining ingredients, let the sauce boil for another 5 minutes, and serve. This is a delicious sauce to serve with boiled batter pudding, and when thus used, should be sent to table poured over the pudding. *Time*.—20 minutes to ½ hour. *Average cost*, 1*s.* 2*d.* *Sufficient* for 4 or 5 persons. *Seasonable* in June, July, and August.

CHERRY TART.

Ingredients.—1½ lb. of cherries, 2 small tablespoonfuls of moist sugar, ½ lb. of short crust. *Mode*.—Pick the stalks from the cherries, put them, with the sugar, into a *deep* pie-dish just capable of holding them, with a small cup placed upside down in the midst of them. Make a short crust with ½ lb. of flour, by either of the recipes for short crust, lay a border round the edge of the dish, put on the cover, and ornament the edges; bake in a brisk oven from ½ hour to 40 minutes; strew finely-sifted sugar over, and serve hot or cold, although the latter is the more usual mode. It is more economical to make two or three tarts at one time, as the trimmings from one tart answer for lining the edges of the dish for another, and so much paste is not required as when they are made singly. Unless for family use, never make fruit pies in very *large* dishes; select them, however, as *deep* as possible. *Time*.—½ hour to 40 minutes. *Average cost*, in full season, 8*d.* *Sufficient* for 5 or 6 persons. *Seasonable* in June, July, and August.

Note.—A few currants added to the cherries will be found to impart a nice piquante taste to them.

CHESTNUT SAUCE, Brown.

Ingredients.—½ lb. of chestnuts, ½ pint of stock, 2 lumps of sugar, 4 tablespoonfuls of Spanish sauce (*see* SAUCES). *Mode*.—Prepare the chestnuts as in the succeeding recipe, by scalding and peeling them; put them in a stewpan with the stock and sugar, and simmer them till tender. When done, add Spanish sauce in the above proportion, and rub the whole through a tammy. Keep this sauce rather liquid, as it is liable to thicken. *Time*.—1½ hour to simmer the chestnuts. *Average cost*, 8*d.*

CHESTNUT SAUCE, for Fowls or Turkey.

Ingredients.—½ lb. of chestnuts, ½ pint of white stock, 2 strips of lemon-peel, cayenne to taste, ¼ pint of cream or milk. *Mode*.—Peel off the outside skin of the chestnuts, and put them into boiling water for a few minutes; take off the thin inside peel, and put them into a saucepan with the white stock and lemon-peel, and let them simmer for 1½ hour, or until the chestnuts are quite tender. Rub the whole through a hair-sieve with a wooden spoon; add seasoning and the cream; let it just simmer, but not boil, and keep stirring all the time. Serve very hot, and quickly. If milk is used instead of cream, a very small quantity of thickening may be required: that, of course, the cook will determine. *Time.*—Altogether, nearly 2 hours. *Average cost,* 8d. *Sufficient,* this quantity for a turkey.

CHESTNUT (Spanish) SOUP.

Ingredients.—¾ lb. of Spanish chestnuts, ¼ pint of cream; seasoning to taste of salt, cayenne, and mace; 1 quart of stock. *Mode.*—Take the outer rind from the chestnuts, and put them into a large pan of warm water. As soon as this becomes too hot for the fingers to remain in it, take out the chestnuts, peel them quickly, and immerse them in cold water, and wipe and weigh them. Now cover them with good stock, and stew them gently for rather more than ¾ of an hour, or until they break when touched with a fork; then drain, pound, and rub them through a fine sieve reversed; add sufficient stock, mace, cayenne, and salt, and stir it often until it boils, and put in the cream. The stock in which the chestnuts are boiled can be used for the soup, when its sweetness is not objected to, or it may, in part, be added to it; and the rule is, that ¾ lb. of chestnuts should be given to each quart of soup. *Time.*—Rather more than 1 hour. *Average cost,* per quart, 1*s.* 6*d.* *Sufficient* for 4 persons. *Seasonable* from October to February.

CHICKENS, Boiled.

Ingredients.—A pair of chickens, water. *Choosing and Trussing.*—In choosing fowls for boiling, it should be borne in mind that those which are not black-legged are generally much whiter when dressed. Pick, draw, singe, wash, and truss them in the following manner, without the livers in the wings; and, in drawing, be careful not to break the gall-bladder:—Cut off the neck, leaving sufficient skin to skewer back. Cut the feet off to the first joint, tuck the stumps into a slit made on each side of the belly, twist the wings over the back of the fowl, and secure the top of the leg and the bottom of the wing together by running a skewer through them and the body. The other side must be done in the same manner. Should the fowl be very large and old, draw the sinews of the legs before tucking them in. Make a slit in the apron of the fowl, large enough to admit the parson's nose, and tie a string on the tops of the legs to keep them in their proper place. *Mode.*—When they are firmly trussed, put them into a stew-pan with plenty of hot water, bring it to boil, and carefully remove all the scum as it rises. *Simmer very gently* until the fowl is tender, and bear in mind that the slower it boils the plumper and whiter

BOILED FOWL.

will the fowl be. Many cooks wrap them in a floured cloth to preserve the colour, and to prevent the scum from clinging to them; in this case, a few slices of lemon should be placed on the breasts, over these a sheet of buttered paper, and then the cloth; cooking them in this manner renders the flesh very white. Boiled ham, bacon, boiled tongue, or pickled pork, are the usual accompaniments to boiled fowls, and they may be served with Béchamel, white sauce, parsley and butter, oyster, lemon, liver, celery, or mushroom sauce. A little should be poured over the fowls after the skewers are removed, and the remainder sent in a tureen to table. *Time.*—Large fowl, 1 hour; moderate-sized one, ¾ hour; chicken, from 20 minutes to ½ hour. *Average cost,* in full season, 5*s.* the pair. *Sufficient* for 7 or 8 persons. *Seasonable* all the year, but scarce in early spring.

CHICKEN BROTH.

Ingredients.—½ fowl, or the inferior joints of a whole one; 1 quart of water, 1 blade of mace, ½ onion, a small bunch of sweet herbs, salt to taste, 10 peppercorns. *Mode.*—An old fowl not suitable for eating may be converted into very good broth; or, if a young one be used, the inferior joints may be put in the broth, and the best pieces reserved for dressing in some other manner. Put the fowl into a saucepan, stew all the ingredients, and simmer gently for 1½ hour, carefully skimming the broth well. When done, strain, and put by in a cool place until wanted; then take all the fat off the top, warm up as much as may be required, and serve. This broth is, of course, only for those invalids whose stomachs are strong enough to digest it, with a flavouring of herbs, &c. It may be made in the same manner as beef tea, with water and salt only, but the preparation will be but tasteless and insipid. When the invalid cannot digest this chicken broth with the flavouring, we would recommend plain beef tea in preference to plain chicken tea, which it would be without the addition of herbs, onions, &c. *Time.*—1½ hour. *Sufficient* to make rather more than 1 pint of broth.

CHICKEN, Curried.

[COLD MEAT COOKERY.] *Ingredients.*—The remains of cold roast fowls, 2 large onions, 1 apple, 2 oz. of butter, 1 dessert-spoonful of curry-powder, 1 teaspoonful of flour, ½ pint of gravy, 1 tablespoonful of lemon-juice. *Mode.*—Slice the onions, peel, core, and chop the apple, and cut the fowl into neat joints; fry these in the butter of a nice brown, then add the curry-powder, flour, and gravy, and stew for about 20 minutes. Put in the lemon-juice, and serve with boiled rice, either placed in a ridge round the dish or separately. Two or three shalots or a little garlic may be added, if approved. *Time.*—Altogether, ½ hour. *Average cost*, exclusive of the cold fowl, 6*d.* *Seasonable* in the winter.

CHICKEN CUTLETS (an Entrée).

Ingredients.—2 chickens; seasoning to taste of salt, white pepper, and cayenne; 2 blades of pounded mace, egg and bread crumbs, clarified butter, 1 strip of lemon-rind, 2 carrots, 1 onion, 2 tablespoonfuls of mushroom ketchup, thickening of butter and flour, 1 egg. *Mode.*—Remove the breast and leg-bones of the chickens; cut the meat into neat pieces after having skinned it, and season the cutlets with pepper, salt, pounded mace, and cayenne. Put the bones, trimmings, &c., into a stewpan with 1 pint of water, adding carrots, onions, and lemon-peel in the above proportion; stew gently for 1½ hour, and strain the gravy. Thicken it with butter and flour, add the ketchup and 1 egg well beaten; stir it over the fire, and bring it to the simmering-point, but do not allow it to boil. In the mean time, egg and bread crumb the cutlets, and give them a few drops of clarified butter; fry them a delicate brown, occasionally turning them; arrange them pyramidically on the dish, and pour over them the sauce. *Time.*—10 minutes to fry the cutlets. *Average cost*, 2*s.* each. *Sufficient* for an entrée. *Seasonable* from April to July.

CHICKEN CUTLETS, French.

[COLD MEAT COOKERY.] *Ingredients.*—The remains of cold roast or boiled fowl, fried bread, clarified butter, the yolk of 1 egg, bread crumbs, ½ teaspoonful of finely-minced lemon-peel; salt, cayenne, and mace to taste. For sauce,—1 oz. of butter, 2 minced shalots, a few slices of carrot, a small bunch of savoury herbs, including parsley, 1 blade of pounded mace, 6 peppercorns, ¼ pint of gravy. *Mode.*—Cut the fowls into as many nice cutlets as possible; take a corresponding number of sippets about the same size, all cut one shape; fry them a pale brown, put them before the fire, then dip the cutlets into clarified butter mixed with the yolk of an egg, cover with bread crumbs seasoned in the above proportion, with lemon-peel, mace, salt, and cayenne; fry them for about 5 minutes, put each piece on one of the sippets, pile them high in the dish, and serve with the following sauce, which should be made ready for the cutlets. Put the butter into a stewpan, add the shalots, carrot, herbs, mace, and peppercorns; fry for 10 minutes, or rather longer; pour in ½ pint of good gravy, made of the chicken-bones; stew gently for 20 minutes, strain it, and serve. *Time.*—5 minutes to fry the cutlets; 35 minutes to make the gravy. *Average cost*, exclusive of the chicken, 9*d.* *Seasonable* from April to July.

CHICKEN, Fricasseed (an Entrée).

Ingredients.—2 small fowls or 1 large one, 3 oz. of butter, a bunch of parsley and green onions, 1 clove, 2 blades of mace, 1 shalot, 1 bay-leaf, salt and white pepper to taste, ¼ pint of cream, the yolks of 3 eggs. *Mode.*—Choose a couple of fat plump chickens, and, after drawing, singeing, and washing them, skin, and carve them into joints; blanch these in boiling water for 2 or 3 minutes, take them out, and immerse them in cold water to render them white. Put the trimmings, with the necks and legs, into a stewpan; add the parsley, onions, clove, mace, shalot, bay-leaf, and a seasoning of pepper and salt; pour to these the water that the chickens were blanched in, and simmer gently for rather more than 1 hour. Have ready another stewpan; put in the joints of fowl, with the above proportion of butter; dredge them with flour, let them get hot, but do not brown them much; then moisten the fricassee with the gravy made from the trimmings, &c., and stew very gently for ½ hour. Lift the fowl into another stewpan, skim the sauce, reduce it quickly over the fire by letting it boil fast, and strain it over them. Add the cream, and a seasoning of pounded mace and cayenne; let it boil up, and when ready to serve, stir to it the well-beaten yolks of 3 eggs; these should not be put in till the last moment, and the sauce should be made *hot*, but must *not boil*, or it will instantly curdle. A few button-mushrooms stewed with the fowl are by many persons considered an improvement. *Time.*—1 hour to make the gravy, ½ hour to simmer the fowl. *Average cost*, 5*s.* the pair. *Sufficient.*—1 large fowl for 1 entrée. *Seasonable* at any time

CHICKEN (or Fowl) PATTIES.

[COLD MEAT COOKERY.] *Ingredients.*—The remains of cold roast chicken or fowl; to every ¼ lb. of meat allow 2 oz. of ham, 3 tablespoonfuls of cream, 2 tablespoonfuls of veal gravy, ½ teaspoonful of minced lemon-peel; cayenne, salt, and pepper to taste; 1 tablespoonful of lemon-juice, 1 oz. of butter rolled in flour, puff paste. *Mode.*—Mince very small the white meat from a cold roast fowl, after removing all the skin; weigh it, and to every ¼ lb. of meat allow the above proportion of minced ham. Put these into a stewpan with the remaining ingredients, stir over the fire for 10 minutes or ¼ hour, taking care that the mixture does not burn. Roll out some puff paste about ¼ inch in thickness, line the patty-pans with this, put upon each a small piece of bread, and cover with another layer of paste; brush over with the yolk of an egg, and bake in a brisk oven for about ¼ hour. When done, cut a round piece out of the top, and, with a small spoon, take out the bread (be particular in not breaking the outside border of the crust), and fill the patties with the mixture. *Time.*—¼ hour to prepare the meat; not quite ¼ hour to bake the crust. *Seasonable* at any time.

CHICKEN (or Fowl) PIE.

Ingredients.—2 small fowls or 1 large one, white pepper and salt to taste, ½ teaspoonful of grated nutmeg, ½ teaspoonful of pounded mace, forcemeat, a few slices of ham, 3 hard-boiled eggs, ½ pint of water, puff crust. *Mode.*—Skin and cut up the fowls into joints, and put the neck, leg, and backbones in a stewpan, with a little water, an onion, a bunch of savoury herbs, and a blade of mace; let these stew for about an hour, and, when done, strain off the liquor: this is for gravy. Put a layer of fowl at the bottom of a pie-dish, then a layer of ham, then one of forcemeat and hard-boiled eggs cut in rings; between the layers put a seasoning of pounded mace, nutmeg, pepper, and salt. Proceed in this manner until the dish is full, and pour in about ½ pint of water; border the edge of the dish with puff crust, put on the cover, ornament the top, and glaze it by brushing over it the yolk of an egg. Bake from 1¼ to 1½ hour, should the pie be very large, and, when done, pour in at the top the gravy made from the bones. If to be eaten cold, and wished particularly nice, the joints of the fowls should be boned, and placed in the dish with alternate layers of forcemeat; sausage-meat may also be substituted for the forcemeat, and is now very much used. When the chickens are boned, and mixed with sausage-meat, the pie will take about 2 hours to bake. It should be covered with a piece of paper when about half-done, to prevent the paste being dried up or scorched. *Time.*—For a pie with unboned meat, 1¼ to 1½ hour; with boned meat and sausage or forcemeat, 1½ to 2 hours. *Average cost*, with 2 fowls, 6*s.* 6*d.* *Sufficient* for 6 or 7 persons. *Seasonable* at any time.

CHICKEN, Potted (a Luncheon or Breakfast Dish).

Ingredients.—The remains of cold roast chicken; to every lb. of meat allow ¼ lb. of fresh butter, salt and cayenne to taste,

1 teaspoonful of pounded mace, ½ small nutmeg. *Mode.*—Strip the meat from the bones of cold roast fowl; when it is freed from gristle and skin, weigh it, and to every lb. of meat allow the above proportion of butter, seasoning, and spices. Cut the meat into small pieces, pound it well with the fresh butter, sprinkle in the spices gradually, and keep pounding until reduced to a perfectly smooth paste. Put it into potting-pots for use, and cover it with clarified butter, about ¼ inch in thickness, and, if to be kept for some time, tie over a bladder: 2 or 3 slices of ham, minced and pounded with the above ingredients, will be found an improvement. It should be kept in a dry place. *Seasonable* at any time.

CHICKEN (or Fowl) SALAD.

Ingredients.—The remains of cold roast or boiled chicken, 2 lettuces, a little endive, 1 cucumber, a few slices of boiled beetroot, salad-dressing. *Mode.*—Trim neatly the remains of the chicken; wash, dry, and slice the lettuces, and place in the middle of a dish; put the pieces of fowl on the top, and pour the salad-dressing over them. Garnish the edge of the salad with hard-boiled eggs cut in rings, sliced cucumber, and boiled beetroot cut in slices. Instead of cutting the eggs in rings, the yolks may be rubbed through a hair sieve, and the whites chopped very finely, and arranged on the salad in small bunches, yellow and white alternately. This should not be made long before it is wanted for table. *Average cost*, exclusive of the cold chicken, 8*d.* *Sufficient* for 4 or 5 persons. *Seasonable* at any time.

CHILI VINEGAR.

Ingredients.—50 fresh red English chilies, 1 pint of vinegar. *Mode.*—Pound or cut the chilies in half, and infuse them in the vinegar for a fortnight, when it will be fit for use. This will be found an agreeable relish to fish, as many people cannot eat it without the addition of an acid and cayenne pepper.

CHINA CHILO.

Ingredients.—1½ lb. of leg, loin, or neck of mutton, 2 onions, 2 lettuces, 1 pint of green peas, 1 teaspoonful of salt, 1 teaspoonful of pepper, ¼ pint of water, ¼ lb. of clarified butter; when liked, a little

cayenne. *Mode.*—Mince the above quantity of undressed leg, loin, or neck of mutton, adding a little of the fat, also minced; put it into a stewpan with the remaining ingredients, previously shredding the lettuce and onion rather fine; closely cover the stewpan, after the ingredients have been well stirred, and simmer gently for rather more than two hours. Serve in a dish, with a border of rice round, the same as for curry. *Time.* —Rather more than two hours. *Average cost*, 1*s.* 6*d.* *Sufficient* for 3 or 4 persons. *Seasonable* from June to August.

CHOCOLATE, to Make.

Ingredients.—Allow ½ oz. of chocolate to each person; to every oz. allow ½ pint of water, ½ pint of milk. *Mode.*—Make the milk-and-water hot; scrape the chocolate into it, and stir the mixture constantly and quickly until the chocolate is dissolved; bring it to the boiling-point, stir it well, and serve directly with white sugar. Chocolate prepared within a mill, as shown in the engraving, is made by putting in the scraped chocolate, pouring over it the boiling milk-and-water, and milling it over the fire until hot and frothy. *Sufficient.*—Allow ½ oz. of cake chocolate to each person.

MILL.

CHOCOLATE CREAM.

Ingredients.—3 oz. of grated chocolate, ¼ lb. of sugar, 1½ pint of cream, 1½ oz. of clarified isinglass, the yolks of 6 eggs. *Mode.*—Beat the yolks of the eggs well, put them into a basin with the grated

CREAM-MOULD.

chocolate, the sugar, and 1 pint of the cream; stir these ingredients well together, pour them into a jug, and set this jug in a saucepan of boiling water; stir it one way until the mixture thickens, but *do not allow it to boil*, or it will curdle. Strain the cream through a sieve into a basin; stir in the isinglass and the other ½ pint of cream, which should be well whipped; mix all well together, and pour it into a mould which has been previously oiled with the purest salad-oil, and, if at hand, set it in ice until wanted for table. *Time.*—About 10 minutes to stir the mixture over the fire. *Average cost*, 4*s.* 6*d.*, with cream at 1*s.* per pint. *Sufficient* to fill a quart mould. *Seasonable* at any time.

CHOCOLATE SOUFFLE.

Ingredients.—4 eggs, 3 teaspoonfuls of pounded sugar, 1 teaspoonful of flour, 3 oz. of the best chocolate. *Mode.*—Break the eggs, separating the whites from the yolks, and put them into different basins; add to the yolks the sugar, flour, and chocolate, which should be very finely grated, and stir these ingredients for 5 minutes. Then well whisk the whites of the eggs in the other basin until they are stiff, and, when firm, mix lightly with the yolks till the whole forms a smooth and light substance; butter a round cake-tin, put in the mixture, and bake in a moderate oven from 15 to 20 minutes. Pin a white napkin round the tin, strew sifted sugar over the top of the soufflé, and send it immediately to table. The proper appearance of this dish depends entirely on the expedition with which it is served; and some cooks, to preserve its lightness, hold a salamander over the soufflé until it is placed on the table. If allowed to stand after it comes from the oven it will be entirely spoiled, as it falls almost immediately. *Time.*—15 to 20 minutes. *Average cost*, 1*s.* *Sufficient* for a moderate-sized soufflé. *Seasonable* at any time.

CLARET-CUP.

Ingredients.—1 bottle of claret, 1 bottle of soda-water, about ½ lb. of pounded ice, 4 tablespoonfuls of powdered sugar, ¼ teaspoonful of grated nutmeg, 1 liqueur-glass of Maraschino, a sprig of green borage. *Mode.*—Put all the ingredients into a silver cup, regulating the proportion of ice by the state of the weather; if very warm, a larger quantity would be necessary. Hand the cup round with a clean napkin passed through one of the handles, that the edge of the cup may be wiped after each guest has partaken of the contents thereof. *Seasonable* in summer.

CLARET-CUP.

COCK-A-LEEKIE.

Ingredients.—A capon or large fowl (sometimes an old cock, from which the recipe takes its name, is used), which should be trussed as for boiling, 2 or 3 bunches of fine leeks, 5 quarts of stock (*see* STOCK), pepper and salt to taste. *Mode.*—Well wash the leeks (and, if old, scald them in boiling water for a few minutes), taking off the roots and part of the heads, and cut them into lengths of about an inch. Put the fowl into the stock, with, at first, one half of the leeks, and allow it to simmer gently. In half an hour add the remaining leeks, and then it may simmer for 3 or 4 hours longer. It should be carefully skimmed, and can be seasoned to taste. In serving, take out the fowl and carve it neatly, placing the pieces in a tureen, and pouring over them the soup, which should be very thick of leeks (a *purée* of leeks, the French would call it). *Time.*—4 hours. *Average cost*, 1*s.* 6*d.* per quart; or with stock, 1*s.* *Sufficient* for 10 persons. *Seasonable* in winter.

Note.—Without the fowl, the above, which would then be merely called leek soup, is very good, and also economical. Cock-a-leekie was largely consumed at the Burns Centenary Festival at the Crystal Palace, Sydenham, in 1859.

COCOA, to Make.

Ingredients.—Allow 2 teaspoonfuls of the prepared cocoa to 1 breakfast-cup; boiling milk and boiling water. *Mode.*—Put the cocoa into a breakfast-cup, pour over it sufficient cold milk to make it into a smooth paste; then add equal quantities of boiling milk and boiling water, and stir all well together. Care must be taken not to allow the milk to get burnt, as it will entirely spoil the flavour of the preparation. The above directions are usually given for making the prepared cocoa. The rock cocoa, or that bought in a solid piece, should be scraped, and made in the same manner, taking care to rub down all the lumps before the boiling liquid is added. *Sufficient.*—2 teaspoonfuls of prepared cocoa for 1 breakfast-cup, or ¼ oz. of the rock cocoa for the same quantity.

COD.

Cod should be chosen for the table when it is plump and round near the tail, when the hollow behind the head is deep, and when the sides are undulated as if they were ribbed. The glutinous parts about the head lose their delicate flavour after the fish has been twenty-four hours out of the water. The great point by which the cod should be judged is the firmness of its flesh; and, although the cod is not firm when it is alive, its quality may be arrived at by pressing the finger into the flesh: if this rises immediately, the flesh is good; if not, it is stale. Another sign of its goodness is, if the fish, when it is cut, exhibits a bronze appearance, like the silver side of a round of beef; when this is the case the flesh will be firm when cooked. Stiffness in a cod, or in any other fish, is a sure sign of freshness, though not always of quality. Sometimes codfish, though exhibiting signs of rough usage, will eat much better than those with red gills, so strongly recommended by many cookery-books. This appearance is generally caused by the fish having been knocked about at sea, in the well-boats, in which they are conveyed from the fishing-grounds to market.

COD à la BECHAMEL.

[COLD MEAT COOKERY.] *Ingredients.*—Any remains of cold cod, 4 tablespoonfuls of béchamel (*see* BECHAMEL SAUCE), 2 oz. of butter; seasoning to taste of pepper and salt; fried bread, a few bread crumbs. *Mode.*—Flake the cod carefully, leaving out all skin and bone; put the béchamel in a stewpan with the butter, and stir it over the fire till the latter is melted; add seasoning, put in the fish, and mix it well with the sauce. Make a border of fried bread round the dish, lay in the fish, sprinkle over with bread crumbs, and baste with butter. Brown either before the fire or with a salamander, and garnish with toasted bread cut in fanciful shapes. *Time.*—½ hour. *Average cost*, exclusive of the fish, 6*d.*

COD à la CREME.

[COLD MEAT COOKERY.] *Ingredients.*—1 large slice of cod, 1 oz. of butter, 1 chopped shalot, a little minced parsley, ¼ teacupful of white stock, ¼ pint of milk or cream, flour to thicken, cayenne and lemon-juice to taste, ¼ teaspoonful of powdered sugar. *Mode.*—Boil the cod, and while hot, break it into flakes; put the butter, shalot, parsley, and stock into a stewpan, and let them boil for 5 minutes. Stir in sufficient flour to thicken, and pour to it the milk or cream. Simmer for 10 minutes, add the cayenne and sugar, and, when liked, a little lemon-juice. Put the fish in the sauce to warm gradually, but do not let it boil. Serve in a dish garnished with croûtons. *Time.*—Rather more than ½ hour. *Average cost*, with cream, 2*s.* *Sufficient* for 3 persons. *Seasonable* from November to March.

Note.—The remains of fish from the preceding day answer very well for this dish.

COD à l'ITALIENNE.

Ingredients.—2 slices of crimped cod, 1 shalot, 1 slice of ham minced very fine, ½ pint of white stock, when liked, ½ teacupful of cream; salt to taste; a few drops of garlic vinegar, a little lemon-juice, ½ teaspoonful of powdered sugar. *Mode.*—Chop the shalots, mince the ham very fine, pour on the stock, and simmer for 15 minutes. If the colour should not be good, add cream in the above proportion, and strain it through a fine sieve; season it, and put in the vinegar, lemon-juice, and sugar. Now boil the cod, take out the middle bone, and skin it; put it on the dish without breaking, and pour the sauce over it. *Time.*—¾ hour. *Average cost*, 3*s.* 6*d.*, with fresh fish. *Sufficient* for 4 persons. *Seasonable* from November to March.

COD à la MAITRE D'HOTEL.

[COLD MEAT COOKERY.] *Ingredients.*—2 slices of cod, ¼ lb. of butter, a little chopped shalot and parsley; pepper to taste; ¼ teaspoonful of grated nutmeg, or rather less when the flavour is not liked; the juice of ¼ lemon. *Mode.*—Boil the cod, and either leave it whole, or, what is still better, flake it from the bone, and take off the skin. Put it into a stewpan with the butter, parsley, shalot, pepper, and nutmeg. Melt the butter gradually, and be very careful that it does not become like oil. When all is well mixed and thoroughly hot, add the lemon-juice, and serve. *Time.*—½ hour. *Average cost*, 2*s*. 6*d*.; with remains of cold fish, 5*d*. *Sufficient* for 4 persons. *Seasonable* from November to March.

Note.—Cod that has been left will do for this.

COD, Curried.

[COLD MEAT COOKERY.] *Ingredients.*—2 slices of large cod, or the remains of any cold fish; 3 oz. of butter, 1 onion sliced, a teacupful of white stock, thickening of butter and flour, 1 *small* teaspoonful of curry-powder, ¼ pint of cream, salt and cayenne to taste. *Mode.*—Flake the fish, and fry it of a nice brown colour with the butter and onions; put this in a stewpan, add the stock and thickening, and simmer for 10 minutes. Stir the curry-powder into the cream; put it, with the seasoning, to the other ingredients; give one boil, and serve. *Time.*—¾ hour. *Average cost*, with fresh fish, 3*s*. *Sufficient* for 4 persons. *Seasonable* from November to March.

COD PIE.

Ingredients.—2 slices of cod; pepper and salt to taste; ½ a teaspoonful of grated nutmeg, 1 large blade of pounded mace, 2 oz. of butter, ½ pint of stock, a paste crust (*see* PASTRY). For sauce,—1 tablespoonful of stock, ¼ pint of cream or milk, thickening of flour or butter, lemon-peel chopped very fine to taste, 12 oysters. *Mode.*—Lay the cod in salt for 4 hours, then wash it and place it in a dish; season, and add the butter and stock; cover with the crust, and bake for 1 hour, or rather more. Now make the sauce, by mixing the ingredients named above; give it one boil, and pour it into the pie by a hole made at the top of the crust, which can easily be covered by a small piece of pastry cut and baked in any fanciful shape,—such as a leaf, or otherwise. *Time.*—1½ hour. *Average cost*, with fresh fish, 2*s*. 6*d*. *Sufficient* for 6 persons. *Seasonable* from November to March.

Note.—The remains of cold fish may be used for this pie.

COD PIE. (Economical.)

[COLD MEAT COOKERY.] *Ingredients.* Any remains of cold cod, 12 oysters, sufficient melted butter to moisten it; mashed potatoes enough to fill up the dish. *Mode.*—Flake the fish from the bone, and carefully take away all the skin. Lay it in a pie-dish, pour over the melted butter and oysters (or oyster sauce, if there is any left), and cover with mashed potatoes. Bake for ½ an hour, and send to table of a nice brown colour. *Time.*—½ hour. *Seasonable* from November to March.

COD, Salt, commonly called "Salt-fish."

Ingredients.—Sufficient water to cover the fish. *Mode.*—Wash the fish, and lay it all night in water, with a ¼ pint of vinegar. When thoroughly soaked, take it out, see that it is perfectly clean, and put it in the fish-kettle with sufficient cold water to cover it. Heat it gradually, but do not let it boil much, or the fish will be hard. Skim well, and when done, drain the fish, and put it on a napkin garnished with hard-boiled eggs cut in rings. *Time.*—About 1 hour. *Average cost*, 6*d*. per lb. *Sufficient* for each person, ¼ lb. *Seasonable* in the spring.

Note.—Serve with egg sauce and parsnips. This is an especial dish on Ash Wednesday.

COD SOUNDS

Should be well soaked in salt and water, and thoroughly washed before dressing them. They are considered a great delicacy, and may either be broiled, fried, or boiled; if they are boiled, mix a little milk with the water.

COD SOUNDS, en Poule.

Ingredients.—For forcemeat, 12 chopped oysters, 3 chopped anchovies, ¼ lb. of bread crumbs, 1 oz. of butter, 2 eggs, seasoning of salt, pepper, nutmeg, and mace to taste; 4 cod sounds. *Mode.*—Make the forcemeat by mixing the ingredients well together. Wash the sounds, and boil them in milk and water for ½ an hour; take them out, and let them cool. Cover each with a layer of forcemeat, roll them up in a nice form, and skewer them. Rub over with lard, dredge with flour, and cook them gently before the fire in a Dutch oven. *Time.*—1 hour. *Average cost*, 6*d*. per lb.

COD'S HEAD & SHOULDERS.

Ingredients.—Sufficient water to cover the fish; 5 oz. of salt to each gallon of water. *Mode.*—Cleanse the fish thoroughly, and rub a little salt over the thick part and inside of the fish 1 or 2 hours before dressing it, as this very much improves the flavour. Lay it in the fish-kettle, with sufficient cold water to cover it. Be very particular not to pour the water on the fish, as it is liable to break it, and only keep it just simmering. If the water should boil away, add a little by pouring it in at the side of the kettle, and not on the fish. Add salt in the above proportion, and bring it gradually to a boil. Skim very carefully, draw it to the side of the fire, and let it gently simmer till done. Take it out and drain it; serve on a hot napkin, and garnish with cut lemon and horseradish. *Time.*—According to size, ½ an hour, more or less. *Average cost,* from 3*s.* to 6*s.* *Sufficient* for 6 or 8 persons. *Seasonable* from November to March.

Note.—Oyster sauce and plain melted butter should be served with this.

COD'S HEAD & SHOULDERS, to Carve.

First run the knife along the centre of the side of the fish, namely, from *d* to *b*, down to the bone; then carve it in un-

broken slices downwards from *d* to *e*, or upwards from *d* to *c*, as shown in the engraving. The carver should ask the guests if they would like a portion of the roe and liver.

Note.—Of this fish, the parts about the backbone and shoulders are the firmest and most esteemed by connoisseurs. The sound, which lines the fish beneath the backbone, is considered a delicacy, as are also the gelatinous parts about the head and neck.

COFFEE, Essence of.

Ingredients.—To every ¼ lb. of ground coffee allow 1 small teaspoonful of powdered chicory, 3 small teacupfuls, or 1 pint, of water. *Mode.*—Let the coffee be freshly ground, and, if possible, freshly roasted; put it into a percolater, or filter, with the chicory, and pour *slowly* over it the above proportion of boiling water. When it has all filtered through, warm the coffee sufficiently to bring it to the simmering-point, but do not allow it to boil; then filter it a second time, put it into a clean and dry bottle, cork it well, and it will remain good for several days. Two tablespoonfuls of this essence are quite sufficient for a breakfast-cupful of hot milk. This essence will be found particularly useful to those persons who have to rise extremely early; and having only the milk to make boiling, is very easily and quickly prepared. When the essence is bottled, pour another 3 teacupfuls of *boiling* water slowly on the grounds, which, when filtered through, will be a very weak coffee. The next time there is essence to be prepared, make this weak coffee boiling, and pour it on the ground coffee instead of plain water: by this means a better coffee will be obtained. Never throw away the grounds without having made use of them in this manner; and always cork the bottle well that contains this preparation, until the day that it is wanted for making the fresh essence. *Time.*—To be filtered once, then brought to the boiling-point, and filtered again. *Average cost,* with coffee at 1*s.* 8*d.* per lb., 6*d.* *Sufficient.*—Allow 2 tablespoonfuls for a breakfast-cupful of hot milk.

COFFEE, Nutritious.

Ingredients.—½ oz. of ground coffee, 1 pint of milk. *Mode.*—Let the coffee be freshly ground; put it into a saucepan with the milk, which should be made nearly boiling before the coffee is put in, and boil together for 3 minutes; clear it by pouring some of it into a cup, and then back again, and leave it on the hob for a few minutes to settle thoroughly. This coffee may be made still more nutritious by the addition of an egg well beaten, and put into the coffee-cup. *Time.*—5 minutes to boil, 5 minutes to settle. *Sufficient* to make 1 large breakfast-cupful of coffee.

COFFEE, Simple Method of Making.

Ingredients.—Allow ½ oz., or 1 tablespoonful, of coffee to each person; to every oz. allow ¼ pint of water. *Mode.*—Have a small iron ring made to fit the top of the coffee-pot inside, and to this ring sew a small muslin bag (the muslin for the purpose must not be too thin). Fit the bag into the pot, warm the pot with some boiling water; throw this away, and put the ground coffee into the bag; pour over as much boiling water as is required, close the lid, and, when all the water has filtered through, remove the bag, and send the coffee to table. Making it in this manner prevents the necessity of pouring the coffee from one vessel to another, which cools and spoils it. The water should be poured on the coffee gradually, so that the infusion may be stronger; and the bag must be well made, that none of the grounds may escape through the seams, and so make the coffee thick and muddy. *Sufficient.*—Allow 1 tablespoonful, or ½ oz., to each person.

COFFEE, to Make.

Ingredients.—Allow ½ oz., or 1 tablespoonful, of ground coffee to each person; to every oz. of coffee allow ⅓ pint of water. *Mode.*—To make coffee good, *it should never be boiled*, but the boiling water merely poured on it, the same as for tea. The coffee should always be purchased in the berry,—if possible, freshly roasted; and it should never be ground long before it is wanted for use.

LOYSEL'S HYDROSTATIC URN.

There are very many new kinds of coffee-pots, but the method of making the coffee is nearly always the same, namely, pouring the boiling water on the powder, and allowing it to filter through. Our illustration shows one of Loysel's Hydrostatic Urns, which are admirably adapted for making good and clear coffee, which should be made in the following manner:—Warm the urn with boiling water, remove the lid and movable filter, and place the ground coffee at the bottom of the urn. Put the movable filter over this, and screw the lid, inverted, tightly on the end of the centre pipe. Pour into the inverted lid the above proportion of boiling water, and when all the water so poured has disappeared from the funnel, and made its way down the centre pipe and up again through the ground coffee by *hydrostatic pressure*, unscrew the lid and cover the urn. Pour back direct into the urn, *not through the funnel*, one, two, or three cups, according to the size of the percolater, in order to make the infusion of uniform strength; the contents will then be ready for use, and should run from the tap strong, hot, and clear. The coffee made in these urns generally turns out very good, and there is but one objection to them,—the coffee runs rather slowly from the tap; this is of no consequence where there is a small party, but tedious where there are many persons to provide for. A remedy for this objection may be suggested, namely, to make the coffee very strong, so that not more than ¼ cup would be required, as the rest would be filled up with milk. Making coffee in filters or percolaters does away with the necessity of using isinglass, white of egg, and various other preparations, to clear it. Coffee should always be served very hot, and, if possible, in the same vessel in which it is made, as pouring it from one pot to another cools, and consequently spoils it. Many persons may think that the proportion of water we have given for each oz. of coffee is rather small; it is so, and the coffee produced from it will be very strong; ¼ of a cup will be found quite sufficient, which should be filled with nice hot milk, or milk and cream mixed. This is the *café au lait* for which our neighbours over the Channel are so justly celebrated. Should the ordinary method of making coffee be preferred, use double the quantity of water, and, in pouring it into the cups, put in more coffee and less milk. *Sufficient.*—For very good coffee, allow ½ oz., or 1 tablespoonful, to each person.

COFFEE, to Roast. (A French Recipe.)

It being an acknowledged fact that French coffee is decidedly superior to that made in England, and as the roasting of the berry is of great importance to the flavour of the preparation, it will be useful and interesting to know how they manage these things in France. In Paris, there are two houses justly celebrated for the flavour of their coffee,—*La Maison Corcellet* and *La Maison Royer de Chartres*; and to obtain this flavour, before roasting, they add to every 3 lbs. of coffee a piece of butter the size of a nut, and a dessertspoonful of powdered sugar: it is then roasted in the usual manner. The addition of the butter and sugar develops the flavour and aroma of the berry; but it must be borne in mind, that the quality of the butter must be of the very best description.

COLLOPS, Scotch.

[COLD MEAT COOKERY.] *Ingredients.*—The remains of cold roast veal, a little butter, flour, ½ pint of water, 1 onion, 1 blade of pounded mace, 1 tablespoonful of lemon-juice, ½ teaspoonful of finely-minced lemon-peel, 2 tablespoonfuls of sherry, 1 tablespoonful of mushroom ketchup. *Mode.*—Cut the veal the same thickness as for cutlets, rather larger than a crown piece; flour the meat well, and fry a light brown in butter; dredge again with flour, and add ½ pint of water, pouring it in by degrees; set it on the fire, and when it boils, add the onion and mace, and let it simmer very gently about ¾ hour; flavour the gravy with lemon-juice, peel, wine, and ketchup, in the above proportion; give one boil, and serve. *Time.*—¾ hour. *Seasonable* from March to October.

COLLOPS, Scotch, White.

[COLD MEAT COOKERY.] *Ingredients.* The remains of cold roast veal, ½ teaspoonful of grated nutmeg, 2 blades of pounded mace, cayenne and salt to taste, a little butter, 1 dessertspoonful of flour, ½ pint of water, 1 teaspoonful of anchovy sauce, 1 tablespoonful of lemon-juice, ¼ teaspoonful of lemon-peel, 1 tablespoonful of mushroom ketchup, 3 tablespoonfuls of cream, 1 tablespoonful of sherry. *Mode.*—Cut the veal into thin slices about 3 inches in width; hack them with a knife, and grate on them the nutmeg, mace, cayenne, and salt, and fry them in a little butter. Dish them, and make a gravy in the pan by putting in the remaining ingredients. Give one boil, and pour it over the collops; garnish with lemon and slices of toasted bacon, rolled. Forcemeat balls may be added to this dish. If cream is not at hand, substitute the yolk of an egg beaten up well with a little milk. *Time.*—About 5 or 7 minutes. *Seasonable* from May to October.

COMPOTE.

A confiture made at the moment of need, and with much less sugar than would be ordinarily put to preserves. They are very wholesome things, suitable to most stomachs which cannot accommodate themselves to raw fruit or a large portion of sugar: they are the happy medium, and far better than ordinary stewed fruit. For Fruit Compôtes refer to the recipes relating to the various Fruits.

CONFECTIONARY.

In speaking of confectionary, it should be remarked that many preparations come under that head; for the various fruits, flowers, herbs, roots, and juices, which, when boiled with sugar, were formerly employed in pharmacy as well as for sweetmeats, were called *confections*, from the Latin word *conficere*, 'to make up;' but the term confectionary embraces a very large class indeed of sweet food, many kinds of which should not be attempted in the ordinary cuisine. The thousand and one ornamental dishes that adorn the tables of the wealthy should be purchased from the confectioner: they cannot profitably be made at home. Apart from these, cakes, biscuits, and tarts, &c., the class of sweetmeats called confections may be thus classified:—1. Liquid confects, or fruits either whole or in pieces, preserved by being immersed in a fluid transparent syrup; as the liquid confects of apricots, green citrons, and many foreign fruits. 2. Dry confects are those which, after having been boiled in the syrup, are taken out and put to dry in an oven, as citron and orange-peel, &c. 3. Marmalade, jams, and pastes, a kind of soft compounds made of the pulp of fruits or other vegetable substances, beat up with sugar or honey; such as oranges, apricots, pears, &c. 4. Jellies are the juices of fruits boiled with sugar to a pretty thick consistency, so as, upon cooling, to form a trembling jelly; as currant, gooseberry, apple jelly, &c. 5. Conserves are a kind of dry confects, made by beating up flowers, fruits, &c., with sugar, not dissolved. 6. Candies are fruits candied over with sugar after having been boiled in the syrup.

COW-HEEL, Fried.

Ingredients. — Ox-feet, the yolk of 1 egg, bread crumbs, parsley, salt and cayenne to taste, boiling butter. *Mode.* —Wash, scald, and thoroughly clean the feet, and cut them into pieces about 2 inches long; have ready some fine bread crumbs mixed with a little minced parsley, cayenne, and salt; dip the pieces of heel into the yolk of egg, sprinkle them with the bread crumbs, and fry them until of a nice brown in boiling butter. *Time.*—¼ hour. *Average cost*, 6*d*. each. *Seasonable* at any time.

Note.—Ox-feet may be dressed in various ways, stewed in gravy or plainly boiled and served with melted butter. When plainly boiled, the liquor will answer for making sweet or relishing jellies, and also to give richness to soups or gravies.

COW-HEEL STOCK, for Jellies (More Economical than Calf's-Feet).

Ingredients.—2 cow-heels, 3 quarts of water. *Mode.* — Procure 2 heels that have only been scalded, and not boiled; split them in two, and remove the fat between the claws; wash them well in warm water, and put them into a saucepan with the above proportion of cold water; bring it gradually to boil, remove all the scum as it rises, and simmer the heels gently from 7 to 8 hours, or until the liquor is reduced one-half; then strain it into a basin, measuring the quantity, and put it in a cool place. Clarify it in the same manner as calf's-feet stock, using, with the other ingredients, about ½ oz. of isinglass to each quart. This stock should be made the day before it is required for use. Two dozen shank-bones of mutton, boiled for 6 or 7 hours, yield a quart of strong firm stock. They should be put on in 2 quarts of water, which should be reduced one-half. Make this also the day before it is required. *Time.*—7 to 8 hours to boil the cow-heels, 6 to 7 hours to boil the shank-bones. *Average cost*, from 4*d*. to 6*d*. each. *Sufficient.*—2 cow-heels should make 3 pints of stock. *Seasonable* at any time.

COWSLIP WINE.

Ingredients.—To every gallon of water allow 3 lbs. of lump sugar, the rind of 2 lemons, the juice of 1, the rind and juice of 1 Seville orange, 1 gallon of cowslip pips. To every 4½ gallons of wine allow 1 bottle of brandy. *Mode.*—Boil the sugar and water together for ½ hour, carefully removing all the scum as it rises. Pour this boiling liquor on the orange and lemon-rinds and the juice, which should be strained; when milk-warm, add the cowslip pips or flowers, picked from the stalks and seeds; and to 9 gallons of wine 3 tablespoonfuls of good fresh brewers' yeast. Let it ferment 3 or 4 days, then put all together in a cask with the brandy, and let it remain for 2 months, when bottle it off for use. *Time.*—To be boiled ½ hour; to ferment 3 or 4 days; to remain in the cask 2 months. *Average cost*, exclusive of the cowslips, which may be picked in the fields, 2*s*. 9*d*. per gallon. *Seasonable.* Make this in April or May.

CRAB, to Choose.

The middle-sized crab is the best; and the crab, like the lobster, should be judged by its weight; for if light, it is watery.

CRAB, to Dress.

Ingredients.—1 crab, 2 tablespoonfuls of vinegar, 1 ditto of oil; salt, white pepper, and cayenne, to taste. *Mode.*—Empty the shells, and thoroughly mix the meat with the above ingredients, and put it in the large shell. Garnish with slices of cut lemon and parsley. The quantity of oil may be increased when it is much liked. *Average cost*, from 10*d*. to 2*s*. *Seasonable* all the year; but not so good in May, June, and July. *Sufficient* for 3 persons.

CRAB, Hot.

Ingredients.—1 crab, nutmeg, salt and pepper to taste, 3 oz. of butter, ¼ lb. of bread crumbs, 3 tablespoonfuls of vinegar. *Mode.* — After having boiled the crab, pick the meat out from the shells, and mix with it the nutmeg and seasoning. Cut up the butter in small pieces, and add the bread crumbs and vinegar. Mix altogether, put the whole in the large shell, and brown before the fire or with a salamander. *Time.*—1 hour. *Average cost*, from 10*d.* to 2*s.* *Sufficient* for 3 persons. *Seasonable* all the year; but not so good in May, June, and July.

CRAB SAUCE, for Fish (equal to Lobster Sauce).

Ingredients.—1 crab; salt, pounded mace, and cayenne to taste; ½ pint of melted butter made with milk. *Mode.*—Choose a nice fresh crab, pick all the meat away from the shell, and cut it into small square pieces. Make ½ pint of melted butter, put in the fish and seasoning; let it gradually warm through, and simmer for 2 minutes: it should not boil. *Average cost*, 1*s.* 2*d.*

CRAYFISH.

Crayfish should be thrown into boiling water, to which has been added a good seasoning of salt and a little vinegar. When done, which will be in ¼ hour, take them out and drain them. Let them cool, arrange them on a napkin, and garnish with plenty of double parsley.

Note.—This fish is frequently used for garnishing boiled turkey, boiled fowl, calf's head, turbot, and all kinds of boiled fish.

CRAYFISH, Potted.

Ingredients.—100 crayfish; pounded mace, pepper, and salt to taste; 2 oz. butter. *Mode.*—Boil the fish in salt and water, pick out all the meat, and pound it in a mortar to a paste. Whilst pounding, add the butter gradually, and mix in the spice and seasoning. Put it in small pots, and pour over it clarified butter, carefully excluding the air. *Time.*—15 minutes to boil the crayfish. *Average cost*, 2*s.* 9*d.* *Seasonable* all the year.

CRAYFISH SOUP.

Ingredients.—50 crayfish, ¼ lb. of butter, 6 anchovies, the crumb of 1 French roll, a little lobster-spawn, seasoning to taste, 2 quarts of medium stock, or fish stock. *Mode.*—Shell the crayfish, and put the fish between two plates until they are wanted; pound the shells in a mortar with the butter and anchovies; when well beaten, add a pint of stock, and simmer for ¾ of an hour. Strain it through a hair sieve, put the remainder of the stock to it, with the crumb of the roll; give it one boil, and rub it through a tammy, with the lobster-spawn. Put in the fish, but do not let the soup boil after it has been rubbed through the tammy. If necessary, add seasoning. *Time.*—1½ hour. *Average cost*, 2*s.* 3*d.* or 1*s.* 9*d.* per quart. *Sufficient* for 8 persons. *Seasonable* from January to July.

CREAM à la VALOIS.

Ingredients.—4 sponge cakes, jam, ¾ pint of cream, sugar to taste, the juice of ½ lemon, ¼ glass of sherry, 1¼ oz. of isinglass. *Mode.*—Cut the sponge-cakes into thin slices, place two together with preserve between them, and pour over them a small quantity of sherry mixed with a little brandy. Sweeten and flavour the cream with the lemon-juice and sherry; add the isinglass, which should be dissolved in a little water, and beat up the cream well. Place a little in an oiled mould; arrange the pieces of cake in the cream, then fill the mould with the remainder, let it cool, and turn it out on a dish. By oiling the mould the cream will have a much smoother appearance, and will turn out more easily than when merely dipped in cold water. *Average cost*, 3*s.* 6*d.* *Sufficient* to fill a 1½ pint mould. *Seasonable* at any time.

CREAM CHEESE.

Cream cheese should be served on a d'oyley, and garnished either with water-cresses or parsley; of the former, a plentiful supply should be given, as they add greatly to the appearance of the dish, besides improving the flavour of the cheese.

CREAM, Devonshire.

The milk should stand 24 hours in the winter, half that time when the weather is very warm. The milkpan is then set on a stove, and should there remain until the milk is quite hot; but it must not boil, or there will be a thick skin on the surface. When it is sufficiently done the undulations on the surface look thick, and small rings appear. The time required for scalding cream depends on the size of the pan and the heat of the fire, but the slower it is done the better. The pan should be placed in the dairy when the cream is sufficiently scalded, and skimmed the following day. This cream is so much esteemed that it is sent to the London markets in small square tins, and is exceedingly delicious eaten with fresh fruit. In Devonshire, butter is made from this cream, and is usually very firm.

CREAM, Italian.

Ingredients.—½ pint of milk, ½ pint of cream, sugar to taste, 1 oz. of isinglass, 1 lemon, the yolks of 4 eggs. *Mode.*—Put the cream and milk into a saucepan, with sugar to sweeten, and the lemon-rind. Boil until the milk is well flavoured, then strain it into a basin and add the beaten yolks of eggs. Put this mixture into a jug, place the jug in a saucepan of boiling water over the fire, and stir the contents until they thicken, but do not allow them to boil. Take the cream off the fire, stir in the lemon-juice and isinglass, which should be melted, and whip well; fill a mould, place it in ice if at hand, and, when set, turn it out on a dish, and garnish as taste may dictate. The mixture may be whipped and drained, and then put into small glasses, when this mode of serving is preferred. *Time.*—From 5 to 8 minutes to stir the mixture in the jug. *Average cost*, with the best isinglass, 2*s.* 6*d.* *Sufficient* to fill 1½ pint mould. *Seasonable* at any time.

CREAM SAUCE, for Fish or White Dishes.

Ingredients.—¼ pint of cream, 2 oz. of butter, 1 teaspoonful of flour, salt and cayenne to taste; when liked, a small quantity of pounded mace or lemon-juice. *Mode.*—Put the butter in a very clean saucepan, dredge in the flour, and keep shaking round till the butter is melted. Add the seasoning and cream, and stir the whole till it boils; let it just simmer for 5 minutes, when add either pounded mace or lemon-juice to taste to give it a flavour. *Time.*—5 minutes to simmer. *Average cost* for this quantity, 7*d.*

Note.—This sauce may be flavoured with very finely-shredded shalot.

CREAM, Stone, of tous les Mois.

Ingredients.—½ lb. of preserve, 1 pint of milk, 2 oz. of lump sugar, 1 heaped tablespoonful of tous les mois, 3 drops of essence of cloves, 3 drops of almond-flavouring. *Mode.*—Place the preserve at the bottom of a glass dish; put the milk into a lined saucepan, with the sugar, and make it boil. Mix to a smooth batter the tous les mois with a very little cold milk; stir it briskly into the boiling milk, add the flavouring, and simmer for 2 minutes. When rather cool, but before turning solid, pour the cream over the jam, and ornament it with strips of red-currant jelly or preserved fruit. *Time.*—2 minutes. *Average cost*, 10*d.* *Sufficient* for 4 or 5 persons. *Seasonable* at any time.

CREAM, Swiss.

Ingredients.—¼ lb. of macaroons or 6 small sponge-cakes, sherry, 1 pint of cream, 5 oz. of lump sugar, 2 large tablespoonfuls of arrowroot, the rind of 1 lemon, the juice of ½ lemon, 3 tablespoonfuls of milk. *Mode.*—Lay the macaroons or sponge-cakes in a glass dish, and pour over them as much sherry as will cover them, or sufficient to soak them well. Put the cream into a lined saucepan, with the sugar and lemon-rind, and let it remain by the side of the fire until the cream is well flavoured, when take out the lemon-rind. Mix the arrowroot smoothly with the cold milk; add this to the cream, and let it boil gently for about 3 minutes, keeping it well stirred. Take it off the fire, stir till nearly cold, when add the lemon-juice, and pour the whole over the cakes. Garnish the cream with strips of angelica, or candied citron cut thin, or bright-coloured jelly or preserve. This cream is exceedingly delicious, flavoured with vanilla instead of lemon: when this flavouring is used the sherry may be omitted, and the mixture poured over the *dry* cakes. *Time.*—About ½ hour to infuse the lemon-rind; 5 minutes to boil the cream. *Average cost*, with cream at 1*s.* per pint, 3*s.* *Sufficient* for 5 or 6 persons. *Seasonable* at any time.

CREAM, Vanilla.

Ingredients.—1 pint of milk, the yolks of 8 eggs, 6 oz. of sugar, 1 oz. of isinglass, flavouring to taste of essence of vanilla. *Mode.*—Put the milk and sugar into a saucepan, and let it get hot over a slow fire; beat up the yolks of the eggs, to which add gradually the sweetened milk;

flavour the whole with essence of vanilla, put the mixture into a jug, and place this jug in a saucepan of boiling water. Stir the contents with a wooden spoon one way until the mixture thickens, but do not allow it to boil, or it will be full of lumps. Take it off the fire; stir in the isinglass, which should be previously dissolved in about ¼ pint of water, and boiled for 2 or 3 minutes; pour the cream into an oiled mould, put it in a cool place to set, and turn it out carefully on a dish. Instead of using the essence of vanilla, a pod may be boiled in the milk until the flavour is well extracted. A pod, or a pod and a half, will be found sufficient for the above proportion of ingredients. *Time.*—About 10 minutes to stir the mixture. *Average cost*, with the best isinglass, 2*s*. 6*d*. *Sufficient* to fill a quart mould. *Seasonable* at any time.

VANILLA-CREAM MOULD.

CREAM, Whipped, for putting on Trifles, serving in Glasses, &c.

Ingredients.—To every pint of cream allow 3 oz. of pounded sugar, 1 glass of sherry or any kind of sweet white wine, the rind of ½ lemon, the white of 1 egg. *Mode.*—Rub the sugar on the lemon-rind, and pound it in a mortar until quite fine, and beat up the white of the egg until quite stiff; put the cream into a large bowl, with the sugar, wine, and beaten egg, and whip it to a froth; as fast as the froth rises take it off with a skimmer, and put it on a sieve to drain in a cool place. This should be made the day before it is wanted, as the whip is then so much firmer. The cream should be whipped in a cool place, and in summer over ice, if it is obtainable. A plain whipped cream may be served on a glass dish, and garnished with strips of angelica, or pastry-leaves, or pieces of bright-coloured jelly: it makes a very pretty addition to the supper-table. *Time.*—About 1 hour to whip the cream. *Average cost*, with cream at 1*s*. per pint, 1*s*. 9*d*. *Sufficient* for 1 dish or 1 trifle. *Seasonable* at any time.

PASTRY-LEAF.

CRUMPETS.

These are made in the same manner as muffins, only, in making the mixture, let it be more like batter than dough. Let it rise for about ½ hour; pour it into iron rings, which should be ready on a hot-plate; bake them, and when one side appears done, turn them quickly on the other. *To toast them*, have ready a very *bright clear* fire; put the crumpet on a toasting-fork, and hold it before the fire, *not too close*, until it is nicely brown on one side, but do not allow it to blacken; turn it, and brown the other side; then spread it with good butter, cut it in half, and, when all are done, pile them on a hot dish, and send them quickly to table. Muffins and crumpets should always be served on separate dishes, and both toasted and served as expeditiously as possible. *Time.*—From 10 to 15 minutes to bake them. *Sufficient.*—Allow 2 crumpets to each person.

CRUST, Butter, for Boiled Puddings.

Ingredients.—To every lb. of flour allow 6 oz. of butter, ½ pint of water. *Mode.*—With a knife, work the flour to a smooth paste with ½ pint of water; roll the crust out rather thin; place the butter over it in small pieces, dredge lightly over it some flour, and fold the paste over; repeat the rolling once more, and the crust will be ready for use. It may be enriched by adding another 2 oz. of butter; but, for ordinary purposes, the above quantity will be found quite sufficient. *Average cost*, 6*d*. per lb.

CRUST, Common, for Raised Pies.

Ingredients.—To every lb. of flour allow ½ pint of water, 1½ oz. of butter, 1½ oz. of lard, ½ saltspoonful of salt. *Mode.*—Put into a saucepan the water; when it boils, add the butter and lard, and when these are melted, make a hole in the middle of the flour; pour in the water gradually, beat it well with a wooden spoon, and be particular in not making the paste too soft. When it is well mixed, knead it with the hands until quite stiff, dredging a little flour over the paste and board to prevent them from sticking. When it is well kneaded, place it before the fire, with a cloth covered over it, for a few minutes; it will then be more easily worked into shape. This paste does not taste so nicely as a richer one, but it is worked with greater facility, and answers just as well for raised pies, for the crust is seldom eaten. *Average cost*, 5*d*. per lb.

CRUST, Dripping, for Kitchen Puddings, Pies, &c.

Ingredients.—To every lb. of flour allow 6 oz. of clarified beef dripping, ½ pint of water. *Mode.*—After having clarified the dripping, weigh it, and to every lb. of flour allow the above proportion of dripping. With a knife, work the flour into a smooth paste with the water, rolling it out three times, each time placing on the crust 2 oz. of the dripping broken into small pieces. If this paste is lightly made, if good dripping is used, and *not too much of it*, it will be found good; and by the addition of two tablespoonfuls of fine moist sugar, it may be converted into a common short crust for fruit pies. *Average cost*, 4*d*. per lb.

CRUST, Lard or Flead.

Ingredients.—To every lb. of flour allow ½ lb. of lard or flead, ½ pint of water, ½ saltspoonful of salt. *Mode.*—Clear the flead from skin, and slice it into thin flakes; rub it into the flour, add the salt, and work the whole into a smooth paste, with the above proportion of water; fold the paste over two or three times, beat it well with the rolling-pin, roll it out, and it will be ready for use. The crust made from this will be found extremely light, and may be made into cakes or tarts; it may also be very much enriched by adding more flead to the same proportion of flour. *Average cost*, 8*d*. per lb.

CRUST, Suet, for Pies or Puddings.

Ingredients.—To every lb. of flour allow 5 or 6 oz. of beef suet, ½ pint of water. *Mode.* —Free the suet from skin and shreds, chop it extremely fine, and rub it well into the flour; work the whole to a smooth paste with the above proportion of water; roll it out, and it is ready for use. This crust is quite rich enough for ordinary purposes, but when a better one is desired, use from ½ to ¾ lb. of suet to every lb. of flour. Some cooks, for rich crusts, pound the suet in a mortar, with a small quantity of butter. It should then be laid on the paste in small pieces, the same as for puff-crust, and will be found exceedingly nice for hot tarts. 5 oz. of suet to every lb. of flour will make a very good crust; and even ¼ lb. will answer very well for children, or where the crust is wanted very plain. *Average cost*, 5*d*. per lb.

CRUST, Common Short.

Ingredients.—To every lb. of flour allow 2 oz. of sifted sugar, 3 oz. of butter, about ½ pint of boiling milk. *Mode.*—Crumble the butter into the flour as finely as possible, add the sugar, and work the whole up to a smooth paste with the boiling milk. Roll it out thin, and bake in a moderate oven. *Average cost*, 6*d*. per lb.

CRUST, Very good Short for Fruit Tarts.

Ingredients.—To every lb. of flour allow ½ or ¾ lb. of butter, 1 tablespoonful of sifted sugar, ⅓ pint of water. *Mode.*—Rub the butter into the flour, after having ascertained that the latter is perfectly dry; add the sugar, and mix the whole into a stiff paste with about ⅓ pint of water. Roll it out two or three times, folding the paste over each time, and it will be ready for use. *Average cost*, 1*s*. 1*d*. per lb.

CRUST, Another good Short.

Ingredients.—To every lb. of flour allow 8 oz. of butter, the yolks of 2 eggs, 2 oz. of sifted sugar, about ¼ pint of milk. *Mode.*—Rub the butter into the flour, add the sugar, and mix the whole as lightly as possible to a smooth paste, with the yolks of the eggs well beaten, and the milk. The proportion of the latter ingredient must be judged of by the size of the eggs; if these are large so much will not be required, and more if the eggs are smaller. *Average cost*, 1*s*. per lb.

CUCUMBER SAUCE.

Ingredients.—3 or 4 cucumbers, 2 oz. of butter, 6 tablespoonfuls of brown gravy. *Mode.*—Peel the cucumbers, quarter them, and take out the seeds; cut them into small pieces, put them in a cloth, and rub them well to take out the water that hangs about them. Put the butter in a saucepan, add the cucumbers, and shake them over a sharp fire until they are of a good colour; then pour over them the gravy, mixed with the cucumbers, and simmer gently for 10 minutes, when it will be ready to serve. *Time.*—Altogether, ½ hour.

CUCUMBER SAUCE, White.

Ingredients.—3 or 4 cucumbers, ½ pint of white stock, cayenne and salt to taste, the yolks of 3 eggs. *Mode.*—Cut the cucumbers into small pieces, after peeling them and taking out the seeds. Put them in the stewpan with the white stock and seasoning; simmer gently till the cucumbers are tender, which will be in about ¼ hour. Then add the yolks of the eggs, well beaten; stir them to the sauce, but do not allow it to boil, and serve very hot. *Time.*—Altogether, ½ hour.

CUCUMBER SOUP (French Recipe).

Ingredients.—1 large cucumber, a piece of butter the size of a walnut, a little chervil and sorrel cut in large pieces, salt and pepper to taste, the yolks of 2 eggs, 1 gill of cream, 1 quart of medium stock. *Mode.*—Pare the cucumber, quarter it, and take out the seeds; cut it in thin slices, put these on a plate with a little salt, to draw the water from them; drain, and put them in your stewpan with the butter. When they are warmed through, without being browned, pour the stock on them. Add the sorrel, chervil, and seasoning, and boil for 40 minutes. Mix the well-beaten yolks of the eggs with the cream, which add at the moment of serving. *Time.* — 1 hour. *Average cost,* 1*s.* 2*d.* per quart. *Sufficient* for 4 persons. *Seasonable* from June to September.

CUCUMBER VINEGAR (a very nice addition to Salads).

Ingredients.—10 large cucumbers, or 12 smaller ones, 1 quart of vinegar, 2 onions, 2 shalots, 1 tablespoonful of salt, 2 tablespoonfuls of pepper, ¼ teaspoonful of cayenne. *Mode.*—Pare and slice the cucumbers, put them in a stone jar or wide-mouthed bottle with the vinegar; slice the onions and shalots, and add them, with all the other ingredients, to the cucumbers. Let it stand 4 or 5 days, boil it all up, and, when cold, strain the liquor through a piece of muslin, and store it away in small bottles well sealed. This vinegar is a very nice addition to gravies, hashes, &c., as well as a great improvement to salads, or to eat with cold meat.

CUCUMBERS, to Dress.

Ingredients.—3 tablespoonfuls of salad-oil, 4 tablespoonfuls of vinegar, salt and pepper to taste. *Mode.*—Pare the cucumber, cut it equally into *very thin*

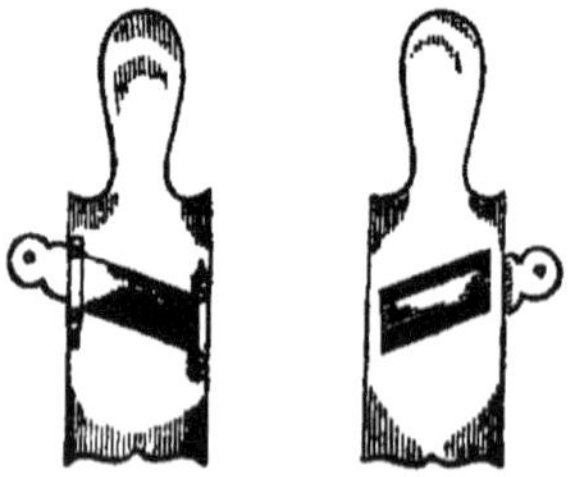

CUCUMBER-SLICES.

slices, and *commence* cutting from the *thick end;* if commenced at the stalk, the cucumber will most likely have an exceedingly bitter taste, far from agreeable. For the purpose of slicing cucumbers evenly and very thin, we recommend the slice in preference to an ordinary knife. Put the slices into a dish, sprinkle over salt and pepper, and pour over oil and vinegar in the above proportion; turn

SLICED CUCUMBERS.

the cucumber about, and it is ready to serve. This is a favourite accompaniment to boiled salmon, is a nice addition to all descriptions of salads, and makes a pretty garnish to lobster salad. *Average cost,* when scarce, 1*s.* to 2*s.* 6*d.*; when cheapest, may be had for 1*d.* each. *Seasonable.*—Forced from the beginning of March to the end of June; in full season in July, August, and September.

CUCUMBERS, Fried.

Ingredients.—2 or 3 cucumbers, pepper and salt to taste, flour, oil or butter. *Mode.*—Pare the cucumbers, and cut them into slices of an equal thickness, commencing to slice from the thick and not the stalk end of the cucumber. Wipe the slices dry with a cloth, dredge them with flour, and put them into a pan of boiling oil or butter; keep turning them about until brown; lift them out of the pan, let them drain, and serve, piled lightly in a dish. These will be found a great improvement to rump-steak: they should be placed on a dish with the steak on the top. *Time.*—5 minutes. *Average cost*, when cheapest, 1*d.* each. *Sufficient* for 4 or 5 persons. *Seasonable.*—Forced from the beginning of March to the end of June; in full season in July and August.

CUCUMBERS à la Poulette.

Ingredients.—2 or 3 cucumbers, salt and vinegar, 2 oz. of butter, flour, ½ pint of broth, 1 teaspoonful of minced parsley, a lump of sugar, the yolks of 2 eggs, salt and pepper to taste. *Mode.*—Pare and cut the cucumbers into slices of an equal thickness, and let them remain in a pickle of salt and vinegar for ½ hour, then drain them in a cloth, and put them into a stewpan with the butter. Fry them over a brisk fire, but do not brown them, and then dredge over them a little flour; add the broth, skim off all the fat, which will rise to the surface, and boil gently until the gravy is somewhat reduced, but the cucumber should not be broken. Stir in the yolks of the eggs, add the parsley, sugar, and a seasoning of pepper and salt; bring the whole to the *point of boiling*, and serve. *Time.*—Altogether, 1 hour. *Average cost*, when cheapest, 1*d.* each. *Sufficient* for 5 or 6 persons. *Seasonable* in July, August, or September; but may be had, forced, from the beginning of March.

CUCUMBERS, Pickled.

Ingredients.—1 oz. of whole pepper, 1 oz. of bruised ginger, sufficient vinegar to cover the cucumbers. *Mode.*—Cut the cucumbers in thick slices, sprinkle salt over them, and let them remain for 24 hours. The next day, drain them well for 6 hours, put them into a jar, pour boiling vinegar over them, and keep them in a warm place. In a short time, boil up the vinegar again, add pepper and ginger in the above proportion, and instantly cover them up. Tie them down with bladder, and in a few days they will be fit for use.

CUCUMBERS, an excellent way of Preserving.

Ingredients.—Salt and water, 1 lb. of lump sugar, the rind of 1 lemon, 1 oz. of ginger, cucumbers. *Mode.*—Choose the greenest cucumbers, and those that are most free from seeds; put them in strong salt and water, with a cabbage-leaf to keep them down; tie a paper over them, and put them in a warm place till they are yellow, then wash them and set them over the fire in fresh water with a very little salt, and another cabbage-leaf over them; cover very closely, but take care they do not boil. If they are not a fine green, change the water again, cover them as before, and make them hot. When they are a good colour take them off the fire and let them cool; cut them in quarters, take out the seeds and pulp, and put them into cold water; let them remain for 2 days, changing the water twice each day, to draw out the salt. Put the sugar, with ½ pint of water, in a saucepan over the fire; remove the scum as it rises, and add the lemon-peel and ginger with the outside scraped off; when the syrup is tolerably thick, take it off the fire, and when *cold*, wipe the cucumbers *dry* and put them in. Boil the syrup once in 2 or 3 days for 3 weeks; strengthen it if required, and let it be quite cold before the cucumbers are put in. Great attention must be paid to the directions in the commencement of this recipe, as, if these are not properly carried out, the result will be far from satisfactory. *Seasonable.*—This recipe should be used in June, July, or August.

CUCUMBERS, German Method of keeping for Winter use.

Ingredients.—Cucumbers, salt. *Mode.*—Pare and slice the cucumbers (as for the table), sprinkle well with salt, and let them remain for 24 hours; strain off the liquor, pack in jars, a thick layer of cucumbers and salt alternately; tie down closely, and, when wanted for use, take out the quantity required. Now wash them well in fresh water, and dress as usual with pepper, vinegar, and oil.

CUCUMBERS, Stewed.

Ingredients.—3 large cucumbers, flour, butter, rather more than ½ pint of good brown gravy. *Mode.*—Cut the cucumbers lengthwise the size of the dish they are intended to be served in; empty them of the seeds, and put them into boiling water with a little salt, and let them simmer for 5 minutes; then take them out, place them in another stewpan, with the gravy, and let them boil over a brisk fire until the cucumbers are tender. Should these be bitter, add a lump of sugar; carefully dish them, skim the sauce, pour over the cucumbers, and serve. *Time.*—Altogether, 20 minutes. *Average cost*, when cheapest, 1*d.* each. *Sufficient* for 3 or 4 persons. *Seasonable* in June, July, and August; but may be had, forced, from the beginning of March.

CUCUMBERS, Stewed with Onions

Ingredients.—6 cucumbers, 3 moderate-sized onions, not quite 1 pint of white stock, cayenne and salt to taste, the yolks of 2 eggs, a very little grated nutmeg. *Mode.*—Pare and slice the cucumbers, take out the seeds, and cut the onions into thin slices; put these both into a stewpan, with the stock, and let them boil for ¼ hour or longer, should the cucumbers be very large. Beat up the yolks of 2 eggs; stir these into the sauce; add the cayenne, salt, and grated nutmeg; bring it to the point of boiling, and serve. Do not allow the sauce to boil, or it will curdle. This is a favourite dish with lamb or mutton chops, rump-steaks, &c. *Time.*—Altogether, 20 minutes. *Average cost*, when cheapest, 1*d.* each. *Sufficient* for 6 or 7 persons. *Seasonable* in July, August, and September; but may be had, forced, from the beginning of March.

CURRANT DUMPLINGS.

Ingredients.—1 lb. of flour, 6 oz. of suet, ½ lb. of currants, rather more than ½ pint of water. *Mode.*—Chop the suet finely, mix it with the flour, and add the currants, which should be nicely washed, picked, and dried; mix the whole to a limp paste with the water (if wanted very nice, use milk); divide it into 7 or ·plings; tie them in cloths, and boil for 1¼ hour. They may be boiled without a cloth: they should then be made into round balls, and dropped into boiling water, and should be moved about at first, to prevent them from sticking to the bottom of the saucepan. Serve with a cut lemon, cold butter, and sifted sugar. *Time.*—In a cloth, 1¼ hour; without, ¾ hour. *Average cost*, 9*d.* *Sufficient* for 6 or 7 persons. *Seasonable* at any time.

CURRANT FRITTERS.

Ingredients.—½ pint of milk, 2 tablespoonfuls of flour, 4 eggs, 3 tablespoonfuls of boiled rice, 3 tablespoonfuls of currants, sugar to taste, a very little grated nutmeg, hot lard or clarified dripping. *Mode.*—Put the milk into a basin with the flour, which should previously be rubbed to a smooth batter with a little cold milk; stir these ingredients together; add the well-whisked eggs, the rice, currants, sugar, and nutmeg. Beat the mixture for a few minutes, and, if not sufficiently thick, add a little more boiled rice; drop it, in small quantities, into a pan of boiling lard or clarified dripping; fry the fritters a nice brown, and, when done, drain them on a piece of blotting-paper, before the fire. Pile them on a white d'oyley, strew over sifted sugar, and serve them very hot. Send a cut lemon to table with them. *Time.*—From 8 to 10 minutes to fry the fritters. *Average cost*, 9*d.* *Sufficient* for 3 or 4 persons. *Seasonable* at any time.

CURRANT JAM, Black.

Ingredients.—To every lb. of fruit, weighed before being stripped from the stalks, allow ¾ lb. of loaf sugar, 1 gill of water. *Mode.*—Let the fruit be very ripe, and gathered on a dry day. Strip it from the stalks, and put it into a preserving-pan, with a gill of water to each lb. of fruit; boil these together for 10 minutes; then add the sugar, and boil the jam again for 30 minutes, reckoning from the time when the jam simmers equally all over, or longer, should it not appear to set nicely when a little is poured on to a plate. Keep stirring it to prevent it from burning, carefully remove all the scum, and when done, pour it into pots. Let it cool, cover the top of the jam with oiled paper, and the top of the jars with a piece of tissue-paper brushed over on both sides with the white of an egg: this, when cold, forms a hard stiff cover, and perfectly excludes the air. Great attention must be paid to the stirring of this jam, as it is very liable to burn, on account of the thickness of the juice. *Time.*—10 minutes to boil the fruit and water; 30 minutes with the sugar, or longer. *Average cost*, from 6*d.* to 8*d.* for a pot capable of holding 1 lb. *Sufficient.*—Allow from 6 to 7 quarts of currants to make 1 dozen pots of jam, each pot to hold 1 lb. *Seasonable.*—Make this in July.

CURRANT JAM, Red.

Ingredients.—To every lb. of fruit allow ¾ lb. of loaf sugar. *Mode.*—Let the fruit be gathered on a fine day; weigh it, and then strip the currants from the stalks; put them into a preserving-pan with sugar in the above proportion; stir them, and boil them for about ¾ hour. Carefully remove the scum as it rises. Put the jam into pots, and, when cold, cover with oiled papers; over these put a piece of tissue-paper brushed over on both sides with the white of an egg; press the paper round the top of the pot, and, when dry, the covering will be quite hard and air-tight. *Time.*—½ to ¾ hour, reckoning from the time the jam boils all over. *Average cost*, for a lb. pot, from 6*d.* to 8*d.* *Sufficient.*—Allow from 6 to 7 quarts of currants to make 12 1-lb. pots of jam. *Seasonable.*—Make this in July.

JAM-POT.

CURRANT JELLY, Black.

Ingredients.—Black currants; to every pint of juice allow ¼ pint of water, 1 lb of loaf sugar. *Mode.*—Strip the currants from the stalks, which may be done in an expeditious manner, by holding the bunch in one hand, and passing a small silver fork down the currants: they will then readily fall from the stalks. Put them into a jar, place this jar in a saucepan of boiling water, and simmer them until their juice is extracted; then strain them, and to every pint of juice allow the above proportion of sugar and water; stir these ingredients together cold until the sugar is dissolved; place the preserving-pan on the fire, and boil the jelly for about ½ hour, reckoning from the time it commences to boil all over, and carefully remove the scum as it rises. If the jelly becomes firm when a little is put on a plate, it is done; it should then be put into *small* pots, and covered the same as the jam in the preceding recipe. If the jelly is wanted very clear, the fruit should not be squeezed dry; but, of course, so much juice will not be obtained. If the fruit is not much squeezed, it may be converted into a jam for immediate eating, by boiling it with a little common sugar: this answers very well for a nursery preserve. *Time.*—About ¾ hour to extract the juice; ½ hour to boil the jelly. *Average cost*, from 8*d.* to 10*d.* per ½-lb. pot. *Sufficient.*—From 3 pints to 2 quarts of fruit should yield a pint of juice. *Seasonable.*—Make this in July.

CURRANT JELLY, Red.

Ingredients.—Red currants; to every pint of juice allow ¾ lb. of loaf sugar. *Mode.*—Have the fruit gathered in fine weather; pick it from the stalks, put it into a jar, and place this jar in a saucepan of boiling water over the fire, and let it simmer gently until the juice is well drawn from the currants; then strain them through a jelly-bag or fine cloth, and if the jelly is wished very clear, do not squeeze them *too much*, as the skin and pulp from the fruit will be pressed through with the juice, and so make the jelly muddy. Measure the juice, and to each pint allow ¾ lb of loaf sugar; put these into a preserving-pan, set it over the fire, and keep stirring the jelly until it is done, carefully removing every particle of scum as it rises, using a wooden or silver spoon for the purpose, as metal or iron ones would spoil the colour of the jelly. When it has boiled from 20 minutes to ½ hour, put a little of the jelly on a plate, and if firm when cool, it is done. Take it off the fire, pour it into small gallipots, cover each of the pots with an oiled paper, and then with a piece of tissue-paper brushed over on both sides with the white of an egg. Label the pots, adding the year when the jelly was made, and store it away in a dry place. A jam may be made with the currants, if they are not squeezed too dry, by adding a few fresh raspberries, and boiling all together, with sufficient sugar to sweeten it nicely. As this jam is not worth storing away, but is only for immediate eating, a smaller proportion of sugar than usual will be found enough: it answers very well for children's puddings, or for a nursery preserve. *Time.*—From ¾ to 1 hour to extract the juice; 20 minutes to ½ hour to boil the jelly. *Average cost*, from 8*d.* to 10*d.* per ½-lb. pot. *Sufficient.*—8 quarts of currants will make from 10 to 12 pots of jelly. *Seasonable.*—Make this in July.

Note.—Should the above proportion of sugar not be found sufficient for some tastes, add an extra ¼ lb. to every pint of juice, making altogether 1lb.

CURRANT JELLY, White.

Ingredients.—White currants; to every pint of juice allow ¾lb. of good loaf sugar. *Mode.*—Pick the currants from the stalks, and put them into a jar; place this jar in a saucepan of boiling water, and simmer until the juice is well drawn from the fruit, which will be in from ¾ to 1 hour. Then strain the currants through a fine cloth or jelly-bag; do not squeeze them too much, or the jelly will not be clear, and put the juice into a very clean preserving-pan, with the sugar. Let this simmer gently over a clear fire until it is firm, and keep stirring and skimming until it is done; then pour it into small pots, cover them, and store away in a dry place. *Time.*—¾ hour to draw the juice; ½ hour to boil the jelly. *Average cost*, from 8*d.* to 10*d.* per ½-lb. pot. *Sufficient.*—From 3 pints to 2 quarts of fruit should yield 1 pint of juice. *Seasonable* in July and August.

CURRANT PUDDING, Boiled (Plain and Economical).

Ingredients.—1 lb. of flour, ½ lb. of suet, ½ lb. of currants, milk. *Mode.*—Wash the currants, dry them thoroughly, and pick away any stalks or grit; chop the suet finely; mix all the ingredients together, and moisten with sufficient milk to make the pudding into a stiff batter; tie it up in a floured cloth, put it into boiling water, and boil for 3½ hours; serve with a cut lemon, cold butter, and sifted sugar. *Time.*—3½ hours. *Average cost*, 10*d.* *Sufficient* for 7 or 8 persons. *Seasonable* at any time.

CURRANT PUDDING, Black or Red.

Ingredients.—1 quart of red or black currants, measured with the stalks, ¼ lb. of moist sugar, suet crust or butter crust (*see* recipes for CRUSTS). *Mode.*—Make, with ¾ lb. of flour, either a suet crust or butter crust (the former is usually made); butter a basin, and line it with part of the crust; add the currants, which should be stripped from the stalks, and sprinkle the sugar over them; put the cover of the pudding on; make the edges very secure, that the juice does not escape; tie it down with a floured cloth, put it into boiling water, and boil from 2½ to 3 hours. Boiled without a basin, allow ½ hour less. We have given rather a large proportion of sugar; but we find fruit puddings are so much more juicy and palatable when *well sweetened* before they are boiled, besides being more economical. A few raspberries added to red-currant pudding are a very nice addition; about ½ pint would be sufficient for the above quantity of fruit. Fruit puddings are very delicious if, when they are turned out of the basin, the crust is browned with a salamander, or put into a very hot oven for a few minutes to colour it: this makes it crisp on the surface. *Time.*—2½ to 3 hours; without a basin, 2 to 2½ hours. *Average cost*, in full season, 8*d.* *Sufficient* for 6 or 7 persons. *Seasonable* in June, July, and August.

CURRANT AND RASPBERRY TART, Red.

Ingredients.—1½ pint of picked currants, ½ pint of raspberries, 3 heaped tablespoonfuls of moist sugar, ½ lb of short crust. *Mode.*—Strip the currants from the stalks, and put them into a deep pie-dish, with a small cup placed in the midst, bottom upwards; add the raspberries and sugar; place a border of paste round the edge of the dish, cover with crust, ornament the edges, and bake from ½ to ¾ hour; strew some sifted sugar over before being sent to table. This tart is more generally served cold than hot. *Time.*—½ to ¾ hour. *Average cost*, 1*s.* *Sufficient* for 5 or 6 persons. *Seasonable* in June, July, and August.

Note.—In tarts of this description carefully avoid washing the fruit.

CURRANTS, Iced, for Dessert.

Ingredients.—½ pint of water, the whites of 2 eggs, currants, pounded sugar. *Mode.*—Select very fine bunches of red or white currants, and well beat the whites of the eggs. Mix these with the water; then take the currants, a bunch at a time, and dip them in; let them drain for a minute or two, and roll them in very fine-pounded sugar. Lay them to dry on paper, when the sugar will crystallize round each currant, and have a very pretty effect. All fresh fruit may be prepared in the same manner; and a mixture of various fruits iced in this manner, and arranged on one dish, looks very well for a summer dessert. *Time.*—½ day to dry the fruit. *Average cost*, 8*d*. for a pint of iced currants. *Seasonable* in summer.

CURRY.

Ingredients.—Veal, mutton, fowl, or rabbit; a large onion, butter, brown gravy or stock, a tablespoonful of curry-powder. *Mode.*—Let the meat be half fried. Cut the onion into small pieces, and fry it in butter till quite brown; add the meat, with a small quantity of brown gravy or stock, also the curry-powder, and stew all for about 20 minutes. This is for a dry curry; more gravy and curry-powder can be used if preferred. *Time.*—20 minutes. *Seasonable* at any time.

CURRY ST. LEONARDS.

Ingredients.—Chicken, or any meat; 2 tablespoonfuls of butter, 2 tablespoonfuls of curry-powder, 4 or 5 leaves of mint, a teacup of good gravy, salt, a dessertspoonful of vinegar, 3 tablespoonfuls of cream. *Mode.*—Fry together for 10 minutes the butter, curry-powder, and mint; then add the meat *cut into dice*, also the gravy, salt, and vinegar. Let all these simmer for 20 minutes, and then pour over the cream, and serve quite hot. *Time.*—30 minutes. *Seasonable* at any time.

CURRY-POWDER (Founded on Dr. Kitchener's Recipe).

Ingredients.—¼ lb. of coriander-seed, ¼ lb. of turmeric, 2 oz. of cinnamon-seed, ½ oz. of cayenne, 1 oz. of mustard, 1 oz. of ground ginger, ½ ounce of allspice, 2 oz. of fenugreek seed. *Mode.*—Put all the ingredients in a cool oven, where they should remain one night; then pound them in a mortar, rub them through a sieve, and mix thoroughly together; keep the powder in a bottle, from which the air should be completely excluded.

CURRY-POWDER (Capt. White's Recipe; most excellent).

Ingredients.—1 lb. of pale turmeric seed, 4 oz. of cumming seed, 8 oz. of coriander seed, 4 oz. of black pepper, 2 oz. of cayenne pepper, 4 oz. of Jamaica ginger, 10 oz. of caraway seed, ¼ oz. of cardamums. *Mode.*—Mix together all these ingredients, well pounded, and then place the mixture in the sun, or before the fire, stirring it frequently. *Average cost*, 5*s*. 2*d*.

Note.—This will be found a most excellent curry-powder, if care be taken to purchase the ingredients at a good druggist's.

CUSTARDS, Boiled.

Ingredients.—1 pint of milk, 5 eggs, 3 oz. of loaf sugar, 3 laurel-leaves, or the rind of ½ lemon, or a few drops of essence of vanilla, 1 tablespoonful of brandy. *Mode.*—Put the milk into a *lined* saucepan, with the sugar and whichever of the above flavourings may be preferred (the lemon-rind flavours custards most deliciously), and let the milk steep by the side of the fire until it is well flavoured. Bring it to the point of boiling, then strain it into a basin;

CUSTARDS IN GLASSES.

whisk the eggs well, and, when the milk has cooled a little, stir in the eggs, and *strain* this mixture into a jug. Place this jug in a saucepan of boiling water over the fire; keep stirring the custard *one way* until it thickens; but on no account allow it to reach the boiling point, as it will instantly curdle and be full of lumps. Take it off the fire, stir in the brandy, and when this is well mixed with the custard, pour it into glasses, which should be rather more than three-parts full; grate a little nutmeg over the top, and the dish is ready for table. To make custards look and eat better, ducks' eggs should be used, when obtainable; they add very much to the flavour and richness, and so many are not required as of the ordinary eggs, 4 ducks' eggs to the pint of milk making a delicious custard. When desired extremely rich and good, cream should be substituted for the milk, and double the quantity of eggs used to those mentioned, omitting the whites. *Time.*—½ hour to infuse the lemon-rind, about 10 minutes to stir the custard. *Average cost*, 8d. *Sufficient* to fill 8 custard-glasses. *Seasonable* at any time.

CUSTARD PUDDING, Baked.

Ingredients.—1½ pint of milk, the rind of ¼ lemon, ¼ lb. of moist sugar, 4 eggs. *Mode.*—Put the milk into a saucepan with the sugar and lemon-rind, and let this infuse for about ½ hour, or until the milk is well flavoured; whisk the eggs, yolks and whites; pour the milk to them, stirring all the while; then have ready a pie-dish, lined at the edge with paste ready baked; strain the custard into the dish, grate a little nutmeg over the top, and bake in a *very slow* oven for about ½ hour, or rather longer. The flavour of this pudding may be varied by substituting bitter almonds for the lemon-rind; and it may be very much enriched by using half cream and half milk, and doubling the quantity of eggs. *Time.*—½ to ¾ hour. *Average cost*, 9d. *Sufficient* for 5 or 6 persons. *Seasonable* at any time.

Note.—This pudding is usually served cold with fruit tarts.

CUSTARD PUDDING, Boiled.

Ingredients.—1 pint of milk, 1 tablespoonful of flour, 4 eggs, flavouring to taste. *Mode.*—Flavour the milk by infusing in it a little lemon-rind or cinnamon; whisk the eggs, stir the flour gradually to these, and pour over them the milk, and stir the mixture well. Butter a basin that will exactly hold it; put in the custard, and tie a floured cloth over; plunge it into boiling water, and turn it about for a few minutes, to prevent the flour from settling in one part. Boil it slowly for ½ hour; turn it out of the basin, and serve. The pudding may be garnished with red-currant jelly, and sweet sauce may be sent to table with it. *Time.*—½ hour. *Average cost*, 7d. *Sufficient* for 5 or 6 persons. *Seasonable* at any time.

CUSTARD SAUCE, for Sweet Puddings or Tarts.

Ingredients.—½ pint of milk, 2 eggs, 3 oz. of pounded sugar, 1 tablespoonful of brandy. *Mode.*—Put the milk in a very clean saucepan, and let it boil. Beat the eggs, stir to them the milk and pounded sugar, and put the mixture into a jug. Place the jug in a saucepan of boiling water; keep stirring well until it thickens, but do not allow it to boil, or it will curdle. Serve the sauce in a tureen, stir in the brandy, and grate a little nutmeg over the top. This sauce may be made very much nicer by using cream instead of milk; but the above recipe will be found quite good enough for ordinary purposes. *Average cost*, 6d. per pint. *Sufficient*, this quantity, for 2 fruit tarts, or 1 pudding.

CUSTARD TARTLETS, or Fanchonnettes.

Ingredients.—For the custard, 4 eggs, ¾ pint of milk, 2 oz. of butter, 2 oz. of pounded sugar, 3 dessertspoonfuls of flour, flavouring to taste; the whites of 2 eggs, 2 oz. of pounded sugar. *Mode.*—Well beat the eggs; stir to them the milk, the butter, which should be beaten to a cream, the sugar, and flour; mix these ingredients well together, put them into a very clean saucepan, and bring them to the simmering point, but do not allow them to boil. Flavour with essence of vanilla, bitter almonds, lemon, grated chocolate, or any flavouring ingredient that may be preferred. Line some round tartlet-pans with good puff-paste; fill them with the custard, and bake in a moderate oven for about 20 minutes; then take them out of the pans; let them cool, and in the meantime whisk the whites of the eggs to a stiff froth; stir into this the pounded sugar, and spread smoothly over the tartlets a little of this mixture. Put them in the oven again to set the icing, but be particular that they do not scorch; when the icing looks crisp, they are done. Arrange them, piled high in the centre, on a white napkin, and garnish the dish, and in between the tartlets, with strips of bright jelly, or very firmly-made preserve. *Time.*—20 minutes to bake the tartlets; 5 minutes after being iced. *Average cost*, exclusive of the paste, 1*s*. *Sufficient* to fill 10 or 12 tartlets. *Seasonable* at any time.

Note.—The icing may be omitted on the top of the tartlets, and a spoonful of any kind of preserve put at the bottom of the custard instead: this varies both the flavour and appearance of this dish.

CUTLET, the Invalid's.

Ingredients.—1 nice cutlet from a loin or neck of mutton, 2 teacupfuls of water, 1 very small stick of celery, pepper and salt to taste. *Mode*.—Have the cutlet cut from a very nice loin or neck of mutton; take off all the fat; put it into a stewpan, with the other ingredients; stew *very gently* indeed for nearly 2 hours, and skim off every particle of fat that may rise to the surface from time to time. The celery should be cut into thin slices before it is added to the meat, and care must be taken not to put in too much of this ingredient, or the dish will not be good. If the water is allowed to boil fast, the cutlet will be hard. *Time*.—2 hours' very gentle stewing. *Average cost*, 6*d*. *Sufficient* for 1 person. *Seasonable* at any time.

CUTLETS, Mutton, Italian.

Ingredients.—About 3 lbs. of the neck of mutton, clarified butter, the yolk of 1 egg, 4 tablespoonfuls of bread crumbs, 1 tablespoonful of minced savoury herbs, 1 tablespoonful of minced parsley, 1 teaspoonful of minced shalot, 1 saltspoonful of finely-chopped lemonpeel; pepper, salt, and pounded mace to taste; flour, ½ pint of hot broth or water, 2 teaspoonfuls of Harvey's sauce, 1 teaspoonful of soy, 2 teaspoonfuls of tarragon vinegar, 1 tablespoonful of port wine. *Mode*.—Cut the mutton into nicely-shaped cutlets, flatten them, and trim off some of the fat, dip them in clarified butter, and then into the beaten yolk of an egg. Mix well together bread crumbs, herbs, parsley, shalot, lemon-peel, and seasoning in the above proportion, and cover the cutlets with these ingredients. Melt some butter in a frying-pan, lay in the cutlets, and fry them a nice brown; take them out, and keep them hot before the fire. Dredge some flour into the pan, and, if there is not sufficient butter, add a little more; stir till it looks brown, then put in the hot broth or water, and the remaining ingredients; give one boil, and pour round the cutlets. If the gravy should not be thick enough, add a little more flour. Mushrooms, when obtainable, are a great improvement to this dish, and when not in season, mushroom-powder may be substituted for them. *Time*.—10 minutes; rather longer, should the cutlets be very thick. *Average cost*, 2*s*. 9*d*. *Sufficient* for 5 or 6 persons. *Seasonable* at any time.

CUTLETS of Cold Mutton.

[COLD MEAT COOKERY.] *Ingredients*.—The remains of cold loin or neck of mutton, 1 egg, bread crumbs, brown gravy or tomato sauce. *Mode*.—Cut the remains of cold loin or neck of mutton into cutlets, trim them, and take away a portion of the fat, should there be too much; dip them in beaten egg, and sprinkle with bread crumbs, and fry them a nice brown in hot dripping. Arrange them on a dish, and pour round them either a good gravy or hot tomato sauce. *Time*.—About 7 minutes. *Seasonable*.—Tomatoes to be had most reasonably in September and October.

DAMPFNUDELN, or German Puddings.

Ingredients.—1 lb. of flour, ¼ lb. of butter, 5 eggs, 2 small tablespoonfuls of yeast, 2 tablespoonfuls of finely-pounded sugar, milk, a very little salt. *Mode*.—Put the flour into a basin, make a hole in the centre, into which put the yeast, and rather more than ¼ pint of warm milk; make this into a batter with the middle of the flour, and let the sponge rise in a warm temperature. When sufficiently risen, mix the eggs, butter, sugar, and salt, with a little more warm milk, and knead the whole well together with the hands, beating the dough until it is perfectly smooth, and it drops from the fingers. Then cover the basin with a cloth, put it in a warm place, and when the dough has nicely risen, knead it into small balls; butter the bottom of a deep sauté-pan, strew over some pounded sugar, and let the dampfnudeln be laid in, but do not let them touch one another; then pour over sufficient milk to cover them, put on the lid, and let them rise to twice their original size by the side of the fire. Now place them in the oven for a few minutes to acquire a nice brown colour, and serve them on a napkin, with custard sauce flavoured with vanilla, or a compôte of any fruit that may be preferred. *Time.*—½ to ¾ hour for the sponge to rise; 10 to 15 minutes for the puddings to rise; 10 minutes to bake them in a brisk oven. *Sufficient* for 10 or 12 dampfnudeln. *Seasonable* at any time.

DAMSON CHEESE.

Ingredients.—Damsons; to every lb. of fruit pulp allow ½ lb. of loaf sugar. *Mode.*—Pick the stalks from the damsons, and put them into a preserving-pan; simmer them over the fire until they are soft, occasionally stirring them, then beat them through a coarse sieve, and put the pulp and juice into the preserving-pan, with sugar in the above proportion, having previously carefully weighed them. Stir the sugar well in, and simmer the damsons slowly for 2 hours. Skim well, then boil the preserve quickly for ½ hour, or until it looks firm and hard in the spoon; put it quickly into shallow pots, or very tiny earthenware moulds, and, when cold, cover it with oiled papers, and the jars with tissue-paper brushed over on both sides with the white of an egg. A few of the stones may be cracked, and the kernels boiled with the damsons, which very much improves the flavour of the cheese. *Time.*—1 hour to boil the damsons without the sugar; 2 hours to simmer them slowly, ½ hour quickly. *Average cost,* from 8*d.* to 10*d.* per ½-lb. pot. *Sufficient.*—1 pint of damsons to make a *very small* pot of cheese. *Seasonable.* —Make this in September or October.

DAMSON JAM.

Ingredients.—Damsons; to every lb. of fruit allow ¾ lb. of loaf sugar. *Mode.*—Have the fruit gathered in dry weather, pick it over, and reject any that is at all blemished. Stone the damsons, weigh them, and to every lb. allow ¾ lb. of loaf sugar. Put the fruit and sugar into a preserving-pan; keep stirring them gently until the sugar is dissolved, and carefully remove the scum as it rises. Boil the jam for about an hour, reckoning from the time it commences to simmer all over alike: it must be well stirred all the time, or it will be liable to burn and stick to the pan, which will cause the jam to have a very disagreeable flavour. When the jam looks firm, and the juice appears to set, it is done; then take it off the fire, put it into pots, cover it down, when quite cold, with oiled and egged papers, and store it away in a dry place. *Time.*—1 hour after the jam simmers all over. *Average cost,* from 6*d.* to 8*d.* per lb. pot. *Sufficient.*—1½ pint of damsons for a lb. pot. *Seasonable.*—Make this in September or October.

DAMSON PUDDING.

Ingredients.—1½ pint of damsons, ¼ lb. of moist sugar, ¾ lb. of suet or butter crust. *Mode.*—Make a suet crust with ¾ lb. of flour by recipe; line a buttered pudding-basin with a portion of it; fill the basin with the damsons, sweeten them, and put on the lid; pinch the edges of the crust together, that the juice does not escape; tie over a floured cloth, put the pudding into boiling water, and boil from 2½ to 3 hours. *Time.*—2½ to 3 hours. *Average cost,* 8*d.* *Sufficient* for 6 or 7 persons. *Seasonable* in September and October.

DAMSON TART.

Ingredients.—1½ pint of damsons, ¼ lb. of moist sugar, ½ lb. of short or puff crust. *Mode.*—Put the damsons, with the sugar between them, into a deep pie-dish, in the midst of which place a small cup or jar turned upside down; pile the fruit high in the middle, line the edges of the dish with short or puff crust, whichever may be preferred; put on the cover, ornament the edges, and bake from ½ to ¾ hour in a good oven. If puff-crust is used, about 10 minutes before the pie is done, take it out of the oven, brush it over with the white of an egg beaten to a froth with the blade of a knife; strew some sifted sugar over, and a few drops of water, and put the tart back to finish baking: with short crust, a little plain sifted sugar, sprinkled over, is all that will be required. *Time.*—½ to ¾ hour. *Average cost,* 10*d.* *Sufficient* for 5 or 6 persons. *Seasonable* in September and October.

DAMSONS, Baked, for Winter use.

Ingredients.—To every lb. of fruit allow 6 oz. of pounded sugar; melted mutton suet. *Mode.*—Choose sound fruit, not too ripe; pick off the stalks, weigh it, and to every lb. allow the above proportion of pounded sugar. Put the fruit into large dry stone jars, sprinkling the sugar amongst it; cover the jars with saucers, place them in a rather cool oven, and bake the fruit until it is quite tender. When cold, cover the top of the fruit with a piece of white paper cut to the size of the jar; pour over this melted mutton suet about an inch thick, and cover the tops of the jars with thick brown paper well tied down. Keep the jars in a cool·dry place, and the fruit will remain good till the following Christmas, but not much longer. *Time.*—From 5 to 6 hours to bake the damsons in a very cool oven. *Seasonable* in September and October.

DAMSONS, Compôte of.

Ingredients.—1 quart of damsons, 1 pint of syrup (*see* SYRUP). *Mode.*—Procure sound ripe damsons, pick the stalks from them, and put them into boiling syrup made by the recipe. Simmer them gently until the fruit is tender, but not sufficiently soft to break; take them up, boil the syrup for 5 minutes, pour it over the damsons, and serve. This should be sent to table in a glass dish. *Time.*—About ¼ hour to simmer the damsons; 5 minutes to boil the syrup. *Average cost*, 9*d*. *Sufficient* for 4 or 5 persons. *Seasonable* in September and October.

DAMSONS, Preserved.

Ingredients.—To every quart of damsons allow ½ lb. of loaf sugar. *Mode.*—Put the damsons (which should be picked from the stalks and quite free from blemishes) into a jar, with pounded sugar sprinkled amongst them in the above proportion; tie the jar closely down, set it in a saucepan of cold water; bring it gradually to boil, and simmer gently until the damsons are soft, without being broken. Let them stand till cold; then strain the juice from them, boil it up well, strain it through a jelly-bag, and pour it over the fruit. Let it cool, cover with oiled papers, and the jars with tissue-paper brushed over on both sides with the white of an egg, and store away in a dry place. *Time.*—About ¾ hour to simmer the fruit after the water boils; ¾ hour to boil the juice. *Seasonable.*—Make this in September or October.

DAMSONS, or any kind of Plums, to Preserve. (Useful in Winter.)

Ingredients.—Damsons or plums; boiling water. *Mode.*—Pick the fruit into clean dry stone jars, taking care to leave out all that are broken or blemished. When full, pour boiling water on the plums, until it stands one inch above the fruit; cut a piece of paper to fit the inside of the jar, over which pour melted mutton-suet; cover down with brown paper, and keep the jars in a dry cool place. When used, the suet should be removed, the water poured off, and the jelly at the bottom of the jar used and mixed with the fruit. *Seasonable* in September and October.

DARIOLES À LA VANILLE. (Sweet Entremets.)

Ingredients.—½ pint of milk, ½ pint of cream, 2 oz. of flour, 3 oz. of pounded sugar, 6 eggs, 2 oz. of butter, puff-paste, flavouring of essence of vanilla. *Mode.*—Mix the flour to a smooth batter, with the milk; stir in the cream, sugar, the eggs, which should be well whisked, and the butter, which should be beaten to a cream. Put in some essence of vanilla, drop by drop, until the mixture is well flavoured; line some dariole-moulds with puff-paste, three-parts fill them with the batter, and bake in a good oven from 25 to 35 minutes. Turn them out of the moulds on a dish, without breaking them; strew over sifted sugar, and serve. The flavouring of the darioles may be varied by substituting lemon, cinnamon, or almonds, for the vanilla. *Time.*—25 to 35 minutes. *Average cost*, 1*s*. 8*d*. *Sufficient* to fill 6 or 7 dariole-moulds. *Seasonable* at any time.

DECEMBER—BILLS OF FARE.

Dinner for 18 persons.

First Course.

Stewed Eels.	Mock-Turtle Soup, removed by Cod's Head & Shoulders and Oyster Sauce. Vase of Flowers. Julienne Soup, removed by Soles aux fines herbes.	Fried Whitings.

December—Bills of Fare

Second Course.

Roast Goose.	Haunch of Mutton. Ham and Brussels Sprouts. Vase of Flowers. Game Pie. Boiled Turkey and Celery Sauce.	Stewed Beef à la Jardinière.

Entrées.

Curried Lobster.	Fillets of Grouse and Sauce Piquante. Vase of Flowers. Sweetbreads.	Mutton Cutlets and Soubise Sauce.

Third Course.

Apricot Tourte. Tipsy Cake.	Lemon Jelly.	Pheasants, removed by Plum-Pudding. Vanilla Cream. Vase of Flowers. Blancmange. Wild Ducks, removed by Iced Pudding.	Champagne Jelly.	Victoria Sandwiches. Mince Pies.

Dessert and Ices.

Dinner for 12 persons.

First Course.—Game soup; clear vermicelli soup; codfish au gratin; fillets of whitings à la maître d'hôtel. *Entrées.*—Filet de bœuf and sauce piquante; fricasseed chicken; oyster patties; curried rabbit. *Second Course.*—Roast turkey and sausages; boiled leg of pork and vegetables; roast goose; stewed beef à la Jardinière. *Third Course.*—Widgeon; partridges; Charlotte aux pommes; mince pies; orange jelly, lemon cream; apple tart; cabinet pudding. Dessert and ices.

December—Dinners for 6 persons.

Dinner for 10 persons.

First Course. — Mulligatawny soup; fried slices of codfish; soles à la crème. *Entrées.*—Croquettes of fowl; pork cutlets and tomato sauce. *Second Course.*—Roast ribs of beef; boiled turkey and celery sauce; tongue, garnished; lark pudding; vegetables. *Third Course.*—Roast hare; grouse; plum-pudding; mince pies; Charlotte à la Parisienne; cheesecakes; apple tart; Nesselrode pudding. Dessert and ices.

Dinner for 8 persons.

First Course.—Carrot soup; crimped cod and oyster sauce; baked soles. *Entrées.*—Mutton kidneys à la Française; oyster patties. *Second Course.*—Boiled beef and vegetables; marrow-bones; roast fowls and water-cresses; tongue, garnished; game pie. *Third Course.*—Partridges; blancmange; compôte of apples; vol-au-vent of pears; almond cheesecakes; lemon pudding. Dessert and ices.

Dinners for 6 persons.

First Course.—Rabbit soup; brill and shrimp sauce. *Entrées.*—Curried fowl; oyster patties. *Second Course.*—Roast turkey and sausages; boiled leg of pork; vegetables. *Third Course.* — Hunters' pudding; lemon cheesecakes; apple tart; custards, in glasses; raspberry cream. Dessert.

First Course.—Ox-tail soup; crimped cod and oyster sauce. *Entrées.*—Savoury rissoles; fowl scollops à la Béchamel. *Second Course.* — Haunch of mutton; boiled chickens and celery sauce; bacon-cheek, garnished with Brussels sprouts; vegetables. *Third Course.* — Snipes; orange jelly; cheesecakes; apples à la Portugaise; apricot-jam tartlets; soufflé of rice. Dessert.

First Course.—Vermicelli soup; soles à la maître d'hôtel; fried eels. *Entrées.*—Pork cutlets and tomato sauce; ragout of mutton à la Jardinière. *Second Course.*—Roast goose; boiled leg of mutton and vegetables. *Third Course.* —Pheasants; whipped cream; meringues; compôte of

Normandy pippins; mince pies; plum-pudding. Dessert.

First Course. — Carrot soup; baked cod; fried smelts. *Entrées.*—Stewed rump-steak à la Jardinière; fricasseed chicken. *Second Course.*—Roast leg of mutton, boned and stuffed; boiled turkey and oyster sauce; vegetables. *Third Course.* — Wild ducks; fancy pastry; lemon cream; damson tart, with bottled fruit; custards, in glasses; cabinet pudding. Dessert.

DECEMBER, Plain Family Dinners for.

Sunday.—1. Carrot soup. 2. Roast beef, horseradish sauce, vegetables. 3. Plum-pudding, mince pies.

Monday.—1. Fried whitings, melted butter. 2. Rabbit pie, cold beef, mashed potatoes. 3. Plum-pudding cut in slices and warmed, apple tart.

Tuesday.—1. Hashed beef and broiled bones, pork cutlets and tomato sauce; vegetables. 2. Baked lemon pudding.

Wednesday.—1. Boiled neck of mutton and vegetables,—the broth served first with a little pearl barley or rice boiled in it. 2. Bakewell pudding.

Thursday.—1. Roast leg of pork, apple sauce; vegetables. 2. Rice snowballs.

Friday.—1. Soles à la crême. 2. Cold pork and mashed potatoes, broiled rump-steaks and oyster sauce. 3. Rolled jam pudding.

Saturday.—1. The remains of cold pork curried, dish of rice, mutton cutlets and mashed potatoes. 2. Baked apple dumplings.

Sunday.—1. Roast turkey and sausages, boiled leg of pork, pease pudding; vegetables. 2. Baked apple pudding, mince pies.

Monday. — 1. Hashed turkey, cold pork, mashed potatoes. 2. Mincemeat pudding.

Tuesday.—1. Pea-soup made from liquor in which pork was boiled. 2. Boiled fowls and celery sauce, vegetables. 3. Baked rice pudding.

Wednesday.—1. Roast leg of mutton, stewed Spanish onions, potatoes. 2. Baked rolled jam pudding.

Thursday.—1. Baked cod's head. 2. Cold mutton, roast hare, gravy and red-currant jelly. 3. Macaroni.

Friday.—1. Hare soup, made with stock and remains of roast hare. 2. Hashed mutton, pork cutlets, and mashed potatoes. 3. Open tarts, rice blancmange.

Saturday.—1. Rumpsteak-and-kidney pudding, vegetables. 2. Mince pies, baked apple dumplings.

DECEMBER, Things in Season.

Fish.—Barbel, brill, carp, cod, crabs, eels, dace, gudgeons, haddocks, herrings, lobsters, oysters, perch, pike, shrimps, skate, sprats, soles, tench, thornback, turbot, whiting.

Meat.—Beef, house lamb, mutton, pork, venison.

Poultry. — Capons, chickens, fowls, geese, pigeons, pullets, rabbits, teal, turkeys, widgeons, wild ducks.

Game.—Hares, partridges, pheasants, snipes, woodcocks.

Vegetables.—Broccoli, cabbages, carrots, celery, leeks, onions, potatoes, parsnips, Scotch kale, turnips, winter spinach.

Fruit. — Apples, chestnuts, filberts, grapes, medlars, oranges, pears, walnuts, dried fruits, such as almonds and raisins, figs, dates, &c.,—crystallized preserves.

DESSERT.

With moderns the dessert is not so profuse, nor does it hold the same relationship to the dinner that it held with the ancients,—the Romans more especially. On ivory tables they would spread hundreds of different kinds of raw, cooked, and preserved fruits, tarts, and cakes, as substitutes for the more substantial comestibles with which the guests were satiated. However, as late as the reigns of our two last Georges, fabulous sums were often expended upon fanciful desserts. The dessert certainly repays, in its general effect, the expenditure upon it of much pains; and it may be said, that if there be any poetry at all in meals, or the process of feeding, there is poetry in the dessert, the materials for which should be selected with taste, and, of course, must depend, in a great measure, upon the season. Pines, melons, grapes, peaches, nectarines, plums, strawberries, apples, pears, oranges, almonds, raisins, figs, walnuts, filberts, medlars, cherries, &c. &c., all kinds of dried fruits, and choice and delicately-flavoured cakes and biscuits, make up the dessert, together with the most costly and *recherché* wines. The shape of the dishes varies at different periods, the prevailing fashion at present being oval and circular dishes on stems. The patterns and colours are also subject to changes of fashion; some persons selecting china, chaste in pattern and colour; others, elegantly-shaped glass dishes on stems, with gilt edges. The beauty of the dessert services at the tables of the wealthy tends to enhance the splendour of the plate. The general mode of putting a dessert on table, now the elegant tazzas are fashionable, is, to place them down the middle of the table, a tall and short dish alternately; the fresh fruits being arranged on the tall dishes, and dried fruits, bon-bons, &c., on small round or oval glass plates. The garnishing needs especial attention, as the contrast of the brilliant-coloured fruits with nicely-arranged foliage is very charming. The garnish *par excellence* for dessert is the ice-plant; its crystallized dewdrops producing a marvellous effect in the height of summer, giving a most inviting sense of coolness to the fruit it encircles. The double-edged mallow, strawberry, and vine leaves have a pleasing effect; and for winter desserts, the bay, cuba, and laurel are sometimes used. In town, the expense and difficulty of obtaining natural foliage is great, but paper and composite leaves are to be purchased at an almost nominal price. Mixed fruits of the larger sort are now frequently served on one dish. This mode admits of the display of much taste in the arrangement of the fruit: for instance, a pine in the centre of the dish, surrounded with large plums of various sorts and colours, mixed with pears, rosy-cheeked apples, all arranged with a due regard to colour, have a very good effect. Again, apples and pears look well mingled with plums and grapes, hanging from the border of the dish in a négligé sort of manner, with a large bunch of the same fruit lying on the top of the apples. A dessert would not now be considered complete without candied and preserved fruits and confections. The candied fruits may be purchased at a less cost than they can be manufactured at home. They are preserved abroad in most ornamental and elegant forms. And since, from the facilities of travel, we have become so familiar with the tables of the French, chocolate in different forms is indispensable to our desserts. Olives, too, should not be omitted; these should be served in a small, deep glass dish, with a little of the liquor, or brine, poured over.

DESSERT DISHES.

The tazza, or dish with stem, the same as that shown in our illustrations, is now the favourite shape for dessert-dishes. The fruit can be arranged and shown to better advantage on these tall high dishes than on the short flat ones. All the dishes are now usually placed down the centre of the table, dried and fresh fruit alternately, the former being arranged on small round or oval glass plates, and the latter on the dishes with stems. The fruit should always be gathered on the same day that it is required for table, and should be tastefully arranged on the dishes, with leaves between and round it. By purchasing fruits that *are in season*, a dessert can be supplied at a very moderate cost. These, with a few fancy biscuits, crystallised fruit, bon-bons, &c., are sufficient for an ordinary dessert. When fresh fruit cannot be obtained, dried and foreign fruits, compôtes, baked pears, stewed Normandy pippins, &c. &c., must supply its place, with the addition of preserves, bon-bons, cakes, biscuits, &c. At fashionable tables, forced fruit is served growing in pots, these pots being hidden in more ornamental ones, and arranged with the other dishes. A few vases of fresh flowers, tastefully arranged, add very much to the appearance of the dessert; and, when these are not obtainable, a few paper ones, mixed with green leaves, answer very well as a substitute. In decorating a table, whether for luncheon, dessert, or supper, a vase or two of flowers should never be forgotten, as they add so much to the elegance of the *tout ensemble*. In summer and autumn, ladies residing in the country can always manage to have a few freshly-gathered flowers on their tables, and should never be without this inexpensive luxury. On the Continent, vases or epergnes filled with flowers are invariably placed down the centre of the dinner-table at regular distances. Ices for dessert are usually moulded; when this is not the case, they are handed round in glasses, with wafers to accompany them. Preserved ginger is frequently handed round after ices, to prepare the palate for the delicious dessert wines. A basin or glass of finely-pounded lump sugar must never be omitted at a dessert, as also a glass jug of fresh cold water (iced, if possible), and two goblets by its side. Grape scissors, a melon-knife and fork, and nutcrackers, should always be put on table, if there are dishes of fruit requiring them. Zests are sometimes served at the close of the dessert; such as anchovy toasts or biscuits. The French often serve plain or grated cheese with a dessert of fresh or dried fruits. At some tables, finger-glasses are placed at the right of each person, nearly half filled with cold spring water, and in winter with tepid water. These precede the dessert. At other tables, a glass or vase is simply handed round, filled with perfumed water, into which each guest dips the corner of his napkin, and, when needful, refreshes his lips and the tips of his fingers. After the dishes are placed, and every one is provided with plates, glasses, spoons, &c., the wine should be put at each end of the table, cooled or otherwise, according to the season. If the party be small, the wine may be placed only at the top of the table, near the host. The following dishes may be introduced at dessert, according to season:—

Dish of Nuts.—These are merely arranged piled high in the centre of the dish, as shown in the engraving, with or without leaves round the edge. Filberts should always be served with the outer skin or husk on them; and walnuts should be well wiped with a damp cloth, and then with a dry one, to remove the unpleasant sticky feeling the shells frequently have. *Seasonable.*—Filberts from September to March; walnuts from September to January.

DISH OF NUTS.

Box of French Plums.—If the box which contains them is exceedingly ornamental, it may be placed on the table; if small, on a glass dish; if large, without one. French plums may also be arranged on a glass plate, and garnished with bright-coloured sweetmeats, which make a very good effect. All fancy boxes of preserved and crystallized fruit may be put on the table or not, at pleasure. These little matters of detail must, of course, be left to individual taste. *Seasonable.*—May be purchased all the year; but are in greater perfection in the winter.

BOX OF FRENCH PLUMS.

Dish of Mixed Fruit.—For a centre dish, a mixture of various fresh fruits has a remarkably good effect, particularly if a pine be added to the list. A high raised appearance should be given to the fruit, which is done in the following manner. Place a tumbler in the centre of the dish, and, in this tumbler, the pine, crown uppermost; round the tumbler put a thick layer of moss, and, over this, apples, pears, plums, peaches, and such fruit as is simultaneously in season. By putting a layer of moss underneath, so much fruit is not required, besides giving a better shape to the dish. Grapes should be placed on the top of the fruit, a portion of some of the bunches hanging over the sides of the dish in a négligé kind of manner, which takes off the formal look of the dish. In arranging the plums, apples, &c., let the colours contrast well. *Seasonable.*—Suitable for a dessert in September or October.

DISH OF MIXED FRUIT.

Box of Chocolate.—This is served in an ornamental box, placed on a glass plate or dish. *Seasonable.* — May be purchased at any time.

BOX OF CHOCOLATE.

Dish of Apples.—The apples should be nicely wiped with a dry cloth, and arranged on a dish, piled high in the centre, with evergreen leaves between each layer. The inferior apples should form the bottom layer, with the bright-coloured large ones at the top. The leaves of the laurel, bay, holly, or any shrub green in winter, are suitable for garnishing dessert dishes. Oranges may be arranged in the same manner; they should also be wiped with a dry cloth before being sent to table.

DISH OF APPLES.

Dish of Mixed Summer Fruit.—This dish consists of cherries, raspberries, currants, and strawberries, piled in different layers, with plenty of leaves between each layer, so that each fruit is well separated. The fruit should be arranged with a due regard to colour, so that they contrast nicely one with the other. Our engraving shows a layer of white cherries at the bottom, then one of red raspberries, over that a layer of white currants, and at the top some fine scarlet strawberries. *Seasonable* in June, July, and August.

DISH OF MIXED SUMMER FRUIT.

Almonds and Raisins.—These are usually served on glass dishes, the fruit piled high in the centre, and the almonds blanched and strewn over. To blanch the almonds, put them into a small mug or teacup, pour over them boiling water, let them remain for 2 or 3 minutes, and the skins may then be easily removed. Figs, dates, French plums, &c., are all served on small glass plates or oval dishes, but without the almonds. *Seasonable* at any time, but more suitable in winter, when fresh fruit is not obtainable.

ALMONDS AND RAISINS.

Dish of Strawberries.—Fine strawberries, arranged in the manner shown in the engraving, look exceedingly well. The inferior ones should be placed at the bottom of the dish, and the others put in rows pyramidically, with the stalks downwards, so that when the whole is completed, nothing but the red part of the fruit is visible. The fruit should be gathered with rather long stalks, as there is then something to support it, and it can be placed more upright in each layer. A few of the finest should be reserved to crown the top.

DISH OF STRAWBERRIES.

DEVONSHIRE JUNKET.

Ingredients.—To every pint of new milk allow 2 dessertspoonfuls of brandy, 1 dessertspoonful of sugar, and 1½ dessertspoonful of prepared rennet; thick cream, pounded cinnamon, or grated nutmeg. *Mode.*—Make the milk bloodwarm; put it into a deep dish with the brandy, sugar, and rennet; stir it altogether, and cover it over until it is set. Then spread some thick or clotted cream over the top, grate some nutmeg, and strew some sugar over, and the dish will be ready to serve. *Time.*—About 2 hours to set the milk. *Seasonable* at any time.

DINNER,

Being the grand solid meal of the day, is a matter of considerable importance; and a well-served table is a striking index of human ingenuity and resource.

The elegance with which a dinner is served depends, of course, partly upon the means, but still more upon the taste of the master and mistress of the house. It may be observed, in general, that there should always be flowers on the table, and, as they form no item of expense where a garden is, there is no reason why they should not be employed every day.

The variety of the dishes which furnish forth a modern dinner-table, does not necessarily imply anything unwholesome, or anything capricious. Food that is not well relished cannot be well digested; and the appetite of the over-worked man of business, or statesman, or of any dweller in towns, whose occupations are exciting and exhausting, is jaded, and requires stimulation. Men and women who are in rude health, and who have plenty of air and exercise, eat the simplest food with relish, and commonly digest it well; but those conditions are out of the reach of many men. They must suit their mode of dining to their mode of living, if they cannot choose the latter. It is in serving up food that is at once appetizing and wholesome that the skill of the modern housewife is severely tasked; and she has scarcely a more important duty to fulfil. It is, in fact, her particular vocation, in virtue of which she may be said to hold the health of the family, and of the friends of the family, in her hands from day to day.

The following aphorisms and short directions in relation to dinner-parties, are well deserving of notice:—"Let the number of your guests never exceed twelve, so that the conversation may be general. Let the temperature of the dining-room be about 68°. Let the dishes be few in number in the first course, but proportionally good. The order of food is from the most substantial to the lightest. The order of drinking wine is from the mildest to the most foamy and most perfumed. To invite a person to your house is to take charge of his happiness so long as he is beneath your roof. The mistress of the house should always be certain that the coffee is excellent; whilst the master should be answerable for the quality of his wines and liqueurs."

Dinners à la Russe differ from ordinary dinners in the mode of serving the various dishes. In a dinner à la Russe, the dishes are cut up on a sideboard, and handed round to the guests, and each dish may be considered a course. The table for a dinner à la Russe should be laid with flowers and plants in fancy flower-pots down the middle, together with some of the dessert dishes. A *menu* or bill of fare should be placed by the side of each guest.

The following are bills of fare for dinners à la Russe, and eatable from July to November: the dishes can easily be varied to suit other months.

SERVICE A LA RUSSE (July).

Julienne Soup, Vermicelli Soup.

Boiled Salmon, Turbot and Lobster Sauce. Soles-Water Souchy, Perch-Water Souchy. Matelote d'Anguilles à la Toulouse, Filets de Soles à la Normandie. Red Mullet, Trout. Lobster Rissoles, Whitebait.

Riz de Veau à la Banquière, Filets de Poulets aux Coucombres. Canards à la Rouennaise, Mutton Cutlets à la Jardinière. Braised Beef à la Flamande, Spring Chickens, Roast Quarter of Lamb, Roast Saddle of Mutton, Tongue, Ham and Peas.

Quails, larded, Roast Ducks, Turkey Poult, larded. Mayonnaise of Chicken, Tomatos, Green Peas à la Française. Suédoise of Strawberries, Charlotte Russe, Compôte of Cherries. Neapolitan Cakes, Pastry, Madeira Wine Jelly. Iced Pudding à la Nesselrode.

Dessert and Ices.

SERVICE A LA RUSSE (November).

Ox-tail Soup, Soup à la Jardinière.

Turbot and Lobster Sauce, Crimped Cod and Oyster Sauce. Stewed Eels, Soles à la Normandie. Pike and Cream Sauce. Fried Fileted Soles.

Filets de Bœuf à la Jardinière, Croquettes of Game aux Champignons. Chicken Cutlets, Mutton Cutlets and Tomato Sauce. Lobster Rissoles, Oyster Patties. Partridges aux fines Herbes, Larded Sweetbreads. Roast Beef, Poulets aux Cressons, Haunch of Mutton, Roast Turkey, Boiled Turkey and Celery Sauce, Ham.

Grouse, Pheasants, Hare. Salad, Artichokes, Stewed Celery. Italian Cream,

Charlotte aux Pommes, Compôte of Pears. Croûtes madrées aux Fruits, Pastry, Punch Jelly. Iced Pudding. Dessert and Ices.

DORMERS.

[COLD MEAT COOKERY.] *Ingredients.* —½ lb. of cold mutton, 2 oz. of beef suet, pepper and salt to taste, 3 oz. of boiled rice, 1 egg, bread crumbs, made gravy. *Mode.*—Chop the meat, suet, and rice finely; mix well together, and add a high seasoning of pepper and salt, and roll into sausages; cover them with egg and bread crumbs, and fry in hot dripping of a nice brown. Serve in a dish with made gravy poured round them, and a little in a tureen. *Time.*—¼ hour to fry the sausages. *Average cost,* exclusive of the meat, 6*d.* *Seasonable* at any time.

DRAUGHT for Summer.

Ingredients.—The juice of 1 lemon, a tumblerful of cold water, pounded sugar to taste, ½ small teaspoonful of carbonate of soda. *Mode.*—Squeeze the juice from the lemon; strain, and add it to the water, with sufficient pounded sugar to sweeten the whole nicely. When well mixed, put in the soda, stir well, and drink while the mixture is in an effervescing state.

DRINK, Pleasant, for Warm Weather.

Ingredients.—To every ½ pint of good ale allow 1 bottle of ginger beer. *Mode.* —For this beverage the ginger beer must be in an effervescing state, and the beer not in the least turned or sour. Mix them together, and drink immediately. The draught is refreshing and wholesome, as the ginger corrects the action of the beer. It does not deteriorate by standing a little, but, of course, is better when taken fresh.

DRIPPING, to Clarify.

Good and fresh dripping answers very well for basting everything except game and poultry, and, when well clarified, serves for frying nearly as well as lard; it should be kept in a cool place, and will remain good some time. To clarify it put the dripping into a basin, pour over it boiling water, and keep stirring the whole to wash away the impurities. Let it stand to cool, when the water and dirty sediment will settle at the bottom of the basin. Remove the dripping, and put it away in jars or basins for use.

Another Way.—Put the dripping into a clean saucepan, and let it boil for a few minutes over a slow fire, and be careful to skim it well. Let it stand to cool a little, then strain it through a piece of muslin into jars for use. Beef dripping is preferable to any other for cooking purposes, as, with mutton dripping, there is liable to be a tallowy taste and smell.

DUCK, Hashed.

[COLD MEAT COOKERY.] *Ingredients.* —The remains of cold roast duck, rather more than 1 pint of weak stock or water, 1 onion, 1 oz. of butter, thickening of butter and flour, salt and cayenne to taste, ½ teaspoonful of minced lemon-peel, 1 dessertspoonful of lemon-juice, ½ glass of port wine. *Mode.*—Cut the duck into nice joints, and put the trimmings into a stewpan; slice and fry the onion in a little butter; add these to the trimmings, pour in the above proportion of weak stock or water, and stew gently for 1 hour. Strain the liquor, thicken it with butter and flour, season with salt and cayenne, and add the remaining ingredients; boil it up and skim well; lay in the pieces of duck, and let them get thoroughly hot through by the side of the fire, but do not allow them to boil: they should soak in the gravy for about ½ hour. Garnish with sippets of toasted bread. The hash may be made richer by using a stronger and more highly-flavoured gravy; a little spice or pounded mace may also be added, when their flavour is liked. *Time.*—1½ hour. *Average cost,* exclusive of cold duck, 4*d.* *Seasonable* from November to February; ducklings from May to August.

DUCKS, Roast.

Ingredients.—A couple of ducks; sage-and-onion stuffing; a little flour. *Choosing and Trussing.*—Choose ducks with plump bellies, and with thick and yellowish feet. They should be trussed with the feet on, which should be scalded, and the skin peeled off, and then turned up close to the legs. Run a skewer through the middle of each leg, after having drawn them as close as possible to the body, to plump up the breast, passing the same quite through the body. Cut off the heads and necks, and the pinions at the first joint; bring these close to the sides, twist the feet

ROAST DUCK.

round, and truss them at the back of the bird. After the duck is stuffed, both ends should be secured with string, so as to keep in the seasoning. *Mode.*—To insure ducks being tender, never dress them the same day they are killed; and, if the weather permits, they should hang a day or two. Make a stuffing of sage and onion sufficient for one duck, and leave the other unseasoned, as the flavour is not liked by everybody. Put them down to a brisk clear fire, and keep them well basted the whole of the time they are cooking. A few minutes before serving, dredge them lightly with flour, to make them froth and look plump; and when the steam draws towards the fire, send them to table hot and quickly, with a good brown gravy poured *round*, but not *over* the ducks, and a little of the same in a tureen. When in season, green peas should invariably accompany this dish. *Time.*—Full-grown ducks from ¾ to 1 hour; ducklings from 25 to 35 minutes. *Average cost*, from 2*s.* 3*d.* to 2*s.* 6*d.* each. *Sufficient.*—A couple of ducks for 6 or 7 persons. *Seasonable.*—Ducklings from April to August; ducks from November to February.

DUCK, Roast, to carve.

No dishes require so much knowledge and skill in their carving as do game and poultry; for it is necessary to be well acquainted with the anatomy of the bird

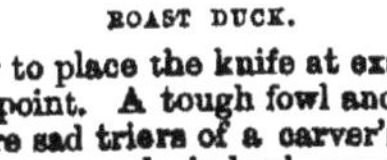

ROAST DUCK.

in order to place the knife at exactly the proper point. A tough fowl and an old goose are sad triers of a carver's powers and temper, and, indeed, sometimes of the good humour of those in the neighbourhood of the carver; for a sudden tilt of the dish may eventuate in the placing of a quantity of the gravy in the lap of the right or left-hand supporter of the host. We will endeavour to assist those who are unacquainted with the "gentle art of carving," and also those who are but slightly acquainted with it, by simply describing the rules to follow, and referring to the distinctly-marked illustrations of each dish, which will further help to bring light to the minds of the uninitiated. If the bird be a young duckling, it may be carved like a fowl, viz., by first taking off the leg and the wing on either side; but in cases where the duckling is very small, it will be as well not to separate the leg from the wing, as they will not then form too large a portion for a single serving. After the legs and wings are disposed of, the remainder of the duck will be also carved in the same manner as a fowl; and not much difficulty will be experienced, as ducklings are tender, and the joints are easily broken by a little gentle forcing, or penetrated by the knife. In cases where the duck is a large bird, the better plan to pursue is then to carve it like a goose, that is, by cutting pieces from the breast in the direction indicated by the lines marked from 1 to 2, commencing to carve the slices close to the wing, and then proceeding upwards from that to the breastbone. If more should be wanted than can be obtained from both sides of the breast, then the legs and wings must be attacked, in the same way as is described in connection with carving a fowl. It may be here remarked, that as the legs of a duck are placed far more backward than those of a fowl, their position causing the waddling motion of the bird, the thigh-bones will be found considerably nearer towards the backbone than in a chicken; this is the only difference worth mentioning. The carver should ask each guest if a portion of stuffing would be agreeable; and in order to get at this, a cut should be made below the breast, as shown by the line from 3 to 4, at the part called the "apron," and the spoon inserted.

LEG, WING, AND NECKBONE OF DUCK.

(As described in the recipe, it is an excellent plan, when a couple of ducks are served, to have one with, and the other without, stuffing.) As to the prime parts of a duck, it has been said that "the wing of a flier and the leg of a swimmer" are severally the best portions. Some persons are fond of the feet of the duck; and, in trussing, these should never be taken off. The leg, wing, and neckbone are here shown; so that it will be easy to see the shape they should be when cut off.

Note.—Ducklings are trussed and roasted in the same manner, and served with the same sauces and accompaniments. When in season, do not omit apple sauce.

DUCK AND PEAS, Stewed.

[COLD MEAT COOKERY.] *Ingredients.*—The remains of cold roast duck, 2 oz. of butter, 3 or 4 slices of lean ham or bacon, 1 tablespoonful of flour, 2 pints of thin gravy, 1, or a small bunch of green onions, 3 sprigs of parsley, 3 cloves, 1 pint of young green peas, cayenne and salt to taste, 1 teaspoonful of pounded sugar. *Mode.*—Put the butter into a stewpan; cut up the duck into joints, lay them in with the slices of lean ham or bacon; make it brown, then dredge in a tablespoonful of flour, and stir this well in before adding the gravy. Put in the onion, parsley, cloves, and gravy, and when it has simmered for ¼ hour, add a pint of young green peas, and stew gently for about ½ hour. Season with cayenne, salt, and sugar; take out the duck, place it round the dish, and the peas in the middle. *Time.*—¾ hour. *Average cost*, exclusive of the cold duck, 1s. *Seasonable* from June to August.

DUCK AND PEAS, Stewed.

[COLD MEAT COOKERY.] *Ingredients.*—The remains of cold roast duck, ½ pint of good gravy, cayenne and salt to taste, ½ teaspoonful of minced lemon-peel, 1 teaspoonful of pounded sugar, 2 oz. of butter rolled in flour, 1½ pint of green peas. *Mode.*—Cut up the duck into joints, lay it in the gravy, and add a seasoning of cayenne, salt, and minced lemon-peel; let this gradually warm through, but not boil. Throw the peas into boiling water slightly salted, and boil them rapidly until tender. Drain them, stir in the pounded sugar, and the

butter rolled in flour; shake them over the fire for two or three minutes, and serve in the centre of the dish, with the duck laid round. *Time.*—15 minutes to boil the peas, when they are full grown. *Average cost*, exclusive of the cold duck, 10*d*. *Seasonable* from June to August.

DUCK, Stewed, in Turnips.

[COLD MEAT COOKERY.] *Ingredients.*—The remains of cold duck, ½ pint of good gravy, 4 shalots, a few slices of carrot, a small bunch of savoury herbs, 1 blade of pounded mace, 1 lb. of turnips weighed after being peeled, 2 oz. of butter, pepper and salt to taste. *Mode.*—Cut up the duck into joints, fry the shalots, carrots, and herbs, and put them with the duck into the gravy. Cut about 1 lb. of turnips into ½ inch squares, put the butter into a stewpan, and stew them till quite tender, which will be in about ½ hour, or rather more; season with pepper and salt, and serve on the centre of the dish, with the duck, &c., laid round. *Time.*—Rather more than ½ hour to stew the turnips. *Average cost*, exclusive of cold duck, 1s. *Seasonable* from November to February.

DUCK, to Ragout a whole.

Ingredients.—1 large duck, pepper and salt to taste, good beef gravy, 2 onions sliced, 4 sage-leaves, a few leaves of lemon thyme, thickening of butter and flour. *Mode.*—After having emptied and singed the duck, season it inside with pepper and salt, and truss it. Roast it before a clear fire for about 20 minutes, and let it acquire a nice brown colour. Put it into a stewpan with sufficient well-seasoned beef gravy to cover it; slice and fry the onions, and add these, with the sage-leaves and lemon thyme, both of which should be finely minced, to the stock. Simmer gently until the duck is tender; strain, skim, and thicken the gravy with a little butter and flour; boil it up, pour over the duck, and serve. When in season, about 1½ pint of young green peas, boiled separately, and put in the ragoût, very much improve this dish. *Time.*—20 minutes to roast the duck; 20 minutes to stew it. *Average cost*, from 2s. 3d. to 2s. 6d. each. *Sufficient* for 4 or 5 persons. *Seasonable* from November to February; ducklings from April to August.

DUCK, Wild, Hashed.

Ingredients.—The remains of cold roast wild duck, 1 pint of good brown gravy, 2 tablespoonfuls of bread crumbs, 1 glass of claret, salt, cayenne, and mixed spices to taste; 1 tablespoonful of lemon or Seville orange-juice. *Mode.*—Cut the remains of the duck into neat joints, put them into a stewpan, with all the above ingredients; let them get gradually hot by the side of the fire, and occasionally stir the contents; when on the point of boiling, serve, and garnish the dish with sippets of toasted bread. *Time.*—About ¼ hour. *Seasonable* from November to February.

DUCK, Wild, Ragout of.

Ingredients.—2 wild ducks, 4 shalots, 1 pint of stock (*see* STOCK), 1 glass of port wine, 1 oz. of butter, a little flour, the juice of ½ lemon, cayenne and salt to taste. *Mode.*—Ducks that have been dressed and left from the preceding day will answer for this dish. Cut them into joints, reserve the legs, wings, and breasts until wanted; put the trimmings into a stewpan with the shalots and stock, and let them simmer for about ½ hour, and strain the gravy. Put the butter into a stewpan; when melted, dredge in a little flour, and pour in the gravy made from the bones; give it one boil, and strain it again; add the wine, lemon-juice, and cayenne; lay in the pieces of duck, and let the whole gradually warm through, but do not allow it to boil, or the duck will be hard. The gravy should not be too thick, and should be very highly seasoned. The squeeze of a Seville orange is a great improvement to this dish. *Time.*—About ½ hour to make the gravy; ¼ hour for the duck gradually to warm through. *Seasonable* from November to February.

DUCK, Wild, Roast.

Ingredients.—Wild duck, flour, butter. *Mode.*—Carefully pluck and draw them; cut off the heads close to the necks, leaving sufficient skin to turn over, and do not cut off the feet; some twist each leg at the knuckle, and rest the claws on each side of the breast; others truss them as shown in our illustration. Roast the birds before a quick fire, and, when they are first put down, let them remain for 5 minutes without basting (this will keep the gravy in); afterwards baste plentifully with butter, and a few minutes before serving dredge them lightly with flour; baste well, and send them to table nicely frothed, and full of gravy. If

ROAST WILD DUCK.

overdone, the birds will lose their flavour. Serve with a good gravy in the dish, or orange gravy, and send to table with them a cut lemon. To take off the fishy taste which wild fowl sometimes have, baste them for a few minutes with hot water to which have been added an onion and a little salt; then take away the pan, and baste with butter. *Time.*—When liked underdressed, 20 to 25 minutes; well done, 25 to 35 minutes. *Average cost*, 4*s.* to 5*s.* the couple.

DUCK, Wild, to Carve.

As game is almost universally served as a dainty, and not as a dish to stand the assaults of an altogether fresh appetite, these dishes are not usually cut up entirely, but only those parts are served of each which are considered the best flavoured and the primest. Of wild fowl, the breast alone is considered by epicures worth eating, and slices are cut from this, in the direction indicated by the lines, from 1 to 2; if necessary, the leg and the wing can be taken off by passing the knife from 3 to 4, and by generally following the directions described for carving boiled fowl.

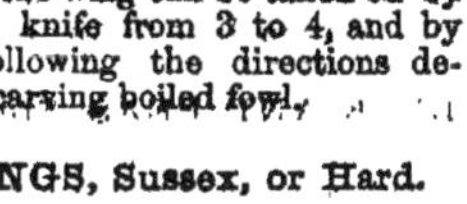

WILD DUCK.

DUMPLINGS, Sussex, or Hard.

Ingredients.—1 lb. of flour, ½ pint of water, ½ saltspoonful of salt. *Mode.*—Mix the flour and water together to a smooth paste, previously adding a small quantity of salt. Form this into small round dumplings; drop them into boiling water, and boil from ½ to ¾ hour. They may be served with roast or boiled meat; in the latter case, they may be cooked with the meat, but should be dropped into the water when it is quite boiling. *Time.*—½ to ¾ hour. *Sufficient* for 10 or 12 dumplings. *Seasonable* at any time.

DUTCH FLUMMERY.

Ingredients.—1½ oz. of isinglass, the rind and juice of 1 lemon, 1 pint of water, 4 eggs, 1 pint of sherry, Madeira, or raisin-wine; sifted sugar to taste. *Mode.*—Put the water, isinglass, and lemon-rind into a lined saucepan, and simmer gently until the isinglass is dissolved; strain this into a basin, stir in the eggs, which should be well beaten, the lemon-juice, which should be strained, and the wine; sweeten to taste with pounded sugar, mix all well together, pour it into a jug, set this jug in a saucepan of boiling water over the fire, and keep stirring it one way until it thickens; but *take care that it does not boil.* Strain it into a mould that has been oiled or laid in water for a short time, and put it in a cool place to set. A tablespoonful of brandy stirred in just before it is poured into the mould, improves the flavour of this dish: it is better if it is made the day before it is required for table. *Time.*—¼ hour to simmer the isinglass; about ¼ hour to stir the mixture over the fire. *Average cost,* 4*s.* 6*d.*, if made with sherry; less with raisin-wine. *Sufficient* to fill a quart mould. *Seasonable* at any time.

EEL BROTH.

Ingredients.—½ lb. of eel, a small bunch of sweet herbs, including parsley, ½ onion, 10 peppercorns, 3 pints of water, 2 cloves, salt and pepper to taste. *Mode.*—After having cleaned and skinned the eel, cut it into small pieces, and put it into a stewpan with the other ingredients; simmer gently until the liquid is reduced to nearly half, carefully removing the scum as it rises. Strain it through a hair sieve: put it by in a cool place, and, when wanted, take off all the fat on the top; warm up as much as is required, and serve with sippets of toasted bread. This is a very nutritious broth, and easy of digestion. *Time.*—To be simmered until the liquor is reduced to half. *Average cost,* 6*d.* *Sufficient* to make 1½ pint of broth. *Seasonable* from June to March.

EEL PIE.

Ingredients.—1 lb. of eels, a little chopped parsley, 1 shalot, grated nutmeg, pepper and salt to taste, the juice of ½ a lemon, small quantity of forcemeat, ¼ pint of Béchamel; puff paste. *Mode.*—Skin and wash the eels, cut them in pieces 2 inches long, and line the bottom of the pie-dish with forcemeat. Put in the eels, and sprinkle them with the parsley, shalots, nutmeg, seasoning, and lemon-juice, and cover with puff-paste. Bake for 1 hour, or rather more; make the Béchamel hot, and pour it into the pie. *Time.*—Rather more than 1 hour. *Seasonable* from August to March.

EEL SOUP.

Ingredients.—3 lbs. of eels, 1 onion, 2 oz. of butter, 3 blades of mace, 1 bunch of sweet herbs, ¼ oz. of peppercorns, salt to taste, 2 tablespoonfuls of flour, ¼ pint of cream, 2 quarts of water. *Mode.*—Wash the eels, cut them into thin slices, and put them into the stewpan with the butter; let them simmer for a few minutes, then pour the water to them, and add the onion, cut in thin slices, the herbs, mace, and seasoning. Simmer till the eels are tender, but do not break the fish. Take them out carefully, mix the flour smoothly to a batter with the cream, bring it to a boil, pour over the eels, and serve. *Time.*—1 hour or rather more. *Average cost,* 10*d.* per quart. *Seasonable* from June to March. *Sufficient* for 8 persons.

Note.—This soup may be flavoured differently by omitting the cream, and adding a little ketchup or Harvey's sauce.

EELS, Boiled.

Ingredients.—4 small eels, sufficient water to cover them; a large bunch of parsley. *Mode.*—Choose small eels for boiling; put them into a stewpan with the parsley, and just sufficient water to cover them; simmer till tender. Take them out, pour a little parsley and butter over them, and serve some in a tureen. *Time.*—½ hour. *Average cost,* 6*d.* per lb. *Seasonable* from June to March. *Sufficient* for 4 persons.

EEL, Collared.

Ingredients.—1 large eel; pepper and salt to taste; 2 blades of mace, 2 cloves, a little allspice very finely pounded, 6 leaves of sage, and a small bunch of herbs minced very small. *Mode.*—Bone the eel and skin it; split it, and sprinkle it over with the ingredients, taking care that the spices are very finely pounded, and the herbs chopped very small. Roll it up and bind with a broad piece of tape, and boil it in water, mixed with a little salt and vinegar, till tender. It may either be served whole or cut in slices; and when cold, the eel should be kept in the liquor it was boiled in, but with a little more vinegar put to it. *Time.*—2 hours. *Average cost*, 6*d.* per lb. *Seasonable* from August to March.

EELS, Fried.

Ingredients.—1 lb. of eels, 1 egg, a few bread crumbs, hot lard. *Mode.*—Wash the eels, cut them into pieces 3 inches long, trim and wipe them very dry; dredge with flour, rub them over with egg, and cover with bread crumbs; fry a nice brown in hot lard. If the eels are small, curl them round, instead of cutting them up. Garnish with fried parsley. *Time.*—20 minutes or rather less. *Average cost*, 6*d.* per lb. *Seasonable* from June to March.

EELS, en Matelote.

Ingredients.—5 or 6 young onions, a few mushrooms, when obtainable; salt, pepper, and nutmeg to taste; 1 laurel leaf, ½ pint of port wine, ½ pint of medium stock, butter and flour to thicken; 2 lbs. of eels. *Mode.*—Rub the stewpan with butter, dredge in a little flour, add the onions cut very small, slightly brown them, and put in all the other ingredients. Wash, and cut up the eels into pieces 3 inches long; put them in the stewpan, and simmer for ½ hour. Make round the dish a border of croûtons, or pieces of toasted bread; arrange the eels in a pyramid in the centre, and pour over the sauce. Serve very hot. *Time.*—¾ hour. *Average cost*, 1*s.* 9*d.* for this quantity. *Seasonable* from August to March. *Sufficient* for 5 or 6 persons.

EELS, Stewed.

Ingredients.—2 lbs. of eels, 1 pint of rich strong stock, 1 onion, 3 cloves, a piece of lemon-peel, 1 glass of port or Madeira, 3 tablespoonfuls of cream; thickening of flour; cayenne and lemon-juice to taste. *Mode.*—Wash and skin the eels, and cut them into pieces about 3 inches long; pepper and salt them, and lay them in a stewpan; pour over the stock, add the onion stuck with cloves, the lemon-peel, and the wine. Stew gently for ½ hour, or rather more, and lift them carefully on a dish, which keep hot. Strain the gravy, stir the cream, sufficient flour to thicken; mix altogether, boil for 2 minutes, and add the cayenne and lemon-juice; pour over the eels and serve. *Time.*—¾ hour. *Average cost* for this quantity, 2*s.* 3*d.* *Seasonable* from June to March. *Sufficient* for 5 or 6 persons.

EELS, Stewed.

Ingredients.—2 lbs. of middling-sized eels, 1 pint of medium stock, ¼ pint of port wine; salt, cayenne, and mace to taste; 1 teaspoonful of essence of anchovy, the juice of ½ a lemon. *Mode.*—Skin, wash, and clean the eels thoroughly; cut them into pieces 3 inches long, and put them into strong salt and water for 1 hour; dry them well with a cloth, and fry them brown. Put the stock on with the heads and tails of the eels, and simmer for ½ hour; strain it, and add all the other ingredients. Put in the eels, and stew gently for ½ hour, when serve. *Time.*—2 hours. *Average cost*, 1*s.* 9*d.* *Seasonable* from June to March. *Sufficient* for 5 or 6 persons.

EELS, à la Tartare.

Ingredients.—2 lbs. of eels, 1 carrot, 1 onion, a little flour, 1 glass of sherry; salt, pepper, and nutmeg to taste; bread-crumbs, 1 egg, 2 tablespoonfuls of vinegar. *Mode.*—Rub the butter on the bottom of the stewpan; cut up the carrot and onion, and stir them over the fire for 5 minutes; dredge in a little flour, add the wine and seasoning, and boil for ½ an hour. Skin and wash the eels, cut them into pieces, put them to the other ingredients, and simmer till tender. When they are done, take them out, let them get cold, cover them with egg and bread crumbs, and fry them of a nice brown. Put them on a dish, pour sauce piquante over, and serve them hot. *Time.*—1½ hour. *Average cost*, 1*s.* 8*d.*, exclusive of the sauce piquante. *Seasonable* from August to March. *Sufficient* for 5 or 6 persons.

EGGS.

There is only one opinion as to the nutritive properties of eggs, although the qualities of those belonging to different birds vary somewhat. Those of the common hen are most esteemed as delicate food, particularly when "new-laid." The quality of eggs depends much upon the food given to the hen. Eggs in general are considered most easily digestible when little subjected to the art of cookery. The lightest way of dressing them is by poaching, which is effected by putting them for a minute or two into brisk boiling water: this coagulates the external white, without doing the inner part too much. Eggs are much better when new-laid than a day or two afterwards. The usual time allotted for boiling eggs in the shell is 3 to 3¾ minutes: less time than that in boiling water will not be sufficient to solidify the white, and more will make the yolk hard and less digestible: it is very difficult to *guess* accurately as to the time. Great care should be employed in putting them into the water, to prevent cracking the shell, which inevitably causes a portion of the white to exude, and lets water into the egg. For the purpose of placing eggs in water, always choose a *large* spoon in preference to a small one. Eggs are often beaten up raw in nutritive beverages.

The eggs of the *turkey* are almost as mild as those of the hen; the egg of the *goose* is large, but well-tasted. *Ducks' eggs* have a rich flavour; the albumen is slightly transparent, or bluish, when set or coagulated by boiling, which requires less time than hens' eggs. *Guinea-fowl eggs* are smaller and more delicate than those of the hen. Eggs of *wild fowl* are generally coloured, often spotted; and the taste generally partakes somewhat of the bird they belong to. Those of land birds that are eaten, as the *plover*, *lapwing*, *ruff*, &c., are in general much esteemed; but those of *sea-fowl* have, more or less, a strong fishy taste. The eggs of the *turtle* are very numerous: they consist of yolk only, without shell, and are delicious.

When fresh eggs are dropped into a vessel *full* of boiling water, they crack, because the eggs being well filled, the shells give way to the efforts of the interior fluids, dilated by heat. If the volume of hot water be small, the shells do not crack, because its temperature is reduced by the eggs before the interior dilation can take place. Stale eggs, again, do not crack, because the air inside is easily compressed.

EGG BALLS, for Soups and made Dishes.

Ingredients.—8 eggs, a little flour; seasoning to taste of salt. *Mode.*—Boil 6 eggs for 20 minutes, strip off the shells, take the yolks and pound them in a mortar. Beat the yolks of the 2 uncooked eggs; add them, with a little flour and salt, to those pounded; mix all well together, and roll into balls. Boil them before they are put into the soup or other dish they may be intended for.

EGG SAUCE, for Salt Fish.

Ingredients.—4 eggs, ½ pint of melted butter, when liked, a very little lemon-juice. *Mode.*—Boil the eggs until quite hard, which will be in about 20 minutes, and put them into cold water for ½ hour. Strip off the shells, chop the eggs into small pieces, not, however, too fine. Make the melted butter very smooth, and, when boiling, stir in the eggs, and serve very hot. Lemon-juice may be added at pleasure. *Time.*—20 minutes to boil the eggs. *Average cost,* 8d. *Sufficient.*—This quantity for 3 or 4 lbs. of fish.

Note.—When a thicker sauce is required, use one or two more eggs to the same quantity of melted butter.

EGG SOUP.

Ingredients.—A tablespoonful of flour, 4 eggs, 2 small blades of finely-pounded mace, 2 quarts of stock. *Mode.*—Beat up the flour smoothly in a teaspoonful of cold stock, and put in the eggs; throw them into boiling stock, stirring all the time. Simmer for ¼ of an hour. Season and serve with a French roll in the tureen or fried sippets of bread. *Time.*—½ an hour. *Average cost,* 11d. per quart. *Seasonable* all the year. *Sufficient* for 8 persons.

EGG WINE.

Ingredients.—1 egg, 1 tablespoonful and ½ glass of cold water, 1 glass of sherry, sugar and grated nutmeg to taste. *Mode.*—Beat the egg, mixing with it a tablespoonful of cold water; make the wine-and-water hot, but not boiling; pour it on the egg, stirring all the time. Add sufficient lump sugar to sweeten the mixture, and a little grated nutmeg; put all into a very clean saucepan, set it on a gentle fire, and stir the contents one way until they thicken, but *do not allow them to boil.* Serve in a glass with sippets of toasted bread or plain crisp biscuits. When the egg is not warmed, the mixture will be found easier of digestion, but it is not so pleasant a drink. *Sufficient* for 1 person.

EGGS, to Boil for Breakfast, Salads, &c.

Eggs for boiling cannot be too fresh, or boiled too soon after they are laid; but rather a longer time should be allowed for boiling a new-laid egg than for one that is three or four days old. Have ready a saucepan of boiling water; put the eggs into it gently with a spoon, letting the spoon touch the bottom of the saucepan before it is withdrawn, that the egg may not fall, and consequently crack. For those who like eggs lightly boiled, 3 minutes will be found sufficient; 3¾ to 4 minutes will be ample time to set the white nicely; and, if liked hard, 6 to 7 minutes will not be found too long. Should

EGG-STAND FOR THE BREAKFAST-TABLE.

the eggs be unusually large, as those of black Spanish fowls sometimes are, allow an extra ½ minute for them. Eggs for salads should be boiled from 10 minutes to ¼ hour, and should be placed in a basin of cold water for a few minutes; they should then be rolled on the table with the hand, and the shell will peel off easily. *Time.*—To boil eggs lightly, for invalids or children, 3 minutes; to boil eggs to suit the generality of tastes, 3¾ to 4 minutes; to boil eggs hard, 6 to 7 minutes; for salads, 10 to 15 minutes.

EGGS, Buttered.

Ingredients.—4 new-laid eggs, 2 oz. of butter. *Mode.*—Procure the eggs new-laid if possible; break them into a basin, and beat them well; put the butter into another basin, which place in boiling water, and stir till the butter is melted. Pour that and the eggs into a lined saucepan; hold it over a gentle fire, and, as the mixture begins to warm, pour it two or three times into the basin, and back again, that the two ingredients may be well incorporated. Keep stirring the eggs and butter one way until they are hot, *without boiling*, and serve on hot buttered toast. If the mixture is allowed to boil, it will curdle, and so be entirely spoiled. *Time.*—About 5 minutes to make the eggs hot. *Average cost*, 7*d.* *Sufficient.*—Allow a slice to each person. *Seasonable* at any time.

EGGS, to Choose.

In choosing eggs, apply the tongue to the large end of the egg, and, if it feels warm, it is new, and may be relied on as a fresh egg. Another mode of ascertaining their freshness is to hold them before a lighted candle or to the light, and, if the egg looks clear, it will be tolerably good; if thick, it is stale; and if there is a black spot attached to the shell, it is worthless. No egg should be used for culinary purposes with the slightest taint in it, as it will render perfectly useless those with which it has been mixed. Eggs that are purchased, and that cannot be relied on, should always be broken in a cup, and then put into a basin: by this means stale or bad eggs may be easily rejected, without wasting the others.

EGGS, Ducks'.

Ducks' eggs are usually so strongly flavoured that, plainly boiled, they are not good for eating; they answer, however, very well for various culinary preparations where eggs are required; such as custards, &c. &c. Being so large and highly-flavoured, 1 duck's egg will go as far as 2 small hen's eggs, besides making whatever they are mixed with exceedingly rich. They also are admirable when used in puddings.

EGGS, Fried.

Ingredients. — 4 eggs, ¼ lb. of lard, butter or clarified dripping. *Mode.*—Place a delicately-clean frying-pan over a gentle fire; put in the fat, and allow it to come to the boiling-point. Break the eggs into cups, slip them into the boiling fat, and let them remain until the whites are delicately set; and, whilst they are frying, ladle a little of the fat over them. Take them up with a slice, drain them for a minute from their greasy moisture, trim them neatly, and serve on slices of fried bacon or ham; or the eggs may be placed in the middle of the dish, with the bacon put round as a garnish. *Time.*—2 to 3 minutes. *Average cost*, 1*d.* each; 2*d.* when scarce. *Sufficient* for 2 persons. *Seasonable* at any time.

FRIED EGGS ON BACON.

EGGS à la Maître d'Hôtel.

Ingredients.—¼ lb. of fresh butter, 1 tablespoonful of flour, ½ pint of milk, pepper and salt to taste, 1 tablespoonful of minced parsley, the juice of ½ lemon, 6 eggs. *Mode.*—Put the flour and half the butter into a stewpan; stir them over the fire until the mixture thickens; pour in the milk, which should be boiling; add a seasoning of pepper and salt, and simmer the whole for 5 minutes. Put the remainder of the butter into the sauce, and add the minced parsley; then boil the eggs hard, strip off the shell, cut the eggs into quarters, and put them on a dish. Bring the sauce to the boiling-point, add the lemon-juice, pour over the eggs and serve. *Time.*—5 minutes to boil the sauce; the eggs, 10 to 15 minutes. *Average cost*, 1*s.* *Sufficient* for 4 or 5 persons. *Seasonable* at any time.

EGGS, to Pickle.

Ingredients. — 16 eggs, 1 quart of vinegar, ½ oz. of black pepper, ½ oz. of Jamaica pepper, ½ oz. of ginger. *Mode.*—Boil the eggs for 12 minutes, then dip them into cold water, and take off the shells. Put the vinegar, with the pepper and ginger, into a stewpan, and let it simmer for 10 minutes. Now place the eggs in a jar, pour over them the vinegar, &c., boiling hot, and, when cold, tie them down with bladder to exclude the air. This pickle will be ready for use in a month. *Average cost*, for this quantity, 1*s.* 9*d.* *Seasonable.*—This should be made about Easter, as at this time eggs are plentiful and cheap. A store of pickled eggs will be found very useful and ornamental in serving with many first and second course dishes.

EGGS AU PLAT, or AU MIROIR, served on the Dish in which they are Cooked.

Ingredients.—4 eggs, 1 oz. of butter, pepper and salt to taste. *Mode.*—Butter a dish rather thickly with good fresh butter; melt it, break the eggs into it the same as for poaching, sprinkle them with white pepper and fine salt, and put the remainder of the butter, cut into very small pieces, on the top of them. Put the dish on a hot plate, or in the oven, or before the fire, and let it remain until the whites become set, but not hard, when serve immediately, placing the dish they were cooked in on another. To hasten the cooking of the eggs, a salamander may be held over them for a minute; but great care must be taken that they are not too much done. This is an exceedingly nice dish, and one very easily prepared for breakfast. *Time.*—3 minutes. *Average cost*, 5*d.* *Sufficient* for 2 persons. *Seasonable* at any time.

EGGS, Plovers'.

Plovers' eggs are usually served boiled hard, and sent to table in a napkin, either hot or cold; they may also be shelled, and served the same as eggs à la Tripe, with a good Béchamel sauce, or brown gravy, poured over them. They are also used for decorating salads, the beautiful colour of the white being generally so much admired.

EGGS, Poached.

Ingredients.—Eggs, water. To every pint of water allow 1 tablespoonful of vinegar. *Mode.* — Eggs for poaching should be perfectly fresh, but not quite new-laid; those that are about 36 hours old are the best for the purpose. If quite new-laid, the white is so milky it is almost impossible to set it; and, on the other hand, if the egg be at all stale, it is equally difficult to poach it nicely. Strain some boiling water into a deep clean frying-pan; break the egg into a cup without damaging the yolk, and, when the water boils, remove the pan to the side of the fire, and gently slip the egg into it. Place the pan over a gentle fire, and keep the water simmering until the white looks nicely set, when the egg is ready. Take it up gently with a slice, cut away the ragged edges of the white, and serve either on toasted bread or on slices of ham or bacon, or on spinach, &c. A poached egg should not be overdone, as its appearance and taste will be quite spoiled if the yolk be allowed to harden.

EGGS POACHED ON TOAST.

When the egg is slipped into the water, the white should be gathered together, to keep it a little in form, or the cup should be turned over it for ½ minute. To poach an egg to perfection is rather a difficult operation; so, for inexperienced cooks, a tin egg-poacher may be purchased, which greatly facilitates this manner of dressing eggs. Our illustration clearly shows what it is: it consists

TIN EGG-POACHER.

of a tin plate with a handle, with a space for three perforated cups. An egg should be broken into each cup, and the machine then placed in a stewpan of boiling water, which has been previously strained. When the whites of the eggs appear set, they are done, and should then be carefully slipped on to the toast or spinach, or with whatever they are served. In poaching eggs in a frying-pan, never do more than four at a time; and, when a little vinegar is liked mixed with the water in which the eggs are done, use the above proportion. *Time.*—2½ to 3½ minutes, according to the size of the egg. *Sufficient.*—Allow 2 eggs to each person. *Seasonable* at any time, but less plentiful in winter.

EGGS, Poached, with Cream.

Ingredients.—1 pint of water, 1 teaspoonful of salt, 4 teaspoonfuls of vinegar, 4 fresh eggs, ½ gill of cream, salt, pepper, and pounded sugar to taste, 1 oz. of butter. *Mode.*—Put the water, vinegar, and salt into a frying-pan, and break each egg into a separate cup; bring the water, &c., to boil, and slip the eggs

gently into it without breaking the yolks. Simmer them from 3 to 4 minutes, but not longer, and, with a slice, lift them out on to a hot dish, and trim the edges. Empty the pan of its contents, put in the cream, add a seasoning to taste of pepper, salt, and pounded sugar; bring the whole to the boiling-point; then add the butter, broken into small pieces; toss the pan round and round till the butter is melted; pour it over the eggs, and serve. To insure the eggs not being spoiled whilst the cream, &c. is preparing, it is a good plan to warm the cream with the butter, &c. before the eggs are poached, so that it may be poured over them immediately after they are dished. *Time.*—3 to 4 minutes to poach the eggs, 5 minutes to warm the cream. *Average cost* for the above quantity, 9*d.* *Sufficient* for 2 persons. *Seasonable* at any time.

EGGS, Scotch.

Ingredients.—6 eggs, 6 tablespoonfuls of forcemeat, hot lard, ½ pint of good brown gravy. *Mode.*—Boil the eggs for 10 minutes; strip them from the shells, and cover them with forcemeat, or substitute pounded anchovies for the ham. Fry the eggs a nice brown in boiling lard, drain them before the fire from their greasy moisture, dish them, and pour round from ¼ to ½ pint of good brown gravy. To enhance the appearance of the eggs, they may be rolled in beaten egg and sprinkled with bread-crumbs; but this is scarcely necessary if they are carefully fried. The flavour of the ham or the anchovy in the forcemeat must preponderate, as it should be very relishing. *Time.*—10 minutes to boil the eggs, 5 to 7 minutes to fry them. *Average cost,* 1*s.* 4*d.* *Sufficient* for 3 or 4 persons. *Seasonable* at any time.

EGGS, Snow, or Œufs à la Neige (a very pretty Supper Dish).

Ingredients.—4 eggs, ¾ pint of milk, pounded sugar to taste, flavouring of vanilla, lemon-rind, or orange-flower water. *Mode.*—Put the milk into a saucepan with sufficient sugar to sweeten it nicely, and the rind of ½ lemon. Let this steep by the side of the fire for ½ hour, when take out the peel; separate the whites from the yolks of the eggs, and whisk the former to a perfectly stiff froth, or until there is no liquid remain-jug; bring the milk to the boiling-point, drop in the snow a tablespoonful at a time, and keep turning the eggs until sufficiently cooked. Then place them on a glass dish, beat up the yolks of the eggs, stir to them the milk, add a little more sugar, and strain this mixture into a jug; place the jug in a saucepan of boiling water, and stir it one way until the mixture thickens, but do not allow it to boil, or it will curdle. Pour this custard over the eggs, when they should rise to the surface. They make an exceedingly pretty addition to a supper, and should be put in a cold place after being made. When they are flavoured with vanilla or orange-flowered water, it is not necessary to steep the milk. A few drops of the essence of either may be poured into the milk just before the whites are poached. In making the custard, a little more flavouring and sugar should always be added. *Time.*—About 2 minutes to poach the whites; 8 minutes to stir the custard. *Average cost,* 8*d.* *Sufficient* for 4 or 5 persons. *Seasonable* at any time.

EGGS, to keep Fresh for several Weeks.

Have ready a large saucepan, capable of holding 3 or 4 quarts, full of boiling water. Put the eggs into a cabbage-net, say 20 at a time, and hold them in the water (which must be kept boiling) *for 20 seconds.* Proceed in this manner till you have done as many eggs as you wish to preserve; then pack them away in sawdust. We have tried this method of preserving eggs, and can vouch for its excellence. They will be found, at the end of 2 or 3 months, quite good enough for culinary purposes; and although the white may be a little tougher than that of a new-laid egg, the yolk will be nearly the same. Many persons keep eggs for a long time by smearing the shells with butter or sweet oil: they should then be packed in plenty of bran or sawdust, and the eggs not allowed to touch each other. Eggs for storing should be collected in fine weather, and should not be more than 24 hours old when they are packed away, or their flavour, when used, cannot be relied on. Another simple way of preserving eggs is to immerse them in lime-water soon after they have been laid, and then to put the vessel containing the lime-water in a cellar or cool outhouse. *Seasonable.*—The best time for preserving eggs is from April to September.

EGGS, à la Tripe.

Ingredients.—8 eggs, ¾ pint of Béchamel sauce, dessertspoonful of finely-minced parsley. *Mode.*—Boil the eggs hard; put them into cold water, peel them, take out the yolks whole, and shred the whites. Make ¾ pint of Béchamel sauce; add the parsley, and, when the sauce is quite hot, put the yolks of the eggs into the middle of the dish, and the shred whites round them; pour over the sauce, and garnish with leaves of puff-paste or fried croûtons. There is no necessity for putting the eggs into the saucepan with the Béchamel; the sauce, being quite hot, will warm the eggs sufficiently. *Time.*—10 minutes to boil the eggs. *Average cost,* 1*s.* *Sufficient* for 5 or 6 persons. *Seasonable* at any time.

ELDER WINE.

Ingredients.—To every 3 gallons of water allow 1 peck of elderberries; to every gallon of juice allow 3 lbs. of sugar, ½ oz. of ground ginger, 6 cloves, 1 lb. of good Turkey raisins; ¼ pint of brandy to every gallon of wine. To every 9 gallons of wine, 3 or 4 tablespoonfuls of fresh brewer's yeast. *Mode.*—Pour the water, quite boiling, on the elderberries, which should be picked from the stalks, and let these stand covered for 24 hours; then strain the whole through a sieve or bag, breaking the fruit to express all the juice from it. Measure the liquor, and to every gallon allow the above proportion of sugar. Boil the juice and sugar with the ginger, cloves, and raisins for 1 hour, skimming the liquor the whole time; let it stand until milk-warm, then put it into a clean dry cask, with 3 or 4 tablespoonfuls of good fresh yeast to every 9 gallons of wine. Let it ferment for about a fortnight; then add the brandy, bung up the cask, and let it stand some months before it is bottled, when it will be found excellent. A bunch of hops suspended to a string from the bung, some persons say, will preserve the wine good for several years. Elder wine is usually mulled, and served with sippets of toasted bread and a little grated nutmeg. *Time.*—To stand covered for 24 hours; to be boiled 1 hour. *Average cost*, when made at home, 3*s.* 6*d.* per gallon. *Seasonable.*—Make this in September.

ENDIVE.

This vegetable, so beautiful in appearance, makes an excellent addition to winter salad, when lettuces and other winter salads are not obtainable. It is usually placed in the centre of the dish, and looks remarkably pretty with slices of beetroot, hard-boiled eggs, and curled celery placed round it, so that the colours contrast nicely. In preparing it, carefully wash and cleanse it free from insects, which are generally found near the heart; remove any decayed or dead leaves, and dry it thoroughly by shaking in a cloth. This vegetable may also be served hot, stewed in cream, brown gravy, or butter; but when dressed thus, the sauce it is stewed in should not be very highly seasoned, as that would destroy and overpower the flavour of the vegetable. *Average cost*, 1*d.* per head. *Sufficient.*—1 head for a salad for 4 persons. *Seasonable* from November to March.

ENDIVE, à la Française.

Ingredients.—6 heads of endive, 1 pint of broth, 3 oz. of fresh butter; salt, pepper, and grated nutmeg to taste. *Mode.*—Wash and boil the endive as in the preceding recipe; chop it rather fine, and put into a stewpan with the broth; boil over a brisk fire until the sauce is all reduced; then put in the butter, pepper, salt, and grated nutmeg (the latter must be very sparingly used); mix all well together, bring it to the boiling point, and serve very hot. *Time.*—10 minutes to boil, 5 minutes to simmer in the broth. *Average cost*, 1*d.* per head. *Sufficient* for 3 or 4 persons. *Seasonable* from November to March.

ENDIVE, Stewed.

Ingredients.—6 heads of endive, salt and water, 1 pint of broth, thickening of butter and flour, 1 tablespoonful of lemon-juice, a small lump of sugar. *Mode.*—Wash and free the endive thoroughly from insects, remove the green part of the leaves, and put it into boiling water, slightly salted. Let it remain for 10 minutes; then take it out, drain it till there is no water remaining, and chop it very fine. Put it into a stewpan with the broth; add a little salt and a lump of sugar, and boil until the endive is perfectly tender. When done, which may be ascertained by squeezing a piece between the thumb and finger, add a thickening of butter and flour and the lemon-juice; let the sauce boil up, and serve. *Time.*—10 minutes to boil, 5 minutes to simmer in the broth. *Average cost*, 1*d.* per head. *Sufficient* for 3 or 4 persons. *Seasonable* from November to March.

ESPAGNOLE, or Brown Spanish Sauce.

Ingredients.—2 slices of lean ham, 1 lb. of veal, 1½ pint of white stock, 2 or 3 sprigs of parsley, ½ a bay-leaf, 2 or 3 sprigs of savoury herbs, 6 green onions, 3 shalots, 2 cloves, 1 blade of mace, 2 glasses of sherry or Madeira, thickening of butter and flour. *Mode.*—Cut up the ham and veal into small square pieces, and put them into a stewpan. Moisten these with ½ pint of the stock, and simmer till the bottom of the stewpan is covered with a nicely-coloured glaze, when put in a few more spoonfuls to detach it. Add the remainder of the stock, with the spices, herbs, shalots, and onions, and simmer very gently for 1 hour. Strain and skim off every particle of fat, and, when required for use, thicken with butter and flour, or with a little roux. Add the wine, and, if necessary, a seasoning of cayenne; when it will be ready to serve. *Time.*—1½ hour. *Average cost*, 2*s.* per pint.

Note.—The wine in this sauce may be omitted, and an onion sliced and fried of a nice brown substituted for it. This sauce or gravy is used for many dishes, and with most people is a general favourite.

FEBRUARY—BILLS OF FARE.

Dinner for 18 persons.

First Course.

Fried Eels.

Hare Soup,
removed by
Tarbot and Oyster Sauce.

Vase of
Flowers.

Oyster Soup,
removed by
Crimped Cod, à la Maître
d'Hôtel.

Fried Whiting.

Second Course.

Braised Capon.
Boiled Ham, garnished.
Roast Fowls, garnished with Water-cresses.
Vase of Flowers.
Boiled Fowls and White Sauce.
Pâté Chaud.
Haunch of Mutton.

Entrées.

Lark Pudding.
Lobster Patties.
Vase of Flowers.
Filets de Perdrix.
Fricasseed Chicken.

Third Course.

Ducklings, removed by Iced Pudding.
Meringues.
Cheese-cakes.
Coffee Cream.
Orange Jelly.
Vase of Flowers.
Clear Jelly.
Blancmange.
Victoria Sandwiches.
Partridges, removed by Cabinet Pudding.
Gâteau de Pommes.

Dessert and Ices.

Dinner for 12 persons.

First Course.—Soup à la reine; clear gravy soup; brill and lobster sauce; fried smelts. *Entrées.*—Lobster rissoles; beef palates; pork cutlets à la soubise; grilled mushrooms. *Second Course.*—Braised turkey; haunch of mutton; boiled capon and oysters; tongue, garnished with tufts of broccoli; vegetables and salads. *Third Course.*—Wild ducks; plovers; orange jelly; clear jelly; Charlotte Russe; Nesselrode pudding; gâteau de riz; sea-kale; maids of honour; dessert and ices.

Dinner for 10 persons.

First Course.—Palestine soup; John Dory, with Dutch sauce; red mullet, with sauce Génoise. *Entrées.*—Sweetbread cutlets, with poivrade sauce; fowl au Béchamel. *Second Course.*—Roast saddle of mutton; boiled capon and oysters; boiled tongue, garnished with Brussels sprouts. *Third Course.*—Guinea-fowls; ducklings; pain de rhubarb; orange jelly; strawberry cream; cheesecakes; almond pudding; fig pudding; dessert and ices.

Dinner for 8 persons.

First Course.—Mock turtle soup; fillets of turbot à la crême; fried filleted soles and anchovy sauce. *Entrées.*—Larded fillets of rabbits; tendrons de veau with purée of tomatoes. *Second Course.*—Stewed rump of beef à la Jardinère; roast fowls; boiled ham. *Third Course.*—Roast pigeons or larks; rhubarb tartlets; meringues; clear jelly; cream; ice pudding; soufflé; dessert and ices.

Dinners for 6 persons.

First Course.—Rice soup; red mullet with Génoise sauce; fried smelts. *Entrées.*—Fowl pudding; sweetbreads. *Second Course.*—Roast turkey and sausages; boiled leg of pork; pease pudding. *Third Course.*—Lemon jelly; Charlotte à la vanille; maids of honour; plum-pudding, removed by ice pudding; dessert.

First Course.—Spring soup; boiled turbot and lobster sauce. *Entrées.*—Fricasseed rabbit; oyster patties. *Second Course.*—Boiled round of beef and marrow-bones; roast fowls, garnished with water-cresses and rolled bacon; vegetables. *Third Course.*—Marrow pudding; cheesecakes; tartlets of greengage jam; lemon cream; rhubarb tart; dessert.

First Course.—Vermicelli soup; fried whitings; stewed eels. *Entrées.*—Poulet à la Marengo; breast of veal stuffed and rolled. *Second Course.*—Roast leg of pork and apple sauce; boiled capon and oysters; tongue, garnished with tufts of broccoli. *Third Course.*—Wild ducks; lobster salad; Charlotte aux pommes; pain de rhubarb; vanilla cream; orange jelly; dessert.

First Course.—Ox-tail soup; cod à la crême; fried soles. *Entrées.*—Lark pudding; fowl scollops. *Second Course.*—Roast leg of mutton; boiled turkey and celery sauce; pigeon pie; small ham, boiled and garnished; vegetables. *Third Course.*—Game, when liked; tartlets of raspberry jam; vol-au-vent of rhubarb; Swiss cream; cabinet pudding; broccoli and sea-kale; dessert.

FEBRUARY, Plain Family Dinners for.

Sunday.—1. Ox-tail soup. 2. Roast beef, Yorkshire pudding, broccoli, potatoes. 3. Plum-pudding, apple tart. Cheese.

Monday.—1. Fried soles, plain melted butter, and potatoes. Cold roast beef, mashed potatoes. 3. The remains of plum-pudding cut in slices, warmed, and served with sifted sugar sprinkled over it. Cheese.

Tuesday.—1. The remains of ox-tail soup from Sunday. 2. Pork cutlets with tomato sauce; hashed beef. 3. Rolled jam pudding. Cheese.

Wednesday.—1. Boiled haddock and plain melted butter. 2. Rump-steak pudding, potatoes, greens. 3. Arrowroot, blancmange, garnished with jam.

Thursday.—1. Boiled leg of pork, greens, potatoes, pease pudding. 2. Apple fritters, sweet macaroni.

Friday.—1. Pea-soup made with liquor that the pork was boiled in. 2. Cold pork, mashed potatoes. 3. Baked rice pudding.

Saturday.—1. Broiled herrings and mustard sauce. 2. Haricot, mutton. 3. Macaroni, either served as a sweet pudding or with cheese.

Sunday.—1. Carrot soup. 2. Boiled leg of mutton and caper sauce, mashed turnips, roast fowls, and bacon. 3. Damson tart made with bottled fruit, ratafia pudding.

Monday.—1. The remainder of fowl curried and served with rice; rump-steaks and oyster sauce, cold mutton. 2. Rolled jam pudding.

Tuesday.—1. Vegetable soup made with liquor the mutton was boiled in on Sunday. 2. Roast surloin of beef, Yorkshire pudding, broccoli, and potatoes. 3. Cheese.

Wednesday.—1. Fried soles, melted butter. Cold beef and mashed potatoes: if there is any cold mutton left, cut it into neat slices and warm it in a little caper sauce. 2. Apple tart.

Thursday.—1. Boiled rabbit and onion sauce, stewed beef and vegetables, made with the remains of cold beef and bones. 2. Macaroni.

Friday.—1. Roast leg of pork, sage and onions and apple sauce, greens and potatoes. 2. Spinach and poached eggs instead of pudding. Cheese and water-cresses.

Saturday.—1. Rump-steak and kidney pudding, cold pork and mashed potatoes. 2. Baked rice pudding.

FEBRUARY, Things in Season.

Fish.—Barbel, brill, carp; cod may be bought, but is not so good as in January; crabs, crayfish, dace, eels, flounders, haddocks, herrings, lampreys, lobsters, mussels, oysters, perch, pike, plaice, prawns, shrimps, skate, smelts, soles, sprats, sturgeon, tench, thornback, turbot, whiting.

Meat.—Beef, house lamb, mutton, pork, veal.

Poultry.—Capons, chickens, ducklings, tame and wild pigeons, pullets with eggs, turkeys, wild-fowl, though now not in full season.

Game.—Grouse, hares, partridges, pheasants, snipes, woodcock.

Vegetables.—Beetroot, broccoli (purple and white), Brussels sprouts, cabbages, carrots, celery, chervil, cresses, cucumbers (forced), endive, kidney-beans, lettuces, parsnips, potatoes, savoys, spinach, turnips—various herbs.

Fruit.—Apples (golden and Dutch pippins), grapes, medlars, nuts, oranges, pears (Bon Chrétien), walnuts, dried fruits (foreign), such as almonds and raisins; French and Spanish plums; prunes, figs, dates, crystallized preserves.

FENNEL SAUCE, for Mackerel.

Ingredients.—½ pint of melted butter, rather more than 1 tablespoonful of chopped fennel. *Mode.*—Make the melted butter very smooth, chop the fennel rather small, carefully cleansing it from any grit or dirt, and put it to the butter when this is on the point of boiling. Simmer for a minute or two, and serve in a tureen. *Time.*—2 minutes. *Average cost*, 4*d.* *Sufficient* to serve with 5 or 6 mackerel.

FIG PUDDING.

Ingredients.—2 lbs. of figs, 1 lb. of suet, ½ lb. of flour, ½ lb. of bread crumbs, 2 eggs, milk. *Mode.*—Cut the figs into small pieces, grate the bread finely, and chop the suet very small; mix these well together, add the flour, the eggs, which should be well beaten, and sufficient milk to form the whole into a stiff paste; butter a mould or basin, press the pudding into it very closely, tie it down with a cloth, and boil for 3 hours, or rather longer; turn it out of the mould, and serve with melted butter, wine-sauce, or cream. *Time.*—3 hours, or longer. *Average cost,* 2s. *Sufficient* for 7 or 8 persons. *Seasonable.*—Suitable for a winter pudding.

FIG PUDDING (Staffordshire Recipe).

Ingredients.—1 lb. of figs, 6 oz. of suet, ¾ lb. of flour, milk. *Mode.*—Chop the suet finely, mix with it the flour, and make these into a smooth paste with milk; roll it out to the thickness of about ½ inch, cut the figs in small pieces, and strew them over the paste; roll it up, make the ends secure, tie the pudding in a cloth, and boil it from 1½ to 2 hours. *Time.*—1½ to 2 hours. *Average cost,* 1s. 1d. *Sufficient* for 5 or 6 persons. *Seasonable* at any time.

FIGS, Compôte of Green.

Ingredients.—1 pint of syrup, 1½ pint of green figs, the rind of ½ lemon. *Mode.*—Make a syrup as directed, boiling with it the lemon-rind, and carefully remove all the scum as it rises. Put in the figs, and simmer them very slowly until tender; dish them on a glass dish; reduce the syrup by boiling it quickly for 5

COMPÔTE OF FIGS.

minutes; take out the lemon-peel, pour the syrup over the figs, and the compôte, when cold, will be ready for table. A little port wine, or lemon-juice, added just before the figs are done, will be found an improvement. *Time.*—2 to 3 hours to stew the figs. *Average cost,* figs, 2s. to 3s. per dozen. *Seasonable* in August and September.

FISH.

Fish shortly before they spawn are, in general, best in condition. When the spawning is just over, they are out of season, and unfit for human food.

When fish is out of season, it has a transparent, bluish tinge, however much it may be boiled; whenever it is in season, its muscles are firm, and boil white and curdy.

As food for invalids, white fish, such as the ling, cod, haddock, coal-fish, and whiting, are the best; flat fish, as soles, skate, turbot, and flounders, are also good.

Salmon, mackerel, herrings, and trout soon spoil or decompose after they are killed; therefore, to be in perfection, they should be prepared for the table on the day they are caught. With flat fish, this is not of such consequence, as they will keep longer. The turbot, for example, is improved by being kept for a few hours.

FISH, General Directions for Dressing.

In dressing fish of any kind, the first point to be attended to, is to see that it is perfectly clean. It is a common error to wash it too much, as by doing so the flavour is diminished. If the fish is to be boiled, a little salt and vinegar should be put into the water, to give it firmness, after it is cleaned. Cod-fish, whiting, and haddock, are none the worse for being a little salted, and kept a day; and, if the weather be not very hot, they will be good for two days.

When fish is cheap and plentiful, and a larger quantity is purchased than is immediately wanted, the overplus of such as will bear it should be potted, or pickled, or salted, and hung up; or it may be fried, that it may serve for stewing the next day. Fresh-water fish, having frequently a muddy smell and taste, should be soaked in strong salt and water, after it has been well cleansed. If of a sufficient size, it may be scalded in salt and water, and afterwards dried and dressed.

Fish should be put into cold water and set on the fire to do very gently, or the outside will break before the inner part is done. Unless the fishes are small, they should never be put into warm water; nor should water, either hot or cold, be poured *on* to the fish, as it is liable to break the skin; if it should be necessary to add a little water whilst the fish is cooking, it ought to be poured in gently at the side of the vessel. The fish-plate may be drawn up, to see if the fish be ready, which may be known by its easily separating from the bone. It should then be immediately taken out of the water, or it will become woolly. The fish-plate should be set crossways over the kettle, to keep hot for serving, and a cloth laid over the fish, to prevent its losing its colour.

In garnishing fish great attention is required, and plenty of parsley, horse-radish, and lemon should be used. If fried parsley be used, it must be washed and picked, and thrown into fresh water. When the lard or dripping boils, throw the parsley into it immediately from the water, and instantly it will be green and crisp, and must be taken up with a slice. When well done, and with very good sauce, fish is more appreciated than almost any other dish. The liver and roe, in some instances, should be placed on the dish, in order that they may be distributed in the course of serving; but to each recipe will be appended the proper mode of serving and garnishing.

If fish is to be fried or broiled it must be dried in a nice soft cloth after it is well cleaned and washed. If for frying, brush it over with egg, and sprinkle it with some fine crumbs of bread. If done a second time with the egg and bread, the fish will look so much the better. If required to be very nice, a sheet of white blotting-paper must be placed to receive it, that it may be free from all grease; it must also be of a beautiful colour, and all the crumbs appear distinct. Butter gives a bad colour; lard and clarified dripping are most frequently used; but oil is the best, if the expense be no objection. The fish should be put into the lard when boiling, and there should be a sufficiency of this to cover it.

When fish is broiled, it must be seasoned, floured, and laid on a very clean gridiron, which, when hot, should be rubbed with a bit of suet, to prevent the fish from sticking. It must be broiled over a very clear fire, that it may not taste smoky; and not too near, that it may not be scorched.

In choosing fish, it is well to remember that it is possible it may be *fresh*, and yet not *good*. Under the head of each particular fish in this work, are appended rules for its choice, and the months when it is in season. Nothing can be of greater consequence to a cook than to have the fish good; as, if this important course in a dinner does not give satisfaction, it is rarely that the repast goes off well.

FISH, General Directions for Carving.

In carving fish, care should be taken to help it in perfect flakes, as, if these are broken, the beauty of the fish is lost. The carver should be acquainted, too, with the choicest parts and morsels; and to give each guest an equal share of these *titbits* should be his maxim. Steel knives and forks should on no account be used in helping fish, as these are liable to impart to it a very disagreeable flavour. When silver fish-carvers are considered too dear to be bought, good electro-plated ones answer very well, and are inexpensive.

FISH CAKE.

Ingredients.—The remains of any cold fish, 1 onion, 1 faggot of sweet herbs; salt and pepper to taste, 1 pint of water, equal quantities of bread-crumbs and cold potatoes, ½ teaspoonful of parsley, 1 egg, bread-crumbs. *Mode.*—Pick the meat from the bones of the fish, which latter put, with the head and fins, into a stewpan with the water; add pepper and salt, the onion and herbs, and stew slowly for gravy about 2 hours; chop the fish fine, and mix it well with bread-crumbs and cold potatoes, adding the parsley and seasoning; make the whole into a cake with the white of an egg, brush it over with egg, cover with bread-crumbs, fry of a light brown; strain the gravy, pour it over, and stew gently for ¼ of an hour, stirring it carefully once or twice. Serve hot, and garnish with thin slices of lemon and parsley. *Time.*—½ an hour after the gravy is made.

FISH AND OYSTER PIE.

[COLD MEAT COOKERY.] *Ingredients.*—Any remains of cold fish, such as cod or haddock; 2 dozen oysters, pepper and salt to taste, bread-crumbs sufficient for the quantity of fish; ½ teaspoonful of grated nutmeg, 1 teaspoonful of finely-chopped parsley. *Mode.*—Clear the fish from the bones, and put a layer of it in a pie-dish, which sprinkle with pepper and salt; then a layer of bread-crumbs, oysters, nutmeg, and chopped parsley. Repeat this till the dish is quite full. You may form a covering either of bread-crumbs, which should be browned, or puff-paste, which should be cut into long strips, and laid in cross-bars over the fish, with a line of the paste first laid round the edge. Before putting on the top, pour in some made melted butter, or a little thin white sauce, and the oyster-liquor, and bake. *Time.*—If made of cooked fish, ¼ hour; if made of fresh fish and puff-paste, ¾ hour. *Average cost,* 1*s.* 6*d.* *Seasonable* from September to April.

Note.—A nice little dish may be made by flaking any cold fish, adding a few oysters, seasoning with pepper and salt, and covering with mashed potatoes; ¼ hour will bake it.

FISH PIE, with Tench and Eels.

Ingredients.—2 tench, 2 eels, 2 onions, a faggot of herbs, 4 blades of mace, 3 anchovies, 1 pint of water, pepper and salt to taste, 1 teaspoonful of chopped parsley, the yokes of 6 hard-boiled eggs, puff-paste. *Mode.*—Clean and bone the tench, skin and bone the eels, and cut them into pieces 2 inches long, and leave the sides of the tench whole. Put the bones into a stewpan with the onions, herbs, mace, anchovies, water, and seasoning, and let them simmer gently for 1 hour. Strain it off, put it to cool, and skim off all the fat. Lay the tench and eels in a pie-dish, and between each layer put seasoning, chopped parsley, and hard-boiled eggs; pour in part of the strained liquor, cover in with puff-paste, and bake for ½ hour or rather more. The oven should be rather quick, and when done, heat the remainder of the liquor, which pour into the pie. *Time.*—½ hour to bake, or rather more if the oven is slow.

FISH SAUCE.

Ingredients.—1½ oz. of cayenne, 2 tablespoonfuls of walnut ketchup, 2 tablespoonfuls of soy, a few shreds of garlic and shalot, 1 quart of vinegar. *Mode.*—Put all the ingredients into a large bottle, and shake well every day for a fortnight. Keep it in small bottles well sealed, and in a few days it will be fit for use. *Average cost,* for this quantity, 1*s.*

FISH, Scalloped.

[COLD MEAT COOKERY.] *Ingredients.*—Remains of cold fish of any sort, ½ pint of cream, ½ tablespoonful of anchovy sauce, ½ teaspoonful of made mustard, ditto of walnut ketchup, pepper and salt to taste (the above quantities are for ½ lb. of fish when picked); bread-crumbs. *Mode.*—Put all the ingredients into a stewpan, carefully picking the fish from the bones; set it on the fire, let it remain till nearly hot, occasionally stir the contents, but do not allow it to boil. When done, put the fish into a deep dish or scallop shell, with a good quantity of bread-crumbs; place small pieces of butter on the top, set in a Dutch oven before the fire to brown, or use a salamander. *Time.*—¼ hour. *Average cost,* exclusive of the cold fish, 10*d.*

FISH, Scalloped.

[COLD MEAT COOKERY.] *Ingredients.*—Any cold fish, 1 egg, milk, 1 large blade of pounded mace, 1 tablespoonful of flour, 1 teaspoonful of anchovy sauce, pepper and salt to taste, bread-crumbs, butter. *Mode.*—Pick the fish carefully from the bones, and moisten with milk and the egg; add the other ingredients, and place in a deep ditch or scallop shells; over with bread-crumbs, butter the top, and brown before the fire; when quite hot, serve. *Time.*—20 minutes. *Average cost,* exclusive of the cold fish, 4*d.*

FISH STOCK.

Ingredients.—2 lbs. of beef or veal (these can be omitted), any kind of white fish trimmings of fish which are to be dressed for table, 2 onions, the rind of ½ a lemon, a bunch of sweet herbs, 2 carrots, 2 quarts of water. *Mode.*—Cut up the fish, and put it, with the other ingredients, into the water. Simmer for 2 hours; skim the liquor carefully, and strain it. When a richer stock is wanted, fry the vegetables and fish before adding the water. *Time.*—2 hours. *Average cost,* with meat, 10*d.* per quart; without, 3*d.*

Note.—Do not make fish stock long before it is wanted, as it soon turns sour.

FLOUNDERS, Boiled.

Ingredients.—Sufficient water to cover the flounders, salt in the proportion of 6 oz. to each gallon, a little vinegar. *Mode.*—Put on a kettle with enough water to cover the flounders, lay in the fish, add salt and vinegar in the above proportions, and when it boils, simmer very gently for 5 minutes. They must not boil fast, or they will break. Serve with plain melted butter, or parsley and butter. *Time.*—After the water boils, 5 minutes. *Average cost*, 3*d.* each. *Seasonable* from August to November.

FLOUNDERS, Fried.

Ingredients.—Flounders, egg, and bread-crumbs; boiling lard. *Mode.*—Cleanse the fish, and, two hours before they are wanted, rub them inside and out with salt, to render them firm; wash and wipe them very dry, dip them into egg, and sprinkle over with bread-crumbs; fry them in boiling lard, dish on a hot napkin, and garnish with crisped parsley. *Time.*—From 5 to 10 minutes, according to size. *Average cost*, 3*d.* each. *Seasonable* from August to November. *Sufficient*, 1 for each person.

FLOWERS, Almond.

Ingredients.—Puff-paste; to every ½ lb. of paste allow 3 oz. of almonds, sifted sugar, the white of an egg. *Mode.*—Roll the paste out to the thickness of ¼ inch, and, with a round fluted cutter, stamp out as many pieces as may be required. Work the paste up again, roll it out, and, with a smaller cutter, stamp out some pieces the size of a shilling. Brush the larger pieces over with the white of an egg, and place one of the smaller pieces on each. Blanch and cut the almonds into strips lengthwise; press them slanting into the paste closely round the rings; and when they are all completed, sift over some pounded sugar, and bake for about ¼ hour or twenty minutes. Garnish between the almonds with strips of apple jelly, and place in centre of the ring a small quantity of strawberry jam; pile them high on the dish, and serve. *Time.*—¼ hour or 20 minutes. *Sufficient.*—18 or 20 for a dish. *Seasonable* at any time.

FLOWERS, to Preserve Cut.

A bouquet of freshly-cut flowers may be preserved alive for a long time by placing them in a glass or vase with fresh water, in which a little charcoal has been steeped, or a small piece of camphor dissolved. The vase should be set upon a plate or dish, and covered with a bell-glass, around the edges of which, when it comes in contact with the plate, a little water should be poured to exclude the air.

FLOWERS, to Revive after Packing.

Plunge the stems into boiling water, and, by the time the water is cold, the flowers will have revived. Then cut afresh the ends of the stems, and keep them in fresh cold water.

FONDUE.

Ingredients.—4 eggs, the weight of 2 in Parmesan or good Cheshire cheese, the weight of 2 in butter; pepper and salt to taste. *Mode.*—Separate the yolks from the whites of the eggs; beat the former in a basin, and grate the cheese, or cut it into *very thin* flakes. Parmesan or Cheshire cheese may be used, whichever is the most convenient, although the former is considered more suitable for this dish; or an equal quantity of each may be used. Break the butter into small pieces, add to it the other ingredients, with sufficient pepper and salt to season nicely, and beat the mixture thoroughly. Well whisk the whites of the eggs, stir them lightly in, and either bake the fondue in a soufflé-dish or small round cake-tin. Fill the dish only half full, as the fondue should rise very much. Pin a napkin round the tin or dish, and serve very hot and very quickly. If allowed to stand after it is withdrawn from the oven, the beauty and lightness of this preparation will be entirely spoiled. *Time.*—From 15 to 20 minutes. *Average cost*, 10*d.* *Sufficient* for 4 or 5 persons. *Seasonable* at any time.

FONDUE, Brillat Savarin's (an excellent Recipe).

Ingredients.—Eggs, cheese, butter, pepper and salt. *Mode.*—Take the same number of eggs as there are guests; weigh the eggs in the shell, allow a third of their weight in Gruyère cheese, and a piece of butter one-sixth of the weight of the cheese. Break the eggs into a basin, beat them well; add the cheese, which should be grated, and the butter, which should be broken into small pieces. Stir these ingredients together with a wooden spoon; put the mixture into a lined saucepan, place it over the fire, and stir until the substance is thick and soft.

Put in a little salt, according to the age of the cheese, and a good sprinkling of pepper, and serve the fondue on a very hot silver or metal plate. Do not allow the fondue to remain on the fire after the mixture is set, as, if it boils, it will be entirely spoiled. Brillat Savarin recommends that some choice Burgundy should be handed round with this dish. We have given this recipe exactly as he recommends it to be made; but we have tried it with good Cheshire cheese, and found it answer remarkably well. *Time.* —About 4 minutes to set the mixture. *Average cost*, for 4 persons, 10*d*. *Sufficient.* —Allow 1 egg, with the other ingredients in proportion, for 1 person. *Seasonable* at any time.

FOOD FOR INFANTS, and its Preparation.

The articles generally employed as food for infants consist of arrowroot, bread, flour, baked flour, prepared groats, farinaceous food, biscuit-powder, biscuits, tops-and-bottoms, and semolina, or manna croup, as it is otherwise called, which, like tapioca, is the prepared pith of certain vegetable substances. Of this list the least efficacious, though, perhaps, the most believed in, is arrowroot, which only as a mere agent, for change, and then only for a very short time, should ever be employed as a means of diet to infancy or childhood. It is a thin, flatulent, and innutritious food, and incapable of supporting infantine life and energy. Bread, though the universal *régime* with the labouring poor, where the infant's stomach and digestive powers are a reflex, in miniature, of the father's, should never be given to an infant under three months, and, even then, however finely beaten up and smoothly made, is a very questionable diet. Flour, when well boiled, though infinitely better than arrowroot, is still only a kind of fermentative paste, that counteracts its own good by after-acidity and flatulence.

Baked flour, when cooked into a pale brown mass, and finely powdered, makes a far superior food to the others, and may be considered as a very useful diet, especially for a change. Prepared groats may be classed with arrowroot and raw flour, as being innutritious. The articles that now follow on our list are all good, and such as we could, with conscience and safety, trust to the health and development of any child whatever.

We may observe in this place, that an occasional change in the character of the food is highly desirable, both as regards the health and benefit of the child; and, though the interruption should only last for a day, the change will be advantageous.

The packets sold as farinaceous food are unquestionably the best aliment that can be given from the first to a baby, and may be continued, with the exception of an occasional change, without alteration of the material, till the child is able to take its regular meals of animal and vegetable food. Some infants are so constituted as to require a frequent and a total change in their system of living, seeming to thrive for a certain time on any food given to them, but if persevered in too long, declining in bulk and appearance as rapidly as they had previously progressed. In such cases, the food should be immediately changed, and when that which appeared to agree best with the child is resumed, it should be altered in its quality, and perhaps in its consistency.

For the farinaceous food there are directions with each packet, containing instructions for the making; but, whatever the food employed is, enough should be made at once to last the day and night; at first, about a pint basinful, but, as the child advances, a quart will hardly be too much. In all cases, let the food boil a sufficient time, constantly stirring, and taking every precaution that it does not get burnt, in which case it is on no account to be used.

The food should always be made with water, the whole sweetened at once, and of such a consistency that, when poured out, and it has had time to cool, it will cut with the firmness of a pudding or custard. One or two spoonfuls are to be put into the pap saucepan and stood on the hob till the heat has softened it, when enough milk is to be added, and carefully mixed with the food, till the whole has the consistency of ordinary cream; it is then to be poured into the nursing-bottle, and the food having been drawn through to warm the nipple, it is to be placed in the child's mouth. For the first month or more, half a bottleful will be quite enough to give the infant at one time; but, as the child grows, it will be necessary not only to increase the quantity given at each time, but also gradually to make its food more consistent, and, after the third month, to add an egg to every pint basin of food made. At night, the mother puts the food into the covered pan of her lamp, instead of the saucepan—that is, enough for one supply, and, having lighted the rush, she will find, on the waking of her child, the food sufficiently hot to bear the cooling addition of the milk. But, whether night or day, the same food should never be heated twice, and what the child leaves should be thrown away.

The biscuit powder is used in the same manner as the farinaceous food, and both prepared much after the fashion of making starch. But when tops-and-bottoms, or the whole biscuit, are employed, they require soaking in cold water for some time previously to boiling. The biscuit or biscuits are then to be slowly boiled in as much water as will, when thoroughly soft, allow of their being beaten by a three-pronged fork into a fine, smooth, and even pulp, and which, when poured into a basin and become cold, will cut out like a custard. If two large biscuits have been so treated, and the child is six or seven months old, beat up two eggs, sufficient sugar to properly sweeten it, and about a pint of skim milk. Pour this on the beaten biscuit in the saucepan, stirring constantly; boil for about five minutes, pour into a basin, and use, when cold, in the same manner as the other.

This makes an admirable food, at once nutritious and strengthening. When tops-and-bottoms or rusks are used, the quantity of the egg may be reduced, or altogether omitted.

Semolina, or manna croup, being in little hard grains, like a fine millet-seed, must be boiled for some time, and the milk, sugar, and egg added to it on the fire, and boiled for a few minutes longer, and, when cold, used as the other preparations.

Many persons entertain a belief that cow's milk is hurtful to infants, and, consequently, refrain from giving it; but this is a very great mistake, for both sugar and milk should form a large portion of every meal an infant takes.

FORCEMEATS.

The points which cooks should, in this branch of cookery, more particularly observe, are the thorough chopping of the suet, the complete mincing of the herbs, the careful grating of the bread-crumbs, and the perfect mixing of the whole. These are the three principal ingredients of forcemeats, and they can scarcely be cut too small, as nothing like a lump or fibre should be anywhere perceptible. To conclude, the flavour of no one spice or herb should be permitted to predominate.

FORCEMEAT BALLS, for Fish Soups.

Ingredients.—1 middling-sized lobster, ½ an anchovy, 1 head of boiled celery, the yolk of a hard-boiled egg; salt, cayenne, and mace to taste; 4 tablespoonfuls of bread-crumbs, 2 oz. of butter, 2 eggs. *Mode.*—Pick the meat from the shell of the lobster, and pound it, with the soft parts, in a mortar; add the celery, the yolk of the hard-boiled egg, seasoning, and bread-crumbs. Continue pounding till the whole is nicely amalgamated. Warm the butter till it is in a liquid state; well whisk the eggs, and work these up with the pounded lobster-meat. Make the balls of about an inch in diameter, and fry of a nice pale brown. *Sufficient,* from 18 to 20 balls for 1 tureen of soup.

FORCEMEAT, French.

It will be well to state, in the beginning of this recipe, that French forcemeat, or quenelles, consist of the blending of three separate processes; namely, panada, udder, and whatever meat you intend using.

Panada. *Ingredients.*—The crumb of 2 penny rolls, 4 tablespoonfuls of white stock, 1 oz. of butter, 1 slice of ham, 1 bay-leaf, a little minced parsley, 2 shalots, 1 clove, 2 blades of mace, a few mushrooms, butter, the yolks of 2 eggs. *Mode.*—Soak the crumb of the rolls in milk for about ½ hour, then take it out, and squeeze so as to press the milk from it; put the soaked bread into a stewpan with the above quantity of white stock, and set it on one side; then put into a separate stewpan 1 oz. of butter, a slice of lean ham cut small, with a bay-leaf, herbs, mushrooms, spices, &c., in the above proportions, and fry them gently over a slow fire. When done, moisten with 2 teacupfuls of white stock, boil for 20 minutes, and strain the whole through a sieve over the panada in the other stewpan. Place it over the fire, keep constantly stirring, to prevent its burning, and, when quite dry, put in a small piece of butter. Let this again dry up by stirring over the fire; then add the yolks of 2 eggs, mix well, put the panada to cool on a clean plate, and use it when required. Panada should always be well flavoured, as the forcemeat receives no taste from any of the other ingredients used in its preparation.

Boiled Calf's Udder for French Forcemeat.—Put the udder into a stewpan with sufficient water to cover it; let it stew gently till quite done, when take it out to cool. Trim all the upper parts, cut it into small pieces, and pound well in a mortar, till it can be rubbed through a sieve. That portion which passes through the strainer is one of the three ingredients of which French forcemeats are generally composed; but many cooks substitute butter for this, being a less troublesome and more expeditious mode of preparation.

FORCEMEAT, for Cold Savoury Pies.

Ingredients.—1 lb. of veal, 1 lb. of fat bacon; salt, cayenne, pepper, and pounded mace to taste; a very little nutmeg, the same of chopped lemon-peel, ½ teaspoonful of chopped parsley, ½ teaspoonful of minced savoury herbs, 1 or 2 eggs. *Mode.*—Chop the veal and bacon together, and put them into a mortar with the other ingredients mentioned above. Pound well, and bind with 1 or 2 eggs which have been previously beaten and strained. Work the whole well together, and the forcemeat will be ready for use. If the pie is not to be eaten immediately, omit the herbs and parsley, as these will prevent it from keeping. Mushrooms or truffles may be added. *Sufficient* for 2 small pies.

FORCEMEAT, for Pike, Carp, Haddock, and various Kinds of Fish.

Ingredients.—1 oz. of fresh butter, 1 oz. of suet, 1 oz. of fat bacon, 1 small teaspoonful of minced savoury herbs, including parsley; a little onion, when liked, shredded very fine; salt, nutmeg, and cayenne to taste; 4 oz. of bread-crumbs, 1 egg. *Mode.*—Mix all the ingredients well together, carefully mincing them very finely; beat up the egg, moisten with it, and work the whole very smoothly together. Oysters or anchovies may be added to this forcemeat, and will be found a great improvement. *Average cost*, 6*d*. *Sufficient* for a moderate-sized haddock or pie.

FORCEMEAT, for Baked Pike.

Ingredients.—3 oz. of bread-crumbs, 1 teaspoonful of minced savoury herbs, 8 oysters, 2 anchovies (these may be dispensed with), 2 oz. of suet; salt, pepper, and pounded mace to taste; 6 tablespoonfuls of cream or milk, the yolks of 2 eggs. *Mode.*—Beard and mince the oysters, prepare and mix the other ingredients, and blend the whole thoroughly together. Moisten with the cream and eggs, put all into a stewpan, and stir it over the fire till it thickens, when put it into the fish, which should have previously been cut open, and sew it up. *Time.*—4 or 5 minutes to thicken. *Average cost*, 10*d*. *Sufficient* for a moderate-sized pike.

FORCEMEAT, or QUENELLES, for Turtle Soup. (Soyer's Recipe.)

Take a pound and a half of lean veal from the fillet, and cut it in long thin slices; scrape with a knife till nothing but the fibre remains; put it into a mortar, pound it 10 minutes, or until in a purée; pass it through a wire sieve (use the remainder in stock); then take 1 pound of good fresh beef suet, which skin, shred, and chop very fine; put it into a mortar and pound it; then add 6 oz. of panada (that is, bread soaked in milk and boiled till nearly dry) with the suet; pound them well together, and add the veal; season with a teaspoonful of salt, a quarter one of pepper, half that of nutmeg; work all well together; then add four eggs by degrees, continually pounding the contents of the mortar. When well mixed, take a small piece in a spoon, and poach it in some boiling water; and if it is delicate, firm, and of a good flavour, it is ready for use.

FORCEMEAT VEAL, or VEAL QUENELLES.

Ingredients.—Equal quantities of veal, panada, and calf's udder, 2 eggs; seasoning to taste of pepper, salt, and pounded mace, or grated nutmeg; a little flour. *Mode.*—Take the fleshy part of veal, scrape it with a knife, till all the meat is separated from the sinews, and allow about ½ lb. for an entrée. Chop the meat, and pound it in a mortar till reduced to a paste; then roll it into a ball; make another of panada the same size, and another of udder, taking care that these three balls be of the same *size*. (It is to be remembered, that equality of *size*, and not of weight, is here necessary.) When the three ingredients are properly prepared, pound them altogether in a mortar for some time; for the more quenelles are pounded, the more delicate they are. Now moisten with the eggs, whites and yolks, and continue pounding, adding a seasoning of pepper, spices, &c. When the whole is well blended together, mould it into balls, or whatever shape is intended, roll them in flour, and poach in boiling water, to which a little salt should have been added. If the quenelles are not firm enough, add the yolk of another egg, but omit the white, which only makes them hollow and puffy inside. In the preparation of this recipe, it would be well to bear in mind that the ingredients are to be well pounded and seasoned, and must be made hard or soft according to the dishes they are intended for. For brown or white ragoûts they should be firm, and when the quenelles are used very small, extreme delicacy will be necessary in their preparation. Their flavour may be varied by using the flesh of rabbit, fowl, hare, pheasant, grouse, or an extra quantity of mushroom, parsley, &c.

FORCEMEAT for Veal, Turkeys, Fowls, Hare, &c.

Ingredients.—2 oz. of ham or lean bacon, ¼ lb. of suet, the rind of half a lemon, 1 teaspoonful of minced parsley, 1 teaspoonful of minced sweet herbs; salt, cayenne, and pounded mace to taste; 6 oz. of bread-crumbs, 2 eggs. *Mode.*—Shred the ham or bacon, chop the suet, lemon-peel, and herbs, taking particular care that all be very finely minced; add a seasoning to taste of salt, cayenne, and mace, and blend all thoroughly together with the bread-crumbs, before wetting. Now beat and strain the eggs; work these up with the other ingredients, and the forcemeat will be ready for use. When it is made into balls, fry of a nice brown, in boiling lard, or put them on a tin and bake for ½ hour in a moderate oven. As we have stated before, no one flavour should predominate greatly, and the forcemeat should be of sufficient body to cut with a knife, and yet not dry and heavy. For very delicate forcemeat, it is advisable to pound the ingredients together before binding with the eggs; but for ordinary cooking, mincing very finely answers the purpose. *Average cost*, 8*d*. *Sufficient* for a turkey, a moderate-sized fillet of veal, or a hare.

Note.—In the forcemeat for Hare, the liver of the animal is sometimes added. Boil for 5 minutes, mince it very small, and mix it with the other ingredients. If it should be in an unsound state, it must be on no account made use of.

FOWLS, Boiled, à la Béchamel.

Ingredients.—A pair of fowls, 1 pint of Béchamel, a few bunches of boiled broccoli or cauliflower. *Mode.*—Truss and boil the flowers; make a pint of Béchamel sauce; pour some of this over the fowls, and the remainder send to table in a tureen. Garnish the dish with bunches of boiled cauliflowers or broccoli, and serve very hot. The sauce should be made sufficiently thick to adhere to the fowls; that for the tureen should be thinned by adding a spoonful or two of stock. *Time.*—From ½ to 1 hour, according to size. *Average cost*, in full season, 5*s*. a pair. *Sufficient* for 6 or 7 persons. *Seasonable* all the year, but scarce in early spring.

FOWLS, Boiled, to Carve.

This will not be found a very difficult member of the poultry family to carve, unless, as may happen, a very old farmyard occupant, useless for egg-laying purposes, has, by some unlucky mischance, been introduced into the kitchen as a "fine young chicken." Skill, however, and the application of a small amount of strength, combined with a fine keeping of the temper, will even get over that difficulty. Fixing the fork firmly in the breast, let the knife be firmly passed along the line shown from 1 to 2; then cut downwards from that line to fig. 3;

BOILED FOWL.

and the wing, it will be found, can be easily withdrawn. The shape of the wing should be like the accompanying engraving. Let the fork be placed inside the leg, which should be gently forced away from the body of the fowl; and the joint, being thus discovered, the carver can readily cut through it, and the leg can be served. When the leg is displaced, it should be of the same shape as that shown in the annexed woodcut. The legs and wings on either side having been taken off, the carver should draw his knife through the flesh in the direction of the line 4 to 5; by this means the knife can be slipped underneath the merrythought, which, being lifted up and pressed backward, will immediately come off. The collar- or neck-bones are the next to consider: these lie on each side of the merry-thought, close under the upper part of the wings; and, in order to free these from the fowl, they must also be raised by the knife at their broad end, and turned from the body towards the breast-bone, until the shorter piece of the bone, as shown in the cut, breaks off. There will now be left only the breast, with the ribs. The breast can be, without difficulty, disengaged from the ribs by cutting through the latter, which will offer little impediment. The side bones are now to be taken off; and to do this, the lower end of the back should be turned from the carver, who should press the point of the knife through the top of the backbone, near the centre, bringing it down towards the end of the back completely through the bone. If the knife be now turned in the opposite direction, the joint will be easily separated from the vertebræ. The backbone being now uppermost, the fork should be pressed firmly down on it, whilst at the same time the knife should be employed in raising up the lower small end of the fowl towards the fork, and thus the back will be dislocated about its middle. The wings, breast, and

LEG, WING, AND NECKBONE OF FOWL.

merrythought are esteemed the prime parts of a fowl, and are usually served to the ladies of the company, to whom legs, except as a matter of paramount necessity, should not be given. Byron gave it as one reason why he did not like dining with ladies, that they always had the wings of the fowls, which he himself preferred. We heard a gentleman who, when he might have had a wing, declare his partiality for a leg, saying that he had been obliged to eat legs for so long a time that he had at last come to like them better than the other more prized parts. If the fowl is, capon-like, very large, slices may be carved from its breast in the same manner as from a turkey's.

FOWL, Boiled, with Oysters. (Excellent.)

Ingredients.—1 young fowl, 3 dozen oysters, the yolks of 2 eggs, ½ pint of cream. *Mode.*—Truss a young fowl as for boiling; fill the inside with oysters which have been bearded and washed in their own liquor; secure the ends of the fowl, put it into a jar, and plunge the jar into a saucepan of boiling water. Keep it boiling for 1½ hour, or rather longer; then take the gravy that has flowed from the oysters and fowl, of which there will be a good quantity; stir in the cream and yolks of eggs, add a few oysters scalded in their liquor; let the sauce get quite *hot*, but do not allow it to *boil*; pour some of it over the fowl, and the remainder send to table in a tureen. A blade of pounded mace added to the sauce, with the cream and eggs, will be found an improvement. *Time.*—1½ hour. *Average cost*, 4*s*. 6*d*. *Sufficient* for 3 or 4 persons. *Seasonable* from September to April.

FOWLS, Broiled, and Mushroom Sauce.

Ingredients.—A large fowl; seasoning, to taste, of pepper and salt, 2 handfuls of button mushrooms, 1 slice of lean ham, ¾ pint of thickened gravy, 1 teaspoonful of lemon juice, ½ teaspoonful of pounded sugar. *Mode.*—Cut the fowl into quarters, roast it until three-parts done, and keep it well basted whilst at the fire. Take the fowl up, broil it for a few minutes over a clear fire, and season it with pepper and salt. Have ready some mushroom sauce made in the following manner. Put the mushrooms into a stewpan with a small piece of butter, the ham, a seasoning of pepper and salt, and the gravy; simmer these gently for ½ hour, add the lemon-juice and sugar, dish the fowl, and pour the sauce round them. *Time.*—To roast the fowl, 35 minutes; to broil it, 10 to 15 minutes. *Average cost*, in full season, 2*s.* 6*d.* *Sufficient* for 4 or 5 persons. *Seasonable.*—In full season from May to January.

FOWL, Boiled, and Rice.

Ingredients.—1 fowl, mutton broth, 2 onions, 2 small blades of pounded mace, pepper and salt to taste, ½ pint of rice, parsley and butter. *Mode.*—Truss the fowl as for boiling, and put it into a stewpan with sufficient clear well-skimmed mutton broth to cover it; add the onion, mace, and a seasoning of pepper and salt; stew very gently for about 1 hour, should the fowl be large, and about ½ hour before it is ready put in the rice, which should be well washed and soaked. When the latter is tender, strain it from the liquor, and put it on a sieve reversed to dry before the fire, and, in the mean time, keep the fowl hot. Dish it, put the rice round as a border, pour a little parsley and butter over the fowl, and the remainder send to table in a tureen. *Time.*—A large fowl, 1 hour. *Average cost*, 2*s.* 6*d.* *Sufficient* for 3 or 4 persons. *Seasonable* all the year.

FOWLS, to Bone, for Fricassees, Curries, and Pies.

First carve them entirely into joints, then remove the bones, beginning with the legs and wings, at the head of the largest bone; hold this with the fingers, and work the knife as directed in the recipe above. The remainder of the birds is too easily done to require any instructions.

FOWL, Croquettes of (an Entrée).

Ingredients.—3 or 4 shalots, 1 oz. of butter, 1 teaspoonful of flour, white sauce; pepper, salt, and pounded mace to taste; ½ teaspoonful of pounded sugar, the remains of cold roast fowls, the yolks of 2 eggs, egg, and bread-crumbs. *Mode.*—Mince the fowl, carefully removing all skin and bone, and fry the shalots in the butter; add the minced fowl, dredge in the flour, put in the pepper, salt, mace, pounded sugar, and sufficient white sauce to moisten it; stir to it the yolks of 2 well-beaten eggs, and set it by to cool. Then make the mixture up into balls, egg and bread-crumb them, and fry a nice brown. They may be served on a border of mashed potatoes, with gravy or sauce in the centre. *Time.*—10 minutes to fry the balls. *Seasonable* at any time.

FOWL AND RICE, Croquettes of (an Entrée).

Ingredients.—¼ lb. of rice, 1 quart of stock or broth, 3 oz. of butter, minced fowl, egg, and bread-crumbs. *Mode.*—Put the rice into the above proportion of cold stock or broth, and let it boil very gently for ½ hour; then add the butter, and simmer it till quite dry and soft. When cold, make it into balls, hollow out the inside, and fill with minced fowl made by recipe. The mince should be rather thick. Cover over with rice, dip the balls into egg, sprinkle them with bread-crumbs, and fry a nice brown. Dish them, and garnish with fried parsley. Oysters, white sauce, or a little cream, may be stirred into the rice before it cools. *Time.*—½ hour to boil the rice, 10 minutes to fry the croquettes. *Average cost*, exclusive of the fowl, 8*d.* *Seasonable* at any time.

FOWL, Curried.

Ingredients.—1 fowl, 2 oz. of butter, 3 onions sliced, 1 pint of white veal-gravy, 1 tablespoonful of curry-powder, 1 tablespoonful of flour, 1 apple, 4 tablespoonfuls of cream, 1 tablespoonful of lemon-juice. *Mode.*—Put the butter into a stewpan, with the onions sliced, the fowl cut into small joints, and the apple peeled, cored, and minced. Fry of a pale brown, add the stock, and stew gently for 20 minutes; rub down the curry-powder and flour with a little of the gravy, quite smoothly, and stir this to the other ingredients; simmer for rather more than ½ hour, and just before serving, add the above proportion of hot cream and lemon-juice. Serve with boiled rice, which may either be heaped lightly on a dish by itself, or put round the curry as a border. *Time.*—50 minutes. *Average cost*, 3*s.* 3*d.* *Sufficient* for 3 or 4 persons. *Seasonable* in the winter.

Note.—This curry may be made of cold

chicken, but undressed meat will be found far superior.

FOWL, Fricasseed.

[COLD MEAT COOKERY.] *Ingredients.*—The remains of cold roast fowl, 1 strip of lemon-peel, 1 blade of pounded mace, 1 bunch of savoury herbs, 1 onion, pepper and salt to taste, 1 pint of water, 1 teaspoonful of flour, ½ pint of cream, the yolks of 2 eggs. *Mode.*—Carve the fowls into nice joints; make gravy of the trimmings and legs, by stewing them with the lemon-peel, mace, herbs, onion, seasoning, and water, until reduced to ½ pint; then strain, and put in the fowl. Warm it through, and thicken with a teaspoonful of flour; stir the yolks of the eggs into the cream; add these to the sauce, let it get thoroughly hot, but do not allow it to boil, or it will curdle. *Time.*—1 hour to make the gravy, ¼ hour to warm the fowl. *Average cost,* exclusive of the cold chicken, 8*d.* *Seasonable* at any time.

FOWLS, Fried.

[COLD MEAT COOKERY.] *Ingredients.*—The remains of cold roast fowls, vinegar, salt and cayenne to taste, 3 or 4 minced shalots. For the batter,—½ lb. of flour, ½ pint of hot water, 2 oz. of butter, the whites of 2 eggs. *Mode.*—Cut the fowl into nice joints; steep them for an hour in a little vinegar, with salt, cayenne, and minced shalots. Make the batter by mixing the flour and water smoothly together; melt in it the butter, and add the whites of egg beaten to a froth; take out the pieces of fowl, dip them in the batter, and fry in boiling lard, a nice brown. Pile them high in the dish, and garnish with fried parsley or rolled bacon. When approved, a sauce or gravy may be served with them. *Time.*—10 minutes to fry the fowl. *Average cost,* exclusive of the cold fowl, 8*d.* *Seasonable* at any time.

FOWLS, Fried.

[COLD MEAT COOKERY.] *Ingredients.*—The remains of cold roast fowl, vinegar, salt and cayenne to taste, 4 minced shalots, yolk of egg; to every teacupful of bread-crumbs allow 1 blade of pounded mace, ½ teaspoonful of minced lemon-peel, 1 saltspoonful of salt, a few grains of cayenne. *Mode.*—Steep the pieces of fowl as in the preceding recipe, then dip them into the yolk of an egg or clarified butter; sprinkle over bread-crumbs with which have been mixed salt, mace, cayenne, and lemon-peel in the above proportion. Fry a light brown, and serve with or without gravy, as may be preferred. *Time.*—10 minutes to fry the fowl. *Average cost,* exclusive of the cold fowl, 6*d.* *Seasonable* at any time.

FOWLS, Fried, and French Beans.

[COLD MEAT COOKERY.] *Ingredients.*—The remains of cold roast fowl; the yolk of 1 egg, 2 oz. of butter, 1 blade of pounded mace, ½ saltspoonful of grated nutmeg, bread-crumbs and chopped parsley. *Mode.*—Cut the fowl into neat joints, brush them over with the yolk of egg, and sprinkle them with bread-crumbs, with which the *parsley, nutmeg,* and *mace* have been well mixed. Fry the fowl in the butter until of a nice brown, and dish the pieces on French beans boiled, and afterwards simmered for a minute or two in butter. The dish should be garnished with rolled bacon. *Time.*—10 minutes to fry the fowl. *Average cost,* exclusive of the cold fowl, 6*d.* *Seasonable* from July to September.

FOWL au Gratin.

[COLD MEAT COOKERY.] *Ingredients.*—The remains of either cold roast or boiled fowl, ½ pint of Béchamel sauce, a dessertspoonful of grated Parmesan cheese, pepper and salt to taste, ½ saltspoonful of grated nutmeg, ½ pint of cream, 2 tablespoonfuls of bread-crumbs, fried potatoes. *Mode.*—Mince the fowl not too finely, and make it hot in the Béchamel sauce, to which the nutmeg, pepper and salt, and cream, have been added. When well mixed, serve the fowl on to a dish, cover it with the bread-crumbs and Parmesan cheese, drop over a little clarified butter, and bake in the oven until of a pale brown. Garnish the dish with fried potatoes. *Time.*—10 minutes to warm the fowl, 10 minutes to bake. *Seasonable* at any time.

FOWL, Hashed. An Entree.

[COLD MEAT COOKERY.] *Ingredients.*—The remains of cold roast fowl, 1 pint of water, 1 onion, 2 or 3 small carrots, 1 blade of pounded mace, pepper and salt to taste, 1 small bunch of savoury herbs, thickening of butter and flour, 1½ tablespoonful of mushroom ketchup. *Mode.*—Cut off the best joints from the fowl, and the remainder make into gravy, by adding to the bones and trimmings a pint of water, an onion sliced and fried of a nice brown, the carrots, mace, seasoning, and herbs. Let these stew gently for 1½ hour, strain the liquor, and thicken with a little flour and butter. Lay in the fowl, thoroughly warm it through, add the ketchup, and garnish with sippets of toasted bread. *Time.*—Altogether 1¾ hour. *Average cost,* exclusive of the cold fowl, 4*d.* *Seasonable* at any time.

FOWL, Hashed, Indian Fashion (an Entree).

[COLD MEAT COOKERY.] *Ingredients.* —The remains of cold roast fowl, 3 or 4 sliced onions, 1 apple, 2 oz. of butter, pounded mace, pepper and salt to taste, 1 tablespoonful of curry-powder, 2 tablespoonfuls of vinegar, 1 tablespoonful of flour, 1 teaspoonful of pounded sugar, 1 pint of gravy. *Mode.* —Cut the onions into slices, mince the apple, and fry these in the butter; add pounded mace, pepper, salt, curry-powder, vinegar, flour, and sugar in the above proportions; when the onion is brown, put in the gravy, which should be previously made from the bones and trimmings of the fowls, and stew for ¾ hour; add the fowl cut into nice-sized joints, let it warm through, and when quite tender, serve. The dish should be garnished with an edging of boiled rice. *Time.*—1 hour. *Average cost,* exclusive of the fowl, 8*d.* *Seasonable* at any time.

FOWL, an Indian Dish of (an Entrée).

[COLD MEAT COOKERY.] *Ingredients.* —The remains of cold roast fowl, 3 or 4 sliced onions, 1 tablespoonful of curry-powder, salt to taste. *Mode.*—Divide the fowl into joints; slice and fry the onions in a little butter, taking care not to burn them; sprinkle over the fowl a little curry-powder and salt; fry these nicely, pile them high in the centre of the dish, cover with the onion, and serve with a cut lemon on a plate. Care must be taken that the onions are not greasy: they should be quite dry, but not burnt. *Time.*—5 minutes to fry the onions, 10 minutes to fry the fowl. *Average cost,* exclusive of the fowl, 4*d.* *Seasonable* during the winter months.

FOWL à la Mayonnaise.

Ingredients.—A cold roast fowl, Mayonnaise sauce, 4 or 5 young lettuces, 4 hard-boiled eggs, a few water-cresses, endive. *Mode.*—Cut the fowl into neat joints, lay them in a deep dish, piling them high in the centre, sauce the fowl with Mayonnaise, and garnish the dish with young lettuces cut in halves, water-cresses, endive, and hard-boiled eggs: these may be sliced in rings, or laid on the dish whole, cutting off at the bottom a piece of the white, to make the egg stand. All kinds of cold meat and solid fish may be dressed à la Mayonnaise, and make excellent luncheon or supper dishes. The sauce should not be poured over the fowls until the moment of serving. Should a very large Mayonnaise be required, use 2 fowls instead of one, with an equal proportion of the remaining ingredients. *Average cost,* with one fowl, 3*s.* 6*d.* *Sufficient* for a moderate-sized dish. *Seasonable* from April to September.

FOWL, Minced (an Entrée).

[COLD MEAT COOKERY.] *Ingredients.* —The remains of cold roast fowl, 2 hard-boiled eggs, salt, cayenne, and pounded mace, 1 onion, 1 faggot of savoury herbs, 6 tablespoonfuls of cream, 1 oz. of butter, two teaspoonfuls of flour, ½ teaspoonful of finely-minced lemon-peel, 1 tablespoonful of lemon-juice. *Mode.*—Cut out from the fowl all the white meat, and mince it finely without any skin or bone; put the bones, skin, and trimmings into a stewpan with an onion, a bunch of savoury herbs, a blade of mace, and nearly a pint of water; let this stew for an hour, then strain the liquor. Chop the eggs small; mix them with the fowl; add salt, cayenne, and pounded mace, put in the gravy and remaining ingredients; let the whole just boil, and serve with sippets of toasted bread. *Time.*—Rather more than 1 hour. *Average cost,* exclusive of the fowl, 8*d.* *Seasonable* at any time.

Note.—Another way to make this is to mince the fowl, and warm it in white sauce or Béchamel. When dressed like this, 3 or 4 poached eggs may be placed on the top: oysters, or chopped mushrooms, or balls of oyster forcemeat, may be laid round the dish.

FOWL, Minced, à la Béchamel.

[COLD MEAT COOKERY.] *Ingredients.*—The remains of cold roast fowl, 6 tablespoonfuls of Béchamel sauce, 6 tablespoonfuls of white stock, the white of 1 egg, bread-crumbs, clarified butter. *Mode.*—Take the remains of roast fowls, mince the white meat very small, and put it into a stewpan with the Béchamel and stock; stir it well over the fire, and just let it boil up. Pour the mince into a dish, beat up the white of egg, spread it over, and strew on it a few grated bread-crumbs; pour a very little clarified butter on the whole, and brown either before the fire or with a salamander. This should be served in a silver dish, if at hand. *Time.*—2 or 3 minutes to simmer in the sauce. *Seasonable* at any time.

FOWL, Ragoût of.

[COLD MEAT COOKERY.] *Ingredients.*—The remains of cold roast fowls, 3 shalots, 2 blades of mace, a faggot of savoury herbs, 2 or 3 slices of lean ham, 1 pint of stock or water, pepper and salt to taste, 1 onion, 1 dessertspoonful of flour, 1 tablespoonful of lemon-juice, ½ teaspoonful of pounded sugar, 1 oz. of butter. *Mode.*—Cut the fowls up into neat pieces, the same as for a fricassee; put the trimmings into a stewpan with the shalots, mace, herbs, ham, onion, and stock (water may be substituted for this). Boil it slowly for 1 hour, strain the liquor, and put a small piece of butter into a stewpan; when melted, dredge in sufficient flour to dry up the butter, and stir it over the fire. Put in the strained liquor, boil for a few minutes, and strain it again over the pieces of fowl. Squeeze in the lemon-juice, add the sugar and a seasoning of pepper and salt, make it hot, but do not allow it to boil; lay the fowl neatly on the dish, and garnish with croûtons. *Time.*—Altogether 1½ hour. *Average cost,* exclusive of the cold fowl, 9*d.* *Seasonable* at any time.

FOWLS, Roast.

Ingredients.—A pair of fowls, a little flour. *Mode.*—Fowls, to be tender, should be killed a couple of days before they are dressed; when the feathers come out easily; then let them be picked and cooked. In drawing them be careful not to break the gall-bag, as, wherever it touches, it would impart a very bitter taste; the liver and gizzard should also be preserved. Truss them in the following manner:—After having carefully picked them, cut off the head, and skewer the skin of the neck down over the back. Cut off the claws, dip the legs in boiling water, and scrape them; turn the pinions under, run a skewer through them and the middle of the legs, which should be passed through the body to the pinion and leg on the other side, one skewer securing the limbs on both sides. The

ROAST FOWL.

liver and gizzard should be placed in the wings, the liver on one side and the gizzard on the other. Tie the legs together by passing a trussing-needle, threaded with twine, through the backbone, and secure it on the other side. If trussed like a capon, the legs are placed more apart. When firmly trussed, singe them all over; put them down to a bright clear fire, paper the breasts with a sheet of buttered paper, and keep the fowls well basted. Roast them for ¾ hour, more or less, according to the size, and 10 minutes before serving, remove the paper, dredge the fowls with a little fine flour, put a piece of butter into the basting-ladle, and as it melts baste the fowls with it; when nicely frothed and of a rich colour, serve with good brown gravy (a little of which should be poured over the fowls), and a tureen of well-made bread sauce. Mushroom, oyster, or egg sauce, are very suitable accompaniments to roast fowl.—Chicken is roasted in the same manner. *Time.*—A very large fowl, quite 1 hour; a medium-sized one, ¾ hour; chicken, ½ hour, or rather longer. *Average cost,* in full season, 5*s.* a pair; when scarce, 7*s.* 6*d.* the pair. *Sufficient* for 6 or 7 persons. *Seasonable* all the year, but scarce in early spring.

FOWL, Roast, to Carve.

A roast fowl is carved in the same manner as a boiled fowl, viz., by cutting along the line from 1 to 2, and then round the leg between it and the wing. The markings and detached pieces, as shown in the engravings under the heading of

"Boiled Fowl," supersede the necessity of our lengthily again describing the operation. It may be added, that the liver, being considered a delicacy, should be divided, and one half served with each wing. In the case of a fowl being stuffed, it will be proper to give each guest a portion, unless it be not agreeable to some one of the party.

ROAST FOWL.

FOWL, Roast, Stuffed.

Ingredients.—A large fowl, forcemeat, a little flour. *Mode.*—Select a large plump fowl, fill the breast with forcemeat, truss it firmly, the same as for a plain roast fowl, dredge it with flour, and put it down to a bright fire. Roast it for nearly or quite an hour, should it be very large; remove the skewers, and serve with a good brown gravy and a tureen of bread sauce. *Time.*—Large fowl, nearly or quite 1 hour. *Average cost*, in full season, 2*s.* 6*d.* each. *Sufficient* for 4 or 5 persons. *Seasonable* all the year, but scarce in early spring.

Note.—Sausage-meat stuffing may be substituted: this is now a very general mode of serving fowl.

FOWL SAUTE with Peas (an Entrée).

[COLD MEAT COOKERY.] *Ingredients.*—The remains of cold roast fowl, 2 oz. of butter, pepper, salt, and pounded mace to taste, 1 dessertspoonful of flour, ½ pint of weak stock, 1 pint of green peas, 1 teaspoonful of pounded sugar. *Mode.*—Cut the fowl into nice pieces; put the butter into a stewpan; sautez or fry the fowl a nice brown colour, previously sprinkling it with pepper, salt, and pounded mace. Dredge in the flour, shake the ingredients well round, then add the stock and peas, and stew till the latter are tender, which will be in about 20 minutes; put in the pounded sugar, and serve, placing the chicken round, and the peas in the middle of the dish. When liked, mushrooms may be substituted for the peas. *Time.*—Altogether 40 minutes. *Average cost*, exclusive of the fowl, 7*d.* *Seasonable* from June to August.

FOWL SCOLLOPS.

[COLD MEAT COOKERY.] *Ingredients.*—The remains of cold roast or boiled fowl, ½ pint of Béchamel, or white sauce. *Mode.*—Strip off the skin from the fowl; cut the meat into thin slices, and warm them in about ½ pint, or rather more, of Béchamel, or white sauce. When quite hot, serve, and garnish the dish with rolled ham or bacon toasted. *Time.*—1 minute to simmer the slices of fowl. *Seasonable* at any time.

FRENCH TERMS used in modern Household Cookery, explained.

ASPIC.—A savoury jelly, used as an exterior moulding for cold game, poultry, fish, &c. This, being of a transparent nature, allows the article which it covers to be seen through it. This may also be used for decorating or garnishing.

ASSIETTE (plate).—*Assiettes* are the small *entrées* and *hors-d'œuvres*, the quantity of which does not exceed what a plate will hold. At dessert, fruits, cheese, chestnuts, biscuits, &c., if served upon a plate, are termed *assiettes*.—ASSIETTE VOLANTE is a dish which a servant hands round to the guests, but is not placed upon the table. Small cheese soufflés and different dishes, which ought to be served very hot, are frequently made *assiettes volantes*.

AU-BLEU.—Fish dressed in such a manner as to have a *bluish* appearance.

BAIN-MARIE.—An open saucepan or kettle of nearly boiling water, in which a smaller vessel can be set for cooking and warming. This is very useful for keeping articles hot, without altering their quantity or quality. If you keep sauce, broth, or soup by the fireside, the soup reduces and becomes too strong, and the sauce thickens as well as reduces; but this is prevented by using the *bain-marie*, in which the water should be very hot, but not boiling.

BÉCHAMEL.—French white sauce, now frequently used in English cookery.

BLANCH.—To whiten poultry, vegetables, fruit, &c., by plunging them into boiling water for a short time, and afterwards plunging them into cold water, there to remain until they are cold.

BLANQUETTE.—A sort of fricassee.

BOUILLI.—Beef or other meat boiled; but, generally speaking, boiled beef is understood by the term.

French Terms

BOUILLIE.—A French dish resembling hasty-pudding.

BOUILLON.—A thin broth or soup.

BRAISE.—To stew meat with fat bacon until it is tender, it having previously been blanched.

BRAISIÈRE.—A saucepan having a lid with ledges, to put fire on the top.

BRIDER.—To pass a packthread through poultry, game, &c., to keep together their members.

CARAMEL (burnt sugar).—This is made with a piece of sugar, of the size of a nut, browned in the bottom of a saucepan; upon which a cupful of stock is gradually poured, stirring all the time, and adding the broth little by little. It may be used with the feather of a quill, to colour meats, such as the upper part of fricandeaux; and to impart colour to sauces. Caramel made with water instead of stock may be used to colour *compôtes* and other *entremets*.

CASSEROLE.—A crust of rice, which, after having been moulded into the form of a pie, is baked, and then filled with a fricassee of white meat or a purée of game.

COMPOTE.—A stew, as of fruit or pigeons.

CONSOMMÉ.—Rich stock, or gravy.

CROQUETTE.—Ball of fried rice or potatoes.

CROÛTONS.—Sippets of bread.

DAUBIÈRE.—An oval stewpan, in which *daubes* are cooked; *daubes* being meat or fowl stewed in sauce.

DÉSOSSER.—To *bone*, or take out the bones from poultry, game, or fish. This is an operation requiring considerable experience.

ENTRÉES.—Small side or corner dishes served with the first course.

ENTREMETS.—Small side or corner dishes served with the second course.

ESCALOPES.—Collops; small, round, thin pieces of tender meat, or of fish, beaten with the handle of a strong knife to make them tender.

FEUILLETAGE.—Puff-paste.

FLAMBER.—To singe fowl or game, after they have been picked.

FONCER.—To put in the bottom of a saucepan slices of ham, veal, or thin broad slices of bacon.

GALETTE.—A broad thin cake.

GÂTEAU.—A cake, correctly speaking; but used sometimes to denote a pudding and a kind of tart.

GLACER.—To glaze, or spread upon hot meats, or larded fowl, a thick and rich sauce or gravy, called *glaze*. This is laid on with a feather or brush, and in confectionary the term means to ice fruits and pastry with sugar, which glistens on hardening.

HORS-D'ŒUVRES.—Small dishes, or *assiettes volantes* of sardines, anchovies, and other relishes of this kind, served to the guests during the first course. (*See* ASSIETTES VOLANTES.)

LIT.—A bed or layer; articles in thin slices are placed in layers, other articles, or seasoning, being laid between them.

MAIGRE.—Broth, soup, or gravy, made without meat.

MATELOTE.—A rich fish-stew, which is generally composed of carp, eels, trout, or barbel. It is made with wine.

MAYONNAISE.—Cold sauce, or salad dressing.

MENU.—The bill of fare.

MERINGUE.—A kind of icing, made of whites of eggs and sugar, well beaten.

MIROTON.—Larger slices of meat than collops; such as slices of beef for a vinaigrette, or ragoût or stew of onions.

MOUILLER.—To add water, broth, or other liquid, during the cooking.

PANER.—To cover with very fine crumbs of bread, meats, or any other articles to be cooked on the gridiron, in the oven, or frying-pan.

PIQUER.—To lard with strips of fat bacon, poultry, game, meat, &c. This should always be done according to the vein of the meat, so that in carving you slice the bacon across as well as the meat.

POELÉE.—Stock used instead of water for boiling turkeys, sweetbreads, fowls, and vegetables, to render them less insipid.—This is rather an expensive preparation.

PURÉE.—Vegetables or meat reduced to a very smooth pulp, which is afterwards mixed with enough liquid to make it of the consistency of very thick soup.

RAGOÛT.—Stew or hash.

REMOULADE.—Salad dressing.

RISSOLES.—Pastry, made of light puff-paste, and cut into various forms, and fried. They may be filled with fish, meat, or sweets.

ROUX.—Brown and white; French thickening.

SALMI.—Ragoût of game previously roasted.

SAUCE PIQUANTE.—A sharp sauce, in which somewhat of a vinegar flavour predominates.

SAUTER.—To dress with sauce in a saucepan, repeatedly moving it about.

TAMIS.—Tammy, a sort of open cloth or sieve through which to strain broth and sauces, so as to rid them of small bones, froth, &c.

TOURTE.—Tart. Fruit pie.

TROUSSER.—To truss a bird; to put together the body and tie the wings and thighs, in order to round it for roasting or boiling, each being tied then with pack-thread, to keep it in the required form.

VOL-AU-VENT.—A rich crust of very fine puff-paste, which may be filled with various delicate ragoûts or fricassees, of fish, flesh, or fowl. Fruit may also be inclosed in a *vol-au-vent*.

FRITTERS, Indian.

Ingredients.—3 tablespoonfuls of flour, boiling water, the yolks of 4 eggs, the whites of 2, hot lard or clarified dripping, jam. *Mode*.—Put the flour into a basin, and pour over it sufficient *boiling* water to make it into a stiff paste, taking care to stir and beat it well, to prevent it getting lumpy. Leave it a little time to cool, and then break into it (*without beating them at first*) the yolks of 4 eggs and the whites of 2, and stir and beat all well together. Have ready some boiling lard or butter; drop a dessertspoonful of batter in at a time, and fry the fritters of a light brown. They should rise so much as to be almost like balls. Serve on a dish, with a spoonful of preserve or marmalade dropped in between each fritter. This is an excellent dish for a hasty addition to dinner, if a guest unexpectedly arrives, it being so easily and quickly made, and it is always a great favourite. *Time*.—From 5 to 8 minutes to fry the fritters. *Average cost*, exclusive of the jam, 5*d*. *Sufficient* for 4 or 5 persons. Seasonable at any time.

FRITTERS, Plain.

Ingredients.—3 oz. of flour, 3 eggs, ⅓ pint of milk. *Mode*.—Mix the flour to a smooth batter with a small quantity of the milk; stir in the eggs, which should be well whisked, and then the remainder of the milk; beat the whole to a perfectly smooth batter, and should it be found not quite thin enough, add two or three tablespoonfuls more milk. Have ready a frying-pan, with plenty of boiling lard in it; drop in rather more than a tablespoonful at a time of the batter, and fry the fritters a nice brown, turning them when sufficiently cooked on one side. Drain them well from the greasy moisture by placing them upon a piece of blotting-paper before the fire; dish them on a white d'oyley, sprinkle over them sifted sugar, and send to table with them a cut lemon and plenty of pounded sugar. *Time*.—From 6 to 8 minutes. *Average cost*, 4*d*. *Sufficient* for 3 or 4 persons. *Seasonable* at any time.

FRUIT, to Bottle Fresh. (Very useful in Winter.)

Ingredients.—Fresh fruits, such as currants, raspberries, cherries, gooseberries, plums of all kinds, damsons, &c.; wide-mouthed glass bottles, new corks to fit them tightly. *Mode*.—Let the fruit be full grown, but not too ripe, and gathered in dry weather. Pick it off the stalks without bruising or breaking the skin, and reject any that is at all blemished: if gathered in the damp, or if the skins are cut at all, the fruit will mould. Have ready some *perfectly dry* glass bottles, and some nice *new* soft corks or bungs; burn a match in each bottle, to exhaust the air, and quickly place the fruit in to be preserved; gently cork the bottles, and put them in a very *cool* oven, where let them remain until the fruit has shrunk away a fourth part. Then take the bottles out; *do not open them*, but immediately beat the corks in tight, cut off the tops, and cover them with melted resin. If kept in a dry place, the fruit will remain good for months; and on this principally depends the success of the preparation; for if stored away in a place that is in the least damp, the fruit will soon spoil. *Time*.—From 5 to 6 hours in a very slow oven.

FRUIT, to Bottle Fresh.

Ingredients.—Any kind of fresh fruit, such as currants, cherries, gooseberries, all kinds of plums, &c.; wide-mouthed glass bottles, new corks to fit them tightly. *Mode*.—The fruit must be full-grown, not too ripe, and gathered on a fine day. Let it be carefully picked and put into the bottles, which must be clean and perfectly dry. Tie over the tops of the bottles pieces of bladder; stand the bottles in a large pot, copper, or boiler, with cold water to reach to their necks; kindle a fire under, let the water boil, and as the bladders begin to rise and puff, prick them. As soon as the water boils, extinguish the fire, and let the bottles remain where they are, to become cold. The next day remove the bladders, and strew over the fruit a thick layer of pounded sugar; fit the bottles with cork, and let each cork lie close at hand to its own bottle. Hold for a few moments, in the neck of the bottle, two or three lighted matches, and when they have filled the bottle neck with gas, and before they go out, remove them very quickly; instantly cork the bottle closely, and dip it in bottle-cement. *Time.*—Altogether about 8 hours.

FRUIT, to Bottle Fresh, with Sugar. (Very useful in Winter.)

Ingredients.—Any kind of fresh fruit; to each quart bottle allow ¼ lb. of pounded sugar. *Mode.*—Let the fruit be gathered in dry weather. Pick it carefully, and drop it into *clean* and *very dry* quart glass bottles, sprinkling over it the above proportion of pounded sugar to each quart. Put the corks in the bottles, and place them in a copper of cold water up to their necks, with small hay-wisps round them, to prevent the bottles from knocking together. Light the fire under, bring the water gradually to boil, and let it simmer gently until the fruit in the bottles is reduced nearly one third. Extinguish the fire, *and let the bottles remain in the water until it is perfectly cold;* then take them out, make the corks secure, and cover them with melted resin or wax. *Time.*—About ½ hour from the time the water commences to boil.

FRUIT TURNOVERS (suitable for Pic-Nics).

Ingredients.—Puff-paste, any kind of fruit, sugar to taste. *Mode.*—Make some puff-paste by recipe; roll it out to the thickness of about ¼ inch, and cut it out in pieces of a circular form; pile the fruit on half of the paste, sprinkle over some sugar, wet the edges and turn the paste over. Press the edges together, ornament them, and brush the turnovers over with the white of an egg; sprinkle over sifted sugar, and bake on tins, in a brisk oven, for about 20 minutes. Instead of putting the fruit in raw, it may be boiled down with a little sugar first, and then inclosed in the crust; or jam, of any kind, may be substituted for fresh fruit. *Time.*—20 minutes. *Sufficient.*—½ lb. of puff-paste will make a dozen turnovers. *Seasonable* at any time.

GAME, Hashed.

[COLD MEAT COOKERY.] *Ingredients.*—The remains of cold game, 1 onion stuck with 3 cloves, a few whole peppers, a strip of lemon-peel, salt to taste, thickening of butter and flour, 1 glass of port wine, 1 tablespoonful of lemon-juice, 1 tablespoonful of ketchup, 1 pint of water or weak stock. *Mode.*—Cut the remains of cold game into joints, reserve the best pieces, and the inferior ones and trimmings put into a stewpan with the onion, pepper, lemon-peel, salt, and water or weak stock; stew these for about an hour, and strain the gravy; thicken it with butter and flour; add the wine, lemon-juice, and ketchup; lay in the pieces of game, and let them gradually warm through by the side of the fire; do not allow it to boil, or the game will be hard. When on the point of simmering, serve, and garnish the dish with sippets of toasted bread. *Time.*—Altogether 1½ hour. *Seasonable* from August to March.

Note.—Any kind of game may be hashed by the above recipe, and the flavour may be varied by adding flavoured vinegars, curry powder, &c.; but we cannot recommend these latter ingredients, as a dish of game should really have a gamy taste; and if too many sauces, essences, &c., are added to the gravy, they quite overpower and destroy the flavour the dish should possess.

GERMAN PUFFS.

Ingredients.—2 oz. of flour, 2 eggs, ½ pint of new milk, 2 oz. of melted butter, little salt and nutmeg. *Mode.*—Let the 2 eggs be well beaten, then mix all the ingredients well together, and heat them up just before they are put into little cups half full for baking. Bake for ¼ hour in a hot oven till the puffs are of a nice brown; turn out on a flat dish, rub a little butter over each puff, and dust on it powdered sugar. *Time.*—¼ hour. *Average cost, 6d.* *Seasonable* at any time.

GHERKINS, Pickled.

Ingredients.—Salt and water, 1 oz. of bruised ginger, ½ oz. of whole black pepper, ¼ oz. of whole allspice, 4 cloves,

2 blades of mace, a little horseradish. This proportion of pepper, spices, &c., for 1 quart of vinegar. *Mode.*—Let the gherkins remain in salt and water for 3 or 4 days, when take them out, wipe perfectly dry, and put them into a stone jar. Boil sufficient vinegar to cover them, with spices and pepper, &c., in the above proportion, for 10 minutes; pour it, quite boiling, over the gherkins, cover the jar with vine-leaves, and put over them a plate, setting them near the fire, where they must remain all night. Next day drain off the vinegar, boil it up again, and pour it hot over them. Cover up with fresh leaves, and let the whole remain till quite cold. Now tie down closely with bladder to exclude the air, and in a month or two they will be fit for use. *Time.*—4 days. *Seasonable* from the middle of July to the end of August.

GIBLET PIE.

Ingredients.—A set of duck or goose giblets, 1 lb. of rump-steak, 1 onion, ½ teaspoonful of whole black pepper, a bunch of savoury herbs, plain crust. *Mode.*—Clean, and put the giblets into a stewpan with an onion, whole pepper, and a bunch of savoury herbs; add rather more than a pint of water, and simmer gently for about 1½ hour. Take them out, let them cool, and cut them into pieces; line the bottom of a pie-dish with a few pieces of rump-steak; add a layer of giblets and a few more pieces of steak; season with pepper and salt, and pour in the gravy (which should be strained), that the giblets were stewed in; cover with a plain crust, and bake for rather more than 1½ hour in a brisk oven. Cover a piece of paper over the pie, to prevent the crust taking too much colour. *Time.*—1½ hour to stew the giblets, about 1 hour to bake the pie. *Average cost*, exclusive of the giblets, 1*s*. 4*d*. *Sufficient* for 5 or 6 persons.

GIBLET SOUP.

Ingredients.—3 sets of goose or duck giblets, 2 lbs. of shin of beef, a few bones, 1 ox-tail, 2 mutton-shanks, 2 large onions, 2 carrots, 1 large faggot of herbs, salt and pepper to taste, ¼ pint of cream, 1 oz. of butter mixed with a dessert-spoonful of flour, 3 quarts of water. *Mode.*—Scald the giblets, cut the gizzards in 8 pieces, and put them in a stew-

pan with the beef, bones, ox-tail, mutton-shanks, onions, herbs, pepper, and salt; add the 3 quarts of water, and simmer till the giblets are tender, taking care to skim well. When the giblets are done, take them out, put them in your tureen, strain the soup through a sieve, add the cream and butter, mixed with a dessert-spoonful of flour, boil it up for a few minutes, and pour it over the giblets. It can be flavoured with port wine and a little mushroom ketchup, instead of cream. Add salt to taste. *Time.*—3 hours. *Average cost*, 9*d*. per quart. *Seasonable* all the year. *Sufficient* for 10 persons.

GINGER, Apple. (A Dessert Dish.)

Ingredients.—2 lbs. of any kind of hard apples, 2 lbs. of loaf sugar, 1½ pint of water, 1 oz. of tincture of ginger. *Mode.*—Boil the sugar and water until they form a rich syrup, adding the ginger when it boils up. Pare, core, and cut the apples into pieces; dip them in cold water to preserve the colour, and boil them in the syrup until transparent; but be careful not to let them break. Put the pieces of apple into jars, pour over the syrup, and carefully exclude the air, by well covering them. It will remain good some time, if kept in a dry place. *Time.*—From 5 to 10 minutes to boil the syrup; about ½ hour to simmer the apples. *Average cost*, 2*s*. *Sufficient* for 7 or 8 persons. *Seasonable.*—Make this in September, October, or November.

GINGER-BEER.

Ingredients.—2½ lbs. of loaf sugar, 1½ oz. of bruised ginger, 1 oz. of cream of tartar, the rind and juice of 2 lemons, 3 gallons of boiling water, two large table-spoonfuls of thick and fresh brewer's yeast. *Mode.*—Peel the lemons, squeeze the juice, strain it, and put the peel and juice into a large earthen pan, with the bruised ginger, cream of tartar, and loaf sugar. Put over these ingredients 3 gallons of *boiling* water; let it stand until just warm, when add the yeast, which should be thick and perfectly fresh. Stir the contents of the pan well, and let them remain near the fire all night, covering the pan over with a cloth. The next day skim off the yeast, and pour the liquor carefully into another vessel, leaving the sediment; then bottle immediately, and tie the corks down, and in 3 days the ginger-beer will be fit for use. For some tastes, the above proportion of sugar may be found rather too large, when it may be diminished; but the beer will not keep so long good. *Average cost* for this quantity, 2*s.*; or ½*d.* per bottle. *Sufficient* to fill 4 dozen ginger-beer bottles. *Seasonable.*—This should be made during the summer months.

GINGER CREAM.

Ingredients.—The yolks of 4 eggs, 1 pint of cream, 3 oz. of preserved ginger, 2 dessertspoonfuls of syrup, sifted sugar to taste, 1 oz. of isinglass. *Mode.*—Slice the ginger finely; put it into a basin with the syrup, the well-beaten yolks of eggs, and the cream; mix these ingredients well together, and stir them over the fire for about 10 minutes, or until the mixture thickens; then take it off the fire, whisk till nearly cold, sweeten to taste, add the isinglass, which should be melted and strained, and serve the cream in a glass dish. It may be garnished with slices of preserved ginger or candied citron. *Time.*—About 10 minutes to stir the cream over the fire. *Average cost,* with cream at 1*s.* per pint, 3*s.* 6*d.* *Sufficient* for a good-sized dish. *Seasonable* at any time.

GINGER, Preserved,

Comes from the West Indies. It is made by scalding the roots when they are green and full of sap, then peeling them in cold water and putting them into jars, with a rich syrup; in which state we receive them. It should be chosen of a deep yellow colour, with a little transparency. What is dark-coloured, fibrous, and stringy, is not good. Ginger roots, fit for preserving and in size equal to West Indian, have been produced in the Royal Agricultural Garden in Edinburgh.

GINGER PUDDING.

Ingredients.—½ lb. of flour, ¼ lb. of suet, ¼ lb. of moist sugar, 2 large teaspoonfuls of grated ginger. *Mode.*—Shred the suet very fine, mix it with the flour, sugar, and ginger; stir all well together; butter a basin, and put the mixture in *dry*; tie a cloth over, and boil for 3 hours. *Time.*—3 hours. *Average cost,* 6*d.* *Sufficient* for 5 or 6 persons. *Seasonable* at any time.

GINGER WINE.

Ingredients.—To 9 gallons of water allow 27 lbs. of loaf sugar, 9 lemons, 12 oz. of bruised ginger, 3 tablespoonfuls of yeast, 2 lbs. of raisins stoned and chopped, 1 pint of brandy. *Mode.*—Boil together for 1 hour in a copper (let it previously be well scoured and beautifully clean) the water, sugar, *lemon-rinds,* and bruised ginger; remove every particle of scum as it rises, and when the liquor is sufficiently boiled, put it into a large tub or pan, as it must not remain in the copper. When nearly cold, add the yeast, which must be thick and very fresh, and, the next day, put all in a dry cask with the strained lemon-juice and chopped raisins. Stir the wine every day for a fortnight; then add the brandy, stop the cask down by degrees, and in a few weeks it will be fit to bottle. *Average cost,* 2*s.* per gallon. *Sufficient* to make 9 gallons of wine. *Seasonable.*—The best time for making this wine is either in March or September.

Note.—Wine made early in March will be fit to bottle in June.

GINGERBREAD, Thick.

Ingredients.—1 lb. of treacle, ¼ lb. of butter, ¼ lb. of coarse brown sugar, 1½ lb. of flour, 1 oz. of ginger, ½ oz. of ground allspice, 1 teaspoonful of carbonate of soda, ¼ pint of warm milk, 3 eggs. *Mode.*—Put the flour into a basin, with the sugar, ginger, and allspice; mix these together; warm the butter, and add it, with the treacle, to the other ingredients. Stir well; make the milk just warm, dissolve the carbonate of soda in it, and mix the whole into a nice smooth dough with the eggs, which should be previously well whisked; pour the mixture into a buttered tin, and bake it from ¾ to 1 hour, or longer, should the gingerbread be very thick. Just before it is done, brush the top over with the yolk of an egg beaten up with a little milk, and put it back in the oven to finish baking. *Time.*—¾ to 1 hour. *Average cost,* 1*s.* per square. *Seasonable* at any time.

GINGERBREAD, White.

Ingredients.—1 lb. of flour, ½ lb. of butter, ½ lb. of loaf sugar, the rind of 1 lemon, 1 oz. of ground ginger, 1 nutmeg grated, ½ teaspoonful of carbonate of soda, 1 gill of milk. *Mode.*—Rub the butter into the flour; add the sugar, which should be finely pounded and sifted, and the minced lemon-rind, ginger, and nutmeg. Mix these well together; make the milk just warm, stir in the soda, and work the whole into a nice smooth paste; roll it out, cut it into cakes, and bake in a moderate oven from 15 to 20 minutes. *Time.*—15 to 20 minutes. *Average cost,* 1*s.* 3*d.* *Seasonable* at any time.

GINGERBREAD-NUTS, Rich Sweetmeats.

Ingredients.—1 lb. of treacle, ¼ lb. of clarified butter, 1 lb. of coarse brown sugar, 2 oz. of ground ginger, 1 oz. of candied orange-peel, 1 oz. of candied angelica, ½ oz. of candied lemon-peel, ½ oz. of coriander seeds, ½ oz. of caraway seeds, 1 egg; flour. *Mode.*—Put the treacle into a basin, and pour over it the butter, melted so as not to oil, the sugar, and ginger. Stir these ingredients well together, and whilst mixing, add the candied peel, which should be cut into very small pieces, but not bruised, and the caraway and coriander seeds, which should be pounded. Having mixed all thoroughly together, break in an egg, and work the whole up with as much fine flour as may be necessary to form a paste. Make this into nuts of any size, and put them on a tin plate, and bake in a slow oven from ¼ to ½ hour. *Time.*—¼ to ½ hour. *Average cost,* from 1*s.* to 1*s.* 4*d.* per lb. *Seasonable* at any time.

GINGERBREAD-NUTS, Sunderland. (An Excellent Recipe.)

Ingredients.—1¾ lb. of treacle, 1 lb. of moist sugar, 1 lb. of butter, 2¾ lbs. of flour, 1½ oz. of ground ginger, 1½ oz. of allspice, 1½ oz. of coriander-seeds. *Mode.*—Let the allspice, coriander-seeds, and ginger be freshly ground; put them into a basin, with the flour and sugar, and mix these ingredients well together; warm the treacle and butter together; then with a spoon work it into the flour, &c. until the whole forms a nice smooth paste. Drop the mixture from the spoon on a piece of buttered paper, and bake in rather a slow oven from 20 minutes to ½ hour. A little candied lemon-peel mixed with the above is an improvement, and a great authority in culinary matters suggests the addition of a little cayenne pepper in gingerbread. Whether it be advisable to use the latter ingredient or not, we leave our readers to decide. *Time.*—20 minutes to ½ hour. *Average cost,* 1*s.* to 1*s.* 4*d.* per lb. *Seasonable* at any time.

GLAZE for covering Cold Hams, Tongues, &c.

Ingredients.—Stock, doubling the quantity of meat in the recipes. *Mode.*—We may remark at the outset, that unless glaze is wanted in very large quantities, it is seldom made expressly. Either of the stocks, boiled down and reduced very considerably, will be found to produce a very good glaze. Put the stock into a stewpan, over a nice clear fire; let it boil till it becomes somewhat stiff, when keep stirring, to prevent its burning. The moment it is sufficiently reduced, and come to a glaze, turn it into the glaze-pot before it gets cold. As, however, this is not to be found in every establishment, a white earthenware jar would answer the purpose; and this may be placed in a vessel of boiling water, to melt the glaze when required. It should never be warmed in a saucepan, except on the principle of the bain marie, lest it should reduce too much, and become black and bitter. If the glaze is wanted of a pale colour, more veal than beef should be used in making the stock; and it is as well to omit turnips and celery, as these impart a disagreeable bitter flavour.

GLAZE-KETTLE.

This is a kettle used for keeping the strong stock boiled down to a jelly, which is known by the name of glaze. It is composed of two tin vessels, as

GLAZE-KETTLE.

shown in the cut, one of which, the upper,—containing the glaze, is inserted into one of larger diameter, and containing boiling water.

GLAZE, to, Cold Joints, &c.

Melt the glaze by placing the vessel which contains it, into the bain marie or saucepan of boiling water; brush it over the meat with a paste-brush, and if in places it is not quite covered, repeat the operation. The glaze should not be too dark a colour.

GOLDEN PUDDING.

Ingredients.—¼ lb. of bread-crumbs, ¼ lb. of suet, ¼ lb. of marmalade, ¼ lb. of sugar, 4 eggs. *Mode.*—Put the bread-crumbs into a basin; mix with them the suet, which should be finely minced, the marmalade, and the sugar; stir all these ingredients well together, beat the eggs to a froth, moisten the pudding with these, and when well mixed put it into a mould or buttered basin; tie down with a floured cloth, and boil for 2 hours. When turned out, strew a little fine-sifted sugar over the top, and serve. *Time.*—2 hours. *Average cost,* 11*d.* *Sufficient* for 5 or 6 persons. *Seasonable* at any time.

Note.—The mould may be ornamented with stoned raisins, arranged in any fanciful pattern, before the mixture is poured in, which would add very much to the appearance of the pudding. For a plainer pudding, double the quantities of the bread-crumbs; and if the eggs do not moisten it sufficiently, use a little milk.

GOOSE, Green.

Ingredients.—Goose, 3 oz. of butter, pepper and salt to taste. *Mode.*—Geese are called green till they are about four months old, and should not be stuffed. After it has been singed and trussed, put into the body a seasoning of pepper and salt, and the butter to moisten it inside. Roast before a clear fire for about ¾ hour, froth and brown it nicely, and serve with a brown gravy, and, when liked, gooseberry-sauce. This dish should be garnished with water-cresses. *Time.*—About ¾ hour. *Average cost,* 4*s.* 6*d.* each. *Sufficient* for 5 or 6 persons. *Seasonable* in June, July, and August.

GOOSE, Hashed.

[COLD MEAT COOKERY.] *Ingredients.*—The remains of cold roast goose, 2 onions, 2 oz. of butter, 1 pint of boiling water, 1 dessertspoonful of flour, pepper and salt to taste, 1 tablespoonful of port wine, 2 tablespoonfuls of mushroom ketchup. *Mode.*—Cut up the goose into pieces of the size required; the inferior joints, trimmings, &c., put into a stewpan to make the gravy; slice and fry the onions in the butter of a very pale brown; add these to the trimmings, and pour over about a pint of boiling water; stew these gently for ¾ hour, then skim and strain the liquor. Thicken it with flour, and flavour with port wine and ketchup in the above proportion; add a seasoning of pepper and salt, and put in the pieces of goose; let these get thoroughly hot through, but do not allow them to boil, and serve with sippets of toasted bread. *Time.*—Altogether, rather more than 1 hour. *Average cost,* exclusive of the cold goose, 4*d.* *Seasonable* from September to March.

GOOSE, Roast.

Ingredients. — Goose, 4 large onions, 10 sage-leaves, ¼ lb. of bread-crumbs, 1½ oz. of butter, salt and pepper to taste, 1 egg. *Choosing and Trussing.*—Select a goose with a clean white skin, plump breast, and yellow feet: if these latter are red, the bird is old. Should the weather permit, let it hang for a few days; by so doing the flavour will be very much improved. Pluck, singe, draw, and carefully wash and wipe the goose; cut off the neck close to the back, leaving the skin long enough to turn over; cut off the feet at the first joint, and separate the pinions at the first joint. Beat the breast-bone flat with a rolling-pin, put a skewer through the under part of each wing, and having drawn up the legs closely, put a skewer into the middle of

ROAST GOOSE.

each, and pass the same quite through the body. Insert another skewer into the small of the leg, bring it close down to the side-bone, run it through, and do the same to the other side. Now cut off the end of the vent, and make a hole in the skin sufficiently large for the passage of the rump, in order to keep in the seasoning. *Mode.*—Make a sage-and-onion stuffing of the above ingredients, put it into the body of the goose, and secure it firmly at both ends by passing the rump through the hole made in the skin, and the other end by tying the skin of the neck to the back: by this means the seasoning will not escape. Put it down to a brisk fire, keep it well basted, and roast from 1½ to 2 hours, according to the size. Remove the skewers, and serve with a tureen of good gravy, and one of well-made apple sauce. Should a very highly-flavoured seasoning be preferred, the onions should not be parboiled, but minced raw: of the two methods the mild seasoning is far superior. A ragoût, or pie, should be made of the giblets, or they may be stewed down to make gravy. Be careful to serve the goose before the breast falls, or its appearance will be spoiled by coming flattened to table. As this is rather a troublesome joint to carve, a *large* quantity of gravy should not be poured round the goose, but sent in a tureen. *Time.*—A large goose, 1¾ hour; a moderate-sized one, 1¼ to 1½ hour. *Seasonable* from September to March; but in perfection from Michaelmas to Christmas. *Average cost,* 5*s.* 6*d.* each. *Sufficient* for 8 or 9 persons.

Note.—A teaspoonful of made mustard, a saltspoonful of salt, a few grains of cayenne, mixed with a glass of port wine, are sometimes poured into the goose by a slit made in the apron. This sauce is by many considered an improvement.

GOOSE, Roast, to Carve.

It would not be fair to say that this dish bodes a great deal of happiness to an inexperienced carver, especially if there is a large party to serve, and the slices off the breast should not suffice to satisfy the desires and cravings of many wholesome appetites, produced, may be, by the various sports in vogue at Michaelmas and Christmas. The beginning of the task, however, is not in any way difficult. Evenly-cut slices, not too thick or too thin, should be carved from the breast in the direction of the line from 2 to 3; after the first slice has been cut,

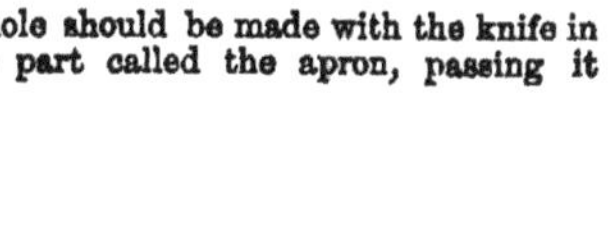

ROAST GOOSE.

a hole should be made with the knife in the part called the apron, passing it round the line as indicated by the figures 1, 1, 1; here the stuffing is located, and some of this should be served on each plate, unless it is discovered that it is not agreeable to the taste of some one guest. If the carver manages cleverly, he will be able to cut a very large number of fine slices off the breast, and the more so if he commences close down by the wing, and carves upwards towards the ridge of the breastbone. As many slices as can be taken from the breast being carved, the wings should be cut off, and the same process as described in carving boiled fowl is made use of in this instance, only more dexterity and greater force will most probably be required. The shape of the leg, when disengaged from the body of the goose, should be like that shown in the accompanying engraving. It will be necessary, perhaps, in taking off the leg, to turn

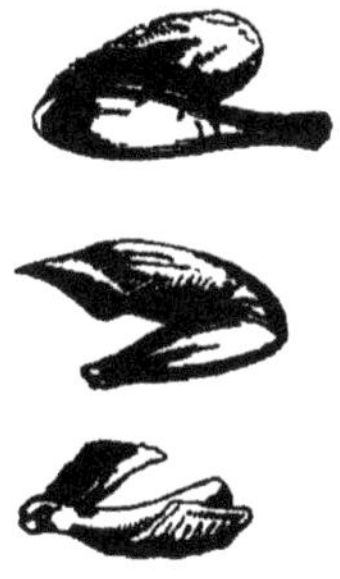

LEG, WING, AND NECK-BONE OF GOOSE.

the goose on its side, and then, pressing down the small end of the leg, the knife should be passed under it from the top quite down to the joint; the leg being now turned back by the fork, the knife must cut through the joint, loosening the thighbone from its socket. The merrythought, which in a goose is not so large as might be expected, is disengaged in the same way as that of a fowl—by passing the knife under it, and pressing it backwards towards the neck. The neck-bones, of which we give a cut, are freed by the same process as are those of a fowl; and the same may be said of all the other parts of this bird. The breast of a goose is the part most esteemed; all parts, however, are good, and full of juicy flavour.

GOOSE STUFFING, Soyer's Recipe for.

Take 4 apples peeled and cored, 4 onions, 4 leaves of sage, and 4 leaves of lemon thyme not broken, and boil them in a stewpan with sufficient water to cover them; when done, pulp them through a sieve, removing the sage and thyme; then add sufficient pulp of mealy potatoes to cause it to be sufficiently dry without sticking to the hand; add pepper and salt, and stuff the bird.

GOOSEBERRIES, Compôte of.

Ingredients.—Syrup; to 1 pint of syrup allow nearly a quart of gooseberries. *Mode.*—Top and tail the gooseberries, which should not be very ripe, and pour over them some boiling water; then take them out and plunge them into cold water with which has been mixed a tablespoonful of vinegar, which will assist to keep the fruit a good colour. Make a pint of syrup, and when it boils drain the gooseberries and put them in; simmer them gently until the fruit is nicely pulped and tender without being broken; then dish the gooseberries on a glass dish, boil the syrup for 2 or 3 minutes, pour over the gooseberries, and serve cold. *Time.*—About 5 minutes to boil the gooseberries in the syrup, 3 minutes to reduce the syrup. *Average cost*, 9*d.* *Sufficient.*—A quart of gooseberries for 5 or 6 persons. *Seasonable* in June.

GOOSEBERRY CHIPS. (Useful for Dessert.)

Ingredients.—Gooseberries unripe and green, but quite full-grown; sifted loaf sugar. *Mode.*—Put the gooseberries, when cleaned of tops and tails, into jars, and boil them in a copper till quite soft. To every lb. of pulp put ½ lb. of loaf sugar sifted: the sugar must be stirred in very gently. Then pour out the sweetened pulp on flat dishes, about ½ inch thick, which must be set in the sun to dry. When sufficiently dried in the sun, the pulp may be cut into strips, and twisted into any fanciful shapes, bows, &c. *Time* for drying, according to the amount of sun. *Seasonable* at all times.

Note.—These chips may be kept for years in tin boxes, if packed quite dry, with layers of paper between the rows.

GOOSEBERRY FOOL.

Ingredients.—Green gooseberries; to every pint of pulp add 1 pint of milk, or ½ pint of cream and ½ pint of milk; sugar to taste. *Mode.*—Cut the tops and tails off the gooseberries, put them into a jar with 2 tablespoonfuls of water and a little good moist sugar; set this jar in a saucepan of boiling water, and let it boil until the fruit is soft enough to mash. When done enough, beat it to a pulp, work this pulp through a colander, and stir to every pint the above proportion of milk, or equal quantities of milk and cream. Ascertain if the mixture is sweet enough, and put in plenty of sugar, or it will not be eatable; and in mixing the milk and gooseberries add the former very gradually to these: serve in a glass dish, or in small glasses. This, although a very old-fashioned and homely dish, is, when well made, very delicious, and, if properly sweetened, a very suitable preparation for children. *Time.*—From ¾ to 1 hour. *Average cost*, 6*d.* per pint, with milk. *Sufficient.*—A pint of milk and a pint of gooseberry pulp for 5 or 6 children. *Seasonable* in May and June.

GOOSEBERRY JAM.

Ingredients.—To every lb. of fruit allow ¾ lb. of loaf sugar; currant-juice. *Mode.*—Select red hairy gooseberries; have them gathered in dry weather, when quite ripe, without being too soft. Weigh them; with a pair of scissors cut off the tops and tails, and to every 6 lbs. of fruit have ready ½ pint of red-currant juice, drawn as for jelly. Put the gooseberries and currant-juice into a preserving-pan, let them boil tolerably quickly, keeping them well stirred; when they begin to break, add to them the sugar, and keep simmering until the jam becomes firm, carefully skimming and stirring it, that it does not burn at the bottom. It should be boiled rather a long time, or it will not keep. Put it into pots (not too large), let it get perfectly cold, then cover the pots down with oiled and egged papers. *Time.*—About 1 hour to boil the gooseberries in the currant-juice, from ½ to ¾ hour with the sugar. *Average cost*, per lb. pot, from 6*d.* to 8*d.* *Sufficient.*—Allow 1½ pint of fruit for a lb. pot. *Seasonable.*—Make this in June or July.

GOOSEBERRY JAM.

Ingredients.—To every 8 lbs. of red, rough, ripe gooseberries allow 1 quart of red-currant juice, 5 lbs. of loaf sugar. *Mode.*—Have the fruit gathered in dry weather, and cut off the tops and tails. Prepare 1 quart of red-currant juice, the same as for red-currant jelly; put it into a preserving-pan with the sugar, and keep stirring until the latter is dissolved.

Keep it boiling for about 5 minutes; skim well; then put in the gooseberries, and let them boil from ½ to ¾ hour; then turn the whole into an earthen pan, and let it remain for 2 days. Boil the jam up again until it looks clear; put it into pots, and when cold, cover with oiled paper, and over the jars put tissue-paper brushed over on both sides with the white of an egg, and store away in a dry place. Care must be taken, in making this, to keep the jam well stirred and well skimmed, to prevent it burning at the bottom of the pan, and to have it very clear. *Time.*—5 minutes to boil the currant-juice and sugar after the latter is dissolved; from ½ to ¾ hour to simmer the gooseberries the first time, ¼ hour the second time of boiling. *Average cost*, from 8*d.* to 10*d.* per lb. pot. *Sufficient.*—Allow 1½ pint of fruit for a lb. pot. *Seasonable.*—Make this in June or July.

GOOSEBERRY JAM, White or Green.

Ingredients.—Equal weight of fruit and sugar. *Mode.*—Select the gooseberries not very ripe, either white or green, and top and tail them. Boil the sugar with water (allowing ½ pint to every lb.) for about ¼ hour, carefully removing the scum as it rises; then put in the gooseberries, and simmer gently till clear and firm: try a little of the jam on a plate; if it jellies when cold, it is done, and should then be poured into pots. When cold, cover with oiled paper, and tissue-paper brushed over on both sides with the unbeaten white of an egg, and stow away in a dry place. *Time.*—¼ hour to boil the sugar and water, ¾ hour the jam. *Average cost*, from 6*d.* to 8*d.* per lb. pot. *Sufficient.*—Allow 1½ pint of fruit for a lb. pot. *Seasonable.*—Make this in June.

GOOSEBERRY JELLY.

Ingredients.—Gooseberries; to every pint of juice allow ¾ lb. of loaf sugar. *Mode.*—Put the gooseberries, after cutting off the tops and tails, into a preserving-pan, and stir them over the fire until they are quite soft; then strain them through a sieve, and to every pint of juice allow ¾ lb. of sugar. Boil the juice and sugar together for nearly ¾ hour, stirring and skimming all the time; and if the jelly appears firm when a little of it is poured on to a plate, it is done, and should then be taken up and put into small pots. Cover the pots with oiled and egged papers, the same as for currant jelly, and store away in a dry place. *Time.*—¾ hour to simmer the gooseberries without the sugar; ¾ hour to boil the juice. *Average cost*, from 8*d.* to 10*d.* per ½-lb. pot. *Seasonable* in July.

GOOSEBERRY PUDDING, Baked.

Ingredients. — Gooseberries, 3 eggs, 1½ oz. of butter, ½ pint of bread-crumbs, sugar to taste. *Mode.*—Put the gooseberries into a jar, previously cutting off the tops and tails; place this jar in boiling water, and let it boil until the gooseberries are soft enough to pulp; then beat them through a coarse sieve, and to every pint of pulp add 3 well-whisked eggs, 1½ oz. of butter, ½ pint of bread-crumbs, and sugar to taste; beat the mixture well, put a border of puff-paste round the edge of a pie-dish, put in the pudding, bake for about 40 minutes, strew sifted sugar over, and serve. *Time.* —About 40 minutes. *Average cost*, 10*d.* *Sufficient* for 4 or 5 persons. *Seasonable* from May to July.

GOOSEBERRY PUDDING, Boiled.

Ingredients.—¾ lb. of suet crust, 1½ pint of green gooseberries, ¼ lb. of moist sugar. *Mode.*—Line a pudding-basin with suet crust rolled out to about ½ inch in thickness, and, with a pair of scissors, cut off the tops and tails of the gooseberries; fill the basin with the fruit, put in the sugar, and cover with crust. Pinch the edges of the pudding together, tie over it a floured cloth, put it into boiling water, and boil from 2½ to 3 hours; turn it out of the basin, and serve with a jug of cream. *Time.*—2½ to 3 hours. *Average cost*, 10*d.* *Sufficient* for 6 or 7 persons. *Seasonable* from May to July.

BOILED FRUIT PUDDING.

GOOSEBERRY SAUCE for Boiled Mackerel.

Ingredients.—1 pint of green gooseberries, 3 tablespoonfuls of Béchamel (veal gravy may be substituted for this), 2 oz. of fresh butter; seasoning to taste of salt, pepper, and grated nutmeg. *Mode.*—Boil the gooseberries in water until quite tender; strain them, and rub them through a sieve. Put into a saucepan the Béchamel or gravy, with the butter and seasoning; add the pulp from the gooseberries, mix all well together, and heat gradually through. A little pounded sugar added to this sauce is by many persons considered an improvement, as the saccharine matter takes off the extreme acidity of the unripe fruit. *Time.*—Boil the gooseberries from 20 minutes to ½ hour. *Sufficient.*—This quantity, for a large dish of mackerel. *Seasonable* from May to July.

GOOSEBERRY TART.

Ingredients.—1½ pint of gooseberries, ½ lb. of short crust, ¼ lb. of moist sugar. *Mode.*—With a pair of scissors cut off the tops and tails of the gooseberries; put them into a deep pie-dish, pile the fruit high in the centre, and put in the sugar; line the edge of the dish with short crust, put on the cover, and ornament the edges of the tart; bake in a good oven for about ¾ hour, and before being sent to table, strew over it some fine-sifted sugar. A jug of cream, or a dish of boiled or baked custards, should always accompany this dish. *Time.*—¾ hour. *Average cost,* 9*d.* *Sufficient* for 5 or 6 persons. *Seasonable* from May to July.

GOOSEBERRY TRIFLE.

Ingredients.—1 quart of gooseberries, sugar to taste, 1 pint of custard, a plateful of whipped cream. *Mode.*—Put the gooseberries into a jar, with sufficient moist sugar to sweeten them, and boil them until reduced to a pulp. Put this pulp at the bottom of a trifle-dish; pour over it a pint of custard made by recipe, and, when cold, cover with whipped cream. The cream should be whipped the day before it is wanted for table, as it will then be so much firmer and more solid; but it should not be added to the fruit until a short time before it is required. The dish may be garnished as fancy dictates. *Time.*—About ¾ hour to boil the gooseberries. *Average cost,* 1*s.* 6*d.* *Sufficient* for 1 trifle. *Seasonable* in May, June, and July.

GOOSEBERRY VINEGAR. (An Excellent Recipe.)

Ingredients.—2 pecks of crystal gooseberries, 6 gallons of water, 12 lbs. of foots sugar of the coarsest brown quality. *Mode.*—Mash the gooseberries (which should be quite ripe) in a tub with a mallet; put to them the water nearly milk-warm; let this stand 24 hours; then strain it through a sieve, and put the sugar to it; mix it well, and tun it. These proportions are for a 9-gallon cask; and if it be not quite full, more water must be added. Let the mixture be stirred from the bottom of the cask two or three times daily for three or four days, to assist the melting of the sugar; then paste a piece of linen cloth over the bunghole, and set the cask in a warm place, *but not in the sun;* any corner of a warm kitchen is the best situation for it. The following spring it should be drawn off into stone bottles, and the vinegar will be fit for use twelve months after it is made. This will be found a most excellent preparation, greatly superior to much that is sold under the name of the best white wine vinegar. Many years' experience has proved that pickle made with this vinegar will keep, when bought vinegar will not preserve the ingredients. The cost per gallon is merely nominal, especially to those who reside in the country and grow their own gooseberries; the coarse sugar is then the only ingredient to be purchased. *Time.*—To remain in the cask 9 months. *Average cost,* when the gooseberries have to be purchased, 1*s.* per gallon; when they are grown at home, 6*d.* per gallon. *Seasonable.*—This should be made the end of June or the beginning of July, when gooseberries are ripe and plentiful.

GOOSEBERRY WINE, Effervescing.

Ingredients.—To every gallon of water allow 6 lbs. of green gooseberries, 3 lbs. of lump sugar. *Mode.*—This wine should be prepared from unripe gooseberries, in order to avoid the flavour which the fruit would give to the wine when in a mature state. Its briskness depends more upon the time of bottling than upon the unripe state of the fruit, for effervescing wine can be made from fruit that is ripe as well as that which is unripe. The fruit should be selected when it has nearly attained its full growth, and consequently before it shows any tendency to ripen. Any bruised or decayed berries, and those that are very small, should be rejected. The blossom and stalk ends should be removed, and the fruit well bruised in a tub or pan, in such quantities as to insure each berry being broken without crushing the seeds. Pour the water (which should be warm) on the fruit, squeeze and stir it with the hand until all the pulp is removed from the skin and seeds, and cover the whole closely for 24 hours; after which, strain it through a coarse bag, and press it with as much force as can be conveniently applied, to extract the whole of the juice and liquor the fruit may contain. To every 40 or 50 lbs. of fruit one gallon more of hot water may be passed through the *marc*, or husks, in order to obtain any soluble matter that may remain, and be again pressed. The juice should be put into a tub or pan of sufficient size to contain all of it, and the sugar added to it. Let it be well stirred until the sugar is dissolved, and place the pan in a warm situation; keep it closely covered, and let it ferment for a day or two. It must then be drawn off into clean casks, placed a little on one side for the scum that arises to be thrown out, and the casks kept filled with the remaining "must," that should be reserved for that purpose. When the active fermentation has ceased, the casks should be plugged upright, again filled, if necessary, the bungs be put in loosely, and, after a few days, when the fermentation is a little more languid (which may be known by the hissing noise ceasing), the bungs should be driven in tight, and a spile-hole made, to give vent if necessary. About November or December, on a clear fine day, the wine should be racked from its lees into clean casks, which may be rinsed with brandy. After a month, it should be examined to see if it is sufficiently clear for bottling; if not, it must be fined with isinglass, which may be dissolved in some of the wine: 1 oz. will be sufficient for 9 gallons. In bottling the wine, it will be necessary to wire the corks down, or to tie them down with string. Old champagne bottles are the best for this wine. In March or April, or when the gooseberry bushes begin to blossom, the wine must be bottled, in order to insure its being effervescing. *Seasonable.*—Make this the end of May or beginning of June, before the berries ripen.

GRAVIES, General Stock for.

By the addition of various store sauces, thickening and flavouring, good stock may be converted into good gravies. It should be borne in mind, however, that the goodness and strength of spices, wines, flavourings, &c., evaporate, and that they lose a great deal of their fragrance if added to the gravy a long time before they are wanted. If this point is attended to, a saving of one half the quantity of these ingredients will be effected, as, with long boiling, the flavour almost entirely passes away. The shank-bones of mutton, previously well soaked, will be found a great assistance in enriching gravies; a kidney or melt, beef skirt, trimmings of meat, &c. &c., answer very well when only a small quantity is wanted, and a good gravy need not necessarily be so very expensive; for economically-prepared dishes are oftentimes found as savoury and wholesome as dearer ones. The cook should also remember that the fragrance of gravies should not be overpowered by too much spice, or any strong essences, and that they should always be warmed in a *bain marie*, after they are flavoured, or else in a jar or jug placed in a saucepan full of boiling water. The remains of roast-meat gravy should always be saved; as, when no meat is at hand, a very nice gravy in haste may be made from it, and when added to hashes, ragoûts, &c., is a great improvement.

GRAVY, a Good Beef, for Poultry, Game, &c.

Ingredients.—½ lb. of lean beef, ½ pint of cold water, 1 shalot or small onion, ½ a teaspoonful of salt, a little pepper, 1 tablespoonful of Harvey's sauce or mushroom ketchup, ½ a teaspoonful of arrowroot. *Mode.*—Cut up the beef into small pieces, and put it, with the water, into a stewpan. Add the shalot and seasoning, and simmer gently for 3 hours, taking care that it does not boil fast. A short time before it is required, take the arrowroot, and having mixed it with a little cold water, pour it into the gravy, which keep stirring, adding the Harvey's sauce, and just letting it boil. Strain off the gravy in a tureen, and serve very hot. *Time.*—3 hours. *Average cost*, 8d. per pint.

GRAVY, Beef, a Quickly Made.

Ingredients.—½ lb. of shin of beef, ½ onion, ¼ carrot, 2 or 3 sprigs of parsley and savoury herbs, a piece of butter about the size of a walnut; cayenne and mace to taste, ¾ pint of water. *Mode.*—Cut up the meat into very small pieces, slice the onion and carrot, and put them into a small saucepan with the butter. Keep stirring over a sharp fire until they have taken a little colour, when add the water and the remaining ingredients. Simmer for ½ hour, skim well, strain, and flavour, when it will be ready for use. *Time.*—½ hour. *Average cost,* for this quantity, *5d.*

GRAVY, Brown.

Ingredients.—2 oz. of butter, 2 large onions, 2 lbs. of shin of beef, 2 small slices of lean bacon (if at hand), salt and whole pepper to taste, 3 cloves, 2 quarts of water. For thickening, 2 oz. of butter, 3 oz. of flour. *Mode.*—Put the butter into a stewpan; set this on the fire, throw in the onions cut in rings, and fry them a light brown; then add the beef and bacon, which should be cut into small square pieces; season, and pour in a teacupful of water; let it boil for about ten minutes, or until it is of a nice brown colour, occasionally stirring the contents. Now fill up with water in the above proportion; let it boil up, when draw it to the side of the fire to simmer very gently for 1½ hour; strain, and when cold, take off all the fat. In thickening this gravy, melt 3 oz. of butter in a stewpan, add 2 oz. of flour, and stir till of a light-brown colour; when cold, add it to the strained gravy, and boil it up quickly. This thickening may be made in larger quantities, and kept in a stone jar for use when wanted. *Time.* — Altogether, 2 hours. *Average cost, 4d.* per pint.

GRAVY, Brown, without Meat.

Ingredients.—2 large onions, 1 large carrot, 2 oz. of butter, 3 pints of boiling water, 1 bunch of savoury herbs, a wineglassful of good beer; salt and pepper to taste. *Mode.*—Slice, flour, and fry the onions and carrots in the butter until of a nice light-brown colour, then add the boiling water and the remaining ingredients; let the whole stew gently for about an hour, then strain, and when cold, skim off all the fat. Thicken it, and, if thought necessary, add a few drops of colouring. *Time.*—1 hour. *Average cost, 2d.* per pint.

Note.—The addition of a small quantity of mushroom ketchup or Harvey's sauce very much improves the flavour of this gravy.

GRAVY, Cheap, for Minced Veal.

Ingredients.—Bones and trimmings of cold roast or boiled veal, 1½ pint of water, 1 onion, ¼ teaspoonful of minced lemon-peel, ¼ teaspoonful of salt, 1 blade of pounded mace, the juice of ¼ lemon; thickening of butter and flour. *Mode.*—Put all the ingredients into a stewpan, except the thickening and lemon-juice, and let them simmer very gently for rather more than 1 hour, or until the liquor is reduced to a pint, when strain through a hair sieve. Add a thickening of butter and flour, and the lemon-juice; set it on the fire, and let it just boil up, when it will be ready for use. It may be flavoured with a little tomato sauce, and, where a rather dark-coloured gravy is not objected to, ketchup, or Harvey's sauce, may be added at pleasure. *Time.*—Rather more than 1 hour. *Average cost, 3d.*

GRAVY, Cheap, for Hashes, &c.

Ingredients.—Bones and trimmings of the cooked joint intended for hashing, ¼ teaspoonful of salt, ¼ teaspoonful of whole pepper, ¼ teaspoonful of whole allspice, a small faggot of savoury herbs, ½ head of celery, 1 onion, 1 oz. of butter, thickening, sufficient boiling water to cover the bones. *Mode.*—Chop the bones in small pieces, and put them in a stewpan, with the trimmings, salt, pepper, spice, herbs, and celery. Cover with boiling water, and let the whole simmer gently for 1½ or 2 hours. Slice and fry the onion in the butter till it is of a pale brown, and mix it gradually with the gravy made from the bones; boil for ¼ hour, and strain into a basin; now put it back into the stewpan; flavour with walnut pickle or ketchup, pickled-onion liquor, or any store sauce that may be preferred. Thicken with a little butter and flour, kneaded together on a plate, and the gravy will be ready for use. After the thickening is added, the gravy should just boil, to take off the rawness of the flour. *Time.*—2 hours, or rather more. *Average cost, 4d.*, exclusive of the bones and trimmings.

GRAVY for Roast Meat.

Ingredients.—Gravy, salt. *Mode.*—Put a common dish with a small quantity of salt in it under the meat, about a quarter of an hour before it is removed from the fire. When the dish is full, take it away, baste the meat, and pour the gravy into the dish on which the joint is to be served.

GRAVY for Venison.

Ingredients.—Trimmings of venison, 3 or 4 mutton shank-bones, salt to taste, 1 pint of water, 2 teaspoonfuls of walnut ketchup. *Mode.*—Brown the trimmings over a nice clear fire, and put them in a stewpan with the shank-bones and water; simmer gently for 2 hours, strain and skim, and add the walnut ketchup and a seasoning of salt. Let it just boil, when it is ready to serve. *Time.*—2 hours.

GRAVY, Jugged (Excellent).

Ingredients.—2 lbs. of shin of beef, $\frac{1}{2}$ lb. of lean ham, 1 onion or a few shalots, 2 pints of water, salt and whole pepper to taste, 1 blade of mace, a faggot of savoury herbs, $\frac{1}{2}$ a large carrot, $\frac{1}{2}$ a head of celery. *Mode.*—Cut up the beef and ham into small pieces, and slice the vegetables; take a jar, capable of holding two pints of water, and arrange therein, in layers, the ham, meat, vegetables, and seasoning, alternately, filling up with the above quantity of water; tie down the jar, or put a plate over the top, so that the steam may not escape; place it in the oven, and let it remain there from 6 to 8 hours; should, however, the oven be very hot, less time will be required. When sufficiently cooked, strain the gravy, and when cold, remove the fat. It may be flavoured with ketchup, wines, or any other store sauce that may be preferred. It is a good plan to put the jar in a cool oven over-night, to draw the gravy; and then it will not require so long baking the following day. *Time.*—From 6 to 8 hours, according to the oven. *Average cost*, 7*d.* per pint.

GRAVY-KETTLE.

This is a utensil which will not be found in every kitchen; but it is a useful one where it is necessary to keep gravies hot for the purpose of pouring over various dishes as they are cooking. It is made of copper, and should, conse-

GRAVY-KETTLE.

quently, be heated over the hot-plate, if there be one, or a charcoal stove.

GRAVY made without Meat for Fowls.

Ingredients.—The necks, feet, livers, and gizzards of the fowls, 1 slice of toasted bread, $\frac{1}{2}$ onion, 1 faggot of savoury herbs, salt and pepper to taste, $\frac{1}{2}$ pint of water, thickening of butter and flour, 1 dessertspoonful of ketchup. *Mode.*—Wash the feet of the fowls thoroughly clean, and cut them and the neck into small pieces. Put these into a stewpan with the bread, onion, herbs, seasoning, livers, and gizzards; pour the water over them and simmer gently for 1 hour. Now take out the liver, pound it, and strain the liquor to it. Add a thickening of butter and flour, and a flavouring of mushroom ketchup; boil it up and serve. *Time.*—1 hour. *Average cost*, 4*d.* per pint.

GRAVY, Rich, for Hashes, Ragouts, &c.

Ingredients.—2 lbs. of shin of beef, 1 large onion or a few shalots, a little flour, a bunch of savoury herbs, 2 blades of mace, 2 or 3 cloves, 4 whole allspice, $\frac{1}{4}$ teaspoonful of whole pepper, 1 slice of lean ham or bacon, $\frac{1}{2}$ a head of celery (when at hand), 2 pints of boiling water; salt and cayenne to taste. *Mode.*—Cut the beef into thin slices, as also the onions, dredge them with flour, and fry of a pale brown, but do not allow them to get black; pour in the boiling water, let it boil up, and skim. Add the remaining ingredients, and simmer the whole very gently for 2 hours, or until all the juices are extracted from the meat; put it by to get cold, when take off all the fat. This gravy may be flavoured with ketchup, store sauces, wine, or, in fact, anything that may give additional and suitable relish to the dish it is intended for.

Time.—Rather more than 2 hours. *Average cost*, 8*d*. per pint.

GRAVY SOUP.

Ingredients.—6 lbs. of shin of beef, a knuckle of veal weighing 5 lbs., a few pieces or trimmings, 2 slices of nicely-flavoured lean ham; ¼ lb. of butter, 4 onions, 4 carrots, 1 turnip, nearly a head of celery, 3 blades of mace, 6 cloves, a bunch of savoury herbs, seasoning of salt and pepper to taste, 3 lumps of sugar, 6 quarts of boiling soft water. It can be flavoured with ketchup, Leamington sauce, Harvey's sauce, and a little soy. *Mode.* — Slightly brown the meat and ham in the butter, but do not let them burn. When this is done, pour to it the water, and as the scum rises, take it off; when no more appears, add all the other ingredients, and let the soup simmer slowly by the fire for 6 hours without stirring it any more from the bottom; take it off, and let it settle; skim off all the fat you can, and pass it through a sieve or cloth. When perfectly cold you can remove all the fat, and leave the sediment untouched, which serves very nicely for thick gravies, hashes, &c. *Time.* —7 hours. *Average cost*, 1*s*. per quart. *Seasonable* all the year. *Sufficient* for 14 persons.

GRAVY, Veal, for White Sauces, Fricassees, &c.

Ingredients. — 2 slices of nicely-flavoured lean ham, any poultry trimmings, 3 lbs. of lean veal, a faggot of savoury herbs, including parsley, a few green onions (or 1 large onion may be substituted for these), a few mushrooms, when obtainable; 1 blade of mace, salt to taste, 3 pints of water. *Mode.*—Cut up the ham and veal into small square pieces, put these in a stewpan, moistening them with a small quantity of water; place them over the fire to draw down. When the bottom of the stewpan becomes covered with a white glaze, fill up with water in the above proportion; add the remaining ingredients, stew very slowly for 3 or 4 hours, and do not forget to skim well the moment it boils. Put it by, and when cold take off all the fat. This may be used for Béchamel, sauce tournée, and many other white sauces. *Time.*—3 or 4 hours. *Average cost*, 9*d*. per pint.

GREENGAGE JAM.

Ingredients. — To every lb. of fruit, weighed before being stoned, allow ¾ lb. of lump sugar. *Mode.*—Divide the greengages, take out the stones, and put them into a preserving-pan. Bring the fruit to a boil, then add the sugar, and keep stirring it over a gentle fire until it is melted. Remove all the scum as it rises, and, just before the jam is done, boil it rapidly for 5 minutes. To ascertain when it is sufficiently boiled, pour a little on a plate, and if the syrup thickens and appears firm, it is done. Have ready half the kernels blanched; put them into the jam, give them one boil, and pour the preserve into pots. When cold, cover down with oiled papers, and, over these, tissue paper brushed over on both sides with the white of an egg. *Time.*—¾ hour after the sugar is added. *Average cost*, from 6*d*. to 8*d*. per lb. pot. *Sufficient.*—Allow about 1¼ pint of fruit for every lb. pot of jam. *Seasonable.*—Make this in August or September.

GREENGAGES, Compote of.

Ingredients.—1 pint of syrup, 1 quart of greengages. *Mode.*—Make a syrup, skim it well, and put in the greengages when the syrup is boiling, having previously removed the stalks and stones from the fruit. Boil gently for ¼ hour, or until the fruit is tender; but take care not to let it break, as the appearance of the dish would be spoiled were the fruit reduced to a pulp. Take the greengages carefully out, place them on a glass dish, boil the syrup for another 5 minutes, let it cool a little, pour over the fruit, and, when cold, it will be ready for use. *Time.* —¼ hour to simmer the fruit, 5 minutes the syrup. *Average cost*, in full season, 10*d*. *Sufficient* for 4 or 5 persons. *Seasonable* in July, August, and September.

GREENGAGES, to Preserve and Dry.

Ingredients. — To every lb. of sugar allow 1 lb. of fruit, ¼ pint of water. *Mode.*—For this purpose, the fruit must be used before it is quite ripe, and part of the stalk must be left on. Weigh the fruit, rejecting all that is in the least degree blemished, and put it into a lined saucepan with the sugar and water, which should have been previously boiled together to a rich syrup. Boil the fruit in this for 10 minutes, remove it from the fire, and drain the greengages. The next day, boil up the syrup and put in the fruit again, and let it simmer for 3 minutes, and drain the syrup away. Continue this process for 5 or 6 days, and the last time place the greengages, when drained, on a hair sieve, and put them in an oven or warm spot to dry; keep them in a box, with paper between each layer, in a place free from damp. *Time.*—10 minutes the first time of boiling. *Seasonable.*—Make this in August or September.

GREENGAGES, Preserved in Syrup.

Ingredients.—To every lb. of fruit allow 1 lb. of loaf sugar, ¼ pint of water. *Mode.*—Boil the sugar and water together for about 10 minutes; divide the greengages, take out the stones, put the fruit into the syrup, and let it simmer gently until nearly tender. Take it off the fire, put it into a large pan, and, the next day, boil it up again for about 10 minutes with the kernels from the stones, which should be blanched. Put the fruit carefully into jars, pour over it the syrup, and, when cold, cover down, so that the air is quite excluded. Let the syrup be well skimmed both the first and second day of boiling, otherwise it will not be clear. *Time.*—10 minutes to boil the syrup; ¼ hour to simmer the fruit the first day, 10 minutes the second day. *Average cost*, from 6*d*. to 8*d*. per lb. pot. *Sufficient.*—Allow about 1 pint of fruit to fill a 1-lb. pot. *Seasonable.*—Make this in August or September.

GREENS, Boiled Turnip.

Ingredients.—To each ½ gallon of water allow 1 heaped tablespoonful of salt; turnip-greens. *Mode.*— Wash the greens well in two or three waters, and pick off all the decayed and dead leaves; tie them in small bunches, and put them into plenty of boiling water, salted in the above proportion. Keep them boiling quickly, with the lid of the saucepan uncovered, and when tender, pour them into a colander; let them drain, arrange them in a vegetable-dish, remove the string that the greens were tied with, and serve. *Time.*—15 to 20 minutes. *Average cost*, 4*d*. for a dish for 3 persons. *Seasonable* in March, April, and May.

GROUSE PIE.

Ingredients.—Grouse; cayenne, salt, and pepper to taste; 1 lb. of rump-steak, ½ pint of well-seasoned broth, puff-paste. *Mode.*—Line the bottom of a pie-dish with the rump-steak cut into neat pieces, and, should the grouse be large, cut them into joints; but, if small, they may be laid in the pie whole; season highly with salt, cayenne, and black pepper; pour in the broth, and cover with a puff-paste; brush the crust over with the yolk of an egg, and bake from ¾ to 1 hour. If the grouse is cut into joints, the backbones and trimmings will make the gravy, by stewing them with an onion, a little sherry, a bunch of herbs, and a blade of mace: this should be poured in after the pie is baked. *Time.*—¾ to 1 hour. *Average cost*, exclusive of the grouse, which are seldom bought, 1*s*. 9*d*. *Seasonable* from the 12th of August to the beginning of December.

GROUSE, Roast.

Ingredients.—Grouse, butter, a thick slice of toasted bread. *Mode.*—Let the birds hang as long as possible; pluck and draw them; wipe, but do not wash them, inside and out, and truss them without the head, the same as for a roast fowl. Many persons still continue to truss them

ROAST GROUSE.

with the head under the wing, but the former is now considered the most approved method. Put them down to a sharp clear fire; keep them well basted the whole of the time they are cooking, and serve them on a buttered toast, soaked in the dripping-pan, with a little melted butter poured over them, or with bread-sauce and gravy. *Time.* — ½ hour; if liked very thoroughly done, 35 minutes. *Average cost*, 2*s*. to 2*s*. 6*d*. the brace; but seldom bought. *Sufficient.*—2 for a dish. *Seasonable* from the 12th of August to the beginning of December.

GROUSE, to Carve.

Grouse may be carved in the way first

described in carving partridge. The backbone of the grouse is highly esteemed by many, and this part of many game birds is considered the finest-flavoured.

ROAST GROUSE.

GROUSE SALAD (Soyer's Recipe improved.)

Ingredients.—8 eggs, butter, fresh salad, 2 or 3 grouse; for the sauce, 1 tablespoonful of minced shalot, 2 tablespoonfuls of pounded sugar, the yolks of 2 eggs, 1 teaspoonful of minced parsley, ¼ oz. of salt, 12 tablespoonfuls of oil, 4 tablespoonfuls of Chili vinegar, 1 gill of cream, 2 tablespoonfuls of chopped tarragon and chervil. *Mode.*—Boil the eggs hard, shell them, throw them into cold water, cut a thin slice off the bottom to facilitate the proper placing of them in the dish, cut each one into four lengthwise, and make a very thin flat border of butter, about one inch from the edge of the dish the salad is to be served on; fix the pieces of egg upright close to each other, the yolk outside, or the yolk and white alternately; lay in the centre a fresh salad of whatever is in season, and, having previously roasted the grouse rather underdone, cut it into eight or ten pieces, and prepare the sauce as follows:—Put the shalots into a basin, with the sugar, the yolk of an egg, the parsley, and salt, and mix in by degrees the oil and vinegar; when all the ingredients are well mixed, put the sauce on ice or in a cool place. When ready to serve, whip the cream rather thick, which lightly mix with it; then lay the inferior parts of the grouse on the salad, sauce over so as to cover each piece, then lay over the salad and the remainder of the grouse, pour the rest of the sauce over, and serve. The eggs may be ornamented with a little dot of radishes or beetroot on the point. Anchovy and gherkin, cut into small diamonds, may be placed between, or cut gherkins in slices, and a border of them laid round. Tarragon or chervil-leaves are also a pretty addition. The remains of cold black-game, pheasant, or partridge may be used in the above manner, and will make a very delicate dish. *Average cost*, 2*s*. 3*d*. *Seasonable* from the 12th of August to the beginning of December.

GRUEL, to make.

Ingredients.—1 tablespoonful of Robinson's patent groats, 2 tablespoonfuls of cold water, 1 pint of boiling water. *Mode.*—Mix the prepared groats smoothly with the cold water in a basin; pour over them the boiling water, stirring it all the time. Put it into a very clean saucepan; boil the gruel for 10 minutes, keeping it well stirred; sweeten to taste, and serve. It may be flavoured with a small piece of lemon-peel, by boiling it in the gruel, or a little grated nutmeg may be put in; but in these matters the taste of the patient should be consulted. Pour the gruel in a tumbler, and serve. When wine is allowed to the invalid, 2 tablespoonfuls of sherry or port make this preparation very nice. In cases of colds, the same quantity of spirits is sometimes added instead of wine. *Time.*—10 minutes. *Sufficient* to make a pint of gruel.

GUDGEONS.

Ingredients.— Egg and bread-crumbs sufficient for the quantity of fish; hot lard. *Mode.* — Do not scrape off the scales, but take out the gills and inside, and cleanse thoroughly; wipe them dry, flour and dip them into egg, and sprinkle over with bread-crumbs. Fry of a nice brown. *Time.*—3 or 4 minutes. *Average cost.* — Seldom bought. *Seasonable* from March to July. *Sufficient.*—3 for each person.

GUINEA-FOWL, Roast, Larded.

Ingredients.—A guinea-fowl, lardoons, flour, and salt. *Mode.*—When this bird is larded, it should be trussed the same as a pheasant; if plainly roasted, truss it like a turkey. After larding and trussing it, put it down to roast at a brisk fire; keep it well basted, and a short time before serving, dredge it with a little flour, and let it froth nicely. Serve with a little gravy in the dish, and a tureen of the same, and one of well-made bread-sauce. *Time.* — Guinea-fowl, larded, 1¼ hour; plainly roasted, about 1 hour. *Sufficient* for 6 persons. *Seasonable* in winter.

Note.—The breast, if larded, should be covered with a piece of paper, and removed about 10 minutes before serving.

GURNET, or GURNARD.

Ingredients.—1 gurnet, 6 oz. of salt to

each gallon of water. *Mode.*—Cleanse the fish thoroughly, and cut off the fins; have ready some boiling water, with salt in the above proportion; put the fish in, and simmer very gently for ¼ hour. Parsley and butter, or anchovy sauce, should be served with it. *Time.*—¼ hour. *Average cost.*—Seldom bought. *Seasonable* from October to March, but in perfection in October. *Sufficient.*—A middling-sized one for two persons.

Note.—This fish is frequently stuffed with forcemeat, and baked.

HADDOCK, Baked.

Ingredients.—A nice forcemeat, butter to taste, egg and bread-crumbs. *Mode.*—Scale and clean the fish, without cutting it open much; put in a nice delicate forcemeat, and sew up the slit. Brush it over with egg, sprinkle over bread-crumbs, and baste frequently with butter. Garnish with parsley and cut lemon, and serve with a nice brown gravy, plain melted butter, or anchovy sauce. The egg and bread-crumbs can be omitted, and pieces of butter placed over the fish. *Time.*—Large haddock, ¾ hour; moderate size, ½ hour. *Seasonable* from August to February. *Average cost,* from 9*d.* upwards.

Note.—Haddocks may be filleted, rubbed over with egg and bread-crumbs, and fried a nice brown; garnish with crisped parsley.

HADDOCK, Boiled.

Ingredients.—Sufficient water to cover the fish; ¼ lb. of salt to each gallon of water. *Mode.*—Scrape the fish, take out the inside, wash it thoroughly, and lay it in a kettle, with enough water to cover it, and salt in the above proportion. Simmer gently from 15 to 20 minutes, or rather more, should the fish be very large. For small haddocks, fasten the tails in their mouths, and put them into boiling water. 10 to 15 minutes will cook them. Serve with plain melted butter, or anchovy sauce. *Time.*—Large haddock, ½ hour; small, ¼ hour, or rather less. *Average cost,* from 9*d.* upwards. *Seasonable* from August to February.

HADDOCK, Dried.

Dried haddock should be gradually warmed through, either before or over a nice clear fire. Rub a little piece of butter over, just before sending it to table.

HADDOCK, Dried.

Ingredients.—1 large thick haddock, 2 bay-leaves, 1 small bunch of savoury herbs, not forgetting parsley, a little butter and pepper; boiling water. *Mode.*—Cut up the haddock into square pieces, make a basin hot by means of hot water, which pour out. Lay in the fish, with the bay-leaves and herbs; cover with boiling water; put a plate over to keep in the steam, and let it remain for 10 minutes. Take out the slices, put them in a hot dish, rub over with butter and pepper, and serve. *Time.*—10 minutes. *Seasonable* at any time, but best in winter.

HAM OMELET (a delicious Breakfast Dish).

Ingredients.—6 eggs, 4 oz. of butter, ½ saltspoonful of pepper, 2 tablespoonfuls of minced ham. *Mode.*—Mince the ham very finely, without any fat, and fry it for 2 minutes in a little butter; then make the batter for the omelet, stir in the ham, and proceed as in the case of a plain omelet. Do not add any salt to the batter, as the ham is usually sufficiently salt to impart a flavour to the omelet. Good lean bacon, or tongue, answers equally well for this dish; but they must also be slightly cooked previously to mixing them with the batter. Serve very hot and quickly, without gravy. *Time.*—From 4 to 6 minutes. *Average cost,* 1*s.* *Sufficient* for 4 persons. *Seasonable* at any time.

HAM, FRIED, AND EGGS (a Breakfast Dish).

Ingredients.—Ham; eggs. *Mode.*—Cut the ham into slices, and take care that they are of the same thickness in every part. Cut off the rind, and if the ham should be particularly hard and salt, it will be found an improvement to soak it for about 10 minutes in hot water, and then dry it in a cloth. Put it into a cold frying-pan, set it over the fire, and turn the slices 3 or 4 times whilst they are cooking. When done, place them on a dish, which should be kept hot in front of the fire during the time the eggs are being poached. Poach the eggs, slip them on to the slices of ham, and serve quickly. *Time.*—7 or 8 minutes to broil the ham. *Average cost,* 8*d.* to 1*s.* per lb. by the whole ham. *Sufficient.*—Allow 2 eggs and a slice of ham to each person. *Seasonable* at any time.

Note.—Ham may also be toasted or broiled; but, with the latter method, to insure its being well cooked, the fire must be beautifully clear, or it will have a smoky flavour far from agreeable.

HAM, Potted, that will keep Good for some time.

Ingredients.—To 4 lbs. of lean ham allow 1 lb. of fat, 2 teaspoonfuls of pounded mace, ½ nutmeg grated, rather more than ½ teaspoonful of cayenne, clarified lard. *Mode.*—Mince the ham, fat and lean together in the above proportion, and pound it well in a mortar, seasoning it with cayenne pepper, pounded mace, and nutmeg; put the mixture into a deep baking-dish, and bake for ½ hour; then press it well into a stone jar, fill up the jar with clarified lard, cover it closely, and paste over it a piece of thick paper. If well seasoned, it will keep a long time in winter, and will be found very convenient for sandwiches, &c. *Time.*—½ hour. *Seasonable* at any time.

HAM, Potted (a nice addition to the Breakfast or Luncheon table).

Ingredients.—To 2 lbs. of lean ham allow ½ lb. of fat, 1 teaspoonful of pounded mace, ½ teaspoonful of pounded allspice, ½ nutmeg, pepper to taste, clarified butter. *Mode.*—Cut some slices from the remains of a cold ham, mince them small, and to every 2 lbs. of lean allow the above proportion of fat. Pound the ham in a mortar to a fine paste, with the fat, gradually add the seasonings and spices, and be very particular that all the ingredients are well mixed and the spices well pounded. Press the mixture into potting-pots, pour over clarified butter, and keep it in a cool place. *Average cost* for this quantity, 2*s.* 6*d.* *Seasonable* at any time.

HAM, to Bake.

Ingredients.—Ham; a common crust. *Mode.*—As a ham for baking should be well soaked, let it remain in water for at least 12 hours. Wipe it dry, trim away any rusty places underneath, and cover it with a common crust, taking care that this is of sufficient thickness all over to keep the gravy in. Place it in a moderately-heated oven, and bake for nearly 4 hours. Take off the crust and skin, and cover with raspings, the same as for boiled ham, and garnish the knuckle with a paper frill. This method of cooking a ham is, by many persons, considered far superior to boiling it, as it cuts fuller of gravy and has a finer flavour, besides keeping a much longer time good. *Time.*—A medium-sized ham, 4 hours. *Average cost*, from 8*d.* to 1*s.* per lb. by the whole ham. *Seasonable* all the year.

HAM, to Boil.

Ingredients.—Ham, water, glaze, or raspings. *Mode.*—In choosing a ham, ascertain that it is perfectly sweet, by running a sharp knife into it, close to the bone; and if, when the knife is withdrawn, it has an agreeable smell, the ham is good; if, on the contrary, the blade has a greasy appearance and offensive smell, the ham is bad. If it has been

BOILED HAM.

long hung, and is very dry and salt, let it remain in soak for 24 hours, changing the water frequently. This length of time is only necessary in the case of its being very hard; from 8 to 12 hours would be sufficient for a Yorkshire or Westmoreland ham. Wash it thoroughly clean, and trim away from the under-side all the rusty and smoked parts, which would spoil the appearance. Put it into a boiling-pot, with sufficient cold water to cover it; bring it gradually to boil, and as the scum rises, carefully remove it. Keep it simmering very gently until tender, and be careful that it does not stop boiling, nor boil too quickly. When done, take it out of the pot, strip off the skin, and sprinkle over it a few fine bread-raspings, put a frill of cut paper round the knuckle, and serve. If to be eaten cold, let the ham remain in the water until nearly cold: by this method the juices are kept in, and it will be found infinitely superior to one taken out of the water hot; it should, however, be borne in mind that the ham must *not* remain in the saucepan *all* night. When the skin is removed, sprinkle over bread-raspings, or, if wanted particularly nice, glaze it. Place a paper frill round the knuckle, and garnish with parsley or cut vegetable flowers. *Time.*—A ham weighing 10 lbs., 4 hours to *simmer gently*; 15 lbs., 5 hours; a very large one, about 6 hours. *Average cost*, from 8*d.* to 1*s.* per lb. by the whole ham. *Seasonable* all the year.

HAM, how to Boil to give it an excellent flavour.

Ingredients. — Vinegar and water, 2 heads of celery, 2 turnips, 3 onions, a large bunch of savoury herbs. *Mode.*—Prepare the ham as in the preceding recipe, and let it soak for a few hours in vinegar and water. Put it on in cold water, and when it boils, add the vegetables and herbs. Simmer very gently until tender, take it out, strip off the skin, cover with bread-raspings, and put a paper ruche or frill round the knuckle. *Time.*—A ham weighing 10 lbs., 4 hours. *Average cost*, 8*d.* to 1*s.* per lb. by the whole ham. *Seasonable* at any time.

HAM, to Carve.

In cutting a ham, the carver must be guided according as he desires to practise economy, or have, at once, fine slices out of the prime part. Under the first supposition, he will commence at the knuckle end, and cut off thin slices towards the thick part of the ham. To reach the choicer portion, the knife, which must be very sharp and thin, should be carried quite down to the bone, in the direction of the line 1 to 2. The slices

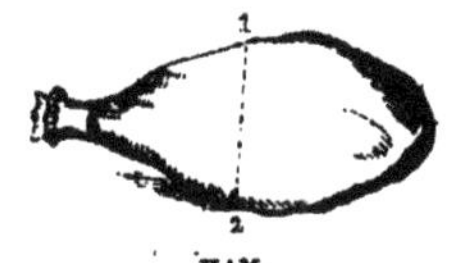

HAM.

should be thin and even, and always cut down to the bone. There are some who like to carve a ham by cutting a hole at the top, and then slicing pieces off inside the hole, gradually enlarging the circle; but we think this is a plan not to be recommended. A ham, when hot, is usually sent to table with a paper ruffle round the knuckle.

HAMS, for Curing (Mons. Ude's Recipe).

Ingredients.—For 2 hams weighing about 16 or 18 lbs. each, allow 1 lb. of moist sugar, 1 lb. of common salt, 2 oz. of saltpetre, 1 quart of good vinegar. *Mode.*—As soon as the pig is cold enough to be cut up, take the 2 hams and rub them well with common salt, and leave them in a large pan for 3 days. When the salt has drawn out all the blood, drain the hams, and throw the brine away. Mix sugar, salt, and saltpetre together in the above proportion, rub the hams well with these, and put them into a vessel large enough to hold them, always keeping the salt over them. Let them remain for 3 days, then pour over them a quart of good vinegar. Turn them in the brine every day for a month, then drain them well, and rub them with bran. Have them smoked over a wood fire, and be particular that the hams are hung as high up as possible from the fire; otherwise the fat will melt, and they will become dry and hard. *Time.*—To be pickled 1 month; to be smoked 1 month. *Sufficient* for 2 hams of 18 lbs. each. *Seasonable* from October to March.

HAMS, to Cure Sweet, in the Westmoreland way.

Ingredients.—3 lbs. of common salt, 3 lbs. of coarse sugar, 1 lb. of bay-salt, 3 quarts of strong beer. *Mode.*—Before the hams are put into pickle, rub them the preceding day well with salt, and drain the brine well from them. Put the above ingredients into a saucepan, and boil for ¼ hour; pour over the hams, and let them remain a month in the pickle. Rub and turn them every day, but do not take them out of the pickling-pan; and have them smoked for a month. *Time.*—To be pickled 1 month; to be smoked 1 month. *Seasonable* from October to March.

HAMS, to Pickle (Suffolk Recipe).

Ingredients.—To a ham from 10 to 12 lbs., allow 1 lb. of coarse sugar, ¾ lb. of salt, 1 oz. of saltpetre, ½ a teacupful of vinegar. *Mode.*—Rub the hams well with common salt, and leave them for a day or two to drain; then rub well in the above proportion of sugar, salt, saltpetre, and vinegar, and turn them every other day. Keep them in the pickle 1 month, drain them, and send them to be smoked over a wood fire for 3 weeks or a month. *Time.*—To remain in the pickle 1 month; to be smoked 3 weeks or 1 month. *Sufficient.*—The above proportion of pickle is sufficient for 1 ham. *Seasonable.*—Hams should be pickled from October to March.

HAMS, to Salt Two, about 12 or 15 lbs. each.

Ingredients.—2 lbs. of treacle, ½ lb. of saltpetre, 1 lb. of bay-salt, 2 pounds of common salt. *Mode.*—Two days before they are put into pickle, rub the hams well with salt, to draw away all slime and blood. Throw what comes from them away, and then rub them with treacle, saltpetre, and salt. Lay them in a deep pan, and let them remain one day; boil the above proportion of treacle, saltpetre, bay-salt, and common salt for ¼ hour, and pour this pickle boiling hot over the hams: there should be sufficient of it to cover them. For a day or two rub them well with it; afterwards they will only require turning. They ought to remain in this pickle for 3 weeks or a month, and then be sent to be smoked, which will take nearly or quite a month to do. An ox-tongue pickled in this way is most excellent, to be eaten either green or smoked. *Time.*—To remain in the pickle 3 weeks or a month; to be smoked about a month. *Seasonable* from October to March.

HAMS, to Smoke, at Home.

Take an old hogshead, stop up all the crevices, and fix a place to put a cross-stick near the bottom, to hang the articles to be smoked on. Next, in the side, cut a hole near the top, to introduce an iron pan filled with sawdust and small pieces of green wood. Having turned the tub upside down, hang the articles upon the cross-stick, introduce the iron pan in the opening, and place a piece of red-hot iron in the pan, cover it with sawdust, and all will be complete. Let a large ham remain 40 hours, and keep up a good smoke. Fish may be smoked in the same manner.

HARE, Broiled (a Supper or Luncheon Dish).

Ingredients.—The legs and shoulders of a roast hare, cayenne and salt to taste, a little butter. *Mode.*—Cut the legs and shoulders from a roast hare, season them highly with salt and cayenne, and broil them over a very clear fire for 5 minutes. Dish them on a hot dish, rub over them a little cold butter, and send to table very quickly. *Time.*—5 minutes. *Seasonable* from September to the end of February.

HARE, Hashed.

[COLD MEAT COOKERY.] *Ingredients.*—The remains of cold roast hare, 1 blade of pounded mace, 2 or 3 allspice, pepper and salt to taste, 1 onion, a bunch of savoury herbs, 3 tablespoonfuls of port wine, thickening of butter and flour, 2 tablespoonfuls of mushroom ketchup. *Mode.*—Cut the cold hare into neat slices, and put the head, bones, and trimmings into a stewpan, with ¾ pint of water; add the mace, allspice, seasoning, onion, and herbs, and stew for nearly an hour, and strain the gravy; thicken it with butter and flour, add the wine and ketchup, and lay in the pieces of hare, with any stuffing that may be left. Let the whole gradually heat by the side of the fire, and, when it has simmered for about 5 minutes, serve, and garnish the dish with sippets of toasted bread. Send red-currant jelly to table with it. *Time.*—Rather more than 1 hour. *Average cost*, exclusive of the cold hare, 6*d.* *Seasonable* from September to the end of February.

HARE, Jugged (very good).

Ingredients.—1 hare, 1½ lb. of gravy beef, ½ lb. of butter, 1 onion, 1 lemon, 6 cloves; pepper, cayenne, and salt to taste; ½ pint of port wine. *Mode.*—Skin, paunch, and wash the hare, cut it into pieces, dredge them with flour, and fry in boiling butter. Have ready 1½ pint of gravy, made from the above proportion of beef, and thickened with a little flour. Put this into a jar; add the pieces of fried hare, an onion stuck with six cloves, a lemon peeled and cut in half, and a good seasoning of pepper, cayenne, and salt; cover the jar down tightly, put it up to the neck into a stewpan of boiling water, and let it stew until the hare is quite tender, taking care to keep the water boiling. When nearly done, pour in the wine, and add a few forcemeat balls: these must be fried or baked in the oven for a few minutes before they are put to the gravy. Serve with red-currant jelly. *Time.*—3½ to 4 hours. If the hare is very old, allow 4½ hours. *Average cost*, 7*s*. *Sufficient* for 7 or 8 persons. *Seasonable* from September to the end of February.

HARE, Jugged (a Quicker and more Economical Way).

Ingredients.—1 hare, a bunch of sweet herbs, 2 onions, each stuck with 3 cloves, 6 whole allspice, ½ teaspoonful of black pepper, a strip of lemon-peel, thickening of butter and flour, 2 tablespoonfuls of mushroom ketchup, ¼ pint of port wine. *Mode*.—Wash the hare nicely, cut it up into joints (not too large), and flour and brown them as in the preceding recipe; then put them into a stewpan with the herbs, onions, cloves, allspice, pepper, and lemon-peel; cover with hot water, and when it boils, carefully remove all the scum, and let it simmer gently till tender, which will be in about 1¾ hour, or longer, should the hare be very old. Take out the pieces of hare, thicken the gravy with flour and butter, add the ketchup and port wine, let it boil for about 10 minutes, strain it through a sieve over the hare, and serve. A few fried forcemeat balls should be added at the moment of serving, or, instead of frying them, they may be stewed in the gravy, about 10 minutes before the hare is wanted for table. Do not omit to serve red-currant jelly with it. *Time*.—Altogether 2 hours. *Average cost*, 5*s*. 6*d*. *Sufficient* for 7 or 8 persons. *Seasonable* from September to the end of February.

Note.—Should there be any left, re-warm it the next day by putting the hare, &c., into a covered jar, and placing this jar in a saucepan of boiling water; this method prevents a great deal of waste.

HARE, Potted (a Luncheon or Breakfast Dish).

Ingredients.—1 hare, a few slices of bacon, a large bunch of savoury herbs, 4 cloves, ½ teaspoonful of whole allspice, 2 carrots, 2 onions, salt and pepper to taste, 1 pint of water, 2 glasses of sherry. *Mode*.—Skin, empty, and wash the hare; cut it down the middle, and put it into a stewpan, with a few slices of bacon under and over it; add the remaining ingredients, and stew very gently until the hare is tender, and the flesh will separate easily from the bones. When done enough, take it up, remove the bones, and pound the meat, *with the bacon*, in a mortar, until reduced to a perfectly smooth paste. Should it not be sufficiently seasoned, add a little cayenne, salt, and pounded mace, but be careful that these are well mixed with the other ingredients. Press the meat into potting-pots, pour over clarified butter, and keep in a dry place. The liquor that the hare was stewed in, should be saved for hashes, soups, &c. &c. *Time*.—About 2½ hours to stew the hare. *Seasonable* from September to the end of February.

HARE, Roast.

Ingredients.—Hare, forcemeat, a little milk, butter. *Choosing and Trussing*.—Choose a young hare; which may be known by its smooth and sharp claws, and by the cleft in the lip not being much spread. To be eaten in perfection, it must hang for some time; and, if properly taken care of, it may be kept for several days. It is better to hang without being paunched; but should it be previously emptied, wipe the inside every day, and sprinkle over it a little pepper and ginger, to prevent the musty taste which long keeping in the damp occasions, and also which affects the stuffing. After it is skinned, wash it well, and soak for an hour in warm water to draw out the blood; if old, let it lie in vinegar for a short time, but wash it well afterwards in several waters. Make a forcemeat, wipe the hare dry, fill the belly with it, and sew it up. Bring the

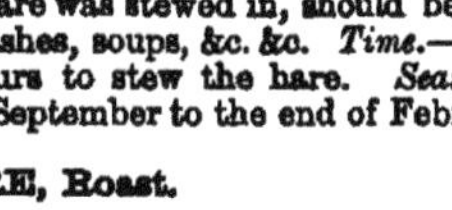

ROAST HARE.

hind and fore legs close to the body towards the head, run a skewer through each, fix the head between the shoulders by means of another skewer, and be careful to leave the ears on. Put a string round the body from skewer to skewer, and tie it above the back. *Mode*.—The hare should be kept at a distance from the fire when it is first laid down, or the outside will become dry and hard before the inside is done. Baste it well with milk for a short time, and afterwards with butter; and particular attention must be paid to the basting, so as to preserve the meat on the back juicy and nutritive. When it is almost roasted enough, flour the hare, and baste well with butter. When nicely frothed, dish it, remove the skewers, and send it to table with a little gravy in the dish, and a tureen of the same. Red-currant jelly must also not be forgotten, as this is an indispensable accompaniment to roast hare. For economy, good beef dripping may be substituted for the milk and butter to baste with; but the basting, as we have before stated, must be continued without intermission. If the liver is good, it may be parboiled, minced, and mixed with the stuffing; but it should not be used unless quite fresh. *Time.*—A middling-sized hare, 1¼ hour; a large hare, 1½ to 2 hours. *Average cost*, from 4*s.* to 6*s.* *Sufficient* for 5 or 6 persons. *Seasonable* from September to the end of February.

HARE, Roast, to Carve.

The "Grand Carver" of olden times, a functionary of no ordinary dignity, was pleased when he had a hare to manipulate, for his skill and grace had an opportunity of display. *Diners à la Russe* may possibly, ere-while, save modern gentlemen the necessity of learning the art which was in auld lang syne one of the necessary accomplishments of the youthful squire; but, until side-tables become universal, or till we see the office of "grand carver" once more instituted, it will be well for all to learn how to assist at the carving of this dish, which, if not the most elegant in appearance, is a very general favourite.

ROAST HARE.

The hare, having its head to the left, as shown in the woodcut, should be first served by cutting slices from each side of the backbone, in the direction of the lines from 3 to 4. After these prime parts are disposed of, the leg should next be disengaged by cutting round the line indicated by the figures 5 to 6. The shoulders will then be taken off by passing the knife round from 7 to 8. The back of the hare should now be divided by cutting quite through its spine, as shown by the line 1 to 2, taking care to feel with the point of the knife for a joint where the back may be readily penetrated. It is the usual plan not to serve any bone in helping hare; and thus the flesh should be sliced from the legs and placed alone on the plate. In large establishments, and where mess-cooks are kept, it is often the case that the backbone of the hare, especially in old animals, is taken out, and then the process of carving is, of course, considerably facilitated. A great point to be remembered in connection with carving hare is, that plenty of gravy should accompany each helping, otherwise this dish, which is naturally dry, will lose half its flavour, and so become a failure. Stuffing is also served with it; and the ears, which should be nicely crisp, and the brains of the hare, are esteemed as delicacies by many connoisseurs.

HARE SOUP.

Ingredients.—A hare fresh-killed, 1 lb. of lean gravy-beef, a slice of ham, 1 carrot, 2 onions, a faggot of savoury herbs, ¼ oz. of whole black pepper, a little browned flour, ¼ pint of port wine, the crumb of two French rolls, salt and cayenne to taste, 3 quarts of water. *Mode.*—Skin and paunch the hare, saving the liver and as much blood as possible. Cut it in pieces, and put it in a stewpan with all the ingredients, and simmer gently for 6 hours. This soup should be made the day before it is wanted. Strain through a sieve, put the best parts of the hare in the soup, and serve.

HARE SOUP.

Proceed as above; but, instead of putting the joints of the hare in the soup, pick the meat from the bones, pound it in a mortar, and add it, with the crumb of two French rolls, to the soup. Rub all through a sieve; heat slowly, but do not let it boil. Send it to table immediately. *Time.*—8 hours. *Average cost*, 1*s.* 9*d.* per quart. *Seasonable* from September to February. *Sufficient* for 10 persons.

HERB POWDER, for Flavouring when Fresh Herbs are not obtainable.

Ingredients.—1 oz. of dried lemon-thyme, 1 oz. of dried winter savory, 1 oz. of dried sweet marjoram and basil, 2 oz. of dried parsley, 1 oz. of dried lemon-peel. *Mode.*—Prepare and dry the herbs, pick the leaves from the stalks, pound them, and sift them through a hair sieve; mix in the above proportions, and keep in glass bottles, carefully excluding the air. This we think a far better method of keeping herbs, as the flavour and fragrance do not evaporate so much as when they are merely put in paper bags. Preparing them in this way, you have them ready for use at a moment's notice. Mint, sage, parsley, &c., dried, pounded, and each put into separate bottles, will be found very useful in winter.

HERBS, to Dry, for Winter Use.

On a very dry day, gather the herbs, just before they begin to flower. If this is done when the weather is damp, the herbs will not be so good a colour. (It is very necessary to be particular in little matters like this, for trifles constitute perfection, and herbs nicely dried will be found very acceptable when frost and snow are on the ground. It is hardly necessary, however, to state that the flavour and fragrance of fresh herbs are incomparably finer.) They should be perfectly freed from dirt and dust, and be divided into small bunches, with their roots cut off. Dry them quickly in a very hot oven, or before the fire, as by this means most of their flavour will be preserved, and be careful not to burn them; tie them up in paper bags, and keep in a dry place. This is a very general way of preserving dried herbs; but we would recommend the plan described in a former recipe. *Seasonable.*—From the month of July to the end of September is the proper time for storing herbs for winter use.

HERRINGS, White, Baked.

Ingredients.—12 herrings, 4 bay-leaves, 12 cloves, 12 allspice, 2 small blades of mace, cayenne pepper and salt to taste, sufficient vinegar to fill up the dish. *Mode.*—Take herrings, cut off the heads, and gut them. Put them in a pie-dish, heads and tails alternately, and, between each layer, sprinkle over the above ingredients. Cover the fish with the vinegar, and bake for ½ hour, but do not use it till quite cold. The herrings may be cut down the front, the backbone taken out, and closed again. Sprats done in this way are very delicious. *Time.*—½ an hour. *Average cost*, 1*d.* each.

To Choose the Herring.—The more scales this fish has, the surer the sign of its freshness. It should also have a bright and silvery look; but if red about the head, it is a sign that it has been dead for some time.

HERRINGS, Red, or YARMOUTH BLOATERS.

The best way to cook these is to make incisions in the skin across the fish, because they do not then require to be so long on the fire, and will be far better than when cut open. The hard roe makes a nice relish by pounding it in a mortar, with a little anchovy, and spreading it on toast. If very dry, soak in warm water 1 hour before dressing.

HIDDEN MOUNTAIN, The (a pretty Supper Dish).

Ingredients.—6 eggs, a few slices of citron, sugar to taste, ¼ pint of cream, a layer of any kind of jam. *Mode.*—Beat the whites and yolks of the eggs separately; then mix them and beat well again, adding a few thin slices of citron, the cream, and sufficient pounded sugar to sweeten it nicely. When the mixture is well beaten, put it into a buttered pan, and fry the same as a pancake; but it should be three times the thickness of an ordinary pancake. Cover it with jam, and garnish with slices of citron and holly-leaves. This dish is served cold. *Time.*—About 10 minutes to fry the mixture. *Average cost*, with the jam, 1*s.* 4*d.* *Sufficient* for 3 or 4 persons. *Seasonable* at any time.

HODGE-PODGE.

Ingredients.—2 lbs. of shin of beef, 3 quarts of water, 1 pint of table-beer, 2 onions, 2 carrots, 2 turnips, 1 head of celery; pepper and salt to taste; thickening of butter and flour. *Mode.*—Put the meat, beer, and water in a stewpan; simmer for a few minutes, and skim carefully. Add the vegetables and seasoning; stew gently till the meat is tender. Thicken with the butter and flour, and serve with turnips and carrots, or spinach and celery. *Time.*—3 hours, or rather more. *Average cost*, 3*d.* per quart. *Seasonable* at any time. *Sufficient* for 12 persons.

HODGE-PODGE.

[COLD MEAT COOKERY.] *Ingredients.*—About 1 lb. of underdone cold mutton, 2 lettuces, 1 pint of green peas, 5 or 6 green onions, 2 oz. of butter, pepper and salt to taste, ½ teacupful of water. *Mode.*—Mince the mutton, and cut up the lettuces and onions in slices. Put these in a stewpan, with all the ingredients except the peas, and let these simmer very gently for ¾ hour, keeping them well stirred. Boil the peas separately, mix these with the mutton, and serve very hot. *Time.*—¾ hour. *Sufficient* for 3 or 4 persons. *Seasonable* from the end of May to August.

HOLLY-LEAVES, to Frost, for Garnishing and Decorating Dessert and Supper Dishes.

Ingredients.—Sprigs of holly, oiled butter, coarsely-powdered sugar. *Mode.*—Procure some nice sprigs of holly; pick the leaves from the stalks, and wipe them with a clean cloth free from all moisture; then place them on a dish near the fire, to get thoroughly dry, but not too near to shrivel the leaves; dip them into oiled butter, sprinkle over them some coarsely-powdered sugar, and dry them before the fire. They should be kept in a dry place, as the least damp would spoil their appearance. *Time.*—About 10 minutes to dry before the fire. *Seasonable.*—These may be made at any time; but are more suitable for winter garnishes, when fresh flowers are not easily obtained.

HONEY CAKE.

Ingredients.—½ breakfast-cupful of sugar, 1 breakfast-cupful of rich sour cream, 2 breakfast-cupfuls of flour, ½ teaspoonful of carbonate of soda, honey to taste. *Mode.*—Mix the sugar and cream together; dredge in the flour, with as much honey as will flavour the mixture nicely; stir it well that all the ingredients may be thoroughly mixed; add the carbonate of soda, and beat the cake well for another 5 minutes; put it into a buttered tin, bake it from ½ to ¾ hour, and let it be eaten warm. *Time.*—½ to ¾ hour. *Average cost*, 8*d*. *Sufficient* for 3 or 4 persons. *Seasonable* at any time.

HORSERADISH.

This root, scraped, is always served with hot roast beef, and is used for garnishing many kinds of boiled fish. Let the horseradish remain in cold water for an hour; wash it well, and with a sharp knife scrape it into very thin shreds, commencing from the thick end of the root. Arrange some of it lightly in a small glass dish, and the remainder use for garnishing the joint; it should be placed in tufts round the border of the dish, with 1 or 2 bunches on the meat. *Average cost*, 2*d*. per stick. *Seasonable* from October to June.

HORSERADISH SAUCE, to serve with Roast Beef.

Ingredients.—4 tablespoonfuls of grated horseradish, 1 teaspoonful of pounded sugar, 1 teaspoonful of salt, ½ tea-spoonful of pepper, 2 teaspoonfuls of made mustard; vinegar. *Mode.*—Grate the horseradish, and mix it well with the sugar, salt, pepper, and mustard; moisten it with sufficient vinegar to give it the consistency of cream, and serve in a tureen; 3 or 4 tablespoonfuls of cream added to the above very much improve the appearance and flavour of this sauce. To heat it to serve with hot roast beef, put it in a *bain marie* or a jar, which place in a saucepan of boiling water; make it hot, but do not allow it to boil, or it will curdle.

Note.—This sauce is a great improvement on the old-fashioned way of serving cold-scraped horseradish with hot roast beef. The mixing of the cold vinegar with the warm gravy cools and spoils everything on the plate. Of course, with cold meat, the sauce should be served cold.

HORSERADISH VINEGAR.

Ingredients.—¼ lb. of scraped horseradish, 1 oz. of minced shalot, 1 drachm of cayenne, 1 quart of vinegar. *Mode.*—Put all the ingredients into a bottle, which shake well every day for a fortnight. When it is thoroughly steeped, strain and bottle, and it will be fit for use immediately. This will be found an agreeable relish to cold beef, &c. *Seasonable.*—This vinegar should be made either in October or November, as horseradish is then in its highest perfection.

HOT SPICE (a Delicious Adjunct to Chops, Steaks, Gravies, &c.)

Ingredients.—3 drachms each of ginger, black pepper, and cinnamon, 7 cloves, ½ oz. mace, ¼ oz. of cayenne, 1 oz. grated nutmeg, 1½ oz. white pepper. *Mode.*—Pound the ingredients, and mix them thoroughly together, taking care that everything is well blended. Put the spice in a very dry glass bottle for use. The quantity of cayenne may be increased, should the above not be enough to suit the palate.

ICE-CREAMS, Fruit.

Ingredients.—To every pint of fruit-juice allow 1 pint of cream; sugar to taste. *Mode.*—Let the fruit be well ripened; pick it off the stalks, and put it into a large earthen pan. Stir it about with a wooden spoon, breaking it until it is well mashed; then, with the back of the spoon, rub it through a hair sieve. Sweeten it nicely with pounded sugar; whip the cream for a few minutes, add it to the fruit, and whisk the whole again for another 5 minutes. Put the mixture into the freezing-pot, and freeze, taking care to stir the cream, &c., two or three times, and to remove it from the sides of the vessel, that the mixture may be equally frozen and smooth. Ices are usually served in glasses, but if moulded, as they sometimes are for dessert, must have a small quantity of melted isinglass added to them, to enable them to keep their shape. Raspberry, strawberry, currant, and all fruit ice-creams, are made in the same manner. A little pounded sugar sprinkled over the fruit before it is mashed assists to extract the juice. In winter, when fresh fruit is not obtainable, a little jam may be substituted for it: it should be melted and worked through a sieve before being added to the whipped cream; and if the colour should not be good, a little prepared cochineal or beetroot may be put in to improve its appearance. *Time.*—½ hour to freeze the mixture. *Average cost,* with cream at 1*s.* per pint, 4*d.* each ice. *Seasonable,* with fresh fruit, in June, July, and August.

ICE, Lemon-water.

Ingredients.—To every pint of syrup, allow ½ pint of lemon-juice; the rind of 4 lemons. *Mode.*—Rub the sugar on the rinds of the lemons, and with it make the syrup. Strain the lemon-juice, add it to the other ingredients, stir well, and put the mixture into a freezing-pot. Freeze as directed for Ice Pudding, and when the mixture is thoroughly and equally frozen, put it into ice-glasses. *Time.*—½ hour to freeze the mixture. *Average cost,* 3*d.* to 4*d.* each. *Seasonable* at any time.

ICED-PUDDING (Parisian Recipe).

Ingredients.—½ lb. of sweet almonds, 2 oz. of bitter ones, ¾ lb. of sugar, 8 eggs, 1½ pint of milk. *Mode.*—Blanch and dry the almonds thoroughly in a cloth, then pound them in a mortar until reduced to a smooth paste; add to these the well-beaten eggs, the sugar, and milk; stir these ingredients over the fire until they thicken, but do not allow them to boil; then strain and put the mixture into the freezing-pot; surround it with ice, and freeze it. When quite frozen, fill an iced-pudding mould, put on the lid, and keep the pudding in ice until required for table; then turn it out on the dish, and garnish it with a *compôte* or

ICED-PUDDING MOULD.

any fruit that may be preferred, pouring a little over the top of the pudding. This pudding may be flavoured with vanilla, Curaçoa, or Maraschino. *Time.*—½ hour to freeze the mixture. *Seasonable.*—Served all the year round.

ICES.

Ices are composed, it is scarcely necessary to say, of congealed cream or water, combined sometimes with liqueurs or other flavouring ingredients, or more generally with the juices of fruits. At desserts, or at some evening parties, ices are scarcely to be dispensed with. The principal utensils required for making ice-creams are ice-tubs, freezing-pots, spaddles, and a cellaret. The tub must be large enough to contain about a bushel of ice, pounded small, when brought out of the ice-house, and mixed very carefully with either *salt*, *nitre*, or *soda*. The freezing-pot is best made of pewter. If it be of tin, as is sometimes the case, the congelation goes on too rapidly in it for the thorough intermingling of its contents, on which the excellence of the ice greatly depends. The spaddle is generally made of copper, kept bright and clean. The cellaret is a tin vessel, in which ices are kept for a short time from dissolving. The method to be pursued in the freezing process must be attended to. When the ice-tub is prepared with fresh-pounded ice and salt, the freezing-pot is put into it up to its cover. The articles to be congealed are then poured into it and covered over; but to prevent the ingredients from separating and the heaviest of them from falling to the bottom of the mould, it is requisite to turn the freezing-pot round and round by the handle, so as to keep its contents moving until the congelation commences. As soon as this is perceived (the cover of the pot being occasionally taken off for the purpose of noticing when freezing takes place), the cover is immediately closed over it, ice is put upon it, and it is left in this state till it is served. The use of the spaddle is to stir up and remove from the sides of the freezing-pot the cream, which in the shaking may have washed against it, and by stirring it in with the rest, to prevent waste of it occurring. Any negligence in stirring the contents of the freezing-pot before congelation takes place, will destroy the whole: either the sugar sinks to the bottom and leaves the ice insufficiently sweetened, or lumps are formed, which disfigure and discolour it.

ICES, to make Fruit-water.

Ingredients.—To every pint of fruit-juice allow 1 pint of syrup. *Mode.*—Select nice ripe fruit; pick off the stalks and put it into a large earthen pan, with a little pounded sugar strewed over; stir it about with a wooden spoon until it is well broken, then rub it through a hair sieve. Make a syrup, without white of egg; let it cool, add the fruit-juice, mix well together, and put the mixture into the freezing-pot. Proceed as directed for Ice Puddings, and when the mixture is equally frozen, put it into small glasses. Raspberry, strawberry, cur-

DISH OF ICES.

rant, and other fresh-fruit-water ices, are made in the same manner. *Time.*—½ hour to freeze the mixture. *Average cost*, 3*d*. to 4*d*. each. *Seasonable*, with fresh fruit, in June, July, and August.

ICING, Almond, for Cakes.

Ingredients.—To every lb. of finely-pounded loaf sugar, allow 1 lb. of sweet almonds, the whites of 4 eggs, a little rosewater. *Mode.*—Blanch the almonds, and pound them (a few at a time) in a mortar to a paste, adding a little rose-water to facilitate the operation. Whisk the whites of the eggs to a strong froth; mix them with the pounded almonds, stir in the sugar, and beat altogether. When the cake is sufficiently baked, lay on the almond icing, and put it into the oven to dry. Before laying this preparation on the cake, great care must be taken that it is nice and smooth, which is easily accomplished by well beating the mixture.

ICING, Sugar, for Cakes.

Ingredients. — To every lb. of loaf sugar allow the whites of 4 eggs, 1 oz. of fine starch. *Mode.*—Beat the eggs to a strong froth, and gradually sift in the sugar, which should be reduced to the finest possible powder, and gradually add the starch, also finely powdered. Beat the mixture well until the sugar is smooth; then with a spoon or broad knife lay the ice equally over the cakes. These should then be placed in a very cool oven, and the icing allowed to dry and harden, but not to colour. The icing may be coloured with strawberry or currant juice, or with prepared cochineal. If it be put on the cakes as soon as they are withdrawn from the oven, it will become firm and hard by the time the cakes are cold. On very rich cakes, such as wedding, christening cakes, &c., a layer of almond icing is usually spread over the top, and over that the white icing as described. All iced cakes should be kept in a very dry place.

INVALID COOKERY.

A few Rules to be observed in Cooking for Invalids.

Let all the kitchen utensils used in the preparation of invalids' cookery be delicately and *scrupulously clean*; if this is not the case, a disagreeable flavour may be imparted to the preparation, which flavour may disgust, and prevent the patient from partaking of the refreshment when brought to him or her.

For invalids, never make a large quantity *of one thing*, as they seldom require much at a time; and it is desirable that variety be provided for them.

[illegible]ys have something in readiness; a little beef tea, nicely made and nicely [illegible]ed, a few spoonfuls of jelly, &c., [illegible] it may be administered as soon [illegible] the invalid wishes for it. If obliged [illegible] wait a long time, the patient loses the desire to eat, and often turns against the food when brought to him or her.

In sending dishes or preparations up to invalids, let everything look as tempting as possible. Have a clean tray-cloth laid smoothly over the tray; let the spoons, tumblers, cups and saucers, &c., be very clean and bright. Gruel served in a tumbler is more appetizing than when served in a basin or cup and saucer.

As milk is an important article of food for the sick, in warm weather let it be kept on ice, to prevent its turning sour. Many other delicacies may also be preserved good in the same manner for some little time.

If the patient be allowed to eat vegetables, never send them up undercooked, or half raw; and let a small quantity only be temptingly arranged on a dish. This rule will apply to every preparation, as an invalid is much more likely to enjoy his food if small delicate pieces are served to him.

Never leave food about a sick-room; if the patient cannot eat it when brought to him, take it away, and bring it to him in an hour or two's time. Miss Nightingale says, "To leave the patient's untasted food by his side from meal to meal, in hopes that he will eat it in the interval, is simply to prevent him from taking any food at all." She says, "I have known patients literally incapacitated from taking one article of food after another by this piece of ignorance. Let the food come at the right time, and be taken away, eaten or uneaten, at the right time, but never let a patient have 'something always standing' by him, if you don't wish to disgust him of everything."

Never serve beef tea or broth with the *smallest particle* of fat or grease on the surface. It is better, after making either of these, to allow them to get perfectly cold, when *all the fat* may be easily removed; then warm up as much as may be required. Two or three pieces of clean whity-brown paper laid on the broth will absorb any greasy particles that may be floating at the top, as the grease will cling to the paper.

Roast mutton, chickens, rabbits, calves' feet or head, game, fish (simply dressed), and simple puddings, are all light food, and easily digested. Of course, these things are only partaken of supposing the patient is recovering.

A mutton chop, nicely cut, trimmed, and broiled to a turn, is a dish to be recommended for invalids; but it must not be served *with all the fat* at the end, nor must it be too thickly cut. Let it be cooked over a fire free from smoke, and sent up with the gravy in it, between two very hot plates. Nothing is more disagreeable to an invalid than *smoked* food.

In making toast-and-water, never blacken the bread, but toast it only a nice brown. Never leave toast-and-water to make until the moment it is required, as it cannot then be properly prepared,—at least the patient will be obliged to drink it warm, which is anything but agreeable.

In boiling eggs for invalids, let the white be just set; if boiled hard, they will be likely to disagree with the patient.

In Miss Nightingale's admirable "Notes on Nursing," a book that no mother or nurse should be without, she says,—"You cannot be too careful as to quality in sick-diet. A nurse should never put before a patient milk that is sour, meat or soup that is turned, an egg that is bad, or vegetables underdone." Yet often, she says, she has seen these things brought in to the sick, in a state perfectly perceptible to every nose or eye except the nurse's. It is here that the clever nurse appears,—she will not bring in the peccant article; but, not to disappoint the patient, she will whip up something else in a few minutes. Remember, that sick-cookery should half do the work of your poor patient's weak digestion.

She goes on to caution nurses, by saying,—"Take care not to spill into your patient's saucer; in other words, take care that the outside bottom rim of his cup shall be quite dry and clean. If, every time he lifts his cup to his lips, he has to carry the saucer with it, or else to drop the liquid upon and to soil his sheet, or bedgown, or pillow, or, if he is sitting up, his dress, you have no idea what a difference this minute want of care on your part makes to his comfort, and even to his willingness for food."

INVALID'S CUTLET.

Ingredients.—1 nice cutlet from a loin or neck of mutton; 2 teacupfuls of water; 1 very small stick of celery; pepper and salt to taste. *Mode.*—Have the cutlet cut from a very nice loin or neck of mutton, take off all the fat, put it into a stewpan with the other ingredients; stew very gently indeed for nearly 2 hours, and skim off every particle of fat that may rise to the surface from time to time. The celery should be cut into thin slices before it is added to the meat, and care must be taken not to put in too much of this, or the dish will not be good. If the water is allowed to boil fast, the cutlet will be hard. *Time.*—2 hours very gentle stewing. *Average cost,* 6d. *Sufficient* for one person. *Seasonable.*—Whenever celery may be had.

INVALID'S JELLY.

Ingredients.—12 shanks of mutton, 3 quarts of water, a bunch of sweet herbs, pepper and salt to taste, 3 blades of mace, 1 onion, 1 lb. of lean beef, a crust of bread toasted brown. *Mode.*—Soak the shanks in plenty of water for some hours, and scrub them well; put them, with the beef and other ingredients, into a saucepan with the water, and let them simmer very gently for 5 hours. Strain the broth, and, when cold, take off all the fat. It may be eaten either warmed up or cold as a jelly. *Time.*—5 hours. *Average cost,* 1*s*. *Sufficient* to make from 1½ to 2 pints of jelly. *Seasonable* at any time.

INVALIDS, Lemonade for.

Ingredients.—½ lemon, lump sugar to taste, 1 pint of boiling water. *Mode.*—Pare off the rind of the lemon thinly; cut the lemon into 2 or 3 thick slices, and remove as much as possible of the white outside pith, and all the pips. Put the slices of lemon, the peel, and lump sugar into a jug; pour over the boiling water; cover it closely, and in 2 hours it will be fit to drink. It should either be strained or poured off from the sediment. *Time.*—2 hours. *Average cost,* 2*d*. *Sufficient* to make 1 pint of lemonade. *Seasonable* at any time.

JAM ROLY-POLY PUDDING.

Ingredients.—¾ lb. of suet-crust, ¾ lb. of any kind of jam. *Mode.*—Make a nice light suet-crust, and roll it out to the thickness of about ½ inch. Spread the jam equally over it, leaving a small margin of paste without any, where the pudding joins. Roll it up, fasten the ends securely, and tie it in a floured cloth; put the pudding into boiling water, and boil for 2 hours. Mincemeat or marmalade may be substituted for the jam, and makes excellent puddings. *Time.*—2 hours. *Average cost,* 9*d*. *Sufficient* for 5 or 6 persons. *Seasonable.*—Suitable for winter puddings, when fresh fruit is not obtainable.

JANUARY—BILLS OF FARE.

Dinner for 18 persons.

First Course.

Mock-Turtle Soup,
removed by
Cod's Head and Shoulders.

Stewed Eels. | Vase of Flowers. | Red Mullet.

Clear Oxtail Soup,
removed by
Fried Filleted Soles.

Entrées.

Ris de Veau aux Tomates.

Ragoût of Lobster. | Vase of Flowers. | Cotelettes de Porc à la Robert.

Poulet à la Marengo.

Second Course.

Roast Turkey.

Boiled Turkey and Celery Sauce.

Pigeon Pie.

Vase of Flowers.

Boiled Ham.

Tongue, garnished.

Saddle of Mutton.

Third Course.

Charlotte à la Parisienne.

Pheasants, removed by Plum-Pudding.

Apricot-Jam Tartlets.

Jelly.

Cream.

Vase of Flowers.

Cream.

Jelly.

Mince Pies.

Snipes, removed by Pommes à la Condé.

Maids of Honour.

Dinner for 12 persons.

First Course.—Carrot soup à la Crécy; ox-tail soup; turbot and lobster sauce; fried smelts, with Dutch sauce. *Entrées.* Mutton cutlets, with Soubise sauce; sweetbreads; oyster patties; fillets of rabbits. *Second Course.*—Roast turkey; stewed rump of beef à la jardinière; boiled ham, garnished with Brussels sprouts; boiled chickens and celery sauce. *Third Course.*—Roast hare; teal; eggs à la neige; vol-au-vent of preserved fruit; 1 jelly; 1 cream; potatoes à la maître d'hôtel; grilled mushrooms; dessert and ices.

Dinner for 10 persons.

First Course.—Soup à la Reine; whitings au gratin; crimped cod and oyster sauce. *Entrées.*—Tendrons de veau; curried fowl and boiled rice. *Second Course.*—Turkey, stuffed with chestnuts, and chestnut sauce; boiled leg of mutton, English fashion, with caper sauce and mashed turnips. *Third Course.*—Woodcocks or partridges; widgeon;

Charlotte à la vanille; cabinet pudding; orange jelly; blancmange; artichoke bottoms; macaroni, with Parmesan cheese; dessert and ices.

Dinner for 8 persons.

First Course.—Mulligatawny soup; brill and shrimp sauce; fried whitings. *Entrées.*—Fricasseed chicken; pork cutlets, with tomato sauce. *Second Course.*—Haunch of mutton; boiled turkey and celery sauce; boiled tongue, garnished with Brussels sprouts. *Third Course.*—Roast pheasants; meringues à la crême; compôte of apples; orange jelly; cheesecakes; soufflé of rice; dessert and ices.

Dinners for 6 persons.

First Course.—Julienne soup; soles à la Normandie. *Entrées.*—Sweetbreads, with sauce piquante; mutton cutlets, with mashed potatoes. *Second Course.*—Haunch of venison; boiled fowls and bacon, garnished with Brussels sprouts. *Third Course.*—Plum-pudding; custards in glasses; apple tart; fondue à la Brillat Savarin; dessert.

First Course.—Vermicelli soup; fried slices of codfish and anchovy sauce; John Dory. *Entrées.* — Stewed rump-steak à la jardinière; rissoles; oyster patties. *Second Course.*—Leg of mutton; curried rabbit and boiled rice. *Third Course.*—Partridges; apple fritters; tartlets of greengage jam; orange jelly; plum-pudding; dessert.

First Course.—Pea-soup; baked haddock; soles à la crême. *Entrées.*—Mutton cutlets and tomato sauce; fricasseed rabbit. *Second Course.*—Roast pork and apple sauce; breast of veal, rolled and stuffed; vegetables. *Third Course.*—Jugged hare; whipped cream; blancmange; mince pies; cabinet pudding.

First Course.—Palestine soup; fried smelts; stewed eels. *Entrées.*—Ragoût of lobster; broiled mushrooms; vol-au-vent of chicken. *Second Course.*—Sirloin of beef; boiled fowls and celery sauce; tongue, garnished with Brussels sprouts. *Third Course.*—Wild ducks; Charlotte aux pommes; cheesecakes; transparent jelly, inlaid with brandy cherries; blancmange; Nesselrode pudding.

JANUARY, Plain Family Dinners for.

Sunday.—1. Boiled turbot and oyster sauce, potatoes. 2. Roast leg or griskin of pork, apple sauce, brocoli, potatoes. 3. Cabinet pudding, and damson tart made with preserved damsons.

Monday.—1. The remains of turbot warmed in oyster sauce, potatoes. 2. Cold pork, stewed steak. 3. Open jam tart, which should have been made with the pieces of paste left from the damson tart; baked arrowroot pudding.

Tuesday.—1. Boiled neck of mutton, carrots, mashed turnips, suet dumplings, and caper sauce: the broth should be served first, and a little rice or pearl barley should be boiled in it along with the meat. 2. Rolled jam pudding.

Wednesday.—1. Roast rolled ribs of beef, greens, potatoes, and horseradish sauce. 2. Bread-and-butter pudding, cheesecakes.

Thursday.—1. Vegetable soup (the bones from the ribs of beef should be boiled down with this soup), cold beef, mashed potatoes. 2. Pheasants, gravy, bread sauce. 3. Macaroni.

Friday.—1. Fried whitings or soles. 2. Boiled rabbit and onion sauce, minced beef, potatoes. 3. Currant dumplings.

Saturday.—1. Rump-steak pudding or pie, greens, and potatoes. 2. Baked custard pudding and stewed apples.

Sunday.—1. Codfish and oyster sauce, potatoes. 2. Joint of roast mutton, either leg, haunch, or saddle; brocoli and potatoes, red-currant jelly. 3. Apple tart and custards, cheese.

Monday.—1. The remains of codfish picked from the bone, and warmed through in the oyster sauce; if there is no sauce left, order a few oysters and make a little fresh; and do not let the fish boil, or it will be watery. 2. Curried rabbit, with boiled rice served separately, cold mutton, mashed potatoes. 3. Somersetshire dumplings with wine sauce.

Tuesday.—1. Boiled fowls, parsley-and-butter; bacon garnished with Brussels sprouts; minced or hashed mutton. 2. Baroness pudding.

Wednesday.—1. The remains of the fowls cut up into joints and fricasseed; joint of roast pork and apple sauce, and, if liked, sage-and-onion, served on a dish by itself; turnips and potatoes. 2. Lemon pudding, either baked or boiled.

Thursday.—1. Cold pork and jugged hare, red-currant jelly, mashed potatoes. 2. Apple pudding.

Friday.—1. Boiled beef, either the aitchbone or the silver side of the round; carrots, turnips, suet dumplings, and potatoes: if there is a marrow-bone, serve the marrow on toast at the same time. 2. Rice snowballs.

Saturday.—1. Pea-soup made from liquor in which beef was boiled; cold beef, mashed potatoes. 2. Baked batter fruit pudding.

JANUARY, Things in Season.

Fish.—Barbel, brill, carp, cod, crabs, crayfish, dace, eels, flounders, haddocks, herrings, lampreys, lobsters, mussels, oysters, perch, pike, plaice, prawns, shrimps, skate, smelts, soles, sprats, sturgeon, tench, thornback, turbot, whitings.

Meat.—Beef, house lamb, mutton, pork, veal, venison.

Poultry.—Capons, fowls, tame pigeons, pullets, rabbits, turkeys.

Game.—Grouse, hares, partridges, pheasants, snipe, wild-fowl, woodcock.

Vegetables.—Beetroot, brocoli, cabbages, carrots, celery, chervil, cresses, cucumbers (forced), endive, lettuces, parsnips, potatoes, savoys, spinach, turnips, various herbs.

Fruit.—Apples, grapes, medlars, nuts, oranges, pears, walnuts, crystallized preserves (foreign), dried fruits, such as almonds and raisins; French and Spanish plums; prunes, figs, dates.

JAUNEMANGE.

Ingredients.—1 oz. of isinglass, 1 pint of water, ½ pint of white wine, the rind and juice of 1 large lemon, sugar to taste, the yolks of 6 eggs. *Mode.*—Put the isinglass, water, and lemon-rind into a saucepan, and boil gently until the former is dissolved; then add the strained lemon-juice, the wine, and sufficient white sugar to sweeten the whole nicely. Boil for 2 or 3 minutes, strain the mixture into a jug, and add the yolks of the eggs, which should be well beaten; place the jug in a saucepan of boiling water; keep stirring the mixture one way until it thickens, *but do not allow it to boil*; then take it off the fire, and keep stirring until nearly cold. Pour it into a mould, omitting the sediment at the bottom of the jug, and let it remain until quite firm. *Time.*—½ hour to boil the isinglass and water; about 10 minutes to stir the mixture in the jug. *Average cost*, with the best isinglass, 2s. 9d. *Sufficient* to fill a quart mould. *Seasonable* at any time.

JELLIES

Are not the nourishing food they were at one time considered to be, and many eminent physicians are of opinion that they are less digestible than the flesh, or muscular part of animals; still, when acidulated with lemon-juice and flavoured with wine, they are very suitable for some convalescents. Vegetable jelly is a distinct principle, existing in fruits, which possesses the property of gelatinizing when boiled and cooled; but it is a principle entirely different from the gelatine of animal bodies, although the name of jelly, common to both, sometimes leads to an erroneous idea on that subject. Animal jelly, or gelatine, is glue, whereas vegetable jelly is rather analogous to gum. Liebig places gelatine very low indeed in the scale of usefulness. He says, "Gelatine, which by itself is tasteless, and when eaten, excites nausea, possesses no nutritive value; that, even when accompanied by the savoury constituents of flesh, it is not capable of supporting the vital process, and when added to the usual diet as a substitute for plastic matter, does not increase, but on the contrary, diminishes the nutritive value of the food, which it renders insufficient in quantity and inferior in quality." It is this substance which is most frequently employed in the manufacture of the jellies supplied by the confectioner; but those prepared at home from calves' feet do possess some nutrition, and are the only sort that should be given to invalids. Isinglass is the purest variety of gelatine, and is prepared from the sounds or swimming-bladders of certain fish, chiefly the sturgeon. From its whiteness it is mostly used for making blancmange and similar dishes.

JELLIES, Bottled, How to Mould.

Uncork the bottle; place it in a saucepan of hot water until the jelly is reduced to a liquid state; taste it, to ascertain whether it is sufficiently flavoured, and if not, add a little wine. Pour the jelly into moulds which have been soaked in water; let it set, and turn it out by placing the mould in hot water for a minute; then wipe the outside, put a dish on the top, and turn it over quickly. The jelly should then slip easily away from the mould, and be quite firm. It may be garnished as taste dictates.

JELLY, Isinglass, or Gelatine. (Substitutes for Calf's Feet.)

Ingredients.—3 oz. of isinglass or gelatine, 2 quarts of water. *Mode.*—Put the isinglass or gelatine into a saucepan with the above proportion of cold water; bring it quickly to boil, and let it boil very fast, until the liquor is reduced one-half. Carefully remove the scum as it rises, then strain it through a jelly-bag, and it will be ready for use. If not required very clear, it may be merely strained through a fine sieve, instead of being run through a bag. Rather more than ½ oz. of isinglass is about the proper quantity to use for a quart of strong calf's-feet stock, and rather more than 2 oz. for the same quantity of fruit juice. As isinglass varies so much in quality and strength, it is difficult to give the exact proportions. The larger the mould, the stiffer should be the jelly; and where there is no ice, more isinglass must be used than if the mixture were frozen. This forms a stock for all kinds of jellies, which may be flavoured in many ways. *Time.*—1½ hour. *Sufficient*, with wine, syrup, fruit, &c., to fill two moderate-sized moulds. *Seasonable* at any time.

Note.—The above, when boiled, should be perfectly clear, and may be mixed warm with wine, flavourings, fruits, &c., and then run through the bag.

JELLY-BAG, How to make a.

The very stout flannel called double-mill, used for ironing-blankets, is the best material for a jelly-bag: those of home manufacture are the only ones to be relied on for thoroughly clearing the jelly. Care should be taken that the seam of the bag be stitched twice, to secure it against unequal filtration. The most convenient mode of using the bag

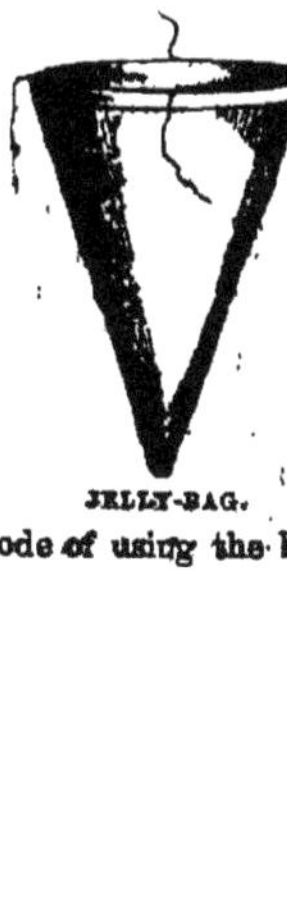

JELLY-BAG.

is to tie it upon a hoop the exact size of the outside of its mouth; and, to do this, strings should be sewn round it at equal distances. The jelly-bag may, of course, be made any size; but one of twelve or fourteen inches deep, and seven or eight across the mouth, will be sufficient for ordinary use. The form of a jelly-bag is the fool's-cap.

JELLY Moulded with fresh Fruit, or Macedoine de Fruits.

Ingredients.—Rather more than 1½ pint of jelly, a few nice strawberries, or red or white currants, or raspberries, or any fresh fruit that may be in season. *Mode.*—Have ready the above proportion of jelly, which must be very clear and rather sweet, the raw fruit requiring an additional quantity of sugar. Select ripe, nice-looking fruit; pick off the stalks, unless currants are used, when they are laid in the jelly as they come from the tree. Begin by putting a little jelly at the bottom of the mould, which must harden; then arrange the fruit

JELLY MOULDED WITH CHERRIES.

round the sides of the mould, recollecting that *it will be reversed when turned out;* then pour in some more jelly to make the fruit adhere, and, when that layer is set, put another row of fruit and jelly until the mould is full. If convenient, put it in ice until required for table, then wring a cloth in boiling water, wrap it round the mould for a minute, and turn the jelly carefully out. Peaches, apricots, plums, apples, &c., are better for being boiled in a little clear syrup before they are laid in the jelly; strawberries, raspberries, grapes, cherries, and currants are put in raw. In winter, when fresh fruits are not obtainable, a very pretty jelly may be made with preserved fruits or brandy cherries: these, in a bright and clear jelly, have a very pretty effect; of course, unless the jelly be *very clear*, the beauty of the dish will be spoiled. It may be garnished with the same fruit as is laid in the jelly; for instance, an open jelly with strawberries might have, piled in the centre, a few of the same fruit prettily arranged, or a little whipped cream might be substituted for the fruit. *Time.*—One layer of jelly should remain 2 hours in a very cool place, before another layer is added. *Average cost,* 2s. 6d. *Sufficient,* with fruit, to fill a quart mould. *Seasonable,* with fresh fruit, from June to October; with dried, at any time.

JELLY, ORANGE, Moulded with slices of Orange.

Ingredients.—1½ pint of orange jelly, 4 oranges, ½ pint of clarified syrup. *Mode.*—Boil ½ lb. of loaf sugar with ½ pint of water until there is no scum left (which must be carefully removed as fast as it rises), and carefully peel the oranges; divide them into thin slices, without breaking the thin skin, and put these pieces of orange into the syrup, where let them remain for about 5 minutes; then take them out, and use the syrup for the jelly. When the oranges are well drained, and the jelly is nearly cold, pour a little of the latter into the bottom of the mould; then lay in a few pieces of orange; over these pour a little jelly, and when this is set, place another layer of oranges, proceeding in this manner until the mould is full. Put it in ice, or in a cool place, and, before turning it out, wrap a cloth round the mould for a minute or two, which has been wrung out in boiling water. *Time.*—5 minutes to simmer the oranges. *Average cost,* 3s. 6d. *Sufficient,* with the slices of orange, to fill a quart mould. *Seasonable* from November to May.

JELLY of Two Colours.

Ingredients.—1½ pint of calf's-feet jelly, a few drops of prepared cochineal. *Mode.*—Make 1½ pint of calf's-feet jelly, or, if wished more economical, of clarified syrup and gelatine, flavouring it in

JELLY OF TWO COLOURS.

any way that may be preferred. Colour one-half of the jelly with a few drops of prepared cochineal, and the other half leave as pale as possible. Have ready a mould well wetted in every part; pour in a small quantity of the red jelly, and let this set; when quite firm, pour on it the same quantity of the pale jelly, and let this set; then proceed in this manner until the mould is full, always taking care to let one jelly set before the other is poured in, or the colours would run one into the other. When turned out, the jelly should have a striped appearance. For variety, half the mould may be filled at once with one of the jellies, and, when firm, filled up with the other: this, also, has a very pretty effect, and is more expeditiously prepared than when the jelly is poured in small quantities into the mould. Blancmange and red jelly, or blancmange and raspberry cream, moulded in the above manner, look very well. The layers of blancmange and jelly should be about an inch in depth, and each layer should be perfectly hardened before another is added. Half a mould of blancmange and half a mould of jelly are frequently served in the same manner. A few pretty dishes may be made, in this way, of jellies or blancmanges left from the preceding day, by melting them separately in a jug placed in a saucepan of boiling water, and then moulding them by the foregoing directions. *Time.*—¾ hour to make the jelly. *Average cost*, with calf's-feet jelly, 2*s.*; with gelatine and syrup, more economical. *Sufficient* to fill 1½-pint mould. *Seasonable* at any time.

Note.—In making the jelly, use for flavouring a very pale sherry, or the colour will be too dark to contrast nicely with the red jelly.

JELLY, Open, with whipped Cream (a very pretty dish).

Ingredients.—1½ pint of jelly, ½ pint of cream, 1 glass of sherry, sugar to taste. *Mode.*—Make the above proportion of calf's-feet or isinglass jelly, colouring and flavouring it in any way that may be preferred; soak a mould, open in the centre, for about ½ hour in cold water; fill it with the jelly, and let it remain in a cool place until perfectly set; then turn it out on a dish; fill the centre with whipped cream, flavoured with sherry and sweetened with pounded sugar; pile this cream high in the centre, and serve. The jelly should be made of rather a dark colour, to contrast nicely with the cream. *Time.*—¾ hour.

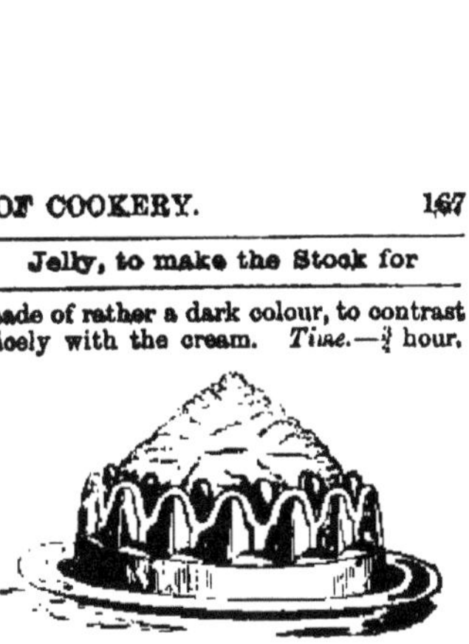

OPEN JELLY WITH WHIPPED CREAM.

Average cost, 3*s.* 6*d.* *Sufficient* to fill 1½-pint mould. *Seasonable* at any time.

JELLY, Savoury, for Meat Pies.

Ingredients.—3 lbs. of shin of beef, 1 calf's-foot, 3 lbs. of knuckle of veal, poultry trimmings (if for game pies, any game trimmings), 2 onions stuck with cloves, 2 carrots, 4 shalots, a bunch of savoury herbs, 2 bay-leaves; when liked, 2 blades of mace and a little spice; 2 slices of lean ham; rather more than 2 quarts of water. *Mode.*—Cut up the meat and put it into a stewpan with all the ingredients except the water; set it over a slow fire to draw down, and, when the gravy ceases to flow from the meat, pour in the water. Let it boil up, then carefully take away all scum from the top. Cover the stewpan closely, and let the stock simmer very gently for 4 hours: if rapidly boiled, the jelly will not be clear. When done, strain it through a fine sieve or flannel bag; and when cold, the jelly should be quite transparent. If this is not the case, clarify it with the whites of eggs. *Time.*—4 hours. *Average cost*, for this quantity, 5*s.*

JELLY, to make the Stock for, and to Clarify it.

Ingredients.—2 calf's feet, 6 pints of water. *Mode.*—The stock for jellies should always be made the day before it is required for use, as the liquor has time to cool, and the fat can be so much more easily and effectually removed when thoroughly set. Procure 2 nice calf's feet; scald them, to take off the hair; slit them in two, remove the fat from between the claws, and wash the feet well in warm water; put them into a stewpan, with the above proportion of cold water, bring it gradually to boil, and remove every particle of scum as it rises. When it is well skimmed, boil it very gently for 6 or 7 hours, or until the liquor is reduced rather more than half;

JELLY-MOULD.

then strain it through a sieve into a basin, and put it in a cool place to set. As the liquor is strained, measure it, to ascertain the proportion for the jelly, allowing something for the sediment and fat at the top. To clarify it, carefully remove all the fat from the top, pour over a little warm water, to wash away any that may remain, and wipe the jelly with a clean cloth; remove the jelly from the sediment, put it into a saucepan, and, supposing the quantity to be a quart, add to it 6 oz. of loaf sugar, the shells and well-whisked whites of 5 eggs, and stir these ingredients together cold; set the saucepan on the fire, but *do not stir the jelly after it begins to warm.* Let it boil about 10 minutes after it rises to a head, then throw in a teacupful of cold water; let it boil 5 minutes longer, then take the saucepan off, cover it closely, and let it remain ½ hour near the fire. Dip the jelly-bag into hot water, wring it out quite dry, and fasten it on to a stand or the back of a chair, which must be placed near the fire, to prevent the jelly from setting before it has run through the bag. Place a basin underneath to receive the jelly; then pour it into the bag, and should it not be clear the first time, run it through the bag again. This stock is the foundation of all *really good* jellies, which may be varied in innumerable ways, by colouring and flavouring with liqueurs, and by moulding it with fresh and preserved fruits. To insure the jelly being firm when turned out, ½ oz. of isinglass clarified might be added to the above proportion of stock. Substitutes for calf's feet are now frequently used in making jellies, which lessen the expense and trouble in preparing this favourite dish, isinglass and gelatine being two of the principal materials employed; but although they may *look* as nicely as jellies made from good stock, they are never so delicate, having very often an unpleasant flavour, somewhat resembling glue, particularly when made with gelatine. *Time.*—About 6 hours to boil the feet for the stock; to clarify it,—¼ hour to boil, ½ hour to stand in the saucepan covered. *Average cost.*—Calf's feet may be purchased for 6*d.* each when veal is in full season, but more expensive when it is scarce. *Sufficient.*—2 calf's feet should make 1 quart of stock. *Seasonable* from March to October, but may be had all the year.

JOHN DORY.

Ingredients.—¼ lb. of salt to each gallon of water. *Mode.*—This fish, which is esteemed by most people a great delicacy, is dressed in the same way as a turbot, which it resembles in firmness, but not in richness. Cleanse it thoroughly and cut off the fins; lay it in a fish-kettle, cover with cold water, and add salt in the above proportion. Bring it gradually to a boil, and simmer gently for ¼ hour, or rather longer, should the fish be very large. Serve on a hot napkin, and garnish with cut lemon and parsley. Lobster, anchovy, or shrimp sauce, and plain melted butter, should be sent to table with it. *Time.*—After the water boils, ¼ to ½ hour, according to size. *Average cost,* 3*s.* to 5*s.* *Seasonable* all the year, but best from September to January.

Note.—Small John Dory are very good baked.

JUNE—BILLS OF FARE.

Dinner for 18 persons.

First Course.

Fillets of Gurnets.	Asparagus Soup, removed by Crimped Salmon. Vase of Flowers. Vermicelli Soup, removed by Whitebait.	Soles aux fines herbes.

June—Bills of Fare.

Entrées.

Lamb Cutlets and Peas.

Lobster Patties. — Vase of Flowers. — Tendrons de Veau à la Jardinière.

Larded Sweetbreads.

Second Course.

Saddle of Lamb.

Tongue.

Roast Spring Chickens. — Vase of Flowers. — Boiled Capons.

Ham.

Boiled Calf's Head.

Third Course.

Leveret, removed by Iced Pudding.

Wine Jelly.

Prawns. — Vol-au-Vent of Strawberries and Cream. — Vase of Flowers. — Custards, in glasses. — Tartlets.

Blancmange.

Cheesecakes. — Goslings, removed by Fondues, in cases. — Plovers' Eggs.

Dessert and Ices.

Dinner for 12 persons.

First Course.—Green-pea soup; rice soup; salmon and lobster sauce; trout à la Genévése; whitebait. *Entrées.*—Lamb cutlets and cucumbers; fricasseed chicken; stewed veal and peas; lobster rissoles. *Second Course.*—Roast quarter of lamb and spinach; filet de bœuf à la Jardinière; boiled fowls; braised shoulder of lamb; tongue; vegetables. *Third Course.*—Goslings; ducklings; Nesselrode pudding; Charlotte à la Parisienne; gooseberry tartlets; strawberry cream; raspberry-and-currant tart; custards; dessert and ices.

Dinner for 10 persons.

First Course.—Julienne soup; salmon trout and parsley-and-butter; red mullet. *Entrées.*—Stewed breast of veal and peas; mutton cutlets à la Maintenon. *Second Course.*—Roast fillet of veal; boiled leg of lamb, garnished with young carrots; boiled bacon-cheek; vegetables. *Third Course.*—Roast ducks; leveret; gooseberry tart; strawberry cream; strawberry tartlets; meringues; cabinet pudding; iced pudding; dessert and ices.

Dinner for 8 persons.

First Course.—Vermicelli soup; trout à la Genévése; salmon cutlets. *Entrées.*—Lamb cutlets and peas; fricasseed chicken. *Second Course.*—Roast ribs of beef; half calf's head, tongue, and brains; boiled ham; vegetables. *Third Course.*—Roast ducks; compôte of gooseberries; strawberry jelly; pastry; iced pudding; cauliflower with cream sauce; dessert and ices.

Dinner for 6 persons.

First Course.—Spring soup; boiled salmon and lobster sauce. *Entrées.*—Veal cutlets and endive; ragoût of duck and green peas. *Second Course.*—Roast loin of veal; boiled leg of lamb and white sauce; tongue, garnished; vegetables. *Third Course.*—Strawberry cream; gooseberry tartlets; almond pudding; lobster salad; dessert.

First Course.—Calf's head soup; mackerel à la maître d'hôtel; whitebait. *Entrées.*—Chicken cutlets; curried lobster. *Second Course.*—Fore-quarter of lamb and salad; stewed beef à la Jardinière; vegetables. *Third Course.*—Goslings; green-currant tart; custards, in glasses; strawberry blancmange; soufflé of rice; dessert.

First Course.—Green-pea soup; baked soles aux fines herbes; stewed trout. *Entrées.*—Calf's liver and bacon; rissoles. *Second Course.*—Roast saddle of lamb and salad; calf's head à la tortue; vegetables. *Third Course.*—Roast ducks; vol-au-vent of strawberries and cream;

strawberry tartlets; lemon blancmange; baked gooseberry pudding; dessert.

First Course.—Spinach soup; soles à la crême; red mullet. *Entrées.*—Roast fillet of veal; braised ham and spinach. *Second Course.*—Boiled fowls and white sauce; vegetables. *Third Course.*—Leveret; strawberry jelly; Swiss cream; cheesecakes; iced pudding; dessert.

JUNE, Plain Family Dinners for.

Sunday.—1. Salmon trout and parsley-and-butter, new potatoes. 2. Roast fillet of veal, boiled bacon-cheek and spinach, vegetables. 3. Gooseberry tart, custard.

Monday.—1. Light gravy soup. 2. Small meat pie, minced veal, garnished with rolled bacon, spinach, and potatoes. 3. Raspberry-and-currant tart.

Tuesday.—1. Baked mackerel, potatoes. 2. Boiled leg of lamb, garnished with young carrots. 3. Lemon pudding.

Wednesday.—1. Vegetable soup. 2. Calf's liver and bacon, peas, hashed lamb from remains of cold joint. 3. Baked gooseberry pudding.

Thursday.—1. Roast ribs of beef, Yorkshire pudding, peas, potatoes. 2. Stewed rhubarb and boiled rice.

Friday.—1. Cold beef and salad, lamb cutlets and peas. 2. Boiled gooseberry pudding and baked custard pudding.

Saturday.—1. Rump-steak pudding, broiled beef-bones and cucumber, vegetables. 2. Bread pudding.

Sunday.—1. Roast fore-quarter of lamb, mint sauce, peas, and new potatoes. 2. Gooseberry pudding, strawberry tartlets. Fondue.

Monday.—1. Cold lamb and salad, stewed neck of veal and peas, young carrots, and new potatoes. 2. Almond pudding.

Tuesday.—1. Green-pea soup. 2. Roast ducks stuffed, gravy, peas, and new potatoes. 3. Baked ratafia pudding.

Wednesday.—1. Roast leg of mutton, summer cabbage, potatoes. 2. Gooseberry and rice pudding.

Thursday.—1. Fried soles, melted butter, potatoes. 2. Sweetbreads, hashed mutton, vegetables. 3. Bread-and-butter pudding.

Friday.—1. Asparagus soup. 2. Boiled beef, young carrots, and new potatoes, suet dumplings. 3. College puddings.

Saturday.—1. Cold boiled beef and salad, lamb cutlets, and green peas. 2. Boiled gooseberry pudding and plain cream.

JUNE, Things in Season.

Fish.—Carp, crayfish, herrings, lobsters, mackerel, mullet, pike, prawns, salmon, soles, tench, trout, turbot.

Meat.—Beef, lamb, mutton, veal, buck venison.

Poultry.—Chickens, ducklings, fowls, green geese, leverets, plovers, pullets, rabbits, turkey poults, wheatears.

Vegetables.—Artichokes, asparagus, beans, cabbages, carrots, cucumbers, lettuces, onions, parsnips, peas, potatoes, radishes, small salads, sea-kale, spinach,—various herbs.

Fruit.—Apricots, cherries, currants, gooseberries, melons, nectarines, peaches, pears, pineapples, raspberries, rhubarb, strawberries.

JULY—BILLS OF FARE.

Dinner for 18 persons.

First Course.

Green-Pea Soup, removed by Salmon and dressed Cucumber.

Whitebait. | Vase of Flowers. | Stewed Trout.

Soup à la Reine, removed by Mackerel à la Maître d'Hotel.

Entrées.

Lamb Cutlets and Peas.

Lobster Curry en Casserole. | Vase of Flowers. | Scollops of Chickens.

Chicken Patties.

Second Course.

	Haunch of Venison.	
	Pigeon Pie.	
Boiled Capons.	Vase of Flowers.	Spring Chickens.
	Braised Ham.	
	Saddle of Lamb.	

Third Course.

Prawns.		Roast Ducks, removed by Vanilla Soufflé.		Custards.
	Cherry Tart.	Raspberry Cream.	Raspberry-and-Currant Tart.	
		Vase of Flowers.		
		Strawberry Cream.		
Creams.		Green Goose, removed by Iced Pudding.		Tartlets.

Dessert and Ices.

Dinner for 12 persons.

First Course.—Soup à la Jardinière; chicken soup; crimped salmon and parsley-and-butter; trout aux fines herbes. in cases. *Entrées.*—Tendrons de veau and peas; lamb cutlets and cucumbers. *Second Course.*—Loin of veal à la Béchamel; roast fore-quarter of lamb; salad; braised ham, garnished with broad beans; vegetables. *Third Course.*—Roast ducks; turkey poult; stewed peas à la Francaise; lobster salad; cherry tart; raspberry-and-currant tart; custards, in glasses; lemon creams; Nesselrode pudding; marrow pudding. Dessert and ices.

Dinner for 8 persons.

First Course.—Green-pea soup; salmon and lobster sauce; crimped perch and Dutch sauce. *Entrées.*—Stewed veal and peas; lamb cutlets and cucumbers. *Second Course.*—Haunch of venison; boiled fowls à la Béchamel; braised

ham; vegetables. *Third Course.*—Roast ducks; peas à la Francaise; lobster salad; strawberry cream; blancmange; cherry tart; cheesecakes; iced pudding. Dessert and ices.

Dinner for 6 persons.

First Course.—Soup à la Jardinière; salmon trout and parsley-and-butter; fillets of mackerel à la maître d'hôtel. *Entrées.*—Lobster cutlets; beef palates, à la Italienne. *Second Course.*—Roast lamb; boiled capon and white sauce; boiled tongue, garnished with small vegetable marrows; bacon and beans. *Third Course.*—Goslings; whipped strawberry cream; raspberry-and-currant tart; meringues; cherry tartlets; iced pudding. Dessert and ices.

First Course.—Julienne soup; crimped salmon and caper sauce; whitebait. *Entrées.*—Croquettes à la Reine; curried lobster. *Second Course.*—Roast lamb; rump of beef à la Jardinière. *Third Course.*—Larded turkey poult; raspberry cream; cherry tart; custards, in glasses; Gâteaux à la Genévése; Nesselrode pudding. Dessert.

JULY, Plain Family Dinners for.

Sunday.—1. Salmon trout and parsley-and-butter. 2. Roast fillet of veal, boiled bacon-cheek, peas, potatoes. 3. Raspberry-and-currant tart, baked custard pudding.

Monday.—1. Green-pea soup. 2. Roast fowls garnished with watercresses; gravy, bread sauce; cold veal and salad. 3. Cherry tart.

Tuesday.—1. John dory and lobster sauce. 2. Curried fowl with remains of cold fowls, dish of rice, veal rolls with remains of cold fillet. 3. Strawberry cream.

Wednesday.—1. Roast leg of mutton, vegetable marrow and potatoes, melted butter. 2. Black-currant pudding.

Thursday.—1. Fried soles, anchovy sauce. 2. Mutton cutlets and tomato sauce, hashed mutton, peas, potatoes. 3. Lemon dumplings.

Friday.—1. Boiled brisket of beef, carrots, turnips, suet dumplings, peas, potatoes. 2. Baked semolina pudding.

Saturday.—1. Cold beef and salad, lamb cutlets and peas. 2. Rolled jam pudding.

Sunday.—1. Julienne soup. 2. Roast lamb, half calf's head, tongue and brains, boiled ham, peas and potatoes. 3. Cherry tart, custards.

Monday.—1. Hashed calf's head, cold lamb and salad. 2. Vegetable marrow and white sauce, instead of pudding.

Tuesday.—1. Stewed veal, with peas, young carrots, and potatoes. Small meat pie. 2. Raspberry-and-currant pudding.

Wednesday.—1. Roast ducks stuffed, gravy, peas, and potatoes; the remains of stewed veal rechauffé. 2. Macaroni served as a sweet pudding.

Thursday.—1. Slices of salmon and caper sauce. 2. Boiled knuckle of veal, parsley-and-butter, vegetable marrow and potatoes. 3. Black-currant pudding.

Friday.—1. Roast shoulder of mutton, onion sauce, peas and potatoes. 2. Cherry tart, baked custard pudding.

Saturday.—1. Minced mutton, rump-steak-and-kidney pudding. 2. Baked lemon pudding.

JULY, Things in Season.

Fish.—Carp, crayfish, dory, flounders, haddocks, herrings, lobsters, mackerel, mullet, pike, plaice, prawns, salmon, shrimps, soles, sturgeon, tench, thornback.

Meat.—Beef, lamb, mutton, veal, buck venison.

Poultry.—Chickens, ducklings, fowls, green geese, leverets, plovers, pullets, rabbits, turkey poults, wheatears, wild ducks (called flappers).

Vegetables. — Artichokes, asparagus, beans, cabbages, carrots, cauliflowers, celery, cresses, endive, lettuces, mushrooms, onions, peas, radishes, small salading, sea-kale, sprouts, turnips, vegetable marrow,—various herbs.

Fruit.—Apricots, cherries, currants, figs, gooseberries, melons, nectarines, pears, pineapples, plums, raspberries, strawberries, walnuts in high season, for pickling.

JULIENNE, Soup à la.

Ingredients.—½ pint of carrots, ½ pint of turnips, ½ pint of onions, 2 or 3 leeks, ½ head of celery, 1 lettuce, a little sorrel and chervil, if liked, 2 oz. of butter, 2 quarts of stock. *Mode.*—Cut the vegetables into strips of about 1¼ inch long, and be particular they are all the same size, or some will be hard whilst the others will be done to a pulp. Cut the lettuce, sorrel, and chervil into larger pieces; fry the carrots in the butter, and pour the stock boiling to them. When this is done, add all the other vegetables and herbs, and stew gently for at least an hour. Skim off all the fat, pour the soup over thin slices of bread, cut round about the size of a shilling, and serve. *Time.* — 1½ hour. *Average cost.*—1*s.* 3*d.* per quart. *Seasonable* all the year. *Sufficient* for 8 persons.

STRIPS OF VEGETABLE.

Note.—In summer, green peas, asparagus-tops, French beans, &c., can be added. When the vegetables are very strong, instead of frying them in butter at first, they should be blanched, and afterwards simmered in the stock.

KALE BROSE (a Scotch Recipe).

Ingredients.—Half an ox-head or cow-heel, a teacupful of toasted oatmeal, salt to taste, 2 handfuls of greens, 3 quarts of water. *Mode.*—Make a broth of the ox-head or cow-heel, and boil it till oil floats on the top of the liquor, then boil the greens, shred, in it. Put the oatmeal, with a little salt, into a basin, and mix with it quickly a teacupful of the fat broth: it should not run into one doughy mass, but form knots. Stir it into the whole, give one boil, and serve very hot. *Time.*—4 hours. *Average cost,* 8*d.* per quart. *Seasonable* all the year, but more suitable in winter. *Sufficient* for 10 persons.

KEGEREE.

Ingredients.—Any cold fish, 1 teacupful of boiled rice, 1 oz. of butter, 1 teaspoonful of mustard, 2 soft-boiled eggs, salt and cayenne to taste. *Mode.*—Pick the fish carefully from the bones, mix with the other ingredients, and serve very hot. The quantities may be varied according to the amount of fish used. *Time.*—¼ hour after the rice is boiled. *Average cost,* 5*d.* exclusive of the fish.

KIDNEYS, Broiled (a Breakfast or Supper Dish).

Ingredients.—Sheep kidneys, pepper and salt to taste. *Mode.*—Ascertain that the kidneys are fresh, and cut them open, very evenly, lengthwise, down to the root; for should one half be thicker than the other, one would be underdone

KIDNEYS.

whilst the other would be dried, but do not separate them; skin them, and pass a skewer under the white part of each half to keep them flat, and broil over a nice clear fire, placing the inside downwards; turn them when done enough on one side, and cook them on the other. Remove the skewers, place the kidneys on a very hot dish, season with pepper and salt, and put a tiny piece of butter in the middle of each; serve very hot and quickly, and send very hot plates to table. *Time.*—6 to 8 minutes. *Average cost*, 1½d. each. *Sufficient.*—Allow 1 for each person. *Seasonable* at any time.

Note.—A prettier dish than the above may be made by serving the kidneys each on a piece of buttered toast cut in any fanciful shape. In this case a little lemon-juice will be found an improvement.

KIDNEYS, Fried.

Ingredients.—Kidneys, butter, pepper, and salt to taste. *Mode.*—Cut the kidneys open without quite dividing them, remove the skin, and put a small piece of butter in the frying-pan. When the butter is melted, lay in the kidneys the flat side downwards, and fry them for 7 or 8 minutes, turning them when they are half done. Serve on a piece of dry toast, season with pepper and salt, and put a small piece of butter in each kidney; pour the gravy from the pan over them, and serve very hot. *Time.*—7 or 8 minutes. *Average cost*, 1½d. each. *Sufficient.*—Allow 1 kidney to each person. *Seasonable* at any time.

KIDNEY OMELET (a favourite French Dish).

Ingredients.—6 eggs, 1 saltspoonful of salt, ½ saltspoonful of pepper, 2 sheep's kidneys, or 2 tablespoonfuls of minced veal kidney, 5 oz. of butter. *Mode.*—Skin the kidneys, cut them into small dice, and toss them in a frying-pan, in 1 oz. of butter, over the fire for 2 or 3 minutes. Mix the ingredients for the omelet, and when the eggs are well whisked, stir in the pieces of kidney. Make the butter hot in the frying-pan,

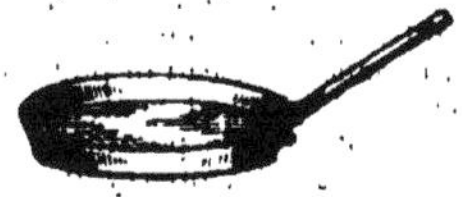

OMELET PAN.

and when it bubbles, pour in the omelet, and fry it over a gentle fire from 4 to 6 minutes. When the eggs are set, fold the edges over, so that the omelet assumes an oval form, and be careful that it is not too much done: to brown the top, hold the pan before the fire for a minute or two, or use a salamander until the desired colour is obtained, but never turn an omelet in the pan. Slip it carefully on to a *very hot* dish, or, what is a much safer method, put a dish on the omelet, and turn the pan quickly over. It should be served the instant it comes from the fire. *Time.*—4 to 6 minutes. *Average cost*, 1s. *Sufficient* for 4 persons. *Seasonable* at any time.

KIDNEYS, Stewed.

Ingredients.—About 8 kidneys, a large dessertspoonful of chopped herbs, 2 oz. butter, 1 dessertspoonful of flour, a little gravy, juice of half a lemon, a teaspoonful of Harvey sauce and mushroom ketchup, cayenne, and salt to taste. *Mode.*—Strew the herbs, with cayenne and salt, over the kidneys, melt the butter in the frying-pan, put in the kidneys, and brown them nicely all round; when nearly done, stir in the flour, and shake them well; now add the gravy and sauce, and stew them for a few minutes, then turn them out into a dish garnished with fried sippets. *Time.*—10 or 12 minutes. *Seasonable* at any time.

LAMB.

The most delicious sorts of lamb are those of the South-Down breed, known by their black feet; and of these, those which have been exclusively suckled on the milk of the parent ewe, are considered the finest. Next to these in estimation are those fed on the milk of several dams; and last of all, though the fattest, the grass-fed lamb: this, however, implies an age much greater than either of the others.

LAMB, in the early part of the season, however reared, is in London, and indeed generally, sold in quarters, divided with eleven ribs to the fore-quarter; but, as the season advances, these are subdivided into two, and the hind-quarter in the same manner; the first consisting of the shoulder, and the neck and breast; the latter, of the leg and the loin.—As lamb, from the juicy nature of its flesh, is especially liable to spoil in unfavourable weather, it should be frequently wiped, so as to remove any moisture that may form on it.

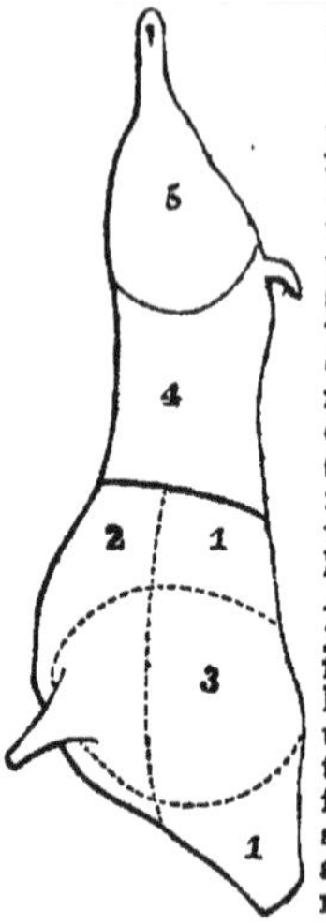

SIDE OF LAMB.

IN THE PURCHASING OF LAMB FOR THE TABLE, there are certain signs by which the experienced judgment is able to form an accurate opinion whether the animal has been lately slaughtered, and whether the joints possess that condition of fibre indicative of good and wholesome meat. The first of these doubts may be solved satisfactorily by the bright and dilated appearance of the eye; the quality of the fore-quarter can always be guaranteed by the blue or healthy ruddiness of the jugular, or vein of the neck; while the rigidity of the knuckle, and the firm, compact feel of the kidney, will answer in an equally positive manner for the integrity of the hind-quarter.

MODE OF CUTTING UP A SIDE OF LAMB IN LONDON.—1. Ribs; 2. Breast; 3. Shoulder; 4. Loin; 5. Leg; 1, 2, 3. Fore Quarter.

LAMB, Breast of, and Green Peas.

Ingredients.—1 breast of lamb, a few slices of bacon, ½ pint of stock, 1 lemon, 1 onion, 1 bunch of savoury herbs, green-

peas. *Mode.*—Remove the skin from a breast of lamb, put it into a saucepan of boiling water, and let it simmer for 5 minutes. Take it out and lay it in cold water. Line the bottom of a stewpan with a few thin slices of bacon; lay the lamb on these; peel the lemon, cut it into slices, and put these on the meat, to keep it white and make it tender; cover with 1 or 2 more slices of bacon; add the stock, onion, and herbs, and set it on a slow fire to simmer very gently until tender. Have ready some green peas, put these on a dish, and place the lamb on the top of them. The appearance of this dish may be much improved by glazing the lamb, and spinach may be substituted for the peas when variety is desired. *Time.*—1½ hour. *Average cost,* 10*d.* per lb. *Sufficient* for 3 persons. *Seasonable.*—Grass lamb, from Easter to Michaelmas.

LAMB, Stewed Breast of.

Ingredients.—1 breast of lamb, pepper and salt to taste, sufficient stock to cover it, 1 glass of sherry, thickening of butter and flour. *Mode.*—Skin the lamb, cut it into pieces, and season them with pepper and salt; lay these in a stewpan, pour in sufficient stock or gravy to cover them, and stew very gently until tender, which will be in about 1½ hour. Just before serving, thicken the sauce with a little butter and flour; add the sherry, give one boil, and pour it over the meat. Green peas, or stewed mushrooms, may be strewed over the meat, and will be found a very great improvement. *Time.*—1½ hour. *Average cost,* 10*d.* per lb. *Sufficient* for 3 persons. *Seasonable.*—Grass lamb, from Easter to Michaelmas.

LAMB, TO CARVE.—Leg, loin, saddle, shoulder, are carved as mutton.

LAMB, Fore-quarter of, to Carve.

We always think that a good and practised carver delights in the manipulation of this joint, for there is a little field for his judgment and dexterity which does not always occur. The separation of the shoulder from the breast is the first point to be attended to; this is done by passing the knife round the dotted line, as shown by the figures 1, 2, 3, 4, and 5, so as to cut through the skin, and then, by raising with a little force the shoulder, into which the fork should be firmly fixed, it will come away with just a little more exercise of the knife. In dividing the shoulder and breast, the carver should take care not to cut away too much of the meat from the latter, as

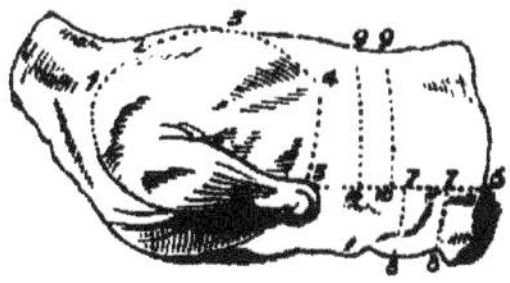

FORE-QUARTER OF LAMB.

that would rather spoil its appearance when the shoulder is removed. The breast and shoulder being separated, it is usual to lay a small piece of butter, and sprinkle a little cayenne, lemon-juice, and salt between them; and when this is melted and incorporated with the meat and gravy, the shoulder may, as more convenient, be removed into another dish. The next operation is to separate the ribs from the brisket, by cutting through the meat on the line 5 to 6. The joint is then ready to be served to the guests; the ribs being carved in the direction of the lines from 9 to 10, and the brisket from 7 to 8. The carver should ask those at the table what parts they prefer—ribs, brisket, or a piece of the shoulder.

LAMB CUTLETS.

Ingredients.—Loin of lamb, pepper and salt to taste. *Mode.*—Trim off the flap from a fine loin of lamb, and cut it into cutlets about ¾ inch in thickness. Have ready a bright clear fire; lay the cutlets on a gridiron, and broil them of a nice pale brown, turning them when required. Season them with pepper and salt; serve very hot and quickly, and garnish with crisped parsley, or place them on mashed potatoes. Asparagus, spinach, or peas are the favourite accompaniments to lamb chops. *Time.*—About 8 or 10 minutes. *Average cost*, 1*s.* per lb. *Sufficient.*—Allow 2 cutlets to each person. *Seasonable* from Easter to Michaelmas.

LAMB, Cutlets and Spinach (an Entrée).

Ingredients.—8 cutlets, egg and bread crumbs, salt and pepper to taste, a little clarified butter. *Mode.*—Cut the cutlets from a neck of lamb, and shape them by cutting off the thick part of the chine-bone. Trim off most of the fat and all the skin, and scrape the top part of the bones quite clean. Brush the cutlets over with egg, sprinkle them with bread crumbs, and season with pepper and salt. Now dip them into clarified butter, sprinkle over a few more bread crumbs, and fry them over a sharp fire, turning them when required. Lay them before the fire to drain, and arrange them on a dish with spinach in the centre, which should be previously well boiled, drained, chopped, and seasoned. *Time.*—About 7 or 8 minutes. *Average cost*, 10*d.* per lb. *Sufficient* for 4 persons. *Seasonable* from Easter to Michaelmas.

Note.—Peas, asparagus, or French beans, may be substituted for the spinach; or lamb cutlets may be served with stewed cucumbers, Soubise sauce, &c., &c.

LAMB, Roast Fore-quarter of.

Ingredients. — Lamb, a little salt. *Mode.*—To obtain the flavour of lamb in perfection, it should not be long kept; time to cool is all that it requires; and though the meat may be somewhat thready, the juices and flavour will be infinitely superior to that of lamb that has been killed 2 or 3 days. Make up

FORE-QUARTER OF LAMB.

the fire in good time, that it may be clear and brisk when the joint is put down. Place it at a sufficient distance to prevent the fat from burning, and baste it constantly till the moment of serving. Lamb should be very *thoroughly* done without being dried up, and not the slightest appearance of red gravy should be visible, as in roast mutton: this rule is applicable to all young white meats. Serve with a little gravy made in the dripping-pan, the same as for other roasts, and send to table with it a tureen of mint sauce, and a fresh salad. A cut lemon, a small piece of fresh butter, and a little cayenne, should also be placed on the table, so that when the carver separates the shoulder from the ribs, they may be ready for his use; if, however, he should not be very expert, we would recommend that the cook should divide these joints nicely before coming to table. *Time.*—Fore-quarter of lamb weighing 10 lbs., 1¾ to 2 hours. *Average cost,* 10*d.* to 1*s.* per lb. *Sufficient* for 7 or 8 persons. *Seasonable.*—Grass lamb, from Easter to Michaelmas.

LAMB'S FRY.

Ingredients.—1 lb. of lamb's fry, 3 pints of water, egg and bread crumbs, 1 teaspoonful of chopped parsley, salt and pepper to taste. *Mode.*—Boil the fry for ¼ hour in the above proportion of water, take it out and dry it in a cloth; grate some bread down finely, mix with it a teaspoonful of chopped parsley and a high seasoning of pepper and salt. Brush the fry lightly over with the yolk of an egg, sprinkle over the bread crumbs, and fry for 5 minutes. Serve very hot on a napkin in a dish, and garnish with plenty of crisped parsley. *Time.*—¼ hour to simmer the fry, 5 minutes to fry it. *Average cost,* 10*d.* per lb. *Sufficient* for 2 or 3 persons. *Seasonable* from Easter to Michaelmas.

LAMB, Hashed, and Broiled Blade-Bone.

[COLD MEAT COOKERY.] *Ingredients.*—The remains of a cold shoulder of lamb, pepper and salt to taste, 2 oz. of butter, about ½ pint of stock or gravy, 1 tablespoonful of shalot vinegar, 3 or 4 pickled gherkins. *Mode.*—Take the blade-bone from the shoulder, and cut the meat into collops as neatly as possible. Season the bone with pepper and salt, pour a little oiled butter over it, and place it in the oven to warm through. Put the stock into a stewpan, add the ketchup and shalot vinegar, and lay in the pieces of lamb. Let these heat gradually through, but do not allow them to boil. Take the blade-bone out of the oven, and place it on a gridiron over a sharp fire to brown. Slice the gherkins, put them into the hash, and dish it with the blade-bone in the centre. It may be garnished with croûtons or sippets of toasted bread. *Time.*—Altogether ½ hour. *Average cost,* exclusive of the meat, 4*d.* *Seasonable.*—House lamb, from Christmas to March; grass lamb, from Easter to Michaelmas.

LAMB, Boiled Leg of, à la Béchamel.

Ingredients.—Leg of lamb, Béchamel sauce. *Mode.*—Do not choose a very large joint, but one weighing about 5 lbs. Have ready a saucepan of boiling water, into which plunge the lamb, and when it boils up again, draw it to the side of the fire, and let the water cool a little. Then stew very gently for about 1¼ hour, reckoning from the time that the water begins to simmer. Make some Béchamel, dish the lamb, pour the sauce over it, and garnish with tufts of boiled cauliflower or carrots. When liked, melted butter may be substituted for the Béchamel: this is a more simple method, but not nearly so nice. Send to table with it some of the sauce in a tureen, and boiled cauliflowers or spinach, with whichever vegetable the dish is garnished. *Time.*—1¼ hour after the water simmers. *Average cost,* 10*d.* to 1*s.* per lb. *Sufficient* for 4 or 5 persons. *Seasonable* from Easter to Michaelmas.

LAMB, Roast Leg of.

Ingredients.—Lamb, a little salt. *Mode.*—Place the joint at a good distance from the fire at first, and baste well the whole time it is cooking. When nearly done, draw it nearer the fire to acquire a nice brown colour. Sprinkle a little fine salt

LEG OF LAMB.

over the meat, empty the dripping-pan of its contents; pour in a little boiling water, and strain this over the meat. Serve with mint sauce and a fresh salad, and for vegetables send peas, spinach, or cauliflowers to table with it. *Time.*—A leg of lamb weighing 5 lbs., 1½ hour. *Average cost,* 10*d.* to 1*s.* a pound. *Sufficient* for 4 or 5 persons. *Seasonable* from Easter to Michaelmas.

LAMB, Braised Loin of.

Ingredients.—1 loin of lamb, a few slices of bacon, 1 bunch of green onions, 5 or 6 young carrots, a bunch of savoury herbs, 2 blades of pounded mace, 1 pint of stock, salt to taste. *Mode.*—Bone a loin of lamb, and line the bottom of a stewpan just capable of holding it, with a few thin slices of fat bacon; add the remaining ingredients, cover the meat with a few more slices of bacon,

LOIN OF LAMB.

pour in the stock, and simmer very gently for 2 hours; take it up, dry it, strain and reduce the gravy to a glaze, with which glaze the meat, and serve it either on stewed peas, spinach, or stewed cucumbers. *Time.*—2 hours. *Average cost,* 11*d.* per lb. *Sufficient* for 4 or 5 persons. *Seasonable* from Easter to Michaelmas.

LAMB, Roast Saddle of.

Ingredients. — Lamb; a little salt. *Mode.*—This joint is now very much in vogue, and is generally considered a nice

SADDLE OF LAMB.

one for a small party. Have ready a clear brisk fire; put down the joint at a little distance, to prevent the fat from scorching, and keep it well basted all

RIBS OF LAMB.

the time it is cooking. Serve with mint sauce and a fresh salad, and send to table with it either peas, cauliflowers, or spinach. *Time.*—A small saddle, 1½ hour; a large one, 2 hours. *Average cost,* 10*d.* to 1*s.* per lb. *Sufficient* for 5 or 6 persons. *Seasonable* from Easter to Michaelmas.

Note.—Loin and ribs of lamb are roasted in the same manner, and served with the same sauces as the above. A loin will take about 1¼ hour; ribs, from 1 to 1¼ hour.

LAMB, Roast Shoulder of.

Ingredients. — Lamb; a little salt. *Mode.*—Have ready a clear brisk fire, and put down the joint at a sufficient distance from it, that the fat may not burn. Keep constantly basting until done, and serve with a little gravy made in the dripping-pan, and send mint sauce to table with it. Peas, spinach, or cauliflowers are the usual vegetables served with lamb, and also a fresh salad. *Time.*—A shoulder of lamb rather more than 1 hour. *Average cost,* 10*d.* to 1*s.* per lb. *Sufficient* for 4 or 5 persons. *Seasonable* from Easter to Michaelmas.

LAMB, Shoulder of, Stuffed.

Ingredients.—Shoulder of lamb, forcemeat, trimmings of veal or beef, 2 onions, ½ head of celery, 1 faggot of savoury herbs, a few slices of fat bacon, 1 quart of stock. *Mode.*—Take the blade-bone out of a shoulder of lamb, fill up its place with forcemeat, and sew it up with coarse thread. Put it into a stewpan with a few slices of bacon under and over the lamb, and add the remaining ingredients. Stew very gently for rather more than 2 hours. Reduce the gravy, with which glaze the meat, and serve with peas, stewed cucumbers, or sorrel sauce. *Time.*—Rather more than 2 hours. *Average cost,* 10*d.* to 1*s.* per lb. *Sufficient* for 4 or 5 persons. *Seasonable* from Easter to Michaelmas.

LANDRAIL, Roast, or Corn-Crake.

Ingredients.—3 or 4 birds, butter, fried bread crumbs. *Mode.*—Pluck and draw the birds, wipe them inside and out with damp cloths, and truss them in the following manner: Bring the head round

LANDRAILS.

under the wing, and the thighs close to the sides; pass a skewer through them and the body, and keep the legs straight. Roast them before a clear fire, keep them well basted, and serve on fried bread crumbs, with a tureen of brown gravy. When liked, bread-sauce may also be sent to table with them. *Time.*—12 to 20 minutes. *Average cost.*—Seldom bought. *Sufficient.*—Allow 4 for a dish. *Seasonable* from August 12th to the middle of September.

LANDRAIL, to Carve.

Landrail, being trussed like Snipe, with the exception of its being drawn, may be carved in the same manner.

LARD, to Melt.

Melt the inner fat of the pig, by putting it in a stone jar, and placing this in a saucepan of boiling water, previously stripping off the skin. Let it simmer gently over a bright fire, and, as it melts, pour it carefully from the sediment. Put it into small jars or bladders for use, and keep it in a cool place. The flead or inside fat of the pig, before it is melted, makes exceedingly light crust, and is particularly wholesome. It may be preserved a length of time by salting it well, and occasionally changing the brine. When wanted for use, wash and wipe it, and it will answer for making into paste as well as fresh lard. *Average cost*, 10*d.* per lb.

LARDING.

Ingredients.—Bacon and larding-needle. *Mode.*—Bacon for larding should be firm and fat, and ought to be cured without any saltpetre, as this reddens white meats. Lay it on a table, the

BACON FOR LARDING, AND LARDING-NEEDLE.

rinds downwards; trim off any rusty part, and cut it into slices of an equal thickness. Place the slices one on the top of another, and cut them evenly into narrow strips, so arranging it that every piece of bacon is of the same size. Bacon for fricandeaux, poultry, and game, should be about 2 inches in length, and rather more than one-eighth of an inch in width. If for larding fillets of beef or loin of veal, the pieces of bacon must be thicker. The following recipe of Soyer is, we think, very explicit; and any cook, by following the directions here given, may be able to lard, if not well, sufficiently for general use:—

"Have the fricandeau trimmed; lay it, lengthwise, upon a clean napkin across your hand, forming a kind of bridge with your thumb at the part where you are about to commence; then with the point of the larding-needle make three distinct lines across, ½ inch apart; run the needle into the third line, at the farther side of the fricandeau, and bring it out at the first, placing one of the lardoons in it; draw the needle through, leaving out ¼ inch of the bacon at each line; proceed thus to the end of the row; then make another line, ½ inch distant, stick in another row of lardoons, bringing them out at the second line, leaving the ends of the bacon out all the same length; make the next row again at the same distance, bringing the ends out between the lardoons of the first row, proceeding in this manner until the whole surface is larded in chequered rows. Everything else is larded in a similar way; and, in the case of poultry, hold the breast over a charcoal fire for one minute, or dip it into boiling water, in order to make the flesh firm."

LARK PIE (an Entrée).

Ingredients.—A few thin slices of beef, the same of bacon, 9 larks, flour; for stuffing, 1 teacupful of bread crumbs, ½ teaspoonful of minced lemon-peel, 1 teaspoonful of minced parsley, 1 egg, salt and pepper to taste, 1 teaspoonful of chopped shalot, ½ pint of weak stock or water, puff-paste. *Mode.*—Make a stuffing of bread crumbs, minced lemon-peel, parsley, and the yolk of an egg, all of which should be well mixed together; roll the larks in flour, and stuff them. Line the bottom of a pie-dish with a few slices of beef and bacon; over these place the larks, and season with salt, pepper, minced parsley, and chopped shalot, in the above proportion. Pour in the stock or water, cover with crust, and bake for an hour in a moderate oven. During the time the pie is baking, shake it 2 or 3 times, to assist in thickening the gravy, and serve very hot. *Time.*—1 hour. *Average cost*, 1*s.* 6*d.* per dozen. *Sufficient* for 5 or 6 persons. *Seasonable.*—In full season in November.

LARKS, Roast.

Ingredients.—Larks, egg and bread crumbs, fresh butter. *Mode.*—These birds are by many persons esteemed a great delicacy, and may be either roasted or broiled. Pick, gut, and clean them; when they are trussed, brush them over with the yolk of an egg; sprinkle with bread crumbs, and roast them before a quick fire; baste them continually with fresh butter, and keep sprinkling with the bread crumbs until the birds are well covered. Dish them on bread crumbs fried in clarified butter, and garnish the dish with slices of lemon. Broiled larks are also very excellent: they should be cooked over a clear fire, and would take about 10 minutes or ¼ hour. *Time.*—¼ hour to roast; 10 minutes to broil. *Seasonable.*—In full season in November.

Note.—Larks may also be plainly roasted, without covering them with egg and bread crumbs; they should be dished on fried crumbs.

LEEK SOUP.

Ingredients.—A sheep's head, 3 quarts of water, 12 leeks cut small, pepper and salt to taste, oatmeal to thicken. *Mode.* Prepare the head, either by skinning or cleaning the skin very nicely; split it in two; take out the brains, and put it into boiling water; add the leeks and seasoning, and simmer very gently for 4 hours. Mix smoothly, with cold water, as much oatmeal as will make the soup tolerably thick; pour it into the soup; continue stirring till the whole is blended and well done, and serve. *Time.*—4½ hours. *Average cost,* 4*d.* per quart. *Seasonable* in winter. Sufficient for 10 persons.

LEMON BISCUITS.

Ingredients.—1¼ lb. of flour, ¾ lb. of loaf sugar, 6 oz. of fresh butter, 4 eggs, 1 oz. of lemon-peel, 2 dessert-spoonfuls of lemon-juice. *Mode.*—Rub the flour into the butter; stir in the pounded sugar and very finely-minced lemon-peel, and when these ingredients are thoroughly mixed, add the eggs, which should be previously well whisked, and the lemon-juice. Beat the mixture well for a minute or two, then drop it from a spoon on to a buttered tin, about 2 inches apart, as the cakes will spread when they get warm; place the tin in the oven, and bake the cakes of a pale brown from 15 to 20 minutes. *Time.*—15 to 20 minutes. *Average cost,* 1*s.* 6*d.* *Seasonable* at any time.

LEMON BLANCMANGE.

Ingredients.—1 quart of milk, the yolks of 4 eggs, 3 oz. of ground rice, 6 oz. of pounded sugar, 1½ oz. of fresh butter, the rind of 1 lemon, the juice of 2, ½ oz. of gelatine. *Mode.*—Make a custard with the yolks of the eggs and ½ pint of the milk, and when done, put it into a basin; put half the remainder of the milk into a saucepan with the ground rice, fresh butter, lemon-rind, and 3 oz. of the sugar, and let these ingredients boil until the mixture is stiff, stirring them continually; when done, pour it into the bowl where the custard is, mixing both well together. Put the gelatine with the rest of the milk into a saucepan, and let it stand by the side of the fire to dissolve; boil for a minute or two, stir carefully into the basin, adding 3 oz. more of pounded sugar. When cold, stir in the lemon-juice, which should be carefully strained, and pour the mixture into a well-oiled mould, leaving out the lemon-peel, and set the mould in a pan of cold water until wanted for table. Use eggs that have rich-looking yolks; and, should the weather be very warm, rather a larger proportion of gelatine must be allowed. *Time.*—Altogether, ½ hour. *Average cost,* 1*s.* 6*d.* *Sufficient* to fill 2 small moulds. *Seasonable* at any time.

BLANCMANGE MOULD.

LEMON CAKE.

Ingredients.—10 eggs, 3 tablespoonfuls of orange-flower water, ¾ lb. of pounded loaf sugar, 1 lemon, ¾ lb. of flour. *Mode.*—Separate the whites from the yolks of the eggs; whisk the former to a stiff froth; add the orange-flower water, the sugar, grated lemon-rind, and mix these ingredients well together. Then beat the yolks of the eggs, and add them, with the lemon-juice, to the whites, &c.; dredge in the flour gradually; keep beating the mixture well; put it into a buttered

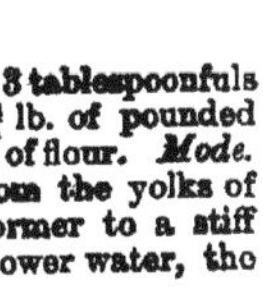

CAKE-MOULD.

mould, and bake the cake about an hour, or rather longer. The addition of a little butter, beaten to a cream, we think, would improve this cake. *Time.*—About 1 hour. *Average cost,* 1*s.* 4*d.* *Seasonable* at any time.

LEMON CHEESECAKES.

Ingredients.—¼ lb. of butter, 1 lb. of loaf sugar, 6 eggs, the rind of 2 lemons and the juice of 3. *Mode.*—Put all the ingredients into a stewpan, carefully grating the lemon-rind and straining the juice. Keep stirring the mixture over the fire until the sugar is dissolved, and it begins to thicken: when of the consistency of honey, it is done; then put it into small jars, and keep in a dry place. This mixture will remain good 3 or 4 months. When made into cheesecakes, add a few pounded almonds, or candied peel, or grated sweet biscuit; line some patty-pans with good puff-paste, rather more than half fill them with the mixture, and bake for about ¼ hour in a good brisk oven. *Time.*—¼ hour. *Average cost,* 1*s.* 4*d.* *Sufficient* for 24 cheesecakes. *Seasonable* at any time.

LEMON CREAM.

Ingredients.—1 pint of cream, the yolks of two eggs, ¼ lb. of white sugar, 1 large lemon, 1 oz. of isinglass. *Mode.*—Put the cream into a *lined* saucepan with the sugar, lemon-peel, and isinglass, and sim-

LEMON-CREAM MOULD.

mer these over a gentle fire for about 10 minutes, stirring them all the time. Strain the cream into a jug, add the yolks of eggs, which should be well beaten, and put the jug into a saucepan of boiling water; stir the mixture one way until it thickens, *but do not allow it to boil;* take it off the fire, and keep stirring it until nearly cold. Strain the lemon-juice into a basin, gradually pour on it the cream, and *stir it well* until the juice is well mixed with it. Have ready a well-oiled mould, pour the cream into it, and let it remain until perfectly set. When required for table, loosen the edges with a small blunt knife, put a dish on the top of the mould, turn it over quickly, and the cream should easily slip away. *Time.*—10 minutes to boil the cream; about 10 minutes to stir it over the fire in the jug. *Average cost,* with cream at 1*s.* per pint, and the best isinglass, 3*s.* 6*d.* *Sufficient* to fill 1½-pint mould. *Seasonable* at any time.

LEMON CREAM, Economical.

Ingredients.—1 quart of milk, 8 bitter almonds, 2 oz. of gelatine, 2 large lemons, ¾ lb. of lump sugar, the yolks of 6 eggs. *Mode.*—Put the milk into a lined saucepan with the almonds, which should be well pounded in a mortar, the gelatine, lemon-rind, and lump sugar, and boil these ingredients for about 5 minutes. Beat up the yolks of the eggs, strain the milk into a jug, add the eggs, and pour the mixture backwards and forwards a few times, until nearly cold; then stir briskly to it the lemon-juice, which should be strained, and keep stirring until the cream is almost cold; put it into an oiled mould, and let it remain until perfectly set. The lemon-juice must not be added to the cream when it is warm, and should be well stirred after it is put in. *Time.*—5 minutes to boil the milk. *Average cost,* 2*s.* 5*d.* *Sufficient* to fill two 1½ pint moulds. *Seasonable* at any time.

LEMON CREAMS, Very Good.

Ingredients.—1 pint of cream, 2 dozen sweet almonds, 3 glasses of sherry, the rind and juice of 2 lemons, sugar to taste. *Mode.*—Blanch and chop the almonds, and put them into a jug with the cream; in another jug put the sherry, lemon-rind, strained juice, and sufficient pounded sugar to sweeten the whole nicely. Pour rapidly from one jug to the other till the mixture is well frothed; then pour it into jelly-glasses, omitting the lemon-rind. This is a very cool and delicious sweet for summer, and may be made less rich by omitting the almonds and substituting orange or raisin wine for the sherry. *Time.*—Altogether, ½ hour. *Average cost,* with cream at 1*s.* per pint, 3*s.* *Sufficient* to fill 12 glasses. *Seasonable* at any time.

LEMON CREAMS, or Custards.

Ingredients.—5 oz. of loaf sugar, 2 pints of boiling water, the rind of 1 lemon and the juice of 3, the yolks of 8 eggs. *Mode.* Make a quart of lemonade in the following manner:—Dissolve the sugar in the boiling water, having previously, with part of the sugar, rubbed off the lemon-rind, and add the strained juice. Strain the lemonade into a saucepan, and add the yolks of the eggs, which should be well beaten; stir this one way over the fire until the mixture thickens, but do not allow it to boil, and serve in custard glasses, or on a glass dish. After the boiling water is poured on the sugar and lemon, it should stand covered for about ½ hour before the eggs are added to it, that the flavour of the rind may be extracted. *Time.*—½ hour to make the lemonade; about 10 minutes to stir the custard over the fire. *Average cost,* 1*s.* *Sufficient* to fill 12 to 14 custard glasses. *Seasonable* at any time.

LEMON DUMPLINGS.

Ingredients.—½ lb. of grated bread, ¼ lb. of chopped suet, ¼ lb. of moist sugar, 2 eggs, 1 large lemon. *Mode.*—Mix the bread, suet, and moist sugar well together, adding the lemon-peel, which should be very finely minced. Moisten with the eggs and strained lemon-juice; stir well, and put the mixture into small buttered cups. Tie them down and boil for ¾ hour. Turn them out on a dish, strew sifted sugar over them, and serve with wine sauce. *Time.*—¾ hour. *Average cost,* 7*d.* *Sufficient* for 6 dumplings. *Seasonable* at any time.

LEMON DUMPLINGS.

LEMON JELLY.

Ingredients.—6 lemons, ¾ lb. of lump sugar, 1 pint of water, 1½ oz. of isinglass, ¼ pint of sherry. *Mode.*—Peel 3 of the lemons, pour ½ pint of boiling water on the rind, and let it infuse for ½ hour; put the sugar, isinglass, and ½ pint of water into a lined saucepan, and boil these ingredients for 20 minutes; then put in the strained lemon-juice, the strained infusion of the rind, and bring the whole to the point of boiling; skim well, add the wine, and run the jelly through a bag; pour it into a mould that has been wetted or soaked in water; put it in ice, if convenient, where let it remain until required for table. Previously to adding the lemon-juice to the other ingredients, ascertain that it is very nicely strained, as, if this is not properly attended to, it is liable to make the jelly thick and muddy. As this jelly is very pale, and almost colourless, it answers very well for moulding with a jelly of any bright hue; for instance, half a jelly bright red, and the other half made of the above, would have a very good effect. Lemon jelly may also be made with calf's-feet stock, allowing the juice of 3 lemons to every pint of stock. *Time.*—Altogether, 1 hour. *Average cost,* with the best isinglass, 3*s.* 6*d.* *Sufficient* to fill 1½ pint mould. *Seasonable* at any time.

LEMON MINCEMEAT.

Ingredients.—2 large lemons, 6 large apples, ½ lb. of suet, 1 lb. of currants, ½ lb. of sugar, 2 oz. of candied lemon-peel, 1 oz. of citron, mixed spice to taste. *Mode.*—Pare the lemons, squeeze them, and boil the peel until tender enough to mash. Add to the mashed lemon-peel the apples, which should be pared, cored, and minced; the chopped suet, currants, sugar, sliced peel, and spice. Strain the lemon-juice to these ingredients, stir the mixture well, and put it in a jar with a closely-fitting lid. Stir occasionally, and in a week or 10 days the mincemeat will be ready for use. *Average cost,* 2*s.* *Sufficient* for 18 large or 24 small pies. *Seasonable.*—Make this about the beginning of December.

LEMON-PEEL.

This contains an essential oil of a very high flavour and fragrance, and is consequently esteemed both a wholesome and agreeable stomachic. It is used, as will be seen by many recipes in this book, as an ingredient for flavouring a number of various dishes. Under the name of candied lemon-peel, it is cleared of the pulp and preserved in sugar, when it becomes an excellent sweetmeat.

LEMON PUDDING, Baked.

Ingredients.—The yolks of 4 eggs, 4 oz. of pounded sugar, 1 lemon, ¼ lb. of butter, puff-crust. *Mode.* —Beat the eggs to a froth; mix with them the sugar and warmed butter; stir these ingredients well together, putting in the grated rind and strained juice of the lemon-peel. Line a shallow dish with puff-paste; put in the mixture, and bake in a moderate oven for 40 minutes; turn the pudding out of the dish, strew over it sifted sugar, and serve. *Time.*—40 minutes. *Average cost*, 10*d.* *Sufficient* for 5 or 6 persons. *Seasonable* at any time.

LEMON PUDDING, Baked.

Ingredients.—10 oz. of bread crumbs, 2 pints of milk, 2 oz. of butter, 1 lemon, ¼ lb. of pounded sugar, 4 eggs, 1 tablespoonful of brandy. *Mode.*—Bring the milk to the boiling point, stir in the butter, and pour these hot over the bread crumbs; add the sugar and very finely-minced lemon-peel; beat the eggs, and stir these in with the brandy to the other ingredients; put a paste round the dish, and bake for ¾ hour. *Time.*—¾ hour. *Average cost*, 1*s.* 2*d.* *Sufficient* for 6 or 7 persons. *Seasonable* at any time.

LEMON PUDDING, Baked (Very Rich).

Ingredients.—The rind and juice of 2 large lemons, ½ lb. of loaf sugar, ¼ pint of cream, the yolks of 8 eggs, 2 oz. of almonds, ½ lb. of butter, melted. *Mode.* —Mix the pounded sugar with the cream and add the yolks of eggs and the butter, which should be previously warmed. Blanch and pound the almonds, and put these, with the grated rind and strained juice of the lemons, to the other ingredients. Stir all well together; line a dish with puff-paste, put in the mixture, and bake for 1 hour. *Time.*—1 hour. *Average cost*, 2*s.* *Sufficient* for 6 or 7 persons. *Seasonable* at any time.

LEMON PUDDING, Boiled.

Ingredients.—½ lb. of chopped suet, ¾ lb. of bread crumbs, 2 small lemons, 6 oz. of moist sugar, ¼ lb. of flour, 2 eggs, milk. *Mode.*—Mix the suet, bread crumbs, sugar, and flour well together, adding the lemon-peel, which should be very finely minced, and the juice, which should be strained. When these ingredients are well mixed, moisten with the eggs and sufficient milk to make the pudding of the consistency of thick batter; put it into a well-buttered mould, and boil for 3½ hours; turn it out, strew sifted sugar over, and serve with wine sauce, or not, at pleasure. *Time.*—3½ hours. *Average cost*, 1*s.* *Sufficient* for 7 or 8 persons. *Seasonable* at any time.

Note.—This pudding may also be baked, and will be found very good. It will take about 2 hours.

LEMON PUDDING, Plain.

Ingredients.—¾ lb. of flour, 6 oz. of lard or dripping, the juice of 1 large lemon, 1 teaspoonful of flour, sugar. *Mode.*—Make the above proportions of flour and lard into a smooth paste, and roll it out to the thickness of about ½ an inch. Squeeze the lemon-juice, strain it into a cup, stir the flour into it, and as much moist sugar as will make it into a stiff and thick paste; spread this mixture over the paste, roll it up, secure the ends, and tie the pudding in a floured cloth. Boil for 2 hours. *Time.*—2 hours. *Average cost*, 7*d.* *Sufficient* for 5 or 6 persons. *Seasonable* at any time.

LEMON SAUCE, for Boiled Fowl.

Ingredients.—1 small lemon, ¾ pint of melted butter. *Mode.*—Cut the lemon into very thin slices, and these again into very small dice. Have ready ¾ pint of melted butter, put in the lemon; let it just simmer, but not boil, and pour it over the fowls. *Time.*—1 minute to simmer. *Average cost*, 6*d.* *Sufficient* for a pair of large fowls.

LEMON WHITE SAUCE, for Fowls, Fricassees, &c.

Ingredients.—½ pint of cream, the rind and juice of 1 lemon, ½ teaspoonful of whole white pepper, 1 sprig of lemon thyme, 3 oz. of butter, 1 dessertspoonful of flour, 1 teacupful of white stock; salt to taste. *Mode.*—Put the cream into a very clean saucepan (a lined one is best), with the lemon-peel, pepper, and thyme, and let these infuse for ½ hour, when simmer gently for a few minutes, or until there is a nice flavour of lemon. Strain it, and add a thickening of butter and flour in the above proportions; stir this well in, and put in the lemon-juice at the moment of serving; mix the stock with the cream, and add a little salt. This sauce should not boil after the cream and stock are mixed together. *Time.*—Altogether, ¾ hour. *Average cost,* 1*s.* 6*d.* *Sufficient,* this quantity, for a pair of large boiled fowls.

Note.—Where the expense of the cream is objected to, milk may be substituted for it. In this case, an additional dessertspoonful, or rather more, of flour must be added.

LEMON SAUCE, for Sweet Puddings.

Ingredients.—The rind and juice of 1 lemon, 1 tablespoonful of flour, 1 oz. of butter, 1 large wineglassful of sherry, 1 wineglassful of water, sugar to taste, the yolks of 4 eggs. *Mode.*—Rub the rind of the lemon on to some lumps of sugar; squeeze out the juice, and strain it; put the butter and flour into a saucepan, stir them over the fire, and when of a pale brown, add the wine, water, and strained lemon-juice. Crush the lumps of sugar that were rubbed on the lemon; stir these into the sauce, which should be very sweet. When these ingredients are well mixed, and the sugar is melted, put in the beaten yolks of 4 eggs; keep stirring the sauce until it thickens, when serve. Do not, on any account, allow it to boil, or it will curdle, and be entirely spoiled. *Time.*—Altogether, 15 minutes. *Average cost,* 1*s.* 2*d.* *Sufficient* for 7 or 8 persons.

LEMON SPONGE.

Ingredients.—2 oz. of isinglass, 1¾ pint of water, ¾ lb. of pounded sugar, the juice of 5 lemons, the rind of 1, the whites of 3 eggs. *Mode.*—Dissolve the isinglass in the water, strain it into a saucepan, and add the sugar, lemon-rind, and juice. Boil the whole from 10 to 15 minutes; strain it again, and let it stand till it is cold and begins to stiffen. Beat the whites of the eggs, put them to it, and whisk the mixture till it is quite white; put it into a mould which has been previously wetted, and let it remain until perfectly set; then turn it out, and garnish it according to taste. *Time.*—10 to 15 minutes. *Average cost,* with the best isinglass, 4*s.* *Sufficient* to fill a quart mould. *Seasonable* at any time.

LEMON SYRUP.

Ingredients.—2 lbs. of loaf sugar, 2 pints of water, 1 oz. of citric acid, ½ drachm of essence of lemon. *Mode.*—Boil the sugar and water together for ¼ hour, and put it into a basin, where let it remain till cold. Beat the citric acid to a powder, mix the essence of lemon with it, then add these two ingredients to the syrup; mix well, and bottle for use. Two tablespoonfuls of the syrup are sufficient for a tumbler of cold water, and will be found a very refreshing summer drink. *Sufficient.*—2 tablespoonfuls of syrup to a tumblerful of cold water.

LEMONS, to Pickle, with the Peel on.

Ingredients. — 6 lemons, 2 quarts of boiling water; to each quart of vinegar allow ½ oz. of cloves, ½ oz. of white pepper, 1 oz. of bruised ginger, ¼ oz. of mace and chillies, 1 oz. of mustard-seed, ½ stick of sliced horseradish, a few cloves of garlic. *Mode.*—Put the lemons into a brine that will bear an egg; let them remain in it 6 days, stirring them every day; have ready 2 quarts of boiling water, put in the lemons, and allow them to boil for ¼ hour; take them out, and let them lie in a cloth until perfectly dry and cold. Boil up sufficient vinegar to cover the lemons, with all the above ingredients, allowing the same proportion as stated to each quart of vinegar. Pack the lemons in a jar, pour over the vinegar, &c. boiling hot, and tie down with a bladder. They will be fit for use in about 12 months, or rather sooner. *Seasonable.*—This should be made from November to April.

LEMONS, to Pickle, without the Peel.

Ingredients.—6 lemons, 1 lb. of fine salt; to each quart of vinegar, the same ingredients as in the last recipe. *Mode.*—Peel the lemons, slit each one down 3 times, so as not to divide them, and rub the salt well into the divisions; place them in a pan, where they must remain for a week, turning them every other day; then put them in a Dutch oven before a clear fire until the salt has become perfectly dry; then arrange them in a jar. Pour over sufficient boiling vinegar to cover them, to which have been added the ingredients mentioned in the foregoing recipe; tie down closely, and in about 9 months they will be fit for use. *Seasonable.*—The best time to make this is from November to April.

Note.—After this pickle has been made from 4 to 5 months, the liquor may be strained and bottled, and will be found an excellent lemon ketchup.

LEMON WINE.

Ingredients.—To 4½ gallons of water allow the pulp of 50 lemons, the rind of 25, 16 lbs. of loaf sugar, ½ oz. of isinglass, 1 bottle of brandy. *Mode.*—Peel and slice the lemons, but use only the rind of 25 of them, and put them into the cold water. Let it stand 8 or 9 days, squeezing the lemons well every day; then strain the water off and put it into a cask with the sugar. Let it work some time, and when it has ceased working, put in the isinglass. Stop the cask down; in about six months put in the brandy and bottle the wine off. *Seasonable.*—The best time to make this is in January or February, when lemons are best and cheapest.

LEMONADE.

Ingredients.—The rind of two lemons, the juice of 3 large or 4 small ones, ½ lb. of loaf sugar, 1 quart of boiling water. *Mode.*—Rub some of the sugar, in lumps, on 2 of the lemons until they have imbibed all the oil from them, and put it with the remainder of the sugar into a jug; add the lemon-juice (but no pips), and pour over the whole a quart of boiling water. When the sugar is dissolved, strain the lemonade through a fine sieve or piece of muslin, and, when cool, it will be ready for use. The lemonade will be much improved by having the white of an egg beaten up in it; a little sherry mixed with it, also, makes this beverage much nicer. *Average cost*, 6*d*. per quart.

LEMONADE, Nourishing.

Ingredients.—1½ pint of boiling water, the juice of 4 lemons, the rinds of 2, ½ pint of sherry, 4 eggs, 6 oz. of loaf sugar. *Mode.*—Pare off the lemon-rind thinly, put it into a jug with the sugar, and pour over the boiling water. Let it cool, then strain it; add the wine, lemon-juice, and eggs, previously well beaten, and also strained, and the beverage will be ready for use. If thought desirable, the quantity of sherry and water could be lessened, and milk substituted for them. To obtain the flavour of the lemon-rind properly, a few lumps of the sugar should be rubbed over it, until some of the yellow is absorbed. *Time.*—Altogether 1 hour to make it. *Average cost*, 1*s*. 8*d*. *Sufficient* to make 2½ pints of lemonade. *Seasonable* at any time.

LETTUCES.

These form one of the principal ingredients to summer salads; they should be blanched, and be eaten young. They are seldom served in any other way, but may be stewed and sent to table in a good brown gravy flavoured with lemon-juice. In preparing them for a salad, carefully wash them free from dirt, pick off all the decayed and outer leaves, and dry them thoroughly by shaking them in a cloth. Cut off the stalks, and either halve or cut the lettuces into small pieces. The manner of cutting them up entirely depends on the salad for which they are intended. In France, the lettuces are sometimes merely wiped with a cloth and not washed, the cooks there declaring that the act of washing them injuriously affects the pleasant crispness of the plant: in this case scrupulous attention must be paid to each leaf, and the grit thoroughly wiped away. *Average cost*, when cheapest, 1*d*. each. *Sufficient.*—Allow 2 lettuces for 4 or 5 persons. *Seasonable* from March to the end of August, but may be had all the year.

LEVERET, to Dress a.

Ingredients.—2 leverets, butter, flour. *Mode.*—Leverets should be trussed in the same manner as a hare, but they do not require stuffing. Roast them before a clear fire, and keep them well basted all the time they are cooking. A few minutes before serving, dredge them lightly with flour, and froth them nicely. Serve with plain gravy in the dish, and send to table red-currant jelly with them. *Time.*—½ to ¾ hour. *Average cost*, in full season, 4*s*. each. *Sufficient* for 5 or 6 persons. *Seasonable* from May to August, but cheapest in July and August.

LIAISON OF EGGS, for Thickening Sauces.

Ingredients.—The yolks of 3 eggs, 8 tablespoonfuls of milk or cream.

Mode.—Beat up the yolks of the eggs, to which add the milk, and strain the whole through a hair-sieve. When the liaison is being added to the sauce it is intended to thicken, care must be exercised to keep stirring it during the whole time, or, otherwise, the eggs will curdle. It should only just simmer, but not boil.

LIQUEUR JELLY.

Ingredients.—1 lb. of lump sugar, 2 oz. of isinglass, 1½ pint of water, the juice of 2 lemons, ¼ pint of liqueur. *Mode.*—Put the sugar, with 1 pint of the water, into a stewpan, and boil them gently by the side of the fire until there is no scum remaining, which must be carefully removed as fast as it rises. Boil the isinglass with the other ½ pint of water, and

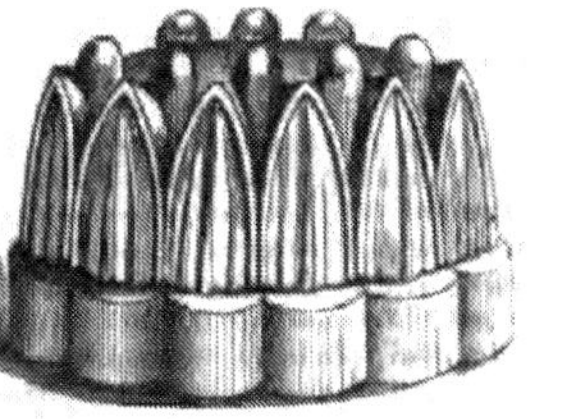

OVAL JELLY MOULD.

skim it carefully in the same manner. Strain the lemon-juice, and add it, with the clarified isinglass, to the syrup; put in the liqueur, and bring the whole to the boiling-point. Let the saucepan remain covered by the side of the fire for a few minutes; then pour the jelly through a bag, put it into a mould, and set the mould in ice until required for table. Dip the mould in hot water, wipe the outside, loosen the jelly by passing a knife round the edges, and turn it out carefully on a dish. Noyeau, Maraschino, Curaçoa, brandy, or any kind of liqueur, answers for this jelly; and, when made with isinglass, liqueur jellies are usually prepared as directed above. *Time.*—10 minutes to boil the sugar and water. *Average cost*, with the best isinglass, 3*s.* 6*d.* *Sufficient* to fill a quart mould. *Seasonable* at any time.

LIVER AND LEMON SAUCE, for Poultry.

Ingredients.—The liver of a fowl, one lemon, salt to taste, ½ pint of melted butter. *Mode.*—Wash the liver, and let it boil for a few minutes; peel the lemon very thin, remove the white part and pips, and cut it into very small dice; mince the liver and a small quantity of the lemon-rind very fine; add these ingredients to ½ pint of smoothly-made melted butter; season with a little salt, put in the cut lemon, heat it gradually, but do not allow it to boil, lest the butter should oil. *Time.*—1 minute to simmer. *Sufficient* to serve with a pair of small fowls.

LIVER AND PARSLEY SAUCE, for Poultry.

Ingredients.—The liver of a fowl, one tablespoonful of minced parsley, ½ pint of melted butter. *Mode.*—Wash and score the liver, boil it for a few minutes, and mince it very fine; blanch or scald a small bunch of parsley, of which there should be sufficient when chopped to fill a tablespoon; add this with the minced liver, to ½ pint of smoothly-made melted butter; let it just boil; when serve. *Time.*—1 minute to simmer. *Sufficient* for a pair of small fowls.

LOBSTERS, to Boil.

Ingredients.—¼ lb. of salt to each gallon of water. *Mode.*—Buy the lobsters alive, and choose those that are heavy and full of motion, which is an indication of their freshness. When the shell is incrusted, it is a sign they are old: medium-sized lobsters are the best. Have ready a stewpan of boiling water, salted in the above proportion; put in the lobster, and keep it boiling quickly from 20 minutes to ¾ hour, according to its size, and do not forget to skim well. If it boils too long, the meat becomes thready, and if not done enough, the spawn is not red: this must be obviated by great attention. Rub the shell over with a little butter or sweet oil, which wipe off again. *Time.*—Small lobster, 20 minutes to ½ hour; large ditto, ½ to ¾ hour. *Average cost*, medium size, 1*s.* 6*d.* to 2*s.* 6*d.* *Seasonable* all the year, but best from March to October.

TO CHOOSE LOBSTERS.—This shell-fish, if it has been cooked alive, as it ought to have been, will have a stiffness in the tail, which, if gently raised, will return with a spring. Care, however, must be taken in thus proving it; for if the tail is pulled straight out, it will not return; when the fish might be pronounced inferior, which, in reality, may not be the case. In order to be good, lobsters should be weighty for their bulk; if light, they will be watery; and those of the medium size, are always the best. Small-sized lobsters are cheapest, and answer very well for sauce. In boiling lobsters, the appearance of the shell will be much improved by rubbing over it a little butter or salad-oil on being immediately taken from the pot.

LOBSTER CURRY (an Entrée).

Ingredients.—1 lobster, 2 onions, 1 oz. butter, 1 tablespoonful of curry-powder, ½ pint of medium stock, the juice of ½ lemon. *Mode.*—Pick the meat from the shell, and cut into nice square pieces; fry the onions of a pale brown in the butter, stir in the curry-powder and stock, and simmer till it thickens, when put in the lobster; stew the whole slowly for ½ hour, stirring occasionally; and just before sending to table, put in the lemon-juice. Serve boiled rice with it, the same as for other curries. *Time.*—Altogether, ¾ hour. *Average cost*, 3*s*. *Seasonable* at any time.

LOBSTER CUTLETS (an Entrée).

Ingredients.—1 large hen lobster, 1 oz. fresh butter, ½ saltspoonful of salt, pounded mace, grated nutmeg, cayenne and white pepper to taste, egg, and bread crumbs. *Mode.*—Pick the meat from the shell, and pound it in a mortar with the butter, and gradually add the mace and seasoning, well mixing the ingredients; beat all to a smooth paste, and add a little of the spawn; divide the mixture into pieces of an equal size, and shape them like cutlets. They should not be very thick. Brush them over with egg, and sprinkle with bread crumbs, and stick a short piece of the small claw in the top of each; fry them of a nice brown in boiling lard, and drain them before the fire, on a sieve reversed; arrange them nicely on a dish, and pour béchamel in the middle, but not over the cutlets. *Time.*—About 8 minutes after the cutlets are made. *Average cost* for this dish, 2*s*. 9*d*. *Seasonable* all the year. *Sufficient* for 5 or 6 persons.

LOBSTERS, to Dress.

☞ When the lobster is boiled, rub it over with a little salad-oil, which wipe off again; separate the body from the tail, break off the great claws, and crack them at the joints, without injuring the meat; split the tail in halves, and arrange all neatly in a dish, with the body upright in the middle, and garnish with parsley.

LOBSTER, Hot.

Ingredients.—1 lobster, 2 oz. of butter, grated nutmeg; salt, pepper, and pounded mace, to taste; bread crumbs, 2 eggs. *Mode.*—Pound the meat of the lobster to a smooth paste with the butter and seasoning, and add a few bread crumbs. Beat the eggs, and make the whole mixture into the form of a lobster; pound the spawn, and sprinkle over it. Bake ¼ hour, and just before serving, lay over it the tail and body shell, with the small claws underneath, to resemble a lobster. *Time.*—¼ hour. *Average cost*, 2*s*. 6*d*. *Seasonable* at any time. *Sufficient* for 4 or 5 persons.

LOBSTER PATTIES (an Entrée).

Ingredients.—Minced lobster, 4 tablespoonfuls of béchamel, 6 drops of anchovy sauce, lemon-juice, cayenne to taste. *Mode.*—Line the patty-pans with puff-paste, and put into each a small piece of bread; cover with paste, brush over with egg, and bake of a light colour. Take as much lobster as is required, mince the meat very fine, and add the above ingredients; stir it over the fire for 5 minutes; remove the lids of the patty-cases, take out the bread, fill with the mixture, and replace the covers. *Seasonable* at any time.

LOBSTER, Potted.

Ingredients.—2 lobsters; seasoning to taste, of nutmeg, pounded mace, white pepper, and salt; ¼ lb. of butter, 3 or 4 bay-leaves. *Mode.*—Take out the meat carefully from the shell, but do not cut it up. Put some butter at the bottom of a dish, lay in the lobster as evenly as possible, with the bay-leaves and seasoning between. Cover with butter, and bake for ¾ hour in a gentle oven. When done, drain the whole on a sieve, and lay the pieces in potting-jars, with the seasoning about them. When cold, pour over it clarified butter, and, if very highly seasoned, it will keep some time. *Time.*—¾ hour. *Average cost* for this quantity, 4*s*. 4*d*. *Seasonable* at any time.

Note.—Potted lobster may be used cold, or as a *fricassee* with cream sauce.

LOBSTER (à la Mode Francaise).

Ingredients.—1 lobster, 4 tablespoonfuls of white stock, 2 tablespoonfuls of cream, pounded mace, and cayenne to taste; bread crumbs. *Mode.*—Pick the meat from the shell, and cut it up into small square pieces; put the stock, cream, and seasoning into a stewpan, add the lobster, and let it simmer gently for 6 minutes. Serve it in the shell, which must be nicely cleaned, and have a border of puff-paste; cover it with bread crumbs, place small pieces of butter over, and brown before the fire, or with a salamander. *Time.*—¼ hour. *Average cost*, 2*s*. 6*d*. *Seasonable* at any time.

LOBSTER SALAD.

Ingredients.—1 hen lobster, lettuces, endive, small salad (whatever is in season), a little chopped beetroot, 2 hard-boiled eggs, a few slices of cucumber. For dressing, 4 tablespoonfuls of oil, 2 do. of vinegar, 1 teaspoonful of made mustard, the yolks of 2 eggs; cayenne and salt to taste; ¼ teaspoonful of anchovy sauce. These ingredients should be mixed perfectly smooth, and form a creamy-looking sauce. *Mode.*—Wash the salad, and thoroughly dry it by shaking it in a cloth. Cut up the lettuces and endive, pour the dressing on them, and lightly throw in the small salad. Mix all well together with the pickings from the body of the lobster; pick the meat from the shell, cut it up into nice square pieces, put half in the salad, the other half reserve for garnishing. Separate the yolks from the whites of 2 hard-boiled eggs; chop the whites very fine, and rub the yolks through a sieve, and afterwards the coral from the inside. Arrange the salad lightly on a glass dish, and garnish, first with a row of sliced cucumber, then with the pieces of lobster, the yolks and whites of the eggs, coral, and beetroot placed alternately, and arranged in small separate bunches, so that the colours contrast nicely. *Average cost*, 3*s*. 6*d*. *Sufficient* for 4 or 5 persons. *Seasonable* from April to October; may be had all the year, but salad is scarce and expensive in winter.

Note.—A few crayfish make a pretty garnishing to lobster salad.

LOBSTER SAUCE, to serve with Turbot, Salmon, Brill, &c. (very Good.)

Ingredients.—1 middling-sized hen lobster, ¾ pint of melted butter, 1 tablespoonful of anchovy sauce, ½ oz. of butter, salt and cayenne to taste, a little pounded mace when liked, 2 or 3 tablespoonfuls of cream. *Mode.*—Choose a hen lobster, as this is indispensable, in order to render this sauce as good as it ought to be. Pick the meat from the shells, and cut it into small square pieces; put the spawn, which will be found under the tail of the lobster, into a mortar with ½ oz. of butter, and pound it quite smooth; rub it through a hair-sieve, and cover up till wanted. Make ¾ pint of melted butter; put in all the ingredients except the lobster-meat, and well mix the sauce before the lobster is added to it, as it should retain its square form, and not come to table shredded and ragged. Put in the meat, let it get thoroughly hot, but do not allow it to boil, as the colour would immediately be spoiled; for it must be remembered that this sauce should always have a bright red appearance. If it is intended to be served with turbot or brill, a little of the spawn (dried and rubbed through a sieve without butter) should be saved to garnish with; but as the goodness, flavour, and appearance of the sauce so much depend on having a proper quantity of spawn, the less used for garnishing the better. *Time.*—1 minute to simmer. *Average cost*, for this quantity, 2*s*. *Seasonable* at any time. *Sufficient* to serve with a small turbot, a brill, or salmon for 6 persons.

Note.—Melted butter made with milk, will be found to answer very well for lobster sauce, as by employing it a nice white colour will be obtained. Less quantity than the above may be made by using a very small lobster, to which add only ½ pint of melted butter, and season as above. Where economy is desired, the cream may be dispensed with, and the remains of a cold lobster left from table, may, with a little care, be converted into a very good sauce.

LOBSTER SOUP.

Ingredients.—3 large lobsters, or 6 small ones; the crumb of a French roll, 2 anchovies, 1 onion, 1 small bunch of sweet herbs, 1 strip of lemon-peel, 2 oz. of butter, a little nutmeg, 1 teaspoonful of flour, 1 pint of cream, 1 pint of milk; forcemeat balls, mace, salt, and pepper to taste, bread crumbs, 1 egg, 2 quarts of water. *Mode.*—Pick the meat from the lobsters, and beat the fins, chine, and small claws in a mortar, previously taking away the brown fin and the bag in the head. Put it in a stewpan, with the crumb of the roll, anchovies, onions, herbs, lemon-peel, and the water; simmer gently till all the goodness is extracted, and strain it off. Pound the spawn in a mortar, with the butter, nutmeg, and flour, and mix with it the cream and milk. Give one boil up, at the same time adding the tails cut in pieces. Make the forcemeat balls with the remainder of the lobster, seasoned with mace, pepper, and salt, adding a little flour, and a few bread crumbs; moisten them with the egg, heat them in the soup, and serve. *Time.*—2 hours, or rather more. *Average cost*, 3*s.* 6*d.* per quart. *Seasonable* from April to October. *Sufficient* for 8 persons.

LUNCHEONS.

The remains of cold joints, nicely garnished, a few sweets, or a little hashed meat, poultry or game, are the usual articles placed on the table for luncheon, with bread and cheese, biscuits, butter, &c. If a substantial meal is desired, rump-steaks or mutton chops may be served, as also veal cutlets, kidneys, or any dish of that kind. In families where there is a nursery, the mistress of the house often partakes of the meal with the children, and makes it her luncheon. In the summer, a few dishes of fresh fruit should be added to the luncheon, or, instead of this, a compôte of fruit or fruit tart, or pudding.

MACARONI, as usually served with the CHEESE COURSE.

I.

Ingredients.—½ lb. of pipe macaroni, ¼ lb. of butter, 6 oz. of Parmesan or Cheshire cheese, pepper and salt to taste, 1 pint of milk, 2 pints of water, bread crumbs. *Mode.*—Put the milk and water into a saucepan with sufficient salt to flavour it; place it on the fire, and, when it boils quickly, drop in the macaroni. Keep the water boiling until it is quite tender; drain the macaroni, and put it into a deep dish. Have ready the grated cheese, either Parmesan or Cheshire; sprinkle it amongst the macaroni and some of the butter cut into small pieces, reserving some of the cheese for the top layer. Season with a little pepper, and cover the top layer of cheese with some very fine bread crumbs. Warm, without oiling, the remainder of the butter, and pour it gently over the bread crumbs. Place the dish before a bright fire to brown the crumbs; turn it once or twice, that it may be equally coloured, and serve very hot. The top of the macaroni may be browned with a salamander, which is even better than placing it before the fire, as the process is more expeditious; but it should never be browned in the oven, as the butter would oil, and so impart a very disagreeable flavour to the dish. In boiling the macaroni, let it be perfectly tender but firm, no part beginning to melt, and the form entirely preserved. It may be boiled in plain water, with a little salt instead of using milk, but should then have a small piece of butter mixed with it. *Time.*—1 to 1½ hour to boil the macaroni, 5 minutes to brown it before the fire. *Average cost*, 1*s.* 6*d.* *Sufficient* for 6 or 7 persons. *Seasonable* at any time.

Note.—Riband macaroni may be dressed in the same manner, but does not require boiling so long a time.

II.

Ingredients.—¼ lb. of pipe or riband macaroni, ½ pint of milk, ½ pint of veal or beef gravy, the yolks of 2 eggs, 4 tablespoonfuls of cream, 3 oz. of grated Parmesan or Cheshire cheese, 1 oz. of butter. *Mode.*—Wash the macaroni, and boil it in the gravy and milk until quite tender, without being broken. Drain it, and put it into rather a deep dish. Beat the yolks of the eggs with the cream and 2 tablespoonfuls of the liquor the macaroni was boiled in; make this sufficiently hot to thicken, but do not allow it to boil; pour it over the macaroni, over which sprinkle the grated cheese and the butter broken into small pieces; brown with a salamander, or before the fire, and serve. *Time.*—1 to 1½ hour to boil the macaroni, 5 minutes to thicken the eggs and cream, 5 minutes to brown. *Average cost*, 1*s.* 2*d.* *Sufficient* for 3 or 4 persons. *Seasonable* at any time.

III.

Ingredients.—¼ lb. of pipe macaroni, ½ pint of brown gravy No. 436, 6 oz. of grated Parmesan cheese. *Mode.*—Wash the macaroni, and boil it in salt and water until quite tender; drain it, and put it into rather a deep dish. Have ready a pint of good brown gravy, pour it hot over the macaroni, and send it to table with grated Parmesan served on a separate dish. When the flavour is liked, a little pounded mace may be added to the water in which the macaroni is boiled; but this must always be sparingly added, as it will impart a very strong flavour. *Time.*—1 to 1½ hour to boil the macaroni. *Average cost*, with the gravy and cheese, 1*s.* 3*d.* *Sufficient* for 3 or 4 persons. *Seasonable* at any time.

MACARONI, Sweet Pudding.

Ingredients.—2½ oz. of macaroni, 2 pints of milk, the rind of ½ lemon, 3 eggs, sugar and grated nutmeg to taste, 2 tablespoonfuls of brandy. *Mode.*—Put the macaroni, with a pint of the milk, into a saucepan with the lemon-peel, and let it simmer gently until the macaroni is tender: then put it into a pie-dish without the peel; mix the other pint of milk with the eggs; stir these well together, adding the sugar and brandy, and pour the mixture over the macaroni. Grate a little nutmeg over the top, and bake in a moderate oven for ½ hour. To make this pudding look nice, a paste should be laid round the edges of the dish, and, for variety, a layer of preserve or marmalade may be placed on the macaroni: in this case, omit the brandy. *Time.*—1 hour to simmer the macaroni; ½ hour to bake the pudding. *Average cost*, 11*d.* *Sufficient* for 5 or 6 persons. *Seasonable* at any time.

MACARONI SOUP.

Ingredients.—3 oz. of macaroni, a piece of butter the size of a walnut, salt to taste, 2 quarts of clear stock. *Mode.*—Throw the macaroni and butter into boiling water, with a pinch of salt, and simmer for ½ an hour. When it is tender, drain and cut it into thin rings or lengths, and drop it into the boiling stock. Stew gently for 15 minutes, and serve grated Parmesan cheese with it. *Time.*—¾ to 1 hour. *Average cost*, 1*s.* per quart. *Seasonable* all the year. *Sufficient* for 8 persons.

MACARONI, a Sweet Dish of.

Ingredients.—¼ lb. of macaroni, 1½ pint of milk, the rind of ½ lemon, 3 oz. of lump sugar, ¾ pint of custard. *Mode.*—Put the milk into a saucepan, with the lemon-peel and sugar; bring it to the boiling-point, drop in the macaroni, and let it gradually swell over a gentle fire, but do not allow the pipes to break. The form should be entirely preserved; and, though tender, should be firm, and not soft, with no part beginning to melt. Should the milk dry away before the macaroni is sufficiently swelled, add a little more. Make a custard, place the macaroni on a dish, and pour the custard over the hot macaroni; grate over it a little nutmeg, and, when cold, garnish the dish with slices of candied citron. *Time.*—From 40 to 50 minutes to swell the macaroni. *Average cost*, with the custard, 1*s.* *Sufficient* for 4 or 5 persons. *Seasonable* at any time.

MACAROONS.

Ingredients.—½ lb. of sweet almonds, ½ lb. of sifted loaf sugar, the whites of three eggs, wafer paper. *Mode.*—Blanch, skin and dry the almonds, and pound them well with a little orange flower or plain water, then add the sifted sugar and the whites of the eggs, which should be beaten to a stiff froth, and mix all the ingredients well together. When the paste looks soft, drop it at equal distances from a biscuit syringe on to sheets of wafer paper: put a strip of almond on the top of each; strew some syrup over, and bake the macaroons in rather a slow oven, of a light brown colour. When hard and set, they are done. They must not be allowed to get very brown, as that would spoil their appearance. If the cakes when baked, appear heavy, add a little more white of egg, which should be well whisked up before it is added to the other ingredients. *Time.*—From 15 to 20 minutes. *Average cost*, 1*s.* 8*d.* per lb.

MACKEREL.

In choosing this fish, purchasers should, to a great extent, be regulated by the brightness of its appearance. If it have a transparent, silvery hue, the flesh is good; but if it be red about the head, it is stale.

MACKEREL, Baked.

Ingredients.—4 middling-sized mackerel, a nice delicate forcemeat, 3 oz. of butter; pepper and salt to taste. *Mode.*—Clean the fish, take out the roes, and fill up with forcemeat, and sew up the slit. Flour, and put them in a dish, heads and tails alternately, with the roes; and, between each layer, put some little pieces of butter, and pepper and salt. Bake for ½ an hour, and either serve with plain melted butter or a *maître d'hôtel* sauce. *Time.*—½ hour. *Average cost* for this quantity, 1*s.* 10*d.* *Seasonable* from April to July. *Sufficient* for 6 persons.

Note.—Baked mackerel may be dressed in the same way as baked herrings, and may also be stewed in wine.

MACKEREL, Boiled.

Ingredients.—¼ lb. of salt to each gallon of water. *Mode.*—Cleanse the inside of the fish thoroughly, and lay it in the kettle with sufficient water to cover it with salt as above; bring it gradually to boil, skim well, and simmer gently till done; dish them on a hot napkin, heads and tails alternately, and garnish with fennel. Fennel sauce and plain melted butter are the usual accompaniments to boiled mackerel; but caper or anchovy sauce is sometimes served with it. *Time.*—After the water boils, 10 minutes; for large mackerel, allow more time. *Average cost*, from 4*d.* *Seasonable* from April to July.

Note.—When variety is desired, fillet the mackerel, boil it, and pour over parsley and butter; send some of this, besides, in a tureen.

MACKEREL, Broiled.

Ingredients.—Pepper and salt to taste, a small quantity of oil. *Mode.*—Mackerel should never be washed when intended to be broiled, but merely wiped very clean and dry, after taking out the gills and insides. Open the back, and put in a little pepper, salt, and oil; broil it over a clear fire, turn it over on both sides, and also on the back. When sufficiently cooked, the flesh can be detached from the bone, which will be in about 10 minutes for a small mackerel. Chop a little parsley, work it up in the butter, with pepper and salt to taste, and a squeeze of lemon-juice, and put it in the back. Serve before the butter is quite melted, with a *maître d'hôtel* sauce in a tureen. *Time.*—Small mackerel 10 minutes. *Average cost*, from 4*d.* *Seasonable* from April to July.

MACKEREL, Fillets of.

Ingredients.—2 large mackerel, 1 oz. butter, 1 small bunch of chopped herbs, 3 tablespoonfuls of medium stock, 3 tablespoonfuls of béchamel; salt, cayenne, and lemon-juice to taste. *Mode.*—Clean the fish, and fillet it; scald the herbs, chop them fine, and put them with the butter and stock into a stewpan. Lay in the mackerel, and simmer very gently for 10 minutes; take them out, and put them on a hot dish. Dredge in a little flour, add the other ingredients, give one boil, and pour it over the mackerel. *Time.*—20 minutes. *Average cost* for this quantity, 1*s.* 6*d.* *Seasonable* from April to July. *Sufficient* for 4 persons.

Note.—Fillets of mackerel may be covered with egg and bread crumbs, and fried of a nice brown. Serve with *maître d'hôtel* sauce and plain melted butter.

MACKEREL, Pickled.

Ingredients.—12 peppercorns, 2 bay-leaves, ½ pint of vinegar, 4 mackerel. *Mode.*—Boil the mackerel, and lay them in a dish; take half the liquor they were boiled in; add as much vinegar, peppercorns, and bay-leaves; boil for 10 minutes, and when cold, pour over the fish. *Time.*—½ hour. *Average cost*, 1*s.* 6*d.*

MACKEREL, Potted.

Ingredients.—Mackerel, a blade of mace, cayenne, salt, and 2 oz. or more butter, according to the quantity of mackerel. *Mode.*—Any remains of cooked mackerel may be potted as follows; pick it well from the bones, break it into very small pieces, and put into a stewpan with the butter, pounded mace, and other ingredients; warm it thoroughly, but do not let it boil; press it into potting pots and pour clarified butter over it.

MAIGRE SOUP (i.e., Soup without Meat).

Ingredients.—6 oz. butter, 6 onions sliced, 4 heads of celery, 2 lettuces, a small bunch of parsley, 2 handfuls of spinach, 3 pieces of bread-crust, 2 blades of mace, salt and pepper to taste, the yolks of 2 eggs, 3 teaspoonfuls of vinegar, 2 quarts of water. *Mode.*—Melt the butter in a stewpan, and put in the onions to stew gently for 3 or 4 minutes; then add the celery, spinach, lettuces, and parsley, cut small. Stir the ingredients well for 10 minutes. Now put in the water, bread, seasoning, and mace. Boil gently for 1½ hour, and, at the moment of serving, beat in the yolks of the eggs and the vinegar, but do not let it boil, or the eggs will curdle. *Time.*—2 hours. *Average cost,* 6*d.* per quart. *Seasonable* all the year. *Sufficient* for 8 persons.

MAIZE, Boiled.

Ingredients.—The ears of young and green Indian wheat; to every ½ gallon of water allow 1 heaped tablespoonful of salt. *Mode.*—This vegetable, which makes one of the most delicious dishes brought to table, is unfortunately very rarely seen in Britain; and we wonder that, in the gardens of the wealthy, it is not invariably cultivated. Our sun, it is true, possesses hardly power sufficient to ripen maize; but, with well-prepared ground, and in a favourable position, it might be sufficiently advanced by the beginning of autumn to serve as a vegetable. The outside sheath being taken off and the waving fibres removed, let the ears be placed in boiling water, where they should remain for about 25 minutes (a longer time may be necessary for larger ears than ordinary); and, when sufficiently boiled and well drained, they may be sent to table whole, and with a piece of toast underneath them. Melted butter should be served with them. *Time.*—25 to 35 minutes. *Average cost.*—Seldom bought. *Sufficient* 1 ear for each person. *Seasonable* in autumn.

MALT WINE.

Ingredients.—5 gallons of water, 28 lbs. of sugar, 6 quarts of sweet-wort, 6 quarts of tun, 3 lbs. of raisins, ½ lb. of candy, 1 pint of brandy. *Mode.*—Boil the sugar and water together for 10 minutes; skim it well, and put the liquor into a convenient-sized pan or tub. Allow it to cool; then mix it with the sweet-wort and tun. Let it stand for 3 days, then put it into a barrel; here it will work or ferment for another three days or more; then bung up the cask, and keep it undisturbed for 2 or 3 months. After this, add the raisins (whole), the candy, and brandy, and, in 6 months' time, bottle the wine off. Those who do not brew, may procure the sweet-wort and tun from any brewer. Sweet-wort is the liquor that leaves the mash of malt before it is boiled with the hops; tun is the new beer after the whole of the brewing operation has been completed. *Time.*—To be boiled 10 minutes; to stand 3 days after mixing; to ferment 3 days; to remain in the cask 2 months before the raisins are added; bottle 6 months after. *Seasonable.*—Make this in March or October.

MANNA KROUP PUDDING.

Ingredients.—3 tablespoonfuls of manna kroup, 12 bitter almonds, 1 pint of milk, sugar to taste, 3 eggs. *Mode.*—Blanch and pound the almonds in a mortar; mix them with the manna kroup; pour over these a pint of boiling milk, and let them steep for about ¼ hour. When nearly cold, add sugar and the well-beaten eggs; mix all well together; put the pudding into a buttered dish, and bake for ½ hour. *Time.*—½ hour. *Average cost,* 8*d.* *Sufficient* for 4 or 5 persons. *Seasonable* at any time.

MARCH—BILLS OF FARE.

Dinner for 18 persons.

First Course.

Red Mullet.	Turtle or Mock Turtle Soup, removed by Salmon and dressed Cucumber. Vase of Flowers. Spring Soup, removed by Boiled Turbot and Lobster Sauce.	Fillets of Whitings.

Entrées.

Vol-au-Vent.	Fricasseed Chicken. Vase of Flowers. Larded Sweetbreads.	Compôte of Pigeons.

March—Bills of Fare

Second Course.

	Fore-quarter of Lamb.	
	Braised Capon.	
Boiled Tongue, garnished.	Vase of Flowers.	Ham.
	Roast Fowls.	
	Rump of Beef à la Jardinière.	

Third Course.

Apricot Tartlets.		Guinea-Fowls, larded, removed by Cabinet Pudding.		Rhubarb Tart.
		Wine Jelly.		
	Custards.	Vase of Flowers.	Jelly, in glasses.	
		Italian Cream.		
Damson Tart.		Ducklings, removed by Nesselrode Pudding.		Cheese-cakes.

Dessert and Ices.

Dinner for 12 persons.

First Course.—White soup; clear gravy soup; boiled salmon, shrimp sauce, and dressed cucumber; baked mullets in paper cases. *Entrées.*—Filet de bœuf and Spanish sauce; larded sweetbreads; rissoles; chicken patties. *Second Course.*—Roast fillet of veal and Béchamel sauce; boiled leg of lamb; roast fowls, garnished with water-cresses; boiled ham, garnished with carrots and mashed turnips; vegetables—sea-kale, spinach, or brocoli. *Third Course.*—Two ducklings; guinea-fowl, larded; orange jelly; Charlotte Russe; coffee cream; ice pudding; macaroni with Parmesan cheese; spinach, garnished with croûtons; dessert and ices.

Dinner for 10 persons.

First Course.—Macaroni soup; boiled turbot and lobster sauce; salmon cutlets. *Entrées.*—Compôte of pigeons; mutton cutlets and tomato sauce. *Second Course.*—Roast lamb; boiled half calf's head, tongue, and brains; boiled bacon-cheek, garnished with spoonfuls of spinach; vegetables. *Third Course.*—Ducklings; plum-pudding; ginger cream; trifle; rhubarb tart; cheesecakes; fondues, in cases; dessert and ices.

Dinner for 8 persons.

First Course.—Calf's-head soup; brill and shrimp sauce; broiled mackerel à la Maître d'Hôtel. *Entrées.*—Lobster cutlets; calf's liver and bacon, aux fines herbes. *Second Course.*—Roast loin of veal; two boiled fowls à la Béchamel; boiled knuckle of ham; vegetables—spinach or brocoli. *Third Course.*—Wild ducks; apple custards; blancmange; lemon jelly; jam sandwiches; ice pudding; potatoes à la Maître d'Hôtel; dessert and ices.

Dinner for 6 persons.

First Course.—Vermicelli soup; soles à la Crême. *Entrées.*—Veal cutlets; small vols-au-vent. *Second Course.*—Small saddle of mutton; half calf's head; boiled bacon-cheek, garnished with Brussels sprouts. *Third Course.*—Cabinet pudding; orange jelly; custards, in glasses; rhubarb tart; lobster salad; dessert.

First Course.—Julienne soup; baked mullets. *Entrées.*—Chicken cutlets; oyster patties. *Second Course.*—Roast lamb and mint sauce; boiled leg of pork; pease pudding; vegetables. *Third Course.*—Ducklings; Swiss cream; lemon jelly; cheesecakes; rhubarb tart; macaroni; dessert.

First Course.—Oyster soup; boiled salmon and dressed cucumber. *Entrées.*—Rissoles; fricasseed chicken. *Second Course.*—Boiled leg of mutton, caper sauce; roast fowls, garnished with water-cresses; vegetables. *Third Course.*—Charlotte aux pommes; orange jelly; lemon cream; soufflé of arrowroot; sea-kale; dessert.

First Course.—Ox-tail soup; boiled mackerel. *Entrées.*—Stewed mutton kidneys; minced veal and oysters. *Second Course.*—Stewed shoulder of veal; roast ribs of beef and horseradish sauce; vegetables. *Third Course.*—Ducklings; tartlets of strawberry jam; cheesecakes; Gâteau de Riz; carrot pudding; sea-kale; dessert.

MARCH, Plain Family Dinners for.

Sunday.—1. Boiled ½ calf's head, pickled pork, the tongue on a small dish with the brains round it; mutton cutlets and mashed potatoes. 2. Plum tart made with bottled fruit, baked custard pudding, Baroness pudding.

Monday.—1. Roast shoulder of mutton and onion sauce, brocoli, baked potatoes. 2. Slices of Baroness pudding warmed, and served with sugar sprinkled over. Cheesecakes.

Tuesday.—1. Mock turtle soup, made with liquor that calf's head was boiled in, and the pieces of head. 2. Hashed mutton, rump-steaks and oyster sauce. 3. Boiled plum-pudding.

Wednesday.—1. Fried whitings, melted butter, potatoes. 2. Boiled beef, suet dumplings, carrots, potatoes, marrow-bones. 3. Arrowroot blancmange, and stewed rhubarb.

Thursday.—1. Pea-soup made from liquor that beef was boiled in. 2. Stewed rump-steak, cold beef, mashed potatoes. 3. Rolled jam pudding.

Friday.—1. Fried soles, melted butter, potatoes. 2. Roast loin of mutton, brocoli, potatoes, bubble-and-squeak. 3. Rice pudding.

Saturday.—1. Rump-steak pie, haricot mutton made with remains of cold loin. 2. Pancakes, ratafia pudding.

Sunday.—1. Roast fillet of veal, boiled ham, spinach and potatoes. 2. Rhubarb tart, custards in glasses, bread-and-butter pudding.

Monday.—1. Baked soles, potatoes. 2. Minced veal and rump-steak pie. 3. Somersetshire dumplings with the remains of custards poured round them; marmalade tartlets.

Tuesday.—1. Gravy soup. 2. Boiled leg of mutton, mashed turnips, suet dumplings, caper sauce, potatoes, veal rissoles made with remains of fillet of veal. 3. Cheese.

Wednesday.—1. Stewed mullet. 2. Roast fowls, bacon, gravy, and bread sauce, mutton pudding, made with a few slices of the cold meat and the addition of two kidneys. 3. Baked lemon pudding.

Thursday.—1. Vegetable soup made with liquor that the mutton was boiled in, and mixed with the remains of gravy soup. 2. Roast ribs of beef, Yorkshire pudding, horseradish sauce, brocoli and potatoes. 3. Apple pudding or macaroni.

Friday.—1. Stewed eels, pork cutlets, and tomato sauce. 2. Cold beef, mashed potatoes. 3. Plum tart made with bottled fruit.

Saturday.—1. Rumpsteak-and-kidney pudding, broiled beef-bones, greens and potatoes. 2. Jam tartlets made with pieces of paste from plum tart, baked custard pudding.

MARCH, Things in Season.

Fish.—Barbel, brill, carp, crabs, crayfish, dace, eels, flounders, haddocks, herrings, lampreys, lobsters, mussels, oysters, perch, pike, plaice, prawns, shrimps, skate, smelts, soles, sprats, sturgeon, tench, thornback, turbot, whiting.

Meat.—Beef, house lamb, mutton, pork, veal.

Poultry.—Capons, chickens, ducklings, tame and wild pigeons, pullets with eggs, turkeys, wild-fowl, though now not in full season.

Game.—Grouse, hares, partridges, pheasants, snipes, woodcock.

Vegetables.—Beetroot, brocoli (purple and white), Brussels sprouts, cabbages, carrots, celery, chervil, cresses, cucumbers (forced), endive, kidney-beans, lettuces, parsnips, potatoes, savoys, seakale, spinach, turnips,—various herbs.

Fruit.—Apples (golden and Dutch pippins), grapes, medlars, nuts, oranges, pears (Bon Chrétien), walnuts, dried fruits (foreign), such as almonds and raisins; French and Spanish plums; prunes, figs, dates, crystallized preserves.

MARMALADE AND VERMICELLI PUDDING.

Ingredients.—1 breakfastcupful of vermicelli, 2 tablespoonfuls of marmalade, ¼ lb. of raisins, sugar to taste, 3 eggs, milk. *Mode.*—Pour some boiling milk on the vermicelli, and let it remain covered for 10 minutes; then mix with it the marmalade, stoned raisins, sugar, and beaten eggs. Stir all well together, put the mixture into a buttered mould, boil for 1½ hour, and serve with custard sauce. *Time.*—1½ hour. *Average cost,* 1*s.* *Sufficient* for 5 or 6 persons. *Seasonable* at any time.

MARROW-BONES, Boiled.

Ingredients.—Bones, a small piece of common paste, a floured cloth. *Mode.*—Have the bones neatly sawed into convenient sizes, and cover the ends with a small piece of common crust, made with flour and water. Over this tie a floured cloth, and place the bones upright in a saucepan of boiling water, taking care there is sufficient to cover them. Boil them for 2 hours, remove the cloth and paste, and serve them upright on a napkin with dry toast. Many persons clear the marrow from the bones after they are cooked, spread it over a slice of toast and add a seasoning of pepper: when served in this manner, it must be very expeditiously sent to table, as it so soon gets cold. *Time.*—2 hours. *Seasonable* at any time.

Note.—Marrow-bones may be baked after preparing them as in the preceding recipe; they should be laid in a deep dish, and baked for 2 hours.

MARROW DUMPLINGS, to serve with Roast Meat, in Soup, with Salad, &c.

(*German Recipe.*)

Ingredients.—1 oz. of beef marrow, 1 oz. of butter, 2 eggs, 2 penny rolls, 1 teaspoonful of minced onion, 1 teaspoonful of minced parsley, salt and grated nutmeg to taste. *Mode.*—Beat the marrow and butter together to a cream; well whisk the eggs, and add these to the other ingredients. When they are well stirred, put in the rolls, which should previously be well soaked in boiling milk, strained, and beaten up with a fork. Add the remaining ingredients, omitting the minced onion where the flavour is very much disliked, and form the mixture into small round dumplings. Drop these into boiling broth, and let them simmer for about 20 minutes or ½ hour. They may be served in soup, with roast meat, or with salad, as in Germany, where they are more frequently sent to table than in this country. They are very good. *Time.*—20 minutes to ½ hour. *Average cost*, 6*d.* *Sufficient* for 7 or 8 dumplings. *Seasonable* at any time.

MARROW PUDDING, Baked or Boiled.

Ingredients.—½ pint of bread crumbs, 1½ pint of milk, 6 oz. of marrow, 4 eggs, ¼ lb. of raisins or currants, or 2 oz. of each; sugar and grated nutmeg to taste. *Mode.*—Make the milk boiling, pour it hot on to the bread crumbs, and let these remain covered for about ½ hour; shred the marrow, beat up the eggs, and mix these with the bread crumbs; add the remaining ingredients, beat the mixture well, and either put it into a buttered mould and boil it for 2¼ hours, or put it into a pie-dish edged with puff-paste, and bake for rather more than ¾ hour. Before sending it to table, sift a little pounded sugar over, after being turned out of the mould or basin. *Time.*—2¼ hours to boil, ¾ hour to bake. *Average cost*, 1*s.* 2*d.* *Sufficient* for 5 or 6 persons. *Seasonable* at any time.

MAY—BILLS OF FARE.

Dinner for 18 persons.

First Course.

Asparagus Soup, removed by Salmon and Lobster Sauce.

Fried Filleted Soles. — Vase of Flowers. — Fillets of Mackerel, à la Maître d'Hôtel.

Ox-tail Soup, removed by Brill & Shrimp Sauce.

Entrées.

Lamb Cutlets and Cucumbers.

Lobster Pudding. — Vase of Flowers. — Curried Fowl.

Veal Ragoût.

Second Course.

Saddle of Lamb.

Raised Pie.

Roast Fowls. — Vase of Flowers. — Boiled Capon and White Sauce.

Braised Ham.

Roast Veal.

Third Course.

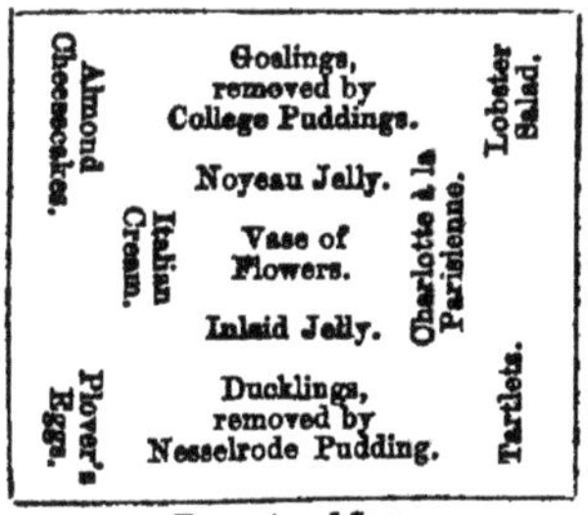

Dessert and Ices.

Dinner for 12 persons.

First Course.—White soup; asparagus soup; salmon cutlets; boiled turbot and lobster sauce. *Entrées.*—Chicken vol-au-vent; lamb cutlets and cucumbers; fricandeau of veal; stewed mushrooms. *Second Course.*—Roast lamb; haunch of mutton; boiled and roast fowls; vegetables. *Third Course.*—Ducklings; goslings; Charlotte Russe; Vanilla cream; gooseberry tart; custards; cheesecakes; cabinet pudding and iced pudding; dessert and ices.

Dinner for 10 persons.

First Course.—Spring soup; salmon à la Genévése; red mullet. *Entrées.*—Chicken vol-au-vent; calf's liver and bacon aux fines herbes. *Second Course.*—Saddle of mutton; half calf's head, tongue, and brains; braised ham; asparagus. *Third Course.*—Roast pigeons; ducklings; sponge-cake pudding; Charlotte à la vanille; gooseberry tart; cream; cheesecakes; apricot-jam tart; dessert and ices.

Dinner for 8 persons.

First Course.—Julienne soup; brill and lobster sauce; fried fillets of mackerel. *Entrées.*—Lamb cutlets and cucumbers; lobster patties. *Second Course.*—Roast fillet of veal; boiled leg of lamb; asparagus. *Third Course.*—Ducklings; gooseberry tart; custards; fancy pastry; soufflé; dessert and ices.

Dinner for 6 persons.

First Course.—Vermicelli soup; boiled salmon and anchovy sauce. *Entrées.*—Fillets of beef and tomato sauce; sweet-

breads. *Second Course.*—Roast lamb; boiled capon; asparagus. *Third Course.*—Ducklings; cabinet pudding; compôte of gooseberries; custards in glasses; blancmange; lemon tartlets; fondue; dessert.

First Course.—Macaroni soup; boiled mackerel à la maître d'hôtel; fried smelts. *Entrées.*—Scollops of fowl; lobster pudding. *Second Course.*—Boiled leg of lamb and spinach; roast sirloin of beef and horseradish sauce; vegetables. *Third Course.*—Roast leveret; salad; soufflé of rice; ramakins; strawberry-jam tartlets; orange jelly; dessert.

First Course.—Julienne soup; trout with Dutch sauce; salmon cutlets. *Entrées.*—Lamb cutlets and mushrooms; vol-au-vent of chicken. *Second Course.*—Roast lamb; calf's head à la tortue; vegetables. *Third Course.*—Spring chickens; iced pudding; Vanilla cream; clear jelly; tartlets; cheesecakes; dessert.

First Course.—Soup à la reine; crimped trout and lobster sauce; baked whitings aux fines herbes. *Entrées.*—Braised mutton cutlets and cucumbers; stewed pigeons. *Second Course.*—Roast fillet of veal; bacon-cheek and greens; fillet of beef à la jardinière. *Third Course.*—Ducklings; soufflé à la vanille; compôte of oranges; meringues; gooseberry tart; fondue; dessert.

MAY, Plain Family Dinners for.

Sunday.—1. Vegetable soup. 2. Saddle of mutton, asparagus and potatoes. 3. Gooseberry tart, custards.

Monday.—1. Fried whitings, anchovy sauce. 2. Cold mutton, mashed potatoes, stewed veal. 3. Fig pudding.

Tuesday.—1. Haricot mutton, made from remains of cold mutton, rump-steak pie. 2. Macaroni.

Wednesday.—1. Roast loin of veal and spinach, boiled bacon, mutton cutlets and tomato sauce. 2. Gooseberry pudding and cream.

Thursday.—1. Spring soup. 2. Roast leg of lamb, mint sauce, spinach, curried veal and rice. 3. Lemon pudding.

Friday.—1. Boiled mackerel and parsley-and-butter. 2. Stewed rump-steak, cold lamb and salad. 3. Baked gooseberry pudding.

Saturday.—1. Vermicelli. 2. Rump-steak pudding, lamb cutlets, and cucumbers. 3. Macaroni.

Sunday.—1. Boiled salmon and lobster or caper sauce. 2. Roast lamb, mint sauce, asparagus, potatoes. 3. Plum-pudding, gooseberry tart.

Monday.—1. Salmon warmed in remains of lobster sauce and garnished with croûtons. 2. Stewed knuckle of veal and rice, cold lamb and dressed cucumber. 3. Slices of pudding warmed, and served with sugar sprinkled over. Baked rice pudding.

Tuesday.—1. Roast ribs of beef, horse-radish sauce, Yorkshire pudding, spinach and potatoes. 2. Boiled lemon pudding.

Wednesday.—1. Fried soles, melted butter. 2. Cold beef and dressed cucumber or salad, veal cutlets and bacon. 3. Baked plum-pudding.

Thursday.—1. Spring soup. 2. Calf's liver and bacon, broiled beef-bones, spinach and potatoes. 3. Gooseberry tart.

Friday.—1. Roast shoulder of mutton, baked potatoes, onion sauce, spinach. 2. Currant dumplings.

Saturday.—1. Broiled mackerel, fennel sauce or plain melted butter. 2. Rump-steak pie, hashed mutton, vegetables. 3. Baked arrowroot pudding.

MAY, Things in Season.

Fish.—Carp, chub, crabs, crayfish, dory, herrings, lobsters, mackerel, red and gray mullet, prawns, salmon, shad, smelts, soles, trout, turbot.

Meat.—Beef, lamb, mutton, veal.

Poultry.—Chickens, ducklings, fowls, green geese, leverets, pullets, rabbits.

Vegetables.—Asparagus, beans, early cabbages, carrots, cauliflowers, cresses, cucumbers, lettuces, pease, early potatoes, salads, sea-kale,—various herbs.

Fruit.—Apples, green apricots, cherries, currants for tarts, gooseberries, melons, pears, rhubarb, strawberries.

MAYONNAISE, a Sauce or Salad-Dressing for cold Chicken, Meat, and other cold Dishes.

Ingredients.—The yolks of 2 eggs, 6 tablespoonfuls of salad oil, 4 tablespoonfuls of vinegar, salt and white pepper to taste, 1 tablespoonful of white stock, 2 tablespoonfuls of cream. *Mode.*—Put the yolks of the eggs into a basin, with a seasoning of pepper and salt; have ready the above quantities of oil and vinegar, in separate vessels; add them *very gradually* to the eggs; continue stirring and rubbing the mixture with a wooden spoon, as herein consists the secret of having a nice smooth sauce. It cannot be stirred too frequently, and it should be made in a very cool place, or, if ice is at hand, it should be mixed over it. When the vinegar and oil are well incorporated with the eggs, add the stock and cream, stirring all the time, and it will then be ready for use.

For a fish Mayonnaise, this sauce may be coloured with lobster-spawn, pounded; and for poultry or meat, where variety is desired, a little parsley-juice may be used to add to its appearance. Cucumber, tarragon, or any other flavoured vinegar, may be substituted for plain, where they are liked. *Average cost*, for this quantity, 7*d*. *Sufficient* for a small salad.

Note.—In mixing the oil and vinegar with the eggs, put in first a few drops of oil, and then a few drops of vinegar, never adding a large quantity of either at one time. By this means, you can be more certain of the sauce not curdling. Patience and practice, let us add, are two essentials for making this sauce good.

MELONS.

This fruit is rarely preserved or cooked in any way, but is sent whole to table on a dish garnished with leaves or flowers, as fancy dictates. A border of any other kind of small fruit, arranged round the melon, has a pretty effect, the colour of the former contrasting nicely with the melon. Plenty of pounded sugar should be served with it; and the fruit should be cut lengthwise, in moderate-sized slices. In America, it is frequently eaten with pepper and salt. *Average cost.*—English, in full season, 3*s*. 6*d*. to 5*s*. each; when scarce, 10*s*. to 15*s*.; *seasonable*, June to August. French, 2*s*. to 3*s*. 6*d*. each; *seasonable*, June and July. Dutch, 9*d*. to 2*s*. each; *seasonable*, July and August.

MERINGUES.

Ingredients.—½ lb. of pounded sugar, the whites of 4 eggs. *Mode.*—Whisk the whites of the eggs to a stiff froth, and, with a wooden spoon, stir in *quickly* the pounded sugar; and have some boards thick enough to put in the oven to prevent the bottom of the meringues from acquiring too much colour. Cut some strips of paper about 2 inches wide; place this paper on the board, and drop a tablespoonful at a time of the mixture on the paper, taking care to let all the meringues be the same size. In dropping it from the spoon, give the mixture the form of an egg, and keep the meringues about 2 inches apart from each other on the paper. Strew over them some sifted sugar, and bake in a moderate oven for ½ hour. As soon as they begin to colour, remove them from the oven; take each slip of paper by the two ends, and turn it gently on the table, and, with a small spoon, take out the soft part of each meringue. Spread some clean paper on the board, turn the meringues upside

MERINGUES.

down, and put them into the oven to harden and brown on the other side. When required for table, fill them with whipped cream, flavoured with liqueur or vanilla, and sweetened with pounded sugar. Join two of the meringues together, and pile them high in the dish, as shown in the annexed drawing. To vary their appearance, finely-chopped almonds or currants may be strewn over them before the sugar is sprinkled over; and they may be garnished with any bright-coloured preserve. Great expedition is necessary in making this sweet dish; as, if the meringues are not put into the oven as soon as the sugar and eggs are mixed, the former melts, and the mixture would run on the paper, instead of keeping its egg-shape. The sweeter the meringues are made, the crisper will they be; but, if there is not sufficient sugar mixed with them, they will most likely be tough. They are sometimes coloured with cochineal; and, if kept well covered in a dry place, will remain good for a month or six weeks. *Time.*—Altogether, about ½ hour. *Average cost*, with the cream and flavouring, 1s. *Sufficient* to make 2 dozen meringues. *Seasonable* at any time.

MILK.

Milk, when of good quality, is of an opaque white colour: the cream always comes to the top; the well-known milky odour is strong; it will boil without altering its appearance in these respects; the little bladders which arise on the surface will renew themselves if broken by the spoon. To boil milk is, in fact, the simplest way of testing its quality. The commonest adulterations of milk are not of a hurtful character. It is a good deal thinned with water, and sometimes thickened with a little starch, or coloured with yolk of egg, or even saffron; but these processes have nothing murderous in them.

MILK AND CREAM, to keep, in hot Weather.

When the weather is very warm, and it is very difficult to prevent milk from turning sour and spoiling the cream, it should be scalded, and it will then remain good for a few hours. It must on no account be allowed to boil, or there will be a skin instead of a cream upon the milk; and the slower the process the safer will it be. A very good plan to scald milk, is to put the pan that contains it into a saucepan or wide kettle of boiling water. When the surface looks thick, the milk is sufficiently scalded, and it should then be put away in a cool place in the same vessel that it was scalded in. Cream may be kept for 24 hours, if scalded without sugar; and by the addition of the latter ingredient, it will remain good double the time, if kept in a cool place. All pans, jugs, and vessels intended for milk, should be kept beautifully clean, and well scalded before the milk is put in, as any negligence in this respect may cause large quantities of it to be spoiled; and milk should never be kept in vessels of zinc or copper. Milk may be preserved good in hot weather, for a few hours, by placing the jug which contains it in ice, or very cold water; or a pinch of bicarbonate of soda may be introduced into the liquid.

MILK AND CREAM, Separation of.

If it be desired that the milk should be freed entirely from cream, it should be poured into a very shallow broad pan or dish, not more than 1½ inch deep, as cream cannot rise through a great depth of milk. In cold and wet weather, milk is not so rich as it is in summer and warm weather, and the morning's milk is always richer than the evening's. The last-drawn milk of each milking, at all times and seasons, is richer than the first-drawn, and on that account should be set apart for cream. Milk should be shaken as little as possible when carried from the cow to the dairy, and should be poured into the pans very gently. Persons not keeping cows, may always have a little cream, provided the milk they purchase be pure and unadulterated. As soon as it comes in, it should be poured into very shallow open pie-dishes, and set by in a very cool place, and in 7 or 8 hours a nice cream should have risen to the surface.

MILK AND CREAM, Substitute for, in Tea and Coffee.

Ingredients.—1 new laid egg to every large breakfastcupful of tea or coffee. *Mode.*—Beat up the whole of the egg in a basin, put it into a cup, and pour over it the tea or coffee quite hot, stirring all the time to prevent the egg from curdling. In point of nourishment, both tea and coffee are much improved by this addition. *Sufficient.*—1 egg to every large breakfastcupful of tea or coffee.

MILK SOUP (a nice Dish for Children).

Ingredients.—2 quarts of milk, 1 saltspoonful of salt, 1 teaspoonful of powdered cinnamon, 3 teaspoonfuls of pounded sugar, or more if liked, 4 thin slices of bread, the yolks of 6 eggs. *Mode.*—Boil the milk with the salt, cinnamon, and sugar; lay the bread in a deep dish, pour over it a little of the milk, and keep it hot over a stove, without burning. Beat up the yolks of the eggs, add them to the milk, and stir it over the fire till it thickens. Do not let it curdle. Pour it upon the bread, and serve. *Time.*—¾ of an hour. *Average cost*, 8*d.* per quart. *Seasonable* all the year. *Sufficient* for 10 children.

MINCE PIES.

Ingredients.—Good puff-paste, mincemeat. *Mode.*—Make some good puff-paste by recipe; roll it out to the thickness of about ¼ inch, and line some good-sized pattypans with it; fill them with mincemeat, cover with the paste, and cut it off all round close to the edge of the tin. Put the pies into a brisk oven, to draw the paste up, and bake for 25 minutes, or longer, should the pies be very large; brush them over with the white of an egg, beaten with the blade of a knife to a stiff froth; sprinkle over pounded sugar, and put them into the oven for a minute or two, to dry the egg; dish the pies on a white d'oyley, and serve hot. They may be merely sprinkled with pounded sugar instead of being glazed, when that mode is preferred. To re-warm them, put the pies on the pattypans, and let them remain in the oven for 10 minutes or ½ hour, and they will be almost as good as if freshly made. *Time.*—25 to 30 minutes; 10 minutes to re-warm them. *Average cost*, 4*d.* each. *Sufficient*—½ lb. of paste for 4 pies. *Seasonable* at Christmas time.

MINCE PIES.

MINCEMEAT.

Ingredients.—2 lbs. of raisins, 3 lbs. of currants, 1½ lb. of lean beef, 3 lbs. of beef suet, 2 lbs. of moist sugar, 2 oz. of citron, 2 oz. of candied lemon-peel, 2 oz. of candied orange-peel, 1 large nutmeg, 1 pottle of apples, the rind of 2 lemons, the juice of 1, ½ pint of brandy. *Mode.*—Stone and *cut* the raisins once or twice across, but do not chop them; wash, dry, and pick the currants free from stalks and grit, and mince the beef and suet, taking care that the latter is chopped very fine; slice the citron and candied peel, grate the nutmeg, and pare, core, and mince the apples; mince the lemon-peel, strain the juice, and when all the ingredients are thus prepared, mix them well together, adding the brandy when the other things are well blended; press the whole into a jar, carefully exclude the air, and the mincemeat will be ready for use in a fortnight.

If an additional quantity of spice be preferred, add ½ teaspoonful of pounded mace, and the same of pounded allspice. We, however, prefer the mincemeat without the latter ingredients, and can vouch for its excellence. *Average cost* for this quantity, 8*s*. *Seasonable.*—Make this about the beginning of December.

MINCEMEAT, Excellent.

Ingredients.—3 large lemons, 3 large apples, 1 lb. of stoned raisins, 1 lb. of currants, 1 lb. of suet, 2 lbs. of moist sugar, 1 oz. of sliced candied citron, 1 oz. of sliced candied orange-peel, and the same quantity of lemon-peel, 1 teacupful of brandy, 2 tablespoonfuls of orange marmalade. *Mode.*—Grate the rinds of the lemons; squeeze out the juice, strain it, and boil the remainder of the lemons until tender enough to pulp or chop very finely. Then add to this pulp the apples, which should be baked, and their skins and cores removed; put in the remaining ingredients one by one, and, as they are added, mix everything very thoroughly together. Put the mincemeat into a stone jar with a closely-fitting lid, and in a fortnight it will be ready for use. *Seasonable.*—This should be made the first or second week in December.

MINT SAUCE, to serve with Roast Lamb.

Ingredients. — 4 dessertspoonfuls of chopped mint, 2 dessertspoonfuls of pounded white sugar, ¼ pint of vinegar. *Mode.*—Wash the mint, which should be young and fresh-gathered, free from grit; pick the leaves from the stalks, mince them very fine, and put them into a tureen; add the sugar and vinegar, and stir till the former is dissolved. This sauce is better by being made 2 or 3 hours before wanted for table, as the vinegar then becomes impregnated with the flavour of the mint. By many persons, the above proportion of sugar would not be considered sufficient; but as tastes vary, we have given the quantity which we have found to suit the general palate. *Average cost,* 3*d*. *Sufficient* to serve with a middling-size joint of lamb.

Note.—Where green mint is scarce and not obtainable, mint vinegar may be substituted for it, and will be found very acceptable in early spring.

MINT VINEGAR.

Ingredients.—Vinegar, mint. *Mode.*—Procure some nice fresh mint, pick the leaves from the stalks, and fill a bottle or jar with them. Add vinegar to them until the bottle is full; *cover closely* to exclude the air, and let it infuse for a fortnight. Then strain the liquor, and put it into small bottles for use, of which the corks should be sealed. *Seasonable.*—This should be made in June, July, or August.

MOCK TURTLE SOUP.

I.

Ingredients.—½ a calf's head, ¼ lb. of butter, ¼ lb. of lean ham, 2 tablespoonfuls of minced parsley, a little minced lemon thyme, sweet marjoram, basil, 2 onions, a few chopped mushrooms (when obtainable), 2 shalots, 2 tablespoonfuls of flour, ¼ bottle of Madeira or sherry, force-meat balls, cayenne, salt and mace to taste, the juice of 1 lemon and 1 Seville orange, 1 dessertspoonful of pounded sugar, 3 quarts of best stock. *Mode.*—Scald the head with the skin on, remove the brain, tie the head up in a cloth, and let it boil for 1 hour. Then take the meat from the bones, cut it into small square pieces, and throw them into cold water. Now take the meat, put it into a stewpan, and cover with stock; let it boil gently for an hour, or rather more, if not quite tender, and set it on one side. Melt the butter in another stewpan, and add the ham, cut small, with the herbs, parsley, onions, shalots, mushrooms, and nearly a pint of stock; let these simmer slowly for 2 hours, and then dredge in as much flour as will dry up the butter. Fill up with the remainder of the stock, add the wine, let it stew gently for 10 minutes, rub it through a tammy, and put it to the calf's head; season with cayenne, and, if required, a little salt; add the juice of the orange and lemon; and when liked, ¼ teaspoonful of pounded mace, and the sugar. Put in the force-meat balls, simmer 5 minutes, and serve very hot. *Time.*—4½ hours. *Average cost,* 3*s*. 6*d*. per quart, or 2*s*. 6*d*. without wine or force-meat balls. *Seasonable* in winter. *Sufficient* for 10 persons.

Note.—The bones of the head should be well stewed in the liquor it was first boiled in, and will make good white stock, flavoured with vegetables, &c.

II.

(*More Economical.*)

Ingredients.—A knuckle of veal weighing 5 or 6 lbs., 2 cowheels, 2 large onions stuck with cloves, 1 bunch of sweet herbs, 3 blades of mace, salt to taste, 12 peppercorns, 1 glass of sherry, 24 force-meat balls, a little lemon-juice, 4 quarts of water. *Mode.*—Put all the ingredients, except the force-meat balls and lemon-juice, in an earthen jar, and stew for 6 hours. Do not open it till cold. When wanted for use, skim off all the fat, and strain carefully; place it on the fire, cut up the meat into inch-and-a-half squares, put it, with the force-meat balls and lemon-juice, into the soup, and serve. It can be flavoured with a tablespoonful of anchovy, or Harvey's sauce. *Time.*—6 hours. *Average cost*, 1*s.* 4*d.* per quart. *Seasonable* in winter. *Sufficient* for 10 persons.

MUFFINS.

Ingredients.—To every quart of milk allow 1½ oz. of German yeast, a little salt; flour. *Mode.*—Warm the milk, add to it the yeast, and mix these well together; put them into a pan, and stir in sufficient flour to make the whole into a dough of rather a soft consistence; cover it over with a cloth, and place it in a warm place to rise, and, when light and nicely risen, divide the dough into pieces, and round them to the proper shape with the hands; place them in a layer of flour about two inches thick, on wooden trays, and let them rise again: when this is effected, they each will exhibit a semi-globular shape. Then place them carefully on a hot plate or stove, and bake them until they are slightly browned, turning them when they are done on one side. Muffins are not easily made, and are more generally purchased than manufactured at home. *To toast them*, divide the edge of the muffin all round, by pulling it open, to the depth of about an inch, with the fingers. Put it on a toasting-fork, and hold it before a very clear fire until one side is nicely browned, but not burnt; turn, and toast it on the other. Do not toast them too quickly, as, if this be done, the middle of the muffin will not be warmed through. When done, divide them by pulling them open; butter them slightly on both sides, put them together again, and cut them into halves: when sufficient are toasted and buttered, pile them on a very hot dish, and send them very quickly to table. *Time.*—From 20 minutes to ½ hour to bake them. *Sufficient.*—Allow 1 muffin to each person.

MUFFINS.

MULBERRIES, Preserved.

Ingredients.—To 2 lbs. of fruit and 1 pint of juice allow 2½ lbs. of loaf sugar. *Mode.*—Put some of the fruit into a preserving pan, and simmer it gently until the juice is well drawn. Strain it through a bag, measure it, and to every pint allow the above proportion of sugar and fruit. Put the sugar into the preserving-pan, moisten it with the juice, boil it up, skim well, and then add the mulberries, which should be ripe, but not soft enough to break to a pulp. Let them stand in the syrup till warm through, then set them on the fire to boil gently; when half done, turn them carefully into an earthen pan, and let them remain till the next day; then boil them as before, and when the syrup is thick, and becomes firm when cold, put the preserve into pots. In making this, care should be taken not to break the mulberries: this may be avoided by very gentle stirring, and by simmering the fruit very slowly. *Time.*—¾ hour to extract the juice; ¼ hour to boil the mulberries the first time, ¼ hour the second time. *Seasonable* in August and September.

MULLAGATAWNY SOUP.

Ingredients.—2 tablespoonfuls of curry powder, 6 onions, 1 clove of garlic, 1 oz. of pounded almonds, a little lemon-pickle, or mango-juice, to taste; 1 fowl or rabbit; 4 slices of lean bacon; 2 quarts of medium stock, or, if wanted very good, best stock. *Mode.*—Slice and fry the onions of a nice colour; line the stewpan with the bacon; cut up the rabbit or fowl into small joints, and slightly brown them; put in the fried onions, the garlic, and stock, and simmer gently till the meat is tender; skim very carefully, and when the meat is done, rub the curry powder to a smooth batter;

add it to the soup with the almonds, which must be first pounded with a little of the stock. Put in seasoning and lemon-pickle or mango-juice to taste, and serve boiled rice with it. *Time.*—2 hours. *Average cost,* 1*s.* 6*d.* per quart. *Seasonable* in winter. *Sufficient* for 8 persons.

Note.—This soup can also be made with breast of veal, or calf's head. Vegetable mullagatawny is made with veal stock, by boiling and pulping chopped vegetable marrow, cucumbers, onions, and tomatoes, and seasoning with curry powder and cayenne. Nice pieces of meat, good curry powder, and strong stock, are necessary to make this soup good.

MULLET, Grey.

Ingredients.—¼ lb. of salt to each gallon of water. *Mode.*—If the fish be very large, it should be laid in cold water, and gradually brought to a boil; if small, put it in boiling water, salted in the above proportion. Serve with anchovy sauce and plain melted butter. *Time.*—According to size, ¼ to ¾ hour. *Average cost,* 8*d.* per lb. *Seasonable* from July to October.

MULLET, Red.

Ingredients.—Oiled paper, thickening of butter and flour, ½ teaspoonful of anchovy sauce, 1 glass of sherry; cayenne and salt to taste. *Mode.*—Clean the fish, take out the gills, but leave the inside, fold in oiled paper, and bake them gently. When done, take the liquor that flows from the fish, add a thickening of butter kneaded with flour; put in the other ingredients, and let it boil for 2 minutes. Serve the sauce in a tureen, and the fish, either with or without the paper cases. *Time.*—About 25 minutes. *Average cost,* 1*s.* each. *Seasonable* at any time, but more plentiful in summer.

Note.—Red mullet may be broiled, and should be folded in oiled paper, the same as in the preceding recipe, and seasoned with pepper and salt. They may be served without sauce; but if any is required, use melted butter, Italian or anchovy sauce. They should never be plain boiled.

MUSHROOM KETCHUP.

Ingredients.—To each peck of mushrooms ½ lb. of salt; to each quart of mushroom-liquor ¼ oz. of cayenne, ½ oz. of allspice, ½ oz. of ginger, 2 blades of pounded mace. *Mode.*—Choose full-grown mushroom flaps, and take care they are perfectly *fresh gathered* when the weather is tolerably dry; for, if they are picked during very heavy rain, the ketchup from which they are made is liable to get musty, and will not keep long. Put a layer of them in a deep pan, sprinkle salt over them, and then another layer of mushrooms, and so on alternately. Let them remain for a few hours, when break them up with the hand; put them in a nice cool place for 3 days, occasionally stirring and mashing them well, to extract from them as much juice as possible. Now measure the quantity of liquor without straining, and to each quart allow the above proportion of spices, &c. Put all into a stone jar, cover it up very closely, put it in a saucepan of boiling water, set it over the fire, and let it boil for 3 hours. Have ready a nice clean stewpan; turn into it the contents of the jar, and let the whole simmer very gently for ½ hour; pour it into a jug, where it should stand in a cool place till the next day; then pour it off into another jug, and strain it into very dry clean bottles, and do not squeeze the mushrooms. To each pint of ketchup add a few drops of brandy. Be careful not to shake the contents, but leave all the sediment behind in the jug; cork well, and either seal or rosin the cork, so as perfectly to exclude the air. When a very clear bright ketchup is wanted, the liquor must be strained through a very fine hair-sieve, or flannel bag, *after* it has been very gently poured off; if the operation is not successful, it must be repeated until you have quite a clear liquor. It should be examined occasionally, and if it is spoiling, should be reboiled with a few peppercorns. *Seasonable* from the beginning of September to the middle of October, when this ketchup should be made.

Note.—This flavouring ingredient, if genuine and well prepared, is one of the most useful store sauces to the experienced cook, and no trouble should be spared in its preparation. Double ketchup is made by reducing the liquor to half the quantity; for example, 1 quart must be boiled down to 1 pint. This goes farther than ordinary ketchup, as so little is required to flavour a good quantity of gravy.

The sediment may also be bottled for immediate use, and will be found to answer for flavouring *thick* soups or gravies.

MUSHROOM POWDER (a valuable addition to Sauces and Gravies, when fresh Mushrooms are not obtainable).

Ingredients.—½ peck of large mushrooms, 2 onions, 12 cloves, ¼ oz. of pounded mace, 2 teaspoonfuls of white pepper. *Mode.*—Peel the mushrooms, wipe them perfectly free from grit and dirt, remove the black fur, and reject all those that are at all worm-eaten; put them into a stewpan with the above ingredients, but without water; shake them over a clear fire, till all the liquor is dried up, and be careful not to let them burn; arrange them on tins, and dry them in a slow oven; pound them to a fine powder, which put into small *dry* bottles; cork well, seal the corks, and keep it in a dry place. In using this powder, add it to the gravy just before serving, when it will merely require one boil-up. The flavour imparted by this means to the gravy, ought to be exceedingly good. *Seasonable.*—This should be made in September, or at the beginning of October.

Note.—If the bottles in which it is stored away are not perfectly dry, as, also, the mushroom powder, it will keep good but a very short time.

MUSHROOM SAUCE, very rich and good, to serve with Fowls or Rabbits.

Ingredients. — 1 pint of mushroom-buttons, salt to taste, a little grated nutmeg, 1 blade of pounded mace, 1 pint of cream, 2 oz. of butter, flour to thicken. *Mode.*—Rub the buttons with a piece of flannel and salt, to take off the skin; cut off the stalks, and put them in a stewpan with the above ingredients, previously kneading together the butter and flour; boil the whole for about ten minutes, stirring all the time. Pour some of the sauce over the fowls, and the remainder serve in a tureen. *Time.*—10 minutes. *Average cost,* 2*s.* *Sufficient* to serve with a pair of fowls. *Seasonable* from August to October.

MUSHROOM SAUCE, Brown, to serve with Roast Meat, &c.

Ingredients.—½ pint of button mushrooms, ½ pint of good beef gravy, 1 tablespoonful of mushroom ketchup (if at hand), thickening of butter and flour. *Mode.*—Put the gravy into a saucepan, thicken it, and stir over the fire until it boils. Prepare the mushrooms by cutting off the stalks, and wiping them free from grit and dirt; the large flap mushrooms cut into small pieces will answer for a brown sauce, when the buttons are not obtainable; put them into the gravy, and let them simmer very gently for about 10 minutes; then add the ketchup, and serve. *Time.*—Rather more than 10 minutes. *Seasonable* from August to October.

Note.—When fresh mushrooms are not obtainable, the powder may be used as a substitute for brown sauce.

MUSHROOM SAUCE, White, to serve with Boiled Fowls, Cutlets, &c.

Ingredients.—Rather more than ½ pint of button mushrooms, lemon-juice, and water, 1 oz. of butter, ½ pint of Béchamel, ¼ teaspoonful of pounded sugar. *Mode.*—Turn the mushrooms white by putting them into lemon-juice and water, having previously cut off the stalks and wiped them perfectly free from grit. Chop them, and put them in a stewpan with the butter. When the mushrooms are softened, add the Béchamel, and simmer for about 5 minutes; should they, however, not be done enough, allow rather more time. They should not boil longer than necessary, as they would then lose their colour and flavour. Rub the whole through a tammy, and serve very hot. After this, it should be warmed in a bain marie. *Time.* — Altogether ¼ hour. *Average cost,* 1*s.* *Seasonable* from August to October.

MUSHROOM SAUCE, White, to serve with Boiled Fowls, Cutlets, &c. (a more simple Method).

Ingredients.—½ pint of melted butter, made with milk, ½ pint of button mushrooms, 1 dessertspoonful of mushroom ketchup, if at hand; cayenne and salt to taste. *Mode.*—Make the melted butter with milk, and add to it the mushrooms, which must be nicely cleaned, and free from grit, and the stalks cut off. Let them simmer gently for about 10 minutes, or until they are quite tender. Put in the seasoning and ketchup; let it just boil, when serve. *Time.*—Rather more than 10 minutes. *Average cost*, 8*d*. *Seasonable* from August to October.

MUSHROOMS, Baked (a Breakfast, Luncheon, or Supper Dish).

Ingredients. — 16 to 20 mushroom-flaps, butter, pepper to taste. *Mode.*—For this mode of cooking, the mushroom-flaps are better than the buttons, and should not be too large. Cut off a portion of the stalk, peel the top, and wipe the mushrooms carefully with a piece of flannel and a little fine salt. Put them into a tin baking-dish, with a very small piece of butter placed on each mushroom; sprinkle over a little pepper, and let them bake for about 20 minutes, or longer should the mushrooms be very large. Have ready a *very hot* dish, pile the mushrooms high in the centre, pour the gravy round, and send them to table quickly, with very *hot* plates. *Time.*—20 minutes; large mushrooms, ½ hour. *Average cost*, 1*d*. each for large mushroom-flaps. *Sufficient* for 5 or 6 persons. *Seasonable.* — Meadow mushrooms in September and October; cultivated mushrooms may be had at any time.

MUSHROOMS, Broiled (a Breakfast, Luncheon, or Supper Dish).

Ingredients.—Mushroom-flaps, pepper and salt to taste, butter, lemon-juice. *Mode.* — Cleanse the mushrooms by wiping them with a piece of flannel and a little salt; cut off a portion of the stalk, and peel the tops; broil them over a clear fire, turning them once, and arrange them on a very hot dish. Put a small piece of butter on each mushroom, season with pepper and salt, and squeeze over them a few drops of lemon-juice. Place the dish before the fire, and when the butter is melted, serve very hot and quickly. Moderate-sized flaps are better suited to this mode of cooking than the buttons: the latter are better in stews. *Time.*—10 minutes for medium-sized mushrooms.

BROILED MUSHROOMS.

Average cost, 1*d*. each for large mushrooms. *Sufficient.*—Allow 3 or 4 mushrooms to each person. *Seasonable.*—Meadow mushrooms in September and October; cultivated mushrooms may be had at any time.

MUSHROOMS, Dried.

Mode.—Wipe them clean, take away the brown part, and peel off the skin; lay them on sheets of paper to dry, in a cool oven, when they will shrivel considerably. Keep them in paper bags, which hang in a dry place. When wanted for use, put them into cold gravy, bring them gradually to simmer, and it will be found that they will regain nearly their usual size.

MUSHROOMS, Pickled.

Ingredients. — Sufficient vinegar to cover the mushrooms; to each quart of mushrooms, 2 blades of pounded mace, 1 oz. of ground pepper, salt to taste. *Mode.*—Choose some nice young button mushrooms for pickling, and rub off the skin with a piece of flannel and salt, and cut off the stalks; if very large, take out the red inside, and reject the black ones, as they are too old. Put them into a stewpan, sprinkle salt over them, with pounded mace and pepper in the above proportion; shake them well over a clear fire until the liquor flows, and keep them there until they are all dried up again; then add as much vinegar as will cover them; just let it simmer for 1 minute, and store it away in stone jars for use. When cold, tie down with bladder and keep in a dry place: they will remain good for a length of time, and are generally considered delicious. *Seasonable.*—Make this the same time as ketchup, from the beginning of September to the middle of October.

MUSHROOMS, to Preserve.

Ingredients.—To each quart of mushrooms, allow 3 oz. butter, pepper and salt to taste, the juice of 1 lemon, clarified butter. *Mode.*—Peel the mushrooms, put them into cold water, with a little lemon-juice; take them out and *dry* them very carefully in a cloth. Put the butter into a stewpan capable of holding the mushrooms; when it is melted, add the mushrooms, lemon-juice, and a seasoning of pepper and salt; draw them down over a slow fire, and let them remain until their liquor is boiled away, and they have become quite dry, but be careful in not allowing them to stick to the bottom of the stewpan. When done, put them into pots, and pour over the top clarified butter. If wanted for immediate use, they will keep good a few days without being covered over. To re-warm them, put the mushrooms into a stewpan, strain the butter from them, and they will be ready for use. *Average cost*, 1*d*. each. *Seasonable*.—Meadow mushrooms in September and October; cultivated mushrooms may be had at any time.

MUSHROOMS, Stewed.

Ingredients.—1 pint mushroom-buttons, 3 oz. of fresh butter, white pepper and salt to taste, lemon-juice, 1 teaspoonful of flour, cream or milk, ¼ teaspoonful of grated nutmeg. *Mode*.—Cut off the ends of the stalks, and pare neatly a pint of mushroom-buttons; put them into a basin of water, with a little lemon juice, as they are done. When all are prepared, take them from the water with the hands, to avoid the sediment, and put them into a stewpan with the fresh butter, white pepper, salt, and the juice of ½ lemon; cover the pan closely, and let the mushrooms stew gently from 20 to 25 minutes; then thicken the butter with the above proportion of flour, add gradually sufficient cream, or cream and milk, to make the sauce of a proper consistency, and put in the grated nutmeg. If the mushrooms are not perfectly tender, stew them for 5 minutes longer, remove every particle of butter which may be floating on the top, and serve. *Time*.—½ hour. *Average cost*, from 9*d*. to 2*s*. per pint. *Sufficient* for 5 or 6 persons. *Seasonable*.—Meadow mushrooms in September and October.

MUSHROOMS, Stewed in Gravy.

Ingredients.—1 pint of mushroom-buttons, 1 pint of brown gravy, ¼ teaspoonful of grated nutmeg, cayenne and salt to taste. *Mode*.—Make a pint of brown gravy, cut nearly all the stalks away from the mushrooms and peel the tops; put them into a stewpan, with the gravy, and simmer them gently from 20 minutes to ½ hour. Add the nutmeg and a seasoning of cayenne and salt, and serve very hot. *Time*.—20 minutes to ½ hour. *Average cost*, 9*d*. to 2*s*. per pint. *Sufficient* for 5 or 6 persons. *Seasonable*.—Meadow mushrooms in September and October.

MUSTARD, How to Mix.

Ingredients.—Mustard, salt and water. *Mode*. — Mustard should be mixed with water that has been boiled and allowed to cool; hot water destroys its essential properties, and raw cold water might cause it to ferment. Put the mustard into a cup, with a small pinch of salt, and mix with it very gradually sufficient boiled water to make it drop from the spoon without being watery. Stir and mix well, and rub the lumps well down with the back of a spoon, as well-mixed mustard should be perfectly free from these. The mustard-pot should not be more than half-full, or rather less if it will not be used for a day or two, as it is so much better when it is freshly mixed.

MUSTARD, Indian, an excellent Relish to Bread and Butter, or any cold Meat.

Ingredients.—¼ lb. of the best mustard, ¼ lb. of flour, ½ oz. of salt, 4 shalots, 4 tablespoonfuls of vinegar, 4 tablespoonfuls of ketchup, ¼ bottle of anchovy sauce. *Mode*.—Put the mustard, flour, and salt into a basin, and make them into a stiff paste with boiling water. Boil the shalots with the vinegar, ketchup, and anchovy sauce, for 10 minutes, and pour the whole, *boiling*, over the mixture in the basin; stir well, and reduce it to a proper thickness; put it into a bottle, with a bruised shalot at the bottom, and store away for use. This makes an excellent relish, and if properly prepared will keep for years.

MUSTARD, Tartar.

Ingredients. — Horseradish vinegar, cayenne, ½ a teacupful of mustard. *Mode*. —Have ready sufficient horseradish vinegar to mix with the above proportion of mustard; put the mustard into a cup, with a slight seasoning of cayenne; mix it perfectly smooth with the vinegar, adding this a little at a time; rub down with the back of a spoon any lumps that may appear, and do not let it be too thin. Mustard may be flavoured in various ways, with Tarragon, shalot, celery, and many other vinegars, herbs, spices, &c.

MUTTON.

Almost every large city has a particular manner of cutting up, or, as it is called, dressing the carcase. In London this process is very simple, and as our butchers have found that much skewering back, doubling one part over another, or scoring the inner cuticle or fell, tends to spoil the meat and shorten the time it would otherwise keep, they avoid all such treatment entirely. The carcase when flayed (which operation is performed while yet warm), the sheep when hung up and the head removed, presents the profile shown in our cut; the small numerals indicating the parts or joints into which one-half of the animal is cut. After separating the hind from the fore quarters, with eleven ribs to the latter, the quarters are usually subdivided in the manner shown in the sketch, in which the several joints are defined by the intervening lines and figures.

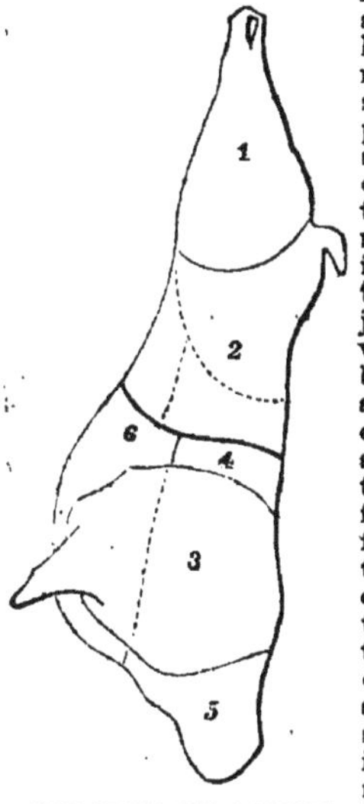

SIDE OF MUTTON, SHOWING THE SEVERAL JOINTS.

Hind quarter: No. 1, the leg; 2, the loin—the two, when cut in one piece, being called the saddle. *Fore quarter:* No. 3, the shoulder; 4 and 5 the neck; No. 5 being called, for distinction, the scrag, which is generally afterwards separated from 4, the lower and better joint; No. 6, the breast. The haunch of mutton, so often served at public dinners and special entertainments, comprises all the leg and so much of the loin, short of the ribs or lap, as is indicated on the upper part of the carcase by a dotted line.

MUTTON, Baked Minced.

[COLD MEAT COOKERY.] *Ingredients.*—The remains of any joint of cold roast mutton, 1 or 2 onions, 1 bunch of savoury herbs, pepper and salt to taste, 2 blades of pounded mace or nutmeg, 1 teacupful of gravy, mashed potatoes. *Mode.*—Mince an onion rather fine, and fry it a light-brown colour; add the herbs and mutton, both of which should be also finely minced and well mixed; season with pepper and salt, and a little pounded mace or nutmeg, and moisten with the above proportion of gravy. Put a layer of mashed potatoes at the bottom of a dish, then the mutton, and then another layer of potatoes, and bake for about ½ hour. *Time.*—½ hour. *Average cost,* exclusive of the meat, 4*d.* *Seasonable* at any time.

Note.—If there should be a large quantity of meat, use 2 onions instead of 1.

MUTTON, Boiled Breast of, and Caper Sauce.

Ingredients.—Breast of mutton, bread crumbs, 2 tablespoonfuls of minced savoury herbs (put a large proportion of parsley), pepper and salt to taste. *Mode.*—Cut off the superfluous fat; bone the meat; sprinkle over a layer of bread crumbs, minced herbs, and seasoning; roll, and bind it up firmly. Boil *gently* for 2 hours, remove the tape, and serve with caper sauce, a little of which should be poured over the meat. *Time.*—2 hours. *Average cost,* 6*d.* per lb. *Sufficient* for 4 or 5 persons. *Seasonable* all the year.

MUTTON, an excellent way to cook a Breast of.

Ingredients.—Breast of mutton, 2 onions, salt and pepper to taste, flour, a bunch of savoury herbs, green peas. *Mode.*—Cut the mutton into pieces about 2 inches square, and let it be tolerably lean; put it into a stewpan, with a little fat or butter, and fry it of a nice brown; then dredge in a little flour, slice the onions, and put it with the herbs in the stewpan; pour in sufficient water *just* to cover the meat, and simmer the whole gently until the mutton is tender. Take out the meat, strain, and skim off all the fat from the gravy, and put both the meat and gravy back into the stewpan; add about a quart of young green peas, and let them boil gently until done. 2 or 3 slices of bacon added and stewed with the mutton give additional flavour; and, to insure the peas being a beautiful green colour, they may be boiled in water separately, and added to the stew at the moment of serving. *Time.*—2½ hours. *Average cost*, 6*d.* per lb. *Sufficient* for 4 or 5 persons. *Seasonable* from June to August.

MUTTON, Broiled, and Tomato Sauce.

[COLD MEAT COOKERY.] *Ingredients.*—A few slices of cold mutton, tomato sauce. *Mode.*—Cut some nice slices from a cold leg or shoulder of mutton; season them with pepper and salt, and broil over a clear fire. Make some tomato sauce, pour it over the mutton, and serve. This makes an excellent dish, and must be served very hot. *Time.*—About 5 minutes to broil the mutton. *Seasonable* in September and October, when tomatoes are plentiful and seasonable.

MUTTON BROTH, to Make.

Ingredients.—1 lb. of the scrag end of the neck of mutton, 1 onion, a bunch of sweet herbs, ½ turnip, 3 pints of water, pepper and salt to taste. *Mode.*—Put the mutton into a stewpan; pour over the water cold, and add the other ingredients. When it boils, skim it very carefully, cover the pan closely, and let it simmer very gently for an hour; strain it, let it cool, take off all the fat from the surface, and warm up as much as may be required, adding, if the patient be allowed to take it, a teaspoonful of minced parsley which has been previously scalded. Pearl barley or rice are very nice additions to mutton broth, and should be boiled as long as the other ingredients. When either of these is added, the broth must not be strained, but merely thoroughly skimmed. Plain mutton broth without seasoning is made by merely boiling the mutton, water, and salt together, straining it, letting the broth cool, skimming all the fat off, and warming up as much as is required. This preparation would be very tasteless and insipid, but likely to agree with very delicate stomachs, whereas the least addition of other ingredients would have the contrary effect. *Time.*—1 hour. *Average cost*, 7*d.* *Sufficient* to make from 1½ to 2 pints of broth. *Seasonable* at any time.

Note.—Veal broth may be made in the same manner; the knuckle of a leg or shoulder is the part usually used for this purpose. It is very good with the addition of the inferior joints of a fowl, or a few shank-bones.

MUTTON BROTH, to Make Quickly.

Ingredients.—1 or 2 chops from a neck of mutton, 1 pint of water, a small bunch of sweet herbs, ¼ of an onion, pepper and salt to taste. *Mode.*—Cut the meat into small pieces; put it into a saucepan with the bones, but no skin or fat; add the other ingredients; cover the saucepan, and bring the water quickly to boil. Take the lid off, and continue the rapid boiling for 20 minutes, skimming it well during the process; strain the broth into a basin; if there should be any fat left on the surface, remove it by laying a piece of thin paper on the top; the greasy particles will adhere to the paper, and so free the preparation from them. To an invalid nothing is more disagreeable than broth served with a quantity of fat floating on the top; to avoid this, it is always better to allow it to get thoroughly cool, the fat can then be so easily removed. *Time.*—20 minutes after the water boils. *Average cost*, 5*d.* *Sufficient* to make ½ pint of broth. *Seasonable* at any time.

MUTTON, Haunch of, to Carve.

A deep cut should, in the first place, be made quite down to the bone, across the knuckle-end of the joint, along the line 1 to 2. This will let the gravy escape; and then it should be carved, in not too thick slices, along the whole

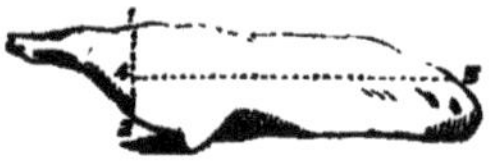

HAUNCH OF MUTTON.

length of the haunch, in the direction of the line from 4 to 3.

MUTTON, Leg of, to Carve.

This homely, but capital English joint, is almost invariably served at table as shown in the engraving. The carving of it is not very difficult: the knife should be carried sharply down in the direction of the line from 1 to 2, and slices taken from either side, as the guests may desire, some liking the knuckle-end, as well done, and others preferring the more underdone part. The fat should be sought near the line 3 to 4. Some connoisseurs are fond of having this joint dished with the under-side uppermost, so as to get at the finely-grained meat lying under that part of the joint, known as the Pope's eye; but this is an extravagant fashion, and one that will hardly find favour in the eyes of many economical British housewives and housekeepers.

LEG OF MUTTON.

MUTTON, Loin of, to Carve.

There is one point in connection with carving a loin of mutton which includes every other; that is, that the joint should be thoroughly well jointed by the butcher before it is cooked. This knack of jointing requires practice and the proper tools; and no one but the butcher is supposed to have these. If the bones be not well jointed, the carving of a loin of mutton is not a gracious business; whereas, if that has been attended to, it is an easy and untroublesome task. The knife should be inserted at fig. 1, and after feeling your way between the bones, it should be carried sharply in the direction of the line 1 to 2. As there are some people who prefer the outside cut, while others do not like it, the question as to their choice of this should be asked.

LOIN OF MUTTON.

MUTTON, Saddle of, to Carve.

Although we have heard, at various intervals, growlings expressed at the inevitable "saddle of mutton" at the dinner-parties of our middle classes, yet we doubt whether any other joint is better liked, when it has been well hung

and artistically cooked. There is a diversity of opinion respecting the mode of sending this joint to table; but it has only reference to whether or no there shall be any portion of the tail, or, if so, how many joints of the tail. Some trim the tail with a paper frill. The carving is not difficult: it is usually cut in the direction of the line from 2 to 1, quite down to the bones, in evenly-sliced pieces. A fashion, however, patronized by some, is to carve it obliquely, in the direction of the line from 4 to 3; in which case the joint would be turned round the other way, having the tail end on the right of the carver.

SADDLE OF MUTTON.

MUTTON, Shoulder of, to Carve.

This is a joint not difficult to carve. The knife should be drawn from the outer edge of the shoulder in the direction of the line from 1 to 2, until the bone of the shoulder is reached. As many slices as can be carved in this manner should be taken, and afterwards the meat lying on each side of the bladebone should be served, by carving in the direction of 3 to 4 and 3 to 4. The uppermost side of the shoulder being now finished, the joint should be turned, and slices taken off along its whole length. There are some who prefer this underside of the shoulder for its juicy flesh, although the grain of the meat is not so fine as that on the other side.

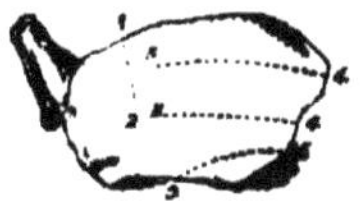

SHOULDER OF MUTTON.

MUTTON CHOPS, Broiled.

Ingredients.—Loin of mutton, pepper and salt, a small piece of butter. *Mode.*—Cut the chops from a well-hung tender loin of mutton, remove a portion of the fat, and trim them into a nice shape; slightly beat and level them; place the gridiron over a bright clear fire, rub the bars with a little fat, and lay on the chops. Whilst broiling, frequently turn them, and in about 8 minutes they will be done. Season with pepper and salt, dish them on a very hot dish, rub a small piece of butter on each chop, and serve very hot and expeditiously. *Time.*—About 8 minutes. *Average cost,* 10*d.* per lb. *Sufficient.*—Allow 1 chop to each person. *Seasonable* at any time.

MUTTON-COLLOPS.

Ingredients.—A few slices of a cold leg or loin of mutton, salt and pepper to taste, 1 blade of pounded mace, 1 small bunch of savoury herbs minced very fine, 2 or 3 shalots, 2 or 3 oz. of butter, 1 dessertspoonful of flour, ½ pint of gravy, 1 tablespoonful of lemon-juice. *Mode.*—Cut some very thin slices from a leg or the chump end of a loin of mutton; sprinkle them with pepper, salt, pounded mace, minced savoury herbs, and minced shalot; fry them in butter, stir in a dessertspoonful of flour, add the gravy and lemon-juice, simmer very gently about 5 or 7 minutes, and serve immediately. *Time.*—5 to 7 minutes. *Average cost,* exclusive of the meat, 6*d.* *Seasonable* at any time.

MUTTON, Curried.

[COLD MEAT COOKERY.] *Ingredients.*—The remains of any joint of cold mutton, 2 onions, ¼ lb. of butter, 1 dessertspoonful of curry-powder, 1 dessertspoonful of flour, salt to taste, ¼ pint of stock or water. *Mode.*—Slice the onions in thin rings, and put them into a stewpan with the butter, and fry of a light brown; stir in the curry-powder, flour, and salt, and mix all together. Cut the meat into nice thin slices (if there is not sufficient to do this, it may be minced), and add it to the other ingredients; when well browned, add the stock or gravy, and stew gently for about ½ hour. Serve in a dish with a border of boiled rice, the same as for other curries. *Time.*—½ hour. *Average cost,* exclusive of the meat, 6*d.* *Seasonable* in winter.

MUTTON CUTLETS, with Mashed Potatoes.

Ingredients.—About 3 lbs. of the best end of the neck of mutton, salt and pepper to taste, mashed potatoes. *Mode.*—Procure a well-hung neck of mutton, saw off about 3 inches of the top of the bones, and cut the cutlets of a moderate thickness. Shape them by chopping off the thick part of the chine-bone; beat them flat with a cutlet-chopper, and scrape quite clean, a portion of the top of the

MUTTON CUTLETS.

bone. Broil them over a nice clear fire for about 7 or 8 minutes, and turn them frequently. Have ready some smoothly-mashed white potatoes; place these in the middle of the dish; when the cutlets are done, season with pepper and salt; arrange them round the potatoes, with the thick end of the cutlets downwards, and serve very hot and quickly. *Time.*—7 or 8 minutes. *Average cost,* for this quantity, 2*s.* 4*d.* *Sufficient* for 5 or 6 persons. *Seasonable* at any time.

Note.—Cutlets may be served in various ways; with peas, tomatoes, onions, sauce piquant, &c.

MUTTON, Braised Fillet of, with French Beans.

Ingredients.—The chump end of a loin of mutton, buttered paper, French beans, a little glaze, 1 pint of gravy. *Mode.*—Roll up the mutton in a piece of buttered paper, roast it for 2 hours, and do not allow it to acquire the least colour. Have ready some French beans, boiled, and drained on a sieve; remove the paper from the mutton, glaze it; just heat up the beans in the gravy, and lay them on the dish with the meat over them. The remainder of the gravy may be strained, and sent to table in a tureen. *Time.*—2 hours. *Average cost,* 8½*d.* per lb. *Sufficient* for 4 or 5 persons. *Seasonable* at any time.

MUTTON, Haricot.

Ingredients.—4 lbs. of the middle or best end of the neck of mutton, 3 carrots, 3 turnips, 3 onions, pepper and salt to taste, 1 tablespoonful of ketchup or Harvey's sauce. *Mode.*—Trim off some of the fat, cut the mutton into rather thin chops, and put them into a frying-pan with the fat trimmings. Fry of a pale brown, but do not cook them enough for eating. Cut the carrots and turnips into dice, and the onions into slices, and slightly fry them in the same fat that the mutton was browned in, but do not allow them to take any colour. Now lay the mutton at the bottom of a stewpan, then the vegetables, and pour over them just sufficient boiling water to cover the whole. Give the boil, skim well, and then set the pan on the side of the fire to simmer gently until the meat is tender. Skim off every particle of fat, add a seasoning of pepper and salt, and a little ketchup, and serve. This dish is very much better if made the day before it is wanted for table, as the fat can be so much more easily removed when the gravy is cold. This should be particularly attended to, as it is apt to be rich and greasy if eaten the same day it is made. It should be served in rather a deep dish. *Time.*—2½ hours to simmer gently. *Average cost,* for this quantity, 3*s*. *Sufficient* for 6 or 7 persons. *Seasonable* at any time.

MUTTON, Haricot.

Ingredients.—Breast or scrag of mutton, flour, pepper, and salt to taste, 1 large onion, 3 cloves, a bunch of savoury herbs, 1 blade of mace, carrots and turnips, sugar. *Mode.*—Cut the mutton into square pieces, and fry them a nice colour; then dredge over them a little flour and a seasoning of pepper and salt. Put all into a stewpan, and moisten with boiling water, adding the onion, stuck with 3 cloves, the mace, and herbs. Simmer gently till the meat is done, skim off all the fat, and then add the carrots and turnips, which should be previously cut in dice and fried in a little sugar to colour them. Let the whole simmer again for 10 minutes; take out the onion and bunch of herbs, and serve. *Time.*—About 3 hours to simmer. *Average cost,* 6*d*. per lb. *Sufficient* for 4 or 5 persons. *Seasonable* at any time.

MUTTON, Haricot.

[COLD MEAT COOKERY.] *Ingredients.*—The remains of cold neck or loin of mutton, 2 oz. of butter, 3 onions, 1 dessertspoonful of flour, ½ pint of good gravy, pepper and salt to taste, 2 tablespoonfuls of port wine, 1 tablespoonful of mushroom ketchup, 2 carrots, 2 turnips, 1 head of celery. *Mode.*—Cut the cold mutton into moderate-sized chops, and take off the fat; slice the onions, and fry them with the chops, in a little butter, of a nice brown colour; stir in the flour, add the gravy, and let it stew gently nearly an hour. In the mean time boil the vegetables until *nearly* tender, slice them, and add them to the mutton about ¼ hour before it is to be served. Season with pepper and salt, add the ketchup and port wine, give one boil, and serve. *Time.*—1 hour. *Average cost,* exclusive of the cold meat, 6*d*. *Seasonable* at any time.

MUTTON, Hashed.

Ingredients.—The remains of cold roast shoulder or leg of mutton, 6 whole peppers, 6 whole allspice, a faggot of savoury herbs, ½ head of celery, 1 onion, 2 oz. of butter, flour. *Mode.*—Cut the meat in nice even slices from the bones, trimming off all superfluous fat and gristle; chop the bones and fragments of the joints, put them into a stewpan with the pepper, spice, herbs, and celery; cover with water, and simmer for 1 hour. Slice and fry the onion of a nice pale-brown colour, dredge in a little flour to make it thick, and add this to the bones, &c. Stew for ¼ hour, strain the gravy, and let it cool; then skim off every particle of fat, and put it, with the meat, into a stewpan. Flavour with ketchup, Harvey's sauce, tomato sauce, or any flavouring that may be preferred, and let the meat gradually warm through, but not boil, or it will harden. To hash meat properly, it should be laid in cold gravy, and only left on the fire just long enough to warm through. *Time.*—1½ hour to simmer the gravy. *Average cost,* exclusive of the meat, 4*d*. *Seasonable* at any time.

MUTTON, Roast Haunch of.

Ingredients.—Haunch of mutton, a little salt, flour. *Mode.*—Let this joint hang as long as possible without becom-

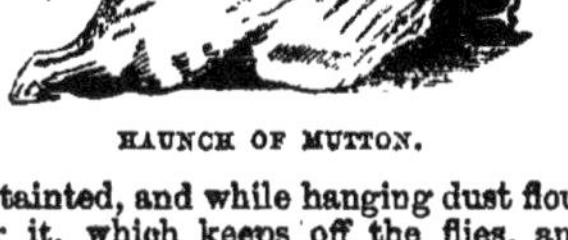

HAUNCH OF MUTTON.

ing tainted, and while hanging dust flour over it, which keeps off the flies, and prevents the air from getting to it. If not well hung, the joint, when it comes to table, will do credit neither to the butcher nor the cook, as it will not be tender. Wash the outside well, lest it should have a bad flavour from keeping; then flour it and put it down to a nice brisk fire, at some distance, so that it may gradually warm through. Keep continually basting, and about ½ hour before it is served, draw it nearer to the fire to get nicely brown. Sprinkle a little fine salt over the meat, pour off the dripping, add a little boiling water slightly salted, and strain this over the joint. Place a paper ruche on the bone, and send red-currant jelly and gravy in a tureen to table with it. *Time.*—About 4 hours. *Average cost,* 10*d.* per lb. *Sufficient* for 8 to 10 persons. *Seasonable.*—In best season from September to March.

MUTTON, Boiled Leg of.

Ingredients. — Mutton, water, salt. *Mode.*—A leg of mutton for boiling should not hang too long, as it will not look a good colour when dressed. Cut off the shank-bone, trim the knuckle, and wash and wipe it very clean; plunge it into sufficient boiling water to cover it; let it boil up, then draw the saucepan to the side of the fire, where it should remain till the finger can be borne in the water. Then place it sufficiently near the fire, that the water may gently simmer, and be very careful that it does not boil fast, or the meat will be hard. Skim well, add a little salt, and in about 2¼ hours after the water begins to simmer, a moderate-sized leg of mutton will be done. Serve with carrots and mashed turnips, which may be boiled with the meat, and send caper sauce to table with it in a tureen. *Time.*—A moderate-sized leg of mutton of 9 lbs., 2¼ hours after the water boils; one of 12 lbs., 3 hours. *Average cost,* 8½*d.* per lb. *Sufficient.*—A moderate-sized leg of mutton for 6 or 8 persons. *Seasonable* nearly all the year, but not so good in June, July, and August.

Note.—When meat is liked very *thoroughly* cooked, allow more time than stated above. The liquor this joint was boiled in should be converted into soup.

MUTTON, Boned Leg of, Stuffed.

Ingredients.—A small leg of mutton, weighing 6 or 7 lbs., forcemeat, 2 shalots finely minced. *Mode.*—Make a forcemeat, to which add 2 finely-minced shalots. Bone the leg of mutton, without spoiling the skin, and cut off a great deal of the fat. Fill the hole up whence the bone was taken with the forcemeat, and sew it up underneath, to prevent its falling out. Bind and tie it up compactly, and roast it before a nice clear fire for about 2½ hours or rather longer; remove the tape and send it to table with a good gravy. It may be glazed or not, as preferred. *Time.*—2½ hours, or rather longer. *Average cost,* 4*s.* 8*d.* *Sufficient* for 6 or 7 persons. *Seasonable* at any time.

MUTTON, Braised Leg of.

Ingredients.—1 small leg of mutton, 4 carrots, 3 onions, 1 faggot of savoury herbs, a bunch of parsley, seasoning to taste of pepper and salt, a few slices of bacon, a few veal trimmings, ½ pint of gravy or water. *Mode.*—Line the bottom of a braising-pan with a few slices of bacon, put in the carrots, onions, herbs, parsley, and seasoning, and over these place the mutton. Cover the whole with a few more slices of bacon and the veal trimmings, pour in the gravy or water, and stew very *gently* for 4 hours. Strain the gravy, reduce it to a glaze over a sharp fire, glaze the mutton with it, and send it to table, placed on a dish of white haricot beans boiled tender, or garnished with glazed onions. *Time.*—4 hours. *Average cost,* 5*s.* *Sufficient* for 6 or 7 persons. *Seasonable* at any time.

MUTTON, Roast Leg of.

Ingredients.—Leg of mutton, a little salt. *Mode.*—As mutton, when freshly killed, is never tender, hang it almost as

LEG OF MUTTON.

long as it will keep; flour it, and put it in a cool airy place for a few days, if the weather will permit. Wash off the flour, wipe it very dry, and cut off the shank-bone; put it down to a brisk clear fire, dredge with flour, and keep continually basting the whole time it is cooking. About 20 minutes before serving, draw it near the fire to get nicely brown; sprinkle over it a little salt, dish the meat, pour off the dripping, add some boiling water slightly salted, strain it over the joint, and serve. *Time.*—A leg of mutton weighing 10 lbs., about 2¼ or 2½ hours; one of 7 lbs., about 2 hours, or rather less. *Average cost*, 8½*d.* per lb. *Sufficient.*—A moderate-sized leg of mutton sufficient for 6 or 8 persons. *Seasonable* at any time, but not so good in June, July, and August.

MUTTON, Roast Loin of.

Ingredients.—Loin of mutton, a little salt. *Mode.*—Cut and trim off the superfluous fat, and see that the butcher joints

LOIN OF MUTTON.

the meat properly, as thereby much annoyance is saved to the carver, when it comes to table. Have ready a nice clear fire (it need not be a very wide large one), put down the meat, dredge with flour, and baste well until it is done. Make the gravy as for roast leg of mutton, and serve very hot. *Time.*—A loin of mutton weighing 6 lbs., 1½ hour, or rather longer. *Average cost*, 8½*d.* per lb. *Sufficient* for 4 or 5 persons. *Seasonable* at any time.

MUTTON, Rolled Loin of (very Excellent).

Ingredients.—About 6 lbs. of a loin of mutton, ½ teaspoonful of pepper, ¼ teaspoonful of pounded allspice, ¼ teaspoonful of mace, ¼ teaspoonful of nutmeg, 6 cloves, forcemeat, 1 glass of port wine, 2 tablespoonfuls of mushroom ketchup. *Mode.*—Hang the mutton till tender, bone it, and sprinkle over it pepper, mace, cloves, allspice, and nutmeg in the above proportion, all of which must be pounded very fine. Let it remain for a day, then make a forcemeat, cover the meat with it, and roll and bind it up firmly. Half bake it in a slow oven, let it grow cold, take off the fat, and put the gravy into a stewpan; flour the meat, put it in the gravy, and stew it till perfectly tender. Now take out the meat, unbind it, add to the gravy wine and ketchup as above, give one boil, and pour over the meat. Serve with red-currant jelly; and, if obtainable, a few mushrooms stewed for a few minutes in the gravy, will be found a great improvement. *Time.*—1½ hour to bake the meat, 1½ hour to stew gently. *Average cost*, 4*s.* 9*d.* *Sufficient* for 5 or 6 persons. *Seasonable* at any time.

Note.—This joint will be found very nice if rolled and stuffed, as here directed, and plainly roasted. It should be well basted, and served with a good gravy and currant jelly.

MUTTON, Boiled Neck of.

Ingredients.—4 lbs. of the middle, or best end of the neck of mutton; a little salt. *Mode.*—Trim off a portion of the fat, should there be too much, and if it is to look particularly nice, the chine-bone should be sawn down, the ribs stripped half-way down, and the ends of the bones chopped off; this is, however, not necessary. Put the meat into sufficient *boiling* water to cover it; when it boils, add a little salt and remove all the scum. Draw the saucepan to the side of the fire, and let the water get so cool that the finger may be borne in it; then simmer very *slowly* and gently until the meat is done, which will be in about 1½ hour, or rather more, reckoning from the time that it begins to simmer. Serve with turnips and caper sauce, and pour a little of it over the meat. The turnips should be boiled with the mutton; and when at hand, a few carrots will also be found an improvement. These, however, if very large and thick, must be cut into long thinnish pieces, or they will not be sufficiently done by the time the mutton is ready. Garnish the dish with carrots and turnips, placed alternately round the mutton. *Time.*—4 lbs. of the neck of mutton, about 1½ hour. *Average cost*, 8½*d.* per lb. *Sufficient* for 6 or 7 persons. *Seasonable* at any time.

MUTTON, Ragout of Cold Neck of.

[COLD MEAT COOKERY.] *Ingredients.*—The remains of a cold neck or loin of mutton, 2 oz. of butter, a little flour, 2 onions sliced, ½ pint of water, 2 small carrots, 2 turnips, pepper and salt to taste. *Mode.*—Cut the mutton into small chops, and trim off the greater portion of the fat; put the butter into a stewpan, dredge in a little flour, add the sliced onions, and keep stirring till brown; then put in the meat. When this is quite brown, add the water, and the carrots and turnips, which should be cut into very thin slices; season with pepper and salt, and stew till quite tender, which will be in about ¾ hour. When in season, green peas may be substituted for the carrots and turnips: they should be piled in the centre of the dish, and the chops laid round. *Time.*—¾ hour. *Average cost,* exclusive of the meat, 4d. *Seasonable,* with peas, from June to August.

MUTTON, Roast Neck of.

Ingredients.—Neck of mutton; a little salt. *Mode.*—For roasting, choose the middle, or the best end, of the neck of mutton, and if there is a very large proportion of fat, trim off some of it, and

NECK OF MUTTON.

1—2. *Best end.* 2—3. *Scrag.*

save it for making into suet puddings, which will be found exceedingly good. Let the bones be cut short, and see that it is properly jointed before it is laid down to the fire, as they will be more easily separated when they come to table. Place the joint at a nice brisk fire, dredge it with flour, and keep continually basting until done. A few minutes before serving, draw it nearer the fire to acquire a nice colour, sprinkle over it a little salt, pour off the dripping, add a little boiling water slightly salted; strain this over the meat and serve. Red-currant jelly may be sent to table with it. *Time.*—4 lbs. of the neck of mutton, rather more than 1 hour. *Average cost,* 8½d. per lb. *Sufficient* for 4 or 5 persons. *Seasonable* at any time.

MUTTON PIE.

[COLD MEAT COOKERY.] *Ingredients.*—The remains of a cold leg, loin, or neck of mutton, pepper and salt to taste, 2 blades of pounded mace, 1 dessertspoonful of chopped parsley, 1 teaspoonful of minced savoury herbs; when liked, a little minced onion or shalot; 3 or 4 potatoes, 1 teacupful of gravy; crust. *Mode.*—Cold mutton may be made into very good pies if well seasoned and mixed with a few herbs; if the leg is used, cut it into very thin slices; if the loin or neck, into thin cutlets. Place some at the bottom of the dish; season well with pepper, salt, mace, parsley, and herbs; then put a layer of potatoes sliced, then more mutton, and so on till the dish is full; add the gravy, cover with a crust, and bake for 1 hour. *Time.*—1 hour. *Seasonable* at any time.

Note.—The remains of an underdone leg of mutton may be converted into a very good family pudding, by cutting the meat into slices, and putting them into a basin lined with a suet crust. It should be seasoned well with pepper, salt, and minced shalot, covered with a crust, and boiled for about three hours.

MUTTON PIE.

Ingredients.—2 lbs. of the neck or loin of mutton, weighed after being boned; 2 kidneys, pepper and salt to taste, 2 teacupfuls of gravy or water, 2 tablespoonfuls of minced parsley; when liked, a little minced onion or shalot; puff crust. *Mode.*—Bone the mutton, and cut the meat into steaks all of the same thickness, and leave but very little fat. Cut up the kidneys, and arrange these with the meat neatly in a pie-dish; sprinkle over them the minced parsley and a seasoning of pepper and salt; pour in the gravy, and cover with a tolerably good puff crust. Bake for 1½ hour, or rather longer, should the pie be very large, and let the oven be rather brisk. A well-made suet crust may be used instead of puff crust, and will be found exceedingly good. *Time.*—1½ hour, or rather longer. *Average cost,* 2s. *Sufficient* for 5 or 6 persons. *Seasonable* at any time.

MUTTON PUDDING.

Ingredients.—About 2 lbs. of the chump end of the loin of mutton, weighed after being boned; pepper and salt to taste, suet crust made with milk, in the proportion of 6 oz. of suet to each pound of flour; a very small quantity of minced onion (this may be omitted when the flavour is not liked). *Mode.*—Cut the meat into rather thin slices, and season them with pepper and salt; line the pudding-dish with crust; lay in the meat, and nearly, but do not quite, fill it up with water; when the flavour is liked, add a small quantity of minced onion; cover with crust, and proceed in the same manner as directed in recipe for rump steak and kidney pudding. *Time.*—About 3 hours. *Average cost,* 1*s.* 9*d.* *Sufficient* for 6 persons. *Seasonable* all the year, but more suitable in winter.

MUTTON, Roast Saddle of.

Ingredients.—Saddle of mutton; a little salt. *Mode.*—To insure this joint being tender, let it hang for ten days or a fortnight, if the weather permits. Cut off the tail and flaps, and trim away every

SADDLE OF MUTTON.

part that has not indisputable pretensions to be eaten, and have the skin taken off and skewered on again. Put it down to a bright, clear fire, and, when the joint has been cooking for an hour, remove the skin and dredge it with flour. It should not be placed too near the fire, as the fat should not be in the slightest degree burnt, but kept constantly basted, both before and after the skin is removed. Sprinkle some salt over the joint; make a little gravy in the dripping-pan; pour it over the meat, which send to table with a tureen of made gravy and red-currant jelly. *Time.*—A saddle of mutton weighing 10 lbs., 2½ hours; 14 lbs., 3¼ hours. When liked underdone, allow rather less time. *Average cost,* 10*d.* per lb. *Sufficient.*—A moderate-sized saddle of 10 lbs. for 7 or 8 persons. *Seasonable* all the year; not so good when lamb is in full season.

MUTTON, Roast Shoulder of.

Ingredients.—Shoulder of mutton; a little salt. *Mode.*—Put the joint down to a bright, clear fire; flour it well, and keep continually basting. About ¼ hour before serving, draw it near the fire, that

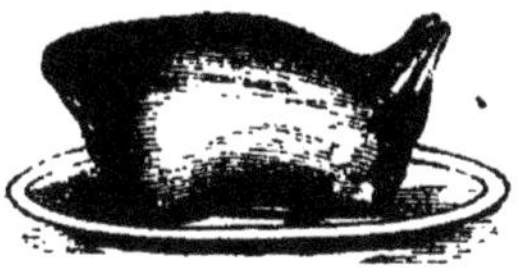

SHOULDER OF MUTTON.

the outside may acquire a nice brown colour, but not sufficiently near to blacken the fat. Sprinkle a little fine salt over the meat, empty the dripping-pan of its contents, pour in a little boiling water slightly salted, and strain this over the joint. Onion sauce, or stewed Spanish onions, are usually sent to table with this dish, and sometimes baked potatoes. *Time.*—A shoulder of mutton weighing 6 or 7 lbs., 1½ hour. *Average cost,* 8*d.* per lb. *Sufficient* for 5 or 6 persons. *Seasonable* at any time.

Note.—Shoulder of mutton may be dressed in a variety of ways; boiled, and served with onion sauce; boned, and stuffed with a good veal forcemeat; or baked, with sliced potatoes in the dripping-pan.

MUTTON SOUP, Good.

Ingredients.—A neck of mutton about 5 or 6 lbs., 3 carrots, 3 turnips, 2 onions, a large bunch of sweet herbs, including parsley; salt and pepper to taste; a little sherry, if liked; 3 quarts of water. *Mode.*—Lay the ingredients in a covered pan before the fire, and let them remain there the whole day, stirring occasionally. The next day put the whole into a stewpan, and place it on a brisk fire. When it commences to boil, take the pan off the fire, and put it on one side to simmer until the meat is done. When ready for use, take out the meat, dish it up with carrots and turnips, and send it to table; strain the soup, let it cool, skim off all the fat, season and thicken it with a tablespoonful, or rather more, of arrowroot; flavour with a little sherry, simmer for 5 minutes, and serve. *Time.*—15 hours. *Average cost,* including the meat, 1*s.* 3*d.* per quart. *Seasonable* at any time. *Sufficient* for 8 persons.

NASTURTIUMS, Pickled (a very good Substitute for Capers).

Ingredients.—To each pint of vinegar, 1 oz. of salt, 6 peppercorns, nasturtiums. *Mode.*—Gather the nasturtium pods on a dry day, and wipe them clean with a cloth; put them in a dry glass bottle, with vinegar, salt, and pepper, in the above proportion. If you cannot find enough ripe to fill a bottle, cork up what you have got until you have some more fit; they may be added from day to day. Bung up the bottles, and seal or rosin the tops. They will be fit for use in 10 or 12 months; and the best way is to make them one season for the next. *Seasonable.*—Look for nasturtium-pods from the end of July to the end of August.

NECTARINES, Preserved.

Ingredients.—To every lb. of sugar allow ¼ pint of water; nectarines. *Mode.*—Divide the nectarines in two, take out the stones, and make a strong syrup with sugar and water in the above proportion. Put in the nectarines, and boil them until they have thoroughly imbibed the sugar. Keep the fruit as whole as possible, and turn it carefully into a pan. The next day boil it again for a few minutes, take out the nectarines, put them into jars, boil the syrup quickly for five minutes, pour it over the fruit, and, when cold, cover the preserve down. The syrup and preserve must be carefully skimmed, or it will not be clear. *Time.*—10 minutes to boil the sugar and water; 20 minutes to boil the fruit the first time, 10 minutes the second time; 5 minutes to boil the syrup. *Seasonable* in August and September, but cheapest in September.

NECTAR, Welsh.

Ingredients.—1 lb. of raisins, 3 lemons, 2 lbs. of loaf sugar, 2 gallons of boiling water. *Mode.*—Cut the peel of the lemons very thin, pour upon it the boiling water, and, when cool, add the strained juice of the lemons, the sugar, and the raisins, stoned and chopped very fine. Let it stand 4 or 5 days, stirring it every day; then strain it through a jelly-bag, and bottle it for present use. *Time.*—4 or 5 days. *Average cost*, 1*s.* 9*d.* *Sufficient* to make 2 gallons.

NEGUS, to make.

Ingredients.—To every pint of port wine allow 1 quart of boiling water, ¼ lb. of sugar, 1 lemon, grated nutmeg to taste. *Mode.*—As this beverage is more usually drunk at children's parties than at any other, the wine need not be very old or expensive for the purpose, a new fruity wine answering very well for it. Put the wine into a jug, rub some lumps of sugar (equal to ¼ lb.) on the lemon-rind until all the yellow part of the skin is absorbed, then squeeze the juice, and strain it. Add the sugar and lemon-juice to the port-wine, with the grated nutmeg; pour over it the boiling water, cover the jug, and, when the beverage has cooled a little, it will be fit for use. Negus may also be made of sherry, or any other sweet white wine, but is more usually made of port than of any other beverage. *Sufficient.*—Allow 1 pint of wine, with the other ingredients in proportion, for a party of 9 or 10 children.

NOVEMBER—BILLS OF FARE.

Dinner for 18 persons.

First Course.

Baked Whitings.	Thick Grouse Soup, removed by Crimped Cod and Oyster Sauce. Vase of Flowers. Clear Ox-tail Soup, removed by Fillets of Turbot à la Crême.	Fried Smelts.

Entrées.

Fillets of Leveret.	Poulet à la Marengo. Vase of Flowers. Mushrooms sautés.	Ragoût of Lobster.

Second Course.

Haunch of Mutton.

Cold Game Pie.

Lark Pudding. — Vase of Flowers. — Roast Fowls.

Boiled Ham.

Boiled Turkey and Celery Sauce.

Third Course.

Apple Tart. — Pommes à la Condé. — Partridges, removed by Plum-pudding. — Wine Jelly. — Vase of Flowers. — Blancmange. — Snipes, removed by Charlotte glacée. — Vol-au-Vent of Pears. — Shell-Fish. — Apricot Tartlets. — Prawns.

Dessert and Ices.

Dinner for 12 persons.

First Course. — Hare soup; Julienne soup; baked cod; soles à la Normandie. *Entrées.*—Riz de veau aux tomates; lobster patties; mutton cutlets and Soubise sauce; croûtades of marrow aux fines herbes. *Second Course.*—Roast sirloin of beef; braised goose; boiled fowls and celery sauce; bacon-cheek, garnished with sprouts. *Third Course.*—Wild ducks; partridges; apples à la Portugaise; Bavarian cream; apricot-jam sandwiches; cheesecakes; Charlotte à la vanille; plum-pudding; dessert and ices.

Dinner for 8 persons.

First Course. — Mulligatawny soup; fried slices of codfish and oyster sauce; eels en matelote. *Entrées.* — Broiled pork cutlets and tomato sauce; tendrons de veau à la jardinière. *Second Course.*

—Boiled leg of mutton and vegetables; roast goose; cold game pie. *Third Course.*—Snipes; teal; apple soufflé; iced Charlotte; tartlets; champagne jelly; coffee cream; mince pies; dessert and ices.

Dinners for 6 persons.

First Course.—Oyster soup; crimped cod and oyster sauce; fried perch and Dutch sauce. *Entrées.*—Pigs' feet à la Béchamel; curried rabbit. *Second Course.* —Roast sucking-pig; boiled fowls and oyster sauce; vegetables. *Third Course.* —Jugged hare; meringues à la crême; apple custard; vol-au-vent of pears; whipped cream; cabinet pudding; dessert.

First Course.—Game soup; slices of codfish and Dutch sauce; fried eels. *Entrées.*—Kidneys à la Maître d'Hôtel; oyster patties. *Second Course.*—Saddle of mutton; boiled capon and rice; small ham; lark pudding. *Third Course.*—Roast hare; apple tart; pineapple cream; clear jelly; cheesecakes; marrow pudding; Nesselrode pudding; dessert.

NOVEMBER, Plain Family Dinners for.

Sunday.—1. White soup. 2. Roast haunch of mutton, haricot beans, potatoes. 3. Apple tart, ginger pudding.

Monday.—1. Stewed eels. 2. Veal cutlets garnished with rolled bacon; cold mutton and winter salad. 3. Baked rice pudding.

Tuesday.—1. Roast fowls, garnished with water-cresses; boiled bacon-cheek; hashed mutton from remains of haunch. 2. Apple pudding.

Wednesday.—1. Boiled leg of pork, carrots, parsnips, and pease-pudding; fowl croquettes made with remainder of cold fowl. 2. Baroness pudding.

Thursday. —1. Cold pork and mashed potatoes; roast partridges, bread sauce and gravy. 2. The remainder of the pudding cut into neat slices, and warmed through, and served with sifted sugar sprinkled over; apple fritters.

them, and in about 8 minutes they will be done. Season with pepper and salt, dish them on a very hot dish, rub a small piece of butter on each chop, and serve very hot and expeditiously. *Time.*—About 8 minutes. *Average cost,* 10*d.* per lb. *Sufficient.*—Allow 1 chop to each person. *Seasonable* at any time.

MUTTON-COLLOPS.

Ingredients.—A few slices of a cold leg or loin of mutton, salt and pepper to taste, 1 blade of pounded mace, 1 small bunch of savoury herbs minced very fine, 2 or 3 shalots, 2 or 3 oz. of butter, 1 dessertspoonful of flour, ½ pint of gravy, 1 tablespoonful of lemon-juice. *Mode.*—Cut some very thin slices from a leg or the chump end of a loin of mutton; sprinkle them with pepper, salt, pounded mace, minced savoury herbs, and minced shalot; fry them in butter, stir in a dessertspoonful of flour, add the gravy and lemon-juice, simmer very gently about 5 or 7 minutes, and serve immediately. *Time.*—5 to 7 minutes. *Average cost,* exclusive of the meat, 6*d.* *Seasonable* at any time.

MUTTON, Curried.

[COLD MEAT COOKERY.] *Ingredients.*—The remains of any joint of cold mutton, 2 onions, ¼ lb. of butter, 1 dessertspoonful of curry-powder, 1 dessertspoonful of flour, salt to taste, ¼ pint of stock or water. *Mode.*—Slice the onions in thin rings, and put them into a stewpan with the butter, and fry of a light brown; stir in the curry-powder, flour, and salt, and mix all together. Cut the meat into nice thin slices (if there is not sufficient to do this, it may be minced), and add it to the other ingredients; when well browned, add the stock or gravy, and stew gently for about ½ hour. Serve in a dish with a border of boiled rice, the same as for other curries. *Time.*—½ hour. *Average cost,* exclusive of the meat, 6*d.* *Seasonable* in winter.

MUTTON CUTLETS, with Mashed Potatoes.

Ingredients.—About 3 lbs. of the best end of the neck of mutton, salt and pepper to taste, mashed potatoes. *Mode.*—Procure a well-hung neck of mutton, saw off about 3 inches of the top of the bones, and cut the cutlets of a moderate thickness. Shape them by chopping off the thick part of the chine-bone; beat them flat with a cutlet-chopper, and scrape quite clean, a portion of the top of the

MUTTON CUTLETS.

bone. Broil them over a nice clear fire for about 7 or 8 minutes, and turn them frequently. Have ready some smoothly-mashed white potatoes; place these in the middle of the dish; when the cutlets are done, season with pepper and salt; arrange them round the potatoes, with the thick end of the cutlets downwards, and serve very hot and quickly. *Time.*—7 or 8 minutes. *Average cost,* for this quantity, 2*s.* 4*d.* *Sufficient* for 5 or 6 persons. *Seasonable* at any time.

Note.—Cutlets may be served in various ways; with peas, tomatoes, onions, sauce piquant, &c.

MUTTON, Braised Fillet of, with French Beans.

Ingredients.—The chump end of a loin of mutton, buttered paper, French beans, a little glaze, 1 pint of gravy. *Mode.*—Roll up the mutton in a piece of buttered paper, roast it for 2 hours, and do not allow it to acquire the least colour. Have ready some French beans, boiled, and drained on a sieve; remove the paper from the mutton, glaze it; just heat up the beans in the gravy, and lay them on the dish with the meat over them. The remainder of the gravy may be strained, and sent to table in a tureen. *Time.*—2 hours. *Average cost,* 8½*d.* per lb. *Sufficient* for 4 or 5 persons. *Seasonable* at any time.

MUTTON, Haricot.

Ingredients.—4 lbs. of the middle or best end of the neck of mutton, 3 carrots, 3 turnips, 3 onions, pepper and salt to taste, 1 tablespoonful of ketchup or Harvey's sauce. *Mode.*—Trim off some of the fat, cut the mutton into rather thin chops, and put them into a frying-pan with the fat trimmings. Fry of a pale brown, but do not cook them enough for eating. Cut the carrots and turnips into dice, and the onions into slices, and slightly fry them in the same fat that the mutton was browned in, but do not allow them to take any colour. Now lay the mutton at the bottom of a stewpan, then the vegetables, and pour over them just sufficient boiling water to cover the whole. Give the boil, skim well, and then set the pan on the side of the fire to simmer gently until the meat is tender. Skim off every particle of fat, add a seasoning of pepper and salt, and a little ketchup, and serve. This dish is very much better if made the day before it is wanted for table, as the fat can be so much more easily removed when the gravy is cold. This should be particularly attended to, as it is apt to be rich and greasy if eaten the same day it is made. It should be served in rather a deep dish. *Time.*—2½ hours to simmer gently. *Average cost,* for this quantity, 3*s.* *Sufficient* for 6 or 7 persons. *Seasonable* at any time.

MUTTON, Haricot.

Ingredients.—Breast or scrag of mutton, flour, pepper, and salt to taste, 1 large onion, 3 cloves, a bunch of savoury herbs, 1 blade of mace, carrots and turnips, sugar. *Mode.*—Cut the mutton into square pieces, and fry them a nice colour; then dredge over them a little flour and a seasoning of pepper and salt. Put all into a stewpan, and moisten with boiling water, adding the onion, stuck with 3 cloves, the mace, and herbs. Simmer gently till the meat is done, skim off all the fat, and then add the carrots and turnips, which should be previously cut in dice and fried in a little sugar to colour them. Let the whole simmer again for 10 minutes; take out the onion and bunch of herbs, and serve. *Time.*—About 3 hours to simmer. *Average cost,* 6*d.* per lb. *Sufficient* for 4 or 5 persons. *Seasonable* at any time.

MUTTON, Haricot.

[COLD MEAT COOKERY.] *Ingredients.*—The remains of cold neck or loin of mutton, 2 oz. of butter, 3 onions, 1 dessertspoonful of flour, ½ pint of good gravy, pepper and salt to taste, 2 tablespoonfuls of port wine, 1 tablespoonful of mushroom ketchup, 2 carrots, 2 turnips, 1 head of celery. *Mode.*—Cut the cold mutton into moderate-sized chops, and take off the fat; slice the onions, and fry them with the chops, in a little butter, of a nice brown colour; stir in the flour, add the gravy, and let it stew gently nearly an hour. In the mean time boil the vegetables until *nearly* tender, slice them, and add them to the mutton about ¼ hour before it is to be served. Season with pepper and salt, add the ketchup and port wine, give one boil, and serve. *Time.*—1 hour. *Average cost,* exclusive of the cold meat, 6*d.* *Seasonable* at any time.

MUTTON, Hashed.

Ingredients.—The remains of cold roast shoulder or leg of mutton, 6 whole peppers, 6 whole allspice, a faggot of savoury herbs, ½ head of celery, 1 onion, 2 oz. of butter, flour. *Mode.*—Cut the meat in nice even slices from the bones, trimming off all superfluous fat and gristle; chop the bones and fragments of the joints, put them into a stewpan with the pepper, spice, herbs, and celery; cover with water, and simmer for 1 hour. Slice and fry the onion of a nice pale-brown colour, dredge in a little flour to make it thick, and add this to the bones, &c. Stew for ¼ hour, strain the gravy, and let it cool; then skim off every particle of fat, and put it, with the meat, into a stewpan. Flavour with ketchup, Harvey's sauce, tomato sauce, or any flavouring that may be preferred, and let the meat gradually warm through, but not boil, or it will harden. To hash meat properly, it should be laid in cold gravy, and only left on the fire just long enough to warm through. *Time.*—1½ hour to simmer the gravy. *Average cost,* exclusive of the meat, 4*d.* *Seasonable* at any time.

MUTTON, Roast Haunch of.

Ingredients. — Haunch of mutton, a little salt, flour. *Mode.*—Let this joint hang as long as possible without becoming tainted, and while hanging dust flour over it, which keeps off the flies, and prevents the air from getting to it. If

HAUNCH OF MUTTON.

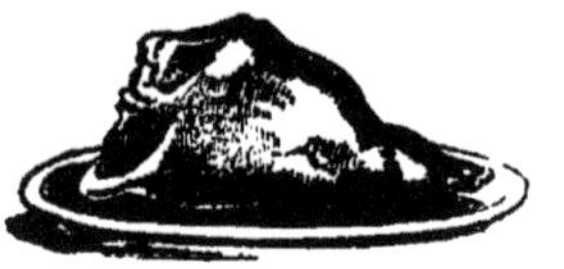

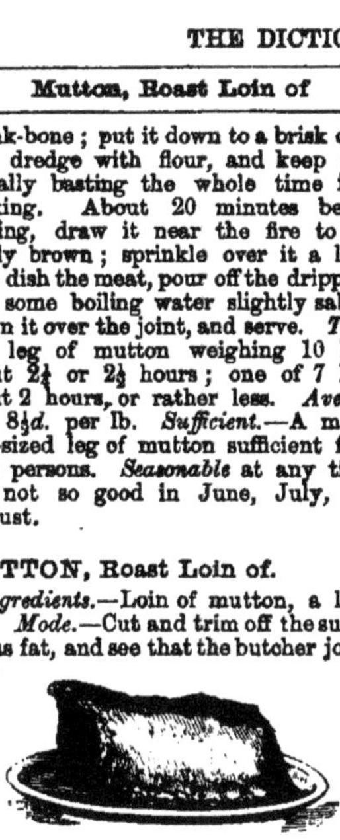

being boned; pepper and salt to taste, suet crust made with milk, in the proportion of 6 oz. of suet to each pound of flour; a very small quantity of minced onion (this may be omitted when the flavour is not liked). *Mode.*—Cut the meat into rather thin slices, and season them with pepper and salt; line the pudding-dish with crust; lay in the meat, and nearly, but do not quite, fill it up with water; when the flavour is liked, add a small quantity of minced onion; cover with crust, and proceed in the same manner as directed in recipe for rump steak and kidney pudding. *Time.*—About 3 hours. *Average cost,* 1s. 9d. *Sufficient* for 6 persons. *Seasonable* all the year, but more suitable in winter.

MUTTON, Roast Saddle of.

Ingredients.—Saddle of mutton; a little salt. *Mode.*—To insure this joint being tender, let it hang for ten days or a fortnight, if the weather permits. Cut off the tail and flaps, and trim away every

SADDLE OF MUTTON.

part that has not indisputable pretensions to be eaten, and have the skin taken off and skewered on again. Put it down to a bright, clear fire, and, when the joint has been cooking for an hour, remove the skin and dredge it with flour. It should not be placed too near the fire, as the fat should not be in the slightest degree burnt, but kept constantly basted, both before and after the skin is removed. Sprinkle some salt over the joint; make a little gravy in the dripping-pan; pour it over the meat, which send to table with a tureen of made gravy and red-currant jelly. *Time.*—A saddle of mutton weighing 10 lbs., 2½ hours; 14 lbs., 3¼ hours. When liked underdone, allow rather less time. *Average cost,* 10*d.* per lb. *Sufficient.*—A moderate-sized saddle of 10 lbs. for 7 or 8 persons. *Seasonable* all the year; not so good when lamb is in full season.

MUTTON, Roast Shoulder of.

Ingredients.—Shoulder of mutton; a little salt. *Mode.*—Put the joint down to a bright, clear fire; flour it well, and keep continually basting. About ¼ hour before serving, draw it near the fire, that

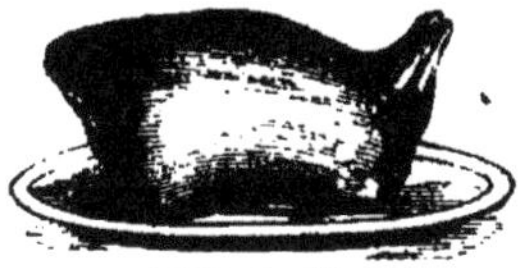

SHOULDER OF MUTTON.

the outside may acquire a nice brown colour, but not sufficiently near to blacken the fat. Sprinkle a little fine salt over the meat, empty the dripping-pan of its contents, pour in a little boiling water slightly salted, and strain this over the joint. Onion sauce, or stewed Spanish onions, are usually sent to table with this dish, and sometimes baked potatoes. *Time.*—A shoulder of mutton weighing 6 or 7 lbs., 1½ hour. *Average cost,* 8*d.* per lb. *Sufficient* for 5 or 6 persons. *Seasonable* at any time.

Note.—Shoulder of mutton may be dressed in a variety of ways; boiled, and served with onion sauce; boned, and stuffed with a good veal forcemeat; or baked, with sliced potatoes in the dripping-pan.

MUTTON SOUP, Good.

Ingredients.—A neck of mutton about 5 or 6 lbs., 3 carrots, 3 turnips, 2 onions, a large bunch of sweet herbs, including parsley; salt and pepper to taste; a little sherry, if liked; 3 quarts of water. *Mode.*—Lay the ingredients in a covered pan before the fire, and let them remain there the whole day, stirring occasionally. The next day put the whole into a stewpan, and place it on a brisk fire. When it commences to boil, take the pan off the fire, and put it on one side to simmer until the meat is done. When ready for use, take out the meat, dish it up with carrots and turnips, and send it to table; strain the soup, let it cool, skim off all the fat, season and thicken it with a tablespoonful, or rather more, of arrowroot; flavour with a little sherry, simmer for 5 minutes, and serve. *Time.*—15 hours. *Average cost,* including the

ONION SOUP, Cheap.

Ingredients.—8 middling-sized onions, 3 oz. of butter, a tablespoonful of rice-flour, salt and pepper to taste, 1 teaspoonful of powdered sugar, thickening of butter and flour, 2 quarts of water. *Mode.*—Cut the onions small, put them into the stewpan with the butter, and fry them well; mix the rice-flour smoothly with the water, add the onions, seasoning, and sugar, and simmer till tender. Thicken with butter and flour, and serve. *Time.*—2 hours. *Average cost*, 4d. per quart. *Seasonable* in winter. *Sufficient* for 8 persons.

ONIONS, Burnt, for Gravies.

Ingredients.—½ lb. of onions, ½ pint of water, ½ lb. of moist sugar, ⅓ pint of vinegar. *Mode.*—Peel and chop the onions fine, and put them into a stewpan (not tinned), with the water; let them boil for 5 minutes, then add the sugar, and simmer gently until the mixture becomes nearly black and throws out bubbles of smoke. Have ready the above proportion of boiling vinegar, strain the liquor gradually to it, and keep stirring with a wooden spoon until it is well incorporated. When cold, bottle for use. *Time.*—Altogether, 1 hour.

ONIONS, Pickled (a very simple Method, and exceedingly Good).

Ingredients.—Pickling onions; to each quart of vinegar, 2 teaspoonfuls of allspice, 2 teaspoonfuls of whole black pepper. *Mode.*—Have the onions gathered when quite dry and ripe, and, with the fingers, take off the thin outside skin; then, with a silver knife (steel should not be used, as it spoils the colour of the onions), remove one more skin, when the onion will look quite clear. Have ready some very dry bottles or jars, and as fast as they are peeled, put them in. Pour over sufficient cold vinegar to cover them, with pepper and allspice in the above proportions, taking care that each jar has its share of the latter ingredients. Tie down with bladder, and put them in a dry place, and in a fortnight they will be fit for use. This is a most simple recipe and very delicious, the onions being nice and crisp. They should be eaten within 6 or 8 months after being done, as the onions are liable to become soft. *Seasonable* from the middle of July to the end of August.

ONIONS, Pickled.

Ingredients.—1 gallon of pickling onions, salt and water, milk; to each ½ gallon of vinegar, 1 oz. of bruised ginger, ¼ tablespoonful of cayenne, 1 oz. of allspice, 1 oz. of whole black pepper, ¼ oz. of whole nutmeg bruised, 8 cloves, ¼ oz. of mace. *Mode.*—Gather the onions, which should not be too small, when they are quite dry and ripe; wipe off the dirt, but do not pare them; make a strong solution of salt and water, into which put the onions, and change this, morning and night, for 3 days, and save the *last* brine they were put in. Then take the outside skin off, and put them into a tin saucepan capable of holding them all, as they are always better done together. Now take equal quantities of milk and the last salt and water the onions were in, and pour this to them; to this add 2 large spoonfuls of salt, put them over the fire, and watch them very attentively. Keep constantly turning the onions about with a wooden skimmer, those at the bottom to the top, and *vice versâ;* and let the milk and water run through the holes of the skimmer. Remember, the onions must never boil, or, if they do, they will be good for nothing; and they should be quite transparent. Keep the onions stirred for a few minutes, and, in stirring them, be particular not to break them. Then have ready a pan with a colander, into which turn the onions to drain, covering them with a cloth to keep in the steam. Place on a table an old cloth, 2 or 3 times double; put the onions on it when quite hot, and over them an old piece of blanket; cover this closely over them, to keep in the steam. Let them remain till the next day, when they will be quite cold, and look yellow and shrivelled; take off the shrivelled skins, when they should be as white as snow. Put them into a pan, make a pickle of vinegar and the remaining ingredients, boil all these up, and pour hot over the onions in the pan. Cover very closely to keep in all the steam, and let them stand till the following day, when they will be quite cold. Put them into jars or bottles well bunged, and a tablespoonful of the best olive-oil on the top of each jar or bottle. Tie them down with bladder, and let them stand in a cool place for a month or six weeks, when they will be fit for use. They should be beautifully white, and eat crisp, without the least softness, and will keep good many months. *Seasonable* from the middle of July to the end of August.

ONIONS, Spanish, Baked.

Ingredients.—4 or 5 Spanish onions, salt, and water. *Mode.*—Put the onions, with their skins on, into a saucepan of boiling water slightly salted, and let them boil quickly for an hour. Then take them out, wipe them thoroughly, wrap each one in a piece of paper separately, and bake them in a moderate oven for 2 hours, or longer, should the onions be very large. They may be served in their skins, and eaten with a piece of cold butter and a seasoning of pepper and salt; or they may be peeled, and a good brown gravy poured over them. *Time.*—1 hour to boil, 2 hours to bake. *Average cost,* medium-sized, 2*d.* each. *Sufficient* for 5 or 6 persons. *Seasonable* from September to January.

ONIONS, Spanish, Pickled.

Ingredients.— Onions, vinegar; salt and cayenne to taste. *Mode.*—Cut the onions in thin slices; put a layer of them in the bottom of a jar; sprinkle with salt and cayenne; then add another layer of onions, and season as before. Proceeding in this manner till the jar is full, pour in sufficient vinegar to cover the whole, and the pickle will be fit for use in a month. *Seasonable.*—May be had in England from September to February.

ONIONS, Spanish, Stewed.

Ingredients.—5 or 6 Spanish onions, 1 pint of good broth or gravy. *Mode.*—Peel the onions, taking care not to cut away too much of the tops or tails, or they would then fall to pieces; put them into a stewpan capable of holding them at the bottom without piling them one on the top of another; add the broth or gravy, and simmer *very gently* until the onions are perfectly tender. Dish them, pour the gravy round, and serve. Instead of using broth, Spanish onions may be stewed with a large piece of butter: they must be done very gradually over a slow fire or hot-plate, and will produce plenty of gravy. *Time.*—To stew in gravy, 2 hours, or longer if very large. *Average cost,* medium-sized, 2*d.* each. *Sufficient* for 6 or 7 persons. *Seasonable* from September to January.

Note.—Stewed Spanish onions are a favourite accompaniment to roast shoulder of mutton.

ORANGE BRANDY. (Excellent.)

Ingredients.—To every ½ gallon of brandy allow ¾ pint of Seville orange-juice, 1¼ lb. of loaf sugar. *Mode.*—To bring out the full flavour of the orange-peel, rub a few lumps of the sugar on 2 or 3 unpared oranges, and put these lumps to the rest. Mix the brandy with the orange-juice, strained, the rinds of 6 of the oranges pared very thin, and the sugar. Let all stand in a closely-covered jar for about 3 days, stirring it 3 or 4 times a day. When clear, it should be bottled and closely corked for a year; it will then be ready for use, but will keep any length of time. This is a most excellent stomachic when taken pure in small quantities; or, as the strength of the brandy is very little deteriorated by the other ingredients, it may be diluted with water. *Time.*—To be stirred every day for 3 days. *Average cost,* 7*s.* *Sufficient* to make 2 quarts. *Seasonable.*—Make this in March.

ORANGE CREAM.

Ingredients.—1 oz. of isinglass, 6 large oranges, 1 lemon, sugar to taste, water, ½ pint of good cream. *Mode.*—Squeeze the juice from the oranges and lemon; strain it, and put it into a saucepan with the isinglass, and sufficient water to make it in all 1½ pint. Rub the sugar on the orange and lemon-rind, add it to the other ingredients, and boil all together for about 10 minutes. Strain

OPEN MOULD.

through a muslin bag, and, when cold, beat up with it ½ pint of thick cream. Wet a mould, or soak it in cold water; pour in the cream, and put it in a cool place to set. If the weather is very cold,

1 oz. of isinglass will be found sufficient for the above proportion of ingredients. *Time.*—10 minutes to boil the juice and water. *Average cost*, with the best isinglass, 3*s*. *Sufficient* to fill a quart mould. *Seasonable* from November to May.

ORANGE CREAMS.

Ingredients.—1 Seville orange, 1 tablespoonful of brandy, ¼ lb. of loaf sugar, the yolks of 4 eggs, 1 pint of cream. *Mode.*—Boil the rind of the Seville orange until tender, and beat it in a mortar to a pulp; add to it the brandy, the strained juice of the orange, and the sugar, and beat all together for about 10 minutes, adding the well-beaten yolks of eggs. Bring the cream to the boiling-point, and pour it very gradually to the other ingredients, and beat the mixture till nearly cold; put it into custard-cups, place the cups in a deep dish of boiling water, where let them remain till quite cold. Take the cups out of the water, wipe them, and garnish the tops of the creams with candied orange-peel or preserved chips. *Time.*—Altogether, ¾ hour. *Average cost*, with cream at 1*s*. per pint, 1*s*. 7*d*. *Sufficient* to make 7 or 8 creams. *Seasonable* from November to May.

Note.—To render this dish more economical, substitute milk for the cream, but add a small pinch of isinglass to make the creams firm.

ORANGE FRITTERS.

Ingredients.—For the batter, ½ lb. of flour, ½ oz. of butter, ½ saltspoonful of salt, 2 eggs, milk, oranges, hot lard or clarified dripping. *Mode.*—Make a nice light batter with the above proportion of flour, butter, salt, eggs, and sufficient milk to make it the proper consistency; peel the oranges, remove as much of the white skin as possible, and divide each orange into eight pieces, without breaking the thin skin, unless it be to remove the pips; dip each piece of orange in the batter. Have ready a pan of boiling lard or clarified dripping; drop in the oranges, and fry them a delicate brown from 8 to 10 minutes. When done, lay them on a piece of blotting-paper before the fire, to drain away the greasy moisture, and dish them on a white d'oyley; sprinkle over them plenty of pounded sugar, and serve quickly. *Time.*—8 to 10 minutes to fry the fritters; 5 minutes

to drain them. *Average cost*, 9*d*. *Sufficient* for 4 or 5 persons. *Seasonable* from November to May.

ORANGE GRAVY, for Wildfowl, Widgeon, Teal, &c.

Ingredients.—½ pint of white stock, 1 small onion, 3 or 4 strips of lemon or orange peel, a few leaves of basil, if at hand, the juice of a Seville orange or lemon, salt and pepper to taste, 1 glass of port wine. *Mode.*—Put the onion, cut in slices, into a stewpan with the stock, orange-peel, and basil, and let them simmer very gently for ¼ hour or rather longer, should the gravy not taste sufficiently of the peel. Strain it off, and add to the gravy the remaining ingredients; let the whole heat through, and, when on the point of boiling, serve very hot in a tureen which should have a cover to it. *Time.*—Altogether ½ hour. *Sufficient* for a small tureen.

ORANGE JELLY.

Ingredients.—1 pint of water, 1½ to 2 oz. of isinglass, ½ lb. of loaf sugar, 1 Seville orange, 1 lemon, about 9 China oranges. *Mode.*—Put the water into a saucepan, with the isinglass, sugar, and the rind of 1 orange, and the same of ½ lemon, and stir these over the fire until

OPEN MOULD.

the isinglass is dissolved, and remove the scum; then add to this the juice of the Seville orange, the juice of the lemon, and sufficient juice of China oranges to make in all 1 pint: from 8 to 10 oranges will yield the desired quantity. Stir all together over the fire until it is just on the point of boiling; skim well; then strain the jelly through a very fine sieve or jelly-bag, and when nearly cold, put it into a mould previously wetted, and, when quite set, turn it out on a dish, and garnish it to taste. To insure this jelly being clear, the orange- and lemon-juice should be well strained, and the isinglass clarified, before they are added to the other ingredients, and, to heighten the colour, a few drops of prepared cochineal may be added. *Time.*—5 minutes to boil without the juice; 1 minute after it is added. *Average cost*, with the best isinglass, 3*s*. 6*d*. *Sufficient* to fill a quart mould. *Seasonable* from November to May.

ORANGE MARMALADE.

Ingredients.—Equal weight of fine loaf sugar and Seville oranges; to 12 oranges allow 1 pint of water. *Mode.*—Let there be an equal weight of loaf sugar and Seville oranges, and allow the above proportion of water to every dozen oranges. Peel them carefully, remove a little of the white pith, and boil the rinds in water 2 hours, changing the water three times to take off a little of the bitter taste. Break the pulp into small pieces, take out all the pips, and cut the boiled rind into chips. Make a syrup with the sugar and water; boil this well, skim it, and, when clear, put in the pulp and chips. Boil all together from 20 minutes to ½ hour; pour it into pots, and, when cold, cover down with bladders or tissue-paper brushed over on both sides with the white of an egg. The juice and grated rind of 2 lemons to every dozen of oranges, added with the pulp and chips to the syrup, are a very great improvement to this marmalade. *Time.*—2 hours to boil the orange-rinds; 10 minutes to boil the syrup; 20 minutes to ½ hour to boil the marmalade. *Average cost*, from 6*d*. to 8*d*. per lb. pot. *Seasonable.*—This should be made in March or April, as Seville oranges are then in perfection.

ORANGE MARMALADE.

Ingredients.—Equal weight of Seville oranges and sugar; to every lb. of sugar allow ½ pint of water. *Mode.*—Weigh the sugar and oranges, score the skin across, and take it off in quarters. Boil these quarters in a muslin bag in water until they are quite soft, and they can be pierced easily with the head of a pin; then cut them into chips about 1 inch long, and as thin as possible. Should there be a great deal of white stringy pulp, remove it before cutting the rind into chips. Split open the oranges, scrape out the best part of the pulp, with the juice, rejecting the white pith and pips. Make a syrup with the sugar and water; boil it until clear; then put in the chips, pulp, and juice, and boil the marmalade from 20 minutes to ½ hour, removing all the scum as it rises. In boiling the syrup, clear it carefully from scum before the oranges are added to it. *Time.*—2 hours to boil the rinds, 10 minutes the syrup, 20 minutes to ½ hour the marmalade. *Average cost*, 6*d*. to 8*d*. per lb. pot. *Seasonable.*—Make this in March or April, when Seville oranges are in perfection.

ORANGE MARMALADE, an easy way of Making.

Ingredients.—To every lb. of pulp allow 1½ lb. of loaf sugar. *Mode.*—Choose some fine Seville oranges; put them whole into a stewpan with sufficient water to cover them, and stew them until they become perfectly tender, changing the water 2 or 3 times; drain them, take off the rind, remove the pips from the pulp, weigh it, and to every lb. allow 1½ of loaf sugar and ½ pint of the water the oranges were last boiled in. Boil the sugar and water together for 10 minutes; put in the pulp, boil for another 10 minutes; then add the peel cut into strips, and boil the marmalade for another 10 minutes, which completes the process. Pour it into jars; let it cool; then cover down with bladders, or tissue-paper brushed over on both sides with the white of an egg. *Time.*—2 hours to boil the oranges; altogether ½ hour to boil the marmalade. *Average cost*, from 6*d*. to 8*d*. per lb. pot. *Seasonable.*—Make this in March or April.

ORANGE MARMALADE, made with Honey.

Ingredients.—To 1 quart of the juice and pulp of Seville oranges allow 1 lb. of the rind, 2 lbs. of honey. *Mode.*—Peel the oranges, and boil the rind in water until tender, and cut it into strips. Take away the pips from the juice and pulp, and put it with the honey and chips into a preserving-pan; boil all together for about ½ hour, or until the marmalade is of the proper consistency; put it into pots, and, when cold, cover down with bladders. *Time.*—2 hours to boil the rind, ½ hour the marmalade.

Average cost, from 7*d.* to 9*d.* per lb. pot. *Seasonable.* —Make this in March or April.

ORANGE MARMALADE, Pounded.

Ingredients.—Weight and ½ in sugar to every lb. of oranges. *Mode.*—Cut some clear Seville oranges in 4 pieces, put all the juice and pulp into a basin, and take out the seeds and skins; boil the rinds in hard water till tender, changing the water 2 or 3 times while boiling; drain them well, and pound them in a mortar; then put them into a preserving-pan with the juice and pulp, and their weight and ½ of sugar; boil rather more than ½ an hour. *Time.*—About 2 hours to boil the rinds, ½ an hour the marmalade.

ORANGE PUDDING, Baked.

Ingredients.—6 oz. of stale sponge cake or bruised ratafias, 6 oranges, 1 pint of milk, 6 eggs, ½ lb. of sugar. *Mode.*—Bruise the sponge cake or ratafias into fine crumbs, and pour upon them the milk, which should be boiling. Rub the rinds of 2 of the oranges on sugar, and add this, with the juice of the remainder, to the other ingredients. Beat up the eggs, stir them in, sweeten to taste, and put the mixture into a pie-dish previously lined with puff-paste. Bake for rather more than ½ hour; turn it out of the dish, strew sifted sugar over, and serve. *Time.*—Rather more than ½ hour. *Average cost*, 1*s.* 6*d.* *Sufficient* for 3 or 4 persons. *Seasonable* from November to May.

ORANGE PUDDING, Seville.

Ingredients.—4 Seville oranges, 6 oz. of fresh butter, 12 almonds, ½ lb. of sifted sugar, the juice of 1 lemon, 8 eggs. *Mode.*—Boil the oranges and chop them finely, taking out all the pips. Put the butter, the almonds, blanched and chopped, and the sugar, into a saucepan, to which add the orange pulp and the lemon-juice. Put it on a hot plate to warm, mixing all together until the butter is thoroughly melted. Turn the mixture out, let it get cold, then add the eggs, which should be well whipped. Put all into a baking-dish, bordered with puff paste, and bake from ½ hour to 40 minutes, according to the heat of the oven. *Time.*—½ hour to 40 minutes. *Seasonable* from November to May.

ORANGE SALAD.

Ingredients.—6 oranges, ¼ lb. of muscatel raisins, 2 oz. of pounded sugar, 4 tablespoonfuls of brandy. *Mode.*—Peel 5 of the oranges; divide them into slices without breaking the pulp, and arrange them on a glass dish. Stone the raisins, mix them with the sugar and brandy, and mingle them with the oranges. Squeeze the juice of the other orange over the whole, and the dish is ready for table. A little pounded spice may be put in when the flavour is liked; but this ingredient must be added very sparingly. *Average cost*, 1*s.* *Sufficient* for 5 or 6 persons. *Seasonable* from November to May.

ORANGE WINE, a very Simple and Easy Method of Making a very Superior.

Ingredients.—90 Seville oranges, 32 lbs. of lump sugar, water. *Mode.*—Break up the sugar into small pieces, and put it into a dry, sweet, 9-gallon cask, placed in a cellar or other storehouse, where it is intended to be kept. Have ready close to the cask two large pans or wooden keelers, into one of which put the peel of the oranges pared quite thin, and into the other the pulp after the juice has been squeezed from it. Strain the juice through a piece of double muslin, and put into the cask with the sugar. Then pour about 1½ gallon of cold spring water on both the peels and the pulp; let it stand for 24 hours, and then strain it into the cask; add more water to the peels and pulp when this is done, and repeat the same process every day for a week: it should take about a week to fill up the cask. Be careful to apportion the quantity as nearly as possible to the seven days, and to stir the contents of the cask each day. On the *third* day after the cask is full—that is, the *tenth* day after the commencement of making—the cask may be securely bunged down. This is a very simple and easy method, and the wine made according to it will be pronounced to be most excellent. There is no troublesome boiling, and all fermentation takes place in the cask. When the above directions are attended to, the wine cannot fail to be good. It should be bottled in 8 or 9 months, and will be fit for use in a twelvemonth after the time of making. Ginger wine may be made in precisely the same manner, only, with the 9-gallon cask for ginger wine, 2 lbs. of the best whole ginger, *bruised*, must be put with the sugar. It will be found convenient to tie the ginger loosely in a muslin bag. *Time.*—Altogether, 10 days to make it. *Average cost*, 2*s*. 6*d*. per gallon. *Sufficient* for 9 gallons. *Seasonable.*—Make this in March, and bottle it in the following January.

ORANGES, Compôte of.

Ingredients.—1 pint of syrup, 6 oranges. *Mode.*—Peel the oranges, remove as much of the white pith as possible, and divide them into small pieces without breaking the thin skin with which they are surrounded. Make the syrup by recipe, adding the rind of the orange cut into thin narrow strips. When the syrup has been well skimmed, and is quite clear, put in the pieces of orange, and simmer them for 5 minutes. Take them out carefully with a spoon without

COMPÔTE OF ORANGES.

breaking them, and arrange them on a glass dish. Reduce the syrup by boiling it quickly until thick; let it cool a little, pour it over the oranges, and, when cold, they will be ready for table. *Time.*—10 minutes to boil the syrup; 5 minutes to simmer the oranges; 5 minutes to reduce the syrup. *Average cost*, 9*d*. *Sufficient* for 5 or 6 persons. *Seasonable* from November to May.

ORANGES, a Pretty Dish of.

Ingredients.—6 large oranges, ½ lb. of loaf sugar, ¼ pint of water, ½ pint of cream, 2 tablespoonfuls of any kind of liquor, sugar to taste. *Mode.*—Put the sugar and water into a saucepan, and boil them until the sugar becomes brittle, which may be ascertained by taking up a small quantity in a spoon, and dipping it in cold water; if the sugar is sufficiently boiled, it will easily snap. Peel the oranges, remove as much of the white pith as possible, and divide them into nice-sized slices, without breaking the thin white skin which surrounds

the juicy pulp. Place the pieces of orange on small skewers, dip them into the hot sugar, and arrange them in layers round a plain mould, which should be well oiled with the purest salad-oil. The sides of the mould only should be lined with the oranges, and the centre left open for the cream. Let the sugar become firm by cooling; turn the oranges carefully out on a dish, and fill the centre with whipped cream, flavoured with any kind of liqueur, and sweetened with pounded sugar. This is an exceedingly ornamental and nice dish for the supper-table. *Time.*—10 minutes to boil the sugar. *Average cost*, 1*s*. 8*d*.—*Sufficient* for 1 mould. *Seasonable* from November to May.

ORANGES, Iced.

Ingredients.—Oranges; to every lb. of pounded loaf sugar allow the whites of 2 eggs. *Mode.*—Whisk the whites of the eggs well, stir in the sugar, and beat this mixture for ¼ hour. Skin the oranges, remove as much of the white pith as possible without injuring the pulp of the fruit; pass a thread through the centre of each orange, dip them into the sugar, and tie them to a stick. Place this stick across the oven, and let the oranges remain until dry, when they will have the appearance of balls of ice. They make a pretty dessert or supper dish. Care must be taken not to have the oven too fierce, or the oranges would scorch and acquire a brown colour, which would entirely spoil their appearance. *Time.*—From ¾ to 1 hour to dry in a moderate oven. *Average cost*, 1½*d*. each. *Sufficient.*—½ lb. of sugar to ice 12 oranges. *Seasonable* from November to May.

ORANGES, Preserved.

Ingredients.—Oranges; to every lb. of juice and pulp allow 2 lbs. of loaf sugar; to every pint of water ½ lb. of loaf sugar. *Mode.*—Wholly grate or peel the oranges, taking off only the thin outside portion of the rind. Make a small incision where the stalk is taken out, squeeze out as much of the juice as can be obtained, and preserve it in a basin with the pulp that accompanies it. Put the oranges into cold water; let them stand for 3 days, changing the water twice; then boil them in fresh water till they are very tender, and put them to drain.

Make a syrup with the above proportion of sugar and water, sufficient to cover the oranges; let them stand in it for 2 or 3 days; then drain them well. Weigh the juice and pulp, allow double their weight of sugar, and boil them together until the scum ceases to rise, which must all be carefully removed; put in the oranges, boil them for 10 minutes, place them in jars, pour over them the syrup, and, when cold, cover down. They will be fit for use in a week. *Time.*—3 days for the oranges to remain in water, 3 days in the syrup; ½ hour to boil the pulp, 10 minutes the oranges. *Seasonable.*—This preserve should be made in February or March, when oranges are plentiful.

OX, The.

The manner in which a side of beef is cut up in London is shown in the engraving on this page. In the metropolis, on account of the large number of its population possessing the means to indulge in the "best of everything," the demand for the most delicate joints of meat is great, the price, at the same time, being much higher for these than for the other parts. The consequence is, that in London the carcass is there divided so as to obtain the greatest quantity of meat on the most esteemed joints. In many places, however, where, from a greater equality in the social condition and habits of the inhabitants, the demand and prices for the different parts of the carcasses are more equalized, there is not the same reason for the butcher to cut the best joints so large.

The meat on those parts of the animal in which the muscles are least called into action is most tender and succulent; as, for instance, along the back, from the rump to the hinder part of the shoulder; whilst the limbs, shoulder, and neck are the toughest, driest, and least-esteemed.

The names of the several joints in the hind and fore quarters of a side of beef, and the purposes for which they are used, are as follows:—

Hind Quarter:—

1. Sirloin,—the two sirloins, cut together in one joint, form a baron; this, when roasted, is the famous national dish of Englishmen, at entertainments, on occasion of rejoicing.
2. Rump,—the finest part for steaks.
3. Aitch-bone,—boiling piece.
4. Buttock,—prime boiling piece.
5. Mouse-round,—boiling or stewing.
6. Hock,—stewing.

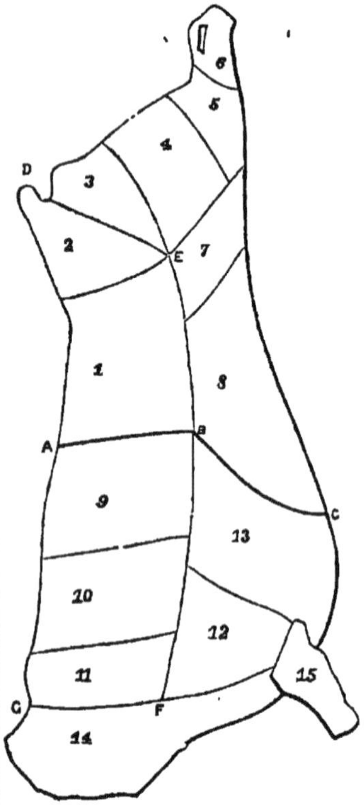

SIDE OF BEEF, SHOWING THE SEVERAL JOINTS.

7. Thick flank, cut with the udder-fat,—primest boiling piece.
8. Thin flank,—boiling.

Fore Quarter:—

9. Five ribs, called the fore-rib.—This is considered the primest roasting piece.

10. Four ribs, called the middle-rib, —greatly esteemed by housekeepers as the most economical joint for roasting.
11. Two ribs, called the chuck-rib, —used for second quality of steaks.
12. Leg-of-mutton piece,—the muscles of the shoulder dissected from the breast.
13. Brisket, or breast,—used for boiling, after being salted.
14. Neck, clod, and sticking-piece, —used for soups, gravies, stocks, pies, and mincing for sausages.
15. Shin,—stewing.

The following is a classification of the qualities of meat, according to the several joints of beef, when cut up in the London manner.

First class—includes the sirloin, with the kidney suet (1), the rump-steak piece (2), the fore-rib (9).

Second class—The buttock (4), the thick flank (7), the middle-rib (10).

Third class—The aitch-bone (3), the mouse-round (5), the thin flank (8), the chuck (11), the leg-of-mutton piece (12), the brisket (13).

Fourth class—The neck, clod, and sticking-piece (14).

Fifth class—The hock (6), the shin (15).

OX-CHEEK SOUP.

Ingredients.—An ox-cheek, 2 oz. of butter, 3 or 4 slices of lean ham or bacon, 1 parsnip, 3 carrots, 2 onions, 3 heads of celery, 3 blades of mace, 4 cloves, a faggot of savoury herbs, 1 bay leaf, a teaspoonful of salt, half that of pepper, 1 head of celery, browning, the crust of a French roll, 5 quarts of water. *Mode.*—Lay the ham in the bottom of the stewpan, with the butter; break the bones of the cheek, wash it clean, and put it on the ham. Cut the vegetables small, add them to the other ingredients, and set the whole over a slow fire for ¼ of an hour. Now put in the water, and simmer gently till it is reduced to 4 quarts; take out the fleshy part of the cheek, and strain the soup into a clean stewpan; thicken with flour, put in a head of sliced celery, and simmer till the celery is tender. If not a good colour, use a little browning. Cut the meat into small square pieces, pour the soup over, and serve with the crust of a French roll in the tureen. A glass of sherry much improves this soup. *Time.*—3 to 4 hours. *Average cost*, 8*d*. per quart. *Seasonable* in winter. *Sufficient* for 12 persons.

OX-CHEEK, Stewed.

Ingredients.—1 cheek, salt and water, 4 or 5 onions, butter and flour, 6 cloves, 3 turnips, 2 carrots, 1 bay-leaf, 1 head of celery, 1 bunch of savoury herbs, cayenne, black pepper, and salt to taste, 1 oz. of butter, 2 dessertspoonfuls of flour, 2 tablespoonfuls of Chili vinegar, 2 tablespoonfuls of mushroom ketchup, 2 tablespoonfuls of port wine, 2 tablespoonfuls of Harvey's sauce. *Mode.*—Have the cheek boned, and prepare it the day before it is to be eaten, by cleaning and putting it to soak all night in salt and water. The next day, wipe it dry and clean, and put it into a stewpan. Just cover it with water, skim well when it boils, and let it gently simmer till the meat is quite tender. Slice and fry 3 onions in a little butter and flour, and put them into the gravy; add 2 whole onions, each stuck with 3 cloves, 3 turnips quartered, 2 carrots sliced, a bay-leaf, 1 head of celery, a bunch of herbs, and seasoning to taste of cayenne, black pepper, and salt. Let these stew till perfectly tender; then take out the cheek, divide into pieces fit to help at table, skim and strain the gravy, and thicken 1½ pint of it with butter and flour in the above proportions. Add the vinegar, ketchup, and port wine; put in the pieces of cheek; let the whole boil up, and serve quite hot. Send it to table in a ragoût-dish.* If the colour of the gravy should not be very good, add a tablespoonful of the browning. *Time.*—4 hours. *Average cost*, 3*d*. per lb. *Sufficient* for 8 persons. *Seasonable* at any time.

OX-TAIL, Broiled (an Entrée).

Ingredients.—2 tails, 1½ pint of stock, salt and cayenne to taste, bread crumbs, 1 egg. *Mode.*—Joint and cut up the tails into convenient-sized pieces, and put them into a stewpan, with the stock, cayenne, and salt, and, if liked very savoury, a bunch of sweet herbs. Let them simmer gently for about 2½ hours; then take them out, drain them, and let them cool. Beat an egg upon a plate; dip in each piece of tail, and, afterwards, sprinkle them well with fine bread crumbs; broil them over a clear fire, until of a brownish colour on both sides, and serve with a good gravy, or any sauce that may be preferred. *Time.*—About 2½ hours. *Average cost*, from 9*d.* to 1*s.* 6*d.*, according to the season. *Sufficient* for 6 persons. *Seasonable* at any time.

Note.—These may be more easily prepared by putting the tails in a brisk oven, after they have been dipped in egg and bread-crumb; and, when brown, they are done. They must be boiled the same time as for broiling.

OX-TAIL SOUP.

Ingredients.—2 ox-tails, 2 slices of ham, 1 oz. of butter, 2 carrots, 2 turnips, 3 onions, 1 leek, 1 head of celery, 1 bunch of savoury herbs, 1 bay-leaf, 12 whole peppercorns, 4 cloves, a tablespoonful of salt, 2 tablespoonfuls of ketchup, ½ glass of port wine, 3 quarts of water. *Mode.*—Cut up the tails, separating them at the joints; wash them, and put them in a stewpan, with the butter. Cut the vegetables in slices, and add them, with the peppercorns and herbs. Put in ½ pint of water, and stir it over a sharp fire till the juices are drawn. Fill up the stewpan with the water, and, when boiling, add the salt. Skim well, and simmer very gently for 4 hours, or until the tails are tender. Take them out, skim and strain the soup, thicken with flour, and flavour with the ketchup and port wine. Put back the tails, simmer for 5 minutes, and serve. *Time.*—4½ hours. *Average cost*, 1*s.* 3*d.* per quart. *Seasonable* in winter. *Sufficient* for 10 persons.

OX-TAILS, Stewed.

Ingredients.—2 ox-tails, 1 onion, 3 cloves, 1 blade of mace, ¼ teaspoonful of whole black pepper, ¼ teaspoonful of allspice, ½ a teaspoonful of salt, a small bunch of savoury herbs, thickening of butter and flour, 1 tablespoonful of lemon-juice, 1 tablespoonful of mushroom ketchup. *Mode.*—Divide the tails at the joints, wash, and put them into a stewpan with sufficient water to cover them, and set them on the fire; when the water boils, remove the scum, and add the onion cut into rings, the spice, seasoning, and herbs. Cover the stewpan closely, and let the tails simmer very gently until tender, which will be in about 2½ hours. Take them out, make a thickening of butter and flour, add it to the gravy, and let it boil for ¼ hour. Strain it through a sieve into a saucepan, put back the tails, add the lemon-juice and ketchup; let the whole just boil up, and serve. Garnish with croûtons or sippets of toasted bread. *Time.*—2½ hours to stew the tails. *Average cost*, 9*d.* to 1*s.* 6*d.*, according to the season. *Sufficient* for 8 persons. *Seasonable* all the year.

OYSTER, Forcemeat for Roast or Boiled Turkey.

Ingredients.—½ pint of bread crumbs, 1½ oz. of chopped suet or butter, 1 faggot of savoury herbs, ¼ saltspoonful of grated nutmeg, salt and pepper to taste, 2 eggs, 18 oysters. *Mode.*—Grate the bread very fine, and be careful that no large lumps remain; put it into a basin with the suet, which must be very finely minced, or, when butter is used, that must be cut up into small pieces. Add the herbs, also chopped as small as possible, and seasoning; mix all these well together, until the ingredients are thoroughly mingled. Open and beard the oysters, chop them, but not too small, and add them to the other ingredients. Beat up the eggs, and, with the hand, work altogether, until it is smoothly mixed. The turkey should not be stuffed too full: if there should be too much forcemeat, roll it into balls, fry them, and use them as a garnish. *Sufficient* for 1 turkey.

OYSTER KETCHUP.

Ingredients.—Sufficient oysters to fill a pint measure, 1 pint of sherry, 3 oz. of salt, 1 drachm of cayenne, 2 drachms of pounded mace. *Mode.*—Procure the oysters very fresh, and open sufficient to fill a pint measure; save the liquor, and scald the oysters in it with the sherry; strain the oysters, and put them in a mortar with the salt, cayenne, and mace; pound the whole until reduced to a pulp, then add it to the liquor in which they were scalded; boil it again five minutes, and skim well; rub the whole through a sieve, and, when cold, bottle and cork closely. The corks should be sealed. *Seasonable* from September to April.

Note.—Cider may be substituted for the sherry.

OYSTER PATTIES (an Entrée).

Ingredients.—2 dozen oysters, 2 oz. of butter, 3 tablespoonfuls of cream, a little lemon-juice, 1 blade of pounded mace; cayenne to taste. *Mode.*—Scald the oysters in their own liquor, beard them, and cut each one into 3 pieces. Put the butter into a stewpan, dredge in sufficient flour to dry it up; add the strained oyster-liquor with the other ingredients; put in the oysters, and let them heat gradually, but not boil fast. Make the patty-cases as directed for lobster patties, fill with the oyster mixture, and replace the covers. *Time.*—2 minutes for the oysters to simmer in the mixture. *Average cost,* exclusive of the patty-cases, 1*s.* 4*d.* *Seasonable* from September to April.

OYSTER SAUCE, to serve with Fish, Boiled Poultry, &c.

Ingredients.—3 dozen oysters, ½ pint of melted butter, made with milk. *Mode.*—Open the oysters carefully, and save their liquor; strain it into a clean saucepan (a lined one is best), put in the oysters, and let them just come to the boiling-point, when they should look plump. Take them off the fire immediately, and put the whole into a basin. Strain the liquor from them, mix with it sufficient melted butter made with milk to make ½ pint altogether. When this is ready and very smooth, put in the oysters, which should be previously bearded, if you wish the sauce to be really nice. Set it by the side of the fire to get thoroughly hot, *but do not allow it to boil,* or the oysters will immediately harden. Using cream instead of milk makes this sauce extremely delicious. When liked, add a seasoning of cayenne or anchovy sauce; but, as we have before stated, a plain sauce *should* be plain, and not be overpowered by highly-flavoured essences; therefore we recommend that the above directions be implicitly followed, and no seasoning added. *Average cost* for this quantity, 2*s.* *Sufficient* for 6 persons. Never allow fewer than 6 oysters to 1 person, unless the party is very large. *Seasonable* from September to April.

A more economical sauce may be made by using a smaller quantity of oysters, and not bearding them before they are added to the sauce: this may answer the purpose, but we cannot undertake to recommend it as a mode for making this delicious adjunct to fish, &c.

OYSTER SOUP.

Ingredients.—6 dozen of oysters, 2 quarts of white stock, ½ pint of cream, 2 oz. of butter, 1½ oz. of flour; salt, cayenne, and mace to taste. *Mode.*—Scald the oysters in their own liquor; take them out, beard them, and put them in a tureen. Take a pint of the stock, put in the beards and the liquor, which must be carefully strained, and simmer for ½ an hour. Take it off the fire, strain it again, and add the remainder of the stock, with the seasoning and mace. Bring it to a boil, add the thickening of butter and flour, simmer for 5 minutes, stir in the boiling cream, pour it over the oysters, and serve. *Time.*—1 hour. *Average cost,* 2*s.* 8*d.* per quart. *Seasonable* from September to April. *Sufficient* for 8 persons.

Note.—This soup can be made less rich by using milk instead of cream, and thickening with arrowroot instead of butter and flour.

OYSTER SOUP.

Ingredients.—2 quarts of good mutton broth, 6 dozen oysters, 2 oz. butter, 1 oz. of flour. *Mode.*—Beard the oysters, and scald them in their own liquor; then add it, well strained, to the broth; thicken with the butter and flour, and simmer for ¼ of an hour. Put in the oysters, stir well, but do not let it boil, and serve very hot. *Time.*—¾ hour. *Average cost,* 2*s.* per quart. *Seasonable* from September to April. *Sufficient* for 8 persons.

OYSTERS, Fried.

Ingredients.—3 dozen oysters, 2 oz. butter, 1 tablespoonful of ketchup, a little chopped lemon-peel, ½ teaspoonful of chopped parsley. *Mode.*—Boil the oysters for 1 minute in their own liquor, and drain them; fry them with the butter, ketchup, lemon-peel, and parsley; lay them on a dish, and garnish with fried potatoes, toasted sippets, and parsley. This is a delicious delicacy, and is a favourite Italian dish. *Time.*—5 minutes. *Average cost* for this quantity, 1*s.* 9*d.* *Seasonable* from September to April. *Sufficient* for 4 persons.

OYSTERS Fried in Batter.

Ingredients.—½ pint of oysters, 2 eggs, ½ pint of milk, sufficient flour to make the batter; pepper and salt to taste;

when liked, a little nutmeg; hot lard. *Mode.*—Scald the oysters in their own liquor, beard them, and lay them on a cloth to drain thoroughly. Break the eggs into a basin, mix the flour with them, add the milk gradually, with nutmeg and seasoning, and put the oysters in the batter. Make some lard hot in a deep frying-pan, put in the oysters, one at a time; when done, take them up with a sharp-pointed skewer, and dish them on a napkin. Fried oysters are frequently used for garnishing boiled fish, and then a few bread crumbs should be added to the flour. *Time.*—5 or 6 minutes. *Average cost* for this quantity, 1*s.* 10*d.* *Seasonable* from September to April. *Sufficient* for 3 persons.

OYSTERS, to Keep.

Put them in a tub, and cover them with salt and water. Let them remain for 12 hours, when they are to be taken out, and allowed to stand for another 12 hours without water. If left without water every alternate 12 hours, they will be much better than if constantly kept in it. Never put the same water twice to them.

OYSTERS, Pickled.

Ingredients.—100 oysters; to each ½ pint of vinegar, 1 blade of pounded mace, 1 strip of lemon-peel, 12 black peppercorns. *Mode.*—Get the oysters in good condition, open them, place them in a saucepan, and let them simmer in their own liquor for about 10 minutes very gently; then take them out one by one, and place them in a jar, and cover them, when cold, with a pickle made as follows:—Measure the oyster-liquor; add to it the same quantity of vinegar, with mace, lemon-peel, and pepper in the above proportion, and boil it for 5 minutes; when cold, pour over the oysters, and tie them down very closely, as contact with the air spoils them. *Seasonable* from September to April.

Note.—Put this pickle away in small jars; because, directly one is opened, its contents should immediately be eaten, as they soon spoil. The pickle should not be kept more than 2 or 3 months.

OYSTERS, Scalloped.

Ingredients.—Oysters, say 1 pint, 1 oz. butter, flour, 2 tablespoonfuls of white stock, 2 tablespoonfuls of cream; pepper and salt to taste; bread crumbs, oiled butter. *Mode.*—Scald the oysters in their own liquor, take them out, beard them, and strain the liquor free from grit. Put 1 oz. of butter into a stewpan; when melted, dredge in sufficient flour to dry it up; add the stock, cream, and strained liquor, and give one boil. Put in the oysters and seasoning; let them gradually heat through, but not boil. Have ready the scallop-shells buttered; lay in the oysters, and as much of the liquid as they will hold; cover them over with bread crumbs, over which drop a little oiled butter. Brown them in the oven, or before the fire, and serve quickly, and very hot. *Time.*—Altogether, ¼ hour. *Average cost,* for this quantity, 3*s.* 6*d.* *Sufficient* for 5 or 6 persons.

OYSTERS, Scalloped.

Prepare the oysters as in the preceding recipe, and put them in a scallop-shell or saucer, and between each layer sprinkle over a few bread crumbs, pepper, salt, and grated nutmeg; place small pieces of butter over, and bake before the fire in a Dutch oven. Put sufficient bread crumbs on the top to make a smooth surface, as the oysters should not be seen. *Time.*—About ¼ hour. *Average cost,* 3*s.* 2*d.* *Seasonable* from September to April.

OYSTERS, Stewed.

Ingredients.—1 pint of oysters, 1 oz. of butter, flour, ⅓ pint of cream; cayenne and salt to taste; 1 blade of pounded mace. *Mode.*—Scald the oysters in their own liquor, take them out, beard them, and strain the liquor; put the butter into a stewpan, dredge in sufficient flour to dry it up, add the oyster-liquor and mace, and stir it over a sharp fire with a wooden spoon; when it comes to a boil, add the cream, oysters, and seasoning. Let all simmer for 1 or 2 minutes, but not longer, or the oysters would harden. Serve on a hot dish, and garnish with croûtons, or toasted sippets of bread. A small piece of lemon-peel boiled with the oyster-liquor, and taken out before the cream is added, will be found an improvement. *Time.*—Altogether 15 minutes. *Average cost* for this quantity, 3*s.* 6*d.* *Seasonable* from September to April. *Sufficient* for 6 persons.

PANCAKES.

Ingredients.—Eggs, flour, milk; to every egg allow 1 oz. of flour, about 1 gill of milk, ½ saltspoonful of salt. *Mode.*—Ascertain that the eggs are fresh; break each one separately in a cup; whisk them well, put them into a basin, with the flour, salt, and a few drops of milk, and beat the whole to a perfectly *smooth* batter; then add by degrees the remainder of the milk. The proportion of this latter ingredient must be regulated by the size of the eggs, &c. &c.; but the batter, when ready for frying, should be of the consistency of thick cream. Place a small frying-pan on the fire to get hot; let it be delicately clean, or the pancakes will stick, and, when quite hot, put into it a small piece of butter, allowing about ½ oz. to each pancake. When it is melted, pour in the batter, about ½ teacupful to a pan 5 inches in diameter, and fry it for about 4 minutes, or until it is nicely brown on one side. By only pouring in a small quantity of batter, and so making the pancakes thin, the necessity of turning them (an operation rather difficult to unskilful cooks) is obviated. When the pancake is done, sprinkle over it some pounded sugar, roll it up in the pan, and take it out with a large slice, and place it on a dish before the fire. Proceed in this manner until sufficient are cooked for a dish; then send them quickly to table, and continue to send in a further quantity, as pancakes are never good unless eaten almost immediately they come from the frying-pan. The batter may be flavoured with a little grated lemon-rind, or the pancakes may have preserve rolled in them instead of sugar. Send sifted sugar and a cut lemon to table with them. To render the pancakes very light, the yolks and whites of the eggs should be beaten separately, and the whites added the last thing to the batter before frying. *Time.*—From 4 to 5 minutes for a pancake that does not require turning; from 6 to 8 minutes for a thicker one. *Average cost* for 3 persons, 6*d.* *Sufficient.*—Allow 3 eggs, with the other ingredients in proportion, for 3 persons. *Seasonable* at any time, but specially served on Shrove Tuesday.

PANCAKES.

PANCAKES.

Ingredients.—6 eggs, 1 pint of cream, ¼ lb. of loaf sugar, 1 glass of sherry, ½ teaspoonful of grated nutmeg, flour. *Mode.*—Ascertain that the eggs are extremely fresh, beat them well, strain and mix with them the cream, pounded sugar, wine, nutmeg, and as much flour as will make the batter nearly as thick as that for ordinary pancakes. Make the frying-pan hot, wipe it with a clean cloth, pour in sufficient batter to make a thin pancake, and fry it for about 5 minutes. Dish the pancakes piled one above the other, strew sifted sugar between each, and serve. *Time.*—About 5 minutes. *Average cost,* with cream at 1*s.* per pint, 2*s.* 3*d.* *Sufficient* to make 8 pancakes. *Seasonable* at any time, but specially served on Shrove Tuesday.

PANCAKES, French.

Ingredients.—2 eggs, 2 oz. of butter, 2 oz. of sifted sugar, 2 oz. of flour, ½ pint of new milk. *Mode.*—Beat the eggs thoroughly, and put them into a basin with the butter, which should be beaten to a cream; stir in the sugar and flour, and when these ingredients are well mixed, add the milk; keep stirring and beating the mixture for a few minutes; put it on buttered plates, and bake in a quick oven for 20 minutes. Serve with a cut lemon and sifted sugar, or pile the pancakes high on a dish, with a layer of preserve or marmalade between each. *Time.*—20 minutes. *Average cost,* 7*d.* *Sufficient* for 3 or 4 persons. *Seasonable* at any time.

PANCAKES, Snow.

Ingredients.—3 tablespoonfuls of flour, 1 egg, 3 tablespoonfuls of snow, about ½ pint of new milk. *Mode.*—Mix the flour with the milk by degrees, add the egg well beaten, and just before frying, the snow, it should then be all beaten up together quickly, and put into the frying-pan immediately. *Sufficient* for 8 pancakes.

PAN KAIL.

Ingredients.—2 lbs. of cabbage, or Savoy greens; ¼ lb. of butter or dripping, salt and pepper to taste, oatmeal for thickening, 2 quarts of water. *Mode.*—Chop the cabbage very fine, thicken the water with oatmeal, put in the cabbage and butter, or dripping; season and simmer for 1½ hour. It can be made sooner by blanching and mashing the greens, adding any good liquor that a joint has been boiled in, and then further thicken with bread or pounded biscuit. *Time.*—1½ hour. *Average cost,* 1½*d.* per quart. *Seasonable* all the year, but more suitable in winter. *Sufficient* for 8 persons.

PARSLEY AND BUTTER, to serve with Calf's Head, Boiled Fowls, &c.

Ingredients. — 2 tablespoonfuls of minced parsley, ½ pint of melted butter. *Mode.*—Put into a saucepan a small quantity of water, slightly salted, and when it boils, throw in a good bunch of parsley which has been previously washed and tied together in a bunch; let it boil for 5 minutes, drain it, mince the leaves *very fine,* and put the above quantity in a tureen; pour over it ½ pint of smoothly-made melted butter; stir once, that the ingredients may be thoroughly mixed, and serve. *Time.*—5 minutes to boil the parsley. *Average cost, 4d. Sufficient* for 1 large fowl; allow rather more for a pair. *Seasonable* at any time.

PARSLEY, Fried, for Garnishing.

Ingredients.—Parsley, hot lard or clarified dripping. *Mode.*—Gather some young parsley; wash, pick, and dry it thoroughly in a cloth; put it into the wire basket of which we have given an engraving, and hold it in boiling lard or dripping for a minute or two. Directly it is done, lift out the basket, and let it stand before the fire, that the parsley may become thoroughly crisp; and the quicker it is fried the better. Should the kitchen not be furnished with the

WIRE BASKET.

above article, throw the parsley into the frying-pan, and when crisp, lift it out with a slice, dry it before the fire, and when thoroughly crisp it will be ready for use.

WIRE BASKET.—For this recipe a wire basket, as shown in the annexed engraving, will be found very useful. It is very light and handy, and may be used for other similar purposes besides that just described.

PARSLEY JUICE, for Colouring various Dishes.

Procure some nice young parsley; wash it and dry it thoroughly in a cloth; pound the leaves in a mortar till all the juice is extracted, and put the juice in a teacup or small jar; place this in a saucepan of boiling water, and warm it on the *bain-marie* principle just long enough to take off its rawness; let it drain, and it will be ready for colouring.

Substitute for. — Sometimes in the middle of winter parsley-leaves are not to be had, when the following will be found an excellent substitute:—Tie up a little parsley-seed in a small piece of muslin, and boil it for 10 minutes in a small quantity of water; use this water to make the melted butter with, and throw into it a little boiled spinach, minced rather fine, which will have an appearance similar to that of parsley.

PARSLEY, to Preserve through the Winter.

Use freshly-gathered parsley for keeping, and wash it perfectly free from grit and dirt; put it into boiling water which has been slightly salted and well skimmed, and then let it boil for 2 or 3 minutes; take it out, let it drain, and lay it on a sieve in front of the fire, when it should be dried as expeditiously as possible. Store it away in a very dry place in bottles, and when wanted for use pour over it a little warm water, and let it stand for about 5 minutes. *Seasonable.*—This may be done at any time between June and October.

PARSNIP SOUP.

Ingredients.—1 lb. of sliced parsnips, 2 oz. of butter, salt and cayenne to taste, 1 quart of stock. *Mode.*—Put the parsnips into the stewpan with the butter, which has been previously melted, and simmer them till quite tender. Then add nearly a pint of stock, and boil together for half an hour. Pass all through a fine strainer, and put to it the remainder of the stock. Season, boil, and serve immediately. *Time.*—2 hours. *Average cost*, 6*d*. per quart. *Seasonable* from October to April. *Sufficient* for 4 persons.

PARSNIPS, Boiled.

Ingredients.—Parsnips; to each ½ gallon of water allow 1 heaped tablespoonful of salt. *Mode.*—Wash the parsnips, scrape them thoroughly, and with the point of the knife remove any black specks about them, and, should they be very large, cut the thick part into quarters. Put them into a saucepan of boiling water salted in the above proportion, boil them rapidly until tender, which may be ascertained by thrusting a fork in them; take them up, drain them, and serve in a vegetable-dish. This vegetable is usually served with salt fish, boiled pork, or boiled beef: when sent to table with the latter, a few should be placed alternately with carrots round the dish as a garnish. *Time.*—Large parsnips, 1 to 1½ hour; small ones, ½ to 1 hour. *Average cost*, 1*d*. each. *Sufficient.*—Allow 1 for each person. *Seasonable* from October to May.

PARTRIDGE, Broiled (a Luncheon, Breakfast, or Supper Dish).

Ingredients.—3 partridges, salt and cayenne to taste, a small piece of butter, brown gravy or mushroom sauce. *Mode.*—Pluck, draw, and cut the partridges in half, and wipe the inside thoroughly with a damp cloth. Season them with salt and cayenne, broil them over a very clear fire, and dish them on a hot dish; rub a small piece of butter over each half, and send them to table with brown gravy or mushroom sauce. *Time.*—About ¼ hour. *Average cost*, 1*s*. 6d. to 2*s*. a brace. *Sufficient* for 3 or four persons. *Seasonable* from the 1st of September to the beginning of February.

PARTRIDGE PIE.

Ingredients.—3 partridges, pepper and salt to taste, 1 teaspoonful of minced parsley (when obtainable, a few mushrooms), ¾ lb. of veal cutlet, a slice of ham, ½ pint of stock, puff paste. *Mode.*—Line a pie-dish with a veal cutlet; over that place a slice of ham and a seasoning of pepper and salt. Pluck, draw, and wipe the partridges; cut off the legs at the first joint, and season them inside with pepper, salt, minced parsley, and a small piece of butter; place them in the dish, and pour over the stock; line the edges of the dish with puff paste, cover with the same, brush it over with the yolk of an egg, and bake for ¾ to 1 hour. *Time.*—¾ to 1 hour. *Average cost*, 1*s*. 6*d*. to 2*s*. a brace. *Sufficient* for 4 or 5 persons. *Seasonable* from the 1st of September to the beginning of February.

Note.—Should the partridges be very large, split them in half, they will then lie in the dish more compactly. When at hand, a few mushrooms should always be added.

PARTRIDGE, Potted.

Ingredients.—Partridges; seasoning to taste of mace, allspice, white pepper, and salt; butter, coarse paste. *Mode.*—Pluck and draw the birds, and wipe them inside with a damp cloth. Pound well some mace, allspice, white pepper, and salt; mix together, and rub every part of the partridges with this. Pack the birds as closely as possible in a baking-pan, with plenty of butter over them, and cover with a coarse flour and water crust. Tie a paper over this, and bake for rather more than 1½ hour; let the birds get cold, then cut them into pieces for keeping, pack them closely into a large potting-pot, and cover with clarified butter. This should be kept in a cool dry place. The butter used for potted things will answer for basting, or for paste for meat pies. *Time.*—1½ hour. *Seasonable* from the 1st of September to the beginning of February.

PARTRIDGE, Roast.

Ingredients. — Partridge; butter. *Choosing and Trussing.*—Choose young birds, with dark-coloured bills and yellowish legs, and let them hang a few days, or there will be no flavour to the

ROAST PARTRIDGE.

flesh, nor will it be tender. The time they should be kept entirely depends on the taste of those for whom they are intended, as what some persons would consider delicious would be to others disgusting and offensive. They may be trussed with or without the head, the latter mode being now considered the most fashionable. Pluck, draw, and wipe the partridge carefully inside and out; cut off the head, leaving sufficient skin on the neck to skewer back; bring the legs close to the breast, between it and the side-bones, and pass a skewer through the pinions and the thick part of the thighs. When the head is left on, it should be brought round and fixed on to the point of the skewer. *Mode.*—When the bird is firmly and plumply trussed, roast it before a nice bright fire; keep it well basted, and a few minutes before serving, flour and froth it well. Dish it, and serve with gravy and bread sauce, and send to table hot and quickly. A little of the gravy should be poured over the bird. *Time.*—25 to 35 minutes. *Average cost,* 1*s.* 6*d.* to 2*s.* a brace. *Sufficient.*—2 for a dish. *Seasonable* from the 1st of September to the beginning of February.

PARTRIDGE SOUP.

Ingredients.—2 partridges, 3 slices of lean ham, 2 shred onions, 1 head of celery, 1 large carrot, and 1 turnip cut into any fanciful shapes, 1 small lump of sugar, 2 oz. of butter, salt and pepper to taste, 2 quarts of medium stock. *Mode.*—Cut the partridges into pieces, and braise them in the butter and ham until quite tender; then take out the legs, wings, and breast, and set them by. Keep the backs and other trimmings in the braise, and add the onions and celery; any remains of cold game can be put in, and 3 pints of stock. Simmer slowly for 1 hour, strain it, and skim the fat off as clean as possible; put in the pieces that were taken out, give it one boil, and skim again to have it quite clear, and add the sugar and seasoning. Now simmer the cut carrot and turnip in 1 pint of stock; when quite tender, put them to the partridges, and serve. *Time.*—2 hours. *Average cost,* 2*s.* or 1*s.* 6*d.* per quart. *Seasonable* from September to February. *Sufficient* for 8 persons.

Note.—The meat of the partridges may be pounded with a crumb of a French roll, and worked with the soup through a sieve. Serve with stewed celery cut in slices, and put in the tureen.

PARTRIDGES, to Carve.

There are several ways of carving this most familiar game bird. The more usual and summary mode is to carry the knife sharply along the top of the breast-bone of the bird, and cut it quite through, thus dividing it into two precisely equal and similar parts, in the same manner as carving a pigeon. Another plan is to cut it into three pieces; viz., by severing a small wing and leg on either side from the body, by following the line 1 to 2 in the upper woodcut; thus making 2 helpings, when the breast will remain for a third plate. The most elegant manner is that of thrusting back the body from the legs, and then cutting through the breast in the direction shown by the line 1 to 2: this plan will give 4 or more small helpings. A little bread-sauce should be served to each guest.

ROAST PARTRIDGE.

PARTRIDGES, Hashed, or Salmi de Perdrix.

Ingredients.—3 young partridges, 3 shallots, a slice of lean ham, 1 carrot, 3 or 4 mushrooms, a bunch of savoury herbs, 2 cloves, 6 whole peppers, ¾ pint of stock, 1 glass of sherry or Madeira, a small lump of sugar. *Mode.*—After the partridges are plucked and drawn, roast them rather underdone, and cover them with paper, as they should not be browned; cut them into joints, take off the skin from the wings, legs, and breasts; put these into a stewpan, cover them up, and set by until the gravy is ready. Cut a slice of ham into small pieces, and put them, with the carrots sliced, the shallots, mushrooms, herbs, cloves, and pepper, into a stewpan; fry them lightly in a little butter, pour in the stock, add the bones and trimming from the partridges, and simmer for ¼ hour. Strain the gravy, let it cool, and skim off every particle of fat; put it to the legs, wings, and breasts, add a glass of sherry or Madeira and a small lump of sugar, let all gradually warm through by the side of the fire, and when on the point of boiling, serve, and garnish the dish with croûtons. The remains of roast partridge answer very well dressed in this way, although not so good as when the birds are in the first instance only half-roasted. This recipe is equally suitable for pheasants, moorgame, &c.; but care must be taken always to skin the joints. *Time.*—Altogether 1 hour. *Sufficient.*—2 or 3 partridges for an entrée. *Seasonable* from the 1st of September to the beginning of February.

PASTE, Common, for Family Pies.

Ingredients.—1¼ lb. of flour, ½ lb. of butter, rather more than ½ pint of water. *Mode.*—Rub the butter lightly into the flour, and mix it to a smooth paste with the water; roll it out 2 or 3 times, and it will be ready for use. This paste may be converted into an excellent short crust for sweet tart by adding to the flour, after the butter is rubbed in, 2 tablespoonfuls of fine-sifted sugar. *Average cost,* 8*d.* per lb.

PASTE, Puff, French, or Feuilletage (Founded on M. Ude's Recipe).

Ingredients.—Equal quantities of flour and butter—say 1 lb. of each; ½ saltspoonful of salt, the yolks of 2 eggs, rather more than ¼ pint of water. *Mode.*—Weigh the flour; ascertain that it is perfectly *dry,* and sift it; squeeze all the water from the butter, and wring it in a clean cloth till there is no moisture remaining. Put the flour on the pasteboard, work lightly into it 2 oz. of the butter, and then make a hole in the centre; into this well put the yolks of 2 eggs, the salt, and about ¼ pint of water (the quantity of this latter ingredient must be regulated by the cook, as it is impossible to give the exact proportion of it); knead up the paste quickly and lightly, and, when quite smooth, roll it out square to the thickness of about ½ inch. Presuming that the butter is perfectly free from moisture, and *as cool* as possible, roll it into a ball, and place this ball of butter on the paste; fold the paste over the butter all round, and secure it by wrapping it well all over. Flatten the paste by rolling it lightly with the rolling-pin until it is quite thin, but not thin enough to allow the butter to break through, and keep the board and paste dredged lightly with flour during the process of making it. This rolling gives it the *first* turn. Now fold the paste in three, and roll out again, and, should the weather be very warm, put it in a cold place on the ground to cool between the several turns; for, unless this is particularly attended to, the paste will be spoiled. Roll out the paste again *twice,* put it by to cool, then roll it out *twice* more, which will make 6 *turnings* in all. Now fold the paste in two, and it will be ready for use. If properly baked and well made, this crust will be delicious, and should rise in the oven about 5 or 6 inches. The paste should be made rather firm in the first instance, as the ball of butter is liable to break through. Great attention must also be paid to keeping the butter very cool, as, if this is in a liquid and soft state, the paste will not answer at all. Should the cook be dexterous enough to succeed in making this, the paste will have a much better appearance than that made by the process of dividing the butter into 4 parts, and placing it over the rolled-out paste; but until experience has been acquired, we recommend puff-paste made by recipe. The above paste is used for vols-au-vent, small articles of pastry, and, in fact, everything that requires very light crust. *Average cost,* 1*s.* 6*d.* per lb.

PASTE, Puff, very Good.

Ingredients.—To every lb. of flour allow 1 lb. of butter, and not quite ½ pint of water. *Mode.*—Carefully weigh the flour and butter, and have the exact proportion; squeeze the butter well, to extract the water from it, and afterwards wring it in a clean cloth, that no moisture may remain. Sift the flour; see that it is perfectly dry, and proceed in the following manner to make the paste, using a very *clean* paste-board and rolling-pin:—Supposing the quantity to be 1 lb. of flour, work the whole into a smooth paste with not quite ½ pint of water, using a knife to mix it with: the proportion of this latter ingredient must be regulated by the discretion of the cook; if too much be added, the paste, when baked, will be tough. Roll it out until it is of an equal thickness of about an inch; break 4 oz. of the butter into small pieces; place these on the paste, sift over it a little flour, fold it over, roll out again, and put another 4 oz. of butter. Repeat the rolling and buttering until the paste has been rolled out 4 times, or equal quantities of flour and butter have been used. Do not omit, every time the paste is rolled out, to dredge a little flour over that and the rolling-pin, to prevent both from sticking. Handle the paste as lightly as possible, and do not press heavily upon it with the rolling-pin. The next thing to be considered is the oven, as the baking of pastry requires particular attention. Do not put it into the oven until it is sufficiently hot to raise the paste; for the best-prepared paste, if not properly baked, will be good for nothing. Brushing the paste as often as rolled out, and the pieces of butter placed thereon, with the white of an egg, assists it to rise in *leaves* or *flakes*. As this is the great beauty of puff-paste, it is as well to try this method. *Average cost*, 1*s*. 4*d*. per lb.

PASTE, Puff, Medium.

Ingredients.—To every lb. of flour allow 8 oz. of butter, 4 oz. of lard, not quite ½ pint of water. *Mode.*—This paste may be made by the directions in the preceding recipe, only using less butter, and substituting lard for a portion of it. Mix the flour to a smooth paste with not quite ½ pint of water; then roll it out 3 times, the first time covering the paste with butter, the second with lard, and the third with butter. Keep the rolling-pin and paste slightly dredged with flour, to prevent them from sticking, and it will be ready for use. *Average cost*, 1*s*. per lb.

PASTE, Puff (Soyer's Recipe).

Ingredients.—To every lb. of flour allow the yolk of 1 egg, the juice of 1 lemon, ½ saltspoonful of salt, cold water, 1 lb. of fresh butter. *Mode.*—Put the flour on to the paste-board; make a hole in the centre, into which put the yolk of the egg, the lemon-juice, and salt; mix the whole with cold water (this should be iced in summer, if convenient) into a soft flexible paste, with the right hand, and handle it as little as possible; then squeeze all the buttermilk from the butter, wring it in a cloth, and roll out the paste; place the butter on this, and fold the edges of the paste over, so as to hide it; roll it out again to the thickness of ¼ inch; fold over one third, over which again pass the rolling-pin; then fold over the other third, thus forming a square; place it with the ends, top, and bottom before you, shaking a little flour both under and over, and repeat the rolls and turns twice again, as before. Flour a baking-sheet, put the paste on this, and let it remain on ice or in some cool place for ½ hour; then roll twice more, turning it as before; place it again upon the ice for ¼ hour, give it 2 more rolls, making 7 in all, and it is ready for use when required. *Average cost*, 1*s*. 6*d*. per lb.

PASTRY AND PUDDINGS, Directions in connection with the making of.

A few general remarks respecting the various ingredients of which puddings and pastry are composed may be acceptable, in addition to the recipes in this department of Household Management.

Flour should be of the best quality, and perfectly dry, and sifted before being used; if in the least damp, the paste made from it will certainly be heavy.

Butter, unless fresh is used, should be washed from the salt, and well squeezed and wrung in a cloth, to get out all the water and buttermilk, which, if left in, assist to make the paste heavy.

Lard should be perfectly sweet, which may be ascertained by cutting the bladder through, and, if the knife smells sweet, the lard is good.

Suet should be finely chopped, perfectly free from skin, and quite sweet; during the process of chopping, it should be lightly dredged with flour, which prevents the pieces from sticking together. Beef suet is considered the best; but veal suet, or the outside fat of a loin or neck of mutton, makes good crusts; as also the skimmings in which a joint of mutton has been boiled, but *without* vegetables.

Clarified Beef Dripping answers very well for kitchen pies, puddings, cakes, or for family use. A very good short crust may be made by mixing with it a small quantity of moist sugar; but care must be taken to use the dripping sparingly, or a very disagreeable flavour will be imparted to the paste.

Strict cleanliness must be observed in pastry-making; all the utensils used should be perfectly free from dust and dirt, and the things required for pastry kept entirely for that purpose.

In mixing paste, add the water very gradually, work the whole together with the knife-blade, and knead it until perfectly smooth. Those who are inexperienced in pastry-making should work

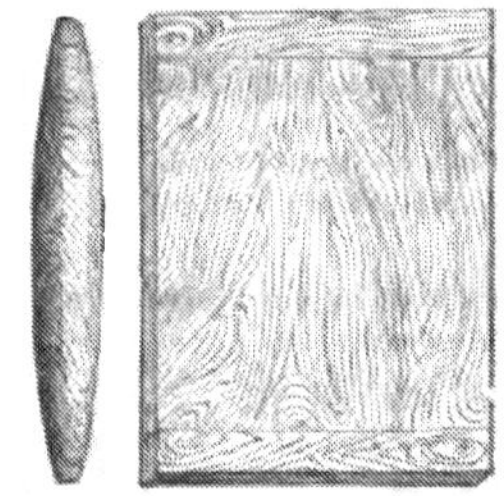

PASTE-BOARD AND ROLLING-PIN.

the butter in by breaking it in small pieces, and covering the paste rolled out. It should then be dredged with flour, and the ends folded over and rolled out very thin again: this process must be repeated until all the butter is used.

PASTE-PINCHERS AND JAGGER, FOR ORNAMENTING THE EDGES OF PIE-CRUSTS.

The art of making paste requires much practice, dexterity, and skill: it should be touched as lightly as possible, made with cool hands and in a cool place (a marble slab is better than a board for the purpose), and the coolest part of the house should be selected for the process during warm weather.

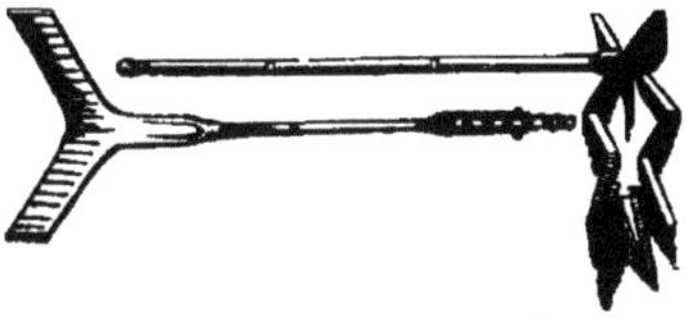

PASTE-CUTTER AND CORNER-CUTTER.

To insure rich paste being light, great expedition must be used in the making and baking; for if it stand long before

it is put in the oven, it becomes flat and heavy.

ORNAMENTAL-PASTE CUTTER.

Puff-paste requires a brisk oven, but not too hot, or it would blacken the crust; on the other hand, if the oven be too slack, the paste will be soddened, and will not rise, nor will it have any colour.

PATTY-PANS, PLAIN AND FLUTED.

Tart-tins, cake-moulds, dishes for baked puddings, patty-pans, &c., should all be buttered before the article intended to

PIE-DISH.

be baked is put in them. Things to be baked on sheets should be placed on buttered paper. Raised-pie paste should have a soaking heat, and paste glazed

RAISED-PIE MOULD.

must have rather a slack oven, that the icing be not scorched. It is

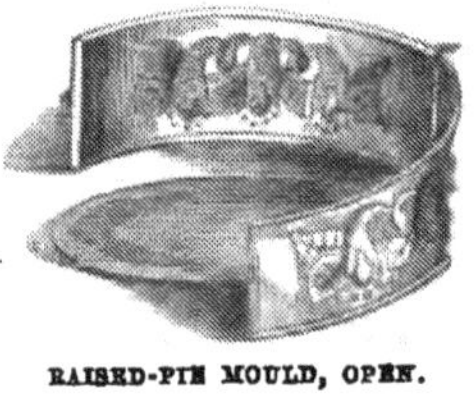

RAISED-PIE MOULD, OPEN.

better to ice tarts, &c., when they are three-parts baked.

Pastry and Puddings

To ascertain when the oven is heated to the proper degree for puff-paste, put a small piece of the paste in previous to baking the whole, and then the heat can thus be judged of.

The freshness of all pudding ingredients is of much importance, as one bad article will taint the whole mixture.

When the *freshness* of eggs is *doubtful*, break each one separately in a cup, before mixing them altogether. Should there be a bad one amongst them, it can be thrown away; whereas, if mixed with the good ones, the entire quantity would be spoiled. The yolks and whites beaten separately make the articles they are put into much lighter.

Raisins and dried fruits for puddings should be carefully picked, and in many cases stoned. Currants should be well washed, pressed in a cloth, and placed on a dish before the fire to get thoroughly dry: they should then be picked carefully over, and *every piece of grit or stone* removed from amongst them. To plump them, some cooks pour boiling water over them, and then dry them before the fire.

Batter pudding should be smoothly mixed and free from lumps. To insure this, first mix the flour with a very small proportion of milk, and add the remainder by degrees. Should the pudding be very lumpy, it may be strained through a hair sieve.

All boiled puddings should be put on in *boiling water*, which must not be allowed to stop simmering, and the pudding must always be covered with the water; if requisite, the saucepan should be kept filled up.

BOILED-PUDDING MOULD.

To prevent a pudding boiled in a cloth from sticking to the bottom of the saucepan, place a small plate or saucer underneath it, and set the pan *on a trivet* over the fire. If a mould is used, this precaution is not necessary; but care must be taken to keep the pudding well covered with water.

For dishing a boiled pudding as soon as it comes out of the pot, dip it into a basin of cold water, and the cloth will then not adhere to it. Great expedition is necessary in sending puddings to table, as by standing they quickly become heavy, batter puddings particularly.

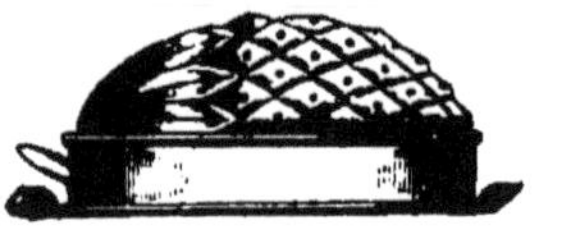

BOILED PUDDING MOULD.

For baked or boiled puddings, the moulds, cups, or basins should be always buttered before the mixture is put in them, and they should be put into the saucepan directly they are filled.

Scrupulous attention should be paid to the cleanliness of pudding-cloths, as from neglect in this particular the outsides of boiled puddings frequently taste very disagreeably. As soon as possible after it is taken off the pudding, it should be soaked in water, and then well washed, without soap, unless it be very greasy. It should be dried out of doors, then folded up and kept in a dry place. When wanted for use, dip it in boiling water, and dredge it slightly with flour.

PUDDING-BASIN.

The dry ingredients for puddings are better for being mixed some time before they are wanted; the liquid portion should only be added just before the pudding is put into the saucepan.

A pinch of salt is an improvement to the generality of puddings; but this ingredient should be added very sparingly, as the flavour should not be detected.

When baked puddings are sufficiently solid, turn them out of the dish they were baked in, bottom uppermost, and strew over them fine-sifted sugar.

When pastry or baked puddings are not done through, and yet the outside is sufficiently brown, cover them over with a piece of white paper until thoroughly cooked: this prevents them from getting burnt.

PASTRY, to Ice or Glaze.

To glaze pastry, which is the usual method adopted for meat or raised pies, break an egg, separate the yolk from the white, and beat the former for a short time. Then, when the pastry is nearly baked, take it out of the oven, brush it over with this beaten yolk of egg, and put it back in the oven to set the glaze.

To ice pastry, which is the usual method adopted for fruit tarts and sweet dishes of pastry, put the white of an egg on a plate, and with the blade of a knife beat it to a stiff froth. When the pastry is nearly baked, brush it over with this, and sift over some pounded sugar; put it back into the oven to set the glaze, and, in a few minutes, it will be done. Great care should be taken that the paste does not catch or burn in the oven, which it is very liable to do after the icing is laid on. *Sufficient.*—Allow 1 egg and 1½ oz. of sugar to glaze 3 tarts.

PASTRY SANDWICHES.

Ingredients.—Puff-paste, jam of any kind, the white of an egg, sifted sugar. *Mode.*—Roll the paste out thin; put half of it on a baking-sheet or tin, and spread equally over it apricot, greengage, or any preserve that may be preferred. Lay over this preserve another thin paste; press the edges together all round; and mark the paste in lines with a knife on the surface, to show where to cut it when baked. Bake from 20 minutes to ½ hour; and, a short time before being done, take the pastry out of the oven, brush it over with the white of an egg, sift over pounded sugar, and put it back in the oven to colour. When cold, cut it into strips; pile these on a dish pyramidically, and serve. These strips, cut about 2 inches long, piled in circular rows, and a plateful of flavoured whipped cream poured in the middle, make a very pretty dish. *Time.*—20 minutes to ½ hour. *Average cost*, with ½ lb. of paste, 1*s.* *Sufficient.*—½ lb. of paste will make 2 dishes of sandwiches. *Seasonable* at any time.

PATE BRISEE, Crust French, for Raised Pies.

Ingredients.—To every lb. of flour allow ½ saltspoonful of salt, 2 eggs, ⅓ pint of water, 6 oz. of butter. *Mode.*—Spread the flour, which should be sifted and thoroughly dry, on the paste-board; make a hole in the centre, into which put the butter; work it lightly into the flour, and when quite fine, add the salt; work the whole into a smooth paste with the eggs (yolks and whites) and water, and make it very firm. Knead the paste well, and let it be rather stiff, that the sides of the pie may be easily raised, and that they do not afterwards tumble or shrink. *Average cost*, 1*s.* per lb.

Note.—This paste may be very much enriched by making it with equal quantities of flour and butter; but then it is not so easily raised as when made plainer.

PATTIES, Fried.

[COLD MEAT COOKERY.] *Ingredients.*—Cold roast veal, a few slices of cold ham, 1 egg boiled hard, pounded mace, pepper and salt to taste, gravy, cream, 1 teaspoonful of minced lemon-peel, good puff-paste. *Mode.*—Mince a little cold veal and ham, allowing one-third ham to two-thirds veal; add an egg boiled hard and chopped, and a seasoning of pounded mace, salt, pepper, and lemon-peel; moisten with a little gravy and cream. Make a good puff-paste; roll rather thin, and cut it into round or square pieces; put the mince between two of them, pinch the edges to keep in the gravy, and fry a light brown. They may also be baked in patty-pans; in that case, they should be brushed over with the yolk of an egg before they are put in the oven. To make a variety, oysters may be substituted for the ham. *Time.*—15 minutes to fry the patties. *Seasonable* from March to October.

PEA SOUP (Inexpensive).

Ingredients.—¼ lb. of onions, ¼ lb. of carrots, 2 oz. of celery, ¾ lb. of split peas, a little mint, shred fine; 1 tablespoonful of coarse brown sugar, salt and pepper to taste, 4 quarts of water, or liquor in which a joint of meat has been boiled. *Mode.*—Fry the vegetables for 10 minutes in a little butter or dripping, previously cutting them up into small pieces; pour the water on them, and when boiling add the peas. Let them simmer for nearly 3 hours, or until the peas are thoroughly done. Add the sugar, seasoning, and mint; boil for ¼ of an hour, and serve. *Time.*—3½ hours. *Average cost*, 1½*d.* per quart. *Seasonable* in winter. *Sufficient* for 12 persons.

PEA SOUP (Green).

Ingredients.—3 pints of green peas, ¼ lb. of butter, 2 or 3 thin slices of ham, 3 onions sliced, 4 shredded lettuces, the crumb of 2 French rolls, 2 handfuls of spinach, 1 lump of sugar, 2 quarts of medium stock. *Mode.*—Put the butter, ham, 1 quart of peas, onions, and lettuces, to a pint of stock, and simmer for an hour; then add the remainder of the stock, with the crumb of the French rolls, and boil for another hour. Now boil the spinach, and squeeze it very dry. Rub the soup through a sieve, and the spinach with it, to colour it. Have ready a pint of *young* peas boiled; add them to the soup, put in the sugar, give one boil, and serve. If necessary, add salt. *Time.*—2½ hours. *Average cost,* 1*s.* 9*d.* per quart. *Seasonable* from June to the end of August. *Sufficient* for 10 persons.

Note.—It will be well to add, if the peas are not quite young, a little more sugar. Where economy is essential, water may be used instead of stock for this soup, boiling in it likewise the pea-shells; but using a double quantity of vegetables.

PEA SOUP, Winter (Yellow).

Ingredients.—1 quart of split peas, 2 lbs. of shin beef, trimmings of meat or poultry, a slice of bacon, 2 large carrots, 2 turnips, 5 large onions, 1 head of celery, seasoning to taste, 2 quarts of soft water, any bones left from roast meat, 2 quarts of common stock, or liquor in which a joint of meat has been boiled. *Mode.*—Put the peas to soak over-night in soft water, and float off such as rise to the top. Boil them in the water till tender enough to pulp; then add the ingredients mentioned above, and simmer for 2 hours, stirring it occasionally. Pass the whole through a sieve, skim well, season, and serve with toasted bread cut in dice. *Time.*—4 hours. *Average cost,* 6*d.* per quart. *Seasonable* all the year round, but more suitable for cold weather. *Sufficient* for 12 persons.

PEACHES, Compote of.

Ingredients.—1 pint of syrup, about 15 small peaches. *Mode.*—Peaches that are not very large, and that would not look well for dessert, answer very nicely for a compote. Divide the peaches, take out the stones, and pare the fruit; make a syrup by recipe, put in the peaches, and stew them gently for about 10 minutes. Take them out without breaking, arrange them on a glass dish, boil the syrup for 2 or 3 minutes, let it cool, pour it over the fruit, and, when cold, it will be ready for table. *Time.*—10 minutes. *Average cost,* 1*s.* 2*d.* *Sufficient* for 5 or 6 persons. *Seasonable* in August and September.

PEACH FRITTERS.

Ingredients.—For the batter, ½ lb. of flour, ½ oz. of butter, ½ saltspoonful of salt, 2 eggs, milk, peaches, hot lard or clarified dripping. *Mode.*—Make a nice smooth batter; skin, halve, and stone the peaches, which should be quite ripe; dip them in the batter, and fry the pieces in hot lard or clarified dripping, which should be boiling before the peaches are put in. From 8 to 10 minutes will be required to fry them; when done, drain them before the fire. Dish them on a white d'oyley. Strew over plenty of pounded sugar and serve. *Time.*—From 8 to 10 minutes to fry the fritters, 5 minutes to drain them. *Average cost,* 1*s.* *Sufficient* for 4 or 5 persons. *Seasonable* in July, August, and September.

PEACHES PRESERVED IN BRANDY.

Ingredients.—To every lb. of fruit weighed before being stoned, allow ¼ lb. of finely-pounded loaf sugar; brandy. *Mode.*—Let the fruit be gathered in dry weather; wipe and weigh it, and remove the stones as carefully as possible, without injuring the peaches much. Put them into a jar, sprinkle amongst them pounded loaf sugar in the above proportion, and pour brandy over the fruit. Cover the jar down closely, place it in a saucepan of boiling water over the fire, and bring the brandy to the simmering-point, but do not allow it to boil. Take the fruit out carefully, without breaking it; put it into small jars, pour over it the brandy, and, when cold, exclude the air by covering the jars with bladders, or tissue-paper brushed over on both sides with the white of an egg. Apricots may be done in the same manner, and, if properly prepared, will be found delicious. *Time.*—From 10 to 20 minutes to bring the brandy to the simmering-point. *Seasonable* in August and September.

PEARS, Baked.

Ingredients.—12 pears, the rind of 1 lemon, 6 cloves, 10 whole allspice; to every pint of water allow ½ lb. of loaf sugar. *Mode.*—Pare and cut the pears into halves, and, should they be very large, into quarters; leave the stalks on, and carefully remove the cores. Place them in a clean baking-jar, with a closely-fitting lid; add to them the lemon-rind cut in strips, the juice of ½ lemon, the cloves, pounded allspice, and sufficient water just to cover the whole, with sugar in the above proportion. Cover the jar down closely, put it into a very cool oven, and bake the pears from 5 to 6 hours, but be very careful that the oven is not too hot. To improve the colour of the fruit, a few drops of prepared cochineal may be added; but this will not be found necessary, if the pears are very gently baked. *Time.*—Large pears, 5 to 6 hours, in a very slow oven. *Average cost,* 1*d.* to 2*d.* each. *Sufficient* for 7 or 8 persons. *Seasonable* from September to January.

PEARS à L'ALLEMANDE.

Ingredients.—6 to 8 pears, water, sugar, 2 oz. of butter, the yolk of an egg, ½ oz. of gelatine. *Mode.*—Peel and cut the pears into any form that may be preferred, and steep them in cold water to prevent them turning black; put them into a saucepan with sufficient cold water to cover them, and boil them with the butter and enough sugar to sweeten them nicely, until tender; then brush the pears over with the yolk of an egg, sprinkle them with sifted sugar, and arrange them on a dish. Add the gelatine to the syrup, boil it up quickly for about 5 minutes, strain it over the pears, and let it remain until set. The syrup may be coloured with a little prepared cochineal, which would very much improve the appearance of the dish. *Time.*—From 20 minutes to ½ hour to stew the pears; 5 minutes to boil the syrup. *Average cost,* 1*s.* 3*d.* *Sufficient* for a large dish. *Seasonable* from August to February.

PEARS, Moulded.

Ingredients.—4 large pears or 6 small ones, 8 cloves, sugar to taste, water, a small piece of cinnamon, ¼ pint of raisin wine, a strip of lemon-peel, the juice of ½ lemon, ½ oz. of gelatine. *Mode.*—Peel and cut the pears into quarters; put them into a jar with ¾ pint of water, cloves, cinnamon, and sufficient sugar to sweeten the whole nicely; cover down the top of the jar, and bake the pears in a gentle oven until perfectly tender, but do not allow them to break. When done, lay the pears in a plain mould, which should be well wetted, and boil ½ pint of the liquor the pears were baked in with the wine, lemon-peel, strained juice, and gelatine. Let these ingredients boil quickly for 5 minutes, then strain the liquid warm over the pears; put the mould in a cool place, and when the jelly is firm, turn it out on a glass dish. *Time.*—2 hours to bake the pears in a cool oven. *Average cost,* 1*s.* 3*d.* *Sufficient* for a quart mould. *Seasonable* from August to February.

PEARS, Preserved.

Ingredients. — Jargonelle pears; to every lb. of sugar allow ½ pint of water. *Mode.*—Procure some Jargonelle pears, not too ripe; put them into a stewpan with sufficient water to cover them, and simmer them till rather tender, but do not allow them to break; then put them into cold water. Boil the sugar and water together for 5 minutes, skim well, put in the pears, and simmer them gently for 5 minutes. Repeat the simmering for 3 successive days, taking care not to let the fruit break. The last time of boiling, the syrup should be made rather richer, and the fruit boiled for 10 minutes. When the pears are done, drain them from the syrup, and dry them in the sun, or in a cool oven; or they may be kept in the syrup, and dried as they are wanted. *Time.*—½ hour to simmer the pears in water, 20 minutes in the syrup. *Average cost,* 1*d.* to 2*d.* each. *Seasonable.*—Most plentiful in September and October.

PEARS, Stewed.

Ingredients. — 8 large pears, 5 oz. of loaf sugar, 6 cloves, 6 whole allspice, ½ pint of water, ¼ pint of port wine, a few drops of prepared cochineal. *Mode.*—

Pare the pears, halve them, remove the cores, and leave the stalks on; put them into a *lined* saucepan with the above ingredients, and let them simmer very gently until tender, which will be in from 3 to 4 hours, according to the quality of the pears. They should be watched, and, when done, carefully lifted

STEWED PEARS.

out on to a glass dish without breaking them. Boil up the syrup quickly for 2 or 3 minutes; allow it to cool a little, pour it over the pears, and let them get perfectly cold. To improve the colour of the fruit, a few drops of prepared cochineal may be added, which rather enhances the beauty of this dish. The fruit must not be boiled fast, but only simmered, and watched that it be not too much done. *Time.*—3 to 4 hours. *Average cost*, 1*s.* 6*d.* *Sufficient* for 5 or 6 persons. *Seasonable* from September to January.

PEAS, Boiled Green.

Ingredients.—Green peas; to each ½ gallon of water allow 1 *small* teaspoonful of moist sugar, 1 heaped tablespoonful of salt. *Mode.*—This delicious vegetable, to be eaten in perfection, should be young, and not *gathered* or *shelled* long before it is dressed. Shell the peas, wash them well in cold water, and drain them; then put them into a saucepan with plenty of *fast-boiling* water, to which salt and *moist sugar* have been added in the above proportion; let them boil quickly over a brisk fire, with the lid of the saucepan uncovered, and be careful that the smoke does not draw in. When tender, pour them into a colander; put them into a hot vegetable-dish, and quite in the centre of the peas place a piece of butter, the size of a walnut. Many cooks boil a small bunch of mint *with* the *peas*, or garnish them with it, by boiling a few sprigs in a saucepan by themselves. Should the peas be very old, and difficult to boil a good colour, a very tiny piece of soda may be thrown in the water previous to putting them in; but this must be very sparingly used, as it causes the peas, when boiled, to have a smashed and broken appearance. With young peas, there is not the slightest occasion to use it. *Time.*—Young peas, 10 to 15 minutes; the large sorts, such as marrowfats, &c., 18 to 24 minutes; old peas, ½ hour. *Average cost*, when cheapest, 6*d.* per peck; when first in season, 1*s.* to 1*s.* 6*d.* per peck. *Sufficient.*—Allow 1 peck of unshelled peas for 4 or 5 persons. *Seasonable* from June to the end of August.

PEAS, Green, à la Francaise.

Ingredients.—2 quarts of green peas, 3 oz. of fresh butter, a bunch of parsley, 6 green onions, flour, a small lump of sugar, ½ teaspoonful of salt, a teaspoonful of flour. *Mode.*—Shell sufficient fresh-gathered peas to fill 2 quarts; put them into cold water, with the above proportion of butter, and stir them about until they are well covered with the butter; drain them in a colander, and put them in a stewpan, with the parsley and onions; dredge over them a little flour, stir the peas well, and moisten them with boiling water; boil them quickly over a large fire for 20 minutes, or until there is no liquor remaining. Dip a small lump of sugar into some water, that it may soon melt; put it with the peas, to which add ½ teaspoonful of salt. Take a piece of butter the size of a walnut, work it together with a teaspoonful of flour, and add this to the peas, which should be boiling when it is put in. Keep shaking the stewpan, and, when the peas are nicely thickened, dress them high in the dish, and serve. *Time.* — Altogether, ¾ hour. *Average cost*, 6*d.* per peck. *Sufficient* for 4 or 5 persons. *Seasonable* from June to the end of August.

PEAS, Stewed Green.

Ingredients.—1 quart of peas, 1 lettuce, 1 onion, 2 oz. of butter, pepper and salt to taste, 1 egg, ½ teaspoonful of powdered sugar. *Mode.*—Shell the peas, and cut the onion and lettuce into slices; put these into a stewpan, with the butter, pepper, and salt, but with no more water than that which hangs around the lettuce from washing. Stew the whole very gently for rather more than 1 hour; then stir in a well-beaten egg, and about ½ teaspoonful of powdered sugar. When the peas, &c., are nicely thickened, serve; but, after the egg is added, do not allow them to boil. *Time.*—1¼ hour.

Average cost, 6*d*. per peck. *Sufficient* for 3 or 4 persons. *Seasonable* from June to the end of August.

PERCH, Boiled.

Ingredients.—¼ lb. of salt to each gallon of water. *Mode*.—Scale the fish, take out the gills and clean it thoroughly; lay it in boiling water, salted as above, and simmer gently for 10 minutes. If the fish is very large, longer time must be allowed. Garnish with parsley, and serve with plain melted butter, or Dutch sauce. Perch do not preserve so good a flavour when stewed as when dressed in any other way. *Time*.—Middling-sized perch, ¼ hour. *Seasonable* from September to November.

Note.—Tench may be boiled the same way, and served with the same sauces.

PERCH, Fried.

Ingredients.—Egg and bread crumbs, hot lard. *Mode*.—Scale and clean the fish, brush it over with egg, and cover with bread crumbs. Have ready some boiling lard; put the fish in, and fry a nice brown. Serve with plain melted butter or anchovy sauce. *Time*.—10 minutes. *Seasonable* from September to November.

Note.—Fry tench in the same way.

PERCH, Stewed with Wine.

Ingredients.—Equal quantities of stock and sherry, 1 bay-leaf, 1 clove of garlic, a small bunch of parsley, 2 cloves, salt to taste; thickening of butter and flour, pepper, grated nutmeg, ½ teaspoonful of anchovy sauce. *Mode*.—Scale the fish and take out the gills, and clean them thoroughly; lay them in a stewpan with sufficient stock and sherry just to cover them. Put in the bay-leaf, garlic, parsley, cloves, and salt, and simmer till tender. When done, take out the fish, strain the liquor, add a thickening of butter and flour, the pepper, nutmeg, and the anchovy sauce, and stir it over the fire until somewhat reduced, when pour over the fish, and serve. *Time*.—About 20 minutes. *Seasonable* from September to November.

PETITES BOUCHÉES.

Ingredients.—6 oz. of sweet almonds, ¼ lb. of sifted sugar, the rind of ½ lemon, the white of 1 egg, puff-paste. *Mode*.—Blanch the almonds, and chop them fine; rub the sugar on the lemon-rind, and pound it in a mortar; mix this with the almonds and the white of the egg. Roll some puff-paste out; cut it in any shape that may be preferred, such as diamonds, rings, ovals, &c., and spread the above mixture over the paste. Bake the bouchées in an oven, not too hot, and serve cold. *Time*.—¼ hour, or rather more. *Average cost*, 1*s*. *Sufficient* for ½ lb. of puff-paste. *Seasonable* at any time.

PHEASANT.

If this bird be eaten three days after it has been killed, it then has no peculiarity of flavour; a pullet would be more relished, and a quail would surpass it in aroma. Kept, however, a proper length of time,—and this can be ascertained by a slight smell and change of colour,—then it becomes a highly-flavoured dish, occupying, so to speak, the middle distance between chicken and venison. It is difficult to define any exact time to "hang" a pheasant; but any one possessed of the instincts of gastronomical science, can at once detect the right moment when a pheasant should be taken down, in the same way as a good cook knows whether a bird should be removed from the spit, or have a turn or two more.

PHEASANT, Broiled (a Breakfast or Luncheon Dish).

Ingredients.—1 pheasant, a little lard, egg and bread crumbs, salt and cayenne to taste. *Mode*.—Cut the legs off at the first joint, and the remainder of the bird into neat pieces; put them into a frying-pan with a little lard, and when browned on both sides, and about half done, take them out and drain them; brush the pieces over with egg, and sprinkle with bread crumbs with which has been mixed a good seasoning of cayenne and salt. Broil them over a moderate fire for about 10 minutes, or rather longer, and serve with mushroom-sauce, sauce piquante, or brown gravy, in which a few game-bones and trimmings have been stewed. *Time*.—Altogether ½ hour. *Sufficient* for 4 or 5 persons. *Seasonable* from the 1st of October to the beginning of February.

PHEASANT, to Carve.

Fixing the fork in the breast, let the carver cut slices from it in the direction of the lines from 2 to 1: these are the prime pieces. If there be more guests to satisfy than these slices will serve, then let the legs and wings be disengaged in the same manner as described

ROAST PHEASANT.

in carving boiled fowl, the point where the wing joins the neckbone being carefully found. The merrythought will come off in the same way as that of a fowl. The most valued parts are the same as those which are most considered in a fowl.

PHEASANT CUTLETS.

Ingredients.—2 or 3 pheasants, egg and bread crumbs, cayenne and salt to taste, brown gravy. *Mode.*—Procure 3 young pheasants that have been hung a few days; pluck, draw, and wipe them inside; cut them into joints; remove the bones from the best of these; and the backbones, trimmings, &c., put into a stewpan, with a little stock, herbs, vegetables, seasoning, &c., to make the gravy. Flatten and trim the cutlets of a good shape, egg and bread-crumb them, broil them over a clear fire, pile them high in the dish, and pour under them the gravy made from the bones, which should be strained, flavoured, and thickened. One of the small bones should be stuck on the point of each cutlet. *Time.*—10 minutes. *Average cost,* 2*s.* 6*d.* to 3*s.* each. *Sufficient* for 2 entrées. *Seasonable* from the 1st of October to the beginning of February.

PHEASANT, Roast.

Ingredients.—Pheasant, flour, butter. *Choosing and trussing.*—Old pheasants may be known by the length and sharp-

ROAST PHEASANT.

ness of their spurs; in young ones they are short and blunt. The cock bird is generally reckoned the best, except when the hen is with egg. They should hang some time before they are dressed, as, if they are cooked fresh, the flesh will be exceedingly dry and tasteless. After the bird is plucked and drawn, wipe the inside with a damp cloth, and truss it in the same manner as partridge. If the head is left on, as shown in the engraving, bring it round under the wing, and fix it on to the point of the skewer. *Mode.*—Roast it before a brisk fire, keep it well basted, and flour and froth it nicely. Serve with brown gravy, a little of which should be poured round the bird, and a tureen of bread sauce. 2 or 3 of the pheasant's best tail-feathers are sometimes stuck in the tail as an ornament; but the fashion is not much to be commended. *Time.*—½ to 1 hour, according to the size. *Average cost,* 2*s.* 6*d.* to 3*s.* each. *Sufficient,*—1 for a dish. *Seasonable* from the 1st of October to the beginning of February.

PHEASANT, Roast, Brillat Savarin's Recipe (à la Sainte Alliance).

When the pheasant is in good condition to be cooked, it should be plucked, and not before. The bird should then be stuffed in the following manner:—Take two snipes, and draw them, putting the bodies on one plate, and the livers, &c., on another. Take off the flesh, and mince it finely with a little beef, lard, a few truffles, pepper and salt to taste, and stuff the pheasant carefully with this. Cut a slice of bread, larger considerably than the bird, and cover it with the liver, &c., and a few truffles: an anchovy and a little fresh butter added to these will do no harm. Put the bread, &c., into the dripping-pan, and, when the bird is roasted, place it on the preparation, and surround it with Florida oranges.

Do not be uneasy, Savarin adds, about your dinner; for a pheasant served in this way is fit for beings better than men. The pheasant itself is a very good bird; and, imbibing the dressing and the flavour of the truffle and snipe, it becomes thrice better.

PHEASANT SOUP.

Ingredients.—2 pheasants, ¼ lb. of butter, 2 slices of ham, 2 large onions sliced, ½ head of celery, the crumb of two French rolls, the yolks of 2 eggs boiled hard, salt and cayenne to taste, a little pounded mace, if liked; 3 quarts of stock medium. *Mode.*—Cut up the pheasants, flour and braise them in the butter and ham till they are of a nice brown, but not burnt. Put them in a stewpan, with the onions, celery, stock, and seasoning, and simmer for 2 hours. Strain the soup; pound the breasts with the crumb of the roll previously soaked, and the yolks of the eggs; put it to the soup, give one boil, and serve. *Time.*—2½ hours. *Average cost,* 2*s.* 10*d.* per quart, or, if made with fragments of cold game, 1*s.* *Seasonable* from October to February. *Sufficient* for 10 persons.

Note.—Fragments, pieces and bones of cold game, may be used to great advantage in this soup, and then 1 pheasant will suffice.

PICKLE, an Excellent.

Ingredients.—Equal quantities of medium-sized onions, cucumbers, and sauce-apples; 1½ teaspoonful of salt, ¾ teaspoonful of cayenne, 1 wineglassful of soy, 1 wineglassful of sherry; vinegar. *Mode.*—Slice sufficient cucumbers, onions, and apples to fill a pint stone jar, taking care to cut the slices very thin; arrange them in alternate layers, adding at the same time salt and cayenne in the above proportion; pour in the soy and wine, and fill up with vinegar. It will be fit for use the day it is made. *Seasonable* in August and September.

PICKLE, Indian (very Superior).

Ingredients.—To each gallon of vinegar allow 6 cloves of garlic, 12 shalots, 2 sticks of sliced horseradish, ¼ lb. of bruised ginger, 2 oz. of whole black pepper, 1 oz. of long pepper, 1 oz. of allspice, 12 cloves, ¼ oz. of cayenne, 2 oz. of mustard-seed, ¼ lb. of mustard, 1 oz. of turmeric; a white cabbage, cauliflowers, radishpods, French beans, gherkins, small round pickling-onions, nasturtiums, capsicums, chilies, &c. *Mode.*—Cut the cabbage, which must be hard and white, into slices, and the cauliflowers into small branches; sprinkle salt over them in a large dish, and let them remain two days; then dry them, and put them into a very large jar, with garlic, shalots, horseradish, ginger, pepper, allspice, and cloves, in the above proportions. Boil sufficient vinegar to cover them, which pour over, and, when cold, cover up to keep them free from dust. As the other things for the pickle ripen at different times, they may be added as they are ready: these will be radish-pods, French beans, gherkins, small onions, nasturtiums, capsicums, chilies, &c., &c. As these are procured, they must, first of all, be washed in a little cold vinegar, wiped, and then simply added to the other ingredients in the large jar, only taking care that they are *covered* by the vinegar. If more vinegar should be wanted to add to the pickle, do not omit first to boil it before adding it to the rest. When you have collected all the things you require, turn all out in a large pan, and thoroughly mix them. Now put the mixed vegetables into smaller jars, without any of the vinegar; then boil the vinegar again, adding as much more as will be required to fill the different jars, and also cayenne, mustard-seed, turmeric, and mustard, which must be well mixed with a little cold vinegar, allowing the quantities named above to each gallon of vinegar. Pour the vinegar, boiling hot, over the pickle, and when cold, tie down with a bladder. If the pickle is wanted for immediate use, the vinegar should be boiled twice more, but the better way is to make it during one season for use during the next. It will keep for years, if care is taken that the vegetables are quite covered by the vinegar.

This recipe was taken from the directions of a lady whose pickle was always pronounced excellent by all who tasted it, and who has, for many years, exactly followed the recipe given above.

Note.—For small families, perhaps the above quantity of pickle will be considered too large; but this may be decreased at pleasure, taking care to properly proportion the various ingredients.

PICKLE, Mixed (very good).

Ingredients.—To each gallon of vinegar allow ¼ lb. of bruised ginger, ¼ lb. of mustard, ¼ lb. of salt, 2 oz. of mustard-seed, 1½ oz. of turmeric, 1 oz. of ground black pepper, ¼ oz. of cayenne, cauliflowers, onions, celery, sliced cucumbers, gherkins, French beans, nasturtiums, capsicums. *Mode.*—Have a large jar, with a tightly-fitting lid, in which put as much vinegar as required, reserving a little to mix the various powders to a smooth paste. Put into a basin the mustard, turmeric, pepper, and cayenne; mix them with vinegar, and stir well until no lumps remain; add all the ingredients to the vinegar, and mix well. Keep this liquor in a warm place, and thoroughly stir every morning for a month with a wooden spoon, when it will be ready for the different vegetables to be added to it. As these come into season, have them gathered on a dry day, and, after merely wiping them with a cloth, to free them from moisture, put them into the pickle. The cauliflowers, it may be said, must be divided into small bunches. Put all these into the pickle raw, and at the end of the season, when there have been added as many of the vegetables as could be procured, store it away in jars, and tie over with bladder. As none of the ingredients are boiled, this pickle will not be fit to eat till 12 months have elapsed. Whilst the pickle is being made, keep a wooden spoon tied to the jar; and its contents, it may be repeated, must be stirred every morning. *Seasonable.*—Make the pickle-liquor in May or June, as the season arrives for the various vegetables to be picked.

PICKLE for Tongues or Beef (Newmarket Recipe).

Ingredients.—1 gallon of soft water, 3 lbs. of coarse salt, 6 oz. of coarse brown sugar, ½ oz. of saltpetre. *Mode.*—Put all the ingredients into a saucepan, and let them boil for ½ an hour, clear off the scum as it rises, and when done pour the pickle into a pickling-pan. Let it get cold, then put in the meat, and allow it to remain in pickle from 8 to 14 days, according to the size. It will keep good for 6 months if well boiled once a fortnight. Tongues will take 1 month or 6 weeks to be properly cured; and, in salting meat, beef and tongues should always be put in separate vessels. *Time.*—A moderate-sized tongue should remain in the pickle about a month, and be turned every day.

PICKLE, Universal.

Ingredients.—To 6 quarts of vinegar allow 1 lb. of salt, ¼ lb. of ginger, 1 oz. of mace, ½ lb. of shalots, 1 tablespoonful of cayenne, 2 oz. of mustard-seed, 1½ oz. of turmeric. *Mode.*—Boil all the ingredients together for about 20 minutes; when cold, put them into a jar with whatever vegetables you choose, such as radish-pods, French beans, cauliflowers, gherkins, &c. &c., as these come into season; put them in fresh as you gather them, having previously wiped them perfectly free from moisture and grit. This pickle will be fit for use in about 8 or 9 months. *Time.*—20 minutes. *Seasonable.*—Make the pickle in May or June, to be ready for the various vegetables.

Note.—As this pickle takes 2 or 3 months to make,—that is to say, nearly that time will elapse before all the different vegetables are added,—care must be taken to keep the jar which contains the pickle well covered, either with a closely-fitting lid, or a piece of bladder securely tied over, so as perfectly to exclude the air.

PICKLES.

Although pickles may be purchased at shops at as low a rate as they can usually be made for at home, or perhaps even for less, yet we would advise all housewives, who have sufficient time and convenience, to prepare their own. The only general rules, perhaps, worth stating here,—as in the recipes all necessary details will be explained—are, that the vegetables and fruits used should be sound, and not over-ripe, and that the very best vinegar should be employed.

PICNIC FOR 40 PERSONS, Bill of Fare for.

A joint of cold roast beef, a joint of cold boiled beef, 2 ribs of lamb, 2 shoulders of lamb, 4 roast fowls, 2 roast ducks, 1 ham, 1 tongue, 2 veal-and-ham pies, 2 pigeon pies, 6 medium-sized lobsters, 1 piece of collared calf's head, 18 lettuces, 6 baskets of salad, 6 cucumbers.

Stewed fruit well sweetened, and put into glass bottles well corked; 3 or 4 dozen plain pastry biscuits to eat with the stewed fruit, 2 dozen fruit turnovers, 4 dozen cheesecakes, 2 cold cabinet puddings in moulds, 2 blancmanges in moulds, a few jam puffs, 1 large cold plum-pudding (this must be good), a few baskets of fresh fruit, 3 dozen plain biscuits, a piece of cheese, 6 lbs. of butter (this, of course, includes the butter for tea), 4 quartern loaves of household bread, 3 dozen rolls, 6 loaves of tin bread (for tea), 2 plain plum cakes, 2 pound cakes,

2 sponge cakes, a tin of mixed biscuits, ½ lb. of tea. Coffee is not suitable for a picnic, being difficult to make.

PICNIC, Things not to be forgotten at.

A stick of horseradish, a bottle of mint-sauce well corked, a bottle of salad dressing, a bottle of vinegar, made mustard, pepper, salt, good oil, and pounded sugar. If it can be managed, take a little ice. It is scarcely necessary to say that plates, tumblers, wine-glasses, knives, forks, and spoons, must not be forgotten; as also teacups and saucers, 3 or 4 teapots, some lump sugar, and milk, if this last-named article cannot be obtained in the neighbourhood. Take 3 corkscrews.

Beverages.—3 dozen quart bottles of ale, packed in hampers; ginger-beer, soda-water, and lemonade, of each 2 dozen bottles; 6 bottles of sherry, 6 bottles of claret, champagne à discrétion, and any other light wine that may be preferred, and 2 bottles of brandy. Water can usually be obtained, so it is useless to take it.

PIG, Sucking, to Carve.

A sucking-pig seems, at first sight, rather an elaborate dish, or rather animal, to carve; but by carefully mastering the details of the business, every difficulty will vanish; and if a partial failure be at first made, yet all embarrassment will quickly disappear on a second trial. A sucking-pig is usually sent to table in the manner shown in the engraving, and the first point to be

SUCKING-PIG.

attended to is to separate the shoulder from the carcase, by carrying the knife quickly and neatly round the circular line, as shown by the figures 1, 2, 3;—the shoulder will then easily come away. The next step is to take off the leg; and this is done in the same way, by cutting round this joint in the direction shown by the figures 1, 2, 3, in the same way

as the shoulder. The ribs then stand fairly open to the knife, which should be carried down in the direction of the line 4 to 5; and two or three helpings will dispose of these. The other half of the pig is served, of course, in the same manner. Different parts of the pig are variously esteemed; some preferring the flesh of the neck; others, the ribs; and others, again, the shoulders. The truth is, the whole of a sucking-pig is delicious, delicate eating; but, in carving it, the host should consult the various tastes and fancies of his guests, keeping the larger joints, generally, for the gentlemen of the party.

PIG, Sucking, Roast.

Ingredients. — Pig, 6 oz. of bread crumbs, 16 sage-leaves, pepper and salt to taste, a piece of butter the size of an egg, salad oil or butter to baste with, about ½ pint of gravy, 1 tablespoonful of lemon-juice. *Mode.*—A sucking-pig, to be eaten in perfection, should not be more than three weeks old, and should be dressed the same day that it is killed. After preparing the pig for cooking, as in the following recipe, stuff it with

ROAST SUCKING-PIG.

finely-grated bread crumbs, minced sage, pepper, salt, and a piece of butter the size of an egg, all of which should be well mixed together, and put into the body of the pig. Sew up the slit neatly, and truss the legs back, to allow the inside to be roasted, and the under part to be crisp. Put the pig down to a bright clear fire, not too near, and let it lay till thoroughly dry; then have ready some butter tied up in a piece of thin cloth, and rub the pig with this in every part. Keep it well rubbed with the butter the whole of the time it is roasting, and do not allow the crackling to become blistered or burnt. When half-done, hang a pig-iron before the middle part (if this is not obtainable, use a flat iron), to prevent its being scorched and dried up before the ends are done. Before it is taken from the fire, cut off the head, and part that and the body down the middle. Chop the brains and mix them with the stuffing; add ½ pint of good gravy, a tablespoonful of lemon-juice, and the gravy that flowed from the pig; put a little of this on the dish with the pig, and the remainder send to table in a tureen. Place the pig back to back in the dish, with one half of the head on each side, and one of the ears at each end, and send it to table as hot as possible. Instead of butter, many cooks take salad oil for basting, which makes the crackling *crisp*; and as this is one of the principal things to be considered, perhaps it is desirable to use it; but be particular that it is very pure, or it will impart an unpleasant flavour to the meat. The brains and stuffing may be stirred into a tureen of melted butter instead of gravy, when the latter is not liked. Apple sauce and the old-fashioned currant sauce are not yet quite obsolete as an accompaniment to roast pig. *Time.*—1½ to 2 hours for a small pig. *Average cost*, 5*s.* to 6*s.* *Sufficient* for 9 or 10 persons. *Seasonable* from September to February.

PIG, Sucking, to Scald a.

Put the pig into cold water directly it is killed; let it remain for a few minutes, then immerse it in a large pan of boiling water for 2 minutes. Take it out, lay it on a table, and pull off the hair as quickly as possible. When the skin looks clean, make a slit down the belly, take out the entrails, well clean the nostrils and ears, wash the pig in cold water, and wipe it thoroughly dry. Take off the feet at the first joint, and loosen and leave sufficient skin to turn neatly over. If not to be dressed immediately, fold it in a wet cloth to keep it from the air.

PIGS' CHEEKS, to Dry.

Ingredients.—Salt, ½ oz. of saltpetre, 2 oz. of bay-salt, 4 oz. of coarse sugar. *Mode.*—Cut out the snout, remove the brains, and split the head, taking off the upper bone to make the jowl a good shape; rub it well with salt; next day take away the brine, and salt it again the following day; cover the head with saltpetre, bay-salt, and coarse sugar, in the above proportion, adding a little common salt. Let the head be often turned, and when it has been in the pickle for 10 days, smoke it for a week or rather longer. *Time.*—To remain in the pickle 10 days; to be smoked 1 week. *Seasonable.*—Should be made from September to March.

Note.—A pig's cheek, or Bath chap, will require two hours' cooking after the water boils.

PIG'S FACE, Collared (a Breakfast or Luncheon Dish).

Ingredients.—1 pig's face; salt. For brine, 1 gallon of spring water, 1 lb. of common salt, ½ handful of chopped juniper-berries, 6 bruised cloves, 2 bay-leaves, a few sprigs of thyme, basil, sage, ¼ oz. of saltpetre. For forcemeat, ½ lb. of ham, ½ lb. bacon, 1 teaspoonful of mixed spices, pepper to taste, ¼ lb. of lard, 1 tablespoonful of minced parsley, 6 young onions. *Mode.*—Singe the head carefully, bone it without breaking the skin, and rub it well with salt. Make the brine by boiling the above ingredients for ½ hour, and letting it stand to cool. When cold, pour it over the head, and let it steep in this for 10 days, turning and rubbing it often. Then wipe, drain, and dry it. For the forcemeat, pound the ham and bacon very finely, and mix with these the remaining ingredients, taking care that the whole is thoroughly incorporated. Spread this equally over the head, roll it tightly in a cloth, and bind it securely with broad tape. Put it into a saucepan with a few meat trimmings, and cover it with stock; let it simmer gently for 4 hours, and be particular that it does not stop boiling the whole time. When quite tender, take it up, put it between 2 dishes with a heavy weight on the top, and when cold, remove the cloth and tape. It should be sent to table on a napkin, or garnished with a piece of deep white paper with a ruche at the top. *Time.*—4 hours. *Average cost*, from 2*s.* to 2*s.* 6*d.* *Seasonable* from October to March.

PIG'S FACE.

PIG'S FRY, to Dress.

Ingredients.—1½ lb. of pig's fry, 2 onions, a few sage leaves, 3 lbs. of potatoes, pepper and salt to taste. *Mode.*—Put the lean fry at the bottom of a pie dish, sprinkle over it some minced sage and onion, and a seasoning of pepper and salt; slice the potatoes; put a layer of these on the seasonings, then the fat-fry, then more seasoning, and a layer of potatoes at the top. Fill the dish with boiling water, and bake for 2 hours, or rather longer. *Time.*—Rather more than 2 hours. *Average cost,* 6*d.* per lb. *Sufficient* for 3 or 4 persons. *Seasonable* from September to March.

PIG'S LIVER (a Savoury and Economical Dish).

Ingredients.—The liver and lights of a pig, 6 or 7 slices of bacon, potatoes, 1 large bunch of parsley, 2 onions, 2 sage leaves, pepper and salt to taste, a little broth or water. *Mode.*—Slice the liver and lights, and wash these perfectly clean, and parboil the potatoes; mince the parsley and sage, and chop the onion rather small. Put the meat, potatoes, and bacon into a deep tin dish, in alternate layers, with a sprinkling of the herbs, and a seasoning of pepper and salt between each; pour on a little water or broth, and bake in a moderately-heated oven for 2 hours. *Time.*—2 hours. *Average cost,* 1*s.* 6*d.* *Sufficient* for 6 or 7 persons. *Seasonable* from September to March.

PIG'S PETTITOES.

Ingredients.—A thin slice of bacon, 1 onion, 1 blade of mace, 6 peppercorns, 3 or 4 sprigs of thyme, 1 pint of gravy, pepper and salt to taste, thickening of butter and flour. *Mode.*—Put the liver, heart, and pettitoes into a stewpan with the bacon, mace, peppercorns, thyme, onion, and gravy, and simmer these gently for ¼ hour; then take out the heart and liver, and mince them very fine. Keep stewing the feet until quite tender, which will be in from 20 minutes to ½ hour, reckoning from the time that they boiled up first; then put back the minced liver, thicken the gravy with a little butter and flour, season with pepper and salt, and simmer over a gentle fire for 5 minutes, occasionally stirring the contents. Dish the mince, split the feet, and arrange them round alternately with sippets of toasted bread, and pour the gravy in the middle. *Time.*—Altogether 40 minutes. *Sufficient* for 3 or 4 persons. *Seasonable* from September to March.

PIGEON, to Carve.

A very straightforward plan is adopted in carving a pigeon: the knife is carried sharply in the direction of the line as shown from 1 to 2, entirely through the bird, cutting it into two precisely equal and similar parts. If it is necessary to make three pieces of it, a small wing should be cut off with the leg on either side, thus serving two guests; and, by this means, there will be sufficient meat left on the breast to send to the third guest.

PIGEON.

PIGEON PIE (Epsom Grand-Stand Recipe).

Ingredients.—1½ lb. of rump-steak, 2 or 3 pigeons, 3 slices of ham, pepper and salt to taste, 2 oz. of butter, 4 eggs, puff crust. *Mode.*—Cut the steak into pieces about 3 inches square, and with it line the bottom of a pie-dish, seasoning it well with pepper and salt. Clean the pigeons, rub them with pepper and salt inside and out, and put into the body of each rather more than ½ oz. of butter; lay them on the steak, and a piece of ham on each pigeon. Add the yolks of four eggs, and half fill the dish with stock; place a border of puff paste round the edge of the dish, put on the cover, and ornament it in any way that may be preferred. Clean three of the feet, and place them in a hole made in the crust at the top: this shows what kind of pie it is. Glaze the crust,—that is to say, brush it over with the yolk of an egg,—and bake it in a well-heated oven for about 1¼ hour. When liked, a seasoning of pounded mace may be added. *Time.*—1¼ hour, or rather less. *Average cost,* 5*s.* 3*d.* *Sufficient* for 5 or 6 persons. *Seasonable* at any time.

PIGEONS, Broiled.

Ingredients.—Pigeons, 3 oz. of butter, pepper and salt to taste. *Mode.*—Take care that the pigeons are quite fresh, and carefully pluck, draw, and wash them; split the backs, rub the birds over with butter, season them with pepper and salt, and broil them over a moderate fire for ¼ hour or 20 minutes. Serve very hot, with either mushroom-sauce or a good gravy. Pigeons may also be plainly boiled, and served with parsley and butter; they should be trussed like boiled fowls, and take from ¼ hour to 20 minutes to boil. *Time.*—To broil a pigeon, from ¼ hour to 20 minutes; to boil one, the same time. *Average cost,* from 6*d.* to 9*d.* each. *Seasonable* from April to September, but in the greatest perfection from Midsummer to Michaelmas.

PIGEONS, Roast.

Ingredients.—Pigeons, 3 oz. of butter, pepper and salt to taste. *Trussing.*—Pigeons, to be good, should be eaten fresh (if kept a little, the flavour goes off), and they should be drawn as soon as killed. Cut off the heads and necks, truss the wings over the backs, and cut off the toes at the first joint: previous to trussing, they should be carefully cleaned, as no bird requires so much washing.

ROAST PIGEON.

Mode.—Wipe the birds very dry, season them inside with pepper and salt, and put about ¾ oz. of butter into the body of each: this makes them moist. Place them at a bright fire, and baste them well the whole of the time they are cooking (they will be done enough in from 20 to 30 minutes); garnish with fried parsley, and serve with a tureen of parsley and butter. Bread sauce and gravy, the same as for roast fowl, are exceedingly nice accompaniments to roast pigeons, as also egg-sauce. *Time.*—From 20 minutes to ½ hour. *Average cost,* 6*d.* to 9*d.* each. *Seasonable* from April to September; but in the greatest perfection from Midsummer to Michaelmas.

PIGEONS, Stewed.

Ingredients.—6 pigeons, a few slices of bacon, 3 oz. of butter, 2 tablespoonfuls of minced parsley, sufficient stock to cover the pigeons, thickening of butter and flour, 1 tablespoonful of mushroom ketchup, 1 tablespoonful of port wine. *Mode.*—Empty and clean the pigeons thoroughly, mince the livers, add to these the parsley and butter, and put it into the insides of the birds. Truss them with the legs inward, and put them into a stewpan, with a few slices of bacon placed under and over them; add the stock, and stew gently for rather more than ½ hour. Dish the pigeons, strain the gravy, thicken it with butter and flour, add the ketchup and port wine, give one boil, pour over the pigeons, and serve. *Time.*—Rather more than ½ hour. *Average cost,* 6*d.* to 9*d.* each. *Sufficient* for 4 or 5 persons. *Seasonable* from April to September.

PIKE, Baked.

Ingredients.—1 or 2 pike, a nice delicate stuffing (*see* Forcemeats), 1 egg, bread crumbs, ¼ lb. butter. *Mode.*—Scale the fish, take out the gills, wash, and wipe it thoroughly dry; stuff it with forcemeat, sew it up, and fasten the tail in the mouth by means of a skewer; brush it over with egg, sprinkle with bread crumbs, and baste with butter, before putting it in the oven, which must be well heated. When the pike is of a nice brown colour, cover it with buttered paper, as the outside would become too dry. If 2 are dressed, a little variety may be made by making one of them green with a little chopped parsley mixed with the bread crumbs. Serve anchovy or Dutch sauce, and plain melted butter with it. *Time.*—According to size, 1 hour, more or less. *Average cost.*—Seldom bought. *Seasonable* from September to March.

Note.—Pike *à la génévese* may be stewed in the same manner as salmon *à la génévese.*

PIKE, Boiled.

Ingredients.—¼ lb. of salt to each gallon of water; a little vinegar. *Mode.*—Scale and clean the pike, and fasten the tail in its mouth by means of a skewer. Lay it in cold water, and when it boils, throw in the salt and vinegar.

The time for boiling depends, of course, on the size of the fish; but a middling-sized pike will take about ½ an hour. Serve with Dutch or anchovy sauce, and plain melted butter. *Time.*—According to size, ½ to 1 hour. *Average cost.*—Seldom bought. *Seasonable* from September to March.

PILLAU FOWL, based on M. Soyer's Recipe (an Indian Dish).

Ingredients.—1 lb. of rice, 2 oz. of butter, a fowl, 2 quarts of stock or good broth, 40 cardamum-seeds, ½ oz. of coriander-seed, ¼ oz. of cloves, ¼ oz. of allspice, ¼ oz. of mace, ¼ oz. of cinnamon, ½ oz. of peppercorns, 4 onions, 6 thin slices of bacon, 2 hard-boiled eggs. *Mode.*—Well wash 1 lb. of the best Patna rice, put it into a fryingpan with the butter, which keep moving over a slow fire until the rice is lightly browned. Truss the fowl as for boiling, put it into a stewpan with the stock or broth; pound the spices and seeds thoroughly in a mortar, tie them in a piece of muslin, and put them in with the fowl. Let it boil slowly until it is nearly done; then add the rice, which should stew until quite tender and almost dry; cut the onions into slices, sprinkle them with flour, and fry, without breaking them, of a nice brown colour. Have ready the slices of bacon curled and grilled, and the eggs boiled hard. Lay the fowl in the form of a pyramid upon a dish, smother with the rice, garnish with the bacon, fried onions, and the hard-boiled eggs cut into quarters, and serve very hot. Before taking the rice out, remove the spices. *Time.*—½ hour to stew the fowl without the rice; ½ hour with it. *Average cost,* 4s. 3d. *Sufficient* for 4 or 5 persons. *Seasonable* at any time.

PINEAPPLE CHIPS.

Ingredients. — Pineapples; sugar to taste. *Mode.*—Pare and slice the fruit thinly, put it on dishes, and strew over it plenty of pounded sugar. Keep it in a hot closet, or very slow oven, 8 or 10 days, and turn the fruit every day until dry; then put the pieces of pine on tins, and place them in a quick oven for 10 minutes. Let them cool, and store them away in dry boxes, with paper between each layer. *Time.*—8 to 10 days. *Seasonable.*—Foreign pines, in July and August.

PINEAPPLE FRITTERS (an elegant dish).

Ingredients. — A small pineapple, a small wineglassful of brandy or liqueur, 2 oz. of sifted sugar; batter as for apple fritters, which see. *Mode.*—This elegant dish, although it may appear extravagant, is really not so if made when pineapples are plentiful. We receive them now in such large quantities from the West Indies, that at times they may be purchased at an exceedingly low rate; it would not, of course, be economical to use the pines which are grown in our English pineries for the purposes of fritters. Pare the pine with as little waste as possible, cut it into rather thin slices, and soak these slices in the above proportion of brandy or liqueur and pounded sugar for 4 hours; then make a batter the same as for apple fritters, substituting cream for the milk, and using a smaller quantity of flour; when this is ready, dip in the pieces of pine, and fry them in boiling lard from 5 to 8 minutes; turn them when sufficiently brown on one side, and, when done, drain them from the lard before the fire, dish them on a white d'oyley, strew over them sifted sugar, and serve quickly. *Time.*—5 to 8 minutes. *Average cost,* when cheap and plentiful, 1*s.* 6*d.* for the pine. *Sufficient* for 3 or 4 persons. *Seasonable* in July and August.

PINEAPPLE, Preserved.

Ingredients. — To every lb. of fruit, weighed after being pared, allow 1 lb. of loaf sugar; ¼ pint of water. *Mode.*—The pines for making this preserve should be perfectly sound but ripe. Cut them into rather thick slices, as the fruit shrinks very much in the boiling. Pare off the rind carefully, that none of the pine be wasted; and, in doing so, notch it in and out, as the edge cannot be smoothly cut without great waste. Dissolve a portion of the sugar in a preserving-pan with ¼ pint of water; when this is melted, gradually add the remainder of the sugar, and boil it until it forms a clear syrup, skimming well. As soon as this is the case, put in the pieces of pine, and boil well for at least ½ hour, or until it looks nearly transparent. Put it into pots, cover down when cold, and store away in a dry place. *Time.*—½ hour to boil the fruit. *Average cost,* 10*d.* to 1*s.* per lb. pot. *Seasonable.*—Foreign pines, in July and August.

PINEAPPLE, Preserved, for present use.

Ingredients.—Pineapple, sugar, water. *Mode.*—Cut the pine into slices ¼ inch in thickness; peel them, and remove the hard part from the middle. Put the parings and hard pieces into a stewpan, with sufficient water to cover them, and boil for ¼ hour. Strain the liquor, and put in the slices of pine. Stew them for 10 minutes, add sufficient sugar to sweeten the whole nicely, and boil again for another ¼ hour; skim well, and the preserve will be ready for use. It must be eaten soon, as it will keep but a very short time. *Time.*—¼ hour to boil the parings in water; 10 minutes to boil the pine without sugar, ¼ hour with sugar. *Average cost.*—Foreign pines, 1*s.* to 3*s.* each; English, from 2*s.* to 12*s.* per lb. *Seasonable.*—Foreign, in July and August; English, all the year.

PIPPINS, Normandy, Stewed.

Ingredients.—1 lb. of Normandy pippins, 1 quart of water, ¼ teaspoonful of powdered cinnamon, ¼ teaspoonful of ground ginger, 1 lb. of moist sugar, 1 lemon. *Mode.*—Well wash the pippins, and put them into 1 quart of water with the above proportion of cinnamon and ginger, and let them stand 12 hours; then put these all together into a stewpan, with the lemon sliced thinly, and half the moist sugar. Let them boil slowly until the pippins are half done; then add the remainder of the sugar, and simmer until they are quite tender. Serve on glass dishes for dessert. *Time.*—2 to 3 hours. *Average cost,* 1*s.* 6*d.* *Seasonable.*—Suitable for a winter dish.

PLAICE, Fried.

Ingredients.—Hot lard, or clarified dripping; egg and bread crumbs. *Mode.*—This fish is fried in the same manner as soles. Wash and wipe them thoroughly dry, and let them remain in a cloth until it is time to dress them. Brush them over with egg, and cover with bread crumbs mixed with a little flour. Fry of a nice brown in hot dripping or lard, and garnish with fried parsley and cut lemon. Send them to table with shrimp-sauce and plain melted butter. *Time.*—About 5 minutes. *Average cost,* 3*d.* each. *Seasonable* from May to November. *Sufficient,* 4 plaice for 4 persons.

Note.—Plaice may be boiled plain, and served with melted butter. Garnish with parsley and cut lemon.

PLAICE, Stewed.

Ingredients.—4 or 5 plaice, 2 onions, ½ oz. ground ginger, 1 pint of lemon-juice, ¼ pint water, 6 eggs; cayenne to taste. *Mode.*—Cut the fish into pieces about 2 inches wide, salt them, and let them remain ¼ hour. Slice and fry the onions a light brown; put them in a stewpan, on the top of which put the fish without washing, and add the ginger, lemon-juice, and water. Cook slowly for ½ hour, and do not let the fish boil, or it will break. Take it out, and when the liquor is cool, add 6 well-beaten eggs; simmer till it thickens, when pour over the fish, and serve. *Time.*—¾ hour. *Average cost* for this quantity, 1*s.* 9*d.* *Seasonable* from May to November. *Sufficient* for 4 or 5 persons; according to the size of the fish.

PLOVERS, to Carve.

Plovers may be carved like quails or woodcock, being trussed and served in the same way as those birds.

PLOVERS, to Dress.

Ingredients.—3 plovers, butter, flour, toasted bread. *Choosing and Trussing.*—Choose those that feel hard at the vent, as that shows their fatness. There are three sorts,—the grey, green, and bastard plover, or lapwing. They will keep good for some time, but if very stale, the feet will be very dry. Plovers are scarcely fit for anything but roasting; they are, however, sometimes stewed, or made into a ragoût, but this mode of cooking is not to be recommended. *Mode.*—Pluck off the feathers, wipe the outside of the birds with a damp cloth, and do not draw them; truss with the head under the wing, put them down to a clear fire, and lay slices of moistened toast in the dripping-pan, to catch the trail. Keep them *well basted,* dredge them lightly with flour a few minutes before they are done, and let them be nicely frothed. Dish them on the toasts, over which the *traill* should be equally spread. Pour round the toast a little good gravy, and send some to table in a tureen. *Time.*—10 minutes to ¼ hour. *Average cost,* 1*s.* 6*d.* the brace, if plentiful. *Sufficient* for 2 persons. *Seasonable.*—In perfection from the beginning of September to the end of January.

PLUM CAKE, Common.

Ingredients.—3 lbs. of flour, 6 oz. of butter or good dripping, 6 oz. of moist sugar, 6 oz. of currants, ½ oz. of pounded allspice, 2 tablespoonfuls of fresh yeast, 1 pint of new milk. *Mode.*—Rub the butter into the flour; add the sugar, currants, and allspice; warm the milk, stir to it the yeast, and mix the whole into a dough; knead it well, and put it into 6 buttered tins; place them near the fire for nearly an hour for the dough to rise, then bake the cakes in a good oven from 1 to 1½ hour. To ascertain when they are done, plunge a clean knife into the middle, and if on withdrawal it comes out clean, the cakes are done. *Time.*—1 to 1½ hour. *Average cost,* 1*s.* 8*d.* *Sufficient* to make 6 small cakes.

PLUM CAKE, a Nice.

Ingredients.—1 lb. of flour, ¼ lb. of butter, ½ lb. of sugar, ½ lb. of currants, 2 oz. of candied lemon-peel, ½ pint of milk, 1 teaspoonful of ammonia or carbonate of soda. *Mode.*—Put the flour into a basin with the sugar, currants, and sliced candied peel; beat the butter to a cream, and mix all these ingredients together with the milk. Stir the ammonia into 2 tablespoonfuls of milk; add it to the dough, and beat the whole well, until everything is thoroughly mixed. Put the dough into a buttered tin, and bake the cake from 1½ to 2 hours. *Time.* 1½ to 2 hours. *Average cost,* 1*s.* 3*d.* *Seasonable* at any time.

PLUM JAM.

Ingredients.—To every lb. of plums, weighed before being stoned, allow ¾ lb. of loaf sugar. *Mode.*—In making plum jam, the quantity of sugar for each lb. of fruit must be regulated by the quality and size of the fruit, some plums requiring much more sugar than others. Divide the plums, take out the stones, and put them on to large dishes, with roughly-pounded sugar sprinkled over them in the above proportion, and let them remain for one day; then put them into a preserving-pan, stand them by the side of the fire to simmer gently for about ½ hour, and then boil them rapidly for another 15 minutes. The scum must be carefully removed as it rises, and the jam must be well stirred all the time, or it will burn at the bottom of the pan, and so spoil the colour and flavour of the preserve. Some of the stones may be cracked, and a few kernels added to the jam just before it is done: these impart a very delicious flavour to the plums. The above proportion of sugar would answer for Orleans plums; the Impératrice, Magnum-bonum, and Winesour would not require quite so much. *Time.* ½ hour to simmer gently, ¼ hour to boil rapidly. *Best plums for preserving.*—Violets, Mussels, Orleans, Impératrice, Magnum-bonum, and Winesour. *Seasonable* from the end of July to the beginning of October.

PLUM PUDDING, Baked.

Ingredients.—2 lbs. of flour, 1 lb. of currants, 1 lb. of raisins, 1 lb. of suet, 2 eggs, 1 pint of milk, a few slices of candied peel. *Mode.*—Chop the suet finely; mix it with the flour, currants, stoned raisins, and candied peel; moisten with the well-beaten eggs, and add sufficient milk to make the pudding of the consistency of very thick batter. Put it into a buttered dish, and bake in a good oven from 2¼ to 2½ hours; turn it out, strew sifted sugar over, and serve. For a very plain pudding, use only half the quantity of fruit, omit the eggs, and substitute milk or water for them. The above ingredients make a large family pudding; for a small one, half the quantity will be found ample; but it must be baked quite 1½ hour. *Time.*—Large pudding, 2¼ to 2½ hours; half the size, 1½ hour. *Average cost,* 2*s.* 6*d.* *Sufficient* for 9 or 10 persons. *Seasonable* in winter.

PLUM PUDDING, Excellent, made without Eggs.

Ingredients.—½ lb. of flour, 6 oz. of raisins, 6 oz. of currants, ¼ lb. of chopped suet, ¼ lb. of brown sugar, ¼ lb. of mashed carrot, ¼ lb. of mashed potatoes, 1 tablespoonful of treacle, 1 oz. of candied lemon-peel, 1 oz. of candied citron. *Mode.*—Mix the flour, currants, suet and sugar well together; have ready the above proportions of mashed carrot and potato, which stir into the other ingredients; add the treacle and lemon-peel; but put no liquid in the mixture, or it will be spoiled. Tie it loosely in a cloth, or, if put in a basin, do not quite fill it, as the pudding should have room to swell, and boil it for 4 hours. Serve with brandy-sauce. This pudding is better for being mixed over-night. *Time*.—4 hours. *Average cost*, 1*s*. 6*d*. *Sufficient* for 6 or 7 persons. *Seasonable* in winter.

PLUM PUDDING, Unrivalled.

Ingredients. — 1½ lb. of muscatel raisins, 1¾ lb. of currants, 1 lb. of sultana raisins, 2 lbs. of the finest moist sugar, 2 lbs. of bread crumbs, 16 eggs, 2 lbs. of finely-chopped suet, 6 oz. of mixed candied peel, the rind of 2 lemons, 1 oz. of ground nutmeg, 1 oz. of ground cinnamon, ½ oz. of pounded bitter almonds, ¼ pint of brandy. *Mode*.—Stone and cut up the raisins, but do not chop them; wash and dry the currants, and cut the candied peel into thin slices. Mix all the dry ingredients well together, and moisten with the eggs, which should be well beaten and strained, to the pudding; stir in the brandy, and, when all is thoroughly mixed, well butter and flour a stout new pudding-cloth; put in the pudding, tie it down very tightly and closely, boil from 6 to 8 hours, and serve with brandy-sauce. A few sweet almonds, blanched and cut in strips, and stuck on the pudding, ornament it prettily. This quantity may be divided and boiled in buttered moulds. For small families this is the most desirable way, as the above will be found to make a pudding of rather large dimensions. *Time*.—6 to 8 hours. *Average cost*, 7*s*. 6*d*. *Seasonable* in winter. *Sufficient* for 12 or 14 persons.

Note.—The muscatel raisins can be purchased at a cheap rate loose (not in bunches): they are then scarcely higher in price than the ordinary raisins, and impart a much richer flavour to the pudding.

PLUM PUDDING, a Plain Christmas, for Children.

Ingredients.—1 lb. of flour, 1 lb. of bread crumbs, ¾ lb. of stoned raisins, ¾ lb. of currants, ¾ lb. of suet, 3 or 4 eggs,

milk, 2 oz. of candied peel, 1 teaspoonful of powdered allspice, ½ saltspoonful of salt. *Mode*.—Let the suet be finely chopped, the raisins stoned, and the currants well washed, picked and dried. Mix these with the other dry ingredients, and stir all well together; beat and strain the eggs to the pudding, stir these in, and add just sufficient milk to make it mix properly. Tie it up in a well-floured cloth, put it into boiling water, and boil for at least 5 hours. Serve with a sprig of holly placed in the middle of the pudding, and a little pounded sugar sprinkled over it. *Time*.—5 hours. *Average cost*, 1*s*. 9*d*. *Sufficient* for 9 or 10 children. *Seasonable* at Christmas.

PLUM PUDDING, Christmas (very good).

Ingredients.—1½ lb. of raisins, ½ lb. of currants, ½ lb. of mixed peel, ¾ lb. of bread-crumbs, ¾ lb. of suet, 8 eggs, 1 wineglassful of brandy. *Mode*.—Stone and cut the raisins in halves, but do not chop them; wash, pick, and dry the currants, and mince the suet finely; cut the candied peel into thin slices, and grate down the bread into fine crumbs. When all these dry ingredients are prepared, mix them well together; then moisten the mixture with the eggs, which should be well beaten,

CHRISTMAS PLUM PUDDING IN MOULD.

and the brandy; stir well, that everything may be very thoroughly blended, and *press* the pudding into a buttered mould; tie it down tightly with a floured cloth, and boil for 5 or 6 hours. It may be boiled in a cloth without a mould, and will require the same time allowed for cooking. As Christmas puddings are usually made a few days before they are required for table, when the pudding is taken out of the pot, hang it up immediately, and put a plate or saucer underneath to catch the water that may drain from it. The day it is to be eaten, plunge it into boiling water, and keep it boiling for at least 2 hours; then turn it out of the mould, and serve with brandy-sauce. On Christmas-day a sprig of holly is usually placed in the middle of the pudding, and about a wine-glassful of brandy poured round it, which, at the moment of serving, is lighted, and the pudding thus brought to table encircled in flame. *Time.*—5 or 6 hours the first time of boiling; 2 hours the day it is to be served. *Average cost,* 4*s.* *Sufficient* for a quart mould for 7 or 8 persons. *Seasonable* on the 25th of December, and on various festive occasions till March.

Note.—Five or six of these puddings should be made at one time, as they will keep good for many weeks, and in cases where unexpected guests arrive, will be found an acceptable and, as it only requires warming through, a quickly-prepared dish. Moulds of every shape and size are manufactured for these puddings, and may be purchased of Messrs. R. & J. Slack, 336, Strand.

PLUM PUDDING (a Pound).

Ingredients.—1 lb. of suet, 1 lb. of currants, 1 lb. of stoned raisins, 8 eggs, ½ grated nutmeg, 2 oz. of sliced candied peel, 1 teaspoonful of ground ginger, ½ lb. of bread crumbs, ½ lb. of flour, ½ pint of milk. *Mode.*—Chop the suet finely; mix with it the dry ingredients; stir

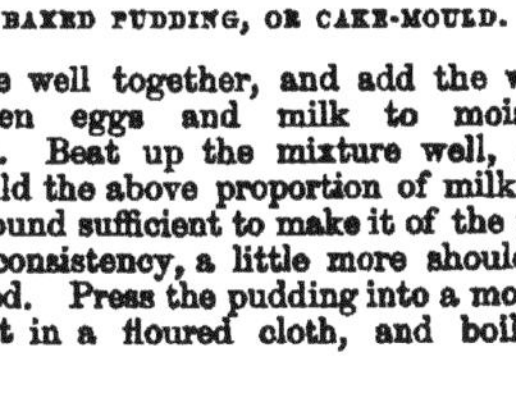

BAKED PUDDING, OR CAKE-MOULD.

these well together, and add the well-beaten eggs and milk to moisten with. Beat up the mixture well, and should the above proportion of milk not be found sufficient to make it of the proper consistency, a little more should be added. Press the pudding into a mould, tie it in a floured cloth, and boil for five hours, or rather longer, and serve with brandy-sauce. *Time.*—5 hours, or longer. *Average cost,* 3*s.* *Sufficient* for 7 or 8 persons. *Seasonable* in winter.

Note.—The above pudding may be baked instead of boiled; it should be put into a buttered mould or tin, and baked for about 2 hours; a smaller one would take about 1½ hour.

PLUM PUDDING (Fresh Fruit).

Ingredients.—¾ lb. of suet crust, 1½ pint of Orleans or any other kind of plum, ¼ lb. of moist sugar. *Mode.*—Line a pudding-basin with suet crust rolled out to the thickness of about ½ inch; fill the basin with the fruit, put in the sugar, and cover with crust. Fold the edges over, and pinch them together, to prevent the juice escaping. Tie over a floured cloth, put the pudding into boiling water, and boil from 2 to 2½ hours. Turn it out of the basin, and serve quickly. *Time.*—2 to 2½ hours. *Average cost,* 10*d.* *Sufficient* for 6 or 7 persons. *Seasonable,* with various kinds of plums, from the beginning of August to the beginning of October.

PLUM TART.

Ingredients.—½ lb. of good short crust, 1½ pint of plums, ¼ lb. of moist sugar. *Mode.*—Line the edges of a deep tart-dish with crust; fill the dish with plums, and place a small cup or jar, upside down, in the midst of them. Put in the sugar, cover the pie with crust, ornament the edges, and bake in a good

PLUM TART.

oven from ½ to ¾ hour. When puff-crust is preferred to short crust, use that made by the given recipe, and glaze the top by brushing it over with the white of an egg beaten to a stiff froth with a knife; sprinkle over a little sifted sugar, and put the pie in the oven to set the glaze. *Time.*—½ to ¾ hour. *Average cost,* 1*s.* *Sufficient* for 5 or 6 persons. *Seasonable,* with various kinds of plums, from the beginning of August to the beginning of October.

PLUMS, French, Stewed (a Dessert dish).

Ingredients.—1½ lb. of French plums, ¾ pint of syrup, 1 glass of port wine, the rind and juice of 1 lemon. *Mode.*—Stew the plums gently in water for 1 hour; strain the water, and with it make the syrup. When it is clear, put in the plums with the port wine, lemon-juice, and rind, and simmer very gently for 1½ hour. Arrange the plums on a glass dish, take out the lemon-rind, pour the syrup over the plums, and, when cold, they will be ready for table. A little allspice stewed with the fruit is by many persons considered an improvement. *Time.*—1 hour to stew the plums in water, 1½ hour in the syrup. *Average cost*, plums sufficiently good for stewing, 1*s.* per lb. *Sufficient* for 7 or 8 persons. *Seasonable* in winter.

PLUMS (Preserved).

Ingredients.—To every lb. of fruit allow ¾ lb. of loaf sugar; for the thin syrup, ¼ lb. of sugar to each pint of water. *Mode.*—Select large ripe plums; slightly prick them, to prevent them from bursting, and simmer them very gently in a syrup made with the above proportion of sugar and water. Put them carefully into a pan, let the syrup cool, pour it over the plums, and allow them to remain for two days. Having previously weighed the other sugar, dip the lumps quickly into water, and put them into a preserving-pan with no more water than hangs about them; and boil the sugar to a syrup, carefully skimming it. Drain the plums from the first syrup; put them into the fresh syrup, and simmer them very gently until they are clear; lift them out singly into pots, pour the syrup over, and, when cold, cover down to exclude the air. This preserve will remain good some time, if kept in a dry place, and makes a very nice addition to a dessert. The magnum-bonum plums answer for this preserve better than any other kind of plum. Greengages are also very delicious done in this manner. *Time.*—¾ hour to 20 minutes to simmer the plums in the first syrup; 20 minutes to ½ hour very gentle simmering in the second. *Seasonable* from August to October.

PLUMS, to Preserve Dry.

Ingredients.—To every lb. of sugar allow ¼ pint of water. *Mode.*—Gather the plums when they are full grown and just turning colour; prick them, put them into a saucepan of cold water, and set them on the fire until the water is on the point of boiling. Then take them out, drain them, and boil them gently in syrup made with the above proportion of sugar and water; and if the plums shrink, and will not take the sugar, prick them as they lie in the pan; give them another boil, skim, and set them by. The next day add some more sugar, boiled almost to candy, to the fruit and syrup; put all together into a wide-mouthed jar, and place them in a cool oven for 2 nights; then drain the plums from the syrup, sprinkle a little powdered sugar over, and dry them in a cool oven. *Time.*—15 to 20 minutes to boil the plums in the syrup. *Seasonable* from August to October.

PORK.

In the country, where, for ordinary consumption, the pork killed for sale is usually both larger and fatter than that supplied to the London consumer, it is customary to remove the skin and fat down to the lean, and, salting that, roast what remains of the joint. Pork goes further, and is consequently a more economical food, than other meats, simply because the texture is closer, and there is less waste in the cooking, either in roasting or boiling.

In fresh pork, the leg is the most economical family joint, and the loin the richest.

Pork, to be preserved, is cured in several ways,—either by covering it with salt, or immersing it in ready-made brine, where it is kept till required; or it is only partially salted, and then hung up to dry, when the meat is called white bacon; or, after salting, it is hung in wood smoke till the flesh is impregnated with the aroma from the wood. The Wiltshire bacon, which is regarded as the finest in the kingdom, is prepared by laying the sides of a hog in large wooden troughs, and then rubbing into the flesh quantities of powdered bay-salt, made hot in a frying-pan. This process is repeated for four days; they are then left for three weeks, merely turning the flitches every other day. After that time they are hung up to dry. The hogs usually killed for purposes of bacon in England average from 18 to 20 stone; on the other hand, the hogs killed in the country for farm-house purposes, seldom weigh less than 26 stone. The legs of boars, hogs, and, in Germany, those of bears, are prepared differently, and called hams.

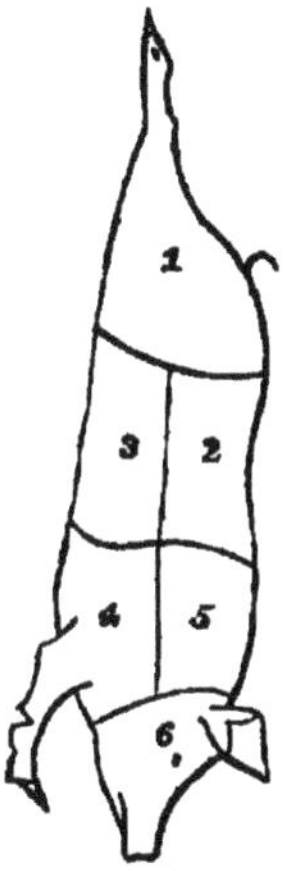

SIDE OF A PIG, SHOWING THE SEVERAL JOINTS.

The practice in vogue formerly in this country was to cut out the hams and cure them separately; then to remove the ribs, which were roasted as "spare-ribs," and, curing the remainder of the side, call it a "gammon of bacon." Small pork to cut for table in joints, is cut up, in most places throughout the kingdom, as represented in the engraving. The side is divided with nine ribs to the fore quarter; and the following is an enumeration of the joints in the two respective quarters:—

HIND QUARTER { 1. The leg.
2. The loin.
3. The spring, or belly.

FORE QUARTER { 4. The hand.
5. The fore-loin.
6. The cheek.

The weight of the several joints of a good pork pig of four stone may be as follows; viz.:—

The leg	8 lbs.
The loin and spring .	7 ,,
The hand	6 ,,
The chine	7 ,,
The cheek . from 2 to 3	,,

Of a bacon pig, the legs are reserved for curing, and when cured are called hams: when the meat is separated from the shoulder-blade and bones and cured, it is called bacon. The bones, with part of the meat left on them, are divided into spare-ribs, griskins, and chines.

PORK CHEESE (an Excellent Breakfast Dish).

Ingredients.—2 lbs. of cold roast pork, pepper and salt to taste, 1 dessertspoonful of minced parsley, 4 leaves of sage, a very small bunch of savoury herbs, 2 blades of pounded mace, a little nutmeg, ½ teaspoonful of minced lemon-peel; good strong gravy, sufficient to fill the mould. *Mode.*—Cut, but do not chop, the pork into fine pieces, and allow ¼ lb. of fat to each pound of lean. Season with pepper and salt; pound well the spices, and chop finely the parsley, sage, herbs, and lemon-peel, and mix the whole nicely together. Put it into a mould, fill up with good strong well-flavoured gravy, and bake rather more than one hour. When cold, turn it out of the mould. *Time.*—Rather more than 1 hour. *Seasonable* from October to March.

Note.—The remains of a pig's head, after the chops are taken off, make most excellent pork cheese.

PORK CUTLETS, or Chops.

Ingredients. — Loin of pork, pepper and salt to taste. *Mode.*—Cut the cutlets from a delicate loin of pork, bone and trim them neatly, and cut away the greater portion of the fat. Season them with pepper; place the gridiron on the fire; when quite hot, lay on the chops, and broil them for about ¼ hour, turning them 3 or 4 times; and be particular that they are *thoroughly* done, but not dry. Dish them, sprinkle over a little fine salt, and serve plain, or with tomato sauce, sauce piquante, or pickled gherkins, a few of which should be laid round the dish as a garnish. *Time.*—About ¼ hour. *Average cost*, 10*d.* per lb. for chops. *Sufficient.*—Allow 6 for 4 persons. *Seasonable* from October to March.

PORK CUTLETS, or Chops.

Ingredients. — Loin, or fore-loin, of pork, egg and bread crumbs, salt and pepper to taste; to every tablespoonful of bread crumbs allow ½ teaspoonful of minced sage; clarified butter. *Mode.*—Cut the cutlets from a loin, or fore-loin, of pork; trim them the same as mutton cutlets, and scrape the top part of the bone. Brush them over with egg, sprinkle with bread crumbs, with which have been mixed minced sage and a seasoning of pepper and salt; drop a little clarified butter on them, and press the crumbs well down. Put the frying-pan on the fire, put in some lard; when this is hot, lay in the cutlets, and fry them a light brown on both sides. Take them out, put them before the fire to dry the greasy moisture from them, and dish them on mashed potatoes. Serve with them any sauce that may be preferred; such as tomato sauce, sauce piquante, sauce Robert, or pickled gherkins. *Time.*—From 15 to 20 minutes. *Average cost,* 10*d.* per lb. for chops. *Sufficient.*—Allow 6 cutlets for 4 persons. *Seasonable* from October to March.

Note.—The remains of roast loin of pork may be dressed in the same manner.

PORK CUTLETS.

[COLD MEAT COOKERY.] *Ingredients.*—The remains of cold roast loin of pork, 1 oz. of butter, 2 onions, 1 dessertspoonful of flour, ½ pint of gravy, pepper and salt to taste, 1 teaspoonful of vinegar and mustard. *Mode.*—Cut the pork into nice-sized cutlets, trim off most of the fat, and chop the onions. Put the butter into a stewpan, lay in the cutlets and chopped onions, and fry a light brown; then add the remaining ingredients, simmer gently for 5 or 7 minutes, and serve. *Time.*—5 to 7 minutes. *Average cost,* exclusive of the meat, 4*d.* *Seasonable* from October to March.

PORK, Roast Griskin of.

Ingredients.—Pork; a little powdered sage. *Mode.*—As this joint frequently comes to table hard and dry, particular care should be taken that it is well basted. Put it down to a bright fire,

SPARE-RIB OF PORK.

and flour it. About 10 minutes before taking it up, sprinkle over some powdered sage; make a little gravy in the dripping-pan, strain it over the meat, and serve with a tureen of apple sauce. This joint will be done in far less time than when the skin is left on, consequently, should have the greatest atten-

GRISKIN OF PORK.

tion that it be not dried up. *Time.*—Griskin of pork weighing 6 lbs., 1½ hour. *Average cost,* 7*d.* per lb. *Sufficient* for 5 or 6 persons. *Seasonable* from September to March.

Note.—A spare-rib of pork is roasted in the same manner as above, and would take 1½ hour for one weighing about 6 lbs.

PORK, Hashed.

Ingredients.—The remains of cold roast pork, 2 onions, 1 teaspoonful of flour, 2 blades of pounded mace, 2 cloves, 1 tablespoonful of vinegar, ½ pint of gravy, pepper and salt to taste. *Mode.*—Chop the onions and fry them of a nice brown; cut the pork into thin slices, season them with pepper and salt, and add these to the remaining ingredients. Stew gently for about ½ hour, and serve garnished with sippets of toasted bread. *Time.*—½ hour. *Average cost,* exclusive of the meat, 3*d.* *Seasonable* from October to March.

PORK, Boiled Leg of.

Ingredients.—Leg of pork; salt. *Mode.*—For boiling, choose a small, compact, well-filled leg, and rub it well with salt; let it remain in pickle for a week or ten days, turning and rubbing it every day. An hour before dressing it, put it into cold water for an hour, which improves the colour. If the pork is purchased ready salted, ascertain how long the meat has been in pickle, and soak it accordingly. Put it into a boiling-pot, with sufficient cold water to cover it; let it gradually come to a boil, and remove the scum as it rises. Simmer it very gently until tender, and do not allow it to boil fast, or the knuckle will fall to pieces before the middle of the leg is done. Carrots, turnips, or parsnips may be boiled with the pork, some of which should be laid round the dish as a garnish. A well-made pease-pudding is an indispensable accompaniment. *Time.*—A leg of pork weighing 8 lbs., 3 hours after the water boils, and to be simmered very gently. *Average cost*, 9*d.* per lb. *Sufficient* for 7 or 8 persons. *Seasonable* from September to March.

Note.—The liquor in which a leg of pork has been boiled makes excellent pea-soup.

PORK, Roast Leg of.

Ingredients. — Leg of pork, a little oil, sage and onion stuffing. *Mode.* — Choose a small leg of pork, and score the skin across in narrow strips, about ¼ inch apart. Cut a slit in the knuckle, loosen the skin, and fill it with a sage-and-onion stuffing.

ROAST LEG OF PORK.

Brush the joint over with a little salad-oil (this makes the crackling crisper, and a better colour), and put it down to a bright, clear fire, not too near, as that would cause the skin to blister. Baste it well, and serve with a little gravy made in the dripping-pan, and do not omit to send to table with it a tureen of well-made apple sauce. *Time.*—A leg of pork weighing 8 lbs., about 3 hours. *Average cost*, 9*d.* per lb. *Sufficient* for 6 or 7 persons. *Seasonable* from September to March.

PORK, Leg of, to Carve.

This joint, which is such a favourite one with many people, is easy to carve. The knife should be carried sharply down to the bone, clean through the crackling, in the direction of the line 1 to 2. Sage and onion and apple sauce are usually sent to table with this dish,—sometimes the leg of pork is stuffed,—and the guests should be asked if they will have either or both. A frequent plan, and we think a good one, is now pursued, of sending sage and onion to table separately from the joint, as it is not everybody to whom the flavour of this stuffing is agreeable.

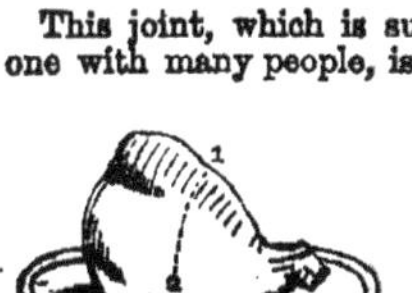

LEG OF PORK.

Note.—The other dishes of pork do not call for any special remarks as to their carving or helping.

PORK, Roast Loin of.

Ingredients. — Pork; a little salt. *Mode.*—Score the skin in strips rather more than ¼ inch apart, and place the joint at a good distance from the fire, on account of the crackling, which would harden before the meat would be heated through, were it placed too near. If very lean, it should be rubbed over with a little salad oil, and kept well basted all the time it is at the fire. Pork should be very thoroughly cooked, but not dry; and be careful never to send it to table the least underdone, as nothing is more unwholesome and disagreeable than under-dressed white meats. Serve with apple sauce and a little gravy made in the dripping-pan. A stuffing of sage and onion may be made separately, and baked in a flat dish: this method is better than putting it in the meat, as many persons have so great an objection to the flavour. *Time.*—A loin of pork weighing 5 lbs., about 2 hours: allow more time should it be very fat. *Average cost*, 9*d.* per lb. *Sufficient* for 5 or 6 persons. *Seasonable* from September to March.

FORE LOIN OF PORK.

HIND LOIN OF PORK.

PORK, to Pickle.

Ingredients.—¼ lb. of saltpetre; salt. *Mode.*—As pork does not keep long without being salted, cut it into pieces of a suitable size as soon as the pig is cold. Rub the pieces of pork well with salt, and put them into a pan with a sprinkling of it between each piece: as it melts on the top, strew on more. Lay a coarse cloth over the pan, a board over that, and a weight on the board, to keep the pork down in the brine. If excluded from the air, it will continue good for nearly 2 years. *Average cost*, 10*d*. per lb. for the prime parts. *Seasonable*.—The best time for pickling meat is late in the autumn.

PORK, Pickled, to Boil.

Ingredients.—Pork; water. *Mode*.—Should the pork be very salt, let it remain in water about 2 hours before it is dressed; put it into a saucepan with sufficient cold water to cover it, let it gradually come to a boil, then gently simmer until quite tender. Allow ample time for it to cook, as nothing is more disagreeable than underdone pork, and when boiled fast, the meat becomes hard. This is sometimes served with boiled poultry and roast veal, instead of bacon: when tender, and not over salt, it will be found equally good. *Time*.—A piece of pickled pork weighing 2 lbs., 1½ hour; 4 lbs., rather more than 2 hours. *Average cost*, 10*d*. per lb. for the primest parts. *Seasonable* at any time.

PORK PIES (Warwickshire Recipe).

Ingredients.—For the crust, 5 lbs. of lard to 14 lbs. of flour; milk, and water. For filling the pies, to every 3 lbs. of meat allow 1 oz. of salt, 2¼ oz. of pepper, a small quantity of cayenne, 1 pint of water. *Mode*.—Rub into the flour a portion of the lard; the remainder put with sufficient milk and water to mix the crust, and boil this gently for ¼ hour. Pour it boiling on the flour, and knead and beat it till perfectly smooth. Now raise the crust in either a round or oval form, cut up the pork into pieces the size of a nut, season it in the above proportion, and press it compactly into the pie, in alternate layers of fat and lean, and pour in a small quantity of water; lay on the lid, cut the edges smoothly round, and pinch them together. Bake in a brick oven, which should be slow, as the meat is very solid. Very frequently, an inexperienced cook finds much difficulty in raising the crust. She should bear in mind that it must not be allowed to get cold, or it will fall immediately: to prevent this, the operation should be performed as near the fire as possible. As considerable dexterity and expertness are necessary to raise the crust with the hand only, a glass bottle or small jar may be placed in the middle of the paste, and the crust moulded on this; but be particular that it is kept warm the whole time. *Sufficient*.—The proportions for 1 pie are 1 lb. of flour and 3 lbs. of meat. *Seasonable* from September to March.

PORK PIES, Little Raised.

Ingredients.—2 lbs. of flour, ½ lb. of butter, ½ lb. of mutton suet, salt and white pepper to taste, 4 lbs. of the neck of pork, 1 dessertspoonful of powdered sage. *Mode*.—Well dry the flour, mince the suet, and put these with the butter into a saucepan, to be made hot, and add a little salt. When melted, mix it up into a stiff paste, and put it before the fire with a cloth over it until ready to make up; chop the pork into small pieces, season it with white pepper, salt, and powdered sage; divide the paste into rather small pieces, raise it in a round or oval form, fill with the meat, and bake in a brick oven. These pies will require a fiercer oven than those in the preceding recipe, as they are made so much smaller, and consequently do not require so soaking a heat. *Time*.—If made small, about 1½ hour. *Seasonable* from September to March.

POTATO FRITTERS.

Ingredients.—2 large potatoes, 4 eggs, 2 tablespoonfuls of cream, 2 ditto of raisin or sweet wine, 1 dessertspoonful of lemon-juice, ½ teaspoonful of grated nutmeg, hot lard. *Mode*.—Boil the potatoes, and beat them up lightly with a fork, but do not use a spoon, as that would make them heavy. Beat the eggs well, leaving out one of the whites; add the other ingredients, and beat all together for at least 20 minutes, or until the batter is extremely light. Put plenty of good lard into a frying-pan, and drop a tablespoonful of the batter at a time into it, and fry the fritters a nice brown. Serve them with the following sauce:—A glass of sherry mixed with the strained juice of a lemon, and sufficient white sugar to sweeten the whole nicely. Warm these ingredients, and serve the sauce separately in a tureen. The fritters should be neatly dished on a white d'oyley, and pounded sugar sprinkled over them. They should be well drained on a piece of blotting-paper before the fire previously to being dished. *Time.*—From 6 to 8 minutes. *Average cost*, 9*d*. *Sufficient* for 3 or 4 persons. *Seasonable* at any time.

POTATO PASTY.

Ingredients.—1½ lb. of rump-steak or mutton cutlets, pepper and salt to taste, ⅓ pint of weak broth or gravy, 1 oz. of butter, mashed potatoes. *Mode.*—Place the meat, cut in small pieces, at the bottom of the pan; season it with pepper and salt, and add the gravy and

POTATO-PASTY PAN.

butter broken into small pieces. Put on the perforated plate, with its valve-pipe screwed on, and fill up the whole space to the top of the tube with nicely-mashed potatoes mixed with a little milk, and finish the surface of them in any ornamental manner. If carefully baked, the potatoes will be covered with a delicate brown crust, retaining all the savoury steam rising from the meat. Send it to table as it comes from the oven, with a napkin folded round it. *Time.*—40 to 60 minutes. *Average cost*, 2*s*. *Sufficient* for 4 or 5 persons. *Seasonable* at any time.

POTATO PUDDING.

Ingredients.—½ lb. of mashed potatoes, 2 oz. of butter, 2 eggs, ¼ pint of milk, 3 tablespoonfuls of sherry, ¼ saltspoonful of salt, the juice and rind of 1 small lemon, 2 oz. of sugar. *Mode.*—Boil sufficient potatoes to make ½ lb. when mashed; add to these the butter, eggs, milk, sherry, lemon-juice, and sugar; mince the lemon-peel very finely, and beat all the ingredients well together. Put the pudding into a buttered pie-dish, and bake for rather more than ½ hour. To enrich it, add a few pounded almonds, and increase the quantity of eggs and butter. *Time.*—½ hour, or rather longer. *Average cost*, 8*d*. *Sufficient* for 5 or 6 persons. *Seasonable* at any time.

POTATO RISSOLES.

Ingredients.—Mashed potatoes, salt and pepper to taste; when liked, a very little minced parsley, egg, and bread crumbs. *Mode.*—Boil and mash the

POTATO RISSOLES.

potatoes; add a seasoning of pepper and salt, and, when liked, a little minced parsley. Roll the potatoes into small balls, cover them with egg and bread crumbs, and fry in hot lard for about 10 minutes; let them drain before the fire, dish them on a napkin, and serve. *Time.*—10 minutes to fry the rissoles. *Seasonable* at any time.

Note.—The flavour of these rissoles may be very much increased by adding finely-minced tongue or ham, or even chopped onions, when these are liked.

POTATO SALAD.

Ingredients.—10 or 12 cold boiled potatoes, 4 tablespoonfuls of tarragon or plain vinegar, 6 tablespoonfuls of salad-oil, pepper and salt to taste, 1 teaspoonful of minced parsley. *Mode.*—Cut the potatoes into slices about ½ inch in thickness; put these into a salad-bowl with oil and vinegar in the above proportion; season with pepper, salt, and a teaspoonful of minced parsley; stir the salad well, that all the ingredients may be thoroughly incorporated, and it is ready to serve. This should be made two or three hours before it is wanted for table. Anchovies, olives, or pickles may be added to this salad, as also slices of cold beef, fowl, or turkey. *Seasonable* at any time.

POTATO SNOW.

Ingredients.—Potatoes, salt, and water. *Mode.*—Choose large white potatoes, as free from spots as possible; boil them in their skins in salt and water until perfectly tender; drain and *dry them thoroughly* by the side of the fire, and peel them. Put a hot dish before the fire, rub the potatoes through a coarse sieve on to this dish; do not touch them afterwards, or the flakes will fall, and serve as hot as possible. *Time.*—½ to ¾ hour to boil the potatoes. *Average cost*, 4*s*. per bushel. *Sufficient*,—6 potatoes for 3 persons. *Seasonable* at any time.

POTATO SOUP.

Ingredients.—4 lbs. of mealy potatoes, boiled or steamed very dry, pepper and salt to taste, 2 quarts of stock. *Mode.*—When the potatoes are boiled, mash them smoothly, that no lumps remain, and gradually put them to the boiling stock; pass it through a sieve, season, and simmer for 5 minutes. Skim well, and serve with fried bread. *Time.*—½ hour. *Average cost*, 10*d*. per quart. *Seasonable* from September to March. *Sufficient* for 8 persons.

POTATO SOUP.

Ingredients.—1 lb. of shin of beef, 1 lb. of potatoes, 1 onion, ½ a pint of peas, 2 oz. of rice, 2 heads of celery, pepper and salt to taste, 3 quarts of water. *Mode.*—Cut the beef into thin slices, chop the potatoes and onion, and put them into a stewpan with the water, peas, and rice. Stew gently till the gravy is drawn from the meat; strain it off, take out the beef, and pulp the other ingredients through a coarse sieve. Put the pulp back into the soup, cut up the celery in it, and simmer till this is tender. Season, and serve with fried bread cut into it. *Time.*—3 hours. *Average cost*, 4*d*. per quart. *Seasonable* from September to March. *Sufficient* for 12 persons.

POTATO SOUP (very Economical).

Ingredients.—4 middle-sized potatoes well pared, a thick slice of bread, 6 leeks peeled and cut into thin slices as far as the white extends upwards from the roots, a teacupful of rice, a teaspoonful of salt, and half that of pepper, and 2 quarts of water. *Mode.*—The water must be completely boiling before anything is put into it; then add the whole of the ingredients at once, with the exception of the rice, the salt, and the pepper. Cover, and let these come to a brisk boil; put in the others, and let the whole boil slowly for an hour, or till all the ingredients are thoroughly done, and their several juices extracted and mixed. *Time.*—2½ hours. *Average cost*, 3*d*. per quart. *Sufficient* for 8 persons. *Seasonable* in winter.

POTATOES, Baked.

Ingredients. — Potatoes. *Mode.* — Choose large potatoes, as much of a size as possible; wash them in lukewarm water, and scrub them well, for the browned skin of a baked potato is by many persons considered the better part of it. Put them into a moderate oven, and bake them for about two hours, turning them three or four times whilst they are cooking. Serve them in a napkin immediately they are done, as, if kept a long time in the oven, they have a shrivelled appearance. Potatoes may also be roasted before the fire, in an American oven; but when thus cooked, they must be done very slowly. Do not forget to send to table with them a piece of cold butter. *Time.*—Large potatoes, in a hot oven, 1½ hour to 2 hours; in a cool oven, 2 to 2½ hours. *Average cost*, 4*s*. per bushel. *Sufficient.*—Allow 2 to each person. *Seasonable* all the year, but not good just before and whilst new potatoes are in season.

BAKED POTATOES SERVED IN NAPKIN.

POTATOES, to Boil.

Ingredients.—10 or 12 potatoes; to each ½ gallon of water allow 1 heaped tablespoonful of salt. *Mode.*—Choose potatoes of an equal size, pare them, take out all the eyes and specks, and as they are peeled, throw them into cold water. Put them into a saucepan, with sufficient *cold* water to cover them, with salt in the above proportion, and let them *boil gently* until tender. Ascertain when they are done by thrusting a fork in them, and take them up the moment they feel soft through; for if they are left in the water afterwards, they become waxy or watery. Drain away the water, put the saucepan by the side of the fire, with the lid partially uncovered, to allow the steam to escape, and let the potatoes get thoroughly dry, and do not allow them to get burnt. Their superfluous moisture will evaporate, and the potatoes, if a good sort, should be perfectly mealy and dry. Potatoes vary so much in quality and size, that it is difficult to give the exact time for boiling; they should be attentively watched, and probed with a fork, to ascertain when they are cooked. Send them to table quickly, and very hot, and with an opening in the cover of the dish, that a portion of the steam may evaporate, and not fall back on the potatoes. *Time.*—Moderate-sized old potatoes, 15 to 20 minutes, after the water boils; large ones, ½ hour to 35 minutes. *Average cost,* 4*s.* per bushel. *Sufficient* for 6 persons. *Seasonable* all the year, but not good just before and whilst new potatoes are in season.

Note.—To keep potatoes hot, after draining the water from them, put a folded cloth or flannel (kept for the purpose) on the top of them, keeping the saucepan-lid partially uncovered. This will absorb the moisture, and keep them hot some time without spoiling.

POTATOES, to Boil in their Jackets.

Ingredients.—10 or 12 potatoes; to each ½ gallon of water, allow 1 heaped tablespoonful of salt. *Mode.*—To obtain this wholesome and delicious vegetable cooked in perfection, it should be boiled and sent to table with the skin on. In Ireland, where, perhaps, the cooking of potatoes is better understood than in any country, they are always served so. Wash the potatoes well, and if necessary, use a clean scrubbing-brush to remove the dirt from them; and, if possible, choose the potatoes so that they may all be as nearly the same size as possible. When thoroughly cleansed, fill the saucepan half full with them, and just cover the potatoes with cold water salted in the above proportion: they are more quickly boiled with a small quantity of water, and, besides, are more savoury than when drowned in it. Bring them to boil, then draw the pan to the side of the fire, and let them simmer gently until tender. Ascertain when they are done by probing them with a fork; then pour off the water, uncover the saucepan, and let the potatoes dry by the side of the fire, taking care not to let them burn. Peel them quickly, put them in a very hot vegetable-dish, either with or without a napkin, and serve very quickly. After potatoes are cooked, they should never be entirely covered up, as the steam, instead of escaping, falls down on them, and makes them watery and insipid. In Ireland they are usually served up with the skins on, and a small plate is placed by the side of each guest. *Time.*—Moderate-sized potatoes, with their skins on, 20 to 25 minutes after the water boils; large potatoes, 25 minutes to ¾ hour, or longer; 5 minutes to dry them. *Average cost,* 4*s.* per bushel. *Sufficient* for 6 persons. *Seasonable* all the year, but not good just before and whilst new potatoes are in season.

POTATOES, New, to Boil.

Ingredients.—Potatoes; to each ½ gallon of water allow 1 heaped tablespoonful of salt. *Mode.*—Do not have the potatoes dug long before they are dressed, as they are never good when they have been out of the ground some time. Well wash them, rub off the skins with a coarse cloth, and put them into *boiling* water salted in the above proportion. Let them boil until tender; try them with a fork, and when done, pour the water away from them; let them stand by the side of the fire with the lid of the saucepan partially uncovered, and when the potatoes are thoroughly dry, put them into a hot vegetable-dish, with a piece of butter the size of a walnut; pile the potatoes over this, and serve. If the potatoes are too old to have the skin rubbed off, boil them in their jackets; drain, peel, and serve them as above, with a piece of butter placed in the midst of them. *Time.*—¼ to ½ hour, according to the size. *Average cost,* in full season, 1*d.* per lb. *Sufficient.*—Allow 3 lbs. for 5 or 6 persons. *Seasonable* in May and June, but may be had, forced, in March.

POTATOES, Fried (French Fashion).

Ingredients.—Potatoes, hot butter or clarified dripping, salt. *Mode.*—Peel and cut the potatoes into thin slices, as nearly the same size as possible; make some butter or dripping *hot* in a frying-pan; put in the potatoes, and fry them on both sides until *nearly* cooked. Now take the potatoes out of the fat, make the fat *quite boiling,* then throw in the potatoes for a minute or two until sufficiently done. The immersion of the vegetable in the grease a second time after it is partially cooked, causes it to puff or "gonfler," as the French say, which is the desired appearance for properly-dressed fried potatoes to posness. When they are crisp and done, take them up, place them on a cloth before the fire to drain the grease from them, and serve very hot, after sprinkling them with salt. These are delicious with rump-steak, and, in France, are frequently served thus as a breakfast dish. The remains of cold potatoes may also be sliced and fried by the above recipe, but the slices must be cut a little thicker. *Time.*—Sliced raw potatoes, 5 minutes; cooked potatoes, 5 minutes. *Average cost,* 4*s.* per bushel. *Sufficient,*—6 sliced potatoes for 3 persons. *Seasonable* at any time.

POTATOES, a German Method of Cooking.

Ingredients.—8 to 10 middling-sized potatoes, 3 oz. of butter, 2 tablespoonfuls of flour, ½ pint of broth, 2 tablespoonfuls of vinegar. *Mode.*—Put the butter and flour into a stewpan; stir over the fire until the butter is of a nice brown colour, and add the broth and vinegar; peel and cut the potatoes into long thin slices, lay them in the gravy, and let them simmer gently until tender, which will be in from 10 to 15 minutes, and serve very hot. A laurel-leaf simmered with the potatoes is an improvement. *Time.*—10 to 15 minutes. *Seasonable* at any time.

POTATOES, à la Maître d'Hôtel.

Ingredients.—Potatoes, salt and water; to every 6 potatoes allow 1 tablespoonful of minced parsley, 2 oz. of butter, pepper and salt to taste, 4 tablespoonfuls of gravy, 2 tablespoonfuls of lemon-juice. *Mode.*—Wash the potatoes clean, and boil them in salt and water; when they are done, drain them, let them cool; then peel and cut the potatoes into thick slices: if these are too thin, they would break in the sauce. Put the butter into a stewpan with the pepper, salt, gravy, and parsley; mix these ingredients well together, put in the potatoes, shake them two or three times, that they may be well covered with the sauce, and, when quite hot through, squeeze in the lemon-juice, and serve. *Time.*—½ to ¾ hour to boil the potatoes; 10 minutes for them to heat in the sauce. *Average cost,* 4*s.* per bushel. *Sufficient* for 3 persons. *Seasonable* all the year.

POTATOES, Mashed.

Ingredients.—Potatoes; to every lb. of mashed potatoes allow 1 oz. of butter, 2 tablespoonfuls of milk, salt to taste. *Mode.*—Boil the potatoes in their skins; when done, drain them, and let them get thoroughly dry by the side of the fire; then peel them, and, as they are peeled, put them into a clean saucepan, and with a *large fork* beat them to a light paste; add butter, milk, and salt in the above proportion, and stir all the ingredients well over the fire. When thoroughly hot, dish them lightly, and draw the fork backwards over the potatoes to make the surface rough, and serve. When dressed in this manner, they may be browned at the top with a salamander, or before the fire. Some cooks press the potatoes into moulds, then turn them out, and brown them in the oven: this is a pretty mode of serving, but it makes them heavy. In whatever way they are sent to table, care must be taken to have them quite free from lumps. *Time.*—From ½ to ¾ hour to boil the potatoes. *Average cost,* 4*s.* per bushel. *Sufficient,*—1 lb. of mashed potatoes for 3 persons. *Seasonable* at any time.

POTATOES, Very Thin-mashed, or, Purée de Pommes de Terre.

Ingredients.—To every lb. of mashed potatoes allow ¼ pint of good broth or stock, 2 oz. of butter. *Mode.*—Boil the potatoes, well drain them, and pound them smoothly in a mortar, or beat them up with a fork; add the stock or broth, and rub the potatoes through a sieve. Put the purée into a very clean saucepan with the butter; stir it well over the fire until thoroughly hot, and it will then be ready to serve. A purée should be rather thinner than mashed potatoes, and is a delicious accompaniment to delicately broiled mutton cutlets. Cream or milk may be substituted for the broth when the latter is not at hand. A casserole of potatoes, which is often used for ragoûts instead of rice, is made by mashing potatoes rather thickly, placing them on a dish, and making an opening in the centre. After having browned the potatoes in the oven, the dish should be wiped clean, and the ragoût or fricassée poured in. *Time.*—About ½ hour to boil the potatoes; 6 or 7 minutes to warm the purée. *Average cost,* 4*s.* per bushel.

Sufficient.—Allow 1 lb. of cooked potatoes for 3 persons. *Seasonable* at any time.

POTATOES, how to use Cold.

Ingredients.—The remains of cold potatoes; to every lb. allow 2 tablespoonfuls of flour, 2 ditto of minced onions, 1 oz. of butter-milk. *Mode.*—Mash the potatoes with a fork until perfectly free from lumps; stir in the other ingredients, and add sufficient milk to moisten them well; press the potatoes into a mould, and bake in a moderate oven until nicely brown, which will be in from 20 minutes to ½ hour. Turn them out of the mould, and serve. *Time.*—20 minutes to ½ hour. *Seasonable* at any time.

POTATOES, to Steam.

Ingredients.—Potatoes; boiling water. *Mode.*—This mode of cooking potatoes is now much in vogue, particularly where they are wanted on a large scale, it being so very convenient. Pare the potatoes, throw them into cold water as they are peeled, then put them into a steamer. Place the steamer over a saucepan of boiling water, and steam the potatoes from 20 to 40 minutes, according to the size and sort. When a fork goes easily through them, they are done; then take them up, dish, and serve very quickly. *Time.*—20 to 40 minutes. *Average cost,* 4*s.* per bushel. *Sufficient.*—Allow 2 large potatoes to each person. *Seasonable* all the year, but not so good whilst new potatoes are in season.

POULET AUX CRESSONS.

Ingredients.—A fowl, a large bunch of water-cresses, 3 tablespoonfuls of vinegar, ¼ pint of gravy. *Mode.*—Truss and roast a fowl by recipe, taking care that it is nicely frothed and brown. Wash and dry the water-cresses, pick them nicely, and arrange them in a flat layer on a dish. Sprinkle over a little salt and the above proportion of vinegar; place over these the fowl, and pour over it the gravy. A little gravy should be served in a tureen. When not liked, the vinegar may be omitted. *Time.*—From ¾ to 1 hour, according to size. *Average cost,* in full season, 2*s.* 6*d.* each. *Sufficient* for 3 or 4 persons. *Seasonable* at any time.

POULET À LA MARENGO.

Ingredients.—1 large fowl, 4 tablespoonfuls of salad oil, 1 tablespoonful of flour, 1 pint of stock or water, about 28 mushroom-buttons, salt and pepper to the taste, 1 teaspoonful of powdered sugar, a very small piece of garlic. *Mode.*—Cut the fowl into 8 or 10 pieces, put them with the oil into a stewpan, and brown them over a moderate fire; dredge in the above proportion of flour, when that is brown, pour in the stock or water, let it simmer very slowly for rather more than ½ an hour, and skim off the fat as it rises to the top; add the mushrooms, season with pepper, salt, garlic, and sugar; take out the fowl, which arrange pyramidically on a dish, with the inferior joints at the bottom. Reduce the sauce by boiling it quickly over the fire, keeping it stirred until sufficiently thick to adhere to the back of the spoon; pour over the fowl, and serve. *Time.*—Altogether 50 minutes. *Average cost,* 3*s.* 6*d.* *Sufficient* for 3 or 4 persons. *Seasonable* at any time.

POUND CAKE.

Ingredients.—1 lb. of butter, 1¼ lb. of flour, 1 lb. of pounded loaf sugar, 1 lb. of currants, 9 eggs, 2 oz. of candied peel, ½ oz. of citron, ½ oz. of sweet almonds; when liked, a little pounded mace. *Mode.*—Work the butter to a cream; dredge in the flour; add the sugar, currants, candied peel, which should be cut into neat slices, and the almonds, which should be blanched and chopped, and mix all these well together; whisk the eggs, and let them be thoroughly blended with the dry ingredients.

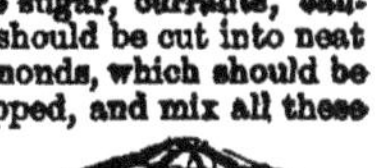

POUND CAKE.

Beat the cake well for 20 minutes, and put it into a round tin, lined at the bottom and sides with a strip of white buttered paper. Bake it from 1½ to 2 hours, and let the oven be well heated when the cake is first put in, as, if this is not the case, the currants will all sink to the bottom of it. To make this preparation light, the yolks and whites of the eggs should be beaten separately, and added separately to the other ingredients. A glass of wine is sometimes added to the mixture; but this is scarcely necessary, as the cake will be found quite rich enough without it. *Time.*—1½ to 2 hours. *Ave-*

rage cost, 3*s*. 6*d*. *Sufficient.*—The above quantity divided in two will make two nice-sized cakes. *Seasonable* at any time.

PRAWN SOUP.

Ingredients.—Two quarts of fish stock, two pints of prawns, the crumb of a French roll, anchovy sauce or mushroom ketchup to taste, one blade of mace, one-fourth pint of vinegar, a little lemon-juice. *Mode.*—Pick out the tails of the prawns, put the bodies in a stewpan with 1 blade of mace, ½ pint of vinegar, and the same quantity of water; stew them for ½ hour, and strain off the liquor. Put the fish stock into a stewpan; add the strained liquor, pound the prawns with the crumb of a roll moistened with a little of the soup, rub them through a tammy, and mix them by degrees with the soup; add ketchup or anchovy sauce to taste with a little lemon-juice. When it is well cooked, put in a few picked prawns; let them get thoroughly hot, and serve. If not thick enough, put in a little butter and flour. *Time.*—Hour. *Average cost*, 2*s*. per quart. *Seasonable* at any time. *Sufficient* for 8 persons.

Note.—This can be thickened with tomatoes, and vermicelli served in it, which makes it a very tasteful soup.

PRAWNS, to Dress.

Cover a dish with a large cup reversed, and over that lay a small white napkin. Arrange the prawns on it in the form of a pyramid, and garnish with plenty of parsley. Sometimes prawns are stuck into a lemon cut in half the long way, and garnished with parsley.

PRESERVES.

From the nature of vegetable substances, and chiefly from their not passing so rapidly into the putrescent state as animal bodies, the mode of preserving them is somewhat different, although the general principles are the same. All the means of preservation are put in practice occasionally for fruits and the various parts of vegetables, according to the nature of the species, the climate, the uses to which they are applied, &c. Some are dried, as nuts, raisins, sweet herbs, &c.; others are preserved by means of sugar, such as many fruits whose delicate juices would be lost by drying; some are preserved by means of vinegar, and chiefly used as condiments or pickles; a few also by salting, as French beans; while others are preserved in spirits. We have, however, in this place to treat of the best methods of preserving fruits. Fruit is a most important item in the economy of health; the epicurean can scarcely be said to have any luxuries without it; therefore, as it is so invaluable, when we cannot have it fresh, we must have it preserved. It has long been a desideratum to preserve fruits by some cheap method, yet by such as would keep them fit for the various culinary purposes, as making tarts and other similar dishes. The expense of preserving them with sugar is a serious objection; for, except the sugar be used in considerable quantities, the success is very uncertain. Sugar also overpowers and destroys the sub-acid taste so desirable in many fruits: those which are preserved in this manner are chiefly intended for the dessert. Fruits intended for preservation should be gathered in the morning, in dry weather, with the morning sun upon them, if possible; they will then have their fullest flavour, and keep in good condition longer than when gathered at any other time. Until fruit can be used, it should be placed in the dairy, an ice-house, or a refrigerator. In an ice-house it will remain fresh and plump for several days. Fruit gathered in wet or foggy weather will soon be mildewed, and be of no service for preserves.

Having secured the first and most important contribution to the manufacture of preserves—the fruit, the next consideration is the preparation of the syrup in which the fruit is to be suspended; and this requires much care. In the confectioner's art there is a great nicety in proportioning the degree of concentration of the syrup very exactly to each particular case; and he knows this by signs, and expresses it by certain technical terms. But to distinguish these properly requires very great attention and considerable experience. The principal thing to be acquainted with is the fact, that, in proportion as the syrup is longer boiled, its water will become evaporated, and its consistency will be thicker. Great care must be taken in the management of the fire, that the syrup does not boil over, and that the boiling is not carried to such an extent as to burn the sugar.

The first degree or consistency is called *the thread*, which is subdivided into the little and great thread. If you dip the finger into the syrup and apply it to the thumb, the tenacity of the syrup will, on separating the finger and thumb, afford a thread, which shortly breaks: this is the little thread. If the thread, from the greater tenacity, and, consequently, greater strength of the syrup, admits of a greater extension of the finger and thumb, it is called the great thread. There are half-a-dozen other terms and experiments for testing the various thickness of the boiling sugar towards the consistency called *caramel;* but that degree of sugar-boiling belongs to the confectioner. A solution of sugar prepared by dissolving two parts of double-refined sugar (the best sugar is the most economical for preserves) in one of water, and boiling this a little, affords a syrup of the right degree of strength, and which neither ferments nor crystallizes. This appears to be the degree called *smooth* by the confectioners, and is proper to be used for the purposes of preserves. The syrup employed should sometimes be clarified, which is done in the following manner:—Dissolve 2 lbs. of loaf sugar in a pint of water; add to this solution the white of an egg, and beat it well. Put the preserving-pan upon the fire with the solution; stir it with a wooden spatula, and when it begins to swell and boil up, throw in some cold water or a little oil to damp the boiling; for, as it rises suddenly, if it should boil over, it would take fire, being of a very inflammable nature. Let it boil up again; then take it off, and remove carefully the scum that has risen. Boil the solution again, throw in a little more cold water, remove the scum, and so on for three or four times successively; then strain it. It is considered to be sufficiently boiled when some taken up in a spoon pours out like oil.

Although sugar passes so easily into the state of fermentation, and is, in fact, the only substance capable of undergoing the vinous stage of that process, yet it will not ferment at all if the quantity be sufficient to constitute a very strong syrup: hence, syrups are used to preserve fruits and other vegetable substances from the changes they would undergo if left to themselves. Before sugar was in use, honey was employed to preserve many vegetable productions, though this substance has now given way to the juice of the sugar-cane.

The fruits that are the most fit for preservation in syrup are apricots, peaches, nectarines, apples, greengages, plums of all kinds, and pears. As an example, take some apricots not too ripe, make a small slit at the stem end, and push out the stone; simmer them in water till they are softened and about half done, and afterwards throw them into cold water. When they have cooled, take them out and drain them. Put the apricots into the preserving-pan with sufficient syrup to cover them; let them boil up three or four times, and then skim them; remove them from the fire, pour them into an earthen pan, and let them cool till next day. Boil them up three days successively, skimming each time, and they will then be finished and in a fit state to be put into pots for use. After each boiling, it is proper to examine into the state of the syrup when cold; if too thin, it will bear additional boiling; if too thick, it may be lowered with more syrup of the usual standard. The reason why the fruit is emptied out of the preserving-pan into an earthen pan is, that the acid of the fruit acts upon the copper, of which the preserving-pans are usually made. From this example the process of preserving fruits by syrup will be easily comprehended. The first object is to soften the fruit by blanching or boiling it in water, in order that the syrup by which it is preserved may penetrate through its substance.

Many fruits, when preserved by boiling, lose much of their peculiar and delicate flavour, as, for instance, pine-apples; and this inconvenience may, in some instances, be remedied by preserving them without heat. Cut the fruit in slices about one-fifth of an inch thick, strew powdered loaf sugar an eighth of an inch thick on the bottom of a jar, and put the slices on it. Put more sugar on this, and then another layer of the slices, and so on till the jar is full. Place the jar with the fruit up to the neck in boiling water, and keep it there till the sugar is completely dissolved, which may take half-an-hour, removing the scum as it rises. Lastly, tie a wet bladder over the mouth of the jar, or cork and wax it.

Any of the fruits that have been preserved in syrup may be converted into dry preserves, by first draining them from the syrup, and then drying them in a stove or very moderate oven, adding to them a quantity of powdered loaf-sugar, which will gradually penetrate the fruit, while the fluid parts of the fruit gently evaporate. They should be dried in the stove or oven on a sieve, and turned every six or eight hours, fresh powdered sugar being sifted over them every time they are turned. Afterwards, they are to be kept in a dry situation, in drawers or boxes. Currants and cherries preserved whole in this manner, in bunches, are extremely elegant, and have a fine flavour. In this way it is, also, that orange and lemon chips are preserved.

Marmalades, jams, and fruit pastes are of the same nature, and are now in very general request. They are prepared without difficulty, by attending to a very few directions; they are somewhat expensive, but may be kept without spoiling for a considerable time. Marmalades and jams differ little from each other: they are preserves of a half-liquid consistency, made by boiling the pulp of fruits, and sometimes part of the rinds, with sugar. The appellation of marmalade is applied to those confitures which are composed of the firmer fruits, as pineapples or the rinds of oranges; whereas jams are made of the more juicy berries, such as strawberries, raspberries, currants, mulberries, &c. Fruit pastes are a kind of marmalades, consisting of the pulp of fruits, first evaporated to a proper consistency, and afterwards boiled with sugar. The mixture is then poured into a mould, or spread on sheets of tin, and subsequently dried in the oven or stove till it has acquired the state of a paste. From a sheet of this paste, strips may be cut and formed into any shape that may be desired, as knots, rings, &c. Jams require the same care and attention in the boiling as marmalade; the slightest degree of burning communicates a disagreeable empyreumatic taste, and if they are not boiled sufficiently, they will not keep. That they may keep, it is necessary not to be sparing of sugar.

In all the operations for preserve-making, when the preserving-pan is used, it should not be placed on the fire, but on a trivet, unless the jam be made on a hot plate, when this is not necessary. If the pan be placed close on to the fire, the preserve is very liable to burn, and the colour and flavour be consequently spoiled.

Fruit jellies are compounds of the juices of fruits combined with sugar, concentrated, by boiling, to such a consistency that the liquid, upon cooling, assumes the form of a tremulous jelly.

Before fruits are candied, they must first be boiled in syrup, after which they are taken out and dried on a stove, or before the fire; the syrup is then to be concentrated, or boiled to a candy height, and the fruit dipped in it, and again laid on the stove to dry and candy; they are then to be put into boxes, and kept dry.

Conserves consist of fresh vegetable matters beat into a uniform mass with refined sugar, and they are intended to preserve the virtues and properties of recent flowers, leaves, roots, peels, or fruits, unaltered, and as near as possible to what they were when fresh gathered, and to give them an agreeable taste.

The last to be mentioned, but not the least important preparation of fruit, is the compôte, which can be made at the moment of need, and with much less sugar than would be ordinarily put to preserves. Compôtes are very wholesome things, suitable to most stomachs which cannot accommodate themselves to raw fruit or a large portion of sugar. They are the happy medium—far better than ordinary stewed fruit.

PTARMIGAN, the, or White Grouse.

This bird is nearly the same size as red grouse, and is fond of lofty situations, where it braves the severest weather, and is found in most parts of Europe, as well as in Greenland. At

THE PTARMIGAN.

Hudson's Bay they appear in such multitudes that so many as sixty or seventy are frequently taken at once in a net.

As they are as tame as chickens, this is done without difficulty. Buffon says that the ptarmigan avoids the solar heat, and prefers the frosts of the summits of the mountains; for, as the snow melts on the sides of the mountains, it ascends till it gains the top, where it makes a hole, and burrows in the snow. In winter, it flies in flocks, and feeds on the wild vegetation of the hills, which imparts to its flesh a bitter, but not altogether an unpalatable taste. It is dark-coloured, has something of the flavour of the hare, and is greatly relished and much sought after by some sportsmen.

PTARMIGAN, to Dress the.

Ingredients.—2 or 3 birds; butter, flour, fried bread crumbs. *Mode.*—The ptarmigan, or white grouse, when young and tender, are exceedingly fine eating, and should be kept as long as possible, to be good. Pluck, draw, and truss them in the same manner as grouse, and roast them before a brisk fire. Flour and froth them nicely, and serve on buttered toast, with a tureen of brown gravy. Bread sauce, when liked, may be sent to table with them, and fried bread crumbs substituted for the toasted bread. *Time.*—About ½ hour. *Sufficient,*—2 for a dish. *Seasonable* from the beginning of February to the end of April.

PTARMIGAN, to Carve.

Ptarmigan, being much of the same size, and trussed in the same manner, as the red bird, may be carved in the manner described, in Partridge and Grouse carving.

PUDDING, Alma.

Ingredients.—½ lb. of fresh butter, ½ lb. of powdered sugar, ½ lb. of flour, ¼ lb. of currants, 4 eggs. *Mode.*—Beat the butter to a thick cream, strew in, by degrees, the sugar, and mix both these well together; then dredge the flour in gradually, add the currants, and moisten with the eggs, which should be well beaten. When all the ingredients are well stirred and mixed, butter a mould that will hold the mixture exactly, tie it down with a cloth, put the pudding into boiling water, and boil for 5 hours; when turned out, strew some powdered sugar over it, and serve. *Time.*—5 hours. *Average cost,* 1s. 6d. *Sufficient* for 5 or 6 persons. *Seasonable* at any time.

PUDDING, Aunt Nelly's.

Ingredients.—½ lb. of flour, ½ lb. of treacle, ½ lb. of suet, the rind and juice of 1 lemon, a few strips of candied lemon-peel, 3 tablespoonfuls of cream, 2 eggs. *Mode.*—Chop the suet finely; mix it with the flour, treacle, lemon-peel minced, and candied lemon-peel; add the cream, lemon-juice, and 2 well-beaten eggs; beat the pudding well, put it into a buttered basin, tie it down with a cloth, and boil from 3½ to 4 hours. *Time.*—3½ to 4 hours. *Average cost,* 1s. 2d. *Sufficient* for 5 or 6 persons. *Seasonable* at any time, but more suitable for a winter pudding.

PUDDING, a Bachelor's.

Ingredients.—4 oz. of grated bread, 4 oz. of currants, 4 oz. of apples, 2 oz. of sugar, 3 eggs, a few drops of essence of lemon, a little grated nutmeg. *Mode.*—Pare, core, and mince the apples very finely, sufficient, when minced, to make 4 oz.; add to these the currants, which should be well washed, the grated bread, and sugar; whisk the eggs, beat these up with the remaining ingredients, and, when all is thoroughly mixed, put the pudding into a buttered basin, tie it down with a cloth, and boil for 3 hours. *Time.*—3 hours. *Average cost,* 9d. *Sufficient* for 4 or 5 persons. *Seasonable* from August to March.

PUDDING, Bakewell (very Rich).

Ingredients.—¼ lb. of puff-paste, 5 eggs, 6 oz. of sugar, ¼ lb. of butter, 1 oz. of almonds, jam. *Mode.*—Cover a dish with thin paste, and put over this a layer of any kind of jam, ½ inch thick; put the yolks of 5 eggs into a basin with the white of 1, and beat these well; add the sifted sugar, the butter, which should be melted, and the almonds, which should be well pounded; beat all together until well mixed, then pour it into the dish over the jam, and bake for an hour in a moderate oven. *Time.*—1 hour. *Average cost,* 1s. 6d. *Sufficient* for 4 or 5 persons. *Seasonable* at any time.

PUDDING, Bakewell.

Ingredients.—¾ pint of bread crumbs, 1 pint of milk, 4 eggs, 2 oz. of sugar,

3 oz. of butter, 1 oz. of pounded almonds, jam. *Mode.*—Put the bread crumbs at the bottom of a pie-dish, then over them a layer of jam of any kind that may be preferred; mix the milk and eggs together; add the sugar, butter, and pounded almonds; beat all well together; pour it into the dish, and bake in a moderate oven for 1 hour. *Time.*—1 hour. *Average cost,* 1*s.* 3*d.* to 1*s.* 6*d.* *Sufficient* for 4 or 5 persons. *Seasonable* at any time.

PUDDING, Baroness (Author's Recipe).

Ingredients.—¾ lb. of suet, ¾ lb. of raisins weighed after being stoned, ¾ lb. of flour, ½ pint of milk, ¼ saltspoonful of salt. *Mode.*—Prepare the suet, by carefully freeing it from skin, and chop it finely; stone the raisins, and cut them in halves, and mix both these ingredients with the salt and flour; moisten the whole with the above proportion of milk, stir the mixture well, and tie the pudding in a floured cloth, which has been previously wrung out in boiling water. Put the pudding into a saucepan of boiling water, and let it boil, without ceasing, 4½ hours. Serve with plain sifted sugar only, a little of which may be sprinkled over the pudding. *Time.*—4½ hours. *Average cost,* 1*s.* 4*d.* *Sufficient* for 7 or 8 persons. *Seasonable* in winter, when fresh fruit is not obtainable.

Note.—This pudding the editress cannot too highly recommend. The recipe was kindly given to her family by a lady who bore the title here prefixed to it; and with all who have partaken of it, it is an especial favourite. Nothing is of greater consequence, in the above directions, than attention to the time of boiling, which should never be *less* than that mentioned.

PUDDING, Royal Coburg.

Ingredients.—1 pint of new milk, 6 oz. of flour, 6 oz. of sugar, 6 oz. of butter, 6 oz. of currants, 6 eggs, brandy and grated nutmeg to taste. *Mode.*—Mix the flour to a smooth batter with the milk, add the remaining ingredients *gradually,* and when well mixed, put it into four basins or moulds half full; bake for ¾ hour, turn the puddings out on a dish, and serve with wine sauce. *Time.*—¾ hour. *Average cost,* 1*s.* 9*d.* *Sufficient* for 7 or 8 persons. *Seasonable* at any time.

PUDDING, Cold.

Ingredients.—4 eggs, 1 pint of milk, sugar to taste, a little grated lemon-rind, 2 oz. of raisins, 4 tablespoonfuls of marmalade, a few slices of sponge cake. *Mode.*—Sweeten the milk with lump sugar, add a little grated lemon-rind, and stir to this the eggs, which should be well whisked; line a buttered mould with the raisins, stoned and cut in half; spread the slices of cake with the marmalade, and place them in the mould; then pour in the custard, tie the pudding down with paper and a cloth, and boil gently for 1 hour: when cold, turn it out, and serve. *Time.*—1 hour. *Average cost,* 1*s.* 2*d.* *Sufficient* for 5 or 6 persons. *Seasonable* at any time.

PUDDING, College.

Ingredients.—1 pint of bread crumbs, 6 oz. of finely-chopped suet, ¼ lb. of currants, a few thin slices of candied peel, 3 oz. of sugar, ¼ nutmeg, 3 eggs, 4 tablespoonfuls of brandy. *Mode.*—Put the bread crumbs into a basin; add the suet, currants, candied peel, sugar, and nutmeg, grated, and stir these ingredients until they are thoroughly mixed. Beat up the eggs, moisten the pudding with these, and put in the brandy; beat well for a few minutes, then form the mixture into round balls or egg-shaped pieces; fry these in hot butter or lard, letting them stew in it until thoroughly done, and turn them two or three times, till of a fine light brown; drain them on a piece of blotting-paper before the fire; dish, and serve with wine sauce. *Time.*—15 to 20 minutes. *Average cost,* 1*s.* *Sufficient* for 7 or 8 puddings. *Seasonable* at any time.

PUDDING, Comarques (Excellent).

Ingredients.—5 eggs, 3 tablespoonfuls of flour, 2 tablespoonfuls of powdered sugar, rind of 1 lemon, ½ pint of cream, different kinds of preserve. *Mode.*—Beat the whites and yolks of the eggs separately, and put them into different basins; stir the flour, sugar, and lemon-peel into the yolks; whip the cream very thick and put it on a sieve to harden; then add it, with the whites of the eggs, to the other ingredients, and pour the mixture into little deep saucers just before putting into the oven. Bake about ½ an hour. When they are taken out, a very thin layer of different kinds of preserve should be put upon each, and they should be piled one above another. A little whipped cream placed here and there on the pudding as a garnish would be found to improve the appearance of this dish. *Time.*—About ½ an hour. *Average cost,* 1*s.* 9*d.* *Sufficient* for 4 or 5 persons. *Seasonable* at any time.

PUDDING, Delhi.

Ingredients.—4 large apples, a little grated nutmeg, 1 teaspoonful of minced lemon peel, 2 large tablespoonfuls of sugar, 6 oz. of currants, ¾ lb. of suet crust. *Mode.*—Pare, core, and cut the apples into slices; put them into a saucepan with the nutmeg, lemon-peel, and sugar, stew them over the fire till soft; then have ready the above quantity of crust, roll it out thin, spread the apples over the paste, sprinkle over the currants, roll the pudding up, closing the ends properly, tie it in a floured cloth, and boil for 2 hours. *Time.*—2 hours. *Average cost,* 1*s.* *Sufficient* for 5 or 6 persons. *Seasonable.*—August to March.

PUDDING, Empress.

Ingredients.—½ lb. of rice, 2 oz. of butter, 3 eggs, jam, sufficient milk to soften the rice. *Mode.*—Boil the rice in the milk until very soft; then add the butter, boil it for a few minutes after the latter ingredient is put in, and set it by to cool. Well beat the eggs, stir these in, and line a dish with puff-paste; put over this a layer of rice, then a thin layer of any kind of jam, then another layer of rice, and proceed in this manner until the dish is full; and bake in a moderate oven for ¾ hour. This pudding may be eaten hot or cold; if the latter, it will be much improved by having a boiled custard poured over it. *Time.*—¾ hour. *Average cost,* 1*s.* *Sufficient* for 6 or 7 persons. *Seasonable* at any time.

PUDDING, Exeter (Very Rich).

Ingredients.—10 oz. of bread-crumbs, 4 oz. of sago, 7 oz. of finely-chopped suet, 6 oz. of moist sugar, the rind of ½ lemon, ¼ pint of rum, 7 eggs, 4 table-spoonfuls of cream, 4 small sponge-cakes, 2 oz. of ratafias, ½ lb. of jam. *Mode.*—Put the bread-crumbs into a basin with the sago, suet, sugar, minced lemon-peel, rum, and 4 eggs; stir these ingredients well together, then add 3 more eggs and the cream, and let the mixture be well beaten. Then butter a mould, strew in a few bread-crumbs, and cover the bottom with a layer of ratafias; then put in a layer of the mixture, then a layer of sliced sponge-cake spread thickly with any kind of jam; then add some ratafias, then some of the mixture and sponge-cake, and so on until the mould is full, taking care that a layer of the mixture is on the top of the pudding. Bake in a good oven from ¾ to 1 hour, and serve with the following sauce:—Put 3 tablespoonfuls of black-currant jelly into a stewpan, add 2 glasses of sherry, and, when warm, turn the pudding out of the mould, pour the sauce over it, and serve hot. *Time.*—From 1 to 1¼ hour. *Average cost,* 2*s.* 6*d.* *Sufficient* for 7 or 8 persons. *Seasonable* at any time.

PUDDING-PIES, Folkestone.

Ingredients.—1 pint of milk, 3 oz. of ground rice, 3 oz. of butter, ¼ lb. of sugar, flavouring of lemon-peel or bay-leaf, 6 eggs, puff-paste, currants. *Mode.*—Infuse 2 laurel or bay leaves, or the rind of ½ lemon, in the milk, and when it is well flavoured, strain it, and add the rice; boil these for ¼ hour, stirring all the time; then take them off the fire, stir in the butter, sugar, and eggs, and let these latter be well beaten before they are added to the other ingredients; when nearly cold, line some patty-pans with puff-paste, fill with the custard, strew over each a few currants, and bake from 20 to 25 minutes in a moderate oven. *Time.*—20 to 25 minutes. *Average cost,* 1*s.* 1*d.* *Sufficient* to fill a dozen patty-pans. *Seasonable* at any time.

PUDDING, German.

Ingredients.—2 teaspoonfuls of flour, 1 teaspoonful of arrowroot, 1 pint of milk, 2 oz. of butter, sugar to taste, the rind of ½ lemon, 4 eggs, 3 tablespoonfuls of brandy. *Mode.*—Boil the milk with the lemon-rind until well flavoured; then strain it, and mix with it the flour, arrowroot, butter, and sugar. Boil these ingredients for a few minutes, keeping them well stirred; then take them off the fire and mix with them the eggs, yolks and whites, beaten separately and added separately. Boil some sugar to candy; line a mould with this, put in the brandy, then the mixture; tie down with a cloth, and boil for rather more than 1 hour. When turned out, the brandy and sugar make a nice sauce. *Time.*—Rather more than 1 hour. *Average cost*, 1*s.* *Sufficient* for 4 or 5 persons. *Seasonable* at any time.

PUDDING, Half-Pay.

Ingredients.—¼ lb. of suet, ¼ lb. of currants, ¼ lb. of raisins, ¼ lb. of flour, ¼ lb. of bread-crumbs, 2 tablespoonfuls of treacle, ½ pint of milk. *Mode.*—Chop the suet finely; mix with it the currants, which should be nicely washed and dried, the raisins, which should be stoned, the flour, bread-crumbs, and treacle; moisten with the milk, beat up the ingredients until all are thoroughly mixed, put them into a buttered basin, and boil the pudding for 3½ hours. *Time.*—3½ hours. *Average cost*, 8*d.* *Sufficient* for 5 or 6 persons. *Seasonable* at any time.

PUDDING, Herodotus.

Ingredients.—½ lb. of bread-crumbs, ½ lb. of good figs, 6 oz. of suet, 6 oz. of moist sugar, ½ saltspoonful of salt, 3 eggs, nutmeg to taste. *Mode.*—Mince the suet and figs very finely; add the remaining ingredients, taking care that the eggs are well whisked; beat the mixture for a few minutes, put it into a buttered mould, tie it down with a floured cloth, and boil the pudding for 5 hours. Serve with wine sauce. *Time.*—5 hours. *Average cost*, 10*d.* *Sufficient* for 5 or 6 persons. *Seasonable* at any time.

PUDDING, Hunter's.

Ingredients.—1 lb. of raisins, 1 lb. of currants, 1 lb. of suet, 1 lb. of bread-crumbs, ½ lb. of moist sugar, 8 eggs, 1 tablespoonful of flour, ¼ lb. of mixed candied peel, 1 glass of brandy, 10 drops of essence of lemon, 10 drops of essence of almonds, ½ nutmeg, 2 blades of mace, 6 cloves. *Mode.*—Stone and shred the raisins rather small, chop the suet finely, and rub the bread until all lumps are well broken; pound the spice to powder, cut the candied peel into thin shreds, and mix all these ingredients well together, adding the sugar. Beat the eggs to a strong froth, and as they are beaten, drop into them the essence of lemon and essence of almonds; stir these to the dry ingredients, mix well, and add the brandy. Tie the pudding firmly in a cloth, and boil it for 6 hours at the least: 7 or 8 hours would be still better for it. Serve with boiled custard, melted red-currant jelly, or brandy sauce. *Time.*—6 to 8 hours. *Average cost*, 3*s.* 6*d.* *Sufficient* for 9 or 10 persons. *Seasonable* in winter.

PUDDING, Manchester (to eat Cold).

Ingredients.—3 oz. of grated bread, ½ pint of milk, a strip of lemon-peel, 4 eggs, 2 oz. of butter, sugar to taste, puff-paste, jam, 3 tablespoonfuls of brandy. *Mode.*—Flavour the milk with lemon-peel, by infusing it in the milk for ½ hour; then strain it on to the bread-crumbs, and boil it for 2 or 3 minutes; add the eggs, leaving out the whites of 2, the butter, sugar, and brandy; stir all these ingredients well together; cover a pie-dish with puff-paste, and at the bottom put a thick layer of any kind of jam; pour the above mixture, cold, on the jam, and bake the pudding for an hour. Serve cold, with a little sifted sugar sprinkled over. *Time.*—1 hour. *Average cost*, 1*s.* *Sufficient* for 5 or 6 persons. *Seasonable* at any time.

PUDDING, Mansfield.

Ingredients.—The crumb of 2 rolls, 1 pint of milk, sugar to taste, 4 eggs, 2 tablespoonfuls of brandy, 6 oz. of chopped suet, 2 tablespoonfuls of flour, ½ lb. of currants, ½ teaspoonful of grated nutmeg, 2 tablespoonfuls of cream. *Mode.*—Slice the roll very then, and pour upon it a pint of boiling milk; let it remain closely covered for ¼ hour, then beat it up with a fork, and sweeten with moist sugar; stir in the chopped suet, flour, currants, and nutmeg. Mix these ingredients well together, moisten with the eggs, brandy, and cream; beat the mixture for 2 or 3 minutes, put it into a buttered dish or mould, and bake in a moderate oven for 1¼ hour. Turn it out, strew sifted sugar over, and serve. *Time.*—1¼ hour. *Average cost*, 1*s.* 3*d.* *Sufficient* for 6 or 7 persons. *Seasonable* at any time.

PUDDING, Marlborough.

Ingredients.—¼ lb. of butter, ¼ lb. of powdered lump sugar, 4 eggs, puff-paste, a layer of any kind of jam. *Mode.*—Beat the butter to a cream, stir in the powdered sugar, whisk the eggs, and add these to the other ingredients. When these are well mixed, line a dish with puff-paste, spread over a layer of any kind of jam that may be preferred, pour in the mixture, and bake the pudding for rather more than ½ hour. *Time.*—Rather more than ½ hour. *Average cost,* 1*s.* *Sufficient* for 5 or 6 persons. *Seasonable* at any time.

PUDDING, Military.

Ingredients.—½ lb. of suet, ½ lb. of bread-crumbs, ½ lb. of moist sugar, the rind and juice of 1 large lemon. *Mode.*—Chop the suet finely, mix it with the bread-crumbs and sugar, and mince the lemon-rind and strain the juice; stir these into the other ingredients, mix well, and put the mixture into small buttered cups, and bake for rather more than ½ hour; turn them out on the dish, and serve with lemon-sauce. The above ingredients may be made into small balls, and boiled for about ½ hour; they should then be served with the same sauce as when baked. *Time.*—Rather more than ½ hour. *Average cost,* 9*d.* *Sufficient* to fill 6 or 7 moderate-sized cups. *Seasonable* at any time.

PUDDING, Monday's.

Ingredients. — The remains of cold plum-pudding, brandy, custard made with 5 eggs to every pint of milk. *Mode.*—Cut the remains of a *good* cold plum-pudding into finger-pieces, soak them in a little brandy, and lay them cross-barred in a mould until full. Make a custard with the above proportion of milk and eggs, flavouring it with nutmeg or lemon-rind; fill up the mould with it; tie it down with a cloth, and boil or steam it for an hour. Serve with a little of the custard poured over, to which has been added a tablespoonful of brandy. *Time.*—1 hour. *Average cost,* exclusive of the pudding, 6*d.* *Sufficient* for 5 or 6 persons. *Seasonable* at any time.

PUDDING, Nesselrode (a fashionable Iced Pudding—Carême's Recipe).

Ingredients. — 40 chestnuts, 1 lb. of sugar, flavouring of vanilla, 1 pint of cream, the yolks of 12 eggs, 1 glass of Maraschino, 1 oz. of candied citron, 2 oz. of currants, 2 oz. of stoned raisins, ½ pint of whipped cream, 3 eggs. *Mode.*—Blanch the chestnuts in the boiling water, remove the husks, and pound them in a mortar until perfectly smooth, adding a few spoonfuls of syrup. Then rub them through a fine sieve, and mix them in a basin with a pint of syrup made from 1 lb. of sugar, clarified, and flavoured with vanilla, 1 pint of cream, and the yolks of 12 eggs. Set this mixture over a slow fire, stirring it *without ceasing,* and just as it begins to boil, take it off and pass it through a tammy. When it is cold, put it into a freezing-pot, adding the Maraschino, and make the mixture set; then add the sliced citron, the currants, and stoned raisins (these two latter should be soaked the day previously in Maraschino and sugar pounded with vanilla); the whole thus mingled, add a plateful of whipped cream mixed with the whites of 3 eggs, beaten to a froth with a little syrup. When the pudding is perfectly frozen, put it into a pine-apple-shaped mould; close the lid, place it again in the freezing-pan, covered over with pounded ice and saltpetre, and let it remain until required for table; then turn the pudding out, and serve. *Time.*—½ hour to freeze the mixture. *Seasonable* from October to February.

PUDDING, Paradise.

Ingredients.—3 eggs, 3 apples, ¼ lb. of bread-crumbs, 3 oz. of sugar, 3 oz. of currants, salt and grated nutmeg to taste, the rind of ½ lemon, ½ wineglassful of brandy. *Mode.*—Pare, core, and mince the apples into small pieces, and mix them with the other dry ingredients; beat up the eggs, moisten the mixture with these, and beat it well; stir in the brandy, and put the pudding into a buttered mould; tie it down with a cloth, boil for 1½ hour, and serve with sweet sauce. *Time.*—1½ hour. *Average cost,* 1*s.* *Sufficient* for 4 or 5 persons.

PUDDING, Peas.

Ingredients.—1½ pint of split peas, 2 oz. of butter, 2 eggs, pepper and salt to taste. *Mode.*—Put the peas to soak over night, in rain-water, and float off any that are worm-eaten or discoloured. Tie them loosely in a clean cloth, leaving a little room for them to swell, and put them on to boil in cold rain-water, allowing 2½ hours after the water has simmered up. When the peas are tender, take them up and drain; rub them through a colander with a wooden spoon; add the butter, eggs, pepper, and salt; beat all well together for a few minutes, until the ingredients are well incorporated; then tie them tightly in a floured cloth; boil the pudding for another hour, turn it on to the dish, and serve very hot. This pudding should always be sent to table with boiled leg of pork, and is an exceedingly nice accompaniment to boiled beef. *Time.*—2½ hours to boil the peas, tied loosely in the cloth; 1 hour for the pudding. *Average cost*, 6*d.* *Sufficient* for 7 or 8 persons. *Seasonable* from September to March.

PUDDING, Quickly-Made.

Ingredients.—¼ lb. of butter, ¼ lb. of sifted sugar, ¼ lb. of flour, 1 pint of milk, 5 eggs, a little grated lemon-rind. *Mode.*—Make the milk hot; stir in the butter, and let it cool before the other ingredients are added to it; then stir in the sugar, flour, and eggs, which should be well whisked, and omit the whites of 2; flavour with a little grated lemon-rind, and beat the mixture well. Butter some small cups, rather more than half fill them; bake from 20 minutes to ½ hour, according to the size of the puddings, and serve with fruit, custard or wine-sauce, a little of which may be poured over them. *Time.*—20 minutes to ½ hour. *Average cost*, 1*s.* 2*d.* *Sufficient* for 6 puddings. *Seasonable* at any time.

PUDDING, Somersetshire.

Ingredients.—3 eggs, their weight in flour, pounded sugar and butter, flavouring of grated lemon-rind, bitter almonds, or essence of vanilla. *Mode.*—Carefully weigh the various ingredients, by placing on one side of the scales the eggs, and on the other the flour; then the sugar, and then the butter. Warm the butter, and with the hands beat it to a cream; gradually dredge in the flour and pounded sugar, and keep stirring and beating the mixture without ceasing until it is perfectly smooth. Then add the eggs, which should be well whisked, and either of the above flavourings that may be preferred; butter some small cups, rather more than half fill them, and bake in a brisk oven for about ½ hour. Turn them out, dish them on a napkin, and serve custard or wine-sauce with them. A pretty little supper-dish may be made of these puddings cold, by cutting out a portion of the inside with the point of a knife, and putting into the cavity a little whipped cream or delicate preserve, such as apricot, greengage, or very bright marmalade. The paste for these puddings requires a great deal of mixing, as the more it is beaten, the better will the puddings be. When served cold, they are usually called *gâteaux à la Madeleine*. *Time.*—½ hour. *Average cost*, 10*d.* *Sufficient* for 6 or 7 puddings. *Seasonable* at any time.

PUDDING, Vicarage.

Ingredients.—¼ lb. of flour, ¼ lb. of chopped suet, ¼ lb. of currants, ¼ lb. of raisins, 1 tablespoonful of moist sugar, ½ teaspoonful of ground ginger, ½ saltspoonful of salt. *Mode.*—Put all the ingredients into a basin, having previously stoned the raisins, and washed, picked, and dried the currants; mix well with a clean knife; dip the pudding-cloth into boiling water, wring it out, and put in the mixture. Have ready a saucepan of boiling water, plunge in the pudding, and boil for 3 hours. Turn it out on the dish, and serve with sifted sugar. *Time.*—3 hours. *Average cost*, 8*d.* *Sufficient* for 5 or 6 persons. *Seasonable.*—Suitable for a winter pudding.

PUDDING, West-Indian.

Ingredients.—1 pint of cream, ½ lb. of loaf-sugar, ½ lb. of Savoy or sponge-cakes, 8 eggs, 3 oz. of preserved green ginger. *Mode.*—Crumble down the cakes, put them into a basin, and pour over them the cream, which should be previously sweetened and brought to the boiling-point; cover the basin, well beat the eggs, and when the cream is soaked up, stir them in. Butter a mould, arrange the ginger round it, pour in the pudding carefully, and tie it down with a cloth; steam or boil it slowly for 1½ hour, and serve with the syrup from the ginger, which should be warmed, and poured over the pudding. *Time.*—1½ hour. *Average cost*, with cream at 1*s.* per pint, 2*s.* 8*d.* *Sufficient* for 5 or 6 persons. *Seasonable* at any time.

PUDDING, Yorkshire, to serve with hot Roast Beef.

Ingredients.—1½ pint of milk, 6 *large* tablespoonfuls of flour, 3 eggs, 1 saltspoonful of salt. *Mode.*—Put the flour into a basin with the salt, and stir gradually to this enough milk to make it into a stiff batter. When this is perfectly smooth, and all the lumps are well

YORKSHIRE PUDDING.

rubbed down, add the remainder of the milk and the eggs, which should be well beaten. Beat the mixture for a few minutes, and pour it into a shallow tin, which has been previously well rubbed with beef dripping. Put the pudding into the oven, and bake it for an hour; then, for another ½ hour, place it under the meat, to catch a little of the gravy that flows from it. Cut the pudding into small square pieces, put them on a hot dish, and serve. If the meat is baked, the pudding may at once be placed under it, resting the meat on a small three-cornered stand. *Time.*—1½ hour. *Average cost,* 7*d.* *Sufficient* for 5 or 6 persons. *Seasonable* at any time.

PUFF-PASTE RINGS, or Puits d'Amour.

Ingredients.—Puff-paste (*see* Paste), the white of an egg, sifted loaf sugar. *Mode.* —Make some good puff-paste by recipe; roll it out to the thickness of about ¼ inch, and, with a round fluted paste-cutter, stamp out as many pieces as may be required; then work the paste up again, and roll it out to the same thickness, and with a *smaller* cutter, stamp out sufficient pieces to correspond with the larger ones. Again stamp out the centre of these smaller rings; brush over the others with the white of an egg, place a small ring on the top of every large circular piece of paste, egg over the tops, and bake from 15 to 20 minutes. Sift over sugar, put them back in the oven to colour them; then fill the rings with preserve of any bright colour. Dish them high on a napkin, and serve. So many pretty dishes of pastry may be made by stamping puff-paste out with fancy cutters, and filling the pieces, when baked, with jelly or preserve, that our space will not allow us to give a separate recipe for each of them; but as they are all made from one paste, and only the shape and garnishing varied, perhaps it is not necessary, and by exercising a little ingenuity, variety may always be obtained. Half-moons, leaves, diamonds, stars, shamrocks, rings, &c., are the most appropriate shapes for fancy pastry. *Time.*—15 to 25 minutes. *Average cost,* with ½ lb. of paste, 1*s.* *Sufficient* for 2 dishes of pastry. *Seasonable* at any time.

PUMPKIN, Preserved.

Ingredients.—To each lb. of pumpkin allow 1 lb. of roughly pounded loaf sugar, 1 gill of lemon-juice. *Mode.*—Obtain a good sweet pumpkin; halve it, take out the seeds, and pare off the rind; cut it into neat slices, or into pieces about the size of a five-shilling piece. Weigh the pumpkin, put the slices in a pan or deep dish in layers, with the sugar sprinkled between them; pour the lemon-juice over the top, and let the whole remain for 2 or 3 days. Boil altogether, adding ½ pint of water to every 3 lbs. of sugar used, until the pumpkin becomes tender; then turn the whole into a pan, where let it remain for a week; then drain off the syrup, boil it until it is quite thick; skim, and pour it, boiling, over the pumpkin. A little bruised ginger and lemon-rind, thinly pared, may be boiled in the syrup to flavour the pumpkin. *Time.*—From ½ to ¾ hour to boil the pumpkin tender. *Average cost,* 5*d.* to 7*d.* per lb. pot. *Seasonable* in September and October; but better when made in the latter month, as the pumpkin is then quite ripe.

Note.—Vegetable marrows are very good prepared in the same manner, but are not quite so rich.

PUNCH, to make Hot.

Ingredients.—½ pint of rum, ½ pint of brandy, ¼ lb. of sugar, 1 large lemon, ½ teaspoonful of nutmeg, 1 pint of boiling water. *Mode.*—Rub the sugar over the lemon until it has absorbed all the yellow part of the skin, then put the sugar into a punchbowl; add the lemon-juice (free from pips), and mix these two ingredients well together. Pour over them the boiling water, stir well together, add the rum, brandy, and nutmeg; mix thoroughly, and the punch will be ready to serve. It is very important in making good punch that all the ingredients are thoroughly incorporated; and to insure success, the processes of mixing must be diligently attended to. *Sufficient.*—Allow a quart for 4 persons; but this information must be taken *cum grano salis;* for the capacities of persons for this kind of beverage are generally supposed to vary considerably.

QUAILS, to Dress.

Ingredients. — Quails, butter, toast. *Mode.*—These birds keep good several days, and should be roasted without drawing. Truss them in the same manner as woodcocks; roast them before a clear fire, keep them well basted, and serve on toast. *Time.*—About 20 minutes. *Average cost.*—Seldom bought. *Sufficient,* 2 for a dish. *Seasonable* from October to December.

QUAILS.

Quails, being trussed and served like Woodcock, may be similarly carved.

QUINCE JELLY.

Ingredients.—To every pint of juice allow 1 lb. of loaf sugar. *Mode.*—Pare and slice the quinces, and put them into a preserving-pan with sufficient water to float them. Boil them until tender, and the fruit is reduced to a pulp; strain off the clear juice, and to each pint allow the above proportion of loaf sugar. Boil the juice and sugar together for about ¾ hour; remove all the scum as it rises, and if the jelly appears firm when a little is poured on a plate, it is done. The residue left on the sieve will answer to make a common marmalade, for immediate use, by boiling it with ½ lb. of common sugar to every lb. of pulp. *Time.*—3 hours to boil the quinces in water; ¾ hour to boil the jelly. *Average cost,* from 8*d.* to 10*d.* per lb. pot. *Seasonable* from August to October.

QUINCE MARMALADE.

Ingredients.—To every lb. of quince pulp allow ¾ lb. of loaf sugar. *Mode.*—Slice the quinces into a preserving-pan, adding sufficient water for them to float; place them on the fire to stew, until reduced to a pulp, keeping them stirred occasionally from the bottom, to prevent their burning; then pass the pulp through a hair sieve, to keep back the skin and seeds. Weigh the pulp, and to each lb. add lump sugar in the above proportion, broken very small. Place the whole on the fire, and keep it well stirred from the bottom of the pan with a wooden spoon, until reduced to a marmalade, which may be known by dropping a little on a cold plate, when, if it jellies, it is done. Put it into jars whilst hot; let it cool, and cover with pieces of oiled paper cut to the size of the mouths of the jars. The tops of them may be afterwards covered with pieces of bladder, or tissue-paper brushed over on both sides with the white of an egg. *Time.*—3 hours to boil the quinces without the sugar; ¾ hour to boil the pulp with the sugar. *Average cost,* from 8*d.* to 9*d.* per lb. pot. *Sufficient.*—Allow 1 pint of sliced quinces for a lb. pot. *Seasonable* in August, September, and October.

RABBIT, Boiled.

Ingredients.—Rabbit; water. *Mode.*—For boiling, choose rabbits with smooth and sharp claws, as that denotes they are young: should these be blunt and rugged, the ears dry and tough, the animal is old. After emptying and skinning it, wash it well in cold water, and let it soak for about ¼ hour in warm

BOILED RABBIT.

water, to draw out the blood. Bring the head round to the side, and fasten it there by means of a skewer run through that and the body. Put the rabbit into sufficient hot water to cover it, let it boil very gently until tender, which will be in from ½ to ¾ hour, according to its size and age. Dish it, and smother it either with onion, mushroom, or liver-sauce, or parsley-and-butter; the former is, however, generally preferred to any of the last-named sauces. When liver-sauce is preferred, the liver should be boiled for a few minutes, and minced very finely, or rubbed through a sieve before it is added to the sauce. *Time.*—A very young rabbit, ½ hour; a large one, ¾ hour; an old one, 1 hour or longer. *Average cost,* from 1*s.* to 1*s.* 6*d.* each. *Sufficient* for 4 persons. *Seasonable* from September to February.

RABBIT, Curried.

Ingredients.—1 rabbit, 2 oz. of butter, 3 onions, 1 pint of stock, 1 tablespoonful of curry powder, 1 tablespoonful of flour, 1 tablespoonful of mushroom powder, the juice of ½ lemon, ½ lb. of rice. *Mode.*—Empty, skin, and wash the rabbit thoroughly, and cut it neatly into joints. Put it into a stewpan with the butter and sliced onions, and let them acquire a nice brown colour, but do not allow them to blacken. Pour in the stock, which should be boiling; mix the curry powder and flour smoothly with a little water, add it to the stock, with the mushroom powder, and simmer gently for rather more than ½ hour; squeeze in the lemon-juice, and serve in the centre of a dish, with an edging of boiled rice all round. Where economy is studied, water may be substituted for the stock; in this case, the meat and onions must be very nicely browned. A little sour apple and rasped cocoa-nut stewed with the curry will be found a great improvement. *Time.*—Altogether ¾ hour. *Average cost,* from 1*s.* to 1*s.* 6*d.* each. *Sufficient* for 4 persons. *Seasonable* in winter.

RABBIT, Fried.

Ingredients.—1 rabbit, flour, dripping, 1 oz. of butter, 1 teaspoonful of minced shalot, 2 tablespoonfuls of mushroom ketchup. *Mode.*—Cut the rabbit into neat joints, and flour them well; make the dripping boil in a fryingpan, put in the rabbit, and fry it a nice brown. Have ready a very hot dish, put in the butter, shalot, and ketchup; arrange the rabbit pyramidically on this, and serve as quickly as possible. *Time.*—10 minutes. *Average cost,* from 1*s.* to 1*s.* 6*d.* each. *Sufficient* for 4 or 5 persons. *Seasonable* from September to February.

Note.—The rabbit may be brushed over with egg, and sprinkled with bread-crumbs, and fried as above. When cooked in this manner, make a gravy in the pan, and pour it round, but not over the pieces of rabbit.

RABBIT, à la Minute.

Ingredients.—1 rabbit, ¼ lb. of butter, salt and pepper to taste, 2 blades of pounded mace, 3 dried mushrooms, 2 tablespoonfuls of minced parsley, 2 teaspoonfuls of flour, 2 glasses of sherry, 1 pint of water. *Mode.*—Empty, skin, and wash the rabbit thoroughly, and cut it into joints. Put the butter into a stewpan with the pieces of rabbit; add salt, pepper, and pounded mace, and let it cook until three parts done; then put in the remaining ingredients, and boil for about 10 minutes; it will then be ready to serve. Fowls or hare may be dressed in the same manner. *Time.*—Altogether, 35 minutes. *Average cost,* from 1*s.* to 1*s.* 6*d.* each. *Sufficient* for 4 or 5 persons. *Seasonable* from September to February.

RABBIT PIE.

Ingredients.—1 rabbit, a few slices of ham, salt and white pepper to taste, 2 blades of pounded mace, ½ teaspoonful of grated nutmeg, a few forcemeat balls, 3 hard-boiled eggs, ½ pint of gravy, puff crust. *Mode.*—Cut up the rabbit (which should be young), remove the breast-bone, and bone the legs. Put the rabbit, slices of ham, forcemeat balls, and hard eggs, by turns, in layers, and season each layer with pepper, salt, pounded mace, and grated nutmeg. Pour in about ½ pint of water, cover with crust, and bake in a well-heated oven for about 1½ hour. Should the crust acquire too much colour, place a piece of paper over it to prevent it from burning. When done, pour in at the top, by means of the hole in the middle of the crust, a little good gravy, which may be made of the breast- and leg-bones of the rabbit, and 2 or 3 shank-bones, flavoured with onion, herbs, and spices. *Time.*—1½ hour. *Average cost,* from 1*s.* to 1*s.* 6*d.* each. *Sufficient* for 4 or 5 persons. *Seasonable* from September to February.

Note.—The liver of the rabbit may be boiled, minced, and mixed with the forcemeat balls, when the flavour is liked.

RABBIT OR HARE, Ragoût of.

Ingredients.—1 rabbit, 3 teaspoonfuls of flour, 3 sliced onions, 2 oz. of butter, a few thin slices of bacon, pepper and salt to taste, 2 slices of lemon, 1 bay-leaf,

1 glass of port wine. *Mode.*—Slice the onions, and put them into a stewpan with the flour and butter; place the pan near the fire, stir well as the butter melts, till the onions become a rich brown colour, and add, by degrees, a little water or gravy till the mixture is of the consistency of cream. Cut some thin slices of bacon; lay in these with the rabbit, cut into neat joints; add a seasoning of pepper and salt, the lemon and bay-leaf, and let the whole simmer until tender. Pour in the port wine, give one boil, and serve. *Time.*—About ½ hour to simmer the rabbit. *Average cost*, from 1*s*. to 1*s*. 6*d*. each. *Sufficient* for 4 or 5 persons. *Seasonable* from September to February.

RABBIT, Roast or Baked.

Ingredients. — 1 rabbit, forcemeat, buttered paper, sausage-meat. *Mode.*—Empty, skin, and thoroughly wash the rabbit; wipe it dry, line the inside with sausage-meat and forcemeat, and to which has been added the minced liver. Sew the stuffing inside, skewer back the head between the shoulders, cut off the fore-joints of the shoulders and legs, bring them close to the body, and secure them by means of a skewer. Wrap the rabbit in buttered paper, and put it

ROAST RABBIT.

down to a bright clear fire; keep it well basted and a few minutes before it is done remove the paper, flour and froth it, and let it acquire a nice brown colour. Take out the skewers, and serve with brown gravy and red-currant jelly. To bake the rabbit, proceed in the same manner as above; in a good oven, it will take about the same time as roasting. *Time.*—A young rabbit, 35 minutes; a large one about ¾ hour. *Average cost*, from 1*s*. to 1*s*. 6*d*. each. *Sufficient* for 4 persons. *Seasonable* from September to February.

RABBIT SOUP.

Ingredients.—2 large rabbits, or 3 small ones; a faggot of savoury herbs, ½ head of celery, 2 carrots, 1 onion, 1 blade of mace, salt and white pepper to taste, a little pounded mace, ½ pint of cream, the yolks of 2 eggs boiled hard, the crumb of a French roll, nearly 3 quarts of water. *Mode.*—Make the soup with the legs and shoulders of the rabbit, and keep the nice pieces for a dish or *entrée*. Put them into warm water, and draw the blood; when quite clean, put them into a stewpan, with a faggot of herbs, and a teacupful, or rather more, of veal stock or water. Simmer slowly till done through, add the three quarts of water, and boil for an hour. Take out the rabbit, pick the meat from the bones, covering it up to keep it white; put the bones back in the liquor, add the vegetables, and simmer for two hours; skim and strain, and let it cool. Now pound the meat in a mortar, with the yolks of the eggs, and the crumb of the roll previously soaked; rub it through a tammy, and gradually add it to the strained liquor, and simmer for 15 minutes. Mix arrowroot or rice-flour with the cream (say 2 dessert-spoonfuls), and stir in the soup; bring it to a boil, and serve. This soup must be very white, and instead of thickening it with arrowroot or rice-flour, vermicelli or pearl barley can be boiled in a little stock, and put in five minutes before serving. *Time.*—Nearly 4 hours. *Average cost*, 1*s*. per quart. *Seasonable* from September to March. *Sufficient* for 10 persons.

RABBIT, Stewed.

Ingredients.—1 rabbit, 2 large onions, 6 cloves, 1 small teaspoonful of chopped lemon-peel, a few forcemeat balls, thickening of butter and flour, 1 large tablespoonful of mushroom ketchup. *Mode.*—Cut the rabbit into small joints; put them into a stewpan, add the onions sliced, the cloves, and minced lemon-peel. Pour in sufficient water to cover the meat, and, when the rabbit is nearly done, drop in a few forcemeat balls, to which has been added the liver, finely chopped. Thicken the gravy with flour and butter, put in the ketchup, give one boil, and serve. *Time.*—Rather more than ½ hour. *Average cost*, 1*s*. to 1*s*. 6*d*. each. *Sufficient* for 4 or 5 persons. *Seasonable* from September to February.

RABBIT STEWED, Larded.

Ingredients.—1 rabbit, a few strips of bacon, rather more than 1 pint of good broth or stock, a bunch of savoury herbs, salt and pepper to taste, thickening of butter and flour, 1 glass of sherry. *Mode.*—Well wash the rabbit, cut it into quarters, lard them with slips of bacon, and fry them; then put them into a stewpan with the broth, herbs, and a seasoning of pepper and salt; simmer gently until the rabbit is tender, then strain the gravy, thicken it with butter and flour, add the sherry, let it boil, pour it over the rabbit, and serve. Garnish with slices of cut lemon. *Time.*—Rather more than ½ hour. *Average cost,* 1*s.* to 1*s.* 6*d.* each. *Sufficient* for 4 or 5 persons. *Seasonable* from September to February.

RABBITS, Stewed in Milk.

Ingredients.—2 very young rabbits, not nearly half grown; 1½ pint of milk, 1 blade of mace, 1 dessertspoonful of flour, a little salt and cayenne. *Mode.*—Mix the flour very smoothly with 4 tablespoonfuls of the milk, and when this is well mixed, add the remainder. Cut up the rabbits into joints, put them into a stewpan, with the milk and other ingredients, and simmer them *very gently* until quite tender. Stir the contents from time to time, to keep the milk smooth and prevent it from burning. ½ hour will be sufficient for the cooking of this dish. *Time.*—½ hour. *Average cost,* from 1*s.* to 1*s.* 6*d.* each. *Sufficient* for 5 or 6 persons. *Seasonable* from September to February.

RABBITS, to carve.

In carving a boiled rabbit, let the knife be drawn on each side of the backbone, the whole length of the rabbit, as shown by the dotted line 3 to 4: thus the rabbit will be in three parts. Now

BOILED RABBIT.

let the back be divided into two equal parts in the direction of the line from 1 to 2; then let the leg be taken off, as shown by the line 5 to 6, and the shoulder, as shown by the line 7 to 8. This, in our opinion, is the best plan to carve a rabbit, although there are other modes which are preferred by some.

A roast rabbit is rather differently trussed from one that is meant to be boiled; but the carving is nearly similar,

ROAST RABBIT.

as will be seen by the cut. The back should be divided into as many pieces as it will give, and the legs and shoulders can then be disengaged in the same manner as those of the boiled animal.

RAISED PIE, of Poultry or Game.

Ingredients.—To every lb. of flour allow ½ lb of butter, ½ pint of water, the yolks of 2 eggs, ½ teaspoonful of salt (these are for the crust); 1 large fowl or pheasant, a few slices of veal cutlet, a few slices of dressed ham, forcemeat, seasoning of nutmeg, allspice, pepper and salt, gravy. *Mode.*—Make a stiff short crust with the above proportion of butter, flour, water, and eggs, and work it up very smoothly; butter a raised-pie mould, and line it with paste. Previously to making the crust, bone the fowl, or whatever bird is intended to be used, lay it, breast downwards, upon a cloth, and season the inside well with pounded mace, allspice, pepper, and salt; then spread over it a layer of forcemeat, then a layer of seasoned veal, and then one of ham, and then another layer of forcemeat, and roll the fowl over, making the skin meet at the back. Line the pie with forcemeat, put in the fowl, and fill up the cavities with slices of seasoned veal, and ham, and forcemeat; wet the edges of the pie, put on the cover, pinch the edges together with the paste-pincers, and decorate it with leaves; brush it over with beaten yolk of egg, and bake in a moderate oven for 4 hours. In the mean time, make a good strong gravy from the bones, pour it through a funnel into the hole at the top; cover this hole with a small leaf, and the pie, when cold, will be ready for use. Let it be remembered that the gravy must be considerably reduced before it is poured into the pie, as, when cold, it should form a firm jelly, and not be the least degree in a liquid state. This recipe is suitable for all kinds of poultry or game, using one or more birds, according to the size of the pie intended to be made;

but the birds must always be boned. Truffles, mushrooms, &c., added to this pie, make it much nicer; and, to enrich it, lard the fleshy parts of the poultry or game with thin strips of bacon. This method of forming raised pies in a mould is generally called a *timbale*, and has the advantage of being more easily made than one where the paste is raised by the hands; the crust, besides, being eatable. *Time.*—Large pie, 4 hours. *Average cost*, 6*s.* 6*d.* *Seasonable*, with poultry, all the year; with game, from September to March.

RAISED PIE, of Veal and Ham.

Ingredients.—3 or 4 lbs. of veal cutlets, a few slices of bacon or ham, seasoning of pepper, salt, nutmeg, and allspice, forcemeat, 2 lbs. of hot-water paste, ½ pint of good strong gravy. *Mode.*—To raise the crust for a pie with the hands is a very difficult task, and can only be accomplished by skilled and experienced cooks. The process should be seen to be satisfactorily learnt, and plenty of practice given to the making of raised pies, as by that means only will success be insured. Make a hot-water paste by

RAISED PIE.

recipe, and from the mass raise the pie with the hands; if this cannot be accomplished, cut out pieces for the top and bottom, and a long piece for the sides; fasten the bottom and side-piece together by means of egg, and pinch the edges well together; then line the pie with forcemeat, put in a layer of veal, and a plentiful seasoning of salt, pepper, nutmeg, and allspice; for, let it be remembered, these pies taste very insipid unless highly seasoned. Over the seasoning place a layer of sliced bacon or cooked ham, and then a layer of forcemeat, veal seasoning, and bacon, and so on until the meat rises to about an inch above the paste; taking care to finish with a layer of forcemeat, to fill all the cavities of the pie, and to lay in the meat firmly and compactly. Brush the top edge of the pie with beaten egg, put on the cover, press the edges, and pinch them round with paste-pincers. Make a hole in the middle of the lid, and ornament the pie with leaves, which should be stuck on with the white of an egg; then brush it all over with the beaten yolk of an egg, and bake the pie in an oven with a soaking heat from 3 to 4 hours. To ascertain when it is done, run a sharp-pointed knife or skewer through the hole at the top into the middle of the pie, and if the meat feels tender, it is sufficiently baked. Have ready about ½ pint of very strong gravy, pour it through a funnel into the hole at the top, stop up the hole with a small leaf of baked paste, and put the pie away until wanted for use. Should it acquire too much colour in the baking, cover it with white paper, as the crust should not in the least degree be burnt. Mushrooms, truffles, and many other ingredients, may be added to enrich the flavour of these pies, and the very fleshy parts of the meat may be larded. These pies are more frequently served cold than hot, and form excellent dishes for cold suppers or breakfasts. The cover of the pie is sometimes carefully removed, leaving the perfect edges, and the top decorated with square pieces of very bright aspic jelly: this has an exceedingly pretty effect. *Time.*—About 4 hours. *Average cost*, 6*s.* 6*d.* *Sufficient* for a very large pie. *Seasonable* from March to October.

RAISIN CHEESE.

Ingredients.—To every lb. of raisins, allow ½ lb. of loaf sugar; pounded cinnamon and cloves to taste. *Mode.*—Stone the raisins; put them into a stewpan with the sugar, cinnamon, and cloves, and let them boil for 1½ hour, stirring all the time. Let the preparation cool a little, pour it into a glass dish, and garnish with strips of candid lemon-peel and citron. This will remain good some time, if kept in a dry place. *Time.*—1½ hour. *Average cost*, 9*d.* *Sufficient.*—1 lb. for 4 or 5 persons. *Seasonable* at any time.

RAISIN PUDDING, Boiled. (Plain and Economical).

Ingredients.—1 lb. of flour, ½ lb. of stoned raisins, ½ lb. of chopped suet, ½ saltspoonful of salt, milk. *Mode.*—After having stoned the raisins and chopped the suet finely, mix them with the flour, add the salt, and when these dry ingredients are thoroughly mixed, moisten the pudding with sufficient milk to make it into a rather stiff paste. Tie it up in a floured cloth, put it into boiling water, and boil for 4 hours: serve with sifted sugar. This pudding may also be made in a long shape, the same as a rolled jam-pudding, and will not require quite so long boiling;—2½ hours would then be quite sufficient. *Time.*—Made round, 4 hours; in a long shape, 2½ hours. *Average cost, 9d. Sufficient* for 8 or 9 persons. *Seasonable* in winter.

RAISIN PUDDING, Baked. (Plain and Economical.)

Ingredients.—1 lb. of flour, ¾ lb. of stoned raisins, ½ lb. of suet, a pinch of salt, 1 oz. of sugar, a little grated nutmeg, milk. *Mode.*—Chop the suet finely; stone the raisins and cut them in halves; mix these with the suet, add the salt, sugar, and grated nutmeg, and moisten the whole with sufficient milk to make it of the consistency of thick batter. Put the pudding into a pie-dish, and bake for 1½ hour, or rather longer. Turn it out of the dish, strew sifted sugar over, and serve. This is a very plain recipe, and suitable where there is a family of children. It, of course, can be much improved by the addition of candied peel, currants, and rather a larger proportion of suet: a few eggs would also make the pudding richer. *Time.*—1½ hour. *Average cost, 9d. Sufficient* for 7 or 8 persons. *Seasonable* in winter.

RAMAKINS, to serve with the Cheese Course.

Ingredients.—¼ lb. of Cheshire cheese, ¼ lb. of Parmesan cheese, ¼ lb. of fresh butter, 4 eggs, the crumb of a small roll; pepper, salt, and pounded mace to taste. *Mode.*—Boil the crumb of the roll in milk for 5 minutes; strain, and put it into a mortar; add the cheese, which should be finely scraped, the butter, the yolks of the eggs, and seasoning, and pound these ingredients well together. Whisk the whites of the eggs, mix them with the paste, and put it into small pans or saucers, which should not be more than half filled. Bake them from 10 to 12 minutes, and serve them very hot and very quickly. This batter answers equally well for macaroni after it is boiled tender. *Time.*—10 or 12 minutes. *Average cost, 1s. 4d. Sufficient* for 7 or 8 persons. *Seasonable* at any time.

RAMAKINS PASTRY, to serve with the Cheese Course.

Ingredients.—Any pieces of very good light puff-paste, Cheshire, Parmesan, or Stilton cheese. *Mode.*—The remains or odd pieces of paste left from large tarts, &c., answer for making these little dishes. Gather up the pieces of paste, roll it out evenly, and sprinkle it with grated cheese of a nice flavour. Fold the paste in three, roll it out again, and sprinkle more cheese over; fold the paste, roll it out, and with a paste-cutter shape it in any way that may be desired. Bake the ramakins in a brisk oven from 10 to 15 minutes, dish them on a hot napkin, and serve quickly. The appearance of this dish may be very much improved by brushing the ramakins over with the yolk of egg before they are placed in the oven. Where expense is not objected to, Parmesan is the best kind of cheese to use for making this dish. *Time.*—10 to 15 minutes. *Average cost,* with ½ lb. of paste, 10*d. Sufficient* for 6 or 7 persons. *Seasonable* at any time.

RASPBERRY CREAM.

Ingredients.—¾ pint of milk, ¾ pint of cream, 1½ oz. of isinglass, raspberry jelly, sugar to taste, 2 tablespoonfuls of brandy. *Mode.*—Boil the milk, cream, and isinglass together for ¼ hour, or until the latter is melted, and strain it through a hair sieve into a basin. Let it cool a little; then add to it sufficient

RASPBERRY-CREAM MOULD.

raspberry jelly, which, when melted, would make ⅓ pint, and stir well till the ingredients are thoroughly mixed. If not sufficiently sweet, add a little pounded sugar with the brandy; whisk the mixture well until nearly cold, put it into a well-oiled mould, and set it in a cool place till perfectly set. Raspberry jam may be substituted for the jelly; but must be melted, and rubbed through a sieve, to free it from seeds: in summer, the juice of the fresh fruit may be used, by slightly mashing it with a wooden spoon, and sprinkling sugar over it; the juice that flows from the fruit should then be used for mixing with the cream. If the colour should not be very good, a few drops of prepared cochineal may be added to improve its appearance. *Time.*—¼ hour to boil the cream and isinglass. *Average cost,* with cream at 1*s.* per pint, and the best isinglass, 3*s.* *Sufficient* to fill a quart mould with fresh fruit in July. *Seasonable,* with jelly, at any time.

Note.—Strawberry cream may be made in precisely the same manner, substituting strawberry jam or jelly for the raspberry.

RASPBERRY JAM.

Ingredients.—To every lb. of raspberries allow 1 lb. of sugar, ¼ pint of red-currant juice. *Mode.*—Let the fruit for this preserve be gathered in fine weather, and used as soon after it is picked as possible. Take off the stalks, put the raspberries into a preserving-pan, break them well with a wooden spoon, and let them boil for ¼ hour, keeping them well stirred. Then add the currant-juice and sugar, and boil again for ½ hour. Skim the jam well after the sugar is added, or the preserve will not be clear. The addition of the currant-juice is a very great improvement to this preserve, as it gives it a piquant taste, which the flavour of the raspberries seems to require. *Time.*—¼ hour to simmer the fruit without the sugar; ½ hour after it is added. *Average cost,* from 6*d.* to 8*d.* per lb. pot. *Sufficient.*—Allow about 1 pint of fruit to fill a 1 lb. pot. *Seasonable* in July and August.

RASPBERRY JELLY.

Ingredients.—To each pint of juice allow ¾ lb. of loaf sugar. *Mode.*—Let the raspberries be freshly gathered, quite ripe, and picked from the stalks; put them into a large jar, after breaking the fruit a little with a wooden spoon, and place this jar, covered, in a saucepan of boiling water. When the juice is well drawn, which will be in from ¾ to 1 hour, strain the fruit through a fine hair sieve or cloth; measure the juice, and to every pint allow the above proportion of loaf sugar. Put the juice and sugar into a preserving-pan, place it over the fire, and boil gently until the jelly thickens when a little is poured on a plate; carefully remove all the scum as it rises, pour the jelly into small pots, cover down, and keep in a dry place. This jelly answers for making raspberry cream, and for flavouring various sweet dishes, when, in winter, the fresh fruit is not obtainable. *Time.*—¾ to 1 hour to draw the juice. *Average cost,* from 9*d.* to 1*s.* per lb. pot. *Sufficient.*—From 3 pints to 2 quarts of fruit should yield 1 pint of juice. *Seasonable.*—This should be made in July or August.

RASPBERRY VINEGAR.

Ingredients.—To every 3 pints of the best vinegar allow 4½ pints of freshly-gathered raspberries; to each pint of liquor allow 1 lb. of pounded loaf sugar, 1 wineglassful of brandy. *Mode.*—Let the raspberries be freshly gathered, pick them from the stalks, and put 1½ pint of them into a stone jar; pour 3 pints of the best vinegar over them, and let them remain for 24 hours; then strain the liquor over another 1½ pint of fresh raspberries. Let them remain another 24 hours, and the following day repeat the process for the third time; then drain off the liquor without pressing, and pass it through a jelly-bag (previously wetted with plain vinegar) into a stone jar. Add to every pint of the liquor 1 lb. of pounded loaf sugar; stir them together, and, when the sugar is dissolved, cover the jar, set it upon the fire in a saucepan of boiling water, and let it boil for an hour, removing the scum as fast as it rises; add to each pint a glass of brandy, bottle it, and seal the corks. This is an excellent drink in cases of fevers and colds: it should be diluted with cold water, according to the taste or requirement of the patient. *Time.*—To be boiled 1 hour. *Average cost,* 1*s.* per pint. *Sufficient* to make 2 quarts. *Seasonable.*—Make this in July or August, when raspberries are most plentiful.

RATAFIAS.

Ingredients.—½ lb. of sweet almonds, ¼ lb. of bitter ones, ¾ lb. of sifted loaf sugar, the white of 4 eggs. *Mode.*—Blanch, skin, and dry the almonds, and pound them in a mortar with the white of an egg; stir in the sugar, and gradually add the remaining whites of eggs, taking care that they are very thoroughly whisked. Drop the mixture, through a small biscuit syringe, on to cartridge-paper, and bake the cakes from 10 to 12 minutes in rather a quick oven. A very small quantity should be dropped on the paper to form one cake, as the mixture spreads; when baked, the ratifias should be about the size of a large button. *Time.*—10 to 12 minutes.—*Average cost,* 1*s.* 8*d.* per lb.

RAVIGOTTE, a French Salad Sauce (Mons. Ude's Recipe).

Ingredients.—1 teaspoonful of mushroom ketchup, 1 teaspoonful of cavice, 1 teaspoonful of Chili vinegar, 1 teaspoonful of Reading sauce, a piece of butter the size of an egg, 3 tablespoonfuls of thick Béchamel, 1 tablespoonful of minced parsley, 3 tablespoonfuls of cream; salt and pepper to taste. *Mode.*—Scald the parsley, mince the leaves very fine, and add to it all the other ingredients; after mixing the whole together thoroughly, the sauce will be ready for use. *Average cost,* for this quantity, 10*d.* *Seasonable* at any time.

REMOULADE, or French Salad-Dressing.

Ingredients.—4 eggs, ½ tablespoonful of made mustard, salt and cayenne to taste, 3 tablespoonfuls of olive-oil, 1 tablespoonful of tarragon or plain vinegar. *Mode.*—Boil 3 eggs quite hard for about ½ hour, put them into cold water, and let them remain in it for a few minutes; strip off the shells, put the yolks in a mortar, and pound them very smoothly; add to them, very gradually, the mustard, seasoning, and vinegar, keeping all well stirred and rubbed down with the back of a wooden spoon. Put in the oil drop by drop, and when this is thoroughly mixed with the other ingredients, add the yolk of a raw egg, and stir well, when it will be ready for use. This sauce should not be curdled; and to prevent this, the only way is to mix a little of everything at a time, and not to cease stirring. The quantities of oil and vinegar may be increased or diminished according to taste, as many persons would prefer a smaller proportion of the former ingredient.

GREEN REMOULADE is made by using tarragon vinegar instead of plain, and colouring with a little parsley-juice. Harvey's sauce, or Chili vinegar, may be added at pleasure. *Time.*—½ hour to boil the eggs. *Average cost,* for this quantity, 7*d.* *Sufficient* for a salad made for 4 or 6 persons.

RHUBARB JAM.

Ingredients.—To every lb. of rhubarb allow 1 lb. of loaf sugar, the rind of ½ lemon. *Mode.*—Wipe the rhubarb perfectly dry, take off the string or peel, and weigh it; put it into a preserving-pan, with sugar in the above proportion; mince the lemon-rind very finely, add it to the other ingredients, and place the preserving-pan by the side of the fire; keep stirring to prevent the rhubarb from burning, and when the sugar is well dissolved, put the pan more over the fire, and let the jam boil until it is done, taking care to keep it well skimmed and stirred with a wooden or silver spoon. Pour it into pots, and cover down with oiled and egged papers. *Time.*—If the rhubarb is young and tender, ¾ hour, reckoning from the time it simmers equally; old rhubarb, 1¼ to 1½ hour. *Average cost,* 5*d.* to 7*d.* per lb. pot. *Sufficient.*—About 1 pint of sliced rhubarb to fill a lb. pot. *Seasonable* from February to May.

RHUBARB AND ORANGE JAM, to resemble Scotch Marmalade.

Ingredients.—1 quart of finely-cut rhubarb, 6 oranges, 1½ lb. of loaf sugar. *Mode.*—Peel the oranges; remove as much of the white pith as possible, divide them, and take out the pips; slice the pulp into a preserving-pan, add the rind of half the oranges cut into thin strips, and the loaf sugar, which should be broken small. Peel the rhubarb, cut it into thin pieces, put it to the oranges, and stir altogether over a gentle fire until the jam is done. Remove all the scum as it rises, put the preserve into pots, and, when cold, cover down. Should the rhubarb be very old, stew it alone for ¼ hour before the other ingredients are added. *Time.*—¾ to 1 hour. *Average cost,* from 6*d.* to 8*d.* per lb. pot. *Seasonable* from February to May.

RHUBARB PUDDING, Boiled.

Ingredients.—4 or 5 sticks of fine rhubarb, ¼ lb. of moist sugar, ¾ lb. of suet-crust. *Mode.*—Make a suet-crust with ¾ lb. of flour, and line a buttered basin with it. Wash and wipe the rhubarb, and, if old, string it—that is so say, pare off the outside skin. Cut it into inch lengths, fill the basin with it, put in the sugar, and cover with crust. Pinch the edges of the pudding together, tie over it a floured cloth, put it into boiling water, and boil from 2 to 2½ hours. Turn it out of the basin, and serve with a jug of cream and sifted sugar. *Time.*—2 to 2½ hours. *Average cost, 7d. Sufficient* for 6 or 7 persons. *Seasonable* from February to May.

RHUBARB TART.

Ingredients.—½ lb. of puff-paste, about 5 sticks of large rhubarb, ¼ lb. of moist sugar. *Mode.*—Make a puff-crust; line the edges of a deep pie-dish with it, and wash, wipe, and cut the rhubarb into pieces about 1 inch long. Should it be old and tough, string it—that is to say, pare off the outside skin. Pile the fruit high in the dish, as it shrinks very much in the cooking; put in the sugar, cover with crust, ornament the edges, and bake the tart in a well-heated oven from ½ to ¾ hour. If wanted very nice, brush it over with the white of an egg beaten to a stiff froth, then sprinkle on it some sifted sugar, and put it in the oven just to set the glaze: this should be done when the tart is nearly baked. A small quantity of lemon-juice, and a little of the peel minced, are by many persons considered an improvement to the flavour of rhubarb tart. *Time.*—½ to ¾ hour. *Average cost, 9d. Sufficient* for 5 persons. *Seasonable* from February to May.

RHUBARB WINE.

Ingredients.—To every 5 lbs. of rhubarb pulp allow 1 gallon of cold spring water; to every gallon of liquor allow 3 lbs. of loaf sugar, ½ oz. of isinglass, the rind of 1 lemon. *Mode.*—Gather the rhubarb about the middle of May; wipe it with a wet cloth, and, with a mallet, bruise it in a large wooden tub or other convenient means. When reduced to a pulp, weigh it, and to every 5 lbs. add 1 gallon of cold spring water; let these remain for 3 days, stirring 3 or 4 times a day; and on the fourth day, press the pulp through a hair sieve; put the liquor into a tub, and to every gallon put 3 lbs. of loaf sugar; stir in the sugar until it is quite dissolved, and add the lemon-rind; let the liquor remain, and, in 4, 5, or 6 days, the fermentation will begin to subside, and a crust or head will be formed, which should be skimmed off, or the liquor drawn from it, when the crust begins to crack or separate. Put the wine into a cask, and if, after that, it ferments, rack it off into another cask, and in a fortnight stop it down. If the wine should have lost any of its original sweetness, add a little more loaf sugar, taking care that the cask is full. Bottle it off in February or March, and in the summer it should be fit to drink. It will improve greatly by keeping; and, should a very brilliant colour be desired, add a little currant-juice. *Seasonable.* Make this about the middle of May.

RICE BISCUITS, or Cakes.

Ingredients.—To every ½ lb. of rice-flour, allow ¼ lb. of pounded lump sugar, ¼ lb. of butter, 2 eggs. *Mode.*—Beat the butter to a cream, stir in the rice-flour and pounded sugar, and moisten the whole with the eggs, which should be previously well beaten. Roll out the paste, shape it with a round paste-cutter into small cakes, and bake them from 12 to 18 minutes in a very slow oven. *Time.*—12 to 18 minutes. *Average cost, 9d. Sufficient* to make about 18 cakes. *Seasonable* at any time.

RICE BLANCMANGE.

Ingredients.—¼ lb. of ground rice, 3 oz. of loaf sugar, 1 oz. of fresh butter, 1 quart of milk, flavouring of lemon-peel, essence of almonds or vanilla, or laurel-leaves. *Mode.*—Mix the rice to a smooth batter with about ½ pint of the milk, and the remainder put into a saucepan, with the sugar, butter, and whichever of the above flavourings may be preferred; bring the milk to the boiling-point, quickly stir in the rice, and let it boil for about 10 minutes, or until it comes easily away from the saucepan, keeping it well stirred the whole time. Grease a mould with pure salad-oil; pour in the rice, and let it get perfectly set, when it should turn out quite easily; garnish it with jam, or pour round a compôte of any kind of fruit, just before it is sent to table. This blancmange is better for being made the day before it is wanted, as it then has time to become firm. If laurel-leaves are used for flavouring, steep 3 of them in the milk, and take them out before the rice is added: about 8 drops of essence of almonds, or from 12 to 16 drops of essence of vanilla, would be required to flavour the above proportion of milk. *Time.*—From 10 to 15 minutes to boil the rice. *Average cost,* 9*d.* *Sufficient* to fill a quart mould. *Seasonable* at any time.

RICE BREAD.

Ingredients.—To every lb. of rice allow 4 lbs. of wheat flour, nearly 3 tablespoonfuls of yeast, ¼ oz. of salt. *Mode.*—Boil the rice in water until it is quite tender; pour off the water, and put the rice, before it is cold, to the flour. Mix these well together with the yeast, salt, and sufficient warm water to make the whole into a smooth dough; let it rise by the side of the fire, then form it into loaves, and bake them from 1½ to 2 hours, according to their size. If the rice is boiled in milk instead of water, it makes very delicious bread or cakes. When boiled in this manner, it may be mixed with the flour without straining the liquid from it. *Time.*—1½ to 2 hours.

RICE, Buttered.

Ingredients.—¼ lb. of rice, 1½ pint of milk, 2 oz. of butter, sugar to taste, grated nutmeg or pounded cinnamon. *Mode.*—Wash and pick the rice, drain, and put it into a saucepan with the milk; let it swell gradually, and, when tender, pour off the milk; stir in the butter, sugar, and nutmeg or cinnamon, and, when the butter is thoroughly melted, and the whole is quite hot, serve. After the milk is poured off, be particular that the rice does not burn: to prevent this, do not cease stirring it. *Time.*—About ¾ hour to swell the rice. *Average cost,* 7*d.* *Sufficient* for 4 or 5 persons. *Seasonable* at any time.

RICE CAKE.

Ingredients.—½ lb. of ground rice, ½ lb. of flour, ½ lb. of loaf sugar, 9 eggs, 20 drops of essence of lemon, or the rind of one lemon, ¼ lb. of butter. *Mode.* —Separate the whites from the yolks of the eggs; whisk them both well, and add to the latter the butter beaten to a cream. Stir in the flour, rice, and lemon (if the rind is used it must be very finely minced), and beat the mixture well; then add the whites of the eggs, beat the cake again for some time, put it into a buttered mould or tin, and bake it for nearly 1½ hour. It may be flavoured with essence of almonds, when this is preferred. *Time.*—Nearly 1½ hour. *Average cost,* 1*s.* 6*d.* *Seasonable* at any time.

CAKE-MOULD.

RICE, SAVOURY CASSEROLE OF; or Rice Border, for Ragoûts, Fricassées, &c. (An Entrée.)

Ingredients.—1½ lb. of rice, 3 pints of weak stock or broth, 2 slices of fat ham, 1 teaspoonful of salt. *Mode.*—A casserole of rice, when made in a mould, is not such a difficult operation as when it is moulded by the hand. It is an elegant and inexpensive entrée, as the remains of cold fish, flesh, or fowl, may be served as ragoûts, fricassées, &c., inclosed in the casserole. It requires great nicety in its preparation, the principal thing to attend to being the boiling of the rice, as, if this is not sufficiently cooked, the casserole, when moulded, will have a rough appearance, which would entirely spoil it. After having washed the rice in two or three waters, drain it well, and put it into a stewpan with the stock, ham, and salt; cover the pan closely, and let the rice gradually swell over a slow fire, occasionally stirring, to prevent its sticking. When it is quite soft, strain it, pick out the pieces of ham, and, with the back of a large wooden spoon, mash the rice to a perfectly smooth paste. Then well grease a mould (moulds are made purposely for rice borders), and turn it upside down for a minute or two, to drain away the fat, should there be too much; put some rice all round the bottom and sides of it; place a piece of soft bread in the middle, and cover it with rice; press it in equally with the spoon,

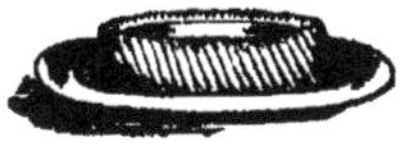

CASSEROLE OF RICE.

and let it cool. Then dip the mould into hot water, turn the casserole carefully on to a dish, mark where the lid is to be formed on the top, by making an incision with the point of a knife about an inch from the edge all round, and put it into a *very hot* oven. Brush it over with a little clarified butter, and bake about ½ hour, or rather longer; then carefully remove the lid, which will be formed by the incision having been made all round, and remove the bread, in small pieces, with the point of a penknife, being careful not to injure the casserole. Fill the centre with the ragoût or fricassée, which should be made thick; put on the cover, glaze it, place it in the oven to set the glaze, and serve as hot as possible. The casserole should not be emptied too much, as it is liable to crack from the weight of whatever is put in; and, in baking it, let the oven be very hot, or the casserole will probably break. *Time.*—About ¾ hour to swell the rice. *Sufficient* for 2 moderate-sized casseroles. *Seasonable* at any time.

RICE, SWEET CASSEROLE OF (an Entremets).

Ingredients.—1½ lb. of rice, 3 pints of milk, sugar to taste, flavouring of bitter almonds, 3 oz. of butter, the yolks of 3 eggs. *Mode.*—This is made in precisely the same manner as a savoury casserole, only substituting the milk and sugar for the stock and salt. Put the milk into a stewpan, with sufficient essence of bitter almonds to flavour it well; then add the rice, which should be washed, picked, and drained, and let it swell gradually in the milk over a slow fire. When it is tender, stir in the sugar, butter, and yolks of eggs; butter a mould, press in the rice, and proceed in exactly the same manner as in preceding recipe. When the casserole is ready, fill it with a compôte of any fruit that may be preferred, or with melted apricot-jam, and serve. *Time.*—From ¾ to 1 hour to swell the rice, ½ to ¾ hour to bake the casserole. *Average cost,* exclusive of the compôte or jam, 1*s.* 9*d.* *Sufficient* for 2 casseroles. *Seasonable* at any time.

RICE CROQUETTES.

Ingredients.—½ lb. of rice, 1 quart of milk, 6 oz. of pounded sugar, flavouring of vanilla, lemon-peel, or bitter almonds, egg and bread-crumbs, hot lard. *Mode.*—Put the rice, milk, and sugar into a saucepan, and let the former gradually swell over a gentle fire until all the milk is dried up; and just before the rice is done, stir in a few drops of essence of any of the above flavourings. Let the rice get cold; then form it into small round balls, dip them into yolk of egg, sprinkle them with bread-crumbs, and fry them in boiling lard for about 10 minutes, turning them about, that they may get equally browned. Drain the greasy moisture from them, by placing them on a cloth in front of the fire for a minute or two; pile them on a white d'oyley, and send them quickly to table. A small piece of jam is sometimes introduced into the middle of each croquette, which adds very much to the flavour of this favourite dish. *Time.*—From ¾ to 1 hour to swell the rice; about 10 minutes to fry the croquettes. *Average cost,* 10*d.* *Sufficient* to make 7 or 8 croquettes. *Seasonable* at any time.

RICE FRITTERS.

Ingredients.—6 oz. of rice, 1 quart of milk, 3 oz. of sugar, 1 oz. of fresh butter, 6 oz. of orange marmalade, 4 eggs. *Mode.*—Swell the rice in the milk, with the sugar and butter, over a slow fire until it is perfectly tender, which will be in about ¾ hour. When the rice is done, strain away the milk, should there be any left, and mix with it the marmalade and well-beaten eggs; stir the whole over the fire until the eggs are set; then spread the mixture on a dish to the thickness of about ½ inch, or rather thicker. When it is perfectly cold, cut it into long strips, dip them in a batter the same as for apple fritters, and fry them a nice brown. Dish them on a white d'oyley, strew sifted sugar over, and serve quickly. *Time.*—About ¾ hour to swell the rice; from 7 to 10 minutes to fry the fritters. *Average cost,* 1*s.* 6*d.* *Sufficient* to make 7 or 8 fritters. *Seasonable* at any time.

RICE-MILK.

Ingredients.—3 tablespoonfuls of rice, 1 quart of milk, sugar to taste; when liked, a little grated nutmeg. *Mode.*—Well wash the rice, put it into a saucepan with the milk, and simmer gently until the rice is tender, stirring it from time to time to prevent the milk from burning; sweeten it, add a little grated nutmeg, and serve. This dish is also very suitable and wholesome for children; it may be flavoured with a little lemon-peel, and a little finely-minced suet may be boiled with it, which renders it more strengthening and more wholesome. Tapioca, semolina, vermicelli, and macaroni, may all be dressed in the same manner. *Time.*—From ¾ to 1 hour. *Seasonable* at any time.

RICE PUDDING, Baked.

Ingredients.—1 small teacupful of rice, 4 eggs, 1 pint of milk, 2 oz. of fresh butter, 2 oz. of beef marrow, ¼ lb. of currants, 2 tablespoonfuls of brandy, nutmeg, ¼ lb. of sugar, the rind of ½ lemon. *Mode.*—Put the lemon-rind and milk into a stewpan, and let it infuse till the milk is well flavoured with the lemon; in the mean time, boil the rice until tender in water, with a very small quantity of salt, and, when done, let it be thoroughly drained. Beat the eggs, stir to them the milk, which should be strained, the butter, marrow, currants, and remaining ingredients; add the rice, and mix all well together. Line the edges of the dish with puff-paste, put in the pudding, and bake for about ¾ hour in a slow oven. Slices of candied-peel may be added at pleasure, or Sultana raisins may be substituted for the currants. *Time.*—¾ hour. *Average cost,* 1*s.* 3*d.* *Sufficient* for 5 or 6 persons. *Seasonable* for a winter pudding, when fresh fruits are not obtainable.

RICE PUDDING, Baked (Plain and Economical; a nice Pudding for Children).

Ingredients.—1 teacupful of rice, 2 tablespoonfuls of moist sugar, 1 quart of milk, ½ oz. of butter or two small tablespoonfuls of chopped suet, ½ teaspoonful of grated nutmeg. *Mode.*—Wash the rice, put it into a pie-dish with the sugar, pour in the milk, and stir these ingredients well together; then add the butter cut up into very small pieces, or, instead of this, the above proportion of finely-minced suet; grate a little nutmeg over the top, and bake the pudding, in a *moderate* oven, from 1½ to 2 hours. As the rice is not previously cooked, care must be taken that the pudding be very slowly baked, to give plenty of time for the rice to swell, and for it to be very

thoroughly done. *Time.*—1½ to 2 hours. *Average cost,* 7*d.* *Sufficient* for 5 or 6 children. *Seasonable* at any time.

RICE PUDDING, Plain Boiled.

Ingredients.—½ lb. of rice. *Mode.*—Wash the rice, tie it in a pudding-cloth, allowing room for the rice to swell, and put it into a saucepan of cold water; boil it gently for two hours, and if, after a time, the cloth seems tied too loosely, take the rice up and tighten the cloth. Serve with sweet melted butter, or cold butter and sugar, or stewed fruit, jam, or marmalade, any of which accompaniments are suitable for plain boiled rice. *Time.*—2 hours after the water boils. *Average cost,* 2*d.* *Sufficient* for 4 or 5 persons. *Seasonable* at any time.

RICE PUDDING, Boiled.

Ingredients.—¼ lb. of rice, 1½ pint of new milk, 2 oz. of butter, 4 eggs, ½ saltspoonful of salt, 4 large tablespoonfuls of moist sugar, flavouring to taste. *Mode.*—Stew the rice very gently in the above proportion of new milk, and, when it is tender, pour it into a basin; stir in the butter, and let it stand to cool; then beat the eggs, add these to the rice with the sugar, salt, and any flavouring that may be approved, such as nutmeg, powdered cinnamon, grated lemon-peel, essence of bitter-almonds, or vanilla. When all is well stirred, put the pudding into a buttered basin, tie it down with a cloth, plunge it into boiling water, and boil for 1¼ hour. *Time.*—1¼ hour. *Average cost,* 1*s.* *Sufficient* for 5 or 6 persons. *Seasonable* at any time.

RICE PUDDING, Boiled (with Dried or Fresh Fruit; a nice Dish for the Nursery).

Ingredients.—½ lb. of rice, 1 pint of any kind of fresh fruit that may be preferred, or ½ lb of raisins or currants. *Mode.*—Wash the rice, tie it in a cloth, allowing room for it to swell, and put it into a saucepan of cold water; let it boil for an hour, then take it up, untie the cloth, stir in the fruit, and tie it up again tolerably tight, and put it into the water for the remainder of the time. Boil for another hour, or rather longer, and serve with sweet sauce if made with dried fruit, and with plain sifted sugar if made with fresh fruit. *Time.*—1 hour to boil the rice without the fruit; 1 hour, or longer, afterwards. *Average cost, 6d.* *Sufficient* for 6 or 7 children. *Seasonable* at any time.

Note.—This pudding is very good made with apples; they should be pared, cored, and cut into thin slices.

RICE PUDDING, French, or Gateau de Riz.

Ingredients.—To every ¼ lb. of rice allow 1 quart of milk, the rind of 1 lemon, ½ teaspoonful of salt, sugar to taste, 4 oz. of butter, 6 eggs, bread crumbs. *Mode.*—Put the milk into a stewpan with the lemon-rind, and let it infuse for ½ hour, or until the former is well flavoured; then take out the peel, have ready the rice washed, picked, and drained; put it into the milk, and let it gradually swell over a very slow fire. Stir in the butter, salt, and sugar, and, when properly sweetened, add the yolks of the eggs, and then the whites, both of which should be well beaten, and added separately to the rice. Butter a mould, strew in some fine bread crumbs, and let them be spread equally over it; then carefully pour in the rice, and bake the pudding in a *slow* oven for 1 hour. Turn it out of the mould, and garnish the dish with preserved cherries, or any bright-coloured jelly or jam. This pudding would be exceedingly nice flavoured with essence of vanilla. *Time.*—¾ to 1 hour for the rice to swell; to be baked 1 hour in a slow oven. *Average cost,* 1*s.* 8d. *Sufficient* for 5 or 6 persons. *Seasonable* at any time.

RICE PUDDING, Baked or Boiled Ground.

Ingredients.—2 pints of milk, 6 tablespoonfuls of ground rice, sugar to taste, 4 eggs, flavouring of lemon-rind, nutmeg, bitter-almonds or bay-leaf. *Mode.*—Put 1½ pint of the milk into a stewpan with any of the above flavourings, and bring it to the boiling point, and, with the other ½ pint of milk, mix the ground rice to a smooth batter; strain the boiling milk to this, and stir over the fire until the mixture is tolerably thick; then pour it into a basin, leave it uncovered, and when nearly or quite cold sweeten it to taste, and add the eggs, which should be previously well beaten, with a little salt. Put the pudding into a well-buttered basin, tie it down with a cloth, plunge it into boiling water, and boil for 1½ hour. For a baked pudding, proceed in precisely the same manner, only using half the above proportion of ground rice, with the same quantity of all the other ingredients: an hour will bake the pudding in a moderate oven. Stewed fruit, or preserves, or marmalade, may be served with either the boiled or baked pudding, and will be found an improvement. *Time.*—1½ hour to boil, 1 hour to bake. *Average cost,* 10*d.* *Sufficient* for 5 or 6 persons. *Seasonable* at any time.

RICE PUDDING, Iced.

Ingredients.—6 oz. of rice, 1 quart of milk, ½ lb. of sugar, the yolks of 6 eggs, 1 small teaspoonful of essence of vanilla. *Mode.*—Put the rice into a stewpan, with the milk and sugar, and let these simmer over a gentle fire until the rice is sufficiently soft to break up into a smooth mass, and should the milk dry away too much, a little more may be added. Stir the rice occasionally, to prevent its burning, then beat it to a smooth mixture; add the yolks of the eggs, which should be well whisked, and the vanilla (should this flavouring not be liked, essence of bitter almonds may be substituted for it); put this rice custard into the freezing-pot, and proceed as directed in the recipe for Iced Pudding. When wanted for table, turn the pudding out of the mould, and pour over the top and round it a compôte of oranges, or any other fruit that may be preferred, taking care that the flavouring in the pudding harmonizes well with the fruit that is served with it. *Time.*—½ hour to freeze the mixture. *Average cost,* 1*s.* 6*d.*; exclusive of the compôte, 1*s.* 4*d.* *Seasonable.*—Served all the year round.

RICE PUDDINGS, Miniature.

Ingredients.—¼ lb. of rice, 1½ pint of milk, 2 oz. of fresh butter, 4 eggs, sugar to taste, flavouring of lemon-peel, bitter almonds, or vanilla; a few strips of candied peel. *Mode.*—Let the rice swell in 1 pint of the milk over a slow fire, putting with it a strip of lemon-peel; stir to it the butter and the other ½ pint of milk, and let the mixture cool. Then add the well-beaten eggs, and a few drops of essence of almonds or essence of vanilla, whichever may be preferred; butter well some small cups or moulds, line them with a few pieces of candied peel sliced very thin, fill them three parts full, and bake for about 40 minutes; turn them out of the cups on to a white d'oyley, and serve with sweet sauce. The flavouring and candied peel might be omitted, and stewed fruit or preserve served instead, with these puddings. *Time.*—40 minutes. *Average cost,* 1*s.* *Sufficient* for 6 puddings. *Seasonable* at any time.

RICE SNOWBALLS (A Pretty Dish for Juvenile Suppers).

Ingredients.—6 oz. of rice, 1 quart of milk, flavouring of essence of almonds, sugar to taste, 1 pint of custard. *Mode.*—Boil the rice in the milk, with sugar and a flavouring of essence of almonds, until the former is tender, adding, if necessary, a little more milk, should it dry away too much. When the rice is quite soft, put it into teacups, or *small* round jars, and let it remain until cold; then turn the rice out on a deep glass dish, pour over a custard, and on the top of each ball place a small piece of bright-coloured preserve or jelly. Lemon-peel or vanilla may be boiled with the rice instead of the essence of almonds, when either of these is preferred; but the flavouring of the custard must correspond with that of the rice. *Time.*—About ¾ hour to swell the rice in the milk. *Average cost,* with the custard, 1*s.* 6*d.* *Sufficient* for 5 or 6 children. *Seasonable* at any time.

RICE SOUFFLE.

Ingredients. — 3 tablespoonfuls of ground rice, 1 pint of milk, 5 eggs, pounded sugar to taste, flavouring of lemon-rind, vanilla, coffee, chocolate, or anything that may be preferred, a piece of butter the size of a walnut. *Mode.*—Mix the ground rice with 6 tablespoonfuls of the milk quite smoothly, and put it into a saucepan with the remainder of the milk and butter, and keep stirring it over the fire for about ¼ hour, or until the mixture thickens. Separate the yolks from the whites of the eggs, beat the former in a basin, and stir to them the rice and sufficient pounded sugar to sweeten the soufflé; but add this latter ingredient as sparingly as possible, as the less sugar there is used the lighter will be the soufflé. Now whisk the whites of the eggs to a stiff froth or snow; mix them with the other preparation, and pour the whole into a soufflé-dish, and put it instantly into the oven; bake it about ½ hour in a moderate oven, take it out, hold a salamander or hot shovel over the top, sprinkle sifted sugar over it, and send the soufflé to table in the dish it was baked in, either with a napkin pinned round, or inclosed in a more ornamental dish. The excellence of this fashionable dish entirely depends on the proper whisking of the whites of the eggs, the manner of baking, and the expedition with which it is sent to table. Soufflés should be served *instantly* from the oven, or they will sink, and be nothing more than an ordinary pudding. *Time.*—About ½ hour. *Average cost,* 1*s.* *Sufficient* for 3 or 4 persons. *Seasonable* at any time.

RICE SOUP.

Ingredients.—4 oz. of Patna rice, salt, cayenne, and mace, 2 quarts of white stock. *Mode.*—Throw the rice into boiling water, and let it boil until tender; then pour it into a sieve, and allow it to drain well. Now add it to the stock boiling, and allow it to simmer a few minutes; season to taste. Serve quickly. *Time.*—1½ hour. *Average cost,* 1*s.* 3*d.* per quart. *Sufficient* for 8 persons. *Seasonable* all the year.

RICE SOUP.

Ingredients.—6 oz. of rice, the yolks of 4 eggs, ½ a pint of cream, rather more than two quarts of stock. *Mode.*—Boil the rice in the stock, and rub half of it through a tammy; put the stock in the stewpan, add all the rice, and simmer gently for 5 minutes. Beat the yolks of the eggs, mix them with the cream (previously boiled), and strain through a hair sieve; take the soup off the fire, add the eggs and cream, stirring frequently. Heat it gradually, stirring all the time; but do not let it boil, or the eggs will curdle. *Time.*—2 hours. *Average cost,* 1*s.* 4*d.* per quart. *Sufficient* for 8 persons. *Seasonable* all the year.

RICE for Curries, &c., Boiled.

Ingredients.—¾ lb. of rice, water, salt. *Mode.*—Pick, wash, and soak the rice in plenty of cold water; then have ready a saucepan of boiling water, drop the rice into it, and keep it boiling quickly, with the lid uncovered, until it is tender, but not soft. Take it up, drain it, and put it on a dish before the fire to dry; do not handle it much with a spoon, but shake it about a little with two forks, that it may all be equally dried, and strew over it a little salt. It is now ready to serve, and may be heaped lightly on a dish by itself, or be laid round the dish as a border, with a curry or fricassee in the centre. Some cooks smooth the rice with the back of a spoon, and then brush it over with the yolk of an egg, and set it in the oven to colour; but the rice, well boiled, white, dry, and with every grain distinct, is by far the more preferable mode of dressing it. During the process of boiling, the rice should be attentively watched, that it be not overdone, as, if this is the case, it will have a mashed and soft appearance. *Time.*—15 to 25 minutes, according to the quality of the rice. *Average cost*, 3*d*. *Sufficient* for a large dish of curry. *Seasonable* at any time.

RICE, To Boil, for Curries, &c. (Soyer's Recipe.)

Ingredients.—1 lb. of the best Carolina rice, 2 quarts of water, 1½ oz. of butter, a little salt. *Mode.*—Wash the rice well in two waters; make 2 quarts of water boiling, and throw the rice into it; boil it until three-parts done, then drain it on a sieve. Butter the bottom and sides of a stewpan, put in the rice, place the lid on tightly, and set it by the side of the fire, until the rice is perfectly tender, occasionally shaking the pan to prevent its sticking. Prepared thus, every grain should be separate and white. Either dish it separately, or place it round the curry as a border. *Time.*—15 to 25 minutes. *Average cost*, 7*d*. *Sufficient* for 2 moderate-sized curries. *Seasonable* at any time.

ROASTING, Memoranda in.

The management of the fire is a point of primary importance in roasting. A radiant fire throughout the operation is absolutely necessary to insure a good result. When the article to be dressed is thin and delicate, the fire may be small; but when the joint is large the fire must fill the grate. Meat must never be put down before a hollow or exhausted fire, which may soon want recruiting; on the other hand, if the heat of the fire become too fierce, the meat must be removed to a considerable distance till it has somewhat abated. Some cooks always fail in roasting, though they succeed in nearly everything else. A French writer on the culinary art says that anybody can learn how to cook, but one must be born a roaster. According to Liebig, beef or mutton cannot be said to be sufficiently roasted, until it has acquired throughout the whole mass a temperature of 158°. But poultry may be well cooked when the inner parts have attained a temperature of 130° to 140°. This depends on the greater amount of blood which beef and mutton contain, the colouring matter of blood not being coagulable under 158°.

ROLLS, Excellent.

Ingredients.—To every lb. of flour allow 1 oz. of butter, ¼ pint of milk, a large teaspoonful of yeast, a little salt. *Mode.*—Warm the butter in the milk, add to it the yeast and salt, and mix these ingredients well together. Put the flour into a pan, stir in the above ingre-

ROLLS.

dients, and let the dough rise, covered in a warm place. Knead it well, make it into rolls, let them rise again for a few minutes, and bake in a quick oven. Richer rolls may be made by adding 1 or 2 eggs and a larger proportion of butter, and their appearance improved by brushing the tops over with yolk of egg or a little milk. *Time.*—1 lb. of flour, divided into 6 rolls, from 15 to 20 minutes.

ROLLS, Hot.

This dish, although very unwholesome and indigestible, is nevertheless a great favourite, and eaten by many persons. As soon as the rolls come from the baker's, they should be put into the oven, which, in the early part of the morning, is sure not to be very hot; and the rolls must not be buttered until wanted. When they are quite hot, divide them lengthwise into three; put some thin flakes of good butter between the slices, press the rolls together, and put them in the oven for a minute or two, but not longer, or the butter would oil; take them out of the oven, spread the butter equally over, divide the rolls in half, and put them on to a very hot clean dish, and send them instantly to table.

ROLLS, Fluted.

Ingredients.—Puff-paste, the white of an egg, sifted sugar, jelly or preserve. *Mode.*—Make some good puff-paste (trimmings answer very well for little dishes of this sort); roll it out to the thickness of ¼ inch, and with a round fluted paste-cutter stamp out as many round pieces as may be required; brush over the upper side with the white of an egg; roll up the pieces, pressing the paste lightly together where it joins; place the rolls on a baking-sheet, and bake for about ¼ hour. A few minutes before they are done, brush them over with the white of an egg; strew over sifted sugar, put them back in the oven; and when the icing is firm and of a pale brown colour, they are done. Place a strip of jelly or preserve across each roll, dish them high on a napkin, and serve cold. *Time.*—¼ hour before being iced; 5 to 10 minutes after. *Average cost,* 1*s.* 3*d.* *Sufficient.*—½ lb. of puff-paste for 2 dishes. *Seasonable* at any time.

ROUX, Brown, a French Thickening for Gravies and Sauces.

Ingredients.—6 oz. of butter, 9 oz. of flour. *Mode.*—Melt the butter in a stewpan over a slow fire, and dredge in, very gradually, the flour; stir it till of a light-brown colour—to obtain this do it very slowly, otherwise the flour will burn and impart a bitter taste to the sauce it is mixed with. Pour it in a jar, and keep it for use: it will remain good some time. *Time.*—About ½ hour. *Average cost,* 7*d.*

ROUX, White, for thickening White Sauces.

Allow the same proportions of butter and flour as in the preceding recipe, and proceed in the same manner as for brown roux, but do not keep it on the fire too long, and take care not to let it colour. This is used for thickening white sauce. Pour it into a jar to use when wanted. *Time.*—½ hour. *Average cost,* 7*d.*

Sufficient.—A dessertspoonful will thicken a pint of gravy.

Note.—Besides the above, sauces may be thickened with potato flour, ground rice, baked flour, arrowroot, &c.: the latter will be found far preferable to the ordinary flour for white sauces. A slice of bread, toasted and added to gravies, answers the two purposes of thickening and colouring them.

RUMP-STEAK, Fried.

Ingredients.—Steaks, butter or clarified dripping.—*Mode.*—Although broiling is a far superior method of cooking steaks to frying them, yet, when the cook is not very expert, the latter mode may be adopted; and, when properly done, the dish may really look very inviting, and the flavour be good. The steaks should be cut rather thinner than for broiling, and with a small quantity of fat to each. Put some butter or clarified dripping into a frying-pan; let it get quite hot, then lay in the steaks. Turn them frequently until done, which will be in about 8 minutes, or rather more, should the steaks be very thick. Serve on a very hot dish, in which put a small piece of butter and a tablespoonful of ketchup, and season with pepper and salt. They should be sent to table quickly, as when cold the steaks are entirely spoiled. *Time.*—8 minutes for a medium-sized steak, rather longer for a very thick one. *Average cost,* 1*s.* per lb. *Seasonable* all the year, but not good in summer, as the meat cannot hang to get tender.

Note.—Where much gravy is liked, make it in the following manner:—As soon as the steaks are done, dish them, pour a little boiling water into the frying-pan, add a seasoning of pepper and salt, a small piece of butter, and a tablespoonful of Harvey's sauce or mushroom ketchup. Hold the pan over the fire for a minute or two, just let the gravy simmer, then pour on the steak, and serve.

RUMP-STEAK AND KIDNEY PUDDING.

Ingredients.—2 lbs. of rump-steak, 2 kidneys, seasoning to taste of salt and black pepper, suet crust made with milk (*see* Pastry), in the proportion of 6 oz. of suet to each 1 lb. of flour. *Mode.*—Procure some tender rump-steak (that which has been hung a little time), and divide it into pieces about an inch square, and cut each kidney into 8 pieces. Line the dish with crust made with suet and flour in the above proportion, leaving a small piece of crust to overlap the edge. Then cover the bottom with a portion of the steak and a few pieces of kidney; season with salt and pepper (some add a little flour to thicken the gravy, but it is not necessary), and then add another layer of steak, kidney, and seasoning. Proceed in this manner till the dish is full, when pour in sufficient water to come within 2 inches of the top of the basin. Moisten the edges of the crust, cover the pudding over, press the two crusts together, that the gravy may not escape, and turn up the overhanging paste. Wring out a cloth in hot water, flour it, and tie up the pudding; put it into boiling water, and let it boil for at least 4 hours. If the water diminishes, always replenish with some hot in a jug, as the pudding should be kept covered all the time, and not allowed to stop boiling. When the cloth is removed, cut out a round piece in the top of the crust, to prevent the pudding bursting, and send it to table in the basin, either in an ornamental dish, or with a napkin pinned round it. Serve quickly. *Time.*—For a pudding with 2 lbs. of steak and 2 kidneys allow 4 hours. *Average cost*, 2*s*. 8*d*. *Sufficient* for 6 persons. *Seasonable* all the year, but more suitable in winter.

Note.—Rump-steak pudding may be very much enriched by adding a few oysters or mushrooms. In Sussex, the inhabitants are noted for their savoury puddings, which are usually made in the manner just described. It differs from the general way of making them, as the meat is cut up into very small pieces and the basin is differently shaped, resembling a very large saucer: on trial, this pudding will be found far nicer, and more full of gravy, than when laid in large pieces in the dish.

RUMP-STEAK AND OYSTER SAUCE.

Ingredients.—3 dozen oysters, ingredients for oyster sauce, 2 lb. of rump-steak, seasoning to taste of pepper and salt. *Mode.*—Make the oyster sauce, and when that is ready, put it by the side of the fire, but do not let it keep boiling. Have the steaks cut of an equal thickness, broil them over a very clear fire, turning them often, that the gravy may not escape. In about 8 minutes they will be done, when put them on a very hot dish; smother with the oyster sauce, and the remainder send to table in a tureen. Serve quickly. *Time.*—About 8 to 10 minutes, according to the thickness of the steak. *Average cost*, 1*s*. per lb. *Sufficient* for 4 persons. *Seasonable* from September to April.

RUMP-STEAK or BEEF-STEAK, Broiled.

Ingredients.—Steaks, a piece of butter the size of a walnut, salt to taste, 1 tablespoonful of good mushroom ketchup or Harvey's sauce. *Mode.*—As the success of a good broil so much depends on the state of the fire, see that it is bright and clear, and perfectly free from smoke, and do not add any fresh fuel just before you require to use the gridiron. Sprinkle a little salt over the fire, put on the gridiron for a few minutes, to get thoroughly hot through; rub it with a piece of fresh suet, to prevent the meat from sticking, and lay on the steaks, which should be cut of an equal thickness, about ¾ of an inch, or rather thinner, and level them by beating them as *little* as possible with a rolling pin. Turn them frequently with steak-tongs (if these are not at hand, stick a fork in the edge of the fat, that no gravy escapes), and in from 8 to 10 minutes they will be done. Have ready a very hot dish, into which put the ketchup, and, when liked, a little minced shalot; dish up the steaks, rub them over with butter, and season with pepper and salt. The exact time for broiling steaks must be determined by taste, whether they are liked underdone or well done; more than from 1 to 10 minutes for a steak ¾ inch in thickness, we think, would spoil and dry up the juices of the meat. Great expedition is necessary in sending broiled steaks to table; and, to have them in perfection, they should not be cooked till everything else prepared for dinner has been dished up, as their excellence entirely depends on their being served very hot. Garnish with scraped horseradish, or slices of cucumber. Oyster, tomato, onion, and many other sauces, are frequent accompaniments to rump-steak, but true lovers of this English dish generally reject all additions but pepper and salt. *Time.*—8 to 10 minutes. *Average cost*, 1*s*. per lb. *Sufficient*.—Allow ½ lb. to each person; if the party consist entirely of gentleman, ¾ lb. will not be too much. *Seasonable* all the year, but not good in the height of summer, as the meat cannot hang long enough to be tender.

RUMP-STEAK PIE.

Ingredients.—3 lbs. of rump-steak, seasoning to taste of salt, cayenne, and black pepper, crust, water, the yolk of an egg. *Mode*.—Have the steaks cut from a rump that has hung a few days, that they may be tender, and be particular that every portion is perfectly sweet. Cut the steaks into pieces about 3 inches long and 2 wide, allowing a *small* piece of fat to each piece of lean, and arrange the meat in layers in a pie-dish. Between each layer sprinkle a seasoning of salt, pepper, and, when liked, a few grains of cayenne. Fill the dish sufficiently with meat to support the crust, and to give it a nice raised appearance when baked, and not to look flat and hollow. Pour in sufficient water to half fill the dish, and border it with paste (*see* Pastry); brush it over with a little water, and put on the cover; slightly press down the edges with the thumb, and trim off close to the dish. Ornament the pie with leaves, or pieces of paste cut in any shape that fancy may direct, brush it over with the beaten yolk of an egg; make a hole in the top of the crust, and bake in a hot oven for about 1½ hour. *Time*.—In a hot oven, 1½ hour. *Average cost*, for this size, 3*s*. 6*d*. *Sufficient* for 6 or 8 persons. *Seasonable* at any time.

RUMP-STEAK PUDDING, Baked.

Ingredients.—6 oz. of flour, 2 eggs, not quite 1 pint of milk, salt to taste, 1½ lb. of rump-steaks, 1 kidney, pepper and salt. *Mode*.—Cut the steaks into nice square pieces, with a small quantity of fat, and the kidney divide into small pieces. Make a batter of flour, eggs, and milk in the above proportion; lay a little of it at the bottom of a pie-dish; then put in the steaks and kidney, which should be well seasoned with pepper and salt, and pour over the remainder of the batter, and bake for 1½ hour in a brisk but not fierce oven.—*Time*.—1½ hour. *Average cost*, 2*s*. *Sufficient* for 4 or 5 persons. *Seasonable* at any time.

RUMP-STEAK, Rolled, Roasted, and Stuffed.

Ingredients.—2 lbs. of rump-steak, forcemeat, pepper and salt to taste, clarified butter. *Mode*.—Have the steaks cut rather thick from a well-hung rump of beef, and sprinkle over them a seasoning of pepper and salt. Make a forcemeat; spread it over *half* of the steak; roll it up, bind and skewer it firmly, that the forcemeat may not escape, and roast it before a nice clear fire for about 1½ hour, or rather longer, should the roll be very large and thick. Keep it constantly basted with butter, and serve with brown gravy, some of which must be poured round the steak, and the remainder sent to table in a tureen. *Time*.—1½ hour. *Average cost*, 1*s*. per lb. *Sufficient* for 4 persons. *Seasonable* all the year, but best in winter.

RUMP-STEAK WITH FRIED POTATOES, or BIFTEK AUX POMMES-DE-TERRE (à la Mode Française).

Ingredients.—2 lb. of steak, 8 potatoes, ¼ lb. of butter, salt and pepper to taste, 1 teaspoonful of minced herbs. *Mode*.—Put the butter into a frying or *sauté* pan, set it over the fire, and let it get very hot; peel, and cut the potatoes into long thin slices; put them into the hot butter, and fry them till of a nice brown colour. Now broil the steaks over a bright clear fire, turning them frequently, that every part may be equally done: as they should not be thick, 5 minutes will broil them. Put the herbs and seasoning in the butter the potatoes were fried in, pour it under the steak, and place the fried potatoes round, as a garnish. To have this dish in perfection, a portion of the fillet of the sirloin should be used, as the meat is generally so much more tender than that of the rump, and the steaks should be cut about ⅓ of an inch in thickness. *Time*.—5 minutes to broil the steaks, and about the same time to fry the potatoes. *Average cost*, 1*s*. per lb. *Sufficient* for 4 persons. *Seasonable* all the year; but not so good in warm weather, as the meat cannot hang to get tender.

RUMP- or BEEF-STEAK, Stewed (an Entrée).

Ingredients.—About 2 lbs. of beef or rump steak, 3 onions, 2 turnips, 3 carrots, 2 or 3 oz. of butter, ½ pint of water, 1 teaspoonful of salt, ½ do. of pepper, 1 tablespoonful of ketchup, 1 tablespoonful of flour. *Mode.*—Have the steaks cut tolerably thick and rather lean; divide them into convenient-sized pieces, and fry them in the butter a nice brown on both sides. Cleanse and pare the vegetables, cut the onions and carrots into thin slices, and the turnips into dice, and fry these in the same fat that the steaks were done in. Put all into a saucepan, add ½ pint of water, or rather more should it be necessary, and simmer very gently for 2½ or 3 hours; when nearly done, skim well, add salt, pepper, and ketchup in the above proportions, and thicken with a tablespoonful of flour mixed with 2 of cold water. Let it boil up for a minute or two after the thickening is added, and serve. When a vegetable-scoop is at hand, use it to cut the vegetables in fanciful shapes; and tomato, Harvey's sauce, or walnut-liquor may be used to flavour the gravy. It is less rich if stewed the previous day, so that the fat may be taken off when cold; when wanted for table, it will merely require warming through. *Time.*—3 hours. *Average cost,* 1*s.* per lb. *Sufficient* for 4 or 5 persons. *Seasonable* at any time.

RUSKS, to make (Suffolk Recipe).

Ingredients.—To every lb. of flour allow 2 oz. of butter, ¼ pint of milk, 2 oz. of loaf sugar, 3 eggs, 1 tablespoonful of yeast. *Mode.*—Put the milk and butter into a saucepan, and keep shaking it round until the latter is melted. Put the flour into a basin with the sugar, mix these well together, and beat the eggs. Stir them with the yeast to the milk and butter, and with this liquid work the flour into a smooth dough. Cover a cloth over the basin, and leave the dough to rise by the side of the fire; then knead it, and divide it into 12 pieces; place them in a brisk oven, and bake for about 20 minutes. Take the rusks out, break them in half, and then set them in the oven to get crisp on the other side. When cold, they should be put into tin canisters to keep them dry; and if intended for the cheese course, the sifted sugar should be omitted. *Time.*—20 minutes to bake the rusks; 5 minutes to render them crisp after being divided. *Average cost,* 8*d.* *Sufficient* to make 2 dozen rusks. *Seasonable* at any time.

RUSKS.

RUSKS, Italian.

A stale Savoy or lemon cake may be converted into very good rusks in the following manner. Cut the cake into slices, divide each slice in two; put them on a baking-sheet, in a slow oven, and when they are of a nice brown and quite hard, they are done. They should be kept in a closed tin canister in a dry place, to preserve their crispness.

SAGE-AND-ONION STUFFING, for Geese, Ducks, and Pork.

Ingredients.—4 large onions, 10 sage-leaves, ¼ lb. of bread crumbs, 1½ oz. of butter, salt and pepper to taste, 1 egg. *Mode.*—Peel the onions, put them into boiling water, let them simmer for 5 minutes or rather longer, and just before they are taken out, put in the sage-leaves for a minute or two to take off their rawness. Chop both these very fine, add the bread, seasoning, and butter, and work the whole together with the yolk of an egg, when the stuffing will be ready for use. It should be rather highly seasoned, and the sage-leaves should be very finely chopped. Many cooks do not parboil the onions in the manner just stated, but merely use them raw. The stuffing then, however, is not nearly so mild, and, to many tastes, its strong flavour would be very objectionable. When made for goose, a portion of the liver of the bird, simmered for a few minutes and very finely minced, is frequently added to this stuffing; and where economy is studied, the egg may be dispensed with. *Time.*—Rather more than 5 minutes to simmer the onions. *Average cost,* for this quantity, 4*d.* *Sufficient* for 1 goose, or a pair of ducks.

SAGO PUDDING.

Ingredients.—1½ pint of milk, 3 tablespoonfuls of sago, the rind of ½ lemon,

3 oz. of sugar, 4 eggs, 1½ oz. of butter, grated nutmeg, puff-paste. *Mode.*—Put the milk and lemon-rind into a stewpan, place it by the side of the fire, and let it remain until the milk is well flavoured with the lemon; then strain it, mix with it the sago and sugar, and simmer gently for about 15 minutes. Let the mixture cool a little, and stir to it the eggs, which should be well beaten, and the butter. Line the edges of a pie-dish with puff-paste, pour in the pudding, grate a little nutmeg over the top, and bake from ¾ to 1 hour. *Time.*—¾ to 1 hour, or longer if the oven is very slow. *Average cost*, 1*s*. Sufficient for 5 or 6 persons. *Seasonable* at any time.

Note.—The above pudding may be boiled instead of baked; but then allow 2 extra tablespoonfuls of sago, and boil the pudding in a buttered basin from 1¼ to 1¾ hour.

SAGO SAUCE FOR SWEET PUDDINGS.

Ingredients.—1 tablespoonful of sago, ⅓ pint of water, ¼ pint of port or sherry, the rind and juice of 1 small lemon, sugar to taste; when the flavour is liked, a little pounded cinnamon. *Mode.*—Wash the sago in two or three waters; then put it into a saucepan, with the water and lemon-peel; let it simmer gently by the side of the fire for 10 minutes, then take out the lemon-peel, add the remaining ingredients, give one boil, and serve. Be particular to strain the lemon-juice before adding it to the sauce. This, on trial, will be found a delicious accompaniment to various boiled puddings, such as those made of bread, raisins, rice, &c. *Time.*—10 minutes. *Average cost*, 9*d*. *Sufficient* for 7 or 8 persons.

SAGO SOUP.

Ingredients.—5 oz. of sago, 2 quarts of stock. *Mode.*—Wash the sago in boiling water, add it, by degrees, to the boiling stock, and simmer till the sago is entirely dissolved, and forms a sort of jelly. *Time.*—Nearly an hour. *Average cost*, 10*d*. per quart. *Sufficient* for 8 persons. *Seasonable* all the year.

Note.—The yolks of 2 eggs, beaten up with a little cream, previously boiled, and added at the moment of serving, much improves this soup.

SALAD, Boiled.

Ingredients.—2 heads of celery, 1 pint of French beans, lettuce, and endive. *Mode.*—Boil the celery and beans separately until tender, and cut the celery into pieces about 2 inches long. Put these into a salad-bowl or dish; pour over either of the salad dressings, and garnish the dish with a little lettuce finely chopped, blanched endive, or a few tufts of boiled cauliflower. This composition, if less agreeable than vegetables in their raw state, is more wholesome; for salads, however they may be compounded, when eaten uncooked, prove to some people indigestible. Tarragon, chervil, burnet, and boiled onion, may be added to the above salad with advantage, as also slices of cold meat, poultry, or fish. *Seasonable.*—From July to October.

SALAD DRESSING (Excellent).

Ingredients.—1 teaspoonful of mixed mustard, 1 teaspoonful of pounded sugar, 2 tablespoonfuls of salad oil, 4 tablespoonfuls of milk, 2 tablespoonfuls of vinegar, cayenne and salt to taste. *Mode.*—Put the mixed mustard into a salad-bowl with the sugar, and add the oil drop by drop, carefully stirring and mixing all these ingredients well together. Proceed in this manner with the milk and vinegar, which must be added very *gradually*, or the sauce will curdle. Put in the seasoning, when the mixture will be ready for use. If this dressing is properly made, it will have a soft creamy appearance, and will be found very delicious with crab, or cold fried fish (the latter cut into dice), as well as with salads. In mixing salad dressings, the ingredients cannot be added *too gradually*, or *stirred too much*. *Average cost*, for this quantity, 3*d*. *Sufficient* for a small salad.

This recipe can be confidently recommended by the editress, to whom it was given by an intimate friend noted for her salads.

SALAD DRESSING (Excellent).

Ingredients.—4 eggs, 1 teaspoonful of mixed mustard, ¼ teaspoonful of white pepper, half that quantity of cayenne, salt to taste, 4 tablespoonfuls of cream, vinegar. *Mode.*—Boil the eggs until hard, which will be in about ¼ hour or 20 minutes; put them into cold water, take off the shells, and pound the yolks in a mortar to a smooth paste. Then add all the other ingredients, except the vinegar, and stir them well until the whole are thoroughly incorporated one with the other. Pour in sufficient vinegar to make it of the consistency of cream, taking care to add but little at a time. The mixture will then be ready for use. *Average cost*, for this quantity, 7*d*. *Sufficient* for a moderate-sized salad.

Note.—The whites of the eggs, cut into rings, will serve very well as a garnishing to the salad.

SALAD DRESSING (Excellent).

Ingredients.—1 egg, 1 teaspoonful of salad oil, 1 teaspoonful of mixed mustard, ¼ teaspoonful of salt, ½ teaspoonful of pounded sugar, 2 tablespoonfuls of vinegar, 6 tablespoonfuls of cream. *Mode.*—Prepare and mix the ingredients by the preceding recipe, and be very particular that the whole is well stirred.

Note.—In making salads, the vegetables, &c., should never be added to the sauce very long before they are wanted for table; the dressing, however, may always be prepared some hours before required. Where salads are much in request, it is a good plan to bottle off sufficient dressing for a few days' consumption, as, thereby, much time and trouble are saved. If kept in a cool place, it will remain good for 4 or 5 days.

Poetic Recipe for Salad.—The Rev. Sydney Smith's recipe.

"Two large potatoes, pass'd through kitchen sieve,
Smoothness and softness to the salad give:
Of mordent mustard add a single spoon,
Distrust the condiment that bites too soon;
But deem it not, thou man of herbs, a fault,
To add a double quantity of salt;
Four times the spoon with oil of Lucca crown,
And twice with vinegar procured from 'town;'
True flavour needs it, and your poet begs,
The pounded yellow of two well-boil'd eggs.
Let onion's atoms lurk within the bowl,
And, scarce suspected, animate the whole;
And, lastly, in the flavour'd compound toss
A magic spoonful of anchovy sauce.
Oh! great and glorious, and herbaceous treat,
'Twould tempt the dying anchorite to eat.
Back to the world he'd turn his weary soul,
And plunge his fingers in the salad-bowl."

SALAD, French.

Ingredients.—Lettuces; a little chopped burnet. To every 4 tablespoonfuls of oil allow 1½ of either Tarragon or plain *French vinegar;* 1 saltspoonful of salt, ½ saltspoonful of pepper. *Mode.*—Wash the lettuces, shake them in a cloth, and cut them into inch lengths. Put the lettuce into a salad-bowl, sprinkle over the chopped burnet, and mix these well together. Put the salt and pepper into the salad-spoon, moisten with the vinegar, disperse this amongst the salad, pour the oil over, and mix the whole well together for at least five minutes, when the preparation will be ready for table. This is the very simple and expeditious mode of preparing a salad generally adopted by our French neighbours, who are so noted for the delicious manner in which they dress their bowl. Success will not be obtained if the right vinegar is not procured, therefore we advise our friends who wish to excel in making a French salad to procure a bottle of the best French vinegar, flavoured with Tarragon or not as the taste may dictate. Those persons living in or near London, can purchase the vinegar of Messrs. Crosse & Blackwell, Soho Square, at whose establishment the quality of this important ingredient in a salad can be relied on. *Time.*—To be stirred at least 5 minutes after all the ingredients are put in. *Sufficient.* Allow 2 moderate-sized lettuces for 4 persons. *Seasonable.* Plentiful in summer, but scarce and dear during the winter season.

SALAD, Fresh Fruit (A Dessert Dish).

Mode.—Fruit salads are made by stripping the fruit from the stalks, piling it on a dish, and sprinkling over it finely pounded sugar. They may be made of strawberries, raspberries, currants, or any of these fruits mixed; peaches also make a very good salad. After the sugar is sprinkled over, about 6 large tablespoonfuls of wine or brandy, or 3 tablespoonfuls of liqueur, should be poured in the middle of the fruit; and, when the flavour is liked, a little pounded cinnamon may be added. In helping the fruit, it should be lightly stirred, that the wine and sugar may be equally distributed. *Sufficient.*—1½ pint of fruit, with 3 oz. of pounded sugar, for 4 or 5 persons. *Seasonable* in summer.

SALAD, Red Cabbage.

Ingredients.—A small red cabbage, 2 teaspoonfuls of salt, ½ pint of vinegar, 3 teaspoonfuls of oil, a small quantity of cayenne pepper. *Mode.*—Take off the outside leaves of a fresh red cabbage, and cut the remainder very finely into small thin slices. Mix with the cabbage the above salad ingredients, and let it remain for two days, when it will be fit for use. This salad will keep very well for a few days. The quantity of the ingredients may of course be a little varied, according to taste. *Time.*—2 days. *Average cost,* from 2*d.* to 3*d.* each. *Seasonable* in July and August.

SALAD, Summer.

Ingredients.—3 lettuces, 2 handfuls of mustard-and-cress, 10 young radishes, a few slices of cucumber. *Mode.*—Let the herbs be as fresh as possible for a salad, and, if at all stale or dead-looking, let them lie in water for an hour or two, which will very much refresh them. Wash and carefully pick them over, remove any decayed or worm-eaten leaves, and drain them thoroughly by swinging them gently in a clean cloth. With a silver knife, cut the lettuces into small pieces, and the radishes and cucumbers into thin slices; arrange all these ingredients lightly on a dish, with the mustard-and-cress, and pour under, but not over the salad, either of the salad dressings, and do not stir it up until it is to be eaten. It may be garnished with hard-boiled eggs, cut in slices, sliced cucumbers, nasturtiums, cut vegetable-flowers, and many other things that taste will always suggest to make a pretty and elegant dish. In making a good salad, care must be taken to have the herbs freshly gathered, and *thoroughly drained* before the sauce is added to them, or it will be watery and thin. Young spring onions, cut small, are by many persons considered an improvement to salads; but, before these are added, the cook should always consult the taste of her employer. Slices of cold meat or poultry added to a salad make a convenient and quickly-made summer luncheon-dish; or cold fish, flaked, will also be found exceedingly nice, mixed with it. *Average cost,* 9*d.* for a salad for 5 or 6 persons; but more expensive when the herbs are forced. *Sufficient* for 5 or 6 persons. *Seasonable* from May to September.

SALAD IN BOWL.

SALAD, Winter.

Ingredients. — Endive, mustard-and-cress, boiled beetroot, 3 or 4 hard-boiled eggs, celery. *Mode.*—The above ingredients form the principal constituents of a winter salad, and may be converted into a very pretty dish, by nicely contrasting the various colours, and by tastefully garnishing it. Shred the celery into thin pieces, after having carefully washed and cut away all worm-eaten pieces; cleanse the endive and mustard-and-cress free from grit, and arrange these high in the centre of a salad-bowl or dish; garnish with the hard-boiled eggs and beetroot, both of which should be cut in slices; and pour into the dish, but not over the salad, either of the salad dressings. Never dress a salad long before it is required for table, as, by standing, it loses its freshness and pretty crisp and light appearance; the sauce, however, may always be prepared a few hours beforehand, and when required to use, the herbs laid lightly over it. *Average cost,* 9*d.* for a salad for 5 or 6 persons. *Sufficient* for 5 or 6 persons. *Seasonable* from the end of September to March.

SALMON (à la Genevese).

Ingredients.—2 slices of salmon, 2 chopped shalots, a little parsley, a small bunch of herbs, 2 bay-leaves, 2 carrots, pounded mace, pepper and salt to taste, 4 tablespoonfuls of Madeira, ½ pint of white stock, thickening of butter and flour, 1 teaspoonful of essence of anchovies, the juice of 1 lemon, cayenne and salt to taste. *Mode.*—Rub the bottom of a stewpan over with butter, and put in the shalots, herbs, bay-leaves, carrots, mace, and seasoning; stir them for 10 minutes over a clear fire, and add the Madeira or sherry; simmer gently for ½ hour, and strain through a sieve over the fish, which stew in this gravy. As soon as the fish is sufficiently cooked, take away all the liquor, except a little to keep the salmon moist, and put it into another stewpan; add the stock, thicken with butter and flour, and put in the anchovies, lemon-juice, cayenne, and salt; lay the salmon on a hot dish, pour over it part of the sauce, and serve the remainder in a tureen. *Time.*—1¼ hour. *Average cost* for this quantity, *3s. 6d.* *Sufficient* for 4 or 5 persons.

SALMON, Boiled.

Ingredients.—6 oz. of salt to each gallon of water,—sufficient water to cover the fish. *Mode.*—Scale and clean the fish, and be particular that no blood is left inside; lay it in the fish-kettle with sufficient cold water to cover it, adding salt in the above proportion. Bring it quickly to a boil, take off all the scum, and let it simmer gently till the fish is done, which will be when the meat separates easily from the bone. Experience alone can teach the cook to fix the time for boiling fish; but it is especially to be remembered, that it should never be under-dressed, as then nothing is more unwholesome. Neither let it remain in the kettle after it is sufficiently cooked, as that would render it insipid, watery, and colourless. Drain it, and if not wanted for a few minutes, keep it warm by means of warm cloths laid over it. Serve on a hot napkin, garnish with cut lemon and parsley, and send lobster or shrimp sauce, and plain melted butter to table with it. A dish of dressed cucumber usually accompanies this fish. *Time.*—8 minutes to each lb. for large thick salmon; 6 minutes for thin fish. *Average cost,* in full season, 1*s.* 3*d.* per lb. *Sufficient,* ½ lb., or rather less, for each person. *Seasonable* from April to August.

Note.—Cut lemon should be put on the table with this fish; and a little of the juice squeezed over it is regarded by many persons as a most agreeable addition. Boiled peas are also, by some connoisseurs, considered especially adapted to be served with salmon.

To CHOOSE SALMON.—To be good, the belly should be firm and thick, which may readily be ascertained by feeling it with the thumb and finger. The circumstance of this fish having *red* gills, though given as a standing rule in most cookery-books, as a sign of its goodness, is not at all to be relied on, as this quality can be easily given them by art.

SALMON AND CAPER SAUCE.

Ingredients.—2 slices of salmon, ¼ lb. butter, ½ teaspoonful of chopped parsley, 1 shalot; salt, pepper, and grated nutmeg to taste. *Mode.*—Lay the salmon in a baking-dish, place pieces of butter over it, and add the other ingredients, rubbing a little of the seasoning into the fish; baste it frequently; when done, take it out and drain for a minute or two; lay it in a dish, pour caper sauce over it, and serve. Salmon dressed in this way, with tomato sauce, is very delicious. *Time.*—About ¾ hour. *Average cost,* 1*s.* 3*d.* per lb. *Sufficient* for 4 or 5 persons. *Seasonable* from April to August.

SALMON, Collared.

Ingredients.—A piece of salmon, say 3 lb., a high seasoning of salt, pounded mace, and pepper; water and vinegar, 3 bay-leaves. *Mode.*—Split the fish; scale, bone, and wash it thoroughly clean; wipe it, and rub in the seasoning inside and out; roll it up, and bind firmly; lay it in a kettle, cover it with vinegar and water (⅓ vinegar, in proportion to the water); add the bay-leaves and a good seasoning of salt and whole pepper, and simmer till done. Do not remove the lid. Serve with melted butter or anchovy sauce. For preserving the collared fish, boil up the liquor in which it was cooked, and add a little more vinegar. Pour over when cold. *Time.*—¾ hour, or rather more.

SALMON, Crimped.

Salmon is frequently dressed in this way at many fashionable tables, but must be very fresh, and cut into slices 2 or 3 inches thick. Lay these in cold salt and water for 1 hour; have ready some boiling water, salted, and well skimmed; put in the fish, and simmer gently for ¼ hour, or rather more; should it be very thick, garnish the same as boiled salmon, and serve with the same sauces. *Time.*—¼ hour, more or less, according to size.

Note.—Never use vinegar with salmon, as it spoils the taste and colour of the fish.

SALMON, Curried.

Ingredients.—Any remains of boiled salmon, ¾ pint of strong or medium stock, 1 onion, 1 tablespoonful of curry-powder, 1 teaspoonful of Harvey's sauce, 1 teaspoonful of anchovy sauce, 1 oz. of butter, the juice of ½ lemon, cayenne and salt to taste. *Mode.*—Cut up the onions into small pieces, and fry them of a pale brown in the butter; add all the ingredients but the salmon, and simmer gently till the onion is tender, occasionally stirring the contents; cut the salmon into small square pieces, carefully take away all skin and bone, lay it in the stewpan, and let it gradually heat through; but do not allow it to boil long. *Time.*—¾ hour. *Average cost*, exclusive of the cold fish, 9*d.*

SALMON CUTLETS.

Cut the slices 1 inch thick, and season them with pepper and salt; butter a sheet of white paper, lay each slice on a separate piece, with their ends twisted; broil gently over a clear fire, and serve with anchovy or caper sauce. When higher seasoning is required, add a few chopped herbs and a little spice. *Time.*—5 to 10 minutes.

SALMON, Pickled.

Ingredients.—Salmon, ½ oz. of whole pepper, ½ oz. of whole allspice, 1 teaspoonful of salt, 2 bay-leaves, equal quantities of vinegar and the liquor in which the fish was boiled. *Mode.*—After the fish comes from table, lay it in a nice dish with a cover to it, as it should be excluded from the air, and take away the bone; boil the liquor and vinegar with the other ingredients for 10 minutes, and let it stand to get cold; pour it over the salmon, and in 12 hours this will be fit for the table. *Time.*—10 minutes.

SALMON, Potted.

Ingredients.—Salmon, pounded mace, cloves, and pepper to taste; 3 bay-leaves, ¼ lb. butter. *Mode.*—Skin the salmon, and clean it thoroughly by wiping with a cloth (water would spoil it); cut it into square pieces, which rub with salt; let them remain till thoroughly drained, then lay them in a dish with the other ingredients, and bake. When quite done, drain them from the gravy, press into pots for use, and, when cold, pour over it clarified butter. *Time.*—½ hour.

SALMON, to Cure.

This process consists in splitting the fish, rubbing it with salt, and then putting it into pickle in tubs provided for the purpose. Here it is kept for about

six weeks, when it is taken out, pressed and packed in casks, with layers of salt.

SALMON, to Help.

First run the knife quite down to the bone, along the side of the fish, from *a* to *b*, and also from *c* to *d*. Then help the thick part lengthwise, that is, in the direction of the lines from *a* to *b*; and the thin part breadthwise, that is, in the direction of the lines from *e* to *f*, as shown in the engraving. A slice of the thick part should always be accompanied by a smaller piece of the thin from the belly, where lies the fat of the fish.

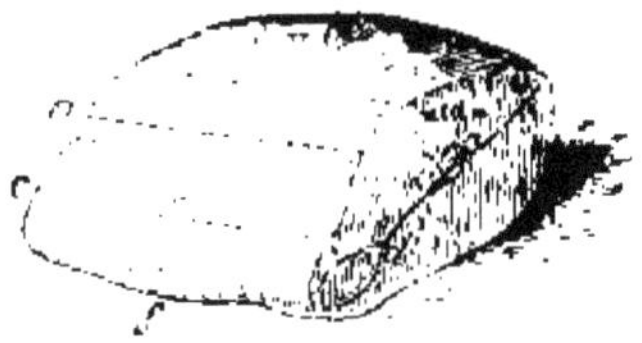

Note. — Many persons, in carving salmon, make the mistake of slicing the thick part of this fish in the opposite direction to that we have stated; and thus, by the breaking of the flakes, the beauty of its appearance is destroyed.

SALSIFY, to Dress.

Ingredients.—Salsify; to each ½ gallon of water allow 1 heaped tablespoonful of salt, 1 oz. of butter, 2 tablespoonfuls of lemon-juice. *Mode.*—Scrape the roots gently, so as to strip them only of their outside peel; cut them into pieces about 4 inches long, and, as they are peeled, throw them into water with which has been mixed a little lemon-juice, to prevent their discolouring. Put them into boiling water, with salt, butter, and lemon-juice in the above proportion, and let them boil rapidly until tender; try them with a fork; and, when it penetrates easily, they are done. Drain the salsify, and serve with a good white sauce or French melted butter. *Time.*—30 to 50 minutes. *Seasonable* in winter.

Note.—This vegetable may be also boiled, sliced, and fried in batter of a nice brown. When crisp and a good colour, they should be served with fried parsley in the centre of the dish, and a little fine salt sprinkled over the salsify.

SANDWICHES, Victoria.

Ingredients.—4 eggs; their weight in pounded sugar, butter, and flour; ¼ saltspoonful of salt, a layer of any kind of jam or marmalade. *Mode.*—Beat the butter to a cream; dredge in the flour and pounded sugar; stir these ingredients well togther, and add the eggs, which should be previously thoroughly whisked. When the mixture has been well beaten for about 10 minutes, butter a Yorkshire-pudding tin, pour in the batter, and bake it in a moderate oven for 20 minutes. Let it cool, spread one half of the cake with a layer of nice preserve, place over it the other half of the cake, press the pieces slightly together, and then cut it into long finger-pieces; pile them in crossbars, on a glass dish, and serve. *Time.*—20 minutes. *Average cost,* 1*s.* 3*d.* *Sufficient* for 5 or 6 persons. *Seasonable* at any time.

SAUCES, General Remarks upon.

The preparation and appearance of sauces and gravies are of the highest consequence, and in nothing does the talent and taste of the cook more display itself. Their special adaptability to the various viands they are to accompany cannot be too much studied, in order that they may harmonize and blend with them as perfectly, so to speak, as does a pianoforte accompaniment with the voice of the singer.

The general basis of most gravies and some sauces is the same stock as that used for soups; and, by the employment of these, with, perhaps, an additional slice of ham, a little spice, a few herbs, and a slight flavouring from some cold sauce or ketchup, very nice gravies may be made for a very small expenditure. A milt (either of a bullock or sheep), the shank-end of mutton that has already been dressed, and the necks and feet of poultry may all be advantageously used for gravy, where much is not required. It may, then, be established as a rule, that there exists no necessity for good gravies to be expensive, and that there is no occasion, as many would have the world believe, to buy ever so many pounds of fresh meat, in order to furnish an ever so little quantity of gravy.

Brown sauces, generally speaking, should scarcely be so thick as white sauces; and it is well to bear in mind, that all those which are intended to mask the various dishes of poultry or meat, should be of a sufficient consistency to slightly adhere to the fowls or joints over which they are poured. For browning and thickening sauces, &c., browned flour may be properly employed.

Sauces should possess a decided character; and whether sharp or sweet, savoury or plain, they should carry out their names in a distinct manner, although, of course, not so much flavoured as to make them too piquant on the one hand, or too mawkish on the other.

Gravies and sauces should be sent to table very hot; and there is all the more necessity for the cook to see to this point, as, from their being usually served in small quantities, they are more liable to cool quickly than if they were in a larger body. Those sauces, of which cream or eggs form a component part, should be well stirred, as soon as these ingredients are added to them, and must never be allowed to boil; as, in that case, they would instantly curdle.

SAUCE à L'AURORE, for Trout, Soles, &c.

Ingredients.—The spawn of 1 lobster, 1 oz. of butter, ½ pint of Béchamel, the juice of ½ lemon, a high seasoning of salt and cayenne. *Mode.*—Take the spawn and pound it in a mortar with the butter, until quite smooth, and work it through a hair sieve. Put the Béchamel into a stewpan, add the pounded spawn, the lemon-juice, which must be strained, and a plentiful seasoning of cayenne and salt; let it just simmer, but do not allow it to boil, or the beautiful red colour of the sauce will be spoiled. A small spoonful of anchovy essence may be added at pleasure. *Time.*—1 minute to simmer. *Average cost,* for this quantity, 1*s.* *Sufficient* for a pair of large soles. *Seasonable* at any time.

SAUCE à la MATELOTE, for Fish.

Ingredients.—½ pint of Espagnole, 3 onions, 2 tablespoonfuls of mushroom ketchup, ½ glass of port wine, a bunch of sweet herbs, ½ bay-leaf, salt and pepper to taste, 1 clove, 2 berries of allspice, a little liquor in which the fish has been boiled, lemon-juice, and anchovy sauce. *Mode.*—Slice and fry the onions of a nice brown colour, and put them into a stewpan with the Espagnole, ketchup, wine, and a little liquor in which the fish has been boiled. Add the seasoning, herbs, and spices, and simmer gently for 10 minutes, stirring well the whole time; strain it through a fine hair sieve, put in the lemon-juice and anchovy sauce, and pour it over the fish. This sauce may be very much enriched by putting in a few small quenelles, or force-meat balls made of fish, and also glazed onions or mushrooms. These, however, should not be added to the matelote till it is dished. *Time.*—10 minutes. *Average cost*, 1s 6d. *Seasonable* at any time.

Note.—This sauce originally took its name as being similar to that which the French sailor (*matelot*) employed as a relish to the fish he caught and ate. In some cases cider and perry were substituted for the wine. The Norman *matelotes* were very celebrated.

SAUCE ALLEMANDE, or German Sauce.

Ingredients.—½ pint of sauce tournée, the yolks of 2 eggs. *Mode.*—Put the sauce into a stewpan, heat it, and stir to it the beaten yolks of 2 eggs, which have been previously strained. Let it just simmer, but not boil, or the eggs will curdle; and after they are added to the sauce, it must be stirred without ceasing. This sauce is a general favourite, and is used for many made dishes. *Time.*—1 minute to simmer. *Average cost*, 6d.

SAUCE ARISTOCRATIQUE (a Store Sauce).

Ingredients.—Green walnuts. To every pint of juice, 1 lb. of anchovies, 1 drachm of cloves, 1 drachm of mace, 1 drachm of Jamaica ginger bruised, 8 shalots. To every pint of the boiled liquor, ½ pint of vinegar, ¼ pint of port wine, 2 tablespoonfuls of soy. *Mode.*—Pound the walnuts in a mortar, squeeze out the juice through a strainer, and let it stand to settle. Pour off the clear juice, and to every pint of it, add anchovies, spices, and cloves in the above proportion. Boil all these together till the anchovies are dissolved, then strain the juice again, put in the shalots (8 to every pint), and boil again. To every pint of the boiled liquor add vinegar, wine, and soy, in the above quantities, and bottle off for use. Cork well and seal the corks. *Seasonable.*—Make this sauce from the beginning to the middle of July, when walnuts are in perfection for sauces and pickling. *Average cost*, 3s. 6d. for a quart.

SAUCE, Benton (to serve with Hot or Cold Roast Beef).

Ingredients. — 1 tablespoonful of scraped horseradish, 1 teaspoonful of made mustard, 1 teaspoonful of pounded sugar, 4 tablespoonfuls of vinegar. *Mode.*—Grate or scrape the horseradish very fine, and mix it with the other ingredients, which must be all well blended together; serve in a tureen. With cold meat, this sauce is a very good substitute for pickles. *Average cost* for this quantity, 2d.

SAUCE, Mango Chetney, Bengal Recipe for Making.

Ingredients. — 1½ lb. of moist sugar, ¾ lb. of salt, ¼ lb. of garlic, ¼ lb. of onions, ¾ lb. of powdered ginger, ¼ lb. of dried chilies, ¾ lb. of mustard-seed, ¾ lb. of stoned raisins, 2 bottles of best vinegar, 30 large unripe sour apples. *Mode.*—The sugar must be made into syrup; the garlic, onions, and ginger be finely pounded in a mortar; the mustard-seed be washed in cold vinegar, and dried in the sun; the apples be peeled, cored, and sliced, and boiled in a bottle and a half of the vinegar. When all this is done, and the apples are quite cold, put them into a large pan, and gradually mix the whole of the rest of the ingredients, including the remaining half-bottle of vinegar. It must be well stirred until the whole is thoroughly blended, and then put into bottles for use. Tie a piece of wet bladder over the mouths of the bottles, after they are well corked. This chetney is very superior to any which can be bought, and one trial will prove it to be delicious.

Note.—This recipe was given by a native to an English lady, who had long been a resident in India, and who, since her return to her native country, has become quite celebrated amongst her friends for the excellence of this Eastern relish.

SAUCE, Bread (to serve with Roast Turkey, Fowl, Game, &c).

Ingredients.—1 pint of milk, ¾ lb. of the crumb of a stale loaf, 1 onion; pounded mace, cayenne, and salt to taste; 1 oz. of butter. *Mode.*—Peel and quarter the onion, and simmer it in the milk till perfectly tender. Break the bread, which should be stale, into small pieces, carefully picking out any hard or side pieces; put it in a very clean saucepan, strain the milk over it, cover it up, and let it remain for an hour to soak. Now beat it up with a fork very smoothly, add a seasoning of pounded mace, cayenne, and salt, with 1 oz. of butter; give the whole one boil, and serve. To enrich this sauce, a small quantity of cream may be added just before sending it to table. *Time.*—Altogether, 1¾ hour. *Average cost* for this quantity, 4*d.* *Sufficient* to serve with a turkey, pair of fowls, or brace of partridges.

SAUCE, Bread (to serve with Roast Turkey, Fowl, Game, &c).

Ingredients.—Giblets of poultry, ¾ lb. of the crumb of a stale loaf, 1 onion, 12 whole peppers, 1 blade of mace, salt to taste, 2 tablespoonfuls of cream or melted butter, 1 pint of water. *Mode.*—Put the giblets, with the head, neck, legs, &c., into a stewpan; add the onion, pepper, mace, salt, and rather more than 1 pint of water. Let this simmer for an hour, when strain the liquor over the bread, which should be previously grated or broken into small pieces. Cover up the saucepan, and leave it for an hour by the side of the fire; then beat the sauce up with a fork until no lumps remain, and the whole is nice and smooth. Let it boil for 3 or 4 minutes; keep stirring it until it is rather thick; when add 3 tablespoonfuls of good melted butter or cream, and serve very hot. *Time.*—2¼ hours. *Average cost*, 6*d.*

SAUCE, Christopher North's, for Meat or Game.

Ingredients.—1 glass of port wine, 2 tablespoonfuls of Harvey's sauce, 1 dessertspoonful of mushroom ketchup, ditto of pounded white sugar, 1 tablespoonful of lemon juice, ½ teaspoonful of cayenne pepper, ditto of salt. *Mode.*—Mix all the ingredients thoroughly together, and heat the sauce gradually, by placing the vessel in which it is made in a saucepan of boiling water. Do not allow it to boil, and serve directly it is ready. This sauce, if bottled immediately, will keep good for a fortnight, and will be found excellent.

SAUCE, Dutch, for Fish.

Ingredients. — ½ teaspoonful of flour, 2 oz. of butter, 2 tablespoonfuls of vinegar, 4 tablespoonfuls of water, the yolks of 2 eggs, the juice of ½ lemon; salt to taste. *Mode.*—Put all the ingredients, except the lemon-juice, into a stewpan; set it over the fire, and keep continually stirring. When it is sufficiently thick, take it off, as it should not boil. If, however, it happens to curdle, strain the sauce through a tammy, add the lemon-juice, and serve. Tarragon vinegar may be used instead of plain, and, by many, is considered far preferable. *Average cost*, 6*d.*

Note.—This sauce may be poured hot over salad, and left to get quite cold, when it should be thick, smooth, and somewhat stiff. Excellent salads may be made of hard eggs, or the remains of salt fish flaked nicely from the bone, by pouring over a little of the above mixture when hot, and allowing it to cool.

SAUCE, Green Dutch, or Hollandaise Verte.

Ingredients. — 6 tablespoonfuls of Béchamel, seasoning to taste of salt and cayenne, a little parsley-green to colour, the juice of ½ a lemon. *Mode.*—Put the Béchamel into a saucepan with the seasoning, and bring it to a boil. Make a green colouring by pounding some parsley in a mortar, and squeezing all the juice from it. Let this just simmer, when add it to the sauce. A moment before serving, put in the lemon-juice, but not before; for otherwise the sauce would turn yellow, and its appearance be thus spoiled. *Average cost*, 4*d.*

SAUCE, Epicurean, for Steaks, Chops, Gravies, or Fish.

Ingredients.—¼ pint of walnut ketchup, ¼ pint of mushroom ditto, 2 tablespoonfuls of Indian soy, 2 tablespoonfuls of port wine; ¼ oz. of white pepper, 2 oz. of shalots, ¼ oz. of cayenne, ¼ oz. of cloves, ¾ pint of vinegar. *Mode.*—Put the whole of the ingredients into a bottle, and let it remain for a fortnight in a warm place, occasionally shaking up the contents. Strain, and bottle off for use. This sauce will be found an agreeable addition to gravies, hashes, stews, &c. *Average cost*, for this quantity, 1*s.* 6*d.*

SAUCE, Genevese, for Salmon, Trout, &c.

Ingredients.—1 small carrot, a small faggot of sweet herbs, including parsley, 1 onion, 5 or 6 mushrooms (when obtainable), 1 bay-leaf, 6 cloves, 1 blade of mace, 2 oz. of butter, 1 glass of sherry, 1½ pint of white stock, thickening of butter and flour, the juice of half a lemon. *Mode.*—Cut up the onion and carrot into small rings, and put them into a stewpan with the herbs, mushrooms, bay-leaf, cloves, and mace; add the butter, and simmer the whole very gently over a slow fire until the onion is quite tender. Pour in the stock and sherry, and stew slowly for 1 hour, when strain it off into a clean saucepan. Now make a thickening of butter and flour, put it to the sauce, stir it over the fire until perfectly smooth and mellow, add the lemon-juice, give one boil, when it will be ready for table. *Time.*—Altogether 2 hours. *Average cost,* 1*s.* 3*d.* per pint. *Sufficient,* half this quantity for two slices of salmon.

SAUCE, Green, for Green Geese or Ducklings.

Ingredients.—¼ pint of sorrel-juice, 1 glass of sherry, ½ pint of green gooseberries, 1 teaspoonful of pounded sugar, 1 oz. of fresh butter. *Mode.*—Boil the gooseberries in water until they are quite tender; mash them and press them through a sieve; put the pulp into a saucepan with the above ingredients; simmer for 3 or 4 minutes, and serve very hot. *Time.*—3 or 4 minutes.

Note.—We have given this recipe as a sauce for green geese, thinking that some of our readers might sometimes require it; but, at the generality of fashionable tables, it is now seldom or never served.

SAUCE, Indian Chetney.

Ingredients.—8 oz. of sharp, sour apples, pared and cored; 8 oz. of tomatoes, 8 oz. of salt, 8 oz. of brown sugar, 8 oz. of stoned raisins, 4 oz. of cayenne, 4 oz. of powdered ginger, 2 oz. of garlic, 2 oz. of shalots, 3 quarts of vinegar, 1 quart of lemon juice. *Mode.*—Chop the apples in small square pieces, and add to them the other ingredients. Mix the whole well together, and put in a well-covered jar. Keep this in a warm place, and stir every day for a month, taking care to put on the lid after this operation; strain, but do not squeeze it dry; store it away in clean jars or bottles for use, and the liquor will serve as an excellent sauce for meat or fish. *Seasonable.*—Make this sauce when tomatoes are in full season, that is, from the beginning of September to the end of October.

SAUCE, Italian (Brown).

Ingredients.—A few chopped mushrooms and shalots, ½ pint of stock, ½ glass of Madeira, the juice of ½ lemon, ½ teaspoonful of pounded sugar, 1 teaspoonful of chopped parsley. *Mode.*—Put the stock into a stewpan with the mushrooms, shalots, and Madeira, and stew gently for ¼ hour, then add the remaining ingredients, and let them just boil. When the sauce is done enough, put it in another stewpan, and warm it in a *bain marie.* The mushrooms should not be chopped long before they are wanted, as they will then become black. *Time.*—¼ hour. *Average cost,* for this quantity, 7*d.* *Sufficient* for a small dish.

SAUCE, Italian (White).

Ingredients.—½ pint of white stock, 2 tablespoonfuls of chopped mushrooms, 1 dessertspoonful of chopped shalots, 1 slice of ham, minced very fine; ¼ pint of Béchamel; salt to taste, a few drops of garlic vinegar, ½ teaspoonful of pounded sugar, a squeeze of lemon-juice. *Mode.*—Put the shalots and mushrooms into a stewpan with the stock and ham, and simmer very gently for ½ hour, when add the Béchamel. Let it just boil up, and then strain it through a tammy; season with the above ingredients, and serve very hot. If this sauce should not have retained a nice white colour, a little cream may be added. *Time.*—½ hour. *Average cost,* for this quantity, 10*d.* *Sufficient* for a moderate-sized dish.

Note.—To preserve the colour of the mushrooms after pickling, throw them into water to which a little lemon-juice has been added.

SAUCE, Leamington (an Excellent Sauce for Flavouring Gravies, Hashes, Soups, &c.—Author's Recipe).

Ingredients.—Walnuts. To each quart of walnut-juice allow 3 quarts of vinegar,

1 pint of Indian soy, 1 oz. of cayenne, 2 oz. of shalots, ¾ oz. of garlic, ½ pint of port wine. *Mode.*—Be very particular in choosing the walnuts as soon as they appear in the market; for they are more easily bruised before they become hard and shelled. Pound them in a mortar to a pulp, strew some salt over them, and let them remain thus for two or three days, occasionally stirring and moving them about. Press out the juice, and to *each quart* of walnut-liquor allow the above proportion of vinegar, soy, cayenne, shalots, garlic, and port wine. Pound each ingredient separately in a mortar, then mix them well together, and store away for use in small bottles. The corks should be well sealed. *Seasonable.*—This sauce should be made as soon as walnuts are obtainable, from the beginning to the middle of July.

SAUCE, Maître d'Hotel (Hot), to serve with Calf's Head, Boiled Eels, and different Fish.

Ingredients.—1 slice of minced ham, a few poultry-trimmings, 2 shalots, 1 clove of garlic, 1 bay-leaf, ¾ pint of water, 2 oz. of butter, 1 dessertspoonful of flour, 1 heaped tablespoonful of chopped parsley; salt, pepper, and cayenne, to taste; the juice of ½ large lemon, ½ teaspoonful of pounded sugar. *Mode.*—Put at the bottom of a stewpan the minced ham, and over it the poultry-trimmings (if these are not at hand, veal should be substituted), with the shalots, garlic, and bay-leaf. Pour in the water, and let the whole simmer gently for 1 hour, or until the liquor is reduced to a full ½ pint. Then strain this gravy, put it in another saucepan, make a thickening of butter and flower in the above proportions, and stir it to the gravy over a nice clear fire, until it is perfectly smooth and rather thick, care being taken that the butter does not float on the surface. Skim well, add the remaining ingredients, let the sauce gradually heat, but do not allow it to boil. If this sauce is intended for an entrée, it is necessary to make it of a sufficient thickness, so that it may adhere to what it is meant to cover. *Time.*—1½ hour. *Average cost,* 1*s.* 2*d.* per pint. *Sufficient* for re-warming the remains of ½ calf's head, or a small dish of cold flaked turbot, cod, &c.

SAUCE, Maigre Maître d'Hotel (Hot.—Made without Meat).

Ingredients.—½ pint of melted butter, 1 heaped tablespoonful of chopped parsley, salt and pepper to taste, the juice of ½ large lemon; when liked, 2 minced shalots. *Mode.*—Make ½ pint of melted butter, stir in the above ingredients, and let them just boil; when it is ready to serve. *Time.*—1 minute to simmer. *Average cost,* 9*d.* per pint.

SAUCE PIQUANTE, for Cutlets, Roast Meat, &c.

Ingredients.—2 oz. of butter, 1 small carrot, 6 shalots, 1 small bunch of savoury herbs, including parsley, ½ a bay-leaf, 2 slices of lean ham, 2 cloves, 6 peppercorns, 1 blade of mace, 3 whole allspice, 4 tablespoonfuls of vinegar, ½ pint of stock, 1 small lump of sugar, ½ saltspoonful of cayenne, salt to taste. *Mode.*—Put into a stewpan the butter, with the carrots and shalots, both of which must be cut into small slices; add the herbs, bay-leaf, spices, and ham (which must be minced rather finely), and let these ingredients simmer over a slow fire, until the bottom of the stewpan is covered with a brown glaze. Keep stirring with a wooden spoon, and put in the remaining ingredients. Simmer very gently for ¼ hour, skim off every particle of fat, strain the sauce through a sieve, and serve very hot. Care must be taken that this sauce be not made too acid, although it should possess a sharpness indicated by its name. Of course the above quantity of vinegar may be increased or diminished at pleasure, according to taste. *Time.*—Altogether ½ hour. *Average cost,* 10*d.* *Sufficient* for a medium-sized dish of cutlets. *Seasonable* at any time.

SAUCE, a Good, for Various Boiled Puddings.

Ingredients.—¼ lb. of butter, ¼ lb. of pounded sugar, a wineglassful of brandy or rum. *Mode.*—Beat the butter to a cream, until no lumps remain; add the pounded sugar, and brandy or rum; stir once or twice until the whole is thoroughly mixed, and serve. This sauce may either be poured round the pudding or served in a tureen, according to the taste or fancy of the cook or mistress. *Average cost*, 8*d*. for this quantity. *Sufficient* for a pudding.

SAUCE, Plum-Pudding.

Ingredients.—1 wineglassful of brandy, 2 oz. of very fresh butter, 1 glass of Madeira, pounded sugar to taste. *Mode*.—Put the pounded sugar in a basin, with part of the brandy and the butter; let it stand by the side of the fire until it is warm and the sugar and butter are dissolved; then add the rest of the brandy, with the Madeira. Either pour it over the pudding, or serve in a tureen. This is a very rich and excellent sauce. *Average cost*, 1*s*. 3*d*. for this quantity. *Sufficient* for a pudding made for 6 persons.

SAUCE, Quin's, an Excellent Fish Sauce.

Ingredients.—½ pint of walnut pickle, ½ pint of port wine, 1 pint of mushroom ketchup, 1 dozen anchovies, 1 dozen shalots, ¼ pint of soy, ½ teaspoonful of cayenne. *Mode*.—Put all the ingredients into a saucepan, having previously chopped the shalots and anchovies very small; simmer for 15 minutes, strain, and, when cold, bottle off for use; the corks should be well sealed to exclude the air. *Time*.—¼ hour. *Seasonable* at any time.

SAUCE, Reading.

Ingredients.—2½ pints of walnut pickle, 1½ oz. of shalots, 1 quart of spring water, ¾ pint of Indian soy, ½ oz. of bruised ginger, ½ oz. of long pepper, 1 oz. of mustard-seed, 1 anchovy, ½ oz. of cayenne, ¼ oz. of dried sweet bay-leaves. *Mode*.—Bruise the shalots in a mortar, and put them in a stone jar with the walnut-liquor; place it before the fire, and let it boil until reduced to 2 pints. Then, into another jar, put all the ingredients except the bay-leaves, taking care that they are well bruised, so that the flavour may be thoroughly extracted; put this also before the fire, and let it boil for 1 hour, or rather more. When the contents of both jars are sufficiently cooked, mix them together, stirring them well as you mix them, and submit them to a slow boiling for ½ hour; cover closely, and let them stand 24 hours in a cool place; then open the jar and add the bay-leaves; let it stand a week longer closed down, when strain through a flannel bag, and it will be ready for use. The above quantities will make ½ gallon. *Time*.—Altogether, 3 hours. *Seasonable*.—This sauce may be made at any time.

SAUCE, Robert, for Steaks, &c.

Ingredients.—2 oz. of butter, 3 onions, 1 teaspoonful of flour, 4 tablespoonfuls of gravy or stock, salt and pepper to taste, 1 teaspoonful of made mustard, 1 teaspoonful of vinegar, the juice of ½ lemon. *Mode*.—Put the butter into a stewpan, set it on the fire, and, when browning, throw in the onions, which must be cut into small slices. Fry them brown, but do not burn them; add the flour, shake the onions in it, and give the whole another fry. Put in the gravy and seasoning, and boil it gently for 10 minutes; skim off the fat, add the mustard, vinegar, and lemon-juice; give it one boil, and pour round the steaks, or whatever dish the sauce has been prepared for. *Time*.—Altogether, ½ hour. *Average cost*, for this quantity, 6*d*. *Sufficient* for about 2 lbs. of steak. *Seasonable* at any time.

Note.—This sauce will be found an excellent accompaniment to roast goose, pork, mutton cutlets, and various other dishes.

SAUCE, Soyer's, for Plum-Pudding.

Ingredients.—The yolks of 3 eggs, 1 tablespoonful of powdered sugar, 1 gill of milk, a very little grated lemon-rind, 2 small wineglassfuls of brandy. *Mode*.—Separate the yolks from the whites of 3 eggs, and put the former into a stewpan; add the sugar, milk, and grated lemon-rind, and stir over the fire until the mixture thickens; but do *not* allow it to *boil*. Put in the brandy; let the sauce stand by the side of the fire, to get quite hot; keep stirring it, and serve in a boat or tureen separately, or pour it over the pudding. *Time*.—Altogether, 10 minutes. *Average cost*, 1*s*. *Sufficient* for 6 or 7 persons.

SAUCE, a Good, for Steaks.

Ingredients.—1 oz. of whole black pepper, ½ oz. of allspice, 1 oz. of salt, ½ oz. grated horseradish, ½ oz. of pickled shalots, 1 pint of mushroom ketchup or walnut pickle. *Mode*.—Pound all the ingredients finely in a mortar, and put them into the ketchup or walnut-liquor. Let them stand for a fortnight, when strain off the liquor and bottle for use. Either pour a little of the sauce over the steaks, or mix it in the gravy. *Seasonable.*—This can be made at any time.

Note.—In using a jar of pickled walnuts, there is frequently left a large quantity of liquor. This should be converted into a sauce like the above, and will be found a very useful relish.

SAUCE, Sweet, for Puddings.

Ingredients.—½ pint of melted butter made with milk, 3 teaspoonfuls of pounded sugar, flavouring of grated lemon-rind or cinnamon. *Mode.*—Make ½ pint of melted butter, omitting any salt; stir in the sugar, add a little grated lemon-rind, nutmeg, or powdered cinnamon, and serve. Previously to making the melted butter, the milk can be flavoured with bitter almonds, by infusing about half a dozen of them in it for about ½ hour; the milk should then be strained before it is added to the other ingredients. This simple sauce may be served for children with rice, batter, or bread pudding. *Time.*—Altogether, 15 minutes. *Average cost*, 4*d*. *Sufficient* for 6 or 7 persons.

SAUCE, Sweet, for Venison.

Ingredients.—A small jar of red-currant jelly, 1 glass of port wine. *Mode.*—Put the above ingredients into a stewpan, set them over the fire, and, when melted, pour in a tureen and serve. It should not be allowed to boil. *Time.*—5 minutes to melt the jelly. *Average cost*, for this quantity, 1*s*.

SAUCE, Tournée.

Ingredients.—1 pint of white stock, thickening of flour and butter, or white roux, a faggot of savoury herbs, including parsley, 6 chopped mushrooms, 6 green onions. *Mode.*—Put the stock into a stewpan with the herbs, onions, and mushrooms, and let it simmer very gently for about ½ hour; stir in sufficient thickening to make it of a proper consistency; let it boil for a few minutes, then skim off all the fat, strain and serve. This sauce, with the addition of a little cream, is now frequently called velouté. *Time.*—½ hour. *Average cost*, for this quantity, 6*d*.

Note.—If poultry trimmings are at hand, the stock should be made of these. The above sauce should not be made too thick, as it does not then admit of the fat being nicely removed.

SAUCE FOR WILDFOWL.

Ingredients.—1 glass of port wine, 1 tablespoonful of Leamington sauce, 1 tablespoonful of mushroom ketchup, 1 tablespoonful of lemon-juice, 1 slice of lemon-peel, 1 large shalot cut in slices, 1 blade of mace, cayenne to taste. *Mode.*—Put all the ingredients into a stewpan, set it over the fire, and let it simmer for about 5 minutes; then strain and serve the sauce in a tureen. *Time.*—5 minutes. *Average cost*, for this quantity, 8*d*.

SAUSAGE-MEAT, Fried.

Ingredients.—To every 1 lb. of lean pork, add ¾ lb. of fat bacon, ½ oz. of salt, 1 saltspoonful of pepper, ¼ teaspoonful of grated nutmeg, 1 teaspoonful of minced parsley. *Mode.*—Remove from the pork all skin, gristle, and bone, and chop it finely with the bacon; add the remaining ingredients, and carefully mix altogether. Pound it well in a mortar, make it into convenient-sized cakes, flour these, and fry them a nice brown for about 10 minutes. This is a very simple method of making sausage-meat, and on trial will prove very good, its great recommendation being, that it is so easily made. *Time.*—10 minutes. *Seasonable* from September to March.

SAUSAGE-MEAT STUFFING FOR TURKEYS.

Ingredients.—6 oz. of lean pork, 6 oz. of fat pork, both weighed after being chopped (beef-suet may be substituted for the latter), 2 oz. of bread-crumbs, 1 small tablespoonful of minced sage, 1 blade of pounded mace, salt and pepper to taste, 1 egg. *Mode.*—Chop the meat and fat very finely, mix with them the other ingredients, taking care that the whole is thoroughly incorporated. Moisten with the egg, and the stuffing will be ready for use. Equal quantities of this stuffing and forcemeat will be found to answer very well, as the herbs, lemon-peel, &c., in the latter, impart a very delicious flavour to the sausage-meat. As preparations, however, like stuffings and forcemeats, are matters to be decided by individual palates, they must be left, to a great extent, to the discrimination of the cook, who should study her employer's taste in this as in every other respect. *Average cost*, 9*d*. *Sufficient* for a small turkey.

SAUSAGE OR MEAT ROLLS.

Ingredients.—1 lb. of puff-paste, sausage-meat, the yolk of 1 egg. *Mode*.—Make 1 lb. of puff-paste; roll it out to the thickness of about ½ inch, or rather less, and divide it into 8, 10, or 12 squares, according to the size the rolls are intended to be. Place some sausage-meat on one-half of each square, wet the edges of the paste, and fold it over the meat; slightly press the edges together, and trim them neatly with a knife. Brush the rolls over with the yolk of an egg, and bake them in a well-heated oven for about ½ hour, or longer should they be very large. The remains of cold chicken and ham, minced and seasoned, as also cold veal or beef, make very good rolls. *Time*.—½ hour, or longer if the rolls are large. *Average cost*, 1*s*. 6*d*. *Sufficient*.—1 lb. of paste for 10 or 12 rolls. *Seasonable*, with sausage-meat, from September to March or April.

SAUSAGES, Beef.

Ingredients.—To every lb. of suet allow 2 lbs. of lean beef, seasoning to taste of salt, pepper, and mixed spices. *Mode*.—Clear the suet from skin, and chop that and the beef as finely as possible; season with pepper, salt, and spices, and mix the whole well together. Make it into flat cakes, and fry of a nice brown. Many persons pound the meat in a mortar after it is chopped; but this is not necessary when the meat is minced finely. *Time*.—10 minutes. *Average cost*, for this quantity, 1*s*. 6*d*. *Seasonable* at any time.

SAUSAGES, Fried.

Ingredients.—Sausages: a small piece of butter. *Mode*.—Prick the sausages with a fork (this prevents them from bursting), and put them into a frying-

FRIED SAUSAGES.

pan with a small piece of butter. Keep moving the pan about, and turn the sausages 3 or 4 times. In from 10 to 12 minutes they will be sufficiently cooked, unless they are *very large*, when a little more time should be allowed for them. Dish them with or without a piece of toast under them, and serve very hot. In some counties, sausages are boiled and served on toast. They should be plunged into boiling water, and simmered for about 10 or 12 minutes. *Time*.—10 to 12 minutes. *Average cost*, 10*d*. per lb. *Seasonable*.—Good from September to March.

Note.—Sometimes, in close warm weather, sausages very soon turn sour; to prevent this, put them in the oven for a few minutes with a small piece of butter to keep them moist. When wanted for table, they will not require so long frying as uncooked sausages.

SAUSAGES, Pork (Author's Oxford Recipe).

Ingredients.—1 lb. of pork, fat and lean, without skin or gristle; 1 lb. of lean veal, 1 lb. of beef suet, ½ lb. of bread-crumbs, the rind of ½ lemon, 1 small nutmeg, 6 sage-leaves, 1 teaspoonful of pepper, 2 teaspoonfuls of salt, ½ teaspoonful of savory, ½ teaspoonful of marjoram. *Mode*.—Chop the pork, veal, and suet finely together, add the bread-crumbs, lemon-peel (which should be well minced), and a small nutmeg grated. Wash and chop the sage-leaves very finely; add these with the remaining ingredients to the sausage-meat, and when thoroughly mixed, either put the meat into skins, or, when wanted for table, form it into little cakes, which should be floured and fried. *Average cost*, for this quantity, 2*s*. 6*d*. *Sufficient* for about 30 moderate-sized sausages. *Seasonable* from October to March.

SAUSAGES, Veal.

Ingredients.—Equal quantities of fat bacon and lean veal; to every lb. of meat, allow 1 teaspoonful of minced-sage, salt and pepper to taste. *Mode*.—Chop the meat and bacon finely, and to every lb. allow the above proportion of very finely-minced sage; add a seasoning of pepper and salt, mix the whole well together, make it into flat cakes, and fry a nice brown. *Seasonable* from March to October.

SAVOY CAKE.

Ingredients.—The weight of 4 eggs in pounded loaf sugar, the weight of 7 in flour, a little grated lemon-rind, or essence of almonds, or orange-flower water. *Mode.*—Break the 7 eggs, putting the yolks into one basin and the whites into another. Whisk the former, and mix with them the sugar, the grated lemon-rind, or any other flavouring to taste; beat them well together, and add the whites of the eggs, whisked to a froth. Put in the flour by degrees, continuing to beat the mixture for ¼ hour, butter a mould, pour in the cake, and bake it from 1¼ to 1½ hour. This is a very nice cake for desert, and may be iced for a supper table, or cut into slices and spread with jam, which converts it into sandwiches. *Time.*—1¼ to 1½ hour. *Average cost,* 1*s.* *Sufficient* for 1 cake. *Seasonable* at any time.

SEA-BREAM, Baked.

Ingredients.—1 bream. Seasoning to taste of salt, pepper, and cayenne; ¼ lb. of butter. *Mode.*—Well wash the bream, but do not remove the scales, and wipe away all moisture with a nice dry cloth. Season it inside and out with salt, pepper, and cayenne, and lay it in a baking-dish. Place the butter, in small pieces, upon the fish, and bake for rather more than ½ an hour. To stuff this fish before baking, will be found a great improvement. *Time.*—Rather more than ½ an hour. *Seasonable* in summer.

Note.—This fish may be broiled over a nice clear fire, and served with a good brown gravy or white sauce, or it may be stewed in wine.

SEA-KALE, Boiled.

Ingredients.—To each ½ gallon of water allow one heaped tablespoonful of salt. *Mode.*—Well wash the kale, cut away any worm-eaten pieces, and tie it into small bunches; put it into *boiling* water, salted in the above proportion, and let it boil quickly until tender. Take it out, drain, untie the bunches, and serve with plain melted butter or white sauce, a little of which may be poured over the kale. Sea-kale may also be parboiled and stewed in good brown gravy: it will then take about ½ hour altogether. *Time.*—15 minutes; when liked very thoroughly done, allow an extra 5 minutes. *Average cost,* in full season, 9*d.* per basket. *Sufficient.*—Allow 12 heads for 4 or 5 persons. *Seasonable* from February to June.

BOILED SEA-KALE.

SEED BISCUITS.

Ingredients.—1 lb. of flour, ¼ lb. of sifted sugar, ¼ lb. of butter, ½ oz. of caraway seeds, 3 eggs. *Mode.*—Beat the butter to a cream; stir in the flour, sugar, and caraway seeds; and when these ingredients are well mixed, add the eggs, which should be well whisked. Roll out the paste, with a round cutter shape out the biscuits, and bake them in a moderate oven from 10 to 15 minutes. The tops of the biscuits may be brushed over with a little milk or the white of an egg, and then a little sugar strewn over. *Time.*—10 or 15 minutes. *Average cost,* 1*s.* *Sufficient* to make 3 dozen biscuits. *Seasonable* at any time.

SEED-CAKE, Common.

Ingredients.—½ quartern of dough, ¼ lb. of good dripping, 6 oz. of moist sugar, ½ oz. of caraway seeds, 1 egg. *Mode.*—If the dough is sent in from the bakers, put it in a basin covered with a cloth, and set it in a warm place to rise. Then with a wooden spoon beat the dripping to a liquid; add it, with the other ingredients, to the dough, and beat it until everything is very thoroughly mixed. Put it into a buttered tin, and bake the cake for rather more than 2 hours. *Time.*—Rather more than 2 hours. *Average cost,* 8*d.* *Seasonable* at any time.

SEED-CAKE, a Very Good.

Ingredients.—1 lb. of butter, 6 eggs, ¾ lb. of sifted sugar, pounded mace and grated nutmeg to taste, 1 lb. of flour, ¾ oz. of caraway seeds, 1 wineglassful of brandy. *Mode.*—Beat the butter to a cream; dredge in the flour; add the sugar, mace, nutmeg, and caraway seeds, and mix these ingredients well together. Whisk the eggs, stir to them the brandy, and beat the cake again for 10 minutes. Put it into a tin lined with buttered paper, and bake it from 1½ to 2 hours. This cake would be equally nice made with currants, and omitting the caraway seeds. *Time.*—1½ to 2 hours. *Average cost*, 2*s.* 6*d.* *Seasonable* at any time.

SEMOLINA PUDDING, Baked.

Ingredients.—3 oz. of semolina, 1½ pint of milk, ¼ lb. of sugar, 12 bitter almonds, 3 oz. of butter, 4 eggs. *Mode.*—Flavour the milk with the bitter almonds, by infusing them in it by the side of the fire for about ½ hour; then strain it, and mix with it the semolina, sugar, and butter. Stir these ingredients over the fire for a few minutes; then take them off, and gradually mix in the eggs, which should be well beaten. Butter a pie-dish, line the edges with puff-paste, put in the pudding, and bake in rather a slow oven from 40 to 50 minutes. Serve with custard sauce or stewed fruit, a little of which may be poured over the pudding. *Time.*—40 to 50 minutes. *Average cost*, 1*s.* 2*d.* *Sufficient* for 5 or 6 persons. *Seasonable* at any time.

SEMOLINA SOUP.

Ingredients.—5 oz. of semolina, 2 quarts of boiling stock. *Mode.*—Drop the semolina into the boiling stock, and keep stirring, to prevent its burning. Simmer gently for half an hour, and serve. *Time.* ¾ an hour. *Average cost*, 10*d.* per quart, or 4*d.* *Sufficient* for 8 persons. *Seasonable* all the year.

SEPTEMBER—BILLS OF FARE.

Dinner for 18 Persons.

First Course.

Red Mullet & Italian Sauce.	Julienne Soup, removed by Brill & Shrimp Sauce.	Fried Eels.
	Vase of Flowers.	
	Giblet Soup, removed by Salmon and Lobster Sauce.	

Entrées.

Fillets of Chicken and Truffles.	Lamb Cutlets and French Beans.	Oysters au gratin.
	Vase of Flowers.	
	Sweetbreads and Tomato Sauce.	

Second Course.

Chickens à la Béchamel.	Saddle of Mutton.	Braised Goose.
	Veal-and-Ham Pie.	
	Vase of Flowers.	
	Broiled Ham, garnished with Cauliflowers.	
	Fillet of Veal.	

Third Course.

Custards.		Partridges, removed by Plum-pudding.		Apple Tart.
	Noyeau Jelly.	Compôte of Greengages.	Lemon Cream.	
		Vase of Flowers.		
Plum Tart.		Pastry Sandwiches.		Custards.
		Grouse & Bread Sauce, removed by Nesselrode Pudding.		

Dessert and Ices.

Dinner for 12 persons.

First Course.—Mock-turtle soup; soup à la Jardinière; salmon and lobster sauce; fried whitings; stewed eels. *Entrées*—Veal cutlets; scalloped oysters; curried fowl; grilled mushrooms. *Second Course.*—Haunch of mutton; boiled calf's head à la Béchamel; braised ham; roast fowls aux Cressons. *Third Course.*—Leveret; grouse; cabinet pudding; iced pudding; compôte of plums; damson tart; cream; fruit jelly; prawns; lobster salad. Dessert and ices.

Dinner for 8 persons.

First Course.—Flemish soup; turbot, garnished with fried smelts; red mullet and Italian sauce. *Entrées.*—Tendrons de veau and truffles; lamb cutlets and sauce piquante. *Second Course.*—Loin of veal à la Béchamel; roast haunch of venison; braised ham; grouse pie; vegetables. *Third Course.* — Roast hare; plum tart; whipped cream; punch jelly; compôte of damsons; marrow pudding; dessert.

Dinner for 6 persons.

First Course.—Game soup; crimped skate; slices of salmon à la genévèse. *Entrées.* — Fricasseed sweetbreads; savoury rissoles. *Second Course.*—Sirloin of beef and horseradish sauce; boiled leg of mutton and caper sauce; vegetables. *Third Course.*—Roast partridges; charlotte Russe; apricots and rice; fruit jelly; cabinet pudding; dessert.

First Course. — Thick gravy soup; fillets of turbot à la crême; stewed eels. *Entrées.*—Vol-au-vent of lobster; salmi of grouse. *Second Course.*—Haunch of venison; rump of beef à la Jardinière; hare, boned and larded, with mushrooms. *Third Course.*—Roast grouse; apricot blancmange; compôte of peaches; plum-tart; custards; plum-pudding; dessert.

SEPTEMBER, Plain Family Dinners for.

Sunday.—1. Julienne soup. 2. Roast ribs of beef, Yorkshire pudding, horseradish sauce, French beans, and potatoes. 3. Greengage pudding, vanilla cream.

Monday.—1. Crimped skate and crab sauce. 2. Cold beef and salad, small veal-and-ham pie. 3. Vegetable marrow and white sauce.

Tuesday. — 1. Fried soles, melted butter. 2. Bowled fowls, parsley-and-butter; bacon-cheek, garnished with French beans; beef rissoles, made from remains of cold beef. 3. Plum tart and cream.

Wednesday.—1. Boiled round of beef, carrots, turnips, and suet dumplings; marrow on toast. 2. Baked damsons and rice.

Thursday.—1. Vegetable soup, made from liquor that beef was boiled in. 2. Lamb cutlets and cucumbers, cold beef and salad. 3. Apple pudding.

Friday.—1. Baked soles. 2. Bubble-and-squeak, made from cold beef; veal cutlets and rolled bacon. 3. Damson tart.

Saturday.—1. Irish stew, rump-steaks and oyster-sauce. 2. Somersetshire dumplings.

Sunday. — 1. Fried filleted soles and anchovy sauce. 2. Roast leg of mutton, brown onion sauce, French beans, and potatoes; half calf's head, tongue, and brains. 3. Plum-tart; custards, in glasses.

Monday.—1. Vegetable-marrow soup. 2. Calf's head à la maître d'hôtel, from remains of cold head; boiled brisket of beef and vegetables. 3. Stewed fruit and baked rice pudding.

Tuesday.—1. Roast fowls and water-cresses; boiled bacon, garnished with tufts of cauliflower; hashed mutton, from remains of mutton of Sunday. 2. Baked plum-pudding.

Wednesday.—1. Boiled knuckle of veal and rice, turnips, potatoes; small ham, garnished with French beans. 2. Baked apple pudding.

Thursday.—1. Brill and shrimp sauce. 2. Roast hare, gravy, and red-currant jelly; mutton cutlets and mashed potatoes. 3. Scalloped oysters, instead of pudding.

Friday. — 1. Small roast loin of mutton; the remains of hare, jugged; vegetable marrow and potatoes. 2. Damson pudding.

Saturday.—1. Rump-steaks, broiled, and oyster-sauce, mashed potatoes; veal-and-ham pie,—the ham may be cut from that boiled on Wednesday, if not all eaten cold for breakfast. 2. Lemon pudding.

SEPTEMBER, Things in Season.

Fish.—Brill, carp, cod, eels, flounders, lobsters, mullet, oysters, plaice, prawns, skate, soles, turbot, whiting, whitebait.

Meat.—Beef, lamb, mutton, pork, veal.

Poultry. — Chickens, ducks, fowls, geese, larks, pigeons, pullets, rabbits, teal, turkeys.

Game. — Blackcock, buck venison, grouse, hares, partridges, pheasants.

Vegetables. — Artichokes, asparagus, beans, cabbage sprouts, carrots, celery, lettuces, mushrooms, onions, pease, potatoes, salads, sea-kale, sprouts, tomatoes, turnips, vegetable marrows,—various herbs.

Fruit.—Bullaces, damsons, figs, filberts, grapes, melons, morella cherries, mulberries, nectarines, peaches, pears, plums, quinces, walnuts.

SHAD, to Dress.

Ingredients.—1 shad, oil, pepper, and salt. *Mode.*—Scale, empty and wash the fish carefully, and make two or three incisions across the back. Season it with pepper and salt, and let it remain in oil for ½ hour. Broil it on both sides over a clear fire, and serve with caper sauce. This fish is much esteemed by the French, and by them is considered excellent. *Time.*—Nearly 1 hour. *Average cost.* —Seldom bought. *Seasonable* from April to June.

SHEEP'S BRAINS, en Matelote (an Entrée).

Ingredients.—6 sheep's brains, vinegar, salt, a few slices of bacon, 1 small onion, 2 cloves, a small bunch of parsley, sufficient stock or weak broth to cover the brains, 1 tablespoonful of lemon-juice, matelote sauce. *Mode.*—Detach the brains from the head without breaking them, and put them into a pan of warm water; remove the skin, and let them remain for two hours. Have ready a saucepan of boiling water, add a little vinegar and salt, and put in the brains. When they are quite firm, take them out and put them into very cold water. Place 2 or 3 slices of bacon in a stewpan, put in the brains, the onion stuck with 2 cloves, the parsley, and a good seasoning of pepper and salt; cover with stock, or weak broth, and boil them gently for about 25 minutes. Have ready some croûtons; arrange these in the dish alternately with the brains, and cover with a matelote sauce, to which has been added the above proportion of lemon-juice. *Time.*—25 minutes. *Average cost,* 1*s.* 6*d.* *Sufficient* for 6 persons. *Seasonable* at any time.

SHEEP'S FEET or TROTTERS (Soyer's Recipe).

Ingredients.—12 feet, ½ lb. of beef or mutton suet, 2 onions, 1 carrot, 2 bay-leaves, 2 sprigs of thyme, 1 oz. of salt, ¼ oz. of pepper, 2 tablespoonfuls of flour, 2½ quarts of water, ¼ lb. of fresh butter, 1 teaspoonful of salt, 1 teaspoonful of flour, ½ teaspoonful of pepper, a little grated nutmeg, the juice of 1 lemon, 1 gill of milk, the yolks of 2 eggs. *Mode.*—Have the feet cleaned, and the long bone extracted from them. Put the suet into a stewpan, with the onions and carrot sliced, the bay-leaves, thyme, salt, and pepper, and let these simmer for 5 minutes. Add 2 tablespoonfuls of flour and the water, and keep stirring till it boils; then put in the feet. Let these simmer for 3 hours, or until perfectly tender, and take them and lay them on a sieve. Mix together, on a plate, with the back of a spoon, butter, salt, flour (1 teaspoonful), pepper, nutmeg, and lemon-juice as above, and put the feet, with a gill of milk, into a stewpan. When very hot, add the butter, &c., and stir continually till melted. Now mix the yolks of 2 eggs with 5 tablespoonfuls of milk; stir this to the other ingredients, keep moving the pan over the fire continually for a minute or two, but do not allow it to boil after the eggs are added. Serve in a very hot dish, and garnish with croûtons, or sippets of toasted bread. *Time.* —3 hours. *Average cost,* 1*s.* 6*d.* *Sufficient* for 4 persons. *Seasonable* at any time.

SHEEP'S HEAD.

Ingredients.—1 sheep's head, sufficient water to cover it, 3 carrots, 3 turnips, 2 or 3 parsnips, 3 onions, a small bunch of parsley, 1 teaspoonful of pepper, 3 teaspoonfuls of salt, ¼ lb. of Scotch oatmeal. *Mode.*—Clean the head well, and let it soak in warm water for 2 hours, to get rid of the blood; put it into a saucepan, with sufficient cold water to cover it, and when it boils, add the vegetables, peeled and sliced, and the remaining ingredients; before adding the oatmeal, mix it to a smooth batter with a little of the liquor. Keep stirring till it boils up; then shut the saucepan closely, and let it stew gently for 1½ or 2 hours. It may be thickened with rice or barley, but oatmeal is preferable. *Time.*—1½ to 2 hours. *Average cost,* 8*d.* each. *Sufficient* for 3 persons. *Seasonable* at any time.

SHORTBREAD, Scotch.

Ingredients.—2 lbs. of flour, 1 lb. of butter, ¼ lb. of pounded loaf sugar, ½ oz. of caraway seeds, 1 oz. of sweet almonds, a few strips of candied orange-peel.

Mode.—Beat the butter to a cream, gradually dredge in the flour, and add the sugar, caraway seeds, and sweet almonds, which should be blanched and cut into small pieces. Work the paste until it is quite smooth, and divide it into six pieces. Put each cake on a separate piece of paper, roll the paste out square to the thickness of about an

SHORTBREAD.

inch, and pinch it upon all sides. Prick it well, and ornament with one or two strips of candied orange-peel. Put the cakes into a good oven, and bake them from 25 to 30 minutes. *Time.*—25 to 30 minutes. *Average cost,* for this quantity, 2*s.* *Sufficient* to make 6 cakes. *Seasonable* at any time.

Note.—Where the flavour of the caraway seeds is disliked, omit them, and add rather a larger proportion of candied peel.

SHRIMP SAUCE, for Various Kinds of Fish.

Ingredients.—½ pint of melted butter, ¼ pint of picked shrimps, cayenne to taste. *Mode.*—Make the melted butter very smoothly, shell the shrimps (sufficient to make ¼ pint when picked), and put them into the butter; season with cayenne, and let the sauce just simmer, but do not allow it to boil. When liked, a teaspoonful of anchovy sauce may be added. *Time.*—1 minute to simmer. *Average cost,* 6*d.* *Sufficient* for 3 or 4 persons.

SHRIMPS OR PRAWNS, to Boil.

Ingredients.—¼ lb. salt to each gallon of water. *Mode.*—Prawns should be very red, and have no spawn under the tail; much depends on their freshness and the way in which they are cooked. Throw them into boiling water, salted as above, and keep them boiling for about 7 or 8 minutes. Shrimps should be done in the same way; but less time must be allowed. It may easily be known when they are done by their changing colour. Care should be taken that they are not over-boiled, as they then become tasteless and indigestible. *Time.*—Prawns, about 8 minutes; shrimps, about 5 minutes. *Average cost,* prawns, 2*s.* per lb.; shrimps, 6*d.* per pint. *Seasonable* all the year.

SHRIMPS OR PRAWNS, Buttered.

Ingredients.—1 pint of picked prawns or shrimps, ¾ pint of stock, thickening of butter and flour; salt, cayenne, and nutmeg to taste. *Mode.*—Pick the prawns or shrimps, and put them in a stewpan with the stock; add a thickening of butter and flour; season, and simmer gently for 3 minutes. Serve on a dish garnished with fried bread or toasted sippets. Cream sauce may be substituted for the gravy. *Time.*—3 minutes. *Average cost* for this quantity, 1*s.* 4*d.*

SHRIMPS, Potted.

Ingredients.—1 pint of shelled shrimps, ¼ lb. of fresh butter, 1 blade of pounded mace, cayenne to taste; when liked, a little nutmeg. *Mode.*—Have ready a pint of picked shrimps, and put them, with the other ingredients, into a stewpan; let them heat gradually in the butter, but do not let it boil. Pour into small pots, and when cold, cover with melted butter, and carefully exclude the air. *Time.*—¼ hour to soak in the butter. *Average cost* for this quantity, 1*s.* 3*d.*

SKATE, to choose.

This fish should be chosen for its firmness, breadth, and thickness, and should have a creamy appearance. When crimped, it should not be kept longer than a day or two, as all kinds of crimped fish soon become sour. Thornback is often substituted for skate, but is very inferior in quality to the true skate.

SKATE, Boiled.

Ingredients.—¼ lb. of salt to each gallon of water. *Mode.*—Cleanse and skin the skate, lay it in a fish-kettle, with sufficient water to cover it, salted in the above proportion. Let it simmer very gently till done; then dish it on a hot napkin, and serve with shrimp, lobster, or caper sauce. *Time.*—According to size, from ½ to 1 hour. *Average cost,* 4*d.* per lb. *Seasonable* from August to April.

SKATE, Crimped.

Ingredients.—½ lb. of salt to each gallon of water. *Mode*.—Clean, skin, and cut the fish into slices, which roll and tie round with string. Have ready some water highly salted, put in the fish, and boil till it is done. Drain well, remove the string, dish on a hot napkin, and serve with the same sauces as above. Skate should never be eaten out of season, as it is liable to produce diarrhœa and other diseases. It may be dished without a napkin, and the sauce poured over. *Time*.—About 20 minutes. *Average cost*, 4*d*. per lb. *Seasonable* from August to April.

SKATE, With Caper Sauce (à la Française).

Ingredients.—2 or 3 slices of skate, ½ pint of vinegar, 2 oz. of salt, ½ teaspoonful of pepper, 1 sliced onion, a small bunch of parsley, 2 bay-leaves, 2 or 3 sprigs of thyme, sufficient water to cover the fish. *Mode*.—Put in a fish-kettle all the above ingredients, and simmer the skate in them till tender. When it is done, skin it neatly, and pour over it some of the liquor in which it has been boiling. Drain it, put it on a hot dish, pour over it caper sauce, and send some of the latter to table in a tureen. *Time*.—½ hour. *Average cost*, 4*d*. per lb. *Seasonable* from August to April.

Note.—Skate may also be served with onion sauce, or parsley and butter.

SKATE, Small, Fried.

Ingredients.—Skate, sufficient vinegar to cover them, salt and pepper to taste, 1 sliced onion, a small bunch of parsley, the juice of ½ lemon, hot dripping. *Mode*.—Cleanse the skate, lay them in a dish, with sufficient vinegar to cover them; add the salt, pepper, onion, parsley, and lemon-juice, and let the fish remain in this pickle for ½ hour. Then drain them well, flour them, and fry of a nice brown, in hot dripping. They may be served either with or without sauce. Skate is not good if dressed too fresh, unless it is crimped; it should, therefore, be kept for a day, but not long enough to produce a disagreeable smell. *Time*.—10 minutes. *Average cost*, 4*d*. per lb. *Seasonable* from August to April.

SMELTS.

When good, this fish is of a fine silvery appearance, and when alive, their backs are of a dark brown shade, which, after death, fades to a light fawn. They ought to have a refreshing fragrance, resembling that of a cucumber.

SMELTS, to Bake.

Ingredients.—12 smelts, bread-crumbs, ¼ lb. of fresh butter, 2 blades of pounded mace; salt and cayenne to taste. *Mode*.—Wash, and dry the fish thoroughly in a cloth, and arrange them nicely in a flat baking-dish. Cover them with fine bread-crumbs, and place little pieces of butter all over them. Season and bake for 15 minutes. Just before serving, add a squeeze of lemon-juice, and garnish with fried parsley and cut lemon. *Time*.—¼ hour. *Average cost*, 2*s*. per dozen. *Seasonable* from October to May. *Sufficient* for 6 persons.

SMELTS, to Fry.

Ingredients.—Egg and bread-crumbs, a little flour; boiling lard. *Mode*.—Smelts should be very fresh, and not washed more than is necessary to clean them. Dry them in a cloth, lightly flour, dip them in egg, and sprinkle over with very fine bread-crumbs, and put them into boiling lard. Fry of a nice pale brown, and be careful not to take off the light roughness of the crumbs, or their beauty will be spoiled. Dry them before the fire on a drainer, and serve with plain melted butter. This fish is often used as a garnishing. *Time*.—5 minutes. *Average cost*, 2*s*. per dozen. *Seasonable* from October to May.

SNIPES, to Dress.

Ingredients. — Snipes, butter, flour, toast. *Mode*.—These, like woodcocks, should be dressed without being drawn. Pluck, and wipe them outside, and truss them with the head under the wing, having previously skinned that and the neck. Twist the legs at the first joint, press the feet upon the thighs, and pass a skewer through these and the body. Place four on a skewer, tie them on to the jack or spit, and roast before a clear fire for about

ROAST SNIPE.

¼ hour. Put some pieces of buttered toast into the dripping-pan to catch the trails; flour and froth the birds nicely, dish the pieces of toast with the snipes on them, and pour round, but not over them, a little good brown gravy. They should be sent to table very hot and expeditiously, or they will not be worth eating. *Time.*—About ¼ hour. *Average cost*, 1s. 6d. to 2s. the brace. *Sufficient.*—4 for a dish. *Seasonable* from November to February.

Note.—Ortolans are trussed and dressed in the same manner.

SNIPES, to Carve.

One of these small but delicious birds may be given, whole, to a gentleman; but, in helping a lady, it will be better to cut them quite through the centre, from 1 to 2, completely dividing them into equal and like portions, and put only one half on the plate.

SNIPE.

SNOW-CAKE.

Ingredients.—½ lb. of *tous-les-mois*, ¼ lb. of white pounded sugar, ¼ lb. of fresh or washed salt butter, 1 egg, the juice of 1 lemon. *Mode.*—Beat the butter to a cream; then add the egg, previously well beaten, and then the other ingredients; if the mixture is not light, add another egg, and beat for ¼ hour, until it turns white and light. Line a flat tin, with raised edges, with a sheet of buttered paper; pour in the cake, and put it into the oven. It must be rather slow, and the cake not allowed to brown at all. If the oven is properly heated, 1 to 1¼ hour will be found long enough to bake it. Let it cool a few minutes, then with a clean sharp knife cut it into small square pieces, which should be gently removed to a large flat dish to cool before putting away. This will keep for several weeks. *Time.*—1 to 1¼ hour. *Average cost*, 1s. 3d. *Seasonable* at any time.

SNOW-CAKE (a genuine Scotch Recipe).

Ingredients.—1 lb. of arrowroot, ½ lb. of pounded white sugar, ½ lb. of butter, the whites of 6 eggs; flavouring to taste, of essence of almonds, or vanilla, or lemon. *Mode.*—Beat the butter to a cream; stir in the sugar and arrowroot gradually, at the same time beating the mixture. Whisk the whites of the eggs to a stiff froth, add them to the other ingredients, and beat well for 20 minutes. Put in whichever of the above flavourings may be preferred; pour the cake into a buttered mould or tin, and bake it in a moderate oven from 1 to 1½ hour. *Time.*—1 to 1½ hour. *Average cost*, with the best Bermuda arrowroot, 4s. 6d.; with St. Vincent ditto, 2s. 9d. *Sufficient* to make a moderate-sized cake. *Seasonable* at any time.

SODA-BISCUITS.

Ingredients.—1 lb. of flour, ½ lb. of pounded loaf sugar, ¼ lb. of fresh butter, 2 eggs, 1 small teaspoonful of carbonate of soda. *Mode.*—Put the flour (which should be perfectly dry) into a basin; rub in the butter, add the sugar, and mix these ingredients well together. Whisk the eggs, stir them into the mixture, and beat it well, until everything is well incorporated. Quickly stir in the soda, roll the paste out until it is about ½ inch thick, cut it into small round cakes with a tin cutter, and bake them from 12 to 18 minutes in rather a brisk oven. After the soda is added, great expedition is necessary in rolling and cutting out the paste, and in putting the biscuits *immediately* into the oven, or they will be heavy. *Time.*—12 to 18 minutes. *Average cost*, 1s. *Sufficient* to make about 3 dozen cakes. *Seasonable* at any time.

SODA-BREAD.

Ingredients.—To every 2 lbs. of flour allow 1 teaspoonful of tartaric acid, 1 teaspoonful of salt, 1 teaspoonful of carbonate of soda, 2 breakfast-cupfuls of cold milk. *Mode.*—Let the tartaric acid and salt be reduced to the finest possible powder; then mix them well with the flour. Dissolve the soda in the milk, and pour it several times from one basin to another, before adding it to the flour. Work the whole quickly into a light dough, divide it into 2 loaves, and put them into a well-heated oven immediately, and bake for an hour. Sour milk or buttermilk may be used, but then a little less acid will be needed. *Time.*—1 hour.

SODA-CAKE.

Ingredients.—½ lb. of butter, 1 lb. of flour, ½ lb. of currants, ½ lb. of moist sugar, 1 teacupful of milk, 3 eggs, 1 teaspoonful of carbonate of soda. *Mode.*—Rub the butter into the flour, add the currants and sugar, and mix these ingredients well together. Whisk the eggs well; stir them to the flour, &c., with the milk, in which the soda should be previously dissolved, and beat the whole up together with a wooden spoon or beater. Divide the dough into two pieces, put them into buttered moulds or cake-tins, and bake in a moderate oven for nearly an hour. The mixture must be extremely well beaten up, and not allowed to stand after the soda is added to it, but must be placed in the oven immediately. Great care must also be taken that the cakes are quite done through, which may be ascertained by thrusting a knife into the middle of them: if the blade looks bright when withdrawn, they are done. If the tops acquire too much colour before the inside is sufficiently baked, cover them over with a piece of clean white paper, to prevent them from burning. *Time.*—1 hour. *Average cost,* 1*s.* 6*d.* *Sufficient* to make 2 small cakes. *Seasonable* at any time.

SOLE OR COD PIE.

Ingredients.—The remains of cold boiled sole or cod, seasoning to taste of pepper, salt, and pounded mace, 1 dozen oysters to each lb. of fish, 3 tablespoonfuls of white stock, 1 teacupful of cream thickened with flour, puff paste. *Mode.*—Clear the fish from the bones, lay it in a pie-dish, and between each layer put a few oysters and a little seasoning; add the stock, and, when liked, a small quantity of butter; cover with puff paste, and bake for ½ hour. Boil the cream with sufficient flour to thicken it; pour in the pie, and serve. *Time.*—½ hour. *Average cost* for this quantity, 10*d.* *Sufficient* for 4 persons. *Seasonable* at any time.

SOLES, to Choose.

This fish should be both thick and firm. If the skin is difficult to be taken off, and the flesh looks grey, it is good.

SOLES, Baked.

Ingredients.—2 soles, ¼ lb. of butter, egg, and bread-crumbs, minced parsley, 1 glass of sherry, lemon-juice; cayenne and salt to taste. *Mode.*—Clean, skin, and well wash the fish, and dry them thoroughly in a cloth. Brush them over with egg, sprinkle with bread-crumbs mixed with a little minced parsley, lay them in a large flat baking-dish, white side uppermost; or if it will not hold the two soles, they may each be laid on a dish by itself; but they must not be put one on the top of the other. Melt the butter, and pour it over the whole, and bake for 20 minutes. Take a portion of the gravy that flows from the fish, add the wine, lemon-juice, and seasoning, give it one boil, skim, pour it *under* the fish, and serve. *Time.*—20 minutes. *Average cost,* 1*s.* to 2*s.* per pair. *Sufficient* for 4 or 5 persons. *Seasonable* at any time.

SOLES, Boiled.

Ingredients.—¼ lb. salt to each gallon of water. *Mode.*—Cleanse and wash the fish carefully, cut off the fins, but do not skin it. Lay it in a fish-kettle, with sufficient cold water to cover it, salted in the above proportion. Let it gradually come to a boil, and keep it simmering for a few minutes, according to the size of the fish. Dish it on a hot napkin after well draining it, and garnish with parsley and cut lemon. Shrimp, or lobster sauce, and plain melted butter, are usually sent to table with this dish. *Time.*—After the water boils, 7 minutes for a middling-sized sole. *Average cost,* 1*s.* to 2*s.* per pair. *Sufficient.*—1 middling-sized sole for two persons. *Seasonable* at any time.

SOLES, Boiled or Fried, to Help.

The usual way of helping this fish is to cut it right through, bone and all, distributing it in nice and not too large pieces. A moderately-sized sole will be sufficient for three slices; namely, the head, middle, and tail. The guests should be asked which of these they prefer. A small one will only give two slices. If the sole is very large, the upper side may be raised from the bone, and then divided into pieces; and the under side afterwards served in the same way.

In helping Filleted Soles, one fillet is given to each person.

SOLES, Filleted, à l'Italienne.

Ingredients. —2 soles; salt, pepper, and grated nutmeg to taste; egg and bread-crumbs, butter, the juice of 1 lemon. *Mode.*—Skin, and carefully wash the soles, separate the meat from the bone, and divide each fillet in two pieces. Brush them over with white of egg, sprinkle with bread-crumbs and seasoning, and put them in a baking-dish. Place small pieces of butter over the whole, and bake for ½ hour. When they are nearly done, squeeze the juice of a lemon over them, and serve on a dish, with Italian sauce (*see* Sauces) poured over. *Time.*—½ hour. *Average cost,* from 1*s.* to 2*s.* per pair. *Sufficient* for 4 or 5 persons. *Seasonable* at any time.

Whiting may be dressed in the same manner, and will be found very delicious.

SOLES, Fricasseed.

Ingredients.—2 middling-sized soles, 1 small one, ½ teaspoonful of chopped lemon-peel, 1 teaspoonful of chopped parsley, a little grated bread; salt, pepper, and nutmeg to taste; 1 egg, 2 oz. butter, ½ pint of good gravy, 2 tablespoonful of port wine, cayenne and lemon-juice to taste. *Mode.*—Fry the soles of a nice brown, and drain them well from fat. Take all the meat from the small sole, chop it fine, and mix with it the lemon-peel, parsley, bread, and seasoning; work altogether, with the yolk of an egg and the butter; make this into small balls, and fry them. Thicken the gravy with a dessertspoonful of flour, add the port wine, cayenne, and lemon-juice; lay in the 2 soles and balls; let them simmer gently for 5 minutes; serve hot, and garnish with cut lemon. *Time.*—10 minutes to fry the soles. *Average cost* for this quantity, 3*s.* *Sufficient* for 4 or 5 persons. *Seasonable* at any time.

SOLES, Fried Filleted.

Soles for filleting should be large, as the flesh can be more easily separated from the bones, and there is less waste. Skin and wash the fish, and raise the meat carefully from the bones, and divide it into nice handsome pieces. The more usual way is to roll the fillets, after dividing each one in two pieces, and either bind them round with twine, or run a small skewer through them. Brush over with egg, and cover with bread-crumbs; fry them as directed in the foregoing recipe, and garnish with fried parsley and cut lemon. When a pretty dish is desired, this is by far the most elegant mode of dressing soles, as they look much better than when fried whole. Instead of rolling the fillets, they may be cut into square pieces, and arranged in the shape of a pyramid on the dish. *Time.*—About 10 minutes. *Average cost,* from 1*s.* to 2*s.* per pair. *Sufficient,* 2 large soles for 6 persons. *Seasonable* at any time.

SOLES, Fried.

Ingredients.—2 middling-sized soles, hot lard or clarified dripping, egg, and bread-crumbs. *Mode.*—Skin and carefully wash the soles, and cut off the fins, wipe them very dry, and let them remain in the cloth until it is time to dress them. Have ready some fine bread-crumbs and beaten egg; dredge the soles with a little flour, brush them over with egg, and cover with bread-crumbs. Put them in a deep pan, with plenty of clarified dripping or lard (when the expense is not objected to, oil is still better) heated, so that it may neither scorch the fish nor make them sodden. When they are sufficiently cooked on one side, turn them carefully, and brown them on the other: they may be considered ready when a thick smoke rises. Lift them out carefully, and lay them before the fire on a reversed sieve and soft paper, to absorb the fat. Particular attention should be paid to this, as nothing is more disagreeable than greasy fish: this may be always avoided by dressing them in good time, and allowing a few minutes for them to get thoroughly crisp, and free from greasy moisture. Dish them on a hot napkin, garnish with cut lemon and fried parsley, and send them to table with shrimp sauce and plain melted butter. *Time.*—10 minutes for large soles; less time for small ones. *Average cost,* from 1*s.* to 2*s.* per pair. *Sufficient* for 4 or 5 persons. *Seasonable* at any time.

SOLES, with Mushrooms.

Ingredients.—1 pint of milk, 1 pint of water, 1 oz. butter, 1 oz. salt, a little lemon-juice, 2 middling-sized soles. *Mode.*—Cleanse the soles, but do not skin them, and lay them in a fish-kettle, with the milk, water, butter, salt, and lemon-juice. Bring them gradually to boil, and let them simmer very gently till done, which will be in about 7 minutes. Take them up, drain them well on a cloth, put them on a hot dish, and pour over them a good mushroom sauce. (*See* Sauces.) *Time.*—After the water boils, 7 minutes. *Sufficient* for 4 persons. *Seasonable* at any time.

SOLES, with Cream Sauce.

Ingredients. — 2 soles; salt, cayenne, and pounded mace to taste; the juice of ½ lemon, salt and water, ½ pint of cream. *Mode.*—Skin, wash, and fillet the soles, and divide each fillet in 2 pieces; lay them in cold salt and water, which bring gradually to a boil. When the water boils, take out the fish, lay it in a delicately clean stewpan, and cover with the cream. Add the seasoning, simmer very gently for ten minutes, and, just before serving, put in the lemon-juice. The fillets may be rolled, and secured by means of a skewer; but this is not so economical a way of dressing them, as double the quantity of cream is required. *Time.*—10 minutes in the cream. *Average cost*, from 1*s.* to 2*s.* per pair. *Sufficient* for 4 or 5 persons. *Seasonable* at any time.

This will be found a most delicate and delicious dish.

SOUFFLE, to make.

Ingredients.—3 heaped tablespoonfuls of potato-flour, rice-flour, arrowroot, or tapioca, 1 pint of milk, 5 eggs, a piece of butter the size of a walnut, sifted sugar to taste, ¼ saltspoonful of salt flavouring. *Mode.*—Mix the potato-flour, or whichever one of the above ingredients is used, with a little of the milk; put it into a saucepan, with the remainder of the milk, the butter, salt, and sufficient pounded sugar to sweeten the whole nicely. Stir these ingredients over the fire until the mixture thickens; then take it off the fire, and let it cool a little. Separate the whites from the yolks of the eggs, beat the latter, and stir them into the soufflé batter. Now whisk the whites of the eggs to the firmest possible froth, for on this depends the excellence of the dish; stir them to the other ingredients, and add a few drops of essence of any flavouring that may be preferred; such as vanilla, lemon, orange, ginger, &c. &c. Pour the batter into a soufflé-dish, put it immediately into the oven, and bake for about ½ hour; then take it out, put the dish into another more ornamental one, such as is made for the purpose; hold a salamander or hot shovel over the soufflé, strew it with sifted sugar, and send it instantly to table. The secret of making a soufflé well, is to have the eggs well whisked, but particularly the whites, the oven not too hot, and to send it to table the moment it comes from the oven. If the soufflé be ever so well made, and it is allowed to stand before being sent to table, its appearance and goodness will be entirely spoiled. Soufflés may be flavoured in various ways, but must be named accordingly. Vanilla is one of the most delicate and recherché flavourings that can be used for this very fashionable dish. *Time.*—About ½ hour in the oven; 2 or 3 minutes to hold the salamander over. *Average cost*, 1*s.* *Sufficient* for 3 or 4 persons. *Seasonable* at any time.

SOUFFLÉ-PAN.

SOUPS, General Directions for Making.

LEAN, JUICY BEEF, MUTTON, AND VEAL form the basis of all good soups; therefore it is advisable to procure those pieces which afford the richest succulence, and such as are fresh-killed. Stale meat renders soups bad, and fat is not well adapted for making them. The principal art in composing good rich soup is so to proportion the several ingredients that the flavour of one shall not predominate over another, and that all the articles of which it is composed shall form an agreeable whole. Care must be taken that the roots and herbs are perfectly well cleaned, and that the water is proportioned to the quantity of meat and other ingredients, allowing a quart of water to a pound of meat for soups, and half that quantity for gravies. In making soups or gravies, gentle stewing or simmering is absolutely necessary. It may be remarked, moreover, that a really good soup can never be made but in a well-closed vessel, although, perhaps, greater wholesomeness is obtained by an occasional exposure to the air. Soups will, in general, take from four to six hours doing, and *are much better prepared the day before they are wanted.* When the soup is cold, the fat may be easily and completely removed; and in pouring it off, care must be taken not to disturb the settlings at the bottom of the vessel, which are so fine that they will escape through a sieve. A very fine hair-sieve or cloth is the best strainer; and if the soup is strained while it is hot, let the tamis or cloth be previously soaked in cold water. Clear soups must be perfectly transparent, and thickened soups about the consistency of cream. To obtain a really clear and transparent soup, it is requisite to continue skimming the liquor until there is not a particle of scum remaining, this being commenced immediately after the water is added to the meat. To thicken and give body to soups and gravies, potato-mucilage, arrowroot, bread-raspings, isinglass, flour and butter, barley, rice, or oatmeal are used. A piece of boiled beef pounded to a pulp, with a bit of butter and flour, and rubbed through a sieve, and gradually incorporated with the soup, will be found an excellent addition. When soups and gravies are kept from day to day in hot weather, they should be warmed up every day, put into fresh-scalded pans or tureens, and placed in a cool larder. In temperate weather, every other day may be sufficient. Stock made from meat only keeps good longer than that boiled with vegetables, the latter being liable to turn the mixture sour, particularly in very warm weather.

VARIOUS HERBS AND VEGETABLES are required for the purpose of making soups and gravies. Of these the principal are,—Scotch barley, pearl barley, wheat flour, oatmeal, bread-raspings, pease, beans, rice, vermicelli, macaroni, isinglass, potato-mucilage, mushroom or mushroom-ketchup, champignons, parsnips, carrots, beetroot, turnips, garlic, shalots, and onions. Sliced onions, fried with butter and flour till they are browned, and then rubbed through a sieve, are excellent to heighten the colour and flavour of brown soups and sauces, and form the basis of many of the fine relishes furnished by the cook. The older and drier the onion, the stronger will be its flavour. Leeks, cucumber, or burnet vinegar; celery or celery seed pounded. The latter, though equally strong, does not impart the delicate sweetness of the fresh vegetable; and when used as a substitute, its flavour should be corrected by the addition of a bit of sugar. Cress-seed, parsley, common thyme, lemon thyme, orange thyme, knotted marjoram, sage, mint, winter savoury, and basil. As fresh green basil is seldom to be procured, and its fine flavour is soon lost, the best way of preserving the extract is by pouring wine on the fresh leaves.

FOR THE SEASONING OF SOUPS, bay-leaves, tomato, tarragon, chervil, burnet, allspice, cinnamon, ginger, nutmeg, clove, mace, black and white pepper, essence of anchovy, lemon peel and juice, and Seville orange juice, are all taken. The latter imparts a finer flavour than the lemon, and the acid is much milder. These materials, with wine, mushroom ketchup, Harvey's sauce, tomato sauce, combined in various proportions, are, with other ingredients, manipulated into an almost endless variety of excellent soups and gravies. Soups, which are intended to constitute the principal part of a meal, certainly ought not to be flavoured like sauces, which are only designed to give a relish to some particular dish.

SOUP-MAKING, the Chemistry and Economy of.

Stock being the basis of all meat soups, and, also, of all the principal sauces, it is essential to the success of these culinary operations, to know the most complete and economical method of extracting, from a certain quantity of meat, the best possible stock, or broth. The theory and philosophy of this process we will, therefore, explain, and then proceed to show the practical course to be adopted.

As all meat is principally composed of fibres, fat, gelatine, osmazome, and albumen, it is requisite to know that the fibres are inseparable, constituting almost all that remains of the meat after it has undergone a long boiling.

FAT is dissolved by boiling; but as it is contained in cells covered by a very fine membrane, which never dissolves, a portion of it always adheres to the fibres. The other portion rises to the surface of the stock, and is that which has escaped from the cells which were not whole, or which have burst by boiling.

GELATINE is soluble; it is the basis and the nutritious portion of the stock. When there is an abundance of it, it causes the stock, when cold, to become a jelly.

OSMAZOME is soluble even when

and is that part of the meat which gives flavour and perfume to the stock. The flesh of old animals contains more *osmazome* than that of young ones. Brown meats contain more than white, and the former make the stock more fragrant. By roasting meat, the osmazome appears to acquire higher properties; so, by putting the remains of roast meats into your stock-pot, you obtain a better flavour.

ALBUMEN is of the nature of the white of eggs; it can be dissolved in cold or tepid water, but coagulates when it is put into water not quite at the boiling-point. From this property in albumen, it is evident that if the meat is put into the stock-pot when the water boils, or after this is made to boil up quickly, the albumen, in both cases, hardens. In the first it rises to the surface, in the second it remains in the meat, but in both it prevents the gelatine and osmazome from dissolving; and hence a thin and tasteless stock will be obtained. It ought to be known, too, that the coagulation of the albumen in the meat always takes place, more or less, according to the size of the piece, as the parts farthest from the surface always acquire *that degree* of heat which congeals it before entirely dissolving it.

BONES ought always to form a component part of the stock-pot. They are composed of an earthy substance,—to which they owe their solidity,—of gelatine, and a fatty fluid, something like marrow. *Two ounces* of them contain as much gelantine as *one pound* of meat; but in them, this is so incased in the earthy substance, that boiling-water can dissolve only the surface of whole bones. By breaking them, however, you can dissolve more, because you multiply their surfaces; and by reducing them to powder or paste, you can dissolve them entirely; but you must not grind them dry. We have said that gelatine forms the basis of stock; but this, though very nourishing, is entirely without taste; and to make the stock savoury, it must contain *osmazome*. Of this, bones do not contain a particle; and that is the reason why stock made entirely of them is not liked; but when you add meat to the broken or pulverized bones, the osmazome contained in it makes the stock sufficiently savoury.

In concluding this part of our subject, the following condensed hints and directions should be attended to in the economy of soup-making:—

BEEF MAKES THE BEST STOCK; veal stock has less colour and taste; whilst mutton sometimes gives it a tallowy smell, far from agreeable, unless the meat has been previously roasted or broiled. Fowls add very little to the flavour of stock, unless they be old and fat. Pigeons, when they are old, add the most flavour to it; and a rabbit or partridge is also a great improvement. From the freshest meat the best stock is obtained.

IF THE MEAT BE BOILED solely to make stock, it must be cut up into the smallest possible pieces; but, generally speaking, if it is desired to have good stock and a piece of savoury meat as well, it is necessary to put a rather large piece into the stock-pot, say sufficient for two or three days, during which time the stock will keep well in all weathers. Choose the freshest meat, and have it cut as thick as possible; for if it is a thin, flat piece, it will not look well, and will be very soon spoiled by the boiling.

NEVER WASH MEAT, as it deprives its surface of all its juices; separate it from the bones, and tie it round with tape, so that its shape may be preserved, then put it into the stock-pot, and for each pound of meat, let there be one pint of water; press it down with the hand, to allow the air, which it contains, to escape, and which often raises it to the top of the water.

PUT THE STOCK-POT ON A GENTLE FIRE, so that it may heat gradually. The albumen will first dissolve, afterwards coagulate; and as it is in this state lighter than the liquid, it will rise to the surface, bringing with it all its impurities. It is this which makes *the scum*. The rising of the hardened albumen has the same effect in clarifying stock as the white of eggs; and, as a rule, it may be said that the more scum there is, the clearer will be the stock. Always take care that the fire is very regular.

REMOVE THE SCUM when it rises thickly, and do not let the stock boil, because then one portion of the scum will be dissolved, and the other go to the bottom of the pot; thus rendering it very difficult to obtain a clear broth. If the fire is regular, it will not be necessary to add cold water in order to make the scum rise; but if the fire is too large at first, it will then be necessary to do so.

WHEN THE STOCK IS WELL SKIMMED, and begins to boil, put in salt and vegetables, which to every 3 lbs. of meat should consist of three carrots, two turnips, one parsnip, a few leeks, and a little celery. You can add, according to taste, a piece of cabbage, two or three cloves stuck in an onion, and a tomato. The latter gives a very agreeable flavour to the stock. If burnt onion be added, it ought, according to the advice of a famous French *chef*, to be tied in a little bag: without this precaution, the colour of the stock is liable to be clouded.

BY THIS TIME we will now suppose that you have chopped the bones which were separated from the meat, and those which were left from the roast meat of the day before. Remember, as was before pointed out, that the more these are broken, the more gelatine you will have. The best way to break them up is to pound them roughly in an iron mortar, adding, from time to time, a little water, to prevent them getting heated. It is a great saving thus to make use of the bones of meat, which, in too many English families, we fear, are entirely wasted; for it is certain, as previously stated, that two ounces of bone contain as much gelatine (which is the nutritive portion of stock) as one pound of meat. In their broken state tie them up in a bag, and put them in the stock-pot; adding the gristly parts of cold meat, and trimmings, which can be used for no other purpose. If, to make up the weight, you have received from the butcher a piece of mutton or veal, broil it slightly over a clear fire before putting it in the stock-pot, and be very careful that it does not contract the least taste of being smoked or burnt.

ADD NOW THE VEGETABLES, which, to a certain extent, will stop the boiling of the stock. Wait, therefore, till it simmers well up again, then draw it to the side of the fire, and keep it gently simmering till it is served, preserving, as before said, your fire always the same. Cover the stock-pot well, to prevent evaporation; do not fill it up, even if you take out a little stock, unless the meat is exposed; in which case a little boiling-water may be added, but only enough to cover it. After six hours' slow and gentle simmering, the stock is done; and it should not be continued on the fire longer than is necessary, or it will tend to insipidity.

Note.—It is on a good stock, or first good broth and sauce, that excellence in cookery depends. If the preparation of this basis of the culinary art is intrusted to negligent or ignorant persons, and the stock is not well skimmed, but indifferent results will be obtained. The stock will never be clear; and when it is obliged to be clarified, it is deteriorated both in quality and flavour. In the proper management of the stock-pot an immense deal of trouble is saved, inasmuch as one stock, in a small dinner, serves for all purposes. Above all things, the greatest economy, consistent with excellence, should be practised, and the price of everything which enters the kitchen correctly ascertained. The *theory* of this part of Household Management may appear trifling, but its practice is extensive, and therefore it requires the best attention.

SOUP, Baked.

Ingredients.—1 lb. of any kind of meat, any trimmings or odd pieces; 2 onions, 2 carrots, 2 oz. of rice, 1 pint of split peas, pepper and salt to taste, 4 quarts of water. *Mode.*—Cut the meat and vegetables in slices, add to them the rice and peas, season with pepper and salt. Put the whole in a jar, fill up with the water, cover very closely, and bake for 4 hours. *Time.*—4 hours. *Average cost*, 2½*d.* per quart. *Seasonable* at any time. *Sufficient* for 10 or 12 persons.

Note.—This will be found a very cheap and wholesome soup, and will be convenient in those cases where baking is more easily performed than boiling.

SOUP, Brilla.

Ingredients.—4 lbs. of shin of beef, 3 carrots, 2 turnips, a large sprig of thyme, 2 onions, 1 head of celery, salt and pepper to taste, 4 quarts water. *Mode.*—Take the beef, cut off all the meat from the bone, in nice square pieces, and boil the bone for 4 hours. Strain the liquor, let it cool, and take off the fat; then put the pieces of meat in the cold liquor; cut small the carrots, turnips, and celery; chop the onions, add them with the thyme and seasoning, and simmer till the meat is tender. If not brown enough, colour it with browning. *Time.*—6 hours. *Average cost*,

5d. per quart. *Seasonable* all the year. *Sufficient* for 10 persons.

SOUP, Chantilly.

Ingredients.—1 quart of young green peas, a small bunch of parsley, 2 young onions, 2 quarts of medium stock. *Mode.*—Boil the peas till quite tender, with the parsley and onions; then rub them through a sieve, and pour the stock to them. Do not let it boil after the peas are added, or you will spoil the colour. Serve very hot. *Time.*—½ hour. *Average cost,* 1*s.* 6*d.* per quart. *Seasonable* from June to the end of August. *Sufficient* for 8 persons.

Note.—Cold peas pounded in a mortar, with a little stock added to them, make a very good soup in haste.

SOUP, Calf's-head.

Ingredients.—½ of calf's head, 1 onion stuck with cloves, a very small bunch of sweet herbs, 2 blades of mace, salt and white pepper to taste, 6 oz. of rice-flour, 3 tablespoonfuls of ketchup, 3 quarts of white stock, or pot-liquor, or water. *Mode.*—Rub the head with salt, soak it for 6 hours, and clean it thoroughly, put it in the stewpan, and cover it with the stock, or pot-liquor, or water, adding the onion and sweet herbs. When well skimmed and boiled for 1½ hour, take out the head, and skim and strain the soup. Mix the rice-flour with the ketchup, thicken the soup with it, and simmer for 5 minutes. Now cut up the head into pieces about two inches long, and simmer them in the soup till the meat and fat are quite tender. Season with white pepper and mace finely pounded, and serve very hot. When the calf's head is taken out of the soup, cover it up or it will discolour. *Time.*—2¼ hours. *Average cost,* 1*s.* 9*d.* per quart, with stock. *Seasonable* from May to October. *Sufficient* for 10 persons.

Note.—Force-meat balls can be added, and the soup may be flavoured with a little lemon-juice, or a glass of sherry or Madeira. The bones from the head may be stewed down again, with a few fresh vegetables, and it will make a very good common stock.

SOUP, à la Cantatrice. (An Excellent Soup, very Beneficial for the Voice.)

Ingredients.—3 oz. of sago, ½ pint of cream, the yolks of 3 eggs, 1 lump of sugar, and seasoning to taste, 1 bay-leaf (if liked), 2 quarts of medium stock.—*Mode.*—Having washed the sago in boiling water, let it be gradually added to the nearly boiling stock. Simmer for ½ hour, when it should be well dissolved. Beat up the yolks of the eggs, add to them the boiling cream; stir these quickly in the soup, and serve immediately. Do not let the soup boil, or the eggs will curdle. *Time.*—40 minutes. *Average cost,* 1*s.* 6*d.* per quart. *Seasonable* all the year. *Sufficient* for 8 persons.

Note.—This is a soup, the principal ingredients of which, sago and eggs, have always been deemed very beneficial to the chest and throat. In various quantities, and in different preparations, these have been partaken of by the principal singers of the day, including the celebrated Swedish Nightingale, Jenny Lind, and, as they have always avowed, with considerable advantage to the voice, in singing.

SOUP, à la Crecy.

Ingredients.—4 carrots, 2 sliced onions, 1 cut lettuce, and chervil; 2 oz. butter, 1 pint of lentils, the crumbs of 2 French rolls, half a teacupful of rice, 2 quarts of medium stock. *Mode.*—Put the vegetables with the butter in the stewpan, and let them simmer 5 minutes; then add the lentils and 1 pint of the stock, and stew gently for half an hour. Now fill it up with the remainder of the stock, let it boil another hour, and put in the crumb of the rolls. When well soaked, rub all through a tammy. Have ready the rice boiled; pour the soup over this, and serve. *Time.*—1¾ hour. *Average cost,* 1*s.* 2*d.* per quart. *Seasonable* all the year. *Sufficient* for 8 persons.

SOUP, à la Flamande (Flemish).

Ingredients.—1 turnip, 1 small carrot, ½ head of celery, 6 green onions shred very fine, 1 lettuce cut small, chervil, ¼ pint of asparagus cut small, ¼ pint of peas, 2 oz. butter, the yolks of 4 eggs, ½ pint of cream, salt to taste, 1 lump of sugar, 2 quarts of stock. *Mode.*—Put the vegetables in the butter to stew gently for an hour with a teacupful of stock; then add the remainder of the stock, and simmer for another hour. Now beat the yolks of the eggs well, mix with the cream (previously boiled), and strain through a hair sieve. Take the soup off the fire, put the eggs, &c., to it and keep stirring it well. Bring it almost to boiling point, but do not leave off stirring, or the eggs will curdle. Season with salt, and add the sugar. *Time.*—2½ hours. *Average cost*, 1*s.* 9*d.* per quart. *Seasonable* from May to August. *Sufficient* for 8 persons.

SOUP, à la Flamande (Flemish).

Ingredients. — 5 onions, 5 heads of celery, 10 moderate-sized potatoes, 3 oz. butter, ½ pint of water, ⅓ pint of cream, 2 quarts of stock. *Mode.* — Slice the onions, celery, and potatoes, and put them with the butter and water into a stewpan, and simmer for an hour. Then fill up the stewpan with stock, and boil gently till the potatoes are done, which will be in about an hour. Rub all through a tammy, and add the cream (previously boiled). Do not let it boil after the cream is put in. *Time.*—2½ hours. *Average cost*, 1*s.* 4*d.* per quart. *Seasonable* from September to May. *Sufficient* for 8 persons.

Note.—This soup can be made with water instead of stock.

SOUP, a Good Family.

Ingredients.—Remains of a cold tongue, 2 lbs. of shin of beef, any cold pieces of meat or beef-bones, 2 turnips, 2 carrots, 2 onions, 1 parsnip, 1 head of celery, 4 quarts of water, ½ teacupful of rice; salt and pepper to taste. *Mode.*—Put all the ingredients in a stewpan, and simmer gently for 4 hours, or until all the goodness is drawn from the meat. Strain off the soup, and let it stand to get cold. The kernels and soft parts of the tongue must be saved. When the soup is wanted for use, skim off all the fat, put in the kernels and soft parts of the tongue, slice in a small quantity of fresh carrot, turnip, and onion; stew till the vegetables are tender, and serve with toasted bread. *Time.*—5 hours. *Average cost*, 3*d.* per quart. *Seasonable* at any time. *Sufficient* for 12 persons.

SOUP, Hessian.

Ingredients.—Half an ox's head, 1 pint of split peas, 8 carrots, 6 turnips, 6 potatoes, 6 onions, 1 head of celery, 1 bunch of savoury herbs, pepper and salt to taste, 2 blades of mace, a little allspice, 4 cloves, the crumb of a French roll, 6 quarts of water. *Mode.*—Clean the head, rub it with salt and water, and soak it for 5 hours in warm water. Simmer it in the water till tender, put it into a pan and let it cool; skim off all the fat; take out the head, and add the vegetables cut up small, and the peas which have been previously soaked; simmer them without the meat, till they are done enough to pulp through a sieve. Put in the seasoning, with the pieces of meat cut up; give one boil, and serve. *Time.*—4 hours. *Average cost*, 6*d.* per quart. *Seasonable* in winter. *Sufficient* for 16 persons.

Note.—An excellent hash or *ragoût* can be made by cutting up the nicest parts of the head, thickening and seasoning more highly a little of the soup, and adding a glass of port wine and 2 tablespoonfuls of ketchup.

SOUP, Portable.

Ingredients. — 2 knuckles of veal, 3 shins of beef, 1 large faggot of herbs, 2 bay-leaves, 2 heads of celery, 3 onions, 3 carrots, 2 blades of mace, 6 cloves, a teaspoonful of salt, sufficient water to cover all the ingredients. *Mode.*—Take the marrow from the bones; put all the ingredients in a stock-pot, and simmer slowly for 12 hours, or more, if the meat be not done to rags; strain it off, and put it in a very cool place; take off all the fat, reduce the liquor in a shallow pan, by setting it over a sharp fire, but be particular that it does not burn; boil it fast and uncovered for 8 hours, and keep it stirred. Put it into a deep dish, and set it by for a day. Have ready a stewpan of boiling water, place the dish in it, and keep it boiling; stir occasionally, and when the soup is thick and ropy, it is done. Form it into little cakes by pouring a small quantity on to the bottom of cups or basins; when cold, turn them out on a flannel to dry. Keep them from the air in tin canisters. *Average cost* of this quantity, 16*s.*

Note.—Soup can be made in 5 minutes with this, by dissolving a small piece, about the size of a walnut, in a pint of warm water, and simmering for 2 minutes. Vermicelli, macaroni, or other Italian pastes, may be added.

SOUP, Prince of Wales's.

Ingredients. — 12 turnips, 1 lump of sugar, 2 spoonfuls of strong veal stock, salt and white pepper to taste, 2 quarts of very bright stock. *Mode.*—Peel the turnips, and with a cutter cut them in balls as round as possible, but very small. Put them in the stock, which must be very bright, and simmer till tender. Add the veal stock and seasoning. Have little pieces of bread cut round, about the size of a shilling; moisten them with stock; put them into a tureen and pour the soup over without shaking, for fear of crumbling the bread, which would spoil the appearance of the soup, and make it look thick. *Time.*—2 hours. *Seasonable* in the winter. *Sufficient* for 8 persons.

SOUP, Regency.

Ingredients.—The bones and remains of any cold game, such as of pheasants, partridges, &c.; 2 carrots, 2 small onions, 1 head of celery, 1 turnip, ¼ lb. of pearl barley, the yolks of 3 eggs boiled hard, ¼ pint of cream, salt to taste, 2 quarts of medium or common stock. *Mode.*—Place the bones or remains of game in the stewpan, with the vegetables sliced; pour over the stock, and simmer for 2 hours; skim off all the fat, and strain it. Wash the barley, and boil it in 2 or 3 waters before putting it to the soup; finish simmering in the soup, and when the barley is done, take out half, and pound the other half with the yolks of the eggs. When you have finished pounding, rub it through a clean tammy, add the cream, and salt if necessary; give one boil, and serve very hot, putting in the barley that was taken out first. *Time.*—2½ hours. *Average cost,* 1*s.* per quart, if made with medium stock, or 6*d.* per quart, with common stock. *Seasonable* from September to March. *Sufficient* for 8 persons.

SOUP, à la Reine.

Ingredients.—1 large fowl, 1 oz. of sweet almonds, the crumb of 1½ French roll, ½ pint of cream, salt to taste, 1 small lump of sugar, 2 quarts of good white veal stock. *Mode.*—Boil the fowl gently in the stock till quite tender, which will be in about an hour, or rather more; take out the fowl, pull the meat from the bones, and put it into a mortar with the almonds, and pound very fine. When beaten enough, put the meat back in the stock, with the crumb of the rolls, and let it simmer for an hour; rub it through a tammy, add the sugar, ½ pint of cream that has boiled, and, if you prefer, cut the crust of the roll into small round pieces, and pour the soup over it, when you serve. *Time.*—2 hours, or rather more. *Average cost,* 2*s.* 7*d.* per quart. *Seasonable* all the year. *Sufficient* for 8 persons.

Note. — All white soups should be warmed in a vessel placed in another of boiling water.

SOUP, à la Reine (Economical).

Ingredients. — Any remains of roast chickens, ½ teacupful of rice, salt and pepper to taste, 1 quart of stock. *Mode.*—Take all the white meat and pound it with the rice, which has been slightly cooked, but not too much. When it is all well pounded, dilute with the stock, and pass through a sieve. This soup should neither be too clear nor too thick. *Time.*—1 hour. *Average cost,* 4*d.* per quart. *Seasonable* all the year. *Sufficient* for 4 persons.

Note.—If stock is not at hand, put the chicken-bones in water, with an onion, carrot, a few sweet herbs, a blade of mace, pepper and salt, and stew for 3 hours.

SOUP, à la Solferino (Sardinian Recipe).

Ingredients.—4 eggs, ½ pint of cream, 2 oz. of fresh butter, salt and pepper to taste, a little flour to thicken, 2 quarts of bouillon. *Mode.*—Beat the eggs, put them into a stewpan, and add the cream, butter, and seasoning; stir in as much flour as will bring it to the consistency of dough; make it into balls, either round or egg-shaped, and fry them in butter; put them in the tureen, and pour the boiling bouillon over them. *Time.*—1 hour. *Average cost,* 1*s.* 3*d.* per quart. *Seasonable* all the year. *Sufficient* for 8 persons.

Note.—This recipe was communicated to the Editress by an English gentleman, who was present at the battle of Solferino, on June 24, 1859, and who was requested by some of Victor Emmanuel's troops, on the day before the battle, to partake of a portion of their *potage.* He willingly enough consented, and found that these clever campaigners had made a palatable dish from very easily-procured materials. In sending the recipe for insertion in this work, he has, however, Anglicised, and somewhat, he thinks, improved it.

SOUP, Spring, or Potage Printanier.

Ingredients.—½ a pint of green peas, if in season, a little chervil, 2 shredded lettuces, 2 onions, a very small bunch of parsley, 2 oz. of butter, the yolks of 3 eggs, 1 pint of water, seasoning to taste, 2 quarts of stock. Put in a clean stewpan the chervil, lettuces, onions, parsley, and butter, to 1 pint of water, and let them simmer till tender. Season with salt and pepper; when done, strain off the vegetables, and put two-thirds of the liquor they were boiled in to the stock. Beat up the yolks of the eggs with the other third, give it a toss over the fire, and at the moment of serving, add this, with the vegetables which you strained off, to the soup. *Time.*—¾ of an hour. *Average cost,* 1*s.* per quart. *Seasonable* from May to October. *Sufficient* for 8 persons.

SOUP, Stew.

Ingredients.—2 lbs. of beef, 5 onions, 5 turnips, ¾ lb. of rice, a large bunch of parsley, a few sweet herbs, pepper and salt, 2 quarts of water. *Mode.*—Cut the beef up in small pieces, add the other ngredients, and boil gently for 2½ hours. Oatmeal or potatoes would be a great improvement. *Time.*—2½ hours. *Average cost,* 6*d.* per quart. *Seasonable* in winter. *Sufficient* for 6 persons.

SOUP, Stew.

Ingredients.—½ lb. of beef, mutton, or pork; ½ pint of split peas, 4 turnips, 8 potatoes, 2 onions, 2 oz. of oatmeal or 3 oz. of rice, 2 quarts of water. *Mode.*—Cut the meat in small pieces, as also the vegetables, and add them, with the peas, to the water. Boil gently for 3 hours; thicken with the oatmeal, boil for another ¼ hour, stirring all the time, and season with pepper and salt. *Time.*—3¼ hours. *Average cost,* 4*d.* per quart. *Seasonable* in winter. *Sufficient* for 8 persons.

Note.—This soup may be made of the liquor in which tripe has been boiled, by adding vegetables, seasoning, rice, &c.

SOUP, Stew, of Salt Meat.

Ingredients.—Any pieces of salt beef or pork, say 2 lbs.; 4 carrots, 4 parsnips, 4 turnips, 4 potatoes, 1 cabbage, 2 oz. of oatmeal or ground rice, seasoning of salt and pepper, 2 quarts of water. *Mode.*—Cut up the meat small, add the water, and let it simmer for 2¾ hours. Now add the vegetables, cut in thin small slices; season, and boil for 1 hour. Thicken with the oatmeal, and serve. *Time.*—2 hours. *Average cost,* 3*d.* per quart without the meat. *Seasonable* in winter. *Sufficient* for 6 persons.

Note.—If rice is used instead of oatmeal, put it in with the vegetables.

SOUP, Useful for Benevolent Purposes.

Ingredients.—An ox-cheek, any pieces of trimmings of beef, which may be bought very cheaply (say 4 lbs.), a few bones, any pot-liquor the larder may furnish, ½ peck of onions, 6 leeks, a large bunch of herbs, ½ lb. of celery (the outside pieces, or green tops, do very well); ½ lb. of carrots, ½ lb. of turnips, ½ lb. of coarse brown sugar, ½ a pint of beer, 4 lbs. of common rice, or pearl barley; ½ lb. of salt, 1 oz. of black pepper, a few raspings, 10 gallons of water. *Mode.*—Divide the meat in small pieces, break the bones, put them in a copper, with the 10 gallons of water, and stew for half an hour. Cut up the vegetables, put them in with the sugar and beer, and boil for 4 hours. Two hours before the soup is wanted, add the rice and raspings, and keep stirring till they are well mixed in the soup, which simmer gently. If the liquor boils away a little, fill up with water. *Time.*—6½ hours. *Average cost,* 1½*d.* per quart.

SOUP, White.

Ingredients.—¼ lb. of sweet almonds, ¼ lb. of cold veal or poultry, a thick slice of stale bread, a piece of fresh lemon-peel, 1 blade of mace, pounded, ¾ pint of cream, the yolks of 2 hard-boiled eggs, 2 quarts of white stock. *Mode.*—Reduce the almonds in a mortar to a paste, with a spoonful of water, and add to them the meat, which should be previously pounded with the bread. Beat all together, and add the lemon-peel, very finely chopped, and the mace. Pour the boiling stock on the whole, and simmer for an hour. Rub the eggs in the cream, put in the soup, bring it to a boil, and serve immediately. *Time.*—1½ hour. *Average cost,* 1*s.* 6*d.* per quart. *Seasonable* all the year. *Sufficient* for 8 persons.

Note.—A more economical white soup may be made by using common veal stock, and thickening with rice, flour, and milk. Vermicelli should be served with it. *Average cost*, 5*d*. per quart.

SPINACH, to Boil (English Mode).

Ingredients.—2 pailfuls of spinach, 2 heaped tablespoonfuls of salt, 1 oz. of of butter, pepper to taste. *Mode.*—Pick the spinach carefully, and see that no stalks or weeds are left amongst it; wash it in several waters, and, to prevent it being gritty, act in the following manner:—Have ready two large pans or tubs filled with water; put the spinach into one of these, and thoroughly wash it; then, *with the hands*, take out the spinach, and put it into the *other tub* of water (by this means all the grit will be left at the bottom of the tub); wash it again, and should it not be perfectly free from dirt, repeat the process. Put it into a very large saucepan, with about ½ pint of water, just sufficient to keep the spinach from burning, and the above proportion of salt. Press it down frequently with a wooden spoon, that it may be done equally; and when it has boiled for rather more than 10 minutes, or until it is perfectly tender, drain it in a colander, squeeze it quite dry, and chop it finely. Put the spinach into a clean stewpan, with the butter and a seasoning of pepper; stir the whole over the fire until quite hot; then put it on a hot dish, and garnish with sippets of toasted bread. *Time.*—10 to 15 minutes to boil the spinach, 5 minutes to warm with the butter. *Average cost* for the above quantity, 8*d*. *Sufficient* for 5 or 6 persons. *Seasonable.*—Spring spinach from March to July; winter spinach from November to March.

SPINACH GARNISHED WITH CROÛTONS.

Note.—Grated nutmeg, pounded mace, or lemon-juice may also be added to enrich the flavour; and poached eggs are also frequently served with spinach: they should be placed on the top of it, and it should be garnished with sippets of toasted bread.

SPINACH dressed with Cream, à la Française.

Ingredients.—2 pailfuls of spinach, 2 tablespoonfuls of salt, 2 oz. of butter, 8 tablespoonfuls of cream, 1 small teaspoonful of pounded sugar, a very little grated nutmeg. *Mode.*—Boil and drain the spinach; chop it fine, and put it into a stewpan with the butter; stir it over a gentle fire, and, when the butter has dried away, add the remaining ingredients, and simmer for about 5 minutes. Previously to pouring in the cream, boil it first, in case it should curdle. Serve on a hot dish, and garnish either with sippets of toasted bread or leaves of puff-paste. *Time.*—10 to 15 minutes to boil the spinach; 10 minutes to stew with the cream. *Average cost* for the above quantity, 8*d*. *Sufficient* for 5 or 6 persons. *Seasonable.*—Spring spinach from March to July; winter spinach from November to March.

SPINACH, French Mode of Dressing.

Ingredients.—2 pailfuls of spinach, 2 tablespoonfuls of salt, 2 oz. of butter, 1 teaspoonful of flour, 8 tablespoonfuls of good gravy; when liked, a very little grated nutmeg. *Mode.*—Pick, wash, and boil the spinach, and when tender, drain and squeeze it perfectly dry from the water that hangs about it. Chop it very fine, put the butter into a stewpan, and lay the spinach over that; stir it over a gentle fire, and dredge in the flour. Add the gravy, and let it boil *quickly* for a few minutes, that it may not discolour. When the flavour of nutmeg is liked, grate some to the spinach, and when thoroughly hot, and the gravy has dried away a little, serve. Garnish the dish with sippets of toasted bread. *Time.*—10 to 15 minutes to boil the spinach; 10 minutes to simmer in the gravy. *Average cost* for the above quantity, 8*d*. *Sufficient* for 5 or 6 persons. *Seasonable.*—Spring spinach from March to July; winter spinach from October to February.

Note.—For an *entremets* or second-course dish, spinach dressed by the above recipe may be pressed into a hot mould; it should then be turned out quickly, and served immediately.

SPINACH-GREEN, for Colouring various Dishes.

Ingredients.—2 handfuls of spinach. *Mode.*—Pick and wash the spinach free from dirt, and pound the leaves in a mortar to extract the juice; then press it through a hair sieve, and put the juice into a small stewpan or jar. Place this in a bain marie, or saucepan of boiling water, and let it set. Watch it closely, as it should not boil; and, as soon as it is done, lay it in a sieve, so that all the water may drain from it, and the green will then be ready for colouring. If made according to this recipe, the spinach-green will be found far superior to that boiled in the ordinary way.

SPINACH SOUP (French Recipe).

Ingredients.—As much spinach as, when boiled, will half fill a vegetable-dish, 2 quarts of very clear medium stock. *Mode.*—Make the cooked spinach into balls the size of an egg, and slip them into the soup-tureen. This is a very elegant soup, the green of the spinach forming a pretty contrast to the brown gravy. *Time.*—1 hour. *Average cost,* 1*s.* per quart. *Seasonable* from October to June.

SPONGE-CAKE.

Ingredients.—The weight of 8 eggs in pounded loaf sugar, the weight of 5 in flour, the rind of 1 lemon, 1 tablespoonful of brandy. *Mode.*—Put the eggs into one side of the scale, and take the weight of 8 in pounded loaf sugar, and the weight of 5 in good *dry* flour. Separate the yolks from the whites of the eggs; beat the former, put them into a saucepan with the sugar, and let them remain over the fire until *milk-warm,* keeping them well stirred. Then put them into a basin, add the grated lemon-rind mixed with the brandy, and stir these well together, dredging in the flour very gradually. Whisk the whites of the eggs to a very stiff froth, stir them to the flour, &c., and beat the cake well for ½ hour.

SPONGE-CAKE.

Put it into a buttered mould strewn with a little fine-sifted sugar, and bake the cake in a quick oven for 1½ hour. Care must be taken that it is put into the oven immediately, or it will not be light. The flavouring of this cake may be varied by adding a few drops of essence of almonds instead of the grated lemon-rind. *Time.*—1½ hour. *Average cost,* 1*s.* 3*d.* *Sufficient* for 1 cake. *Seasonable* at any time.

SPONGE-CAKE.

Ingredients.—½ lb. of loaf sugar, not quite ¼ pint of water, 5 eggs, 1 lemon, ½ lb. of flour, ¼ teaspoonful of carbonate of soda. *Mode.*—Boil the sugar and water together until they form a thick syrup; let it cool a little, then pour it to the eggs, which should be previously well whisked; and after the eggs and syrup are mixed together, continue beating them for a few minutes. Grate the lemon-rind, mix the carbonate of soda with the flour, and stir these lightly to the other ingredients; then add the lemon-juice, and, when the whole is thoroughly mixed, pour it into a buttered mould, and bake in rather a quick oven for rather more than 1 hour. The remains of sponge or Savoy cakes answer very well for trifles, light puddings, &c.; and a very stale one (if not mouldy) makes an excellent tipsy cake. *Time.*—Rather more than 1 hour. *Average cost,* 10*d.* *Sufficient* to make 1 cake. *Seasonable* at any time.

SPONGE-CAKES, Small.

Ingredients.—The weight of 5 eggs in flour, the weight of 8 in pounded loaf sugar; flavouring to taste. *Mode.*—Let the flour be perfectly dry, and the sugar well pounded and sifted. Separate the whites from the yolks of the eggs, and beat the latter up with the sugar; then whisk the whites until they become rather stiff, and mix them with the yolks, but do not stir them more than is just necessary to mingle the ingredients well together. Dredge in the flour by degrees, add the flavouring; butter the tins well, pour in the batter, sift a little sugar over the cakes, and bake them in rather a quick oven, but do not allow them to take too much colour, as they should be rather pale. Remove them from the tins before they get cold, and turn them on their faces, where let them remain until quite cold, when store them away in a closed tin canister or wide-mouthed glass bottle. *Time.*—10 to 15 minutes in a quick oven. *Average cost,* 1*d.* each. *Seasonable* at any time.

SPRATS.

Sprats should be cooked very fresh, which can be ascertained by their bright and sparkling eyes. Wipe them dry; fasten them in rows by a skewer run through the eyes; dredge with flour, and broil them on a gridiron over a nice clear fire. The gridiron should be rubbed with suet. Serve very hot. *Time.*—3 or 4 minutes. *Average cost*, 1*d*. per lb. *Seasonable* from November to March.

TO CHOOSE SPRATS. — Choose these from their silvery appearance, as the brighter they are, so are they the fresher.

SPRATS, Dried.

Dried sprats should be put into a basin, and boiling water poured over them; they may then be skinned and served, and this will be found a much better way than boiling them.

SPRATS, Fried in Batter.

Ingredients. — 2 eggs, flour, bread-crumbs; seasoning of salt and pepper to taste. *Mode.*—Wipe the sprats, and dip them in a batter made of the above ingredients. Fry of a nice brown, serve very hot, and garnish with fried parsley. Sprats may be baked like herrings.

SPROUTS, to Boil Young.

Ingredients.—To each ½ gallon of water allow 1 heaped tablespoonful of salt; a *very small* piece of soda. *Mode.*—Pick away all the dead leaves, and wash the greens well in cold water; drain them in a colander, and put them into fast-boiling water, with salt and soda in the above proportion. Keep them boiling quickly, with the lid uncovered, until tender; and the moment they are done, take them up, or their colour will be spoiled; when well drained, serve. The great art in cooking greens properly, and to have them a good colour, is to put them into *plenty of fast-boiling* water, to let them boil very quickly, and to take them up the moment they become tender. *Time.*—Brocoli sprouts, 10 to 12 minutes; young greens, 10 to 12 minutes; sprouts, 12 minutes, after the water boils. *Seasonable.*—Sprouts of various kinds may be had all the year.

STEW, Irish.

Ingredients.—3 lbs. of the loin or neck of mutton, 5 lbs. of potatoes, 5 large onions, pepper and salt to taste, rather more than 1 pint of water. *Mode.*—Trim off some of the fat of the above quantity of loin or neck of mutton, and cut it into chops of a moderate thickness. Pare and halve the potatoes, and cut the onions into thick slices. Put a layer of potatoes at the bottom of a stewpan, then a layer of mutton and onions, and season with pepper and salt; proceed in this manner until the stewpan is full, taking care to have plenty of vegetables at the top. Pour in the water, and let it stew very gently for 2½ hours, keeping the lid of the stewpan closely shut the *whole* time, and occasionally shaking the preparation to prevent its burning. *Time.*—2½ hours. *Average cost*, for this quantity, 2*s*. 8*d*. *Sufficient* for 5 or 6 persons. *Seasonable.*—Suitable for a winter dish.

STEW, Irish.

Ingredients.—2 or 3 lbs. of the breast of mutton, 1½ pint of water, salt and pepper to taste, 4 lbs. of potatoes, 4 large onions. *Mode.*—Put the mutton into a stewpan with the water and a little salt, and let it stew gently for an hour; cut the meat into small pieces, skim the fat from the gravy, and pare and slice the potatoes and onions. Put all the ingredients into the stewpan, in layers, first a layer of vegetables, then one of meat, and sprinkle seasoning of pepper and salt between each layer; cover closely, and let the whole stew very gently for 1 hour, or rather more, shaking it frequently to prevent its burning. *Time.*—Rather more than 2 hours. *Average cost*, 1*s*. 6*d*. *Sufficient* for 5 or 6 persons. *Seasonable.*—Suitable for a winter dish.

Note.—Irish stew may be prepared in the same manner as above, but baked in a jar instead of boiled. About 2 hours or rather more in a moderate oven will be sufficient time to bake it.

STILTON CHEESE.

Stilton cheese, or British Parmesan, as it is sometimes called, is generally preferred to all other cheeses by those whose authority few will dispute. Those made in May or June are usually served at Christmas; or, to be in prime order, should be kept from 10 to 12 months, or even longer. An artificial ripeness in Stilton cheese is

STILTON CHEESE.

sometimes produced by inserting a small piece of decayed Cheshire into an aperture at the top. From 3 weeks to a month is sufficient time to ripen the cheese. An additional flavour may also be obtained by scooping out a piece from the top, and pouring therein port, sherry, Madeira, or old ale, and letting the cheese absorb these for two or three weeks. But that cheese is the finest which is ripened without any artificial aid, is the opinion of those who are judges in these matters. In serving a Stilton cheese, the top of it should be cut off to form a lid, and a napkin or piece of white paper, with a frill at the top, pinned round. When the cheese goes from table, the lid should be replaced.

STOCKS for all kinds of Soups (Rich Strong Stock).

Ingredients.—4 lbs. of shin of beef, 4 lbs. of knuckle of veal, ½ lb. of good lean ham; any poultry trimmings; 2 oz. of butter; 3 onions, 3 carrots, 2 turnips (the latter should be omitted in summer, lest they ferment), 1 head of celery, a few chopped mushrooms, when obtainable; 1 tomato, a bunch of savoury herbs, not forgetting parsley; 1½ oz. of salt, 3 lumps of sugar, 12 white peppercorns, 6 cloves, 3 small blades of mace, 4 quarts of water. *Mode.*—Line a delicately clean stewpan with the ham cut in thin broad slices, carefully trimming off all its rusty fat; cut up the beef and veal in pieces about 3 inches square, and lay them on the ham; set it on the stove, and draw it down, and stir frequently. When the meat is equally browned, put in the beef and veal bones, the poultry trimmings, and pour in the cold water. Skim well, and occasionally add a little cold water, to stop its boiling, until it becomes quite clear; then put in all the other ingredients, and simmer very slowly for 5 hours. Do not let it come to a brisk boil, that the stock be not wasted, and that its colour may be preserved. Strain through a very fine hair sieve, or cloth, and the stock will be fit for use. *Time.* — 5 hours. *Average cost,* 1*s.* 3*d.* per quart.

STOCK, Economical.

Ingredients.—The liquor in which a joint of meat has been boiled, say 4 quarts; trimmings of fresh meat or poultry, shank-bones, &c., roast-beef bones, any pieces the larder may furnish; vegetables, spices, and the same seasoning as in the foregoing recipe. *Mode.*—Let all the ingredients simmer gently for 6 hours, taking care to skim carefully at first. Strain it off, and put by for use. *Time.*—6 hours. *Average cost,* 3*d.* per quart.

STOCK, Medium.

Ingredients.—4 lbs. of shin of beef, or 4 lbs. of knuckle of veal, or 2 lbs. of each; any bones, trimmings of poultry, or fresh meat, ½ lb. of lean bacon or ham, 2 oz. of butter, 2 large onions, each stuck with 3 cloves; 1 turnip, 3 carrots, 1 head of celery, 3 lumps of sugar, 2 oz. of salt, ½ a teaspoonful of whole pepper, 1 large blade of mace, 1 bunch of savoury herbs, 4 quarts and ½ pint of cold water. *Mode.*—Cut up the meat and bacon or ham into pieces of about 3 inches square; rub the butter on the bottom of the stewpan; put in ½ a pint of water, the meat, and all the other ingredients. Cover the stewpan, and place it on a sharp fire, occasionally stirring its contents. When the bottom of the pan becomes covered with a pale, jelly-like substance, add the 4 quarts of cold water, and simmer very gently for 5 hours. As we have said before, do not let it boil quickly. Remove every particle of scum whilst it is doing, and strain it through a fine hair sieve. This stock is the basis of most of the soups mentioned in this dictionary, and will be found quite strong enough for ordinary purposes. *Time.*—5½ hours. *Average cost,* 9*d.* per quart.

STOCK, To Clarify.

Ingredients.—The whites of 2 eggs, ½ pint of water, 2 quarts of stock. *Mode.*—Supposing that by some accident the soup is not quite clear, and that its quantity is 2 quarts, take the whites of 2 eggs, carefully separated from their yolks, whisk them well together with the water, and add gradually the 2 quarts of boiling stock, still whisking. Place the soup on the fire, and when boiling and well skimmed, whisk the eggs with it till nearly boiling again; then draw it from the fire, and let it settle, until the whites of the eggs become separated. Pass through a fine cloth, and the soup should be clear.

Note.—The rule is, that all clear soups should be of a light straw-colour, and should not savour too strongly of the meat; and that all white or brown thick soups should have no more consistency than will enable them to adhere slightly to the spoon when hot. All *purées* should be somewhat thicker.

STOCK, White (to be used in the preparation of White Soups).

Ingredients.—4 lbs. of knuckle of veal, any poultry trimmings, 4 slices of lean ham, 3 carrots, 2 onions, 1 head of celery, 12 white peppercorns, 2 oz. of salt, 1 blade of mace, a bunch of herbs, 1 oz. butter, 4 quarts of water. *Mode.*—Cut up the veal, and put it with the bones and trimmings of poultry, and the ham, into the stewpan, which has been rubbed with the butter. Moisten with ½ a pint of water, and simmer till the gravy begins to flow. Then add the 4 quarts of water and the remainder of the ingredients; simmer for 5 hours. After skimming and straining it carefully through a very fine hair sieve, it will be ready for use. *Time.*—5½ hours. *Average cost*, 9*d.* per quart.

Note.—When stronger stock is desired, double the quantity of veal, or put in an old fowl. The liquor in which a young turkey has been boiled, is an excellent addition to all white stock or soups.

STOCK, Consommé or White, for many Sauces.

Consommé is made precisely in the same manner as white stock, and, for ordinary purposes, will be found quite good enough. When, however, a stronger stock is desired, either put in half the quantity of water, or double that of the meat. This is a very good foundation for all white sauces.

STRAWBERRY JAM.

Ingredients.—To every lb. of fruit allow ⅓ pint of red-currant juice, 1¼ lb. of loaf sugar. *Mode.*—Strip the currants from the stalks, put them into a jar; place this jar in a saucepan of boiling water, and simmer until the juice is well drawn from the fruit; strain the currants, measure the juice, put it into a preserving pan, and add the sugar. Select well-ripened but sound strawberries; pick them from the stalks, and when the sugar is dissolved in the currant-juice, put in the fruit. Simmer the whole over a moderate fire, from ½ to ¾ hour, carefully removing the scum as it rises. Stir the jam only enough to prevent it from burning at the bottom of the pan, as the fruit should be preserved as whole as possible. Put the jam into jars, and when cold, cover down. *Time.*—½ to ¾ hour, reckoning from the time the jam simmers all over. *Average cost*, from 7*d.* to 8*d.* per lb. pot. *Sufficient.*—12 pints of strawberries will make 12 lbs. of jam. *Seasonable* in June and July.

STRAWBERRY JELLY.

Ingredients.—Strawberries, pounded sugar; to every pint of juice allow 1¼ oz. of isinglass. *Mode.*—Pick the strawberries, put them into a pan, squeeze them well with a wooden spoon, add sufficient pounded sugar to sweeten them nicely, and let them remain for 1 hour, that the juice may be extracted; then add ½ pint of water to every pint of juice. Strain the strawberry-juice and water through a bag; measure it, and to every pint allow 1¼ oz. of isinglass, melted and clarified in ¼ pint of water. Mix this with the juice; put the jelly into a mould, and set the mould in ice. A little lemon-juice added to the strawberry-juice improves the flavour of the jelly, if the fruit is very ripe; but it must be well strained before it is put to the other ingredients, or it will make the jelly muddy. *Time.*—1 hour to draw the juice. *Average cost*, with the best isinglass, 3*s.* *Sufficient.*—Allow 1½ pint of jelly for 5 or 6 persons. *Seasonable* in June, July, and August.

STRAWBERRIES and CREAM.

Ingredients.—To every pint of picked strawberries allow ⅓ pint of cream, 2 oz. of finely-pounded sugar. *Mode.*—Pick the stalks from the fruit, place it on a glass dish, sprinkle over it pounded sugar, and slightly stir the strawberries, that they may all be equally sweetened; pour the cream over the top, and serve. Devonshire cream, when it can be obtained, is exceedingly delicious for this dish; and, if very thick indeed, may be diluted with a little thin cream or milk. *Average cost* for this quantity, with cream at 1*s.* per pint, 1*s.* *Sufficient* for 2 persons. *Seasonable* in June and July.

STRAWBERRIES, Preserved in Wine.

Ingredients.—To every quart bottle allow ¼ lb. of finely-pounded loaf sugar; sherry or Madeira. *Mode.*—Let the fruit be gathered in fine weather, and used as soon as picked. Have ready some perfectly dry glass bottles, and some nice soft corks or bungs. Pick the stalks from the strawberries, drop them into the bottles, sprinkling amongst them pounded sugar in the above proportion, and when the fruit reaches to the neck of the bottle, fill up with sherry or Madeira. Cork the bottles down with new corks, and dip them into melted resin. *Seasonable.*—Make this in June or July.

STRAWBERRIES, to Preserve Whole.

Ingredients.—To every lb. of fruit allow 1½ lb. of good loaf sugar, 1 pint of red-currant juice. *Mode.*—Choose the strawberries not too ripe, of a fine large sort and of a good colour. Pick off the stalks, lay the strawberries in a dish, and sprinkle over them half the quantity of sugar, which must be finely pounded. Shake the dish gently, that the sugar may be equally distributed and touch the under-side of the fruit, and let it remain for 1 day. Then have ready the currant-juice, drawn as for red-currant jelly; boil it with the remainder of the sugar until it forms a thin syrup, and in this simmer the strawberries and sugar, until the whole is sufficiently jellied. Great care must be taken not to stir the fruit roughly, as it should be preserved as whole as possible. Strawberries prepared in this manner are very good served in glasses and mixed with thin cream. *Time.*—½ hour to 20 minutes to simmer the strawberries in the syrup. *Seasonable* in June and July.

STRAWBERRY, Open Tart of, or any other Kind of Preserve.

Ingredients.—Trimmings of puff-paste, any kind of jam. *Mode.*—Butter a tart-pan of the shape shown in the engraving, roll out the paste to the thickness of ⅓ an inch, and line the pan with it; prick a few holes at the bottom with a fork, and bake the tart in a brisk oven from 10 to 15 minutes. Let the paste cool a little; then fill it with preserve, place a few stars or leaves on it, which have been previously cut out of the paste and baked, and the tart is ready for table.

OPEN TART.

By making it in this manner, both the flavour and colour of the jam are preserved, which would otherwise be lost,

OPEN-TART MOULD.

were it baked in the oven on the paste; and, besides, so much jam is not required. *Time.*—10 to 15 min. *Average cost*, 8*d*. *Sufficient.*—1 tart for 3 persons. *Seasonable* at any time.

STURGEON, Baked.

Ingredients.—1 small sturgeon, salt and pepper to taste, 1 small bunch of herbs, the juice of ½ lemon, ¼ lb. of butter, 1 pint of white wine. *Mode.*—Cleanse the fish thoroughly, skin it, and split it along the belly without separating it; have ready a large baking-dish, in which lay the fish, sprinkle over the seasoning and herbs very finely minced, and moisten it with the lemon-juice and wine. Place the butter in small pieces over the whole of the fish, put it in the oven, and baste frequently; brown it nicely, and serve with its own gravy. *Time.*—Nearly 1 hour. *Average cost*, 1*s*. to 1*s*. 6*d*. per lb. *Seasonable* from August to March.

STURGEON, Roast.

Ingredients.—Veal stuffing, buttered paper, the tail-end of a sturgeon. *Mode.*—Cleanse the fish bone and skin it; make a nice veal stuffing (*see* Forcemeats), and fill it with the part where the bones came from; roll it in buttered paper, bind it up firmly with tape, like a fillet of veal, and roast it in a Dutch oven before a clear fire. Serve with good brown gravy, or plain melted butter. *Time.*—About 1 hour. *Average costs*, 1*s.* to 1*s.* 6*d.* per lb. *Seasonable* from August to March.

Note.—Sturgeon may be plainly boiled, and served with Dutch sauce. The fish is very firm, and requires long boiling.

SUET PUDDING, to serve with Roast Meat.

Ingredients.—1 lb. of flour, 6 oz. of finely-chopped suet, ½ saltspoonful of salt, ½ saltspoonful of pepper, ½ pint of milk or water. *Mode.*—Chop the suet very finely, after freeing it from skin, and mix it well with the flour; add the salt and pepper (this latter ingredient may be omitted if the flavour is not liked), and make the whole into a smooth paste with the above proportion of milk or water. Tie the pudding in a floured cloth, or put it into a buttered basin, and boil from 2½ to 3 hours. To enrich it, substitute 3 beaten eggs for some of the milk or water, and increase the proportion of suet. *Time.*—2½ to 3 hours. *Average cost*, 6*d.* *Sufficient* for 5 or 6 persons. *Seasonable* at any time.

Note.—When there is a joint roasting or baking, this pudding may be boiled in a long shape, and then cut into slices a few minutes before dinner is served; these slices should be laid in the dripping-pan for a minute or two, and then browned before the fire. Most children like this accompaniment to roast-meat.

SUGAR, to Boil, to Caramel.

Ingredients. — To every lb. of lump sugar allow 1 gill of spring water. *Mode.* —Boil the sugar and water together very quickly over a clear fire, skimming it very carefully as soon as it boils. Keep it boiling until the sugar snaps when a little of it is dropped in a pan of cold water. If it remains hard, the sugar has attained the right degree; then squeeze in a little lemon-juice, and let it remain an instant on the fire. Set the pan into another of cold water, and the caramel is then ready for use. The insides of well-oiled moulds are often ornamented with this sugar, which with a fork should be spread over them in fine threads or network. A dish of light pastry, tastefully arranged, looks very pretty with this sugar spun lightly over it.

SUPPERS.

Much may be done in the arrangement of a supper-table, at a very small expense, provided *taste* and *ingenuity* are exercised. The colours and flavours of the various dishes should contrast nicely; there should be plenty of fruit and flowers on the table, and the room should be well lighted. We have endeavoured to show how the various dishes may be placed; but of course these little matters entirely depend on the length and width of the table used, on individual taste, whether the tables are arranged round the room, whether down the centre, with a cross one at the top, or whether the supper is laid in two separate rooms, &c., &c. The garnishing of the dishes has also much to do with the appearance of a supper-table. Hams and tongues should be ornamented with cut vegetable flowers, raised pies with aspic jelly cut in dice, and all the dishes garnished sufficiently to be in good taste without looking absurd. The eye, in fact, should be as much gratified as the palate. Hot soup is now often served at suppers, but is not placed on the table. The servants fill the plates from a tureen on the buffet, and then hand them to the guests: when these plates are removed, the business of supper commences.

Where small rooms and large parties necessitate having a standing supper, many things enumerated in the following bill of fare may be placed on the buffet. Dishes for these suppers should be selected which may be eaten standing without any trouble. The following list may, perhaps, assist our readers in the arrangement of a buffet for a standing supper.

Beef, ham, and tongue-sandwiches, lobster and oyster-patties, sausage-rolls, meat-rolls, lobster-salad, dishes of fowls, the latter *all cut up*; dishes of sliced ham, sliced tongue, sliced beef, and galantine of veal; various jellies, blancmanges, and creams; custards in glasses, compôtes of fruit, tartlets of jam, and several dishes of small fancy pastry; dishes of fresh fruit, bonbons, sweetmeats, two or three sponge-cakes, a few plates of biscuits, and the buffet ornamented with vases of fresh or artificial flowers. The above dishes are quite sufficient for a standing supper; where more are desired, a supper must then be laid and arranged in the usual manner.

SUPPER, BILL OF FARE FOR A BALL, FOR 60 PERSONS (for Winter).

Lobster Salad. Two Roast Fowls, cut up. Lobster Salad. Two Roast Fowls, cut up. Lobster Salad.

	Boar's Head, garnished with Aspic Jelly.	
Fruited Jelly.	Mayonnaise of Fowl.	Charlotte Russe.
Small Pastry.	Small Ham, garnished.	Biscuits.
	Iced Savoy Cake.	
Vanilla Cream.	Epergne, with Fruit.	Fruited Jelly.
Prawns.	Two Boiled Fowls, with Béchamel Sauce.	Prawns.
Biscuits.		Small Pastry.
	Tongue, ornamented.	
Custards, in glasses.	Trifle, ornamented.	Custards, in glasses.
	Raised Chicken Pie.	
Fruited Jelly.	Tipsy Cake.	Swiss Cream.
	Roast Pheasant.	
Meringues.	Epergne, with Fruit.	Meringues.
	Galantine of Veal.	
Raspberry Cream.	Tipsy Cake.	Fruited Jelly.
Small Pastry.	Raised Game Pie.	Biscuits.
Custards, in glasses.	Trifle, ornamented.	Custards, in glasses.
	Tongue, ornamented.	
Prawns.	Two Boiled Fowls, with Béchamel Sauce.	Prawns.
Biscuits.		Small Pastry.
	EPERGNE, WITH FRUIT.	
Fruited Jelly.	Iced Savoy Cake.	Blancmange.
	Small Ham, garnished.	
	Mayonnaise of Fowl.	
Charlotte Russe.	Larded Capon.	Fruited Jelly.

Lobster Salad. Two Roast Fowls, cut up. Lobster Salad. Two Roast Fowls, cut up. Lobster Salad.

Note.—When soup is served from the buffet, Mock Turtle and Julienne may be selected. Besides the articles enumerated above, Ices, Wafers, Biscuits, Tea, Coffee, Wines, and Liqueurs will be required. Punch à la Romaine may also be added to the list of beverages.

SUPPER, BILL OF FARE FOR A BALL,

Or a Cold Collation for a Summer Entertainment, or Wedding or Christening Breakfast for 70 or 80 Persons (July).

4 Blancmanges, to be placed down the table.
3 Dishes of Small Pastry.
3 Compôtes of Fruit.
3 English Pines.
3 Fruit Tarts.
4 Jellies, to be placed down the table.
3 Cheesecakes.
20 Small Dishes of various Summer Fruits.

Dish of Lobster, cut up.	Tongue. Ribs of Lamb. Two Roast Fowls. Mayonnaise of Salmon.	Veal-and-Ham Pie.
Charlotte Russe à la Vanille.	Lobster Salad. — Epergne, with Flowers. — Lobster Salad.	Savoy Cake.
Pigeon Pie.	Mayonnaise of Trout. Tongue, garnished. Boiled Fowls and Béchamel Sauce. Collared Eel. Ham. Raised Pie.	Dish of Lobster, cut up.
Lobster Salad.	Two Roast Fowls. Shoulder of Lamb, stuffed. Mayonnaise of Salmon.	Lobster Salad.
Dish of Lobster, cut up.	Larded Capon. — Epergne, with Flowers. — Boar's Head.	Pigeon Pie.
Lobster Salad.	Mayonnaise of Trout. Tongue. Boiled Fowls and Béchamel Sauce. Raised Pie.	Lobster Salad.
Pigeon Pie.	Ham, decorated. Shoulder of Lamb, stuffed. Two Roast Fowls. Mayonnaise of Salmon.	Dish of Lobster, cut up.
Dish of Lobster, cut up. Savoy Cake.	Lobster Salad. — Epergne, with Flowers. — Lobster Salad.	Charlotte Russe à la Vanille. Veal and Ham Pie.
	Mayonnaise of Trout. Tongue, garnished. Boiled Fowls and Béchamel Sauce. Collared Eel.	Dish of Lobster, cut up.

4 Blancmanges, to be placed down the table.
3 Fruit Tarts.
3 Cheesecakes.
20 Small Dishes of various Summer Fruits.
4 Jellies, to be placed down the table.
3 Dishes of Small Pastry.
3 English Pines.
3 Compôtes of Fruit.

Note—The length of the page will not admit of our giving the dishes as they should be placed on the table; they should be arranged with the large and high dishes down the centre, and the spaces filled up with the smaller dishes, fruit, and flowers, taking care that the flavours and colours contrast nicely, and that no two dishes of a sort come together. This bill of fare may be made to answer three or four purposes, placing a wedding cake or christening cake in the centre on a high stand, if required for either of these occasions. A few dishes of fowls, lobster salads, &c. &c., should be kept in reserve to replenish those that are most likely to be eaten first. A joint of cold roast and boiled beef should be placed on the buffet, as being something substantial for the gentlemen of the party to partake of. Besides the articles enumerated in the bill of fare, biscuits and wafers will be required, cream-and-water ices, tea, coffee, wines, liqueurs, soda-water, ginger-beer, and lemonade.

SWEETBREADS, Baked (an Entrée).

Ingredients.—3 sweetbreads, egg and bread-crumbs, oiled butter, 3 slices of toast, brown gravy. *Mode.* — Choose large white sweetbreads; put them into warm water to draw out the blood, and to improve their colour; let them remain for rather more than 1 hour; then put them into boiling water, and allow them to simmer for about 10 minutes, which

SWEETBREADS.

renders them firm. Take them up, drain them, brush over with egg, sprinkle with bread-crumbs; dip them in egg again, and then into more bread-crumbs. Drop on them a little oiled butter, and put the sweetbreads into a moderately-heated oven, and let them bake for nearly ¾ hour. Make 3 pieces of toast; place the sweetbreads on the toast, and pour round, but not over them, a good brown gravy. *Time.*—To soak 1 hour, to be boiled 10 minutes, baked 40 minutes. *Average cost*, 1*s.* to 5*s.* *Sufficient* for an entrée. *Seasonable.*—In full season from May to August.

SWEETBREADS, Fried (à la Maître d'Hôtel), an Entrée.

Ingredients.—3 sweetbreads, egg and bread-crumbs, ¼ lb. of butter, salt and pepper to taste, rather more than ½ pint of maître-d'hôtel sauce. *Mode.*—Soak the sweetbreads in warm water for an hour; then boil them for 10 minutes; cut them in slices, egg and bread-crumb them, season with pepper and salt, and put them into a frying-pan, with the above proportion of butter. Keep turning them until done, which will be in about 10 minutes; dish them, and pour over them a maître-d'hôtel sauce. The dish may be garnished with slices of cut lemon. *Time.*—To soak 1 hour, to be broiled 10 minutes, to be fried about 10 minutes. *Average cost*, 1*s.* to 5*s.*, according to the season. *Sufficient* for an entrée. *Seasonable.*—In full season from May to August.

Note.—The egg and bread-crumb may be omitted, and the slices of sweetbread dredged with a little flour instead, and a good gravy may be substituted for the maître-d'hôtel sauce. This is a very simple method of dressing them.

SWEETBREADS, Stewed (an Entrée).

Ingredients.—3 sweetbreads, 1 pint of white stock, thickening of butter and flour, 6 tablespoonfuls of cream, 1 tablespoonful of lemon-juice, 1 blade of pounded mace, white pepper and salt to taste. *Mode.*—Soak the sweetbreads in warm water for 1 hour, and boil them for 10 minutes; take them out, put them into cold water for a few minutes; lay them in a stewpan with the stock, and simmer them gently for rather more than ½ hour. Dish them; thicken the gravy with a little butter and flour; let it boil up, add the remaining ingredients, allow the sauce to get quite *hot*, but *not boil*, and pour it over the sweetbreads. *Time.*—To soak 1 hour, to be boiled 10 minutes, stewed rather more than ½ hour. *Average cost*, from 1*s.* to 5*s.*, according to the season. *Sufficient* for an entrée. *Seasonable.*—In full season from May to August.

Note.—A few mushrooms added to this dish, and stewed with the sweetbreads, will be found an improvement.

SWEETBREADS, Lambs', larded, and Asparagus (an Entrée).

Ingredients. —2 or 3 sweetbreads, ½ pint of veal stock, white pepper and salt to taste, a small bunch of green onions, 1 blade of pounded mace, thickening of butter and flour, 2 eggs, nearly ½ pint of cream, 1 teaspoonful of minced parsley, a very little grated nutmeg. *Mode.*—Soak the sweetbreads in lukewarm water, and put them into a saucepan with sufficient boiling water to cover them, and let them simmer for 10 minutes; then take them out and put them into cold water. Now lard them, lay them in a stewpan, add the stock, seasoning, onions, mace, and a thickening of butter and flour, and stew gently for ¼ hour or 20 minutes. Beat up the egg with the cream, to which add the minced parsley and a very little grated nutmeg. Put this to the other ingredients; stir it well till quite hot, but do not let it boil after the cream is added, or it will curdle. Have ready some asparagus-tops, boiled; add these to the sweetbreads, and serve. *Time.*—Altogether ½ hour. *Average cost*,

2*s.* 6*d.* to 3*s.* 6*d.* each. *Sufficient.*—3 sweetbreads for 1 entrée. *Seasonable* from Easter to Michaelmas.

SWEETBREADS, another Way to Dress (an Entrée).

Ingredients. — Sweetbreads, egg and bread-crumbs, ½ pint of gravy, ½ glass of sherry. *Mode.*—Soak the sweetbreads in water for an hour, and throw them into boiling water to render them firm. Let them stew gently for about ¼ hour, take them out and put them into a cloth to drain all the water from them. Brush them over with egg, sprinkle them with bread-crumbs, and either brown them in the oven or before the fire. Have ready the above quantity of gravy, to which add ½ glass of sherry; dish the sweetbreads, pour the gravy under them, and garnish with water-cresses. *Time.* — Rather more than ½ hour. *Average cost,* 2*s.* 6*d.* to 3*s.* 6*d.* each. *Sufficient*—3 sweetbreads for 1 entrée. *Seasonable,* from Easter to Michaelmas.

SYLLABUB.

Ingredients.—1 pint of sherry or white wine, ½ grated nutmeg, sugar to taste, 1½ pint of milk. *Mode.*—Put the wine into a bowl, with the grated nutmeg and plenty of pounded sugar, and milk into it the above proportion of milk from the cow. Clouted cream may be laid on the top, with pounded cinnamon or nutmeg and sugar; and a little brandy may be added to the wine before the milk is put in. In some counties, cider is substituted for the wine: when this is used, brandy must always be added. Warm milk may be poured on from a spouted jug or teapot; but it must be held very high. *Average cost,* 2*s.* *Sufficient* for 5 or 6 persons. *Seasonable* at any time.

SYLLABUBS, Whipped.

Ingredients. — ½ pint of cream, ¼ pint of sherry, half that quantity of brandy, the juice of ½ lemon, a little grated nutmeg, 3 oz. of pounded sugar, whipped cream the same as for trifle. *Mode.*—Mix all the ingredients together, put the syllabub into glasses, and over the top of them heap a little whipped cream, made in the same manner as for trifle. Solid syllabub is made by whisking or milling the mixture to a stiff froth, and putting it in the glasses, without the whipped cream at the top. *Average cost,* 1*s.* 8*d.* *Sufficient* to fill 8 or 9 glasses. *Seasonable* at any time.

SYRUP for Jellies, to Clarify.

Ingredients.—To every quart of water allow 2 lbs. of loaf sugar; the white of 1 egg. *Mode.*—Put the sugar and water into a stewpan; set it on the fire, and, when the sugar is dissolved, add the white of the egg, whipped up with a little water. Whisk the whole well together, and simmer very gently until it has thrown up all the scum. Take this off as it rises, strain the syrup through a fine sieve or cloth into a basin, and keep it for use.

TAPIOCA PUDDING.

Ingredients.—3 oz. of tapioca, 1 quart of milk, 2 oz. of butter, ¼ lb. of sugar, 4 eggs, flavouring of vanilla, grated lemon-rind, or bitter almonds. *Mode.*—Wash the tapioca, and let it stew gently in the milk by the side of the fire for ¼ hour, occasionally stirring it; then let it cool a little; mix with it the butter, sugar, and eggs, which should be well beaten, and flavour with either of the above ingredients, putting in about 12 drops of the essence of almonds or vanilla, whichever is preferred. Butter a pie-dish, and line the edges with puff-paste; put in the pudding, and bake in a moderate oven for an hour. If the pudding is boiled, add a little more tapioca, and boil it in a buttered basin 1½ hour. *Time.*—1 hour to bake, 1½ hour to boil. *Average cost,* 1*s.* 2*d.* *Sufficient* for 5 or 6 persons. *Seasonable* at any time.

TAPIOCA SOUP.

Ingredients.—5 oz. of tapioca, 2 quarts of stock. *Mode.*—Put the tapioca into cold stock, and bring it gradually to a boil. Simmer gently till tender, and serve. *Time.*—Rather more than 1 hour. *Average cost,* 1*s.* 6*d.* per quart. *Seasonable* all the year. *Sufficient* for 8 persons.

TARTLETS.

Ingredients.—Trimmings of puff-paste, any jam or marmalade that may be preferred. *Mode.*—Roll out the paste to the thickness of about ½ inch; butter some small round patty-pans, line them with it, and cut off the superfluous paste close to the edge of the pan. Put a small piece of bread into each tartlet (this is to keep them in shape), and bake in a brisk oven for about 10 minutes, or rather longer. When they are done, and are of a nice colour, take the pieces of bread out carefully, and replace them by a spoonful of jam or marmalade. Dish them high on a white d'oyley, piled high in the centre, and serve. *Time.*—10 to 15 minutes. *Average cost,* 1*d.* each. *Sufficient.*—1 lb. of paste will make 2 dishes of tartlets. *Seasonable* at any time.

DISH OF TARTLETS.

TARTLETS, Polish.

Ingredients.—Puff-paste, the white of an egg, pounded sugar. *Mode.*—Roll some good puff-paste out thin, and cut it into 2½-inch squares; brush each square over with the white of an egg, then fold down the corners, so that they all meet in the middle of each piece of paste; slightly press the two pieces together, brush them over with the egg, sift over sugar, and bake in a nice quick oven for about ¼ hour. When they are done, make a little hole in the middle of the paste, and fill it up with apricot jam, marmalade, or red-currant jelly. Pile them high in the centre of a dish, on a napkin, and garnish with the same preserve the tartlets are filled with. *Time.*—¼ hour or 20 minutes. *Average cost,* with ½ lb. of puff-paste, 1*s.* *Sufficient* for 2 dishes of pastry. *Seasonable* at any time.

Note.—It should be borne in mind, that, for all dishes of small pastry, such as the preceding, trimmings of puff-paste, left from larger tarts, answer as well as making the paste expressly.

TEA, to make.

There is very little art in making good tea; if the water is boiling, and there is no sparing of the fragrant leaf, the beverage will almost invariably be good. The old-fashioned plan of allowing a teaspoonful to each person, and one over, is still practised. Warm the teapot with boiling water; let it remain for two or three minutes for the vessel to become thoroughly hot, then pour it away. Put in the tea, pour in from ½ to ¾ pint of *boiling* water, close the lid, and let it stand for the tea to draw from 5 to 10 minutes; then fill up the pot with water. The tea will be quite spoiled unless made with water that is actually *boiling*, as the leaves will not open, and the flavour not be extracted from them; the beverage will consequently be colourless and tasteless,—in fact, nothing but tepid water. Where there is a very large party to make tea for, it is a good plan to have two teapots, instead of putting a large quantity of tea into one pot; the tea, besides, will go farther. When the infusion has been once completed, the addition of fresh tea adds very little to the strength; so, when more is required, have the pot emptied of the old leaves, scalded, and fresh tea made in the usual manner. Economists say that a few grains of carbonate of soda, added before the boiling water is poured on the tea, assist to draw out the goodness; if the water is very hard, perhaps it is a good plan, as the soda softens it; but care must be taken to use this ingredient sparingly, as it is liable to give the tea a soapy taste if added in too large a quantity. For mixed tea, the usual proportion is four spoonfuls of black to one of green; more of the latter when the flavour is very much liked; but strong green tea is highly pernicious, and should never be partaken of too freely. *Time.*—2 minutes to warm the teapot, 5 to 10 minutes to draw the strength from the tea. *Sufficient.*—Allow 1 teaspoonful to each person.

TEA-CAKES.

Ingredients.—2 lbs. of flour, ½ teaspoonful of salt, ¼ lb. of butter or lard, 1 egg, a piece of German yeast the size of a walnut, warm milk. *Mode.*—Put the flour (which should be perfectly dry) into a basin; mix with it the salt, and rub in the butter or lard; then beat the egg well, stir to it the yeast, and add these to the flour with as much warm milk as will make the whole into a smooth paste, and knead it well. Let it rise near the fire, and, when well risen, form it into cakes; place them on tins, let them rise again for a few minutes before putting them into the oven, and bake from ¼ to ½ hour in a moderate oven. These are very nice with a few currants and a little sugar added to the other ingredients, they should be put in after the butter is rubbed in. These cakes should be buttered, and eaten hot as soon as baked; but, when stale, they are very nice split and toasted; or, if dipped in milk, or even water, and covered with a basin in the oven till hot, they will be almost equal to new. *Time.*—½ to ½ hour. *Average cost,* 10*d.* *Sufficient* to make 8 tea-cakes. *Seasonable* at any time.

TEA-CAKES, to toast.

Cut each tea-cake into three or four slices, according to its thickness; toast them on both sides before a nice clear fire, and as each slice is done, spread it with butter on both sides. When a cake is toasted, pile the slices one on the top of the other, cut them into quarters, put them on a very hot plate, and send the cakes immediately to table. As they are wanted, send them in hot, one or two at a time, as, if allowed to stand, they spoil, unless kept in a muffin-plate over a basin of boiling water.

TEA-CAKES.

TEAL, Roast.

Ingredients.—Teal, butter, a little flour. *Mode.*—Choose fat, plump birds, after the frost has set in, as they are generally better flavoured; truss them in the same manner as wild duck; roast them before a brisk fire, and keep them well basted. Serve with brown or orange gravy, water-cresses, and a cut lemon. The remains of teal make excellent hash. *Time.*—From 9 to 15 minutes. *Average cost,* 1*s.* each; but seldom bought. *Sufficient.*—2 for a dish. *Seasonable* from October to February.

TEAL.

TEAL, being of the same character as widgeon and wild duck, may be treated, in carving, in the same style.

TENCH, Matelot of.

Ingredients.—½ pint of stock, ½ pint of port wine, 1 dozen button onions, a few mushrooms, a faggot of herbs, 2 blades of mace, 1 oz. of butter, 1 teaspoonful of minced parsley, thyme, 1 shalot, 2 anchovies, 1 teacupful of stock, flour, 1 dozen oysters, the juice of ½ lemon; the number of tench, according to size. *Mode.*—Scale and clean the tench, cut them into pieces, and lay them in a stewpan; add the stock, wine, onions, mushrooms, herbs, and mace, and simmer gently for ½ hour. Put into another stewpan all the remaining ingredients but the oysters and lemon-juice, and boil slowly for 10 minutes, when add the strained liquor from the tench, and keep stirring it over the fire until somewhat reduced. Rub it through a sieve, pour it over the tench with the oysters, which must be previously scalded in their own liquor, squeeze in the lemon-juice, and serve. Garnish with croûtons. *Time.*—¾ hour. *Seasonable* from October to June.

TENCH, Stewed with Wine.

Ingredients.—½ pint of stock, ½ pint of Madeira or sherry, salt and pepper to taste, 1 bay-leaf, thickening of butter and flour. *Mode.*—Clean and crimp the tench, carefully lay it in a stewpan with the stock, wine, salt and pepper, and bay-leaf, let it stew gently for ½ hour; then take it out, put it on a dish, and keep hot. Strain the liquor, and thicken it with butter and flour kneaded together, and stew for 5 minutes. If not perfectly smooth, squeeze it through a tammy, add a very little cayenne, and pour over the fish. Garnish with balls of veal forcemeat. *Time.*—Rather more than ½ hour. *Seasonable* from October to June.

TENDRONS DE VEAU, Stewed (an Entrée).

Ingredients.—The gristles from 2 breasts of veal, white stock, 1 faggot of savoury herbs, 2 blades of pounded mace, 4 cloves, 2 carrots, 2 onions, a strip of lemon-peel. *Mode.*—The *tendrons* or gristles, which are found round the front of a breast of veal, are now very frequently served as an entrée, and when well dressed, make a nice and favourite dish. Detach the gristles from the bone, and cut them neatly out, so as not to spoil the joint for roasting or stewing. Put them into a stewpan, with sufficient stock to cover them; add the herbs, mace, cloves, carrots, onions, and lemon, and simmer these for nearly, or quite, 4 hours. They should be stewed until a fork will enter the meat easily. Take them up, drain them, strain the gravy, boil it down to a glaze, with which glaze the meat. Dish the *tendrons* in a circle with croûtons fried of a nice colour placed between each; and put mushroom sauce, or a purée of green peas or tomatoes, in the middle. *Time.*—4 hours. *Sufficient* for 1 entrée. *Seasonable.*—With peas, from June to August.

TENDRONS DE VEAU (an Entrée).

Ingredients. — The gristles from 2 breasts of veal, white stock, 1 faggot of savoury herbs, 1 blade of pounded mace, 4 cloves, 2 carrots, 2 onions, a strip of lemon-peel, egg and bread-crumbs, 2 tablespoonfuls of chopped mushrooms, salt and pepper to taste, 2 tablespoonfuls of sherry, the yolk of 1 egg, 3 tablespoonfuls of cream. *Mode.*—After removing the gristles from a breast of veal, stew them for 4 hours, as in the preceding recipe, with stock, herbs, mace, cloves, carrots, onions, and lemon-peel. When perfectly tender, lift them out and remove any bones or hard parts remaining. Put them between two dishes, with a weight on the top, and when cold, cut them into slices. Brush these over with egg, sprinkle with bread-crumbs, and fry a pale brown. Take ½ pint of the gravy they were boiled in, add 2 tablespoonfuls of chopped mushrooms, a seasoning of salt and pepper, the sherry, and the yolk of an egg beaten with 3 tablespoonfuls of cream. Stir the sauce over the fire until it thickens; when it is on the *point of boiling*, dish the tendrons in a circle, and pour the sauce in the middle. Tendrons are dressed in a variety of ways,—with sauce à l'Espagnole, vegetables of all kinds: when they are served with a purée, they should always be glazed. *Time.*—4½ hours. *Average cost.*—Usually bought with breast of veal. *Sufficient* for an entrée. *Seasonable* from March to October.

TETE DE VEAU EN TORTUE (an Entrée).

Ingredients.—Half a calf's head, or the remains of a cold boiled one; rather more than 1 pint of good white stock, 1 glass of sherry or Madeira, cayenne and salt to taste, about 12 mushroom-buttons (when obtainable), 6 hard-boiled eggs, 4 gherkins, 8 quenelles, or forcemeat balls, 12 crayfish, 12 croûtons. *Mode.*—Half a calf's head is sufficient to make a good entrée, and if there are any remains of a cold one left from the preceding day, it will answer very well for this dish. After boiling the head until tender, remove the bones, and cut the meat into neat pieces; put the stock into a stewpan, add the wine, and a seasoning of salt and cayenne; fry the mushrooms in butter for 2 or 3 minutes, and add these to the gravy. Boil this quickly until somewhat reduced; then put in the yolks of the hard-boiled eggs *whole*, and the whites cut in small pieces, and the gherkins chopped. Have ready a few veal quenelles, add these, with the slices of head, to the other ingredients, and let the whole get thoroughly hot, *without boiling*. Arrange the pieces of head as high in the centre of the dish as possible; pour over them the ragoût, and garnish with the crayfish and croûtons placed alternately. A little of the gravy should also be served in a tureen. *Time.*—About ½ hour to reduce the stock. *Sufficient* for 6 or 7 persons. *Average cost*, exclusive of the calf's head, 2*s.* 9*d.* *Seasonable* from March to October.

TIPSY CAKE.

Ingredients.—1 moulded sponge or Savoy cake, sufficient sweet wine or sherry to soak it, 6 tablespoonfuls of brandy, 2 oz. of sweet almonds, 1 pint of rich custard. *Mode.*—Procure a cake that is three or four days old, — either sponge, Savoy, or rice answering for the purpose of a tipsy cake. Cut the bottom of the cake level, to make it stand firm in the dish; make a small hole in the centre, and pour in and over the cake sufficient sweet wine or sherry, mixed with the above proportion of brandy, to soak it nicely. When the cake is well soaked, blanch and cut the almonds into strips, stick them all over the cake, and pour round it a good custard, made by our recipe, allowing 8 eggs instead of 5 to the pint of milk. The cakes are sometimes crumbled and soaked, and a whipped cream heaped over them, the same as for trifles. *Time.*—About 2 hours to soak the cake. *Average cost*, 4*s.* 6*d.* *Sufficient* for 1 dish. *Seasonable* at any time.

TIPSY CAKE.

TIPSY CAKE, an easy way of making.

Ingredients.—12 stale small sponge-cakes, raisin wine, ½ lb. of jam, 1 pint of custard (see Custard). *Mode.*—Soak the sponge-cakes, which should be stale (on this account they should be cheaper), in a little raisin wine; arrange them on a deep glass dish in four layers, putting a layer of jam between each, and pour round them a pint of custard, made by recipe, decorating the top with cut preserved-fruit. *Time.*—2 hours to soak the cakes. *Average cost,* 2*s.* 6*d.* *Sufficient* for 1 dish. *Seasonable* at any time.

TOAD-IN-THE-HOLE (Cold Meat Cookery).

Ingredients.—6 oz. of flour, 1 pint of milk, 3 eggs, butter, a few slices of cold mutton, pepper and salt to taste, 2 kidneys. *Mode.*—Make a smooth batter of flour, milk, and eggs in the above proportion; butter a baking-dish, and pour in the batter. Into this place a few slices of cold mutton, previously well seasoned, and the kidneys, which should be cut into rather small pieces; bake about 1 hour, or rather longer, and send it to table in the dish it was baked in. Oysters or mushrooms may be substituted for the kidneys, and will be found exceedingly good. *Time.*—Rather more than 1 hour. *Average cost,* exclusive of the cold meat, 8*d.* *Seasonable* at any time.

TOAD-IN-THE-HOLE (a Homely but Savoury Dish).

Ingredients.—1½ lb. of rump-steak, 1 sheep's kidney, pepper and salt to taste. For the batter, 3 eggs, 1 pint of milk, 4 tablespoonfuls of flour, ½ salt-spoonful of salt. *Mode.*—Cut up the steak and kidney into convenient-sized pieces, and put them into a pie-dish, with a good seasoning of salt and pepper; mix the flour with a small quantity of milk at first, to prevent its being lumpy; add the remainder, and the 3 eggs, which should be well beaten; put in the salt, stir the batter for about 5 minutes, and pour it over the steak. Place it in a tolerably brisk oven immediately, and bake for 1½ hour. *Time.*—1½ hour. *Average cost,* 1*s.* 9*d.* *Sufficient* for 4 or 5 persons. *Seasonable* at any time.

Note.—The remains of cold beef, rather underdone, may be substituted for the steak, and, when liked, the smallest possible quantity of minced onion or shalot may be added.

TOAST, to make Dry.

To make dry toast properly, a great deal of attention is required; much more, indeed, than people generally suppose. Never use new bread for making any kind of toast, as it eats heavy, and, besides, is very extravagant. Procure a loaf of household bread about two days old; cut off as many slices as may be required, not quite ¼ inch in thickness; trim off the crusts and ragged edges, put the bread on a toasting-fork, and hold it before a very clear fire. Move it backwards and forwards until the bread is nicely coloured; then turn it and toast the other side, and do not place it so near the fire that it blackens. Dry toast should be more gradually made than buttered toast, as its great beauty consists in its crispness, and this cannot be attained unless the process is slow and the bread is allowed gradually to colour. It should never be made long before it is wanted, as it soon becomes tough, unless placed on the fender in front of the fire. As soon as each piece is ready, it should be put into a rack, or stood upon its edges, and sent quickly to table.

TOAST, to make Hot Buttered.

A loaf of household bread about two days old answers for making toast better than cottage bread, the latter not being a good shape, and too crusty for the purpose. Cut as many nice even slices as may be required, rather more than ¼ inch in thickness, and toast them before a very bright fire, without allowing the bread to blacken, which spoils the appearance and flavour of all toast. When of a nice colour on both sides, put it on a hot plate; divide some good butter into small pieces, place them on the toast, set this before the fire, and when the butter is just beginning to melt, spread it lightly over the toast. Trim off the crust and ragged edges, divide each round into 4 pieces, and send the toast quickly to table. Some persons cut the slices of toast across from corner to corner, so making the pieces of a three-cornered shape. Soyer recommends that each slice should be cut into pieces as soon as it is buttered, and when all are ready, that they should be piled lightly on the dish they are intended to be served on. He says that by cutting through 4 or 5 slices at a time, all the butter is squeezed out of the upper ones, while the bottom one is swimming in fat liquid. It is highly essential to use good butter for making this dish.

TOAST-AND-WATER.

Ingredients.—A slice of bread, 1 quart of boiling water. *Mode.*—Cut a slice from a stale loaf (a piece of hard crust is better than anything else for the purpose), toast it of a nice brown on every side, but *do not allow it to burn or blacken.* Put it into a jug, pour the boiling water over it, cover it closely, and let it remain until cold. When strained, it will be ready for use. Toast-and-water should always be made a short time before it is required, to enable it to get cold: if drunk in a tepid or lukewarm state, it is an exceedingly disagreeable beverage. If, as is sometimes the case, this drink is wanted in a hurry, put the toasted bread into a jug, and only just cover it with the boiling water; when this is cool, cold water may be added in the proportion required, the toast-and-water strained; it will then be ready for use, and is more expeditiously prepared than by the above method.

TOAST SANDWICHES.

Ingredients. —Thin cold toast, thin slices of bread-and-butter, pepper and salt to taste. *Mode.* —Place a very thin piece of cold toast between 2 slices of thin bread-and-butter in the form of a sandwich, adding a seasoning of pepper and salt. This sandwich may be varied by adding a little pulled meat, or very fine slices of cold meat, to the toast, and in any of these forms will be found very tempting to the appetite of an invalid.

TOFFEE, Everton.

Ingredients.—1 lb. of powdered loaf sugar, 1 teacupful of water, ¼ lb. of butter, 6 drops of essence of lemon. *Mode.*—Put the water and sugar into a brass pan, and beat the butter to a cream. When the sugar is dissolved, add the butter, and keep stirring the mixture over the fire until it sets, when a little is poured on to a buttered dish; and just before the toffee is done, add the essence of lemon. Butter a dish or tin, pour on it the mixture, and when cool, it will easily separate from the dish. Butter-Scotch, an excellent thing for coughs, is made with brown, instead of white sugar, omitting the water, and flavoured with ⅓ oz. of powdered ginger. It is made in the same manner as toffee. *Time.*—18 to 35 minutes. *Average cost,* 10*d.* *Sufficient* to make a lb. of toffee.

TOMATO SAUCE for Keeping (Excellent).

Ingredients.—To every quart of tomato-pulp allow 1 pint of cayenne vinegar, ¾ oz. of shalots, ¾ oz. of garlic, peeled and cut in slices; salt to taste. To every six quarts of liquor, 1 pint of soy, 1 pint of anchovy-sauce. *Mode.*—Gather the tomatoes quite ripe; bake them in a slow oven till tender; rub them through a sieve, and to every quart of pulp add cayenne vinegar, shalots, garlic, and salt, in the above proportion; boil the whole together till the garlic and shalots are quite soft; then rub it through a sieve, put it again into a saucepan, and, to every six quarts of the liquor, add 1 pint of soy and the same quantity of anchovy-sauce, and boil altogether for about 20 minutes; bottle off for use, and carefully seal or resin the corks. This will keep good for 2 or 3 years, but will be fit for use in a week. A useful and less expensive sauce may be made by omitting the anchovy and soy. *Time.*—Altogether 1 hour. *Seasonable.*—Make this from the middle of September to the end of October.

TOMATO SAUCE for Keeping (Excellent).

Ingredients.—1 dozen tomatoes, 2 teaspoonfuls of the best powdered ginger, 1 dessertspoonful of salt, 1 head of garlic chopped fine, 2 tablespoonfuls of vinegar, 1 dessertspoonful of Chili vinegar (a small quantity of cayenne may be substituted for this). *Mode.*—Choose ripe tomatoes, put them into a stone jar, and stand them in a cool oven until quite tender; when cold, take the skins and stalks from them, mix the pulp with the liquor which is in the jar, but do not strain it; add all the other ingredients, mix well together, and put it into well-sealed bottles. Stored away in a cool, dry place, it will keep good for years. It is ready for use as soon as made, but the flavour is better after a week or two. Should it not appear to keep, turn it out, and boil it up with a little additional ginger and cayenne. For immediate use, the skins should be put into a wide-mouthed bottle with a little of the different ingredients, and they will be found very nice for hashes or stews. *Time.*—4 or 5 hours in a *cool* oven. *Seasonable* from the middle of September to the end of October.

TOMATO SAUCE for Keeping (Excellent).

Ingredients. — 3 dozen tomatoes; to every pound of tomato-pulp allow 1 pint of Chili vinegar, 1 oz. of garlic, 1 oz. of shalot, 2 oz. of salt, 1 large green capsicum, ½ teaspoonful of cayenne, 2 pickled gherkins, 6 pickled onions, 1 pint of common vinegar, and the juice of 6 lemons. *Mode.* — Choose the tomatoes when quite ripe and red; put them in a jar with a cover to it, and bake them till tender. The better way is to put them in the oven overnight, when it will not be too hot, and examine them in the morning to see if they are tender. Do not allow them to remain in the oven long enough to break them; but they should be sufficiently soft to skin nicely and rub through the sieve. Measure the pulp, and to each pound of pulp add the above proportion of vinegar and other ingredients, taking care to chop very fine the garlic, shalot, capsicum, onion, and gherkins. Boil the whole together till everything is tender; then again rub it through a sieve, and add the lemon-juice. Now boil the whole again till it becomes as thick as cream, and keep continually stirring; bottle it when quite cold, cork well, and seal the corks. If the flavour of garlic and shalot is very much disliked, diminish the quantities. *Time.*—Bake the tomatoes in a *cool* oven all night. *Seasonable* from the middle of September to the end of October.

Note. — A quantity of liquor will flow from the tomatoes, which must be put through the sieve with the rest. Keep it well stirred whilst on the fire, and use a wooden spoon.

TOMATO SAUCE, Hot, to serve with Cutlets, Roast Meats, &c.

Ingredients. — 6 tomatoes, 2 shalots, 1 clove, 1 blade of mace, salt and cayenne to taste, ¼ pint of gravy or stock. *Mode.*—Cut the tomatoes in two, and squeeze the juice and seeds out; put them in a stew-pan with all the ingredients, and let them

simmer *gently* until the tomatoes are tender enough to pulp; rub the whole through a sieve, boil it for a few minutes, and serve. The shalots and spices may be omitted when their flavour is objected to. *Time.*—1 hour, or rather more, to simmer the tomatoes. *Average cost*, for this quantity, 1*s*. *In full season* in September and October.

TOMATOES, Baked (Excellent).

Ingredients.—8 or 10 tomatoes, pepper and salt to taste, 2 oz. of butter, bread-crumbs. *Mode.* — Take off the stalks from the tomatoes; cut them into thick slices, and put them into a deep baking-dish; add a plentiful seasoning of pepper and salt, and butter in the above proportion; cover the whole with bread-crumbs; drop over these a little clarified butter; bake in a moderate oven from 20 minutes to ½ hour, and serve very hot. This vegetable, dressed as above, is an exceedingly nice accompaniment to all kinds of roast meat. The tomatoes, instead of being cut in slices, may be baked whole; but they will take rather longer time to cook. *Time.*—20 minutes to ½ hour. *Average cost*, in full season, 9*d*. per basket. *Sufficient* for 5 or 6 persons. *Seasonable* in August, September, and October; but may be had, forced, much earlier.

TOMATOES, Baked (another Mode).

Ingredients.—Some bread-crumbs, a little butter, onion, cayenne, and salt. *Mode.*—Bake the tomatoes whole, then scoop out a small hole at the top; fry the bread crumbs, onion, &c., and fill the holes with this as high up as possible; then brown the tomatoes with a salamander, or in an oven, and take care that the skin does not break.

TOMATOES, Stewed.

Ingredients.—8 tomatoes, pepper and salt to taste, 2 oz. of butter, 2 tablespoonfuls of vinegar. *Mode.*—Slice the tomatoes into a *lined* saucepan; season them with pepper and salt, and place small pieces of butter on them. Cover the lid down closely, and stew from 20 to 25 minutes, or until the tomatoes are perfectly tender; add the vinegar, stir two or three times, and serve with any kind of roast meat, with which they will be found a delicious accompaniment. *Time.*—20 to 25 minutes. *Average cost,*

STEWED TOMATOES.

in full season, 9*d.* per basket. *Sufficient* for 4 or 5 persons. *Seasonable* from August to October; but may be had, forced, much earlier.

TOMATOES, Stewed.

Ingredients.—8 tomatoes, about ½ pint of good gravy, thickening of butter and flour, cayenne and salt to taste. *Mode.*—Take out the stalks of the tomatoes; put them into a wide stewpan, pour over them the above proportion of good brown gravy, and stew gently until they are tender, occasionally *carefully* turning them, that they may be equally done. Thicken the gravy with a little butter and flour worked together on a plate; let it just boil up after the thickening is added, and serve. If it be at hand, these should be served on a silver or plated vegetable-dish. *Time.*—20 to 25 minutes, very gentle stewing. *Average cost,* in full season, 9*d.* per basket. *Sufficient* for 4 or 5 persons. *Seasonable* in August, September, and October; but may be had, forced, much earlier.

TONGUE, Boiled.

Ingredients.—1 tongue, a bunch of savoury herbs, water. *Mode.*—In choosing a tongue, ascertain how long it has been dried or pickled, and select one with a smooth skin, which denotes its being young and tender. If a dried one, and rather hard, soak it at least for 12 hours previous to cooking it; if, however, it is fresh from the pickle, 2 or 3 hours will be sufficient for it to remain in soak. Put the tongue into a stewpan with plenty of cold water and a bunch of savoury herbs; let it gradually come to a boil, skim well, and simmer very gently until tender. Peel off the skin, garnish with tufts of cauliflowers or Brussels sprouts, and serve. Boiled tongue is frequently sent to table with boiled poultry, instead of ham, and is, by many persons, preferred. If to serve cold, peel it, fasten it down to a piece of board by sticking a fork through the root, and another through the top, to straighten it. When cold, glaze it, and

put a paper ruche round the root, and garnish with tufts of parsley. *Time.*—A large smoked tongue, 4 to 4½ hours; a small one, 2½ to 3 hours. A large unsmoked tongue, 3 to 3½ hours; a small one, 2 to 2½ hours. *Average cost,* for a moderate-sized tongue, 3*s.* 6*d.* *Seasonable* at any time.

TONGUES, to Cure.

Ingredients.—For a tongue of 7 lbs., 1 oz. of saltpetre, ½ oz. of black pepper, 4 oz. of sugar, 3 oz. of juniper berries, 6 oz. of salt. *Mode.*—Rub the above ingredients well into the tongue, and let it remain in the pickle for 10 days or a fortnight; then drain it, tie it up in brown paper, and have it smoked for about 20 days over a wood fire; or it may be boiled out of this pickle. *Time.*—From 10 to 14 days to remain in the pickle; to be smoked 24 days. *Average cost,* for a medium-sized uncured tongue, 2*s.* 6*d.* *Seasonable* at any time.

Note.—If not wanted immediately, the tongue will keep 3 or 4 weeks without being too salt; then it must not be rubbed, but only turned in the pickle.

TONGUES, to Cure.

Ingredients.—9 lbs. of salt, 8 oz. of sugar, 9 oz. of powdered saltpetre. *Mode.*—Rub the above ingredients well into the tongues, and keep them in this curing mixture for 2 months, turning them every day. Drain them from the pickle, cover with brown paper, and have them smoked for about 3 weeks. *Time.*—The tongues to remain in pickle 2 months; to be smoked 3 weeks. *Sufficient.*—The above quantity of brine sufficient for 12 tongues, of 5 lbs. each. *Seasonable* at any time.

TONGUE, to Pickle and Dress a, to Eat Cold.

Ingredients.—6 oz. of salt, 2 oz. of bay-salt, 1 oz. of saltpetre, 3 oz. of coarse sugar; cloves, mace, and allspice to taste; butter, common crust of flour and water. *Mode.*—Lay the tongue for a fortnight in the above pickle, turn it every day, and be particular that the spices are well pounded; put it into a small pan just large enough to hold it, place some pieces of butter on it, and cover with a common crust. Bake in a slow oven until so tender that a straw would penetrate it;

take off the skin, fasten it down to a piece of board by running a fork through the root, and another through the tip, at the same time straightening it and putting it into shape. When cold, glaze it, put a paper ruche round the root, which is generally very unsightly, and garnish with tufts of parsley. *Time.*—From 3 to 4 hours in a slow oven, according to size. *Average cost*, for a medium-sized uncured tongue, 2*s.* 6d. *Seasonable* at any time.

TREACLE PUDDING, Rolled.

Ingredients.—1 lb. of suet crust, ½ lb. of treacle, ½ teaspoonful of grated ginger. *Mode.*—Make, with 1 lb. of flour, a suet crust by our given recipe, roll it out to the thickness of ½ inch, and spread the treacle equally over it, leaving a small margin where the paste joins; close the ends securely, tie the pudding in a floured cloth, plunge it into boiling water, and boil for 2 hours. We have inserted this pudding, being economical, and a favourite one with children; it is, of course, only suitable for a nursery, or very plain family dinner. Made with a lard instead of a suet crust, it would be very nice baked, and would be sufficiently done in from 1½ to 2 hours. *Time.*—Boiled pudding, 2 hours; baked pudding, 1½ to 2 hours. *Average cost*, *7d.* *Sufficient* for 5 or 6 persons. *Seasonable* at any time.

TRIFLE, to make a.

Ingredients.—For the whip, 1 pint of cream, 3 oz. of pounded sugar, the white of 2 eggs, a small glass of sherry or raisin wine. For the trifle, 1 pint of custard, made with 8 eggs to a pint of milk; 6 small sponge cakes, or 6 slices of sponge-cake; 12 macaroons, 2 dozen ratafias, 2 oz. of sweet almonds, the grated rind of 1 lemon, a layer of raspberry or strawberry jam, ½ pint of sherry or sweet wine, 6 tablespoonfuls of brandy.

Mode.—The whip to lay over the top of the trifle should be made the day before it is required for table, as the flavour is better, and it is much more solid than when prepared the same day. Put into a large bowl the pounded sugar, the whites of the eggs, which should be beaten to a stiff froth, a glass of sherry or sweet wine, and the cream. Whisk these ingredients well in a cool place, and take off the froth with a skimmer as fast as it rises, and put it on a sieve to drain; continue the whisking till there is sufficient of the whip, which must be put away in a cool place to drain. The next day, place the sponge-cakes, macaroons, and ratafias at the bottom of a trifle-dish; pour over them ½ pint of sherry or sweet wine, mixed with 6 tablespoonfuls of brandy, and, should this proportion of wine not be found quite sufficient, add a little more, as the cakes should be well soaked. Over the cakes put the grated lemon-rind, the sweet almonds, blanched and cut into strips, and a layer of raspberry or strawberry jam. Make a good custard, by recipe, using 8 instead of 5 eggs to the pint of milk, and let this cool a little; then pour it over the cakes, &c. The whip being made the day previously, and the trifle prepared, there remains nothing to do now but heap the whip lightly over the top: this should stand as high as possible, and it may be garnished with strips of bright currant jelly (see illustration), crystallized sweetmeats, or flowers; the small coloured comfits are sometimes used for the purpose of garnishing a trifle, but they are now considered rather old-fashioned. *Average cost*, with cream at 1*s.* per pint, 5*s.* 6*d.* *Sufficient* for 1 trifle. *Seasonable* at any time.

TRIFLE.

TRIFLE, Indian.

Ingredients.—1 quart of milk, the rind of ½ large lemon, sugar to taste, 5 heaped tablespoonfuls of rice-flour, 1 oz. of sweet almonds, ½ pint of custard.

Mode.—Boil the milk and lemon-rind together until the former is well flavoured; take out the lemon-rind and stir in the rice-flour, which should first be moistened with cold milk, and add sufficient loaf sugar to sweeten it nicely. Boil gently for about 5 minutes, and keep the mixture stirred; take it off the fire, let it cool *a little*, and pour it into a glass dish. When cold, cut the rice out in the form of a star, or any other shape that may be preferred; take out the spare rice, and fill the space with boiled custard. Blanch and cut the almonds into strips; stick them over the trifle, and garnish it with pieces of bright-coloured jelly, or preserved fruits, or candied citron. *Time.*—¼ hour to simmer the milk, 5 minutes after the rice is added. *Average cost*, 1s. *Sufficient* for 1 trifle. *Seasonable* at any time.

TRIPE, to Dress.

Ingredients.—Tripe, onion sauce, milk and water. *Mode.*—Ascertain that the tripe is quite fresh, and have it cleaned and dressed. Cut away the coarsest fat, and boil it in equal proportions of milk and water for ¾ hour. Should the tripe be entirely undressed, more than double that time should be allowed for it. Have ready some onion sauce, made by our given recipe, dish the tripe, smother it with the sauce, and the remainder send to table in a tureen. *Time.*—¾ hour; for undressed tripe, from 2½ to three hours. *Average cost*, 7*d.* per lb. *Seasonable* at any time.

Note.—Tripe may be dressed in a variety of ways: it may be cut in pieces and fried in batter, stewed in gravy with mushrooms, or cut into collops, sprinkled with minced onion and savoury herbs, and fried a nice brown in clarified butter.

TROUT, Stewed.

Ingredients.—2 middling-sized trout, ½ onion cut in thin slices, a little parsley, 2 cloves, 1 blade of mace, 2 bay-leaves, a little thyme, salt and pepper to taste, 1 pint of medium stock, 1 glass of port wine, thickening of butter and flour. *Mode.*—Wash the fish very clean, and wipe it quite dry. Lay it in a stewpan, with all the ingredients but the butter and flour, and simmer gently for ½ hour, or rather more, should not the fish be quite done. Take it out, strain the gravy, add the thickening, and stir it over a sharp fire for 5 minutes; pour it over the trout, and serve. *Time.*—According to size, ½ hour or more. *Average cost.*—Seldom bought. *Seasonable* from May to September, and fatter from the middle to the end of August than at any other time. *Sufficient* for 4 persons. Trout may be served with anchovy or caper sauce, baked in buttered paper, or fried whole like smelts. Trout dressed à la Génévese is extremely delicate; for this proceed the same as with salmon.

TRUFFLES, to Dress, with Champagne.

Ingredients.—12 fine black truffles, a few slices of fat bacon, 1 carrot, 1 turnip, 2 onions, a bunch of savoury herbs, including parsley, 1 bay-leaf, 2 cloves, 1 blade of pounded mace, 2 glasses of champagne, ½ pint of stock. *Mode.*—Carefully select the truffles, reject those that have a musty smell, and wash them well with a brush, in cold water only, until perfectly clean. Put the bacon into a stewpan, with the truffles and the remaining ingredients; simmer these gently for an hour, and let the whole cool in the stewpan. When to be served, rewarm them, and drain them on a clean cloth; then arrange them on a delicately white napkin, that it may contrast as strongly as possible with the truffles, and serve. The trimmings of truffles are used to flavour gravies, stock, sauces, &c.; and are an excellent addition to ragoûts, made dishes of fowl, &c. *Time.*—1 hour. *Average cost.*—Not often bought in this country. *Seasonable* from November to March.

TRUFFLES A L'ITALIENNE.

Ingredients.—10 truffles, 1 tablespoonful of minced parsley, 1 minced shalot, salt and pepper to taste, 2 oz. of butter, 2 tablespoonfuls of good brown gravy, the juice of ½ lemon, cayenne to taste. *Mode.*—Wash the truffles and cut them into slices about the size of a penny-piece; put them into a frying-pan, with the parsley, shalot, salt, pepper, and 1 oz. of butter; stir them over the fire, that they may all be equally done, which will be in about 10 minutes, and drain off some of the butter; then add a little more fresh butter, 2 tablespoonfuls of good gravy, the juice of ½ lemon, and a little cayenne; stir over the fire until the whole is on the point of boiling, when serve. *Time.*—Altogether, 20 minutes. *Average cost.*—Not often bought in this country. *Seasonable* from November to March.

TRUFFLES, Italian Mode of Dressing.

Ingredients.—10 truffles, ¼ pint of salad-oil, pepper and salt to taste, 1 tablespoonful of minced parsley, a very little finely minced garlic, 2 blades of pounded mace, 1 tablespoonful of lemon-juice. *Mode.*—After cleansing and brushing the truffles, cut them into thin slices, and put them in a baking-dish, on a seasoning of oil, pepper, salt, parsley, garlic, and mace in the above proportion. Bake them for nearly an hour, and, just before serving, add the lemon-juice, and send them to table very hot. *Time.*—Nearly 1 hour. *Average cost.*—Not often bought in this country. *Seasonable* from November to March.

TRUFFLES AU NATUREL.

Ingredients.—Truffles, buttered paper. *Mode.*—Select some fine truffles; cleanse them, by washing them in several waters with a brush, until not a particle of sand or grit remains on them; wrap each truffle in buttered paper, and bake in a hot oven for quite an hour; take off the paper, wipe the truffles, and serve them in a hot napkin. *Time.*—1 hour. *Average cost.*—Not often bought in this country. *Seasonable* from November to March.

TURBOT.

In choosing turbot see that it is thick, and of a yellowish white; for if of a bluish tint, it is not good. The turbot-kettle, as will be seen by our cut, is made

TURBOT-KETTLE.

differently from ordinary fish kettles, it being less deep, whilst it is wider, and more pointed at the sides; thus exactly answering to the shape of the fish which it is intended should be boiled in it.

TURBOT, Boiled.

Ingredients.—6 oz. of salt to each gallon of water. *Mode.*—Choose a middling-sized turbot; for they are invariably the most valuable: if very large, the meat will be tough and thready. Three or four hours before dressing, soak the fish in salt and water to take off the slime; then thoroughly cleanse it, and with a knife make an incision down the middle of the back, to prevent the skin of the belly from cracking. Rub it over with lemon, and be particular not to cut off the fins. Lay the fish in a very clean turbot-kettle, with sufficient cold water to cover it, and salt in the above proportion. Let it gradually come to a boil, and skim very carefully; keep it gently simmering, and on no account let it boil fast, as the fish would have a very unsightly appearance. When the meat separates easily from the bone, it is done; then take it out, let it drain well, and dish it on a hot napkin. Rub a little lobster spawn through a sieve, sprinkle it over the fish, and garnish with tufts of parsley and cut lemon. Lobster or shrimp sauce, and plain melted butter, should be sent to table with it. *Time.*—After the water boils, about ½ hour for a large turbot; middling size, about 20 minutes. *Average cost,*—large turbot, from 10*s.* to 12*s.*; middling size, from 12*s.* to. 15*s.* *Seasonable* at any time. *Sufficient,* 1 middling-sized turbot for 8 persons.

TURBOT, to Help.

First run the fish-slice down the thickest part of the fish lengthwise, quite through to the bone, and then cut handsome and regular slices across the fish until all the meat on the upper side is helped. When the carver has removed all the meat from the upper side of the fish, the backbone should be raised, put on one side of the dish, and the under side helped as the upper.

TURBOT A LA CREME.

Ingredients. —The remains of cold turbot. For sauce, 2 oz. of butter, 4 tablespoonfuls of cream; salt, cayenne, and pounded mace to taste. *Mode.*—Clear away all skin and bone from the flesh of the turbot, which should be done when it comes from table, as it causes less waste when trimmed hot. Cut the flesh into nice square pieces, as equally as possible; put into a stewpan the butter, let it melt, and add the cream and seasoning; let it just simmer for one minute, but not boil. Lay in the fish to warm, and serve it garnished with croûtons or a paste border. *Time.*—10 minutes. *Seasonable* at any time.

Note.—The remains of cold salmon may be dressed in this way, and the above mixture may be served in a *vol-au-vent.*

TURBOT, Baked Fillets of.

Ingredients.—The remains of cold turbot, lobster sauce left from the preceding day, egg, and bread-crumbs; cayenne and salt to taste; minced parsley, nutmeg, lemon-juice. *Mode.*—After having cleared the fish from all skin and bone, divide it into square pieces of an equal size; brush them over with egg, sprinkle with bread-crumbs mixed with a little minced parsley and seasoning. Lay the fillets in a baking-dish, with sufficient butter to baste with. Bake for ¼ hour, and do not forget to keep them well moistened with the butter. Put a little lemon-juice and grated nutmeg to the cold lobster sauce; make it hot, and pour over the fish, which must be well drained from the butter. Garnish with parsley and cut lemon. *Time.*—Altogether, ½ hour. *Seasonable* at any time.

Note.—Cold turbot thus warmed in the remains of lobster sauce will be found much nicer than putting the fish again in water.

TURBOT A L'ITALIENNE, Fillets of.

Ingredients.—The remains of cold turbot, Italian sauce. *Mode.*—Clear the fish carefully from the bone, and take away all skin, which gives an unpleasant flavour to the sauce. Make the sauce hot, lay in the fish to warm through, but do not let it boil. Garnish with croûtons. *Time.*—5 minutes. *Seasonable* all the year.

TURBOT, or other Large Fish, Garnish for.

Take the crumb of a stale loaf, cut it into small pyramids with flat tops, and on the top of each pyramid put rather more than a tablespoonful of white of egg beaten to a stiff froth. Over this, sprinkle finely-chopped parsley and fine raspings of a dark colour. Arrange these on the napkin round the fish, one green and one brown alternately.

TURBOT AU GRATIN.

Ingredients.—Remains of cold turbot, béchamel (*see* Sauces), bread-crumbs, butter. *Mode.*—Cut the fish of the turbot into small dice, carefully freeing it from all skin and bone. Put them into a stewpan, and moisten with 4 or 5 tablespoonfuls of béchamel. Let it get thoroughly hot, but do not allow it to boil. Spread the mixture on a dish, cover with finely-grated bread-crumbs, and place small pieces of butter over the top. Brown it in the oven, or with a salamander. *Time.*—Altogether, ½ hour. *Seasonable* at any time.

TURKEY, Boiled.

Ingredients.—Turkey; forcemeat. *Choosing and Trussing.*—Hen turkeys are preferable for boiling, on account of their whiteness and tenderness, and one of moderate size should be selected, as a large one is not suitable for this mode of cooking. They should not be dressed until they have been killed 3 or 4 days, as they will neither look white, nor will they be tender. Pluck the bird, carefully draw, and singe it with a piece of white paper; wash it inside and out, and wipe it thoroughly dry with a cloth. Cut off the head and neck, draw the strings or sinews of the thighs, and cut off the legs at the first joint; draw the legs into the body, fill the breast with forcemeat; run a skewer through the

BOILED TURKEY.

wing and the middle joint of the leg, quite into the leg and wing on the opposite side; break the breastbone, and make the bird look as round and as compact as possible. *Mode.*—Put the turkey into sufficient *hot* water to cover it; let it come to a boil, then carefully remove all the scum: if this is attended to, there is no occasion to boil the bird in a floured cloth; but it should be well covered with the water. Let it simmer very gently for about 1½ hour to 1¾ hour, according to the size, and serve with either white, celery, oyster, or mushroom sauce, or parsley-and-butter, a little of which should be poured over the turkey. Boiled ham, bacon, tongue, or pickled pork, should always accompany this dish; and when oyster sauce is served, the turkey should be stuffed with oyster forcemeat. *Time.*—A small turkey, 1½ hour; a large one, 1¾ hour.

Average cost, 5*s*. 6*d*. to 7*s*. 6*d*. each, but more expensive at Christmas, on account of the great demand. *Sufficient* for 7 or 8 persons. *Seasonable* from December to February.

TURKEY, Croquettes of (Cold Meat Cookery).

Ingredients. — The remains of cold turkey; to every ½ lb. of meat allow 2 oz. of ham or bacon, 2 shalots, 1 oz. of butter, 1 tablespoonful of flour, the yolks of 2 eggs, egg and bread-crumbs. *Mode.*—The smaller pieces, that will not do for a fricassée or hash, answer very well for this dish. Mince the meat finely with ham or bacon in the above proportion; make a gravy of the bones and trimmings, well seasoning it; mince the shalots, put them into a stewpan with the butter, add the flour; mix well, then put in the mince, and about ½ pint of the gravy made from the bones. (The proportion of the butter must be increased or diminished according to the quantity of mince.) When just boiled, add the yolks of 2 eggs; put the mixture out to cool, and then shape it in a wineglass. Cover the croquettes with egg and bread-crumbs, and fry them a delicate brown. Put small pieces of parsley-stems for stalks, and serve with rolled bacon cut very thin. *Time.*—8 minutes to fry the croquettes. *Seasonable* from December to February.

TURKEY, Fricasseed (Cold Meat Cookery).

Ingredients.—The remains of cold roast or boiled turkey; a strip of lemon-peel, a bunch of savoury herbs, 1 onion, pepper and salt to taste, 1 pint of water, 4 tablespoonfuls of cream, the yolk of an egg. *Mode.*—Cut some nice slices from the remains of a cold turkey, and put the bones and trimmings into a stewpan, with the lemon-peel, herbs, onion, pepper, salt, and the water; stew for an hour, strain the gravy, and lay in the pieces of turkey. When warm through, add the cream and the yolk of an egg; stir it well round, and, when getting thick, take out the pieces, lay them on a hot dish, and pour the sauce over. Garnish the fricassée with sippets of toasted bread. Celery or cucumbers, cut into small pieces, may be put into the sauce; if the former, it must be boiled first. *Time.*—1 hour to make the gravy. *Average cost*, exclusive of the cold turkey, 4*d*. *Seasonable* from December to February.

TURKEY, Hashed.

Ingredients.—The remains of cold roast turkey, 1 onion, pepper and salt to taste, rather more than 1 pint of water, 1 carrot, 1 turnip, 1 blade of mace, a bunch of savoury herbs, 1 tablespoonful of mushroom ketchup, 1 tablespoonful of port wine, thickening of butter and flour. *Mode.*—Cut the turkey into neat joints; the best pieces reserve for the hash, the inferior joints and trimmings put into a stewpan with an onion cut in slices, pepper and salt, a carrot, turnip, mace, herbs, and water in the above proportion; simmer these for an hour, then strain the gravy, thicken it with butter and flour, flavour with ketchup and port wine, and lay in the pieces of turkey to warm through; if there is any stuffing left, put that in also, as it so much improves the flavour of the gravy. When it boils, serve, and garnish the dish with sippets of toasted bread. *Time.*—1 hour to make the gravy. *Seasonable* from December to February.

TURKEY, Roast.

Ingredients. — Turkey; forcemeat. *Choosing and Trussing.* — Choose cock turkeys by their short spurs and black legs, in which case they are young; if the spurs are long, and the legs pale and rough, they are old. If the bird has been long killed, the eyes will appear sunk and the feet very dry; but, if fresh, the contrary will be the case. Middling-sized fleshy turkeys are by many persons considered superior to those of an immense growth, as they are, generally speaking, much more tender. They should never be dressed the same day they are killed; but, in cold weather, should hang at least 8 days; if the weather is mild, 4 or 5 days will be found sufficient. Carefully pluck the bird, singe it with white paper, and wipe it thoroughly with a cloth; draw it, preserve the liver and gizzard, and be particular not to break the gall-bag, as no washing will remove the bitter taste it imparts where it once touches. Wash it *inside* well, and wipe it thoroughly dry with a cloth; the *outside* merely requires nicely wiping, as we have just stated. Cut off the neck close to the back, but leave enough of the crop-skin to turn over; break the leg-bone close below the knee, draw out the strings from the thighs, and flatten the breastbone to make it look plump. Have ready a forcemeat; fill the breast with this, and, if a trussing-needle is used, sew the neck over to the back; if a needle is not at hand, a skewer will answer the purpose. Run a skewer through the pinion and thigh into the body to the pinion and thigh on the other side, and press the

ROAST TURKEY.

legs as much as possible between the breast and the side-bones, and put the liver under one pinion and the gizzard under the other. Pass a string across the back of the bird, catch it over the points of the skewer, tie it in the centre of the back, and be particular that the turkey is very firmly trussed. This may be more easily accomplished with a needle and twine than with skewers. *Mode.*—Fasten a sheet of buttered paper on to the breast of the bird, put it down to a bright fire, at some little distance *at first* (afterwards draw it nearer), and keep it well basted the whole of the tim it is cooking. About ¼ hour before e.ving, remove the paper, dredge the turkey lightly with flour, and put a piece of butter into the basting-ladle; as the butter melts, baste the bird with it. When of a nice brown and well frothed, serve with a tureen of good brown gravy and one of bread sauce. Fried sausages are a favourite addition to roast turkey; they make a pretty garnish, besides adding very much to the flavour. When these are not at hand, a few forcemeat balls should be placed round the dish as a garnish. Turkey may also be stuffed with sausage-meat, and a chestnut forcemeat with the chestnut sauce is, by many persons, very much esteemed as an accompaniment to this favourite dish. *Time.*—Small turkey, 1½ hour; moderate-sized one, about 10 lbs., 2 hours; large turkey, 2½ hours, or longer. *Average cost,* from 10*s.* to 12*s.*, but expensive at Christmas, on account of the great demand. *Sufficient.*—A moderate-sized turkey for 7 or 8 persons. *Seasonable* from December to February.

TURKEY, Roast.

A noble dish is a turkey, roast or boiled. A Christmas dinner, with the middle-classes of this empire, would scarcely be a Christmas dinner without its turkey; and we can hardly imagine an object of greater envy than is presented by a respected portly pater-familias carving, at the season devoted to good cheer and genial charity, his own fat turkey, and carving it well. The only art consists, as in the carving of a goose, in getting from the breast as many fine slices as possible; and all must have remarked the very great difference in the large number of people whom a good carver will find slices for, and the comparatively few that a bad carver will succeed in serving. As we have stated

ROAST TURKEY.

in both the carving of a duck and goose, the carver should commence cutting slices to the wing, from 2 to 3, and then proceed upwards towards the ridge of the breastbone: this is not the usual plan, but, in practice, will be found the best. The breast is the only part which is looked on as fine in a turkey, the legs being very seldom cut off and eaten at table: they are usually removed to the kitchen, where they are taken off, as here marked, to appear only in a form which seems to have a special attraction at a bachelor's supper-table,—we mean devilled: served in this way, they are especially liked and relished. A boiled turkey is carved in the same manner as when roasted.

TURKEY POULTS, Roast.

Ingredients. —Turkey poult; butter. *Choosing and Trussing.*—Choose a plump bird, and truss it in the following manner:—After it has been carefully plucked, drawn, and singed, skin the neck, and fasten the head under the wing; turn the legs at the first joint, and bring the feet close to the thighs, as a woodcock should be trussed, *and do not stuff it*. *Mode.*—Put it down to a bright fire, keep it well basted, and at first place a piece of paper on the breast to prevent its taking too much colour. About 10 minutes before serving, dredge it lightly with flour, and baste well; when nicely frothed, send it to table immediately, with a little gravy in the dish, and some in a tureen. If at hand, a few water-cresses may be placed round the turkey as a garnish, or it may be larded. *Time.*—About 1 hour. *Average cost*, 7*s.* to 8*s.* each. *Sufficient* for 6 or 7 persons. *Seasonable.*—In full season from June to October.

TURKEY SOUP (a Seasonable Dish at Christmas).

Ingredients.—2 quarts of medium stock, the remains of a cold roast turkey, 2 oz. of rice-flour or arrowroot, salt and pepper to taste, 1 tablespoonful of Harvey's sauce or mushroom ketchup. *Mode.*—Cut up the turkey in small pieces, and put it in the stock; let it simmer slowly until the bones are quite clean. Take the bones out, and work the soup through a sieve; when cool, skim well. Mix the rice-flour or arrowroot to a batter with a little of the soup; add it with the seasoning and sauce, or ketchup. Give one boil, and serve. *Time.*—4 hours. *Average cost*, 10*d.* per quart. *Seasonable* at Christmas. *Sufficient* for 8 persons.

Note.—Instead of thickening this soup, vermicelli or macaroni may be served in it.

TURNIP SOUP.

Ingredients.—3 oz. of butter, 9 good-sized turnips, 4 onions, 2 quarts of stock, seasoning to taste. *Mode.*—Melt the butter in the stewpan, but do not let it boil; wash, drain, and slice the turnips and onions very thin; put them in the butter, with a teacupful of stock, and stew very gently for an hour. Then add the remainder of the stock, and simmer another hour. Rub it through a tammy, put it back into the stewpan, but do not let it boil. Serve very hot. *Time.*—2½ hours. *Average cost*, 8*d.* per quart. *Seasonable* from October to March. *Sufficient* for 8 persons.

Note.—By adding a little cream, this soup will be much improved.

TURNIPS, Boiled.

Ingredients. — Turnips; to each ½ gallon of water allow 1 heaped tablespoonful of salt. *Mode.* — Pare the turnips, and, should they be very large, divide them into quarters; but, unless this is the case, let them be cooked whole. Put them into a saucepan of boiling water, salted in the above proportion, and let them boil gently until tender. Try them with a fork, and, when done, take them up in a colander; let them thoroughly drain, and serve. Boiled turnips are usually sent to table with boiled mutton, but are infinitely nicer when mashed than served whole: unless nice and young, they are scarcely worth the trouble of dressing plainly as above. *Time.*—Old turnips, ¾ to 1¼ hour; young ones, about 18 to 20 minutes. *Average cost*, 4*d.* per bunch. *Sufficient.*—Allow a bunch of 12 turnips for 5 or 6 persons. *Seasonable.*—May be had all the year; but in spring only useful for flavouring gravies, &c.

TURNIPS, German Mode of Cooking.

Ingredients.—8 large turnips, 3 oz. of butter, pepper and salt to taste, rather more than ½ pint of weak stock or broth, 1 tablespoonful of flour. *Mode.*—Make the butter hot in a stewpan, lay in the turnips, after having pared and cut them into dice, and season them with pepper and salt. Toss them over the fire for a few minutes, then add the broth, and simmer the whole gently till the turnips are tender. Brown the above proportion of flour with a little butter; add this to the turnips, let them simmer another 5 minutes, and serve. Boiled mutton is usually sent to table with this vegetable, and may be cooked with the turnips by placing it in the midst of them: the meat would then be very delicious, as, there being so little liquid with the turnips, it would almost be steamed, and, consequently, very tender. *Time.*—20 minutes. *Average cost*, 4*d.* per bunch. *Sufficient* for 4 persons. *Seasonable.*—May be had all the year.

TURNIPS, Mashed.

Ingredients.—10 or 12 large turnips; to each ½ gallon of water allow 1 heaped tablespoonful of salt, 2 oz. of butter, cayenne or white paper to taste. *Mode.*—

Pare the turnips, quarter them, and put them into boiling water, salted in the above proportion; boil them until tender; then drain them in a colander, and squeeze them as dry as possible by pressing them with the back of a large plate. When quite free from water, rub the turnips with a wooden spoon through the colander, and put them into a very clean saucepan; add the butter, white pepper, or cayenne, and, if necessary, a little salt. Keep stirring them over the fire until the butter is well mixed with them, and the turnips are thoroughly hot; dish, and serve. A little cream or milk added after the turnips are pressed through the colander, is an improvement to both the colour and flavour of this vegetable. *Time.*—From ½ to ¾ hour to boil the turnips; 10 minutes to warm them through. *Average cost*, 4*d*. per bunch. *Sufficient* for 4 or 5 persons. *Seasonable.*—May be had all the year; but in early spring only good for flavouring gravies.

TURNIPS IN WHITE SAUCE. (An Entremets, or to be served with the Second Course as a Side-dish.)

Ingredients.—7 or 8 turnips, 1 oz. of butter, ½ pint of white sauce. *Mode.*—Peel and cut the turnips in the shape of pears or marbles; boil them in salt and water, to which has been added a little butter, until tender; then take them out, drain, arrange them on a dish, and pour over the white sauce made by either of the recipes, and to which has been added a small lump of sugar. In winter, when other vegetables are scarce, this will be found a very good and pretty-looking dish: when approved, a little mustard may be added to the sauce. *Time.*—About ¾ hour to boil the turnips. *Average cost*, 4*d*. per bunch. *Sufficient* for 1 side dish. *Seasonable* in winter.

VANILLA CUSTARD SAUCE, to serve with Puddings.

Ingredients.—½ pint of milk, 2 eggs, 2 oz. of sugar, 10 drops of essence of vanilla. *Mode.*—Beat the eggs, sweeten the milk; stir these ingredients well together, and flavour them with essence of vanilla, regulating the proportion of this latter ingredient by the strength of the essence, the size of the eggs, &c. Put the mixture into a small jug, place this jug in a saucepan of boiling water, and stir the sauce *one way* until it thickens; but do not allow it to boil, or it will instantly curdle. Serve in a boat or tureen separately, with plum, bread, or any kind of dry pudding. Essence of bitter almonds or lemon-rind may be substituted for the vanilla, when they are more in accordance with the flavouring of the pudding with which the sauce is intended to be served. *Time.*—To be stirred in the jug from 8 to 10 minutes. *Average cost*, 4*d*. *Sufficient* for 4 or 5 persons.

VEAL, Baked (Cold Meat Cookery).

Ingredients.—½ lb. of cold roast veal, a few slices of bacon, 1 pint of bread-crumbs, ½ pint of good veal gravy, ½ teaspoonful of minced lemon-peel, 1 blade of pounded mace, cayenne and salt to taste, 4 eggs. *Mode.*—Mince finely the veal and bacon; add the bread-crumbs, gravy, and seasoning, and stir these ingredients well together. Beat up the eggs thoroughly; add these, mix the whole well together, put into a dish, and bake from ¾ to 1 hour. When liked, a little good gravy may be served in a tureen as an accompaniment. *Time.*—from ¾ to 1 hour. *Average cost*, exclusive of the cold meat, 6*d*. *Sufficient* for 3 or 4 persons. *Seasonable* from March to October.

VEAL, Roast Breast of.

Ingredients. — Veal; a little flour. *Mode.*—Wash the veal, well wipe it, and dredge it with flour; put it down to a bright fire, not too near, as it should not be scorched. Baste it plentifully until done; dish it, pour over the meat some good melted butter, and send to table with it a piece of boiled bacon and a cut lemon. *Time.*—From 1½ to 2 hours. *Average cost*, 8½*d*. per lb. *Sufficient* for 5 or 6 persons. *Seasonable* from March to October.

VEAL, Breast of, to Carve.

The carving of a breast of veal is not dissimilar to that of a fore-quarter of lamb, when the shoulder has been taken off. The breast of veal consists of two parts, — the rib-bones and the gristly brisket. These two parts should first be separated by sharply passing the knife in the direction of the lines 1, 2; when they are entirely divided, the rib-bones should be carved in the direction of the lines 5 to 6; and the brisket can be helped by cutting pieces in the direction

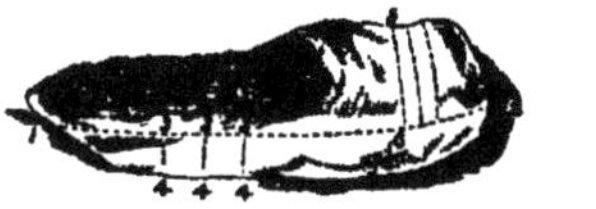

BREAST OF VEAL.

3 to 4. The carver should ask the guests whether they have a preference for the brisket or ribs; and if there be a sweetbread served with the dish, as it often is with roast breast of veal, each person should receive a piece.

VEAL, Stewed Breast of, and Peas.

Ingredients.—Breast of veal, 2 oz. of butter, a bunch of savoury herbs, including parsley; 2 blades of pounded mace, 2 cloves, 5 or 6 young onions, 1 strip of lemon-peel, 6 allspice, ¼ teaspoonful of pepper, 1 teaspoonful of salt, thickening of butter and flour, 2 tablespoonfuls of sherry, 2 tablespoonfuls of tomato sauce, 1 tablespoonful of lemon-juice, 2 tablespoonfuls of mushroom ketchup, green peas. *Mode.*—Cut the breast in half, after removing the bone underneath, and divide the meat into convenient-sized pieces. Put the butter into a frying-pan, lay in the pieces of veal, and fry until of a nice brown colour. Now place these in a stewpan with the herbs, mace, cloves, onions, lemon-peel, allspice, and seasoning; pour over them just sufficient boiling water to cover the meat; well close the lid, and let the whole simmer very gently for about 2 hours. Strain off as much gravy as is required, thicken it with butter and flour, add the remaining ingredients, skim well, let it simmer for about 10 minutes, then pour it over the meat. Have ready some green peas, boiled separately; sprinkle these over the veal, and serve. It may be garnished with forcemeat balls, or rashers of bacon curled and fried. Instead of cutting up the meat, many persons prefer it dressed whole; — in that case it should be half-roasted before the water, &c. are put to it. *Time.*—2½ hours. *Average cost,* 8½*d.* *Sufficient* for 5 or 6 persons. *Seasonable* from March to October.

VEAL, à la Bourgeoise (Excellent).

Ingredients.—2 to 3 lbs. of the loin or neck of veal, 10 or 12 young carrots, a bunch of green onions, 2 slices of lean bacon, 2 blades of pounded mace, 1 bunch of savoury herbs, pepper and salt to taste, a few new potatoes, 1 pint of green peas. *Mode.*—Cut the veal into cutlets, trim them, and put the trimmings into a stewpan with a little butter; lay in the cutlets and fry them a nice brown colour on both sides. Add the bacon, carrots, onions, spice, herbs, and seasoning; pour in about a pint of boiling water, and stew gently for 2 hours on a very slow fire. When done, skim off the fat, take out the herbs, and flavour the gravy with a little tomato sauce and ketchup. Have ready the peas and potatoes, boiled *separately;* put them with the veal, and serve. *Time.*—2 hours. *Average cost,* 2*s.* 9*d.* *Sufficient* for 5 or 6 persons. *Seasonable* from June to August with peas; — rather earlier when these are omitted.

VEAL CAKE (a Convenient Dish for a Picnic).

Ingredients.—A few slices of cold roast veal, a few slices of cold ham, 2 hard-boiled eggs, 2 tablespoonfuls of minced parsley, a little pepper, good gravy. *Mode.*—Cut off all the brown outside from the veal, and cut the eggs into slices. Procure a pretty mould; lay veal, ham, eggs, and parsley in layers, with a little pepper between each, and when the mould is full, get some *strong* stock, and fill up the shape. Bake for ½ hour, and when cold, turn it out. *Time.*—½ hour. *Seasonable* at any time.

VEAL, Curried (Cold Meat Cookery).

Ingredients.—The remains of cold roast veal, 4 onions, 2 apples sliced, 1 tablespoonful of curry-powder, 1 dessertspoonful of flour, ½ pint of broth or water, 1 tablespoonful of lemon-juice. *Mode.*—Slice the onions and apples, and fry them in a little butter; then take them out, cut the meat into neat cutlets, and fry these of a pale brown; add the curry-powder and flour, put in the onion, apples, and a little broth or water, and stew gently till quite tender; add the lemon-juice, and serve with an edging of boiled rice. The curry may be ornamented with pickles, capsicums, and gherkins, arranged prettily on the top. *Time.*—¾ hour. *Average cost,* exclusive of the meat, 4*d.* *Seasonable* from March to October.

VEAL CUTLETS (an Entrée).

Ingredients.—About 3 lbs. of the prime part of the leg of veal, egg and bread-crumbs, 3 tablespoonfuls of minced savoury herbs, salt and pepper to taste, a small piece of butter. *Mode.*—Have the veal cut into slices about ¾ of an inch in thickness, and, if not cut perfectly even, level the meat with a cutlet-bat or rolling-pin. Shape and trim the cutlets, and brush them over with egg. Sprinkle with bread-crumbs, with which have been mixed minced herbs and a seasoning of pepper and salt, and press the crumbs down. Fry them of a delicate brown in fresh lard or butter, and be careful not to burn them. They should be very thoroughly done, but not dry. If the cutlets be thick, keep the pan covered for a few minutes at a good distance from the fire, after they have acquired a good colour: by this means, the meat will be done through. Lay the cutlets in a dish, keep them hot, and make a gravy in the pan as follows:—Dredge in a little flour, add a piece of butter the size of a walnut, brown it, then pour as much boiling water as is required over it, season with pepper and salt, add a little lemon-juice, give one boil, and pour it over the cutlets. They should be garnished with slices of broiled bacon, and a few forcemeat balls will be found a very excellent addition to this dish. *Time.*—For cutlets of a moderate thickness, about 12 minutes; if very thick, allow more time. *Average cost,* 10*d.* per lb. *Sufficient* for 6 persons. *Seasonable* from March to October.

VEAL CUTLETS.

Note.—Veal cutlets may be merely floured and fried of a nice brown: the gravy and garnishing should be the same as in the preceding recipe. They may also be cut from the loin or neck, as shown in the engraving.

VEAL CUTLETS, Broiled, à la Italienne (an Entrée).

Ingredients.—Neck of veal, salt and pepper to taste, the yolk of 1 egg, bread-crumbs, ½ pint of Italian sauce. *Mode.*—Cut the veal into cutlets, flatten and trim them nicely; powder over them a little salt and pepper; brush them over with the yolk of an egg, dip them into bread-crumbs, then into clarified butter, and, afterwards, in the bread-crumbs again; boil or fry them over a clear fire, that they may acquire a good brown colour. Arrange them in the dish alternately with rashers of broiled ham, and pour the sauce (made by recipe for Italian sauce, p. 305) in the middle. *Time.*—10 to 15 minutes, according to the thickness of the cutlets. *Average cost,* 10*d.* per lb. *Seasonable* from March to October.

VEAL CUTLETS, à la Maintenon (an Entrée).

Ingredients.—2 or 3 lbs. of veal cutlets, egg and bread-crumbs, 2 tablespoonfuls of minced savoury herbs, salt and pepper to taste, a little grated nutmeg. *Mode.*—Cut the cutlets about ¾ inch in thickness, flatten them, and brush them over with the yolk of an egg; dip them into bread-crumbs and minced herbs, season with pepper and salt and grated nutmeg, and fold each cutlet in a piece of buttered paper. Broil them, and send them to table with melted butter or a good gravy. *Time.*—From 15 to 18 minutes. *Average cost,* 10*d.* per lb. *Sufficient* for 5 or 6 persons. *Seasonable* from March to October.

VEAL, Fillet of, au Béchamel (Cold Meat Cookery).

Ingredients.—A small fillet of veal, 1 pint of béchamel sauce, a few bread-crumbs, clarified butter. *Mode.*—A fillet of veal that has been roasted the preceding day will answer very well for this dish. Cut the middle out rather deep, leaving a good margin round, from which to cut nice slices, and if there should be any cracks in the veal, fill them up with forcemeat. Mince finely the meat that was taken out, mixing with it a little of the forcemeat to flavour, and stir to it sufficient béchamel to make it of a proper consistency. Warm the veal in the oven for about an hour, taking care to baste it well, that it may not be dry;

put the mince in the place where the meat was taken out, sprinkle a few bread-crumbs over it, and drop a little clarified butter on the bread-crumbs; put it into the oven for ¼ hour to brown, and pour béchamel round the sides of the dish. *Time.*—Altogether 1½ hour. *Seasonable* from March to October.

VEAL, Roast Fillet of.

Ingredients.—Veal, forcemeat, melted butter. *Mode.*—Have the fillet cut according to the size required; take out the bone, and after raising the skin from the meat, put under the flap a nice forcemeat. Prepare sufficient of this, as there should be some left to eat cold, and to season and flavour a mince if required. Skewer and bind the veal up in a

FILLET OF VEAL.

round form; dredge well with flour, put it down at some distance from the fire at first, and baste continually. About ½ hour before serving, draw it nearer the fire, that it may acquire more colour, as the outside should be of a rich brown, but not burnt. Dish it, remove the skewers, which replace by a silver one; pour over the joint some good melted butter, and serve with either boiled ham, bacon, or pickled pork. Never omit to send a cut lemon to table with roast veal. *Time.*—A fillet of veal weighing 12 lbs., about 4 hours. *Average cost,* 9*d.* per lb. *Sufficient* for 9 or 10 persons. *Seasonable* from March to October.

VEAL, Fillet of.

The carving of this joint is similar to that of a round of beef. Slices, not too thick, in the direction of the line 1 to 2 are cut; and the only point to be careful about is, that the veal be *evenly* carved. Between the flap and the meat the stuffing is inserted, and

FILLET OF VEAL.

a small portion of this should be served to every guest. The persons whom the host wishes most to honour should be asked if they like the delicious brown outside slice, as this, by many, is exceedingly relished.

VEAL, Stewed Fillet of.

Ingredients.—A small fillet of veal, forcemeat, thickening of butter and flour, a few mushrooms, white pepper to taste, 2 tablespoonfuls of lemon-juice, 2 blades of pounded mace, ½ glass of sherry *Mode.*—If the whole of the leg is purchased, take off the knuckle to stew, and also the square end, which will serve for cutlets or pies. Remove the bone, and fill the space with a forcemeat. Roll and skewer it up firmly; place a few skewers at the bottom of a stewpan to prevent the meat from sticking, and cover the veal with a little weak stock. Let it simmer very *gently* until tender, as the more slowly veal is stewed, the better. Strain and thicken the sauce, flavour it with lemon-juice, mace, sherry, and white pepper; give one boil, and pour it over the meat. The skewers should be removed, and replaced by a silver one, and the dish garnished with slices of cut lemon. *Time.*—A fillet of veal weighing 6 lbs., 3 hours' very gentle stewing. *Average cost,* 9*d.* per lb. *Sufficient* for 5 or 6 persons. *Seasonable* from March to October.

VEAL, Fricandeau of (an Entrée).

Ingredients.—A piece of the fat side of a leg of veal (about 3 lbs.), lardoons, 2 carrots, 2 large onions, a faggot of savoury herbs, 2 blades of pounded mace, 6 whole allspice, 2 bay-leaves, pepper to taste, a few slices of fat bacon, 1 pint of stock. *Mode.*—The veal for a

FRICANDEAU OF VEAL.

fricandeau should be of the best quality, or it will not be good. It may be known by the meat being white and not thready. Take off the skin, flatten the veal on the table, then at one stroke of the knife, cut off as much as is required, for a fricandeau with an uneven surface never looks well. Trim it, and with a sharp knife make two or three slits in the middle, that it may taste more of the seasoning. Now lard it thickly with fat bacon, as lean gives a red colour to the fricandeau. Slice the vegetables, and put these, with the herbs and spices, in the *middle* of a stewpan, with a few slices of bacon at the top: these should form a sort of mound in the centre for the veal to rest upon. Lay the fricandeau over the bacon, sprinkle over it a little salt, and pour in just sufficient stock to cover the bacon, &c., without touching the veal. Let it gradually come to a boil; then put it over a slow and equal fire, and let it *simmer very* gently for about 2½ hours, or longer should it be very large. Baste it frequently with the liquor, and a short time before serving, put it into a brisk oven, to make the bacon firm, which otherwise would break when it was glazed. Dish the fricandeau, keep it hot, skim off the fat from the liquor, and reduce it quickly to a glaze, with which glaze the fricandeau, and serve with a purée of whatever vegetable happens to be in season—spinach, sorrel, asparagus, cucumbers, peas, &c. *Time.*—2½ hours. If very large, allow more time. *Average cost,* 3*s.* 6*d.* *Sufficient* for an entrée. *Seasonable* from March to October.

VEAL, Fricandeau of (more economical).

Ingredients.—The best end of a neck of veal (about 2½ lbs.), lardoons, 2 carrots, 2 onions, a faggot of savoury herbs, 2 blades of mace, 2 bay-leaves, a little whole white pepper, a few slices of fat bacon. *Mode.*—Cut away the lean part of the best end of a neck of veal with a sharp knife, scooping it from the bones. Put the bones in with a little water, which will serve to moisten the fricandeau: they should stew about 1½ hour. Lard the veal, proceed in the same way as in the preceding recipe, and be careful that the gravy does not touch the fricandeau. Stew very gently for 3 hours; glaze, and serve it on sorrel, spinach, or with a little gravy in the dish. *Time.*—3 hours. *Average cost,* 2*s.* 6*d.* *Sufficient* for an entrée. *Seasonable* from March to October.

Note.—When the prime part of the leg is cut off, it spoils the whole; consequently, to use this for a fricandeau is rather extravagant. The best end of the neck answers the purpose nearly or quite as well.

VEAL, to Carve a Knuckle of.

The engraving, showing the dotted line from 1 to 2, sufficiently indicates the direction which should be given to the knife in carving this dish. The best slices are those from the thickest part of the knuckle, that is, outside the line 1 to 2.

KNUCKLE OF VEAL.

VEAL, to Ragout a Knuckle of.

Ingredients.—Knuckle of veal, pepper and salt to taste, flour, 1 onion, 1 head of celery, or a little celery-seed, a faggot of savoury herbs, 2 blades of pounded mace, thickening of butter and flour, a few young carrots, 1 tablespoonful of tomato sauce, 3 tablespoonfuls of sherry, the juice of ½ lemon. *Mode.*—Cut the meat from a knuckle of veal into neat slices, season with pepper and salt, and dredge them with flour. Fry them in a little butter of a pale brown, and put them into a stewpan with the bone (which should be chopped in several places); add the celery, herbs, mace, and carrots; pour over all about 1 pint of hot water, and let it simmer very gently for 2 hours over a slow but clear fire. Take out the slices of meat and carrots, strain and thicken the gravy with a little butter rolled in flour; add the remaining ingredients, give one boil, put back the meat and carrots, let these get hot through, and serve. When in season, a few green peas, *boiled separately*, and added to this dish at the moment of serving, would be found a very agreeable addition. *Time.*—2 hours. *Average cost,* 5*d.* to 6*d.* per lb. *Sufficient* for 4 or 5 persons.

VEAL, Stewed Knuckle of, and Rice.

Ingredients.—Knuckle of veal, 1 onion, 2 blades of mace, 1 teaspoonful of salt, ½ lb. of rice. *Mode.*—Have the knuckle cut small, or cut some cutlets from it, that it may be just large enough to be eaten the same day it is dressed, as cold boiled veal is not a particularly tempting dish. Break the shank-bone, wash it clean, and put the meat into a stewpan with sufficient water to cover it. Let it gradually come to a boil, put in the salt, and remove the scum as fast as it rises. When it has simmered gently for

KNUCKLE OF VEAL.

about ¾ hour, add the remaining ingredients, and stew the whole gently for 2½ hours. Put the meat into a deep dish, pour over it the rice, &c., and send boiled bacon, and a tureen of parsley and butter to table with it. *Time.*—A knuckle of veal weighing 6 lbs., 3 hours' gentle stewing. *Average cost*, 5*d.* to 6*d.* per lb. *Sufficient* for 5 or 6 persons. *Seasonable* from March to October.

Note. — Macaroni, instead of rice, boiled with the veal, will be found good; or the rice and macaroni may be omitted, and the veal sent to table smothered in parsley and butter.

VEAL, Roast Loin of.

Ingredients. — Veal; melted butter. *Mode.* — Paper the kidney fat; roll in and skewer the flap, which makes the joint a good shape; dredge it well with flour, and put it down to a bright fire. Should the loin be very large, skewer the kidney back for a time to roast

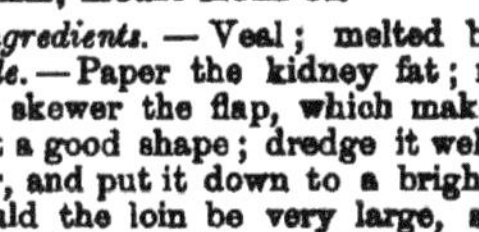

LOIN OF VEAL.

thoroughly. Keep it well basted, and a short time before serving, remove the paper from the kidney, and allow it to acquire a nice brown colour, but it should not be burnt. Have ready some melted butter, put it into the dripping-pan after it is emptied of its contents, pour it over

the veal, and serve. Garnish the dish with slices of lemon and forcemeat balls, and send to table with it boiled bacon, ham, pickled pork, or pig's cheek. *Time.* —A large loin, 3 hours. *Average cost*, 9½*d.* per lb. *Sufficient* for 7 or 8 persons. *Seasonable* from March to October.

Note.—A piece of toast should be placed under the kidneys when the veal is dished.

VEAL, Loin of, au Béchamel (Cold Meat Cookery).

Ingredients.—Loin of veal, ½ teaspoonful of minced lemon-peel, rather more than ½ pint of béchamel or white sauce. *Mode.*—A loin of veal which has come from table with very little taken off, answers well for this dish. Cut off the meat from the inside, mince it, and mix with it some minced lemon-peel; put it into sufficient béchamel to warm it through. In the mean time, wrap the joint in buttered paper, and place it in the oven to warm. When thoroughly hot, dish the mince, place the loin above it, and pour over the remainder of the béchamel. *Time.*—1½ hour to warm the meat in the oven. *Seasonable* from March to October.

VEAL, Loin of, à la Daube.

Ingredients.—The chump end of a loin of veal, forcemeat, a few slices of bacon, a bunch of savoury herbs, 2 blades of mace, ½ teaspoonful of whole white pepper, 1 pint of veal stock or water, 5 or 6 green onions. *Mode.*—Cut off the chump from a loin of veal, and take out the bone; fill the cavity with forcemeat, tie it up tightly, and lay it in a stewpan with the bones and trimmings, and cover the veal with a few slices of bacon. Add the herbs, mace, pepper, and onions, and stock or water; cover the pan with a closely-fitting lid, and simmer for 2 hours, shaking the stewpan occasionally. Take out the bacon, herbs, and onions; reduce the gravy, if not already thick enough, to a glaze, with which glaze the meat, and serve with tomato, mushroom, or sorrel sauce. *Time.*—2 hours. *Average cost*, 9*d.* per lb. *Sufficient* for 4 or 5 persons. *Seasonable* from March to October.

VEAL, to Carve Loin of.

As is the case with a loin of mutton, the careful jointing of a loin of veal is more than half the battle in carving it. If the butcher be negligent in this matter, he should be admonished; for there is nothing more annoying or irritating to an inexperienced carver than to be obliged to turn his knife in all directions to find the exact place where it should be inserted in order to divide the bones. When the jointing is properly performed, there is little difficulty in carrying the knife down in the direction of the line 1 to 2. To each guest should be given a piece of the kidney and kidney fat, which lie underneath, and are considered great delicacies.

LOIN OF VEAL.

VEAL, Minced, with Béchamel Sauce (Cold Meat Cookery, very good).

Ingredients.—The remains of a fillet of veal, 1 pint of béchamel sauce, ½ tea-spoonful of minced lemon-peel, forcemeat balls. *Mode.*—Cut—but do not *chop*—a few slices of cold roast veal as finely as possible, sufficient to make rather more than 1 lb., weighed after being minced. Make the above proportion of béchamel, by recipe; add the lemon-peel, put in the veal, and let the whole gradually warm through. When it is at the point of simmering, dish it, and garnish with forcemeat balls and fried sippets of bread. *Time.*—To simmer 1 minute. *Average cost,* exclusive of the cold meat, 1*s.* 4*d.* *Sufficient* for 5 or 6 persons. *Seasonable* from March to October.

VEAL, Minced (more economical).

Ingredients. — The remains of cold roast fillet or loin of veal, rather more than 1 pint of water, 1 onion, ½ tea-spoonful of minced lemon-peel, salt and white pepper to taste, 1 blade of pounded mace, 2 or 3 young carrots, a faggot of sweet herbs, thickening of butter and flour, 1 tablespoonful of lemon-juice, 3 tablespoonfuls of cream or milk. *Mode.*—Take about 1 lb. of veal, and should there be any bones, dredge them with flour, and put them into a stewpan with the brown outside, and a few meat trimmings; add rather more than a pint of water, the onion cut in slices, lemon-peel, seasoning, mace, carrots, and herbs; simmer these well for rather more than 1 hour, and strain the liquor. Rub a little flour into some butter; add this to the gravy, set it on the fire, and, when it boils, skim well. Mince the veal finely by *cutting,* and not chopping it; put it in the gravy; let it get warmed through gradually; add the lemon-juice and cream, and, when it is on the point of boiling, serve. Garnish the dish with sippets of toasted bread and slices of bacon rolled and toasted. Forcemeat balls may also be added. If more lemon-peel is liked than is stated above, put a little very finely minced to the veal, after it is warmed in the gravy. *Time.*—1 hour to make the gravy. *Average cost,* exclusive of the cold meat, 6*d.* *Seasonable* from March to October.

VEAL, Minced, and Macaroni (a pretty side or corner dish).

Ingredients.—¾ lb. of minced cold roast veal, 3 oz. of ham, 1 tablespoonful of gravy, pepper and salt to taste, ½ tea-spoonful of grated nutmeg, ¼ lb. of bread-crumbs, ¼ lb. of macaroni, 1 or 2 eggs to bind, a small piece of butter. *Mode.*—Cut some nice slices from a cold fillet of veal, trim off the brown outside, and mince the meat finely with the above proportion of ham: should the meat be very dry, add a spoonful of good gravy. Season highly with pepper and salt, add the grated nutmeg and bread-crumbs, and mix these ingredients with 1 or 2 eggs well beaten, which should bind the mixture and make it like forcemeat. In the mean time, boil the macaroni in salt and water, and drain it; butter a mould, put some of the macaroni at the bottom and sides of it, in whatever form is liked; mix the remainder with the forcemeat, fill the mould up to the top, put a plate or small dish on it, and steam for ½ hour. Turn it out carefully, and serve with good gravy poured round, but not over, the meat. *Time.*—½ hour. *Average cost,* exclusive of the cold meat, 10*d.* *Seasonable* from March to October.

Note.—To make a variety, boil some carrots and turnips separately in a little salt and water; when done, cut them into pieces about ⅛ inch in thickness; butter an oval mould, and place these in it, in white and red stripes alternately, at the bottom and sides. Proceed as in the foregoing recipe, and be very careful in turning it out of the mould.

VEAL, Moulded Minced (Cold Meat Cookery).

Ingredients.—¾ lb. of cold roast veal, a small slice of bacon, ⅓ teaspoonful of minced lemon-peel, ½ onion chopped fine, salt, pepper, and pounded mace to taste, a slice of toast soaked in milk, 1 egg. *Mode.*—Mince the meat very fine, after removing from it all skin and outside pieces, and chop the bacon; mix these well together, adding the lemon-peel, onion, seasoning, mace, and toast. When all the ingredients are thoroughly incorporated, beat up an egg, with which bind the mixture. Butter a shape, put in the meat, and bake for ¾ hour; turn it out of the mould carefully, and pour round it a good brown gravy. A sheep's head dressed in this manner is an economical and savoury dish. *Time.* ¾ hour. *Average cost,* exclusive of the meat, 6*d.* *Seasonable* from March to October.

VEAL, Braised Neck of.

Ingredients.—The best end of the neck of veal (from 3 to 4 lbs.), bacon, 1 tablespoonful of minced parsley, salt, pepper, and grated nutmeg to taste; 1 onion, 2 carrots, a little celery (when this is not obtainable, use the seed), ½ glass of sherry, thickening of butter and flour, lemon-juice, 1 blade of pounded mace. *Mode.*—Prepare the bacon for larding, and roll it in minced parsley, salt, pepper, and grated nutmeg; lard the veal, put it into a stewpan with a few slices of lean bacon or ham, an onion, carrots, and celery; and do not quite cover it with water. Stew it gently for 2 hours, or until it is quite tender; strain off the liquor; stir together over the fire, in a stewpan, a little flour and butter until brown; lay the veal in this, the upper side to the bottom of the pan, and let it remain till it is a nice brown colour. Place it in the dish; pour into the stewpan as much gravy as is required, boil it up, skim well, add the wine, pounded mace, and lemon-juice; simmer for 3 minutes, pour it over the meat, and serve. *Time.* — Rather more than 2 hours. *Average cost,* 8*d.* per lb. *Sufficient* for 5 or 6 persons. *Seasonable* from March to October.

VEAL, Roast Neck of.

Ingredients. — Veal, melted butter, forcemeat balls. *Mode.*—Have the veal cut from the best end of the neck; dredge it with flour, and put it down to a bright clear fire; keep it well basted; dish it, pour over it some melted butter, and garnish the dish with fried forcemeat balls; send to table with a cut lemon. The scrag may be boiled or stewed in various ways, with rice, onion-sauce, or parsley and butter. *Time.*—About 2 hours. *Average cost,* 8*d.* per lb. *Sufficient.*—4 or 5 lbs. for 5 or 6 persons. *Seasonable* from March to October.

VEAL OLIVE PIE (Cold Meat Cookery).

Ingredients.—A few thin slices of cold fillet of veal, a few thin slices of bacon, forcemeat, a cupful of gravy, 4 tablespoonfuls of cream, puff-crust. *Mode.*—Cut thin slices from a fillet of veal, place on them thin slices of bacon, and over them a layer of forcemeat, made by recipe, with an additional seasoning of shalot and cayenne; roll them tightly, and fill up a pie-dish with them; add the gravy and cream, cover with a puff-crust, and bake for 1 to 1½ hour: should the pie be very large, allow 2 hours. The pieces of rolled veal should be about 3 inches in length, and about 3 inches round. *Time.*—Moderate-sized pie, 1 to 1½ hour. *Seasonable* from March to October.

VEAL PIE.

Ingredients.—2 lbs. of veal cutlets, 1 or 2 slices of lean bacon or ham, pepper and salt to taste, 2 tablespoonfuls of minced savoury herbs, 2 blades of pounded mace, crust, 1 teacupful of gravy. *Mode.* — Cut the cutlets into square pieces, and season them with pepper, salt, and pounded mace; put them in a pie-dish with the savoury herbs sprinkled over, and 1 or 2 slices of lean bacon or ham placed at the top: if possible, this should be previously cooked, as undressed bacon makes the veal red, and spoils its appearance. Pour in a little water, cover with crust, ornament it in any way that is approved; brush it over with the yolk of an egg, and bake in a well-heated oven for about 1½ hour. Pour in a good gravy after baking, which is done by removing the top ornament, and replacing it after the gravy is added. *Time.*—About 1½ hour. *Average cost,* 2*s.* 6*d.* *Sufficient* for 5 or 6 persons. *Seasonable* from March to October.

VEAL AND HAM PIE.

Ingredients.—2 lbs. of veal cutlets, ½ lb. of boiled ham, 2 tablespoonfuls of minced savoury herbs, ¼ teaspoonful of grated nutmeg, 2 blades of pounded mace, pepper and salt to taste, a strip of lemon-peel finely minced, the yolks of 2 hard-boiled eggs, ½ pint of water, nearly ½ pint of good strong gravy, puff-crust. *Mode.*—Cut the veal into nice square pieces, and put a layer of them at the bottom of a pie-dish; sprinkle over these a portion of the herbs, spices, seasoning, lemon-peel, and the yolks of the eggs cut in slices; cut the ham very thin, and put a layer of this in. Proceed in this manner until the dish is full, so arranging it that the ham comes at the top. Lay a puff paste on the edge of the dish, and pour in about ½ pint of water; cover with crust, ornament it with leaves, brush it over with the yolk of an egg, and bake in a well-heated oven for 1 to 1½ hour, or longer, should the pie be very large. When it is taken out of the oven, pour in at the top, through a funnel, nearly ½ pint of strong gravy: this should be made sufficiently good that, when cold, it may cut in a firm jelly. This pie may be very much enriched by adding a few mushrooms, oysters, or sweetbreads; but it will be found very good without any of the last-named additions. *Time.*—1½ hour, or longer, should the pie be very large. *Average cost,* 3*s.* *Sufficient* for 5 or 6 persons. *Seasonable* from March to October.

VEAL, Potted (for Breakfast).

Ingredients. — To every lb. of veal allow ¼ lb. of ham, cayenne and pounded mace to taste, 6 oz. of fresh butter; clarified butter. *Mode.*—Mince the veal and ham together as finely as possible, and pound well in a mortar, with cayenne, pounded mace, and fresh butter in the above proportion. When reduced to a perfectly smooth paste, press it into potting-pots, and cover with clarified butter. If kept in a cool place, it will remain good some days. *Seasonable* from March to October.

VEAL, Ragout of Cold (Cold Meat Cookery).

Ingredients.—The remains of cold veal, 1 oz. of butter, ½ pint of gravy, thickening of butter and flour, pepper and salt to taste, 1 blade of pounded mace, 1 tablespoonful of mushroom ketchup, 1 tablespoonful of sherry, 1 dessertspoonful of lemon-juice, forcemeat balls. *Mode.*—Any part of veal will make this dish. Cut the meat into nice-looking pieces, put them in a stewpan with 1 oz. of butter, and fry a light brown; add the gravy (hot water may be substituted for this), thicken with a little butter and flour, and stew gently about ¼ hour; season with pepper, salt, and pounded mace; add the ketchup, sherry, and lemon-juice; give one boil, and serve. Garnish the dish with forcemeat balls and fried rashers of bacon. *Time.*—Altogether ½ hour. *Average cost,* exclusive of cold meat, 6*d.* *Seasonable* from March to October.

Note.—The above recipe may be varied, by adding vegetables, such as peas, cucumbers, lettuces, green onions cut in slices, a dozen or two of green gooseberries (not seedy), all of which should be fried a little with the meat, and then stewed in the gravy.

VEAL RISSOLES (Cold Meat Cookery).

Ingredients.—A few slices of cold roast veal, a few slices of ham or bacon, 1 tablespoonful of minced parsley, 1 tablespoonful of minced savoury herbs, 1 blade of pounded mace, a very little grated nutmeg, cayenne and salt to taste, 2 eggs well beaten, bread-crumbs. *Mode.*—Mince the veal very finely with a little ham or bacon; add the parsley, herbs, spices, and seasoning; mix into a paste with an egg; form into balls or cones; brush these over with egg, sprinkle with bread-crumbs, and fry a rich brown. Serve with brown gravy, and garnish the dish with fried parsley. *Time.*—About 10 minutes to fry the rissoles. *Seasonable* from March to October.

VEAL ROLLS (Cold Meat Cookery).

Ingredients.—The remains of a cold fillet of veal, egg and bread-crumbs, a few slices of fat bacon, forcemeat. *Mode.*—Cut a few slices from a cold fillet of veal

½ inch thick; rub them over with egg; lay a thin slice of fat bacon over each piece of veal; brush these with the egg, and over this spread the forcemeat thinly; roll up each piece tightly, egg and bread-crumb them, and fry them a rich brown. Serve with mushroom sauce or brown gravy. *Time.*—10 to 15 minutes to fry the rolls. *Seasonable* from March to October.

VEAL, Stuffed and Stewed Shoulder of.

Ingredients. — A shoulder of veal, a few slices of ham or bacon, forcemeat, 3 carrots, 2 onions, salt and pepper to taste, a faggot of savoury herbs, 3 blades of pounded mace, water, thickening of butter and flour. *Mode.*—Bone the joint by carefully detaching the meat from the blade-bone on one side, and then on the other, being particular not to pierce the skin; then cut the bone from the knuckle, and take it out. Fill the cavity whence the bone was taken with a forcemeat. Roll and bind the veal up tightly; put it into a stewpan with the carrots, onions, seasoning, herbs, and mace; pour in just sufficient water to cover it, and let it stew *very gently* for about 5 hours. Before taking it up, try if it is properly done by thrusting a larding-needle in it: if it penetrates easily, it is sufficiently cooked. Strain and skim the gravy, thicken with butter and flour, give one boil, and pour it round the meat. A few young carrots may be boiled and placed round the dish as a garnish, and, when in season, green peas should always be served with this dish. *Time.*—5 hours. *Average cost*, 7*d.* per lb. *Sufficient* for 8 or 9 persons. *Seasonable* from March to October.

VEAL, Stewed with Peas, Young Carrots, and New Potatoes.

Ingredients.—3 or 4 lbs. of the loin or neck of veal, 15 young carrots, a few green onions, 1 pint of green peas, 12 new potatoes, a bunch of savoury herbs, pepper and salt to taste, 1 tablespoonful of lemon-juice, 2 tablespoonfuls of tomato sauce, 2 tablespoonfuls of mushroom ketchup. *Mode.* — Dredge the meat with flour, and roast or bake it for about ¾ hour: it should acquire a nice brown colour. Put the meat into a stewpan with the carrots, onions, potatoes, herbs, pepper, and salt; pour over it sufficient boiling water to cover it, and stew gently for 2 hours. Take out the meat and herbs, put it in a deep dish, skim off all the fat from the gravy, and flavour it with lemon-juice, tomato sauce, and mushroom ketchup, in the above proportion. Have ready a pint of green peas boiled *separately*; put these with the meat, pour over it the gravy, and serve. The dish may be garnished with a few forcemeat balls. The meat, when preferred, may be cut into chops, and floured and fried instead of being roasted; and any part of veal dressed in this way will be found extremely savoury and good. *Time.* — 3 hours. *Average cost*, 9*d.* per lb. *Sufficient* for 6 or 7 persons. *Seasonable*, with peas, from June to August.

VEGETABLE MARROW, Boiled.

Ingredients. — To each ½ gallon of water, allow 1 heaped tablespoonful of salt; vegetable marrows. *Mode.*—Have ready a saucepan of boiling water, salted in the above proportion; put in the marrows after peeling them, and boil them until quite tender. Take them up with a slice, halve, and, should they be very large, quarter them. Dish them on toast, and send to table with them a tureen of melted butter, or, in lieu of this, a small pat of salt butter. Large vegetable marrows may be preserved throughout the winter by storing them in a dry place; when wanted for use, a few slices should be cut and boiled in the same manner as above; but, when once begun, the marrow must be eaten quickly, as it keeps but a short time after it is cut. Vegetable marrows are also very delicious mashed: they should be boiled, then drained, and mashed smoothly with a wooden spoon. Heat them in a saucepan, add a seasoning of salt and pepper, and a small piece of butter, and dish with a few sippets of toasted bread placed round as a garnish. *Time.*—Young vegetable marrows, 10 to 20 minutes; old ones, ½ to ¾ hour. *Average cost*, in full season, 1*s.* per dozen. *Sufficient.*—Allow 1 moderate-sized marrow for each person. *Seasonable* in July,

VEGETABLE MARROW ON TOAST.

August, and September; but may be preserved all the winter.

VEGETABLE MARROW, Fried.

Ingredients. — 3 medium-sized vegetable marrows, egg and bread-crumbs, hot lard. *Mode.*—Peel, and boil the marrows until tender in salt and water; then drain them and cut them in quarters, and take out the seeds. When thoroughly drained, brush the marrows over with egg, and sprinkle with bread-crumbs; have ready some hot lard, fry the marrow in this, and, when of a nice brown, dish; sprinkle over a little salt and pepper, and serve. *Time.*—About ½ hour to boil the marrow, 7 minutes to fry it. *Average cost*, in full season, 1*s.* per dozen. *Sufficient* for 4 persons. *Seasonable* in July, August, and September.

VEGETABLE MARROWS IN WHITE SAUCE.

Ingredients. —4 or 5 moderate-sized marrows, ½ pint of white sauce. *Mode.* —Pare the marrows; cut them in halves, and shape each half at the top in a point, leaving the bottom end flat for it to stand upright in the dish. Boil the marrows in salt and water until tender; take them up very carefully, and arrange them on a hot dish. Have ready ½ pint of white sauce; pour this over the marrows, and serve. *Time.*—From 15 to 20 minutes to boil the marrows. *Average cost*, in full season, 1*s.* per dozen. *Sufficient* for 5 or 6 persons. *Seasonable* in July, August, and September.

VEGETABLE MARROW IN WHITE SAUCE.

VEGETABLE MARROW SOUP.

Ingredients.—4 young vegetable marrows, or more, if very small, ½ pint of cream, salt and white pepper to taste, 2 quarts of white stock. *Mode.*—Pare and slice the marrows, and put them in the stock boiling. When done almost to a mash, press them through a sieve, and at the moment of serving, add the boiling cream and seasoning. *Time.*—1 hour. *Average cost*, 1*s.* 2*d.* per quart. *Seasonable* in summer. *Sufficient* for 8 persons.

VEGETABLE SOUP.

Ingredients.—7 oz. of carrot, 10 oz. of parsnip, 10 oz. of potato, cut into thin slices; 1¼ oz. of butter, 5 teaspoonfuls of flour, a teaspoonful of made mustard, salt and pepper to taste, the yolks of 2 eggs, rather more than 2 quarts of water. *Mode.*—Boil the vegetables in the water 2½ hours; stir them often, and if the water boils away too quickly, add more, as there should be 2 quarts of soup when done. Mix up in a basin the butter and flour, mustard, salt, and pepper, with a teacupful of cold water; stir in the soup, and boil 10 minutes. Have ready the yolks of the eggs in the tureen; pour on, stir well, and serve. *Time.*—3 hours. *Average cost*, 4*d.* per quart. *Seasonable* in winter. *Sufficient* for 8 persons.

VEGETABLE SOUP.

Ingredients. — Equal quantities of onions, carrots, turnips; ¼ lb. of butter, a crust of toasted bread, 1 head of celery, a faggot of herbs, salt and pepper to taste, 1 teaspoonful of powdered sugar, 2 quarts of common stock or boiling water. Allow ¾ lb. of vegetables to 2 quarts of stock. *Mode.*—Cut up the onions, carrots, and turnips; wash and drain them well, and put them in the stewpan with the butter and powdered sugar. Toss the whole over a sharp fire for 10 minutes, but do not let them brown, or you will spoil the flavour of the soup. When done, pour the stock or boiling water on them; add the bread, celery, herbs, and seasoning; stew for 3 hours; skim well and strain it off. When ready to serve, add a little sliced carrot, celery, and turnip, and flavour with a spoonful of Harvey's sauce, or a little ketchup. *Time.*—3½ hours. *Average cost*, 6*d.* per quart. *Seasonable* all the year. *Sufficient* for 8 persons.

VEGETABLE SOUP.
(*Good and Cheap, made without Meat.*)

Ingredients.—6 potatoes, 4 turnips, or 2 if very large; 2 carrots, 2 onions; if obtainable, 2 mushrooms; 1 head of celery, 1 large slice of bread, 1 small saltspoonful of salt, ½ saltspoonful of ground black pepper, 2 teaspoonfuls of Harvey's sauce, 6 quarts of water. *Mode.*—Peel the vegetables, and cut them up into small pieces; toast the bread rather brown, and put all into a stewpan with the water and seasoning. Simmer gently for 3 hours, or until all is reduced to a pulp, and pass it through a sieve in the same way as pea-soup, which it should resemble in consistence; but it should be a dark brown colour. Warm it up again when required; put in the Harvey's sauce, and, if necessary, add to the flavouring. *Time.*—3 hours, or rather more. *Average cost*, 1d. per quart. *Seasonable* at any time. *Sufficient* for 16 persons.

Note.—This recipe was forwarded to the Editress by a lady in the county of Durham, by whom it was strongly recommended.

VEGETABLES, Cut for Soups, &c.

The annexed engraving represents a cutter for shaping vegetables for soups, ragoûts, stews, &c.; carrots and turnips being the usual vegetables for which this utensil is used. Cut the vegetables into slices about ¼ inch in thickness, stamp them out with the cutter, and boil them for a few minutes in salt and water, until tender. Turnips should be cut in rather thicker slices than carrots, on account of the former boiling more quickly to a pulp than the latter.

VEGETABLE-CUTTER.

VENISON, Hashed.

Ingredients. — The remains of roast venison, its own or mutton gravy, thickening of butter and flour. *Mode.* —Cut the meat from the bones in neat slices, and, if there is sufficient of its own gravy left, put the meat into this, as it is preferable to any other. Should there not be enough, put the bones and trimmings into a stewpan, with about a pint of mutton gravy; let them stew gently for an hour, and strain the gravy. Put a little flour and butter into the stewpan, keep stirring until brown, then add the strained gravy, and give it a boil up; skim and strain again, and, when a little cool, put in the slices of venison. Place the stewpan by the side of the fire, and, when on the point of simmering, serve: do not allow it to boil, or the meat will be hard. Send red-currant jelly to table with it. *Time.* —Altogether, 1½ hour. *Seasonable.*—Buck venison, from June to Michaelmas; doe venison, from November to the end of January.

Note.—A small quantity of Harvey's sauce, ketchup, or port wine, may be added to enrich the gravy: these ingredients must, however, be used very sparingly, or they will overpower the flavour of the venison.

VENISON, Roast Haunch of.

Ingredients. — Venison, coarse flour-and-water paste, a little flour. *Mode.*—Choose a haunch with clear, bright, and thick fat, and the cleft of the hoof smooth and close; the greater quantity of fat there is, the better quality will the meat be. As many people object to venison when it has too much *haut goût*, ascertain how long it has been kept, by running a sharp skewer into the meat close to the bone: when this is withdrawn, its sweetness can be judged of. With care and attention, it will keep good a fortnight, unless the weather is very mild. Keep it perfectly dry by wiping it with clean cloths till not the least damp remains, and sprinkle over powdered ginger or pepper, as a preventive against the fly. When required for use,

ROAST HAUNCH OF VENISON.

wash it in warm water, and *dry* it *well* with a cloth; butter a sheet of white paper, put it over the fat, lay a coarse paste, about ½ inch in thickness, over this, and then a sheet or two of strong paper. Tie the whole firmly on to the haunch with twine, and put the joint down to a strong close fire; baste the venison immediately, to prevent the paper and string from burning, and continue this operation, without intermission, the whole of the time it is cooking. About 20 minutes before it is done, carefully remove the paste and paper, dredge the joint with flour, and baste well with *butter* until it is nicely frothed, and of a nice pale-brown colour; garnish the knuckle-bone with a frill of white paper, and serve with a good, strong, but unflavoured gravy, in a tureen, and currant jelly; or melt the jelly with a little port wine, and serve that also in a tureen. As the principal object in roasting venison is to preserve the fat, the above is the best mode of doing so where expense is not objected to; but, in ordinary cases, the paste may be dispensed with, and a double paper placed over the roast instead: it will not require so long cooking without the paste. Do not omit to send very hot plates to table, as the venison fat so soon freezes: to be thoroughly enjoyed by epicures, it should be eaten on hot-water plates. The neck and shoulder may be roasted in the same manner. *Time.*—A large haunch of buck venison, with the paste, 4 to 5 hours; haunch of doe venison, 3¼ to 3½ hours. Allow less time without the paste. *Average cost*, 1*s.* 4*d.* to 1*s.* 6*d.* per lb. *Sufficient* for 18 persons. *Seasonable.*—Buck venison in greatest perfection from June to Michaelmas; doe venison from November to the end of January.

VENISON, to Carve Haunch of.

Here is a grand dish for a knight of the carving-knife to exercise his skill upon, and, what will be pleasant for many to know, there is but little difficulty in the performance. An incision being made completely down to the bone, in the direction of the line 1 to 2, the gravy will then be able easily to flow; when slices, not too thick, should be cut

HAUNCH OF VENISON.

along the haunch, as indicated by the line 4 to 3; that end of the joint marked 3 having been turned towards the carver, so that he may have a more complete command over the joint. Although some epicures affect to believe that some parts of the haunch are superior to others, yet we doubt if there is any difference between the slices cut above and below the line. It should be borne in mind to serve each guest with a portion of fat; and the most expeditious carver will be the best carver, as, like mutton, venison soon begins to chill, when it loses much of its charm.

VENISON, Stewed.

Ingredients.—A shoulder of venison, a few slices of mutton fat, 2 glasses of port wine, pepper and allspice to taste, 1½ pint of weak stock or gravy, ½ teaspoonful of whole pepper, ½ teaspoonful of whole allspice. *Mode.*—Hang the venison till tender; take out the bone, flatten the meat with a rolling-pin, and place over it a few slices of mutton fat, which have been previously soaked for 2 or 3 hours in port wine; sprinkle these with a little fine allspice and pepper, roll the meat up, and bind and tie it securely. Put it into a stewpan with the bone and the above proportion of weak stock or gravy, whole allspice, black pepper, and port wine; cover the lid down closely, and simmer, very gently, from 3½ to 4 hours. When quite tender, take off the tape, and dish the meat; strain the gravy over it, and send it to table with red currant jelly. Unless the joint is very fat, the above is the best mode of cooking it. *Time.*—3½ to 4 hours. *Average cost,* 1*s.* 4*d.* to 1*s.* 6*d.* per lb. *Sufficient* for 10 or 12 persons. *Seasonable.* — Buck venison, from June to Michaelmas; doe venison, from November to the end of January.

VERMICELLI PUDDING.

Ingredients.—4 oz. of vermicelli, 1½ pint of milk, ½ pint of cream, 3 oz. of butter, 3 oz. of sugar, 4 eggs. *Mode.*—Boil the vermicelli in the milk until it is tender; then stir in the remaining ingredients, omitting the cream, if not obtainable. Flavour the mixture with grated lemon-rind, essence of bitter almonds, or vanilla; butter a pie-dish; line the edges with puff-paste, put in the pudding, and bake in a moderate oven for about ¾ hour. *Time.* — ¾ hour. *Average cost,* 1*s.* 2*d.* without cream. *Sufficient* for 5 or 6 persons. *Seasonable* at any time.

VERMICELLI SOUP.

Ingredients.—1½ lb. of bacon, stuck with cloves; ½ oz. of butter, worked up in flour; 1 small fowl, trussed for boiling; 2 oz. of vermicelli, 2 quarts of white stock. *Mode.* — Put the stock, bacon, butter, and fowl, into the stewpan, and stew for ¾ of an hour. Take the vermicelli, add it to a little of the stock, and set it on the fire, till it is quite tender. When the soup is ready, take out the fowl and bacon, and put the bacon on a dish. Skim the soup as clean as possible; pour it, with the vermicelli, over the fowl. Cut some bread thin, put in the soup, and serve. *Time.* —2 hours. *Average cost,* exclusive of the fowl and bacon, 10*d.* per quart. *Seasonable* in winter. *Sufficient* for 4 persons.

VERMICELLI SOUP.

Ingredients. — ¼ lb. of vermicelli, 2 quarts of clear gravy stock. *Mode.*— Put the vermicelli in the soup, boiling; simmer very gently for ½ an hour, and stir frequently. *Time.* — ½ an hour. *Average cost,* 1*s.* 3*d.* per quart. *Seasonable* all the year. *Sufficient* for 8 persons.

VOL-AU-VENT (an Entrée).

Ingredients.—¾ to 1 lb. of puff-paste, fricasseed chickens, rabbits, ragoûts, or the remains of cold fish, flaked and warmed in thick white sauce. *Mode.*— Make from ¾ to 1 lb. of puff-paste, taking care that it is very evenly rolled out each time, to ensure its rising properly; and if the paste is not extremely light, and put into a good hot oven, this cannot be accomplished, and the *vol-au-vent* will look very badly. Roll out the paste to the thickness of about 1½ inch, and, with a fluted cutter, stamp it out to the desired shape, either round or oval, and, with the point of a small knife, make a slight incision in the paste all round the top, about an inch from the edge, which, when baked, forms the lid. Put the *vol-au-vent* into a good brisk oven, and keep the door shut for a few minutes after it is put in. Particular attention should be paid to the heating of the oven, for the paste *cannot* rise without a tolerable degree of heat. When of a

VOL-AU-VENT.

nice colour, without being scorched, withdraw it from the oven, instantly remove the cover where it was marked, and detach all the soft crumb from the centre: in doing this, be careful not to break the edges of the *vol-au-vent;* but should they look thin in places, stop them with small flakes of the inside paste, stuck on with the white of an egg. This precaution is necessary to prevent the fricassee or ragoût from bursting the case, and so spoiling the appearance of the dish. Fill the *vol-au-vent* with a rich mince, or fricassee, or ragoût, or the remains of cold fish flaked and warmed in a good white sauce, and do not make them very liquid, for fear of the gravy bursting the crust: replace the lid, and serve. To improve the appearance of the crust, brush it over with the yolk of an egg *after* it has risen properly. *Time.*—¾ hour to bake the *vol-au-vent. Average cost,* exclusive of the interior, 1*s.* 6*d.* *Seasonable* at any time.

Note.—Small *vol-au-vents* may be made like those shown in the engraving, and filled with minced veal, chicken, &c. They should be made of the same paste as the larger ones, and stamped out with a small fluted cutter.

SMALL VOL-AU-VENTS.

VOL-AU-VENT OF FRESH STRAWBERRIES, WITH WHIPPED CREAM.

Ingredients. — ¾ lb. of puff-paste, 1 pint of freshly-gathered strawberries, sugar to taste, a plateful of whipped cream. *Mode.*—Make a *vol-au-vent* case, only not quite so large nor so high as for a savoury one. When nearly done, brush the paste over with the white of an egg, then sprinkle on it some pounded sugar, and put it back in the oven to set the glaze. Remove the interior, or soft crumb, and, at the moment of serving, fill it with the strawberries, which should be picked, and broken up with sufficient sugar to sweeten them nicely. Place a few spoonfuls of whipped cream on the top and serve. *Time.*—½ hour to 40 minutes to bake the *vol-au-vent. Average cost,* 2*s.* 3*d.* *Sufficient* for 1 *vol-au-vent.* *Seasonable* in June and July.

VOL-AU-VENT, Sweet, of Plums, Apples, or any other Fresh Fruit.

Ingredients.—¾ lb. of puff-paste, about 1 pint of fruit compôte. *Mode.*—Make ¾ lb. of puff-paste, taking care to bake it in a good brisk oven, to draw it up nicely and make it look light. Have ready sufficient stewed fruit, the syrup of which must be boiled down until very thick; fill the *vol-au-vent* with this, and pile it high in the centre; powder a little sugar over it, and put it back in the oven to glaze, or use a salamander for the purpose: the *vol-au-vent* is then ready to serve. It may be made with any fruit that is in season, such as rhubarb, oranges, gooseberries, currants, cherries, apples, &c.; but care must be taken not to have the syrup too thin, for fear of its breaking through the crust. *Time.*—½ hour to 40 minutes to bake the *vol-au-vent*. *Average cost*, exclusive of the compôte, 1s. 1d. *Sufficient* for 1 entremets.

WAFERS, Geneva.

Ingredients.—2 eggs, 3 oz. butter, 3 oz. flour, 3 oz. pounded sugar. *Mode.*—Well whisk the eggs; put them into a basin, and stir to them the butter, which should be beaten to a cream; add the flour and sifted sugar gradually, and then mix all well together. Butter a baking-sheet, and drop on it a teaspoonful of the mixture at a time, leaving a space between each. Bake in a cool oven; watch the pieces of paste, and, when half done, roll them up like wafers, and put in a small wedge of bread or piece of wood, to keep them in shape. Return them to the oven until crisp. Before serving, remove the bread, put a spoonful of preserve in the widest end, and fill up with whipped cream. This is a very pretty and ornamental dish for the supper-table, and is very nice and easily made. *Time.*—Altogether from 20 to 25 minutes. *Average cost*, exclusive of the preserve and cream, 7d. *Sufficient* for a nice-sized dish. *Seasonable* at any time.

WALNUT KETCHUP.

Ingredients.—100 walnuts, 1 handful of salt, 1 quart of vinegar, ¼ oz. of mace, ¼ oz. of nutmeg, ¼ oz. of cloves, ¼ oz. of ginger, ¼ oz. of whole black pepper, a small piece of horseradish, 20 shalots, ¼ lb. of anchovies, 1 pint of port wine. *Mode.*—Procure the walnuts at the time you can run a pin through them, slightly bruise, and put them into a jar with the salt and vinegar; let them stand 8 days, stirring every day; then drain the liquor from them, and boil it, with the above ingredients, for about ½ hour. It may be strained or not, as preferred, and, if required, a little more vinegar or wine can be added, according to taste. When bottled well, seal the corks. *Time.*—½ hour. *Seasonable.*—Make this from the beginning to the middle of July, when walnuts are in perfection for pickling purposes.

WALNUT KETCHUP.

Ingredients.—½ sieve of walnut-shells, 2 quarts of water, salt, ½ lb. of shalots, 1 oz. of cloves, 1 oz. of mace, 1 oz. of whole pepper, 1 oz. of garlic. *Mode.*—Put the walnut-shells into a pan, with the water, and a large quantity of salt; let them stand for 10 days, then break the shells up in the water, and let it drain through a sieve, putting a heavy weight on the top to express the juice; place it on the fire, and remove all scum that may arise. Now boil the liquor with the shalots, cloves, mace, pepper, and garlic, and let all simmer till the shalots sink; then put the liquor into a pan, and, when cold, bottle, and cork closely. It should stand 6 months before using: should it ferment during that time, it must be again boiled and skimmed. *Time.* — About ¾ hour. *Seasonable* in September, when the walnut-shells are obtainable.

WALNUTS, to have Fresh throughout the Season.

Ingredients.—To every pint of water allow 1 teaspoonful of salt. *Mode.*—Place the walnuts in the salt and water for 24 hours at least; then take them out, and rub them dry. Old nuts may be freshened in this manner; or walnuts, when first picked, may be put into an earthen pan with salt sprinkled amongst them, and with damped hay placed on the top of them, and then covered down with a lid. They must be well wiped before they are put on table. *Seasonable.*—Should be stored away in September or October.

WALNUTS, Pickled (very Good).

Ingredients. — 100 walnuts, salt and water. To each quart of vinegar allow 2 oz. of whole black pepper, 1 oz. of allspice, 1 oz. of bruised ginger. *Mode.*—Procure the walnuts while young; be careful they are not woody, and prick them well with a fork; prepare a strong brine of salt and water (4 lbs. of salt to each gallon of water), into which put the walnuts, letting them remain 9 days, and changing the brine every third day; drain them off, put them on a dish, place it in the sun until they become perfectly black, which will be in 2 or 3 days; have ready dry jars, into which place the walnuts, and do not quite fill the jars. Boil sufficient vinegar to cover them, for 10 minutes, with spices in the above proportion, and pour it hot over the walnuts, which must be quite covered with the pickle; tie down with bladder, and keep in a dry place. They will be fit for use in a month, and will keep good 2 or 3 years. *Time.*—10 minutes. *Seasonable.* — Make this from the beginning to the middle of July, before the walnuts harden.

Note.—When liked, a few shalots may be added to the vinegar, and boiled with it.

WATER SOUCHY.

Perch, tench, soles, eels, and flounders are considered the best fish for this dish. For the souchy, put some water into a stewpan with a bunch of chopped parsley, some roots, and sufficient salt to make it brackish. Let these simmer for 1 hour, and then stew the fish in this water. When they are done, take them out to drain, have ready some finely-chopped parsley, and a few roots cut into slices of about one inch thick and an inch in length. Put the fish in a tureen or deep dish, strain the liquor over them, and add the minced parsley and roots. Serve with brown bread and butter.

WHEATEARS, to Dress.

Ingredients.—Wheatears; fresh butter. *Mode.* — After the birds are picked, gutted, and cleaned, truss them like larks, put them down to a quick fire, and baste them well with fresh butter. When done, which will be in about 20 minutes, dish them on fried bread-crumbs, and garnish the dish with slices of lemon. *Time.* — 20 minutes. *Seasonable* from July to October.

WHISKEY CORDIAL.

Ingredients.—1 lb. of ripe white currants, the rind of 2 lemons, ¼ oz. of grated ginger, 1 quart of whiskey, 1 lb. of lump sugar. *Mode.*—Strip the currants from the stalks; put them into a large jug; add the lemon-rind, ginger, and whiskey; cover the jug closely, and let it remain covered for 24 hours. Strain through a hair-sieve, add the lump sugar, and let it stand 12 hours longer; then bottle, and cork well. *Time.*—To stand 24 hours before being strained; 12 hours after the sugar is added. *Seasonable.*—Make this in July.

WHITEBAIT, to Dress.

Ingredients.—A little flour, hot lard, seasoning of salt. *Mode.* — This fish should be put into iced water as soon as bought, unless they are cooked immediately. Drain them from the water in a colander, and have ready a nice clean dry cloth, over which put 2 good handfuls of flour. Toss in the whitebait, shake them lightly in the cloth, and put them in a wicker-sieve to take away the superfluous flour. Throw them into a pan of boiling lard, very few at a time, and let them fry till of a whitey-brown colour. Directly they are done, they must be taken out, and laid before the fire for a minute or two on a sieve reversed, covered with blotting-paper to absorb the fat. Dish them on a hot napkin, arrange the fish very high in the centre, and sprinkle a little salt over the whole. *Time.*—3 minutes. *Seasonable* from April to August.

WHITE SAUCE, Good.

Ingredients.—½ pint of white stock, ½ pint of cream, 1 dessertspoonful of flour, salt to taste. *Mode.* — Have ready a delicately-clean saucepan, into which put the stock, which should be well flavoured with vegetables, and rather savoury; mix the flour smoothly with the cream, add it to the stock, season with a little salt, and boil all these ingredients very gently for about 10 minutes, keeping them well stirred the whole time, as this sauce is very liable to burn. *Time.*—10 minutes. *Average cost*, 1*s*. *Sufficient* for a pair of fowls. *Seasonable* at any time.

top ornament, and replacing it after the gravy is added. *Time.*—About 1½ hour. *Average cost,* 2*s.* 6*d.* *Sufficient* for 5 or 6 persons. *Seasonable* from March to October.

VEAL AND HAM PIE.

Ingredients.—2 lbs. of veal cutlets, ½ lb. of boiled ham, 2 tablespoonfuls of minced savoury herbs, ¼ teaspoonful of grated nutmeg, 2 blades of pounded mace, pepper and salt to taste, a strip of lemon-peel finely minced, the yolks of 2 hard-boiled eggs, ½ pint of water, nearly ½ pint of good strong gravy, puff-crust. *Mode.*—Cut the veal into nice square pieces, and put a layer of them at the bottom of a pie-dish; sprinkle over these a portion of the herbs, spices, seasoning, lemon-peel, and the yolks of the eggs cut in slices; cut the ham very thin, and put a layer of this in. Proceed in this manner until the dish is full, so arranging it that the ham comes at the top. Lay a puff-paste on the edge of the dish, and pour in about ½ pint of water; cover with crust, ornament it with leaves, brush it over with the yolk of an egg, and bake in a well-heated oven for 1 to 1½ hour, or longer, should the pie be very large. When it is taken out of the oven, pour in at the top, through a funnel, nearly ½ pint of strong gravy: this should be made sufficiently good that, when cold, it may cut in a firm jelly. This pie may be very much enriched by adding a few mushrooms, oysters, or sweetbreads; but it will be found very good without any of the last-named additions. *Time.*— 1½ hour, or longer, should the pie be very large. *Average cost,* 3*s.* *Sufficient* for 5 or 6 persons. *Seasonable* from March to October.

VEAL, Potted (for Breakfast).

Ingredients. — To every lb. of veal allow ¼ lb. of ham, cayenne and pounded mace to taste, 6 oz. of fresh butter; clarified butter. *Mode.*—Mince the veal and ham together as finely as possible, and pound well in a mortar, with cayenne, pounded mace, and fresh butter in the above proportion. When reduced to a perfectly smooth paste, press it into potting-pots, and cover with clarified butter. If kept in a cool place, it will remain good some days. *Seasonable* from March to October.

VEAL, Ragout of Cold (Cold Meat Cookery).

Ingredients.—The remains of cold veal, 1 oz. of butter, ½ pint of gravy, thickening of butter and flour, pepper and salt to taste, 1 blade of pounded mace, 1 tablespoonful of mushroom ketchup, 1 tablespoonful of sherry, 1 dessertspoonful of lemon-juice, forcemeat balls. *Mode.*—Any part of veal will make this dish. Cut the meat into nice-looking pieces, put them in a stewpan with 1 oz. of butter, and fry a light brown; add the gravy (hot water may be substituted for this), thicken with a little butter and flour, and stew gently about ¼ hour; season with pepper, salt, and pounded mace; add the ketchup, sherry, and lemon-juice; give one boil, and serve. Garnish the dish with forcemeat balls and fried rashers of bacon. *Time.*— Altogether ½ hour. *Average cost,* exclusive of cold meat, 6*d.* *Seasonable* from March to October.

Note.—The above recipe may be varied, by adding vegetables, such as peas, cucumbers, lettuces, green onions cut in slices, a dozen or two of green gooseberries (not seedy), all of which should be fried a little with the meat, and then stewed in the gravy.

VEAL RISSOLES (Cold Meat Cookery).

Ingredients.—A few slices of cold roast veal, a few slices of ham or bacon, 1 tablespoonful of minced parsley, 1 tablespoonful of minced savoury herbs, 1 blade of pounded mace, a very little grated nutmeg, cayenne and salt to taste, 2 eggs well beaten, bread-crumbs. *Mode.* —Mince the veal very finely with a little ham or bacon; add the parsley, herbs, spices, and seasoning; mix into a paste with an egg; form into balls or cones; brush these over with egg, sprinkle with bread-crumbs, and fry a rich brown. Serve with brown gravy, and garnish the dish with fried parsley. *Time.*—About 10 minutes to fry the rissoles. *Seasonable* from March to October.

VEAL ROLLS (Cold Meat Cookery).

Ingredients.—The remains of a cold fillet of veal, egg and bread-crumbs, a few slices of fat bacon, forcemeat. *Mode.* —Cut a few slices from a cold fillet of veal

½ inch thick; rub them over with egg; lay a thin slice of fat bacon over each piece of veal; brush these with the egg, and over this spread the forcemeat thinly; roll up each piece tightly, egg and bread-crumb them, and fry them a rich brown. Serve with mushroom sauce or brown gravy. *Time.*—10 to 15 minutes to fry the rolls. *Seasonable* from March to October.

VEAL, Stuffed and Stewed Shoulder of.

Ingredients. — A shoulder of veal, a few slices of ham or bacon, forcemeat, 3 carrots, 2 onions, salt and pepper to taste, a faggot of savoury herbs, 3 blades of pounded mace, water, thickening of butter and flour. *Mode.*—Bone the joint by carefully detaching the meat from the blade-bone on one side, and then on the other, being particular not to pierce the skin; then cut the bone from the knuckle, and take it out. Fill the cavity whence the bone was taken with a forcemeat. Roll and bind the veal up tightly; put it into a stewpan with the carrots, onions, seasoning, herbs, and mace; pour in just sufficient water to cover it, and let it stew *very gently* for about 5 hours. Before taking it up, try if it is properly done by thrusting a larding-needle in it: if it penetrates easily, it is sufficiently cooked. Strain and skim the gravy, thicken with butter and flour, give one boil, and pour it round the meat. A few young carrots may be boiled and placed round the dish as a garnish, and, when in season, green peas should always be served with this dish. *Time.*—5 hours. *Average cost*, 7*d.* per lb. *Sufficient* for 8 or 9 persons. *Seasonable* from March to October.

VEAL, Stewed with Peas, Young Carrots, and New Potatoes.

Ingredients.—3 or 4 lbs. of the loin or neck of veal, 15 young carrots, a few green onions, 1 pint of green peas, 12 new potatoes, a bunch of savoury herbs, pepper and salt to taste, 1 tablespoonful of lemon-juice, 2 tablespoonfuls of tomato sauce, 2 tablespoonfuls of mushroom ketchup. *Mode.* — Dredge the meat with flour, and roast or bake it for about ¾ hour: it should acquire a nice brown colour. Put the meat into a stewpan with the carrots, onions, potatoes, herbs, pepper, and salt; pour over it sufficient boiling water to cover it, and stew gently for 2 hours. Take out the meat and herbs, put it in a deep dish, skim off all the fat from the gravy, and flavour it with lemon-juice, tomato sauce, and mushroom ketchup, in the above proportion. Have ready a pint of green peas boiled *separately*; put these with the meat, pour over it the gravy, and serve. The dish may be garnished with a few forcemeat balls. The meat, when preferred, may be cut into chops, and floured and fried instead of being roasted; and any part of veal dressed in this way will be found extremely savoury and good. *Time.* — 3 hours. *Average cost*, 9*d.* per lb. *Sufficient* for 6 or 7 persons. *Seasonable*, with peas, from June to August.

VEGETABLE MARROW, Boiled.

Ingredients. — To each ½ gallon of water, allow 1 heaped tablespoonful of salt; vegetable marrows. *Mode.*—Have ready a saucepan of boiling water, salted in the above proportion; put in the marrows after peeling them, and boil them until quite tender. Take them up with a slice, halve, and, should they be very large, quarter them. Dish them on toast, and send to table with them a tureen of melted butter, or, in lieu of this, a small pat of salt butter. Large vegetable marrows may be preserved throughout the winter by storing them in a dry place; when wanted for use, a few slices should be cut and boiled in the same manner as above; but, when once begun, the marrow must be eaten quickly, as it keeps but a short time after it is cut. Vegetable marrows are also very delicious mashed: they should be boiled, then drained, and mashed smoothly with a wooden spoon. Heat them in a saucepan, add a seasoning of salt and pepper, and a small piece of butter, and dish with a few sippets of toasted bread placed round as a garnish. *Time.*—Young vegetable marrows, 10 to 20 minutes; old ones, ½ to ¾ hour. *Average cost*, in full season, 1*s.* per dozen. *Sufficient.*—Allow 1 moderate-sized marrow for each person. *Seasonable* in July,

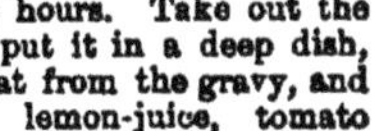

VEGETABLE MARROW ON TOAST.

is on the point of simmering; but do not allow it to boil, or it will instantly curdle. This sauce is delicious with plum, marrow, or bread puddings; but should be served separately, and not poured over the pudding. *Time.*—From 5 to 7 minutes to thicken the butter; about 5 minutes to stir the sauce over the fire. *Average cost,* 1*s.* 10*d.* *Sufficient* for 7 or 8 persons.

WINE, to Mull.

Ingredients.—To every pint of wine allow 1 large cupful of water, sugar, and spice to taste. *Mode.*—In making preparations like the above, it is very difficult to give the exact proportions of ingredients like sugar and spice, as what quantity might suit one person would be to another quite distasteful. Boil the spice in the water until the flavour is extracted, then add the wine and sugar, and bring the whole to the boiling-point, when serve with strips of crisp dry toast, or with biscuits. The spices usually used for mulled wine are cloves, grated nutmeg, and cinnamon or mace. Any kind of wine may be mulled, but port and claret are those usually selected for the purpose; and the latter requires a very large proportion of sugar. The vessel that the wine is boiled in must be delicately clean, and should be kept exclusively for the purpose. Small tin warmers may be purchased for a trifle, which are more suitable than saucepans, as, if the latter are not scrupulously clean, they will spoil the wine, by imparting to it a very disagreeable flavour. These warmers should be used for no other purposes.

WOODCOCK, Roast.

Ingredients. — Woodcocks; butter, flour, toast. *Mode.*—Woodcocks should not be drawn, as the trails are, by epicures, considered a great delicacy. Pluck, and wipe them well outside; truss them

ROAST WOODCOCK.

with the legs close to the body, and the feet pressing upon the thighs; skin the neck and head, and bring the beak round under the wing. Place some slices of toast in the dripping-pan to catch the trails, allowing a piece of toast for each bird. Roast before a clear fire from 15 to 25 minutes; keep them well basted, and flour and froth them nicely. When done, dish the pieces of toast with the birds upon them, and pour round a very little gravy; send some more to table in a tureen. These are most delicious birds when well cooked; but they should not be kept too long: when the feathers drop, or easily come out, they are fit for for table. *Time.*—When liked underdone, 15 to 20 minutes; if liked well done, allow an extra 5 minutes. *Average cost.*—Seldom bought. *Sufficient.*—2 for a dish. *Seasonable* from November to February.

WOODCOCK.

This bird, like a partridge, may be carved by cutting it exactly into two like portions, or made into three helpings, as described in carving partridge. The backbone is considered the tit-bit of a woodcock, and by many the thigh is also thought a great delicacy. This bird is served in the manner advised by Brillat Savarin, in connection with the pheasant, viz., on toast which has received its drippings whilst roasting; and a piece of this toast should invariably accompany each plate.

WOODCOCK.

WOODCOCK, SCOTCH.

Ingredients. — A few slices of hot buttered toast; allow 1 anchovy to each slice. For the sauce,—½ pint of cream, the yolks of 3 eggs. *Mode.*—Separate the yolks from the whites of the eggs; beat the former, stir to them the cream, and bring the sauce to the boiling-point, but do not allow it to boil, or it will curdle. Have ready some hot buttered toast, spread with anchovies pounded to a paste; pour a little of the hot sauce on the top, and serve very hot and very quickly. *Time.*—5 minutes to make the sauce hot. *Sufficient.*—Allow ½ slice to each person. *Seasonable* at any time.

YEAST-CAKE.

Ingredients.—1½ lb. of flour, ½ lb. of butter, ½ pint of milk, 1½ tablespoonful of good yeast, 3 eggs, ¾ lb. of currants, ½ lb. of white moist sugar, 2 oz. of candied peel. *Mode*.—Put the milk and butter into a saucepan, and shake it round over a fire until the butter is melted, but do not allow the milk to get very hot. Put the flour into a basin, stir to it the milk and butter, the yeast and eggs, which should be well beaten, and form the whole into a smooth dough. Let it stand in a warm place, covered with a cloth, to rise, and, when sufficiently risen, add the currants, sugar, and candied peel cut into thin slices. When all the ingredients are thoroughly mixed, line 2 moderate-sized cake-tins with buttered paper, which should be about six inches higher than the tin; pour in the mixture, let it stand to rise again for another ½ hour, and then bake the cakes in a brisk oven for about 1½ hour. If the tops of them become too brown, cover them with paper until they are done through. A few drops of essence of lemon, or a little grated nutmeg, may be added when the flavour is liked. *Time*.—From 1¼ to 1½ hour. *Average cost*, 2*s*. *Sufficient* to make 2 moderate-sized cakes. *Seasonable* at any time.

YEAST-DUMPLINGS.

Ingredients.—½ quartern of dough, boiling water. *Mode*.—Make a very light dough as for bread, using to mix it, milk, instead of water; divide it into 7 or 8 dumplings; plunge them into boiling water, and boil them for 20 minutes. Serve the instant they are taken up, as they spoil directly, by falling and becoming heavy; and in eating them do not touch them with a knife, but tear them apart with two forks. They may be eaten with meat gravy, or cold butter and sugar; and if not convenient to make the dough at home, a little from the baker's answers as well, only it must be placed for a few minutes near the fire, in a basin with a cloth over it, to let it rise again before it is made into dumplings. *Time*.—20 minutes. *Average cost*, 4*d*. *Sufficient* for 5 or 6 persons. *Seasonable* at any time.

YEAST, to Make, for Bread.

Ingredients.—1½ oz. of hops, 3 quarts of water, 1 lb. of bruised malt, ½ pint of yeast. *Mode*.—Boil the hops in the water for 20 minutes; let it stand for about 5 minutes, then add it to 1 lb. of bruised malt prepared as for brewing. Let the mixture stand covered till about lukewarm; then put in not quite ½ pint of yeast; keep it warm, and let it work 3 or 4 hours; then put it into small ½-pint bottles (ginger-beer bottles are the best for the purpose), cork them well, and tie them down. The yeast is now ready for use; it will keep good for a few weeks, and 1 bottle will be found sufficient for 18 lbs. of flour. When required for use, boil 3 lbs. of potatoes without salt, mash them in the same water in which they were boiled, and rub them through a colander. Stir in about ½ lb. of flour; then put in the yeast, pour it in the middle of the flour, and let it stand warm on the hearth all night, and in the morning let it be quite warm when it is kneaded. The bottles of yeast require very careful opening, as it is generally exceedingly ripe. *Time*.—20 minutes to boil the hops and water, the yeast to work 3 or 4 hours. *Sufficient*.—½ pint sufficient for 18 lbs. of flour.

YEAST, Kirkleatham.

Ingredients.—2 oz. of hops, 4 quarts of water, ½ lb. of flour, ½ pint of yeast. *Mode*.—Boil the hops and water for 20 minutes; strain, and mix with the liquid ½ lb. of flour and not quite ½ pint of yeast. Bottle it up, and tie the corks down. When wanted for use, boil potatoes according to the quantity of bread to be made (about 3 lbs. are sufficient for about a peck of flour); mash them, add to them ½ lb. of flour, and mix about ½ pint of the yeast with them; let this mixture stand all day, and lay the bread to rise the night before it is wanted. *Time*.—20 minutes to boil the hops and water. *Sufficient*.—½ pint of this yeast sufficient for a peck of flour, or rather more.

Usque ad Finem.

HER Hand has lost its cunning—the firm, true hand that wrote these *formulæ*, and penned the information contained in this little book. Cold in the silent tomb lie the once nimble, useful fingers,—now nerveless, unable for anything, and ne'er to do work more in this world! Exquisite palate, unerring judgment, sound common sense, refined tastes,—all these had the dear Lady who has gone ere her youth had scarcely come. But four times seven years were all she passed in this world; and since the day she became wedded wife—now nearly nine years past—her greatest, chiefest aims were to provide for the comfort and pleasure of those she loved and had around her, and to employ her best faculties for the use of her sisters, Englishwomen generally. Her surpassing affection and devotion led her to find her happiness in aiding, with all her heart and soul, the Husband whom she richly blessed and honoured with her abounding love.

Her Works speak for themselves; and, although taken from this world in the very height of health and strength, and in the early days of womanhood, she felt that satisfaction—so great to all who strive with good intent and warm will—of knowing herself regarded with respect and gratitude.

Her labours are ended here; in a purer atmosphere she dwells; and may be, in the land beyond the skies, she has nobler work to accomplish. Her plans for the future cannot be wholly carried out: her Husband knew them all, and will diligently devote himself to their execution, as far as may be. The remembrance of her wishes,—always for the private and public welfare,—and the companionship of her two little boys,—too young to know the virtues of their good Mother,—this memory, this presence, will nerve the Father, left alone, to continue to do his duty: in which he will follow the example of his Wife, for her duty no woman has ever better accomplished than the late

Isabella Mary Beeton.

THE END.

London:
Cox & Wyman, Classical and General Printers,
Great Queen Street, W.C.

www.ingramcontent.com/pod-product-compliance
Ingram Content Group UK Ltd.
Pitfield, Milton Keynes, MK11 3LW, UK
UKHW021502020725
6662UKWH00056B/45

9 781015 826236